THE ULTIMATE A-Z BOOK ON MUSCLE BUILDING!

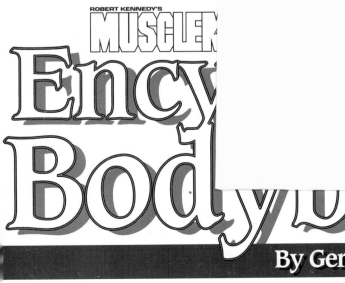

ROBERT KENNEDY'S MUSCLEMAG Encyclopedia of Bodybuilding

By Gerard Thorne and Phil Embleton

Published by MuscleMag International
6465 Airport Road
Mississauga, Ontario
Canada L4V 1E4

Designed by Jackie Kydyk
Edited by Mandy Morgan

Printed in Canada

10 9 8 7 6 5 4 3 2 1 Pbk.

Canadian Cataloging in Publication Data

Thorne, Gerard J., 1963-
    Robert Kennedy's Musclemag International encyclopedia of bodybuilding: the ultimate A-Z book on muscle building

Includes index.
ISBN 1-55210-001-4

    1. Bodybuilding--Encyclopedias. I. Embleton, Phil J., 1963- II. Title. III. Title: Musclemag International encyclopedia of bodybuilding. IV. Title: Encyclopedia of bodybuilding.

GV546.5.T48 1996   646.7'5   C95-920923-9

Distributed in Canada by
Canbook Warehouse
c/o E.A Milley
1220 Nicholson Road
Newmarket, ON
Canada L3Y 7V1
800-399-6858

Distributed in the United States by
BookWorld Services
1933 Whitfield Park Loop
Sarasota FL 34243
800-444-2524

This book is not intended as medical advice, nor is it offered for use in the diagnosis of any health condition or as a substitute for medical treatment and/or counsel. Its purpose is to explore advanced topics on sports nutirition and exercise. All data are for information only. Use of any of the programs within this book is at the sole risk and choice of the reader.

THE ULTIMATE A-Z BOOK ON MUSCLE BUILDING!

Encyclopedia of Bodybuilding

A *MUSCLEMAG* INTERNATIONAL PUBLICATION

DEDICATION...

This book is dedicated to the memories of Debbie Dobbins, Don "Ripper" Ross, Candy Csencsits, Bill Reynolds, and others whose guiding light helped develop bodybuilding into the sport it is today.

ACKNOWLEDGMENTS...

The compilation of this book has been the work of many people, and the authors wish to thank the following individuals for their generous support in this endeavor:

To the gang at the Y – Rick Martin, Melanie Hiscock and John Thorne, our sincere thanks for their advice and words of encouragement.

Thanks to Dr. Maureen "Mo" Connolly, for her invaluable recommendations and criticisms of the early versions of our manuscript (justly deserved, we might add!).

To Bertha Thorne, whose financial advice we continue to seek, and whose vacation plans we will no doubt be funding in the future.

To *MuscleMag's* Gina Logan, for her "answering all the questions." Despite her own hectic schedule, Gina always had time to lend a helping hand (and, yes, Gina, the weather's great here today).

To Drs. Colin Higgs and William McKim, who gave us invaluable advice on the joys and perils of writing.

We are especially grateful to Dr. Elliot Leyton, who invited us into his home and gave freely of his time and 20 years of expertise in the writing game.

Finally, to the man who actually started it all, Robert Kennedy. With little more than a dream and an abundance of perseverance, Bob has developed *MuscleMag International* into the internationally respected organization it is today. In short, Robert Kennedy represents the embodiment of the immigrant dream and we are proud to be given the chance to contribute in our own modest way.

Our thanks to you all!
– Gerard Thorne, Phil Embleton

Table of Contents

Joe Spinello

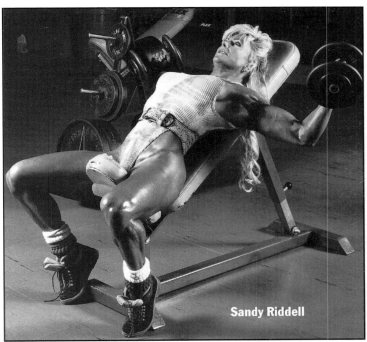

Sandy Riddell

Bruce Patterson

Milos Sarcev

Mia Finnegan

Matt McLaughlin, Sue Price and Dave Fisher

The phrase "chance of a lifetime" gets tossed around pretty loosely these days, but this is what we, the authors, were presented with in January of 1995. It didn't require much deliberation on our part to jump at the chance being offered by Robert Kennedy. "Could you write *MuscleMag International's Encyclopedia of Bodybuilding?*" he asked. "Is Arnold the Terminator?" we responded!

We hope that many readers will recognize our names from our initial foray into the literary world a few years back. We began our writing careers during the fall of 1988 at the height of the Ben Johnson steroid scandal. The fallout from the 1988 Seoul Olympics made drug use by athletes front-page news around the world. Our book, *Steroid Myths,* was conceived after we recognized the need for a comprehensive treatment of the subject.

After many years of research we discovered that, like most issues, steroid use is a multifaceted phenomenon. We could have jumped on the antisteroid bandwagon and written a scalding condemnation of steroid use, but this would fly in the face of our research. Instead, *Steroid Myths* took a neutral stance. We endeavored to simply present the evidence and let readers make up their own minds. With few exceptions, the feedback indicates that we accomplished our objective.

All of the previous brings us to this our latest book – *MuscleMag International's Encyclopedia of Bodybuilding.* First conceived by Robert Kennedy during the summer of 1994, the text is a comprehensive bodybuilding manual drawn from more than 24 years of *MuscleMag* history.

For your convenience we have grouped similar chapters into "books." Followed sequentially, the chapters will take you from beginner to the competitive stages of bodybuilding. In most cases we have attempted to make the chapters distinct entities that can stand on their own, but we realize that there is some overlap between chapters. For example, the nutrition chapter is presented immediately after the beginner's chapter; nevertheless, the information it contains is applicable to all stages of bodybuilding – especially the competitive level. In fact, given the importance of diet to bodybuilding, we have written what we feel is one of the most thorough treatments of the subject.

In order to address the concerns of the competitive bodybuilder, we have outlined the various stages of contest preparation. Everything from carbohydrate loading and shaving down to posing and music selection is found in the three relevant chapters.

In keeping with *MuscleMag's* philosophy of presenting topics in an unbiased manner, we have included a comprehensive chapter on anabolic steroids. It is not meant to be a guide for steroid use, but we realize some readers may be considering the use of these drugs, so it is better to be informed than ignorant of their potential physiological and psychological side effects.

We realize that the baby boomer generation is approaching middle age, and have included a chapter that addresses some of the concerns facing the older bodybuilder. Unlike many sports which may be dangerous for aging athletes, bodybuilding is 100 percent safe, provided you use common sense and follow the advice laid down in the following pages.

The book's largest section is devoted to training with the superstars of the sport. Rather than just give a few exercises for each bodypart, we have presented a comprehensive look at how the champs employ them in their workouts. Wherever possible we have included stars who are famous for the bodypart relevant to that chapter (Arnold's chest, DeMayo's legs, Haney's back, etc.). Rounding out the text are chapters on circuit training, training at home, aerobics for the bodybuilder, training on the road, and the business of bodybuilding.

To conclude, we present a look back at the history of *MuscleMag.* One chapter is a question-and-answer section that addresses the more common bodybuilding problems. Another, *MuscleMag's* Gallery of Stars, profiles some of the sport's major players who have graced the pages of *MMI* over the years. Most profiled are bodybuilders, but a few others have been included because of their contribution to the sport.

Finally, all information presented in this book applies as much to females as it does to males, even though we have a full chapter devoted to women. Gone are the days of male dominance in bodybuilding gyms. Women's bodybuilding is an integral part of the sport, and although recently being somewhat upstaged by women's fitness contests, has developed superstars with followings comparable to those of their male counterparts.

Rare authors, indeed, are they who claim their book to be the most definitive summary of a given topic, and we make no such declarations. We do, however, believe that this text is the most up-to-date bodybuilding manual currently available – whether for competitive bodybuilding, supplementing another sport or sports, or simply looking better at the beach. We feel every conceivable topic is found within the pages of this text, and no matter what your individual goals, we wish you all the best in your future endeavors.

– *Gerard Thorne, Phil Embleton*
St. John's, Newfoundland, Canada

"Every man dies, but not every man truly lives."
– Mel Gibson in the movie *Braveheart*

As a young boy growing up in England, I dreamt of becoming a professional bodybuilder. Money was scarce – I had to save up to buy the latest magazines, to learn all I could about my idols who lived in magical places called California and Venice Beach. My training in oil painting and sculpture landed me a teaching position at a British college. Most people would have been content with that achievement; I felt that there was something *more* I could do. After I produced a series of illustrations for *Health and Strength* magazine (for the princely sum of $1.69!), it dawned on me that I could reach more people through the written word than through gallery pieces. My fingers began to fly across my battered typewriter (which only a bodybuilder could carry – it was a prewar model), and my thoughts on bodybuilding took the form of articles in British bodybuilding magazines. The more I wrote the more I was hooked. I knew I didn't have the genetics to be a professional bodybuilder, but possibly I had what it took to be a writer… and the key to success is not just finding your talents, but being honest enough to admit your own limitations.

I wanted to break into the North American market. My childhood dream of visiting those magical places became a reality when I moved to Canada. And then, having established myself as a writer, I decided to bet everything I had on being a publisher. Thus, in 1974, *MuscleMag International* was born.

Admittedly I was a bit green in the beginning. After writing almost the entire first issue myself, producing the artwork, and having 100,000 copies run off, I suddenly realized that I had forgotten to set up a distribution system. It was kind of like getting ready for the Normandy Invasion and, the night before D-Day, realizing that you forgot the ships! Managing to locate an international distributor, I showed him a couple of copies and crossed my fingers. I will never forget what he said to me. "You mean to tell me, Mr. Kennedy, you have 100,000 of these with no place to go?" Having learned long ago that stupid mistakes are only compounded by lame excuses (and because I couldn't think of a lame excuse, let alone a good one), I answered, "Yes, that's right."

There was a pause. Now you must understand that time is a subjective experience. You know how, when people are in an accident, they report that everything went in slow motion? Well, for me time came to a complete stop – I kid you not. I've waited for hours in airports since then,

Bob Kennedy with "The Myth" Sergio Oliva.

Tonya Knight and Bob Kennedy.

Franco Columbu, Ed Corney, Bob Kennedy and Robby Robinson

With little more than a dream and much determination, Robert Kennedy started *MuscleMag International*, which has become one of bodybuilding's premier publications.

but those delays are short compared to that one moment when I literally stepped out of time. And I remember how time started again when he replied, "Okay, we'll take them!"

That was the definitive moment in my life, the birth of *MuscleMag*. Make no mistake – it has been a long struggle. It was only a few years ago that we started to make money! But it was that same struggle that has shaped *MMI* into the magazine it is today.

MuscleMag has always been different from the other bodybuilding mags because early on we chose to behave like journalists. Other magazines put on a happy face and publish stories that could have been written by Barney. They simply exist as a platform to market supplements, or to glorify certain individuals with an intensity that brings brown-nosing to an artform.

From the start *MuscleMag* has always told it like it is: the latest techniques in training and diet, rising and falling stars, supplements that work and don't work, and the inside story on the bodybuilding world. And we included the dark side – diet disorders, prima donnas and drug use. Our readers get the full story – warts and all.

But honesty is just not enough in the publishing business. Anyone can present information, but people also want to be entertained. I believe that the key to the success of *MuscleMag* has been our sense of humor. Despite the popular image bodybuilders are not just intelligent people. They can be downright hilarious! I can't tell you the number of interviews during which I had to stop the tape because we were laughing so hard! Half the reason people go to work out is to take part in the gym banter, so we adopted that as part of the *MMI* style, which brings me to this book – *Robert Kennedy's MuscleMag International Encyclopedia of Bodybuilding*. It's long overdue. We have compiled for you a comprehensive review of the training techniques covered by *MuscleMag* throughout its 20-year history, and it also contains loads of brand-new information.

We didn't pull any punches with this volume – our readers aren't interested in political correctness. Not reporting on an issue won't make it go away. From drug use to crude behavior in the gym, we've got it all here. This book can be used as a reference guide for experienced bodybuilders, or as a training manual for newcomers.

The last part written for a book is usually the foreword, and to be honest it is the most difficult to compose. You basically have to blow your own horn to establish your credibility, and then summarize the book in a few brief paragraphs – kind of a book report/advertisement, if you will. As I reread the manuscript, I kept trying to think of a quote that reflected both my life and the contents of this book. My wife, a patient woman, convinced me that I needed to relax with a movie. We saw *Braveheart*. Despite the anti-English propaganda (even I was rooting for the Scots by the end of it), there was a quote that struck me like a thunderbolt! I kissed my wife, took out my pen and notepad, and started writing.

I could have gone through life quietly, doing all the conventional things that were expected, daydreaming about a life as publisher of an international magazine. Instead, I left my country (just as Columbu and Schwarzenegger left theirs) to pursue a goal that most people would have dismissed as fantasy. Like many immigrants before me, I worked hard, invested everything I had in my business, and almost went broke several times in the process. But I knew in my heart that my dream would become a reality – I am happy to say it did.

Bodybuilding has given me a lifetime of experiences that no other profession could have provided. I've traveled the world, met all the top bodybuilders, and I'm on a first-name basis with the movers and shakers of the bodybuilding industry. My job is never dull! For me bodybuilding has been proven the path to success. We at *MuscleMag* hope that this book will put you on the road to a healthy and successful life, and that greater success will be yours. I envy your chances!

– Robert Kennedy, Publisher
MuscleMag International

One of the many perks of Bob Kennedy's job is to work with some of the world's most beautiful women, like Marjo Selin.

Bob with fellow publishing mogul Joe Weider.

HOW BODYBUILDING CAME TO BE

HISTORICAL PERSPECTIVES

Attempting to pinpoint the exact time at which bodybuilding became a sport is like trying to determine who invented any given training principle – check with three different people and chances are you will get three different answers! In this introductory section we trace the history of bodybuilding from its earliest roots to its international status of today.

Eugen Sandow

THE ANCIENTS

Many believe the sport of bodybuilding began with the ancient Romans and Greeks, who placed strong emphasis on physical development and conditioning. The survival of a Roman gladiator literally depended on his physical prowess. The Colosseum was no place for the weak and mild mannered, and to get an idea of the daily life of such warriors, one has only to view the classic movie *Spartacus.*

Those who find the Roman ancestral analogy too barbaric may find that of the Greeks more fitting. The Roman ideal often involved public dismemberment. The Greeks emphasized friendly competition with neighboring countries. Instead of using a spear to fight wild animals, Greek competitors used the lance to see who could throw the farthest. Roman gladiators used swords to slay one another; Greek athletes used their hands to wrestle. In fact, the athletes became so successful and popular that a new term was coined to distinguish them from all others – *Olympians!*

THE MIDDLE AGES

One of the most popular forms of entertainment in middle-century Europe was the traveling carnival. Such troupes featured an assortment of acts, one of the most popular being the strongman. These prodigious, beefy characters routinely thrilled audiences with their exploits of great physical strength. The focus of their popularity was how much they could lift. Such physical concerns as proportion and bodyfat percentage were all but ignored.

This disregard of physical health persisted until the late 18th century, when a particular side effect of the Industrial Revolution began to surface. One group that attempted to reverse the public's sedentary lifestyle was the "physical culturists."

Consisting of only a handful of individuals, the physical culturists were dedicated to improving health by stressing the need for better eating habits and more exercise. Aside from the many positives that came out of the Industrial Revolution, negative attributes such as processed food and automation began to creep into the lives of both Europeans and Americans. Recognizing the need for a role model to promote their cause, the physical culturists finally found such an individual on the European strongman circuit. His name was Eugen Sandow, and for many he was bodybuilding's first star.

THE LATE 1800s AND EARLY 1900s

With a reputation as one of Europe's greatest strongmen, Sandow was convinced by promoter Florenz Ziegfeld to come to America and go on tour. What set Sandow apart from his beer-hall contemporaries was his outstanding physique. With a bodyfat level of about five percent, and well proportioned from head to toe, Sandow thrilled audiences by stepping into a glass booth and posing. After a century of Victorian bashfulness Sandow's fig-leaf exhibitions were welcomed by his adoring fans.

Charles Atlas

Throughout the next couple of decades Sandow earned thousands of dollars a week on a regular basis by posing and competing. With his popularity soaring by leaps and bounds, the sale of barbells and dumbells went through the roof. Numerous physical-culture contests took place, the winner receiving a statue of the great man himself. This is a trend that continues today with the presenting of the Sandow statue to the winner of the Mr. Olympia. Although he died of a brain hemorrhage (believed to have been brought on by hauling a stuck car out of mud), Sandow left behind a legacy of competition and promotion.

Throughout the early 20th century other individuals added unique flavor to physical culture. The "Russian Lion," George Hackenschmidt, captured the Russian weightlifting championship in 1898. Later he emigrated to Britain and made a fortune as a professional strongman (he had won numerous weightlifting and wrestling championships) and as an intellectual writer and orator.

One of the most influential ancestors of bodybuilding, Bernarr Macfadden, founded the magazine *Physical Culture.* Not a strongman himself, Macfadden initiated a series of contests to select America's Most Perfectly Developed Man. The first was held in 1903 at New York's Madison Square Garden, and the winner received the (then) princely sum of $1,000.

During the next few decades Macfadden's contests were the epitome of physical culture. They were judged from a bodybuilding perspective, emphasizing not only strength, but also the quality of a competitor's physique. The winner in 1921 was a young man named Angelo Siciliano, and few at the time could have imagined the impact that he would have on American society.

CHARLES ATLAS –
THE WORLD ON HIS SHOULDERS

Within just a few years of winning Macfadden's title, Angelo Siciliano changed his name to Charles Atlas… and a legend in bodybuilding entrepreneurship began.

The venture started as a small mail-order fitness course, but by the early 1970s Atlas's Dynamic Tension program had sold over six million copies. This training course was based on the principles of dynamic tension – a series of exercises that utilized static (tensed but unmoving) muscular contraction. Atlas's marketing gimmick was a stroke of genius. Realizing the biggest

Charles Atlas pulls the *Broadway Express*

consumer base was teenage males, Atlas placed a small advertisement in the popular comic books of the time. The ad consisted of a few cartoons showing a skinny kid being beaten up by a bully and losing his girl. A few weeks and many muscular pounds later he returns to the beach to punch out the bully and reclaim his girl. How did this transformation take place? Why, by following Atlas's Dynamic Tension program, of course! For 50 years the slogan "Don't get sand kicked in your face" became the motto of teenage males everywhere.

Siegmund Klein

THE EMERGENCE OF BODYBUILDING

It is ironic that the principles of dynamic tension laid down by Atlas were rarely followed by the great man himself! Charles Atlas, like most of his colleagues, built his physique almost entirely with the aid of weights. Soon others began to follow suit, and before long *bodybuilders* (as they were beginning to be called) could be found comparing their physiques to those of the preceding generation's strongmen.

One of the most popular stars of the '20s and '30s was Siegmund Klein. With his great shape, thick musculature and extreme definition, Klein set the standard for the next decade or so. Besides his competitive exploits, he became very successful as a gym owner and as a writer. Together with promoter Bernarr Macfadden, Klein convinced many that physical appearance was just as important as physical strength – but with the added benefit of overall good health.

Even though there was still an anti-physique-only element to the world of physical culture, physique contests continued to grow through the 1930s. Competitors still had to perform some sort of athletic event (much the same as lotto winners having to answer a skill-testing question), but the emphasis began to shift so that physical appearance was the primary goal. In 1930 two Mr. America contests were held, including the AAU (American Athletic Union) version, and even though competitors came from varied athletic backgrounds (boxing, judo, wrestling, gymnastics, etc.), it soon became apparent that weightlifters had the advantage.

Bodybuilding's first *real* Mr. America was John Carl Grimek, who took the prestigious title in 1940 and '41. John was the first major bodybuilder who built his physique almost entirely with the aid of weights. Once the word spread, athletes were left with three choices – adopt Grimek's methods, continue on as normal but be outclassed, or give up entirely. Most decided to follow Grimek's lead, and before long physical culture centers (starting to be called *gyms)* were bustling with aspiring Mr. Americas.

THE FIRST SUPERSTARS

If John Grimek was the first true bodybuilder in terms of how he built his physique, then the title of the first *massive* bodybuilder goes to 1943 Mr. America, Clancy Ross. Unlike those who relied on weightlifting to build strength (the great physique just happened to be a side effect), Ross used weights for the sole purpose of

John Grimek

Reg Park

Steve Reeves

Clancy Ross

THE '50s and '60s

The 1950s can be considered a transition period in the history of bodybuilding. Most of the pioneers of the previous two decades had retired from competition and a new generation of bodybuilding stars had emerged. Where previously the emphasis had been on symmetry, such new stars as Reg Park, Bill Pearl and Chuck Sipes brought new meaning to the word *mass*. In fact, Reg was an idol to a young Austrian boy named Arnold Schwarzenegger!

The 1960s witnessed an explosion in bodybuilding stars. Besides the still-competitive Park and Pearl, there were Rick Wayne, Freddy Ortiz, Harold Poole, Dave Draper, Dennis Tinerino, Chet Yorton and Frank Zane. The biggest star of the early to mid-'60s was Larry Scott. In 1965 and 1966 Larry won the sport's first two Mr. Olympia titles. With his Californian good looks and 20-inch arms, he personified the bodybuilding ideal.

Scott was succeeded as Mr. Olympia by a relative newcomer, named Sergio Oliva, who was a refugee from Castro's Cuba. (He defected to the US while representing his country at the 1961 Pan American Games.) With his tiny waist and unheard-of muscle density, Sergio dominated the sport during the late 1960s, winning the Mr. Olympia title from 1967 to 1969.

Oliva's last Mr. O victory deserves mention as it was the first Olympia appearance by the one competitor who would

shaping his body. With his wide shoulders, tiny waist, thick musculature and great definition, he could probably hold his own at a present-day city championship.

Ross was so dominant during the 1940s that he served as inspiration for the next generation of stars, including the one man who brought bodybuilding to the doorstep of the general public – Steve Reeves.

When he walked Muscle Beach, crowds stopped and stared at his every move. Steve Reeves was the first bodybuilder to have mass public appeal, and until his arrival bodybuilding was still a relatively obscure sport. Other than Charles Atlas with his Dynamic Tension course, the general public had little knowledge of the sport or of its practitioners.

Reeves changed all that with his boyish good looks, outstanding physique, and most of all his charismatic personality. After winning both the Mr. America and Mr. Universe titles, he went on to become one of Hollywood's biggest attractions, with starring roles in movies such as *Hercules* and *Thief of Baghdad*.

Bill Pearl

INTRODUCTION – HOW BODYBUILDING CAME TO BE

Arnold
Schwarzenegger

Arnold reigned as king of the sport from 1970 until his retirement in 1975. His domination was so complete that the question asked was not who would win the Olympia, but who would place second!

THE *PUMPING IRON* YEARS

Although he was the dominating personality of body-building in the 1970s, Arnold shared the competitive stage with a host of other great bodybuilders. From Sardinia came Franco Columbu, a 5'5", 185-pound powerhouse. Like Arnold, Franco came to America after dominating the European bodybuilding scene. The two became best friends in Germany, and once Arnold became established in the United States, Franco decided to join him. Besides his bodybuilding titles (including the 1976 and 1981 Mr. Olympias), Franco was recognized as one of the sport's strongest individuals, having won many powerlifting competitions and competed in a number of World's Strongest Man championships.

Franco Columbu

become the sport's most famous star – the "Austrian Oak," Arnold Schwarzenegger.

SHADOW OF AN OAK

Although he placed second to Oliva at the 1969 Mr. Olympia, most in the audience agreed that it was only a matter of time before the "young Austrian kid" would take his place at the top of bodybuilding's hierarchy.

Arnold's competitive career started with his win at the 1965 Junior Mr. Europe competition. Over the next few years he won all the major contests including five Mr. Universe titles. If Arnold's career had a turning point, it was the 1968 Mr. Universe, where he was beaten by a much smaller Frank Zane. Most competitors would have called it quits, but not Arnold. Utilizing the determination that would one day see him conquer Hollywood, Arnold transformed his physique from a massive but smooth 250 pounds to an ultraripped 235 pounds.

Other bodybuilders who made their mark in the 1970s were Boyer Coe, Mike Mentzer, Danny Padilla, Roy Callender, Mike Katz, Albert Beckles, Lou Ferrigno, Ken Waller and Robby Robinson.

THE BIRTH OF *MUSCLEMAG*

From a bodybuilding perspective, one of the more significant events of the early 1970s was the arrival in Canada of a young immigrant named Robert Kennedy. Although he had a secure teaching position at a British arts college, Kennedy felt that life had more to offer. With little more than the shirt on his back and a few dollars in his pocket, Bob left merry old England and headed across the Atlantic.

After taking up residence just outside Toronto, Bob went to work making his dream of establishing an

Frank Zane

Sergio Oliva

Arnold Schwarzenegger

night bodybuilding went from an obscure art form to a legitimate sport.

THE ZANE LOOK

With Arnold retired from competition, bodybuilding's top prize was seemingly within reach of everyone. After winning the event in 1976, Franco Columbu retired and began his very successful chiropractic practice. At the 1977 contest Frank Zane emerged as the winner, and in doing so set the standard for the next three years.

Zane was a perfect example of what an individual could accomplish if he knew his strengths and weaknesses. Realizing that he could never compare in mass with some of the larger opponents, Frank set out to create the world's most balanced, symmetrical and defined physique. And he took the art of posing to new heights. Frank Zane used all of these qualities to capture the Mr. Olympia crown from 1977 to 1979.

THE EARLY 1980s

The 1980s started with much controversy as Arnold Schwarzenegger came out of a five-year retirement to take his seventh Mr. Olympia title. The dispute was not over Arnold's winning so much as *how* he won. Arnold made the comeback after preparing for his first major Hollywood movie, *Conan the Barbarian.* Aside from his decreased mass (down anywhere from 10 to 15 pounds), Arnold's posing was mediocre compared to the routines of his fellow competitors. His deficiencies were highlighted by the outstanding condition of his opponents. The new generation of superstars, led by Mike Mentzer, Boyer Coe and Chris Dickerson, all showed up in the best shape of their lives. Yet, when the final score was in, the Austrian Oak had once again captured the sport's most coveted crown.

international bodybuilding magazine come true. First conceived in 1974, *MuscleMag International* has now grown to be one of the world's largest, and throughout its 20-year history has featured every top star of the sport. As well as publishing this monthly magazine of over 300 pages, Bob has written hundreds of articles relating to bodybuilding, and has also authored (at last count) over 40 books on the subject.

INTO THE LIMELIGHT...

In 1975 two unknown filmmakers, George Butler and Jerome Gary, became part of bodybuilding history when they produced (and Butler directed) a documentary that followed many of the stars through their precontest preparations for the Mr. Universe and Mr. Olympia contests that year. The documentary, called *Pumping Iron,* was based on the 1974 groundbreaking book of the same name that Butler had done with Charles Gaines.

Besides receiving widespread acclaim for its accurate portrayal of a previously little-known sport, this movie featured such stars as Arnold, Franco Columbu, Lou Ferrigno, Ed Corney, Mike Katz and Ken Waller. Prior to *Pumping Iron* most bodybuilding contests were held in school gyms. After its success nothing but the best in contest venues was acceptable. Almost over-

Tom Platz

Chris Dickerson

Samir Bannout

The 1981 Mr. Olympia crown was taken by Franco Columbu, and while many questioned the win of Schwarzenegger in 1980, Franco's 1981 victory created a storm of controversy that is still talked about. Even with new stars such as Chris Dickerson, Tom Platz, Roy Callender and Danny Padilla (all in outstanding shape), Franco Columbu walked away with the Sandow statue. Once again the contention was that a less than worthy winner had stolen the crown.

The Mr. Olympias of 1982 and 1983 were Chris Dickerson and Samir Bannout, respectively. For Dickerson it was the high point of a long career that saw him win more titles than any other bodybuilder in history. After placing second to both Franco and Arnold at the previous Olympias, Chris came close to retiring. But operating on the assumption that lightning couldn't strike a third time, he gave it one more try and was rewarded with the '82 Olympia victory.

In 1983 the O was taken by one of the most perfectly proportioned bodybuilders ever to grace a posing dais. Samir Bannout was born in Lebanon, but like Arnold, Franco and Sergio before him, he decided his future lay in the United States of America. It is interesting to note that the third-place winner in '83 was a relative newcomer named Lee Haney, who, over the next eight years, did what was previously thought impossible. He broke Arnold Schwarzenegger's record of seven Mr. Olympia titles!

A NEW DIRECTION

The early 1980s saw the bodybuilding tree branch out in many new directions. Perhaps the most surprising new element was the creation of women's bodybuilding competitions. Fitness contests for women had long been associated with male bodybuilding events, but it was the emergence of Lisa Lyon that started the change. Unlike previous female contestants, Lyon used weight training to build a muscular physique. Although she was at first considered a curiosity, it wasn't long before others started to copy her training methods.

To address the growing popularity of female bodybuilding, the IFBB instigated the Ms. America and Ms. Olympia contests, and soon female bodybuilding had its own stars, including Rachel McLish (the first Ms. Olympia), Lynn Conkwright, Laura Combes, Stacy Bentley, Georgia Miller Fudge, Carla Dunlap, Shelley Gruwell and Candy Csencsits.

Lisa Lyon

Another major change in the early '80s was the reorganization of the names of IFBB titles. To keep bodybuilding in line with other sports, the once-familiar Mr. and Ms. titles were replaced by "championship" titles. For example, Mr. California became the California Championships, the Mr. America became the US Nationals, and the amateur Mr. Universe became the World Championships. Women's titles changed in the same manner. The only major IFBB titles that kept their old designations were the Ms. and Mr. Olympias, and the Ms. International. We should add that many other bodybuilding federations are still using the old naming system (e.g. NABBA Mr. Universe), and bodybuilders themselves often refer to

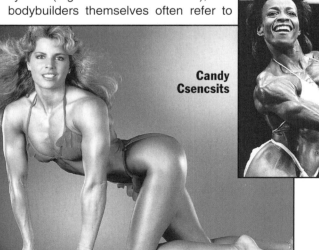

Candy Csencsits

Carla Dunlap

the old titles. Somehow the title of National Championship winner doesn't hold the same aura as Mr. America.

The third major change in the late 1970s and early 1980s was the creation of a Grand Prix circuit. Instead of just one or two major titles up for grabs each year, professionals were given the chance to compete in a number of contests held in both Europe and North America. Each Grand Prix event awarded thousands of dollars in prize money.

BODYBUILDERS SUPREME

After Arnold won his seventh Mr. Olympia title in 1980, most were of the opinion that the Oak's record would never be broken. This attitude began to change in 1983 when Atlanta's 250-pound Lee Haney burst onto the scene. After winning the 1982 Nationals, Lee placed third behind Samir Bannout at the 1983 Mr. Olympia. His assault on Arnold's record began the next year, and by 1991, with eight straight Mr. O wins, he had become the new king of bodybuilding.

Like Schwarzenegger before him, Haney dominated the sport with his own particular combination of size, muscularity and presentation. Other competitors may have had the edge in one category, but no one blended the entire package in the same manner as did Haney.

Lee Labrada

Despite Lee Haney's record run of victories, hungry new contenders were arriving every year. New Jersey's Rich Gaspari quickly developed a reputation for his incredible muscularity and density. Others such as Mike Christian and Berry DeMey rivaled Haney in size, and on numerous occasions forced Big Lee to the limit. Perhaps Haney's greatest challenger was a former Cuban named Lee Labrada.

Nicknamed "Mass With Class," Labrada took a page from Zane's book of strategy and used his 185 pounds to regularly strike fear in the hearts of opponents who outweighed him by as much as 50 pounds. On three separate occasions he took Haney to the limit by placing second at the Mr. Olympia.

CORY'S REIGN

Just as men's bodybuilding was dominated by a single individual, so too was the top female bodybuilding title monopolized for most of the 1980s. Cory Everson's dominance began in 1984 and continued until 1989 when she claimed her sixth straight Ms. Olympia title.

Unlike some female competitors who had carried the degree of muscularity to the extreme, Cory combined the best of both worlds. She had good muscle size and separation, a fantastic posing routine, and yet there was no mistaking Cory for what she was — a beautifully proportioned female bodybuilder.

Six-time Ms.Olympia Cory Everson.

THE NEXT GENERATION

Despite Haney's continued dominance of the sport, by 1990 it was obvious that there was a whole new generation of stars on the horizon. Bodybuilders such as Shawn Ray, Gary Strydom, Vince Comerford, Aaron Baker, Mike Ashley and Vince Taylor began jockeying for position, in line for the throne of Lee Haney. Likewise, Cory Everson's retirement in 1989 left the door wide open for the next generation of female superstars.

As bodybuilding moves through the 1990s, our sport is witnessing some of the greatest physique battles in history. Dorian Yates has picked up where Lee Haney left off.

Standing 5'11" and weighing 265 pounds in contest condition, Britain's first Mr. Olympia has set new standards for muscle size and density. Yates gave a hint of

Eight-time Mr. Olympia Lee Haney.

took the '96 Olympia away from her), Laura Creavalle, Sue Price, Debbie Muggli, Diana Dennis, Sandy Riddell and Yolanda Hughes.

Not to be outdone by other sports, the IFBB inaugurated the Masters Olympia in 1994. This was won by Robby Robinson, and featured such stars as Boyer Coe, Ed Corney, Chris Dickerson, Danny Padilla, Bill Grant and Lou Ferrigno. Sonny Schmidt raised the overall profile of the event by giving Robby a run for his money and taking the title in '95. In 1996 the quality of the contest had been raised yet another notch up the credibility ladder by Vince "The Prince" Taylor's win. By all accounts these competitions were a tremendous success, and no doubt many other former greats will run the Masters gantlet in the future.

FUTURE PERSPECTIVES

With the prize money for professional bodybuilding contests now in the hundreds of thousands of dollars, the sport has seen a virtual avalanche of new competitors. Each year a new crop of hungry young lions emerge on the scene, and with increased numbers has come a whole new set of standards. In their heyday Arnold Schwarzenegger (240 pounds) and Sergio Oliva (230 pounds) were regarded as "mass freaks." Today city and state winners are stepping onstage weighing a ripped 250 pounds.

Six-time Ms. Olympia Lenda Murray.

The new generation of bodybuilding stars– (clockwise) Dorian Yates, Michael Francois and Paul DeMayo.

things to come when he placed second to Lee Haney at the 1991 Mr. O, and since then has added an unheard-of 20 pounds a year to his physique. It seemed there was no upper limit to his development, as each year he showed up larger than the year before, until 1995 when he refined and defined his incredible physique, but kept his bodyweight at 265 pounds.

Nipping closely at Yates's heels are the greatest bodybuilders of all time, the list of which includes Flex Wheeler, Lee Priest, Shawn Ray, Michael Francois, Paul Dillett (all 6'5", 275 pounds of him), Aaron Baker, Kevin Levrone and Vince Taylor.

On the women's front, Lenda Murray has firmly established herself as Cory's successor. With six Ms. Olympia wins to her credit, Lenda is an odds-on favorite to beat Cory's record of six. Lenda has her rivals too, and leading the way are Kim Chizevsky (who

And as for the pros, witness Dorian Yates, Lou Ferrigno, Paul Dillett, Nasser El Sonbaty and Achim Albrecht, all weighing over 260 pounds in contest condition (300-plus pounds in the off-season). As if this were not enough, the next generation promises to be

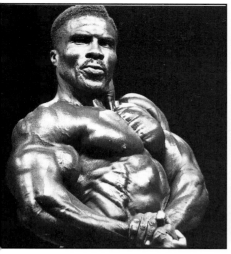

Robby Robinson and Sonny Schmidt

even bigger. For example, 1994 US Nationals champion Paul "Quadzilla" DeMayo weighs over 250 pounds in contest condition while standing just 5'9"!

There are a number of factors contributing to the increase in the size of competitors. First and foremost is the available gene pool. Whereas 30 years ago the only people who took up bodybuilding were those individuals lacking size to begin with, nowadays you have guys strolling into the gym weighing a solid 200 pounds before they even touch a weight. Also, it's a statistical fact that the more people involved in an activity, the greater the genetic selection pool for that particular sport.

A second reason for these bigger bodybuilders is nutritional advancement. Athletes of today have the benefit of the latest nutritional supplements and ergogenic aids. Athletes of 20 years ago depended on protein powders and vitamin tablets. Now there is a multitude of performance and recovery enhancers. One glance through a recent copy of *MuscleMag* will give you some idea of the scope of this billion-dollar-a-year industry.

A final reason for the increased quality of today's and tomorrow's stars is knowledge. In fact, this book illustrates the point quite well. Bodybuilders once had to depend on gym small talk and a few magazine articles to obtain information. Today a visit to the local bookstore shows just how much the situation has changed.

Through the efforts of such individuals as Robert Kennedy, Joe Weider, Arnold Schwarzenegger, Bill Reynolds and Dr. Ellington Darden, the modern bodybuilder has hundreds of books from which to choose. In addition, each month there are eight to 10 top-quality magazines loaded with the latest information on training, nutrition and competition. Instead of spending five to 10 years gathering information, a beginning bodybuilder has such knowledge right at his or her fingertips.

Lou Ferrigno

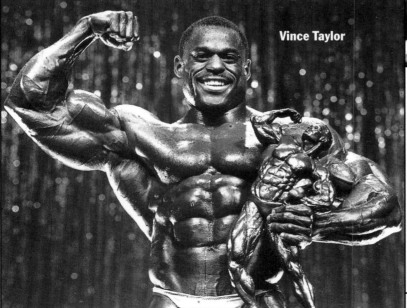

Vince Taylor

A FINAL WORD...

In this chapter we have attempted to give you an idea of bodybuilding's unique history. The sport you have chosen is not some obscure activity that pertains to a select group of individuals. As it stands now, bodybuilding is the fifth most popular sport worldwide. If you train properly, eat correctly and, most importantly, have a champion's dedication, there is a possibility that a few years down the road you too will become part of bodybuilding history. The fact that you are reading this book means you're on the right track.

Achim Albrecht

BOOK ONE

First Reps

1

THE TRUTH ABOUT BODYBUILDING

Joe (left) and Ben Weider (right), shown here with six-time Ms.Olympia Cory Everson, have shaped bodybuilding into the popular sport it is today.

LAYING THE FOUNDATION... IS BODYBUILDING A SPORT?

Perhaps at one time, because of the limited clientele and a lack of organization, bodybuilding technically was not a sport. But through the ongoing efforts of individuals such as the Weider brothers, Joe and Ben, Arnold Schwarzenegger and *MuscleMag's* own Robert Kennedy, bodybuilding is fast becoming one of the world's most popular sports. The Arnold Schwarzenegger Classic and Mr. Olympia contests are regularly covered on ESPN sport networks worldwide, and every year professional bodybuilders win thousands of dollars in prize money.

If bodybuilding is not a sport, then perhaps figure skating and gymnastics are not either. Stop for a moment and think... Athletes from all three disciplines train year round, create routines consisting of a variety of poses set to music, and perform compulsory poses during competition. Winners are chosen by a panel of judges. All three sports are virtually identical in training, organization and competition.

With the recent inclusion of bodybuilding in the Pan American Games, it is only a matter of time before the sport becomes part of the Olympics. Ben Weider and many others will soon have their dream become reality – bodybuilders representing their countries in Olympic competition. Yes, Virginia, there is a Santa Claus... and yes, Virginia, bodybuilding is a sport!

BODYBUILDING MYTHS

"Quite contrary to the stereotypical opinion that most people have of weightlifters – thinking of them as slow, ponderous individuals slowly raising a great weight – well-conditioned weightlifters perform at a speed that must be seen to be appreciated; literally they must do so... the production of much in the way of power is impossible without speed of movement."

– Dr. Arthur Jones
Creator of the Nautilus
line of training machines.

"IT WILL ALL TURN TO FAT!"

If you haven't heard this before, allow us to be the first to warn you! Of all the criticism leveled at bodybuilders, this is the most persistent. It seems many in the general public have a misconception as to what bodybuilding is all about. Muscle cannot turn to fat any more than fat can turn to muscle. If the two were interchangeable, there would be a lot of people out there with great muscle potential – given the number of 45-inch waists around!

We're not sure where this myth originated. It could be that some people, perhaps out of jealousy, take great pride in trying to put bodybuilders down. A more plausible explanation is that some bodybuilders do gain weight when they get older or retire, and there is a biological explanation for this. Our metabolism slows

The awesome Aaron Baker.

down as we age, and this means the body needs fewer calories per day to maintain itself. Unfortunately most people don't reduce their caloric intake to compensate for this slowdown and the end result is a buildup around the midsection.

Closely related to this reasoning is the fact that bodybuilders, in hard training, develop huge appetites. This is not a problem while they're working out, but if their intake stays the same, as soon as training volume is reduced, the unburned calories get stored as fat.

The end product in either case is overweight body-builders. The excess fat was gained in the normal manner – too many calories! Their muscles did not turn to fat and yours will not either.

"THESE PEOPLE LOOK STRONG, BUT THEY'RE NOT!"

Another misconception is that bodybuilders are show-pieces – they may *look* herculean, but they are not very strong at all. This myth may have developed because bodybuilders never performed feats of strength in public as did Soviet weightlifters and overweight strongmen. Even the best boxers (with a few exceptions) did not have well-developed physiques. The muscular bodybuilders who stepped onstage, flexing to the sound of music, were perceived by the general public to be human trophies with few positive attributes.

Rest assured that this myth has been all but dispelled over the past 20 years or so. Now virtually every boxer stepping into the ring has a muscular physique. Powerlifters and Olympic lifters no longer appear fat and overweight. In fact, many have physiques that rival the best bodybuilders.

Finally, be it known that top bodybuilding superstars – Dorian Yates, Kevin Levrone, Flex Wheeler, Michael Francois, Chris Cormier, etc. – have the brute strength to train with poundages that would make any person cringe.

"BODYBUILDERS ARE ALL MUSCLEBOUND AND HAVE NO FLEXIBILITY!"

While it is true that one or two of the sport's larger specimens may have trouble combing their hair, most bodybuilders are no more or less flexible than the average person. Flexibility is just a measure of the range of motion of a joint. Having large muscles does not hinder movement. A well-exercised muscle will in fact *enhance* movement. True, most bodybuilders cannot do the splits, but neither can the average nonbodybuilder. If you train for greater flexibility, then you will

develop it. The presence or absence of muscles makes little difference.

Perhaps the greatest endorsement for bodybuilding comes from those who were once its most vocal foes – athletic coaches. For years coaches had forbidden their athletes to undertake a program of weight training. They subscribed to the old adage that weights would slow you down. How things have changed! Few boxers these days train without the benefit of a weight-training coach. (Evander Holyfield regularly trained with eight-time Mr. Olympia Lee Haney.) Mike Weaver would not have looked out of place in a bodybuilding contest. Even George Foreman, who gets the occasional tease about his weight, sports 20-inch-plus muscular arms. Other sports such as football, hockey and even basketball make regular use of weight training. Suffice it to say that bodybuilding won't make you musclebound or slow you down. On the contrary nothing moves like a well-conditioned physique.

"THEY LOOK GROSS!"

This statement may be myth or fact, depending on your taste. Some people find highly defined muscles and prominent veins a turn-off. It's interesting to note, however, that the most popular movie stars sport muscular physiques. From Arnold Schwarzenegger and Steven Seagal, to Jean-Claude Van Damme and Sylvester Stallone, they all show the results of many years in the gym. If muscles are a turn-off, why do these actors make it a point to regularly remove their shirts at the drop of a hat in their movies? Why? Because their physiques are a major drawing card. Still for many, no amount of persuasion will change their opinion. Nevertheless, the muscular look is fast replacing the soft look.

To dispel the myth that bodybuilders are not flexible, one need look no further than Flex Wheeler!

Before performing a heavy set of side lateral dumbell raises, as shown, Mike Francois makes sure he properly warms up.

Start

Finish

"TRAINING WITH WEIGHTS WILL MAKE WOMEN LOOK LIKE MEN."

One of the major concerns of women who take up weight training is the issue of becoming too masculine. After seeing a female bodybuilder who sports 17-inch muscular arms, many women feel it's just a matter of a few biceps curls and look out – 20-inch arms and a part in Arnold's next movie!

For those females reading this book, let us state here and now that it is impossible for women to develop the same degree of muscle mass as men. Female biochemistry just doesn't allow it. The extremely muscular females sometimes seen in bodybuilding contests are the result of anabolic steroid use – drugs that mimic the actions of the hormone testosterone. In effect, these women are changing their body chemistry from female to male. Unfortunately, besides the extra muscle mass, such nasty side effects as facial hair, a deepened voice and an enlarged clitoris may develop.

Our purpose here is not to promote or condemn anabolic steroid use (we will address this topic in more detail in the chapter on anabolic steroids), but to reassure female weight trainers that a few months or years of bodybuilding will not turn them into Schwarzenegger.

SAFETY...

Before looking at the actual bodybuilding principles and techniques, we must first lay out the ground rules concerning safety in the gym. In preparing this text, we have taken every measure to ensure that your training is as safe as possible. But no matter how many safety rules we outline, conduct in the gym is ultimately *your* responsibility.

The following is not an all-encompassing list of rules. It's merely a guide for reducing the chances of serious injury. The better gyms will have most of these (plus others) posted on the wall. Please follow them.

SAFETY RULES FOR PROPER GYM CONDUCT

1. Always warm up. Most injuries are the result of jumping to heavy poundages too quickly. A warm muscle is more flexible and pliable. A warmup will take only a few minutes, but it can save you a lifetime of pain.
2. Use a spotter. Where necessary, have someone (called a spotter) stand behind you to provide quick assistance with the weight you're lifting. A number of bodybuilders have been found dead under a barbell after attempting heavy bench presses alone. Squats are another exercise in which a spotter is an absolute necessity. You will not need a spot (for safety reasons) when using dumbells or machines. Most machines are designed with safety in mind – it's just a matter of releasing your grip if you get into trouble. (The one possible exception is the Smith machine.) Always use a spotter when performing any exercise in which you may end up pinned beneath the bar.
3. Use collars on all barbells. Even with the best of form most bodybuilders move the bar on a slight angle (i.e. one side lower than the other). If you forget the collars, the plates on the lower end may fall off. The

plates on the other end will then wrench the bar in your hand, and they too will fall off. This violent twisting can pull tendons, tear muscles, and even break bones. So remember, always use collars!

4. Use a weightlifting belt. The human spine was not designed to have heavy loads placed on it. Many of the basic bodybuilding exercises play havoc with the lower back. A wide, tight-fitting belt secures the muscles and bones of the lower back, thus helping to prevent serious injury. Always wear a belt on such exercises as squats, deadlifts, rowing and various pressing movements.

5. Put your weights back when finished. This rule will be rigidly enforced by gym employees. It's very dangerous to have plates and dumbells strewn about the gym floor. Sooner or later someone will trip and fall. If that person happens to be under a barbell at the time, the outcome could be grievous. When finished with your equipment, return it to the correct location. Not only is it good gym etiquette, but more importantly, you are helping to prevent accidents.

6. When unsure of an exercise, ask someone. Most gym instructors are very knowledgeable about exercise technique. If one is not available, consult another experienced gym member. Just about every exercise you'll ever perform is described in this text. If you are trying something new, read the relevant section in this book beforehand. You might want to put a copy in your gym bag (make sure your gym locker is secure) for quick reference.

7. Follow good exercise style. It's no good to read about proper exercise form and then train in a haphazard fashion. Perform all exercises according to the biomechanical technique described in this text. This will not only help prevent injuries, but also ensure you get the most from your efforts.

8. Where applicable, use weight racks. It will only be a matter of time before you are performing such exercises as squats and bench presses with hundreds of pounds. If you lose control, a catch rack will prevent the weight from crashing down on you. Many squat racks have a series of pins arranged in a graded fashion. No matter at what point in the exercise you get in trouble, there will be a set of support pins at that height.

9. Dress appropriately. If it is midsummer, don't wear two or three sweat shirts. This will only speed up water loss, possibly leading to dehydration. The opposite applies as well. A T-shirt and shorts are not sufficient for most winter temperatures. A cold muscle is more susceptible to injury.

With the possible exception of calf raises, wear some sort of footwear during all exercises. Many leg exercises (e.g. leg presses and squats) place tremendous stress on the foot region. A good sturdy sneaker will help support the small bones and muscles of this area.

There is a less obvious but equally important reason for wearing footwear. In a typical workout you will handle dozens if not hundreds of plates. Sooner or later you will drop one. It's nice to have a protective layer between the plate and your foot. A 45-pound plate dropped from an average height of two to three feet can do serious damage. At the very least it will cut the skin, but in all probability it will break the foot. Granted, a sneaker will not provide immunity, but it will reduce the injury.

10. Learn everything you can about bodybuilding. This may seem redundant, but it's a fact that the more you know, the less likely you are to incur a serious injury. Pay special attention to biomechanics and kinesiology. Obtain as many books as possible on exercise form. Read as much biochemistry (nutrition and supplementation) as you can handle. Finally, every issue of *MuscleMag International* provides valuable advice for making your workouts safer and more beneficial. Either take out a subscription or check the newsstand every month. You can never have too much good information.

11. Have a medical checkup before beginning bodybuilding. An athletic 20-year-old may not need a stress test, but individuals living a sedentary lifestyle over the past few years should definitely consult their physician before training, especially if there is a history of stroke or heart disease in the family.

Also, if your family background has a high incidence of stroke, avoid such exercises as lying vertical leg presses. These movements cause a great pressure buildup in the head region and could lead to medical problems.

Dave Fisher hitting a most-muscular pose.

WHAT CAN BODYBUILDING LEAD TO?

The monstrous Victor Richards

HOW FAR?

"I've done the best that I could possibly do with my genetics, and that's what success in this sport is all about."
— *Sonny Schmidt*
IFBB Professional Bodybuilder

One of the advantages of bodybuilding is that programs can be tailored to meet individual goals. Most people who start training don't want to be Mr. Olympia. In fact, most competitive bodybuilders will admit they never intended to enter contests. Only after the iron bug had bitten did competing enter their minds.

How far you want to go in the sport depends on your personal goals. If you're like 90 percent of bodybuilders, you want to lose a few pounds, reshape your body and improve your overall level of fitness. In

other words, competition does not enter into your scheme of things. Keep in mind that as your physique changes and compliments start coming your way (and they certainly will), competitive bodybuilding may suddenly seem to be a realistic pursuit. If you have the genetics, have trained diligently and followed a well-balanced diet, it's only a matter of time before you're up onstage displaying your physique to an enthusiastic audience.

For many of you bodybuilding will be a means to improve performance in other sports. Wrestlers, boxers and judoists all require a combination of speed and power to be successful. Others, such as rowers and cyclists, also find regular weight training to be a great asset.

Whether you intend to compete someday or just want to add a few inches to your chest (you might as well add a few inches to the rest of your body also), you will find all the required information within the covers of this encyclopedia.

GENETICS

"I'm different from any bodybuilder of the past or present. People can tell the difference between me and the bodybuilders who hold the greatest titles. I don't need a title to prove that I'm one of the top bodybuilders in the world."
— *Victor Richards*
IFBB Professional Bodybuilder

You can change the weight on the barbell, your brand of amino acids and even the color of your hair, but there is nothing you can do to alter the hand that fate has dealt you. In simple terms, from the moment of conception your genetics were determined. As you begin to spend more time in the gym, it will become evident that people progress at different rates. Some will pack on 20 to 30 pounds of muscle in a few short months. Others will need years of training to accomplish the same gains. Even between individual bodyparts there is variation. You may get your lower chest to grow by simply looking at a barbell, while the upper chest can be pounded with everything in your training arsenal, yet stubbornly refuse to improve. Tom Platz developed what are considered the greatest thighs in bodybuilding history, but his upper body lagged behind. As a group, many African-Americans have poor calf development, despite many years of blasting them with calf raises. Conversely, some of the greatest calves, in bodybuilding history belong to African-Americans. Witness the calves on Flex Wheeler, Chris Dickerson and Vince Taylor.

A PERSONAL THING

"Well, yeah, he's a muscular guy. He's about my height and pretty muscular. He looked big enough to me when I was young to keep me in line." **– Henderson Thorne IFBB Professional Bodybuilder (commenting on his father's genetics)**

In comparing bodybuilding's top stars, we see that no two physiques are identical. All have outstanding development, but most have bodyparts that are their own trademarks. Casey Viator could never compare abdominals with Serge Nubret, but conversely, Serge's thighs were never in the same league as Casey's massive quadriceps. Sergio Oliva's rear double-biceps shot is in a class of its own. Arnold's one-arm biceps pose has yet to be duplicated. (Check the cover of *Arnold: The Education of a Bodybuilder.*) The most-muscular pose is best demonstrated by Lou Ferrigno.

Cory Everson

Henderson Thorne

While other bodybuilders do look excellent from these angles, the above individuals have physiques that best typify these poses.

Genetics is the science that looks at heredity, or how characteristic traits are passed from generation to generation. Remember Aunt Matilda saying when you were a kid, "Oh my gracious, doesn't he look just like his father?" ...or your grandmother saying, "She has her mother's eyes." Perhaps those comparisons were annoying at the time, but what your well-intentioned relatives were implying was that you "took after" one parent more than the other – some of that parent's genetics were very visible in you.

Genetics can be both beneficial and detrimental. If you come from a family that has a high incidence of cancer, you are at greater risk for developing the disease than someone whose family has a low incidence. That doesn't mean that you *will* get cancer, only that you have a higher chance of developing it. Likewise, if most of your relatives live into their 80s and 90s, then the odds are you'll be dancing at your grandchild's wedding!

"I believe my small joints also add to the appearance of my thighs… If you were to examine the top female bodybuilders with thick thighs, you would notice that many of them have large knee joints."

**– Cory Everson
Six-time Ms. Olympia**

What has all this to do with bodybuilding? Generally speaking, there is a direct relationship between skeleton size and the amount of muscle mass that can be carried. A small-boned individual will probably never carry the same amount of muscle mass as would his or her large-boned counterpart. Look at the contest pictures in a recent copy of *MuscleMag International*. Two bodybuilders of the same height may appear to have a difference in bodyweight of 20 to 30 pounds.

While bones are not the only factor determining muscle size, they are a good indicator. Many authorities of our sport, including Robert Kennedy, have suggested that wrist circumference is indicative of upper-arm size. On average, an individual can expect to develop an upper arm that measures about 10 inches greater than his wrist. For example, a seven-inch wrist will probably lead to a 17-inch arm, but it is highly unlikely that 20-inch arms will be developed on a frame with six-inch wrists. This is not gospel, however, a few bodybuilders (such as Serge Nubret) have developed 20-plus-inch arms with wrists measuring only seven inches. So, even if you have small bones, don't despair!

There is one advantage to having small bones. Nothing looks as impressive as large, full muscles separated by small joints. Many large-boned bodybuilders have that chunky appearance, whereas their smaller-boned colleagues exhibit far better symmetry and proportion.

Another genetic factor that influences your potential is the number of muscle cells contained in a particular muscle. The scientific community generally accepts that individuals are born with a fixed number of muscle

The phenomenal Shawn Ray.

cells, this figure remaining relatively constant over a lifetime. Working out in the gym is not believed to increase the number of muscle fibers, only their size. (We say *believed* because the most recent research suggests that very strenuous activity may split individual muscle fibers.) All things being equal, a person with 200 million muscle cells will develop a larger arm than someone with 100 million muscle cells. This is a very crude analogy as there are many factors that influence muscle growth.

Many of us have seen guys walk into the gym sporting 17-inch arms and yet they've never picked up a barbell in their life. We remark that they're *naturally* well built. No doubt they were blessed with an abundance of muscle cells and, if they remain devoted to their training, in the future may even grace the cover of *MuscleMag International* or some other bodybuilding magazine.

Besides bones and muscle cells, hormone levels are a third factor that may influence muscle-building potential. (See section on bodybuilding biology.) A direct relationship exists between the level of circulating testosterone (male sex hormone) and muscle size. On average, men are bigger and stronger than women because their bodies contain higher levels of testosterone. A male with an overabundance of it will make faster and greater gains than an individual with a lower testosterone level.

In addition to the physiological benefits, testosterone often produces higher aggression levels. Instead of lifting the weights, some guys *attack* them. (The increased aggression levels of anabolic steroid users is one of the side effects of these testosterone-mimicking drugs.) Greater training intensity leads to heavier weights lifted, which in turn leads to greater gains in muscle size and strength.

Recent research suggests that heavy exercises like squats and deadlifts boost natural testosterone production. This is one reason why bodybuilders who make these exercises the mainstay of their workouts show greater gains than those who rely solely on isolation movements.

BEING REALISTIC
Although most people don't like to admit it, genetics do play a major role in the quality of physique you can develop, placing limits on what's achievable in competitive bodybuilding. The bad news is that no matter how much training or dieting is involved, a muscular 240-pound physique is out of reach for most bodybuilders. The good news is that everyone – we repeat, *everyone* – can make tremendous gains in muscle size, strength and level of fitness. Don't let anyone tell you otherwise. Genetics may set your limitations, but we feel safe in saying that no one has yet reached his or her full genetic capability. Who are we to assert that you will never walk on an Olympia stage? Many of today's top stars weren't blessed with great genetics, but with intelligent training and dieting they have proved their doubters wrong.

BODY TYPES
Closely related to genetics is the topic of somatotypes. One method of classifying body types is to use Dr.

William Herbert Sheldon's three-category system. By photographing 46,000 men and women, Sheldon came up with 88 distinct categories, calling them somatotypes. For simplicity he proposed grouping these types into three major categories – ectomorph, mesomorph and endomorph.

The ectomorph is characterized by long thin bones. Ectomorphs tend to be taller than persons of the other two categories. Because of their low levels of bodyfat, ectomorphs are routinely described as *skinny*.

Mesomorphs have a greater than average rate of muscle growth. With their large bones and low fat levels, mesomorphs have wide shoulders and small waists.

Endomorphs, perhaps the type most commonly seen in today's society, have relatively more fat cells than the other two groups. They appear rounded and shorter in stature.

It would be nice and convenient if we all fit neatly into one of these categories. Unfortunately we don't, and most individuals are a combination of all three. Taking this fact into account, Sheldon devised a scale to rank the dominance of each somatotype. Within each of the three major divisions, there are seven degrees of dominance; therefore, the scale ranges from one to seven, with seven being dominant. For example, a person with ectomorphic 1, mesomorphic 5, and endomorphic 4 would be endo-mesomorphic, a muscular type with a moderate amount of bodyfat. Someone who was ectomorphic 5, mesomorphic 3 and endomorphic 1 would be ecto-mesomorphic, a lean individual who has trouble gaining muscle mass.

Although other factors play a role, the following generalizations can be made:

Ectomorphs – As ectomorphs have trouble gaining muscle mass, we suggest they keep workouts short. Perform basic exercises only, with an emphasis on low-rep sets of 6 to 8. If at all possible avoid aerobics. A couple of 20-minute sessions a week would probably not hurt, but calories should be saved for building muscle tissue. When a decent amount of muscle mass has been gained, start adding the occasional run or swim.

As for nutrition, ectomorphs can pay the least attention to diet and get away with it – at least from the point of view of gaining fat. Optimum nutrition, however, is still needed to gain quality muscle mass. Because of high metabolism, ectomorphs burn calories at a very fast rate, so when offered a second piece of meatloaf, take it! As well, supplement meals with a good protein drink.

Endomorphs – With their tendency towards fat storage, endomorphs should keep the rep range high and the time between sets low. This approach helps burn off excess calories.

Unlike ectomorphs, endomorphs have no problem finding calories to work with. On the contrary, they have too many! To combat this excess, add an aerobic exercise such as swimming or jogging two or three times per week.

Endomorphs would be wise to modify eating patterns, keeping fat intake as low as possible. Simple sugars should be avoided. Keep calorie intake low and don't be afraid to leave the table slightly hungry. This way the body will rely on stored fat as an energy source.

Mesomorphs – Ah, the lucky devils! With their capacity for developing muscle tissue, and ability to keep fat levels low, this group is the most suited of the three for bodybuilding. These individuals can handle the long, intense workouts necessary for building a championship physique. For maximum effect mesomorphs can combine a variety of exercises in their training routine.

No matter what your somatotype, you can achieve great results with a regular training program combined with a well-balanced diet.

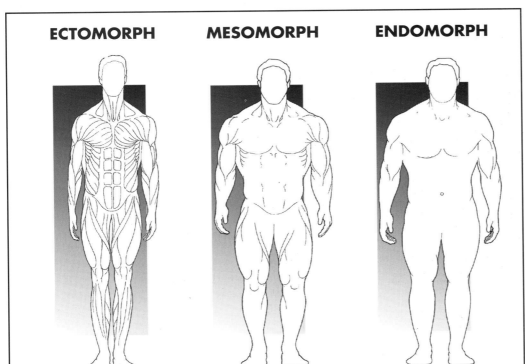

ECTOMORPH   MESOMORPH   ENDOMORPH

Germany's Andreas Munzer was a classic ecto-mesomorph.

activity you can choose, but merely helps guide you to those which are more suited to your body type. The following table lists the three somatotypes and various sports applicable to each. To reach the top in any of the following sports, you probably need to fit predominantly into one somatotype, but only in the extreme case (i.e. championship level). The average person should not feel limited to these suggestions. In fact, engaging in sports that are mainly applicable to other somatotypes could be beneficial as you are ensuring that your muscles are worked from many different angles.

ENDOMORPH:	MESOMORPH:	ECTOMORPH:
Wrestling	Judo	Volleyball
Rowing	Swimming	Running
Powerlifting	Sprinting	Basketball
Bodybuilding	Bodybuilding	Bodybuilding

We must point out that the foregoing table is a generalization. There have been outstanding basketball players who were mesomorphs, and many powerlifting records have been achieved by ectomorphs.

You will notice that we have included bodybuilding under all three categories. This is because there have been champion bodybuilders from all three somatotypes.

Here is a final word on somatotypes. Don't despair if you are an ectomorph or endomorph. Most of the top bodybuilders have characteristics of all three groups. Dorian Yates would fall into the endo-mesomorph category, while Andreas Munzer is a classic ecto-mesomorph. Even the greats like Lee Haney and Schwarzenegger have ectomorphic attributes (long limbs, tendency to leanness). No matter what your somatotype, a regular training program, when combined with a well-balanced diet, will provide greater results than any "2-5-4" classification!

DO I HAVE WHAT IT TAKES?

Do you think you have what it takes to reach the top of the competitive bodybuilding ladder? The following list of prerequisites (edited and condensed for this book) was compiled by *MuscleMag* writer, consultant and former editor, Greg Zulak. It outlines the characteristics that are necessary to become a top bodybuilder.

1. Structure and Frame – The ideal structure for the competitive bodybuilder is the X-frame – wide shoulders, narrow hips, a small waist and a great V-taper. Such superstars as Lee Haney, Lenda Murray, Brian Buchanan and Cory Everson all have outstanding V-tapers. The reverse of an X-frame is the thick-waisted, narrow-shouldered bodybuilder who shows little V-taper and is less aesthetically pleasing to the eye when compared to X-framed bodybuilders.

2. Ideal Muscle Shape – Do your muscles have pleasing lines and shape? Are your biceps full and peaked? Are your lats long and wide? Are your triceps long and horseshoe-shaped? Are your calves full and diamond-shaped? Do your thighs have sweep and flare?

In order to best take advantage of the great muscle-building potential, mesomorphs should follow a balanced diet supplemented with protein and multi-vitamins.

IS IT ANY USE?

Of what use is somatotyping to bodybuilders? Certainly one's body type should figure into one's goals, but there is much more to bodybuilding success than a grab bag of genes. Desire and personality are the real indicators of achievement. Other factors such as nutrition and metabolism are also important.

Determining body type is relatively easy. A quick glance in the mirror gives your first indication. Do you have wide or narrow shoulders? Do you have an excess of fat? Are your bones relatively thick or thin? Your answers will give you a general feeling for body type.

Besides influencing training and eating habits, body type can also be used as a guide for choosing various sports. That doesn't mean you are limited in the type of

3. Joint Size – Are your ankles, knees and elbows small? Do your muscles dwarf your joints, or do your joints overshadow your muscle development?

4. Muscle Size and Mass – Every competitive bodybuilder needs plenty of size and mass that is evenly distributed over the body. Granted, this will be related to height and bone structure, but the following generalizations can be made: Any bodybuilder over 5'8" who doesn't weigh at least 200 pounds in contest condition, does not have arms in the range of 18 to 19 inches, a chest of at least 50 inches, thighs in the 27-inch range, and 18-inch calves, will probably never win a major contest. In the modern bodybuilding arena, only those sporting the best combination of size, muscularity and shape will take home the winner's trophy.

5. Symmetry, Balance and Proportion – From top to bottom and from side to side your body must be developed evenly and be well balanced. Your calves must be in proper proportion with your arms and neck, and your thighs in balance with your torso. Everything should flow and look pleasing and graceful. One bodypart should not stand out from the others. Every muscle must be in proportion.

6. Long Muscle Bellies and Full Muscle Insertions – Once again, this requirement is related to structure and shape. Is there a large gap between your lower biceps and your elbow, or does your biceps extend the full length of your upper arm? And likewise, do you have high lats, short triceps and high calves? For bodybuilding success your muscles should be long and full.

7. Muscular Definition – All things being equal, the bodybuilder with the least amount of bodyfat will win. You will be at a serious disadvantage if you have difficulty losing fat and your muscles don't display veins and striations. A few bodybuilders do become champions while neglecting their diets, but the vast majority must be diligent to reach contest condition.

8. Vascularity – By this we mean how well the veins stand out under the skin. Vascularity is related to definition in that you must have a low level of bodyfat for veins to be seen. For some, no matter how defined, few veins are visible. Others start displaying veins weeks before a contest. (A few genetically gifted bodybuilders have this appearance year round!) Vascularity is not essential to winning, but in today's competitive realm, it may be the difference between first and second place.

9. Muscle Separation – This quality is also closely related to definition. Muscles tend to be not one large belly, but many smaller subunits. Notice the split in Boyer Coe's biceps, the freakiness in Paul Dillett's deltoids, the cross-striations in the triceps of Andreas Munzer, the separation in Dorian Yates's quadriceps. All these bodybuilders have physiques displaying deep

Three of the greatest female bodybuilders ever – Laura Creavalle, Kim Chizevsky and Debbie Muggli.

muscle cuts and great separation. To be competitive your muscles should not appear as one large mass. They must show clear lines of separation between them. The heads of the individual muscles should also stand out. All three triceps heads should be visible. The thighs should be seen as four distinct muscles – not one large lump. Muscle separation is one of the areas in which a bodybuilder of small stature can hold his own against a much larger opponent.

10. Muscle Density – Only years of heavy training will build muscles with a thick, dense look. One of the disadvantages of relying on anabolic steroids is that they give muscles a soft, bloated look. A solid foundation is essential to give your physique that rock-hard, muscular appearance.

11. High Energy Levels – Reaching the top in the bodybuilding world requires thousands of high-energy workouts. Only those with the stamina to undertake this perilous journey will stand on the victor's podium. The typical champion bodybuilder must be able to undergo two to four hours of training, four to six days a week. During the contest season these workouts must be performed while on a calorie-reduced diet. To compound the situation, often three 30-minute aerobic workouts are included in the regimen each week. Enormous amounts of energy are needed to maintain such a rigorous schedule.

12. Natural Strength Levels – Most (if not all) of today's top bodybuilders are immensely strong. All can bench press over 400, squat over 500, and curl 200-plus pounds. Heavy weight builds mass and density. If, from day one, you could hold your own with bodybuilders who have trained for years, the odds are good to excellent that you have the potential to build a large, muscular physique. Although there are some exceptions, light weights will usually not build a championship physique.

13. Metabolism – Are you able to consistently eat appropriate volumes of nutritious food and not have digestive problems? Are you inclined to gain muscle mass and not fat? All the top bodybuilders can answer yes to these questions. So must you… if you wish to become a professional.

14. High Pain Threshold – To stimulate maximum muscle growth you *must* be able to carry your sets to the pain barrier. All top bodybuilders shut out the pain and train their muscles to the max. If you can't handle aching, burning muscles, forget becoming a champ.

15. A Strong Constitution – Does your lifestyle reflect your desire to be a champion bodybuilder? Do you consistently make excuses to miss workouts or do your workouts take priority over everything else? While bodybuilding should not be an obsession, reaching the top will mean total dedication. You must stick to your diet and avoid junk food. Champions are not lazy bodybuilders. Workouts should be missed for only the most serious of reasons (illnesses, family responsibility, etc.).

The champs may have the occasional lethargic day, but in the overall scheme of things, bodybuilding is their focus in life.

16. Positive Mental Attitude – All champion bodybuilders have the ability to greatly improve and reach new goals. Negative thoughts seldom enter their minds. Do you find it easy to focus on training or would you prefer to be doing something else? You can't reach the top with a half-hearted approach – it takes 100 percent all the time, every time.

Lee "Mass with Class" Labrada personifies perfect proportion.

CONCLUSION

The issue of genetics is complex and complicated. You will never know your genetic potential until you start to train, and even then you will never reach your maximum potential. Some individuals who started out with what appeared to be limited genetics went on to bodybuilding greatness. Others who seemed destined for the Olympia stage peaked after four or five years and have never been heard of since.

After years of constant training, adequate nutrition, and proper rest, you may come to the conclusion that your potential falls in the range of average. You will have some outstanding qualities (excellent muscle size, fast recovery time) and some not-so-great attributes (poor definition, weak symmetry). You may be able to compare chests with a recent state or provincial champion, but your leg development is two or three years behind.

You may also realize that, while your potential is high, practical matters make attainment virtually impossible. Maybe your job limits the amount of time available for training. Perhaps weak joints, nagging injuries or recurring tendonitis prevents the type of consistent training necessary to achieve a championship physique.

After realistically assessing your potential as average, should you discontinue training? Absolutely not! For starters, your assessment may be wrong. How many potential bodybuilding superstars gave up because they (or someone else) felt they had no future in the sport? Plenty. If you give up training, an integral part of your life will be lost. Your social life is reduced, your health and fitness levels are impeded, and – perhaps more importantly – you will never know just how far you could have gone.

There are a few guidelines to follow if you feel your genetic ability is limited. By following these guidelines you may find your potential is in fact *unlimited!*

Don't make bodybuilding your whole life. Of all the bodybuilders training worldwide (the figure is in the millions), only a few hundred make their living from the sport, and for most of these the real money is not from winning contests (i.e. prize money), but from doing seminars and posing exhibitions. Try devoting some of your energy to furthering your education. This will make a far greater impact on your life than spending hours in a gym. Trust us on that. If you have outstanding genetics, they will come through no matter what.

Unless you have a superfast recovery system, limit your workouts to about an hour a day, three or four times a week. Granted, training is fun, but too much can be counterproductive. Try to make training as productive as possible. Performing the same routine months (or even years) on end is, for the most part, boring! Of course, if it continually brings results and you like doing the same routine for extended periods of time, then keep going. Who are we to tell you to change a system that works?

As a final note, even if your genetics are limited, your ability to learn is not. Absorb everything you can about the sport. Instead of a case of beer (about $15), pick up the latest bodybuilding book (also about $15). Try to assemble a library of information. Perhaps your problem is not so much a case of limited genetics as limited knowledge. Finally, avoid drugs (anabolic steroids) that promise you wondrous results. All the drugs in the world will not turn you into Mr. Olympia. At the most they will give you about 10 to 20 percent improvement. This edge may be needed at the elite level, but for the average person the risks (acne, increased aggression levels, endocrine problems, etc.) outweigh the possible benefits.

Lee Haney being congratulated by **IFBB** president **Ben Weider** on another Olympia victory. Lee won the Mr. Olympia title for a record eight consecutive years. (1984–1991).

EVERYTHING YOU NEED TO KNOW

Sandy Riddell

BODYBUILDING 101

"When I began training a little more than 10 years ago, I immediately knew that bodybuilding was for me. I read as much as I could about training, nutrition and anything else that would help me succeed as a bodybuilder. Once I found the things that interested me, I'd give them a try in the gym. Through a lot of trial and error I found the training system and diet that worked best for me."
– Dorian Yates, Five-time Mr. Olympia

Bodybuilding is no different from other sports – it too has its own language. Just as tennis has *serves* and *love,* bodybuilding has *sets* and *reps.* Where baseball players talk of *steals* and *RBIs,* bodybuilders discuss *pre-exhaustion* and obtaining the *ripped look.* Over the years every sport, including bodybuilding, has evolved to have its own lingo. Some of the terms in this chapter may seem like a foreign language at first, but don't be alarmed. We will explain each term in an easy-to-comprehend manner. The training programs that follow assume a general knowledge of the basic bodybuilding

terms. So sit back, have your favorite energizer drink close by, and let's improve your vocab!

SETS AND REPS

Go into any gym and no doubt the most commonly heard words will be *sets* and *reps.* No other words are as fundamental to the foundation of bodybuilding.

The word *rep* is an abbreviation for *repetition,* and one rep is one complete movement of a particular exercise. For example, if you are doing bench presses, one rep would involve taking the bar (or handle of the machine) from the rack, lowering it in a controlled manner to the chest, and then pushing it back to the starting position. That entire movement is called a *rep.* Bodybuilders seldom do one rep of an exercise. Usually reps are grouped together in bunches of 6, 8, 10 or more. A group of consecutive reps is called a *set.* If you perform 10 consecutive reps without stopping, you have performed one set of 10 reps. (We'll look at sets in more detail later in the chapter.)

REPS – HOW MANY?

"You just haven't lived until you try doing 4 to 6 sets of 100 reps in various quadriceps and hamstring exercises." **– Diana Dennis, top Pro Bodybuilder**

If you were to draw up a list of the most frequently asked bodybuilding questions, there's no doubt that *How many reps should I do?* would fall at or near the top. It seems just about every bodybuilder is looking for that magical rep range that will put the most muscle mass on over the shortest period of time. Even experienced bodybuilders find themselves frequently questioning their rep ranges. It would be nice if we had all the answers, but bodybuilding is not that simple.

"For the best results you should train holistically. This means that for each bodypart you should do sets of high reps with light weight, medium reps with medium weight, and low reps with heavy weight. This is the only way you can definitely obtain optimum all-round muscular development."
– Albert "The Ageless Wonder" Beckles IFBB Professional, former Mr. Universe

There are three broad categories of rep ranges – those for building muscle mass, those for muscular shape and definition, and those for strength. Unfortunately there is no rep range that will produce maximum gains in all three categories at once. You must decide what aspect of bodybuilding you want to focus on.

Most bodybuilders (especially powerlifters) find that low reps are best for increasing muscular strength. For

One of bodybuilding's greats – Albert Beckles.

HIT THE PEAK

AL BECKLES

example, 5 to 7 reps seems optimal for the lower back and legs, while the upper body can be trained effectively with 3 to 5 reps.

Professional bodybuilder turned fitness competitor, Sharon Bruneau.

If muscle mass is the desired goal (most bodybuilders fall into this category), then 6 to 8 reps is considered the norm. Anything above 10 to 12 reps is reserved for precontest training when improving shape and separation is the main concern.

Finally, there may be times when maintaining muscle mass is the desired goal (e.g. on vacation, during exams). Reps in the 12 to 15 range would then be appropriate, although the lower body would be trained using higher reps (20 to 25).

Please understand that these rep ranges are averages. There is much variation to be found in the bodybuilding world. Many, such as Canada's Nimrod King, find high reps best for gaining muscle mass. Others find they get all the shape and hardness they need from their diet, so high reps are seldom performed.

Although there is no magic number, we suggest that beginners follow a slightly higher rep range – somewhere between 10 and 15 reps. The higher reps necessitate the use of less weight, which in turn means less chance of injury and more attention to correct form. After a few months you can proportionately increase the weight and decrease the reps.

For all the exercise routines presented in this book we have set down the number of reps you should perform. As time moves on, and you become more in tune with your body, you'll discover what rep range works best for you. For now, follow the rep ranges outlined within, at least until you have a good foundation under your weightlifting belt. (A little bodybuilding humor. Very little!) After a few months you can start experimenting with your own program.

STRICT REPS

"Form is very important. Anyone can go into the gym and lift a weight. The trick is using the proper form to make your muscles give you the results you want. Keeping the motion slow and controlled is essential for feeling the muscle work."
– Sharon Bruneau
Canadian Pro Bodybuilder

The most basic form of rep performance is what is called *strict reps*. There are two primary reasons for performing reps in a strict manner – safety and exercise benefit.

The safety aspect cannot be stressed enough. Contrary to popular belief, it's not the amount of weight that causes injuries, but the *style* of the exercise. An exercise using 10 pounds in an uncontrolled manner can do more damage than the same exercise using 100 pounds in a controlled manner. The body's muscles, joints, tendons, etc., were not designed to have tremendous loads placed on them, especially sudden ones. Bouncing or jerking the weight around in an uncontrolled manner is a shortcut to disaster! Orthopedic surgeons and chiropractors may appreciate the business, but seriously, bodybuilding is meant to be fun, productive and, above all, *safe!*

But go into any gym and observe the various patrons. You'll see guys trying to swing hundreds of pounds in the biceps barbell curl. Others will be squatting to the floor as fast as gravity can carry them, and then reversing direction using the knees as an elastic band! Is it any wonder that such individuals tear biceps tendons or "throw their backs out" (a polite way of saying spinal-cord injury!)? Let us state here and now that no matter what exercise you are performing, always – we repeat, *always* – maintain control of the weight.

Besides the safety aspect, there's another reason to perform strict reps. The purpose of an exercise is to work a particular muscle or muscle group. While it's not possible to totally isolate an individual muscle, the goal is to try to reduce the number of secondary muscles being utilized. For example, the barbell curl is designed to work the biceps. Swinging a heavy barbell with the help of the legs and lower back is defeating the purpose of the movement. The objective is to work the biceps, not the lower back. There are other exercises (and safer ones, we might add) for working the lower back. Swinging a barbell loaded with too much weight may impress a few uninformed observers, but it's doing very little in the way of biceps stimulation. Remember, it's the *muscle* you want to work, not the ego!

In his prime Arnold used 60- to 70-pound dumbells for biceps curls. Others were swinging up 90-pounders and yet had *half* Arnold's development, and they could not understand why. The reason was simple – Arnold performed each rep in a slow, controlled manner. There was no bouncing or jerking the weight up for the Oak. He felt every rep. That 60-pound dumbell was stimulating many more muscle fibers than if he had swung up 90 pounds.

This brings us to another point. The vast majority of champion bodybuilders *do not* use heavier and heavier poundages every year. In fact, most are using less now than when they started out. Instead of 600-pound squats, most keep the weight in the 350 to 400 range. Instead of getting the weight up at all cost, they emphasize using only the thigh muscles. A combination of injuries and better technique has resulted in a change in training philosophy. Most champs are quick to point out that they get far better stimulation using moderate weights in good style than haphazardly throwing around heavy poundages.

Yates – shown here at the 1994 Olympia – is one of the greatest bodybuilders of all time.

With time you'll realize that *light* and *heavy* are relative terms and relate to the style of the exercise being performed. By using slow, controlled movements, you can make a 40-pound dumbell feel like 60 pounds. (Of course, you can carry this to the extreme and use a 10-pound dumbell, spending 15 to 20 seconds on every rep, but we doubt you'll get the same results as using a 50-pound dumbell for 10 reps.)

If the top bodybuilders are using moderate weights when they are strong enough to lift more, why should you be any different? Remember, weights are a tool to stimulate growth and, as such, should be lifted by the muscles.

"The Golden Eagle," Tom Platz, shown here performing triceps pushdowns, always gives 110 percent to each and every set.
Start

Finish

FORCED REPS

"When you perform a set of reps, each successive rep becomes more beneficial than the previous one. Never terminate a set when you can perform another rep in good style. Forced reps and negatives are not an essential part of muscle-building because the recuperation factor comes into play. Muscle can only grow if it can recuperate from training. You do not have to include forced reps in every workout. Many successful bodybuilders never employ forced reps."
– Robert Kennedy
Publisher, MuscleMag International

One of the first advanced training techniques learned by bodybuilders is what is called *forced reps*. Instead of terminating a set at the last possible rep, you have a training partner or spotter assist you in completing a couple of additional reps. In gym jargon this is called *providing a spot*. The theory behind spotting is quite simple. If you fail on, say, the 10th rep with 150 pounds, the odds are that you could force out another rep or two with 140 pounds. As soon as you complete the last rep, have your spotter apply just enough assistance to keep the bar moving. A good spot consists of placing the hands under the bar, palms up, and lifting just enough to keep it moving. Most regular gym members know how to spot correctly. If you do not have a regular training partner, don't be shy in asking a stranger for a spot.

REPS – CONCLUSION

Reps are probably the most important aspect in your bodybuilding training. For ultimate success you must choose the rep style that allows the attainment of your goals in the shortest period of time. As no two people respond in the same manner, a certain amount of individual experimentation needs to be carried out. We can provide guidelines, but only *you* can determine which rep style suits your particular needs.

SETS – HOW MANY?

"Physically I don't finish a set until I literally can't work the fatigued muscle any longer. I more or less continue a set until the bar actually drops from my momentarily paralyzed fingers." – **Tom Platz, Mr. Universe Winner**

Bodybuilders agree on the number of sets as much as they agree on the number of reps – that is, they don't! With time the top bodybuilders have discovered the number of sets that provides best results, and in most cases the discovery was made through trial and error. As with reps, there are different schools of thought on the optimal number of sets.

"My training has changed slightly from last year. I'm now training my whole body once every seven days, compared to once every five days. I feel that, as I am getting bigger and stronger now, I need more rest and recuperation." – **Dorian Yates, Five-time Mr. Olympia**

Chris Cormier

Generally speaking, we can divide set numbers into two categories – low (heavy duty) or high (classical). Champion bodybuilders use both styles, but the classical system is far and away the most popular.

HEAVY DUTY

The low-set, high-intensity system (1 to 3 sets per bodypart) was popularized by Dr. Arthur Jones, inventor of the Nautilus equipment. In the late '70s and early '80s, it received a boost from former Mr. Universe Mike Mentzer as he based his heavy-duty system on it. Nowadays its biggest proponent is five-time Mr. Olympia, Dorian Yates, who, while not following the heavy-duty theory in its strictest sense (1 or 2 sets per bodypart), nevertheless keeps sets to a maximum of 4 to 6 per muscle group.

The theory involves performing as few high-intensity sets per bodypart as possible. Many bodybuilders find standard numbers (10 to 20 per bodypart) too taxing on their recovery systems. With a few brief but intense sets they get all the stimulation they need without the energy depletion associated with higher sets – in and out of the gym in half an hour, and on with your life. (We should add that not one champion bodybuilder has used the low-set system exclusively in his/her training. A few may follow the low-

set practice now, but early in their careers used the classical system.)

THE CLASSICAL SYSTEM

The high-set or classical system is the most popular routine followed by bodybuilders. Starting with one or two exercises per bodypart, the bodybuilder graduates to performing four to five exercises per bodypart, and from 2 or 3 sets per exercise to 4 or 5 sets per exercise. By the time they reach the advanced stage of training, many bodybuilders are performing 20 to 25 sets per bodypart. The most frequently asked question is, *Is this necessary?*

Bodybuilders who follow the classical system will respond that to keep improving they must increase the number of sets. Opponents of the high-set system say that these individuals are blessed with great genetics and would grow no matter what they did. Perhaps this is so, but we cannot deny that the high-set system has produced virtually all champion bodybuilders.

PERSONAL PREFERENCE

What's the conclusion to all this? Once again personal preference plays a major role because there are advantages and disadvantages to both systems. The low-set system, performed in 30 minutes or less, does not greatly deplete the body's energy reserves. On the other hand it does not stimulate capillary development or burn many calories. Further, to get the full effect, the poundages used tend to be on the heavy side. This can play havoc with weak or underdeveloped muscles, bones and connective tissues.

Conversely, the classical system ensures adequate muscle stimulation, but it often leaves the individual immensely fatigued. Great genetics, food and (in many cases) performance-enhancing drugs are needed to perform the workouts consisting of 20 to 25 sets per bodypart.

Which system you use will ultimately depend on personal experience. Once you have a good foundation under your belt, try elements of both, adopting the method that works better for you.

TIME BETWEEN SETS

"I take plenty of time between sets for complete recovery. My weight training is for strength and muscle density. I save cardio work for the bike and the treadmill." **– Chris "The Real Deal" Cormier IFBB Professional Bodybuilder**

With regard to time between sets, you want to rest long enough to recover from the last set, but not so long that the muscle cools down before the next set. This works out to an average rest interval of 60 to 90 seconds, which allows enough time to recover between sets. Rest longer and you run the risk of incurring an injury. Conversely, move too quickly and your energy levels will not recover adequately.

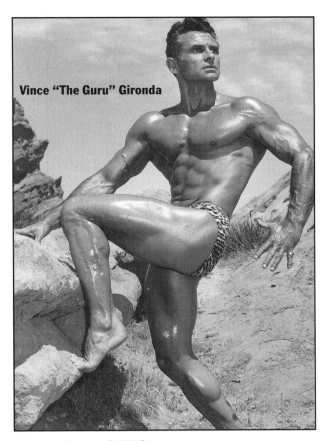

Vince "The Guru" Gironda

PYRAMID SETS

Many bodybuilders find they get the best results by varying the number of reps in subsequent sets. Pyramiding involves starting with a light weight for 15 to 20 reps. This is followed by sets of decreasing reps, but increasing weight. The *peak of the pyramid* is reached with the maximum weight and fewest reps. From here you begin to move down the other side of the pyramid, increasing the reps and decreasing the weight. Generally speaking, the lighter sets are performed for 15 to 20 reps, and the heavier for 4 to 6 reps. The following is a sample bench press routine:

1 x 135 pounds for 20 reps
1 x 225 pounds for 12 reps
1 x 275 pounds for 8 reps (peak of pyramid)
1 x 225 pounds for 10 reps
1 x 135 pounds for 15 reps

DESCENDING SETS OF HALF PYRAMIDS

Because a muscle tires with each set, most individuals find they need to start with the heaviest weights, then lower the weight with each successive set. Unlike regular pyramids, half-pyramids start at the peak and work their way down the back side. You should still perform a few light warmup sets. The following is a sample shoulder press routine:

1-2 light warmup sets
1 x 150 for 6-8 reps
1 x 135 for 8-10 reps
1 x 100 for 12-15 reps
1 x 70 for 20 reps

STRAIGHT SETS

As the name implies, straight sets are performed in a direct and forthright manner. A given number of sets is performed with a chosen weight for a given number of reps. The straight-set pattern is the most common training method used by bodybuilders. Most of the advanced patterns owe their origins to straight sets.

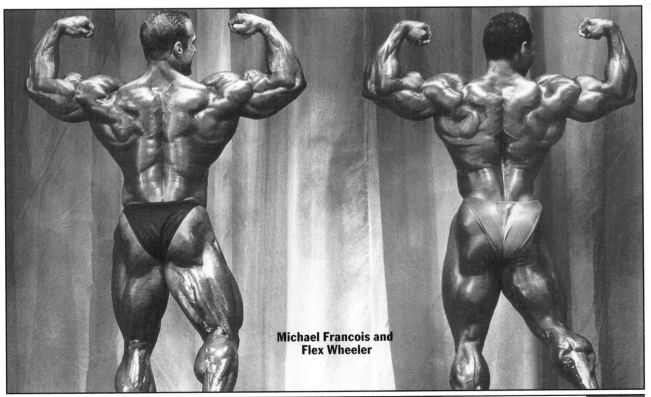

Michael Francois and Flex Wheeler

CHAPTER THREE - EVERYTHING YOU NEED TO KNOW

HOW MUCH WEIGHT?

"One important difference between the bodybuilder who wins titles and the one who tries but fails is that the pro uses barbells as tools for gaining muscle, not as weights that have to be heaved up."– **Robert Kennedy Publisher, MuscleMag International**

The superfreaky Paul Dillett.

"Those who keep their egos under control are rewarded with a better-looking physique. Witness Serge Nubret, a man who can bench press 500 pounds, but who chooses to lower the bar to his neck with his elbows wide apart, using only 250. And Arnold Schwarzenegger, a man able to deadlift more than 600 pounds, exercises with only a third of that weight."

– Vince "The Iron Guru" Gironda

There is no way one person can tell another (just by looking at him) how much weight he should use in a given exercise. It's possible, however, to give general advice on determining workout poundages.

To choose your workout weight, first decide on the number of reps to be performed. For the sake of argument, let's use 10 as our base number. The goal is to pick a weight that enables you to execute 10 good reps, but no more. This means no matter how hard you try, that 11th rep is virtually impossible. There will be days when you can grind out 11 or 12 reps with the same weight. Fine. Take advantage of such days because on others you may manage only 7 or 8 reps. Eventually you will reach a point where performing 11 or 12 reps (or more) every workout is no problem. Congratulations. Now add five pounds to the bar and follow the same procedure.

"A good rule of thumb in bodybuilding is that if you do an exercise in such a way that you have to use less weight than you did before, you're probably doing it better." **– Achim Albrecht, IFBB Pro champion**

If you use different rep ranges in your workout (as most bodybuilders do), you are going to have to vary the poundage. Don't worry. It's not that complicated. After a few workouts you'll have a good idea of how much weight you can lift on the various exercises. As your strength increases, add five to 10 pounds to the movement. Don't sacrifice good form for weight. It's much more effective (and more importantly, safer) to use less weight and good form than heavier weight and sloppy form. If Joe Flex next to you is using 400 pounds in the bench press, don't despair. We assure you that he didn't start out using that weight. Be patient and always use good style. Cheating may get you a few extra reps, but at what cost? It's not necessarily increasing your performance, and unless done in a correct manner could lead to injury. Always *feel* the weight throughout the movement.

Another warning – always warm up before using your top poundages. A muscle not warmed up is more susceptible to injury, even though it may feel stronger or more energetic at this point. As a final note, keep in mind that the words *heavy* and *light* are relative. Some bodybuilders consider 4 to 6 reps as low while others view 1 to 3 reps as low. One bodybuilder may see 10 to 12 reps as high, whereas another would call this moderate. The bottom line is to choose the rep/weight combination that works for you.

You will notice that the exercise programs in this manual outline the number of reps and sets to be performed. The amount of weight used is left to you. Follow the above guidelines and you will have no problem determining workout poundages.

EXERCISE SPEED

"The secret formula for success is quite simple. Use a combination of explosive movements and rhythmic movements to hit a bodypart. The explosive movements stimulate development of the white muscle cells; the rhythmic movements stimulate development of the red muscle cells." **– Lee Haney IFBB Professional Bodybuilder Eight-time Mr.Olympia**

The body's muscles were not designed to be jolted or jerked suddenly. Most injuries are the result of placing too much stress on a muscle too rapidly. Yanking a bar from the floor in a sudden, uncontrolled manner is dangerous. Look at it this way – if you were driving in a car that went from 60 mph to 0 mph in a few seconds, you would probably go through the windshield (provided you were not wearing a seatbelt). Why? Because your body has suddenly been decelerated from 60 to 0. Much the same situation applies to weightlifting. Exercises must be performed in a smooth and controlled manner. It should take anywhere from three to six seconds to perform each rep. (You can go faster on light, warmup sets.) Keep the tension on the bar (cable, dumbell, machine, etc.) at all times. Don't lift the weight nice and slow, only to drop it as fast as gravity can carry it! Many a biceps or pectoral tendon has been torn in this manner.

As a rep is divided into two distinct parts – positive and negative, there is much debate on the speed of each. Some argue that the positive (lifting) segment should take up the bulk of the rep time. Others argue that the negative (lowering) part of the movement is more important and should take longer.

During the '70s Dr. Arthur Jones proposed the two-up-four-down system of reps. Using this style, a bodybuilder would take two seconds to lift the weight (positive) and four seconds to lower it (negative). The theory is that because you are stronger in the lower phase of a rep, lowering the weight in ultraslow fashion tricks the muscle into believing the weight is heavier than it actually is. This in turn leads to more muscle fibers contracting. On paper this sounds fine, but in practice there are limitations, chief of which is the amount of weight used. While it's true that slowly lowering a weight makes the muscle contractions more intense, for maximum potential the weight must be as heavy as possible. Here's the problem: To get the maximum out of the negative part of the movement, you would need more weight than you could lift in the positive phase.

One of bodybuilding's most popular stars – Dennis Newman.

(There is a form of training that is based on negative only training, which will be discussed later.) Therefore the positive part of the movement becomes the limiting phase of the rep.

In recent years many bodybuilding researchers and writers have suggested a reversal of the above. The emphasis is placed on the positive phase of the rep. Instead of four seconds down / two seconds up, the opposite takes place. Take about two seconds to lower the weight and four seconds to raise it. By slowly lifting the weight the muscles are believed to work harder.

Faced with these varying options, the reader is no doubt in a quandary as to which style to use. Don't take out a stop-watch and time the phases of each rep! The numbers are only approximations. The bottom line is to make the exercise as smooth and as comfortable as

CHAPTER THREE - EVERYTHING YOU NEED TO KNOW

possible without bouncing and jerking the weights through the movement.

Whether to place emphasis on the positive or on the negative is ultimately a personal preference, and there are different ways to approach the issue. You can emphasize negatives one day and positives the next. Or you might want to combine the two during one workout. In either case make sure you are controlling the weight and not the other way around.

EXERCISE ORDER

Personal preference also plays a major role in exercise order. In general you should train the larger muscles first and leave the smaller ones for last. There are a couple of reasons for this rule. Exercising the large muscle groups (thighs, chest, back, shoulders) will take most of your energy; therefore, it only makes sense to train them first when energy levels are high. You will still have enough energy left to train the smaller muscles, such as biceps and triceps.

There is another reason to leave the biceps and triceps till last. These muscles are used when training the larger upper-body muscles. Tiring the triceps early in a workout will adversely affect your chest exercises because most of these movements involve the triceps. The same logic applies to back exercises. The biceps are a significant part of most back movements and, in a manner of speaking, they are the weak link in the chain.

Training order is less important for large muscle groups. Initially it will not make much difference whether you train chest first or back first. After a few months evaluate your physique. If your back development is lagging behind your chest, use what is called the muscle-priority system. Change your routine to work the back first and chest second. Muscle priority is not limited to the chest and back. You may find the shoulders need more attention than the legs, or that the chest needs to be worked before the shoulders. In either case change your routine to accommodate the different growth rates of your muscles.

TRAINING TO FAILURE

"The name of the game in bodybuilding is intensity. There's absolutely no question that increased training intensity develops more massive muscles and better muscle quality." **– Tom Platz, IFBB Professional, former Mr.Universe**

How often have you heard bodybuilders suggesting that "you must train to failure on every set?" This sounds great in theory (and would in fact work if you had the recovery system), but let's face it, no one – not even the top professionals – can give 100 percent on *every* set. If they did, within a few weeks they'd be nervous wrecks. For most a few sets to failure at the end of a bodypart is sufficient, and often this is done only once a week.

Repeated all-out workouts don't provide the body with enough time to recover and may actually cause a regression in strength and muscular development. Yet this is the trap into which many bodybuilding beginners fall. They hear about their favorite star training to failure, and reason, *what's good for him is good for me.* Before long our budding superstar is training to failure on each and every set.

Two basic principles must be observed if you expect to make progress with your training program:
1. Your body and muscles must be subjected to greater stress than they are accustomed to.
2. Sufficient recovery time must be allowed between workouts.

The ultraripped Terry Mitsos.

Charles Clairmonte,
Flex Wheeler and
Michael Francois

What's interesting about these two principles is that they must go hand in hand. The muscles that are subjected to a slightly greater stress than usual will respond by getting stronger or larger. They adapt during the recovery period and are prepared for the next workout. If, however, the stress is too great or the recovery period is insufficient, your muscles will not adapt and no improvement will occur. Training to failure too frequently is one sure way of holding back progress.

BREATHING

Do you breathe when training? Yes, absolutely! When? This one is a bit trickier to answer. Most exercise texts suggest breathing in on the downward part of the movement and breathing out on the upward part. Put another way, when gravity is helping you (e.g. lowering the bar on the biceps curl), breathe in, and when fighting against gravity (curling up in the biceps curl), breathe out. The advantage to a good breathing pattern is that it helps your exercise rhythm. For every rep inhale and exhale once. In this way, not only are you pacing yourself correctly, but your muscles are not deprived of an adequate oxygen supply.

As you advance in your training you will find that a few of the heavier exercises necessitate deviating from this routine. The squat is a good example. Breathing in and out in a controlled manner is relatively easy when you're using light weights, but it's virtually impossible when lifting heavy weight. Most bodybuilders find they unconsciously hold their breath when coming out of the movement (rising from the floor).

When performing intense exercise the body obviously needs enormous amounts of oxygen. If you hold your breath, the body is deprived of this valuable gas. If you hold your breath on every rep, it's quite possible you may put the body into a state of oxygen debt – with one of the results being fainting. On the other hand, holding your breath on the last couple of reps should not interfere with the body's oxygen supply.

Breathing is an involuntary physiological condition. No matter what you do, the body's breathing center will keep telling the lungs to inhale and exhale. Even if you hold your breath to the point of unconsciousness (please do not try this at home!), the body will restart the breathing cycle after you pass out. What's the conclusion to all of this? On your warmup sets it might be a good idea to follow the traditional breathing pattern. Once you start using heavier weight, let the body worry about breathing. Trust us – it will do an excellent job!

TIME BETWEEN WORKOUTS

The amount of time needed to recover between workouts depends on several factors. One of the most important is level of training experience. For a beginner, who is unaccustomed to strenuous exercise, a longer time period is usually required. In fact, beginners often need 48 to 72 hours between workouts. The most convenient training split for the novice bodybuilder is three times a week, or every second day. The whole body should be trained during the same workout, and you should never exceed one or two exercises per bodypart.

As your bodybuilding experience expands, increase the frequency of your workouts. The general consensus is to go from a three-times-per-week routine to one where you hit the body four times per week. Instead of

The awesome physique of Geir Borgen Paulsen.

thought. Many factors must be taken into account when explaining muscle recovery intervals.

First and foremost is how much damage is done to the muscle. Performing two or three high-rep sets using 100 pounds places nowhere near the drain on the body's recovery ability that the same number of sets done for 6 to 8 reps to failure using 200 pounds would inflict. Scientific evidence is consistent with the old bodybuilding theory that weight training tears down muscle tissue. Obviously the more you tear down, the longer it takes to regrow.

Muscle growth is a compensation process by which damaged body tissue is replaced by a slightly stronger version of itself. Over years of training such rebuilding produces much larger and stronger muscles. The type of training that seems to do the most damage is negative training, where the emphasis is placed on lowering the weight as slowly as possible. Such training can cause muscle soreness lasting from 10 to 14 days.

With the increased training intensity of today's top stars, the trend is to do fewer but more intense sets. Bodybuilders such as Dorian Yates, Lee Labrada and Mike Mentzer have taken this philosophy to new heights. Mentzer has influenced millions with his heavy-duty system. Many disagree, saying that just 1 or 2 sets per bodypart is insufficient; nevertheless, much of what Mike says makes sense. It is more productive to do 5 superintense sets than 20 subpar moderate sets. Not only are the muscles being stimulated to the maximum, but your recovery system is not taxed to and beyond its limits.

Besides training style, diet can play an important role in determining rest intervals. Although it's a much debated issue among nutritionists, the general feeling within the bodybuilding community is that bodybuilders need more protein than the average individual. If we believe that muscle growth involves a building up of new tissue, then it only makes sense that the building blocks of such growth be present in adequate amounts.

In addition to protein, the amount of carbohydrate consumed is also very important. To complete a strenuous workout, muscle glycogen levels must be high. Also, proper muscle recovery after a workout is very dependent on glycogen levels. The bodybuilder who reduces carbohydrate levels while continuing to exercise intensely will quickly fall into a state of overtraining.

A final factor determining recovery time is the amount of sleep. Contrary to popular belief, muscles do *not* grow during training – they grow after you leave the gym. We humans spend about one-third of our lives asleep. Knowing this, we can assume that anything that takes up this much time must be important. For an athlete rest ranks right up there with training and nutrition. Spending all night watching television or frequenting the bar scene is contradictive to success. Sure, the occasional late Friday or Saturday is not

training the whole body, you split it up into muscle groups and train half of them in alternate workouts. Such a routine allows you to increase the intensity of your training without depleting your energy. In most cases the four-times-a-week routine consists of training two days on, one day off, then two days on again.

Perhaps the ultimate in training volume is working out six days a week. Such routines as three on / one off or four on / one off have become the norm in modern bodybuilding. Even these programs can be expanded by training twice a day! Most bodybuilders, however, limit this type of schedule to the precontest phase of their training cycles.

It would be fine if you could take all this advice at face value, but like most sports, bodybuilding is continuously evolving. In the past five to 10 years much research has been carried out to determine how much time is needed for muscle recovery. Although not universally accepted, the evidence suggests that a muscle takes longer to recover than was previously

harmful, but if you habitually operate on two or three hours' sleep, you are not going to obtain the success you desire. It's that simple.

Of course, it's easy for us to recommend six to eight hours in bed, but your circumstances may not permit such an arrangement. We understand that many people hold two jobs. Students often have to juggle studying, classes and a part-time job, and staying in bed is just not practical. Try to make the most of your situation. If at all possible take a cat nap during the day or early evening. A nap of 30 to 60 minutes produces wonders in terms of mental and physical readiness. Even a couple of 15-minute powernaps spread over a day can boost your energy reserves – giving your body a break from the rigors of daily living. In fact, there is evidence that the human body works more efficiently if the sleep cycle is broken down into smaller units (e.g. two three-hour naps versus one six-hour sleep). Perhaps this is why older people nap frequently during the day!

The quality of sleep also influences the number of workouts you can perform each week. During sleep the body breaks down many of the fatigue and stress toxins produced by strenuous exercise. For example the catabolic hormone cortisol, released in response to stress (of which exercise is an example), is neutralized during the sleep cycle. Perhaps more important is the fact that during the first 90 minutes of deep sleep the body releases the greatest concentration of growth hormone. If you impede the deep-sleep process, the body's natural anabolic properties are hindered.

How much sleep is necessary? The general belief is that adults need a minimum of six hours per day. Some individuals can operate on four hours and others need eight. For the teenagers reading this book, we recommend at least eight hours a day. Besides your muscle recovery, keep in mind that your whole body is still growing (bones, hormones, nerves, etc.). If you want to make the most of your bodybuilding training, get to bed!

Milos Sarcev

Chapter Five

WHERE SHOULD I TRAIN?

WHERE TO TRAIN

Now that you've decided to begin working out, the next thing is to figure out *where*. You have two choices – at home or at a commercial gym – and there are advantages and disadvantages to both.

AT HOME

If you decide to train at home, the first order of business is buying equipment. For $500 to $1000 you can outfit your basement with the latest in training gear. You need a room to set it up in, but this is usually not a problem as most houses have one or two rooms that are nothing more than large storage closets. With a bit of creative decorating (and permission from your spouse or your parents!) you can set up a nice little training area. The advantages include convenience, no waiting for equipment, and no parking hassles. The disadvantages are: no spotters available, no one around for encouragement and motivation, little variety in equipment (unless you have ample money and room), and most important – distractions. By *distractions* we mean a ringing phone, the TV and the ever-beckoning refrigerator.

Still, when all is said and done, training at home can be very productive. Some of today's top bodybuilding superstars started their careers in house basements.

THE GYM

At Temple Gym, Birmingham, Great Britain, Yates comments on his training establishment... "The gym is very basic in terms of equipment, but it's sort of small. The ambiance and accessories of large gyms are nice but not critical. What you need are the drive to succeed and the basics."

– Dorian Yates
Five-time Mr. Olympia

Start

Geir Borgen Paulsen blasts his pecs with incline dumbell presses. *Finish*

If time, money and transportation allow, the commercial gym is the best place to train. Besides the assortment of equipment, you'll be surrounded by knowledgeable people. You get encouragement, advice and variety – all in one neat package.

Gyms can be divided into three main types: general workout facilities like the YMCA, upper-class health spas, and hardcore bodybuilding gyms such as Gold's, Powerhouse and World Gym. There are a number of factors to keep in mind when choosing a gym, the most important of which are location, membership, hours of operation and availability of equipment. Clientele and change-room facilities come next. Health spas tend to be the most expensive, followed by hardcore gyms and general-facility gyms. If your main interest is competitive bodybuilding, and money and location are no object, go to a hardcore gym. They usually have the best equipment and by far the most knowledgeable members, and you will need both if your goal is competitive bodybuilding.

At the other end of the spectrum we have the health spas. These facilities tend to cater mostly to upper-class business executives. Most spas have a small weight gym, a sauna, and often a pool and aerobics room. Membership fees tend to be on the pricey side. Keep in mind that most spas cater to individuals interested in overall fitness as opposed to competitive bodybuilders. Giving that deep grunt on a final set of squats may not sit well with spa members (or owners). Whether it's intimidation or sensitivity, who knows? But be aware of this distinction before joining a spa.

Health spas tend to have limited equipment, often just the basics. If you're planning to develop your physique to the maximum, eventually you will need the type of equipment that spas don't provide.

Your third option lies somewhere between these two. General-fitness facilities are designed for the mainstream population. Such organizations as the YMCA or YWCA provide an assortment of facilities that address most forms of physical fitness. They usually have a large indoor gymnasium, a large weight room and an aerobics room. Many of the larger Ys contain a swimming pool. Prices are reasonable, and discounts are often available to students and seniors. For your dollar, Ys and similar facilities offer as good a bargain as you'll find.

If you've decided to join a gym, great. But be aware of a few disadvantages. Potentially one of the biggest is the time required to get there. Unless you live near one, or work close by, on average it may take 20 to 30 minutes to drive there. Throw in the occasional traffic jams and bad weather, and you could easily chew up an hour or more commuting to and from the gym. Then you have the cost of gas on top of that. One hour a day, four to six times a week, 50 to 52 weeks a year, and it all adds up to an extra $1000 to $2000 a year.

Another disadvantage is the gym's hours of operation. Most hardcore gyms are open from 6 a.m. to 12 midnight, but mainstream facilities often keep little more than normal business hours. This means adjusting your workout around the gym's open hours.

Craig Titus recharges his body between sets with ice-cold water.

Perhaps the biggest drawback to commercial gyms is how crowded they get at peak times. Most are like zoos between 5 and 7 p.m. One sideways glance and your dumbells are headed across the floor. Or after doing that set of leg extensions you head to the squat rack, only to find that two guys have commandeered it. So much for Bob Kennedy's pre-exhaustion principle today!

Then you have those individuals who can be called "equipment hogs." Nothing less than 20 sets of leg extensions or leg curls seems to satisfy these people. Of course, you can ask to work in, but don't be surprised if your good-natured request gets rejected.

The final disadvantage to joining a commercial gym is cost of membership. With prices ranging from a few hundred to a few thousand dollars a year, many individuals prefer to invest the money in home equipment. Not only is this a one-shot deal, but you also avoid the risk of having the gym close down after only a few months of operation.

Where you choose to work out is ultimately a personal decision. A suggestion would be to take a one-month membership at a commercial gym and see how it goes. This will give you enough time to evaluate such factors as equipment, ease in getting there, and the general training atmosphere. Chances are that if you stick it out for four or five weeks, you're hooked. Bodybuilding is an activity that either bites you or not, and if it does, the odds are good to excellent that you will want to train in the best facility – and for the most part that means a gym.

TRAINING OUTDOORS

If you are lucky enough to have access to an outdoor training facility, take advantage of it. Many of the larger California gyms have outdoor weight pens that allow users the benefit of training in fresh air. (In some cities notorious for smog this benefit may be debatable!) The weight pit in Venice beach, California is famous with bodybuilders the world over.

There are a number of advantages to outdoor training. Besides the fresh-air factor you have the added perception of freedom. Being cooped up in a hot, sweaty gym on a hot summer day can drain even the most energetic bodybuilders. When you're performing

squats, staring at the ocean is far more pleasant than facing a wall. Likewise, when you're bench pressing, the blue sky has definite advantages over a ceiling.

Another benefit is the attention you will receive. Most outdoor weight pens attract onlookers. You have worked hard building your physique, so it's understandable that you might want to show it off. Also, people tend to go for that extra rep when they know they're being watched.

Of course, there are a few disadvantages to training outdoors. Two or three hours in the sun can play havoc with your skin. Time passes quickly during training, so always wear a strong sun block to prevent sunburn. Avoid outdoor training between the hours of 12 noon and 4 p.m. when the sun is at its highest and hottest. If at all possible, train before or after these times.

Proper clothing for outdoor training is also essential. Cotton is the coolest natural fabric since it allows absorption and ventilation. Many of the new lycra gym suits are good as they are light and allow perspiration to evaporate rapidly. Don't forget a headband, whether homemade or commercially bought, as nothing

Paul "Quadzilla" DeMayo performs a set of leg extensions outdoors in Venice Beach, California.

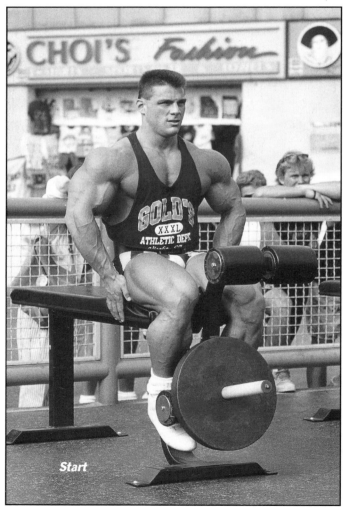

Start

Finish

aggravates the eyes like salty sweat. If you sweat a lot – and most people do when training outdoors – bring an old towel with you. Not only can you wipe up after the last person, but you can also prevent the person following you having to do the same.

Speaking of perspiration, an average adult male could lose eight to 10 quarts a day if stuck outdoors in the heat for several hours. Yes, this is extreme. Nevertheless, a couple of hours' training in the sun will cause large amounts of fluid to be lost. For this reason drink plenty of water. If there's no water fountain available, bring your own water. Fill a bottle before your workout and sip from it between sets. Electrolyte drinks are fine, but many contain sugar and other substances that need water for proper dissolving. By drinking these you may be placing a bigger water demand on the body. Our advice is to save these electrolyte drinks for after the workout and stick to water while training.

With the increased heat you may think it's all right to skip the warmup, but we advise against this shortcut. Just because the air is warm doesn't mean your muscles are. Also, as heat tends to drain most individuals, it would be a good idea to take extra time between sets. Don't tear into the weights like a lunatic only to end up dehydrated, or worse, suffering from heat exhaustion or heat stroke.

If at any time you begin to feel dizzy or lightheaded during the workout, stop training and find a shaded area. Take a few extra sips of water and lower your head to improve blood circulation to the brain. After a while you can try walking around to see how you feel. If you still experience dizziness, terminate training for the day. It probably means you're dehydrated and are bordering on heat exhaustion. Replace liquids and bring body temperature down. Left untreated heat stroke can sometimes develop into a life-threatening condition.

Another point to consider is the quality of air you're breathing. Large cities tend to have high levels of environmental pollutants. During the hot summer months environmental agencies issue smog alerts. If these warnings are available in your area, pay attention to them. The human body does not take kindly to breathing in pollutants for extended periods of time, and training only compounds the problem as you are breathing much harder.

Paul DeMayo shows the results of his years of hard work in the gym.

After your workout head immediately for the showers. Besides the social aspects, showering helps lower the body's temperature. Avoid the temptation to take a cold shower as the cool water could shock the warm muscles and force them to cramp. Keep the water lukewarm, and use a good soap to help remove salt and other byproducts released by sweating. For those whose bodies are unaccustomed to hot weather, an unscented after-shower powder will help keep you dry in your street clothes.

As a final note on outdoor training, since most people do not have access to a commercial outdoor facility, we suggest the following: Get two or three of your friends together and pool your resources. Even if you all train at a gym, most bodybuilders have a few weights and bars kicking around the basement. Combine all of the equipment in the backyard. (Arnold tells of going to the forest with three or four pals on leg days, and squatting until they could hardly walk.) The only rules to follow are your own, which no doubt will be limited. Shout out that extra few reps. Yell and scream if you like. (Of course, be mindful of the neighbors.) You

CHAPTER FOUR – WHERE SHOULD I TRAIN?

The awesome physique of Germany's late Andreas Munzer.

The body will quickly get accustomed to working out at a specific time – whether it be 6 a.m. or 7 p.m.

Although biology may play a role in determining workout times, sociology has the biggest influence. Most North Americans have designed their lives around the 9-to-5 work day. Since a typical class or work day ends at about 4 or 5 p.m., most people like to hit the gym and then head for supper. Although a few like to eat first, exercising after a meal is generally uncomfortable. There are variations – a few bodybuilders like to train early in the morning. Former great, Bill Pearl, finds training at 4 to 5 a.m. the most beneficial. Others like to end their day with a workout.

The best advice we can give is to pick your training time according to your daily schedule. If you're limited to a late-night workout, so be it. You may find that the only solution is to work out before work or school. Most gyms open early and close late to accommodate the variation in workout times. No matter what time you train, the bottom line is to do it regularly and at a time of the day that fits your schedule.

TRAINING – HOW OFTEN?

"Unless you are so ill that you must remain in bed, you should never miss a scheduled workout. One missed workout can set your progress back by as much as a week because you actually experience negative results from missing a training session. Therefore, it takes another workout just to bring yourself back up to the point where you were physically before missing a session, and a second workout to induce any new progress."
— ***Boyer Coe, Mr. Universe and Grand Prix winner***

will be amazed at the quality of your workout, and at the same time it's a nice change of pace. Give it a try.

WHEN TO TRAIN

The most popular training period is between 4 and 8 p.m. The reasoning is more sociology than biology. Before looking at the sociological aspects, let's see if there's a biological basis for favoring one time over another.

Researchers tell us that hormone levels peak in the early morning hours. By training at this time you are taking advantage of the body's natural rhythms. Besides, you're not already drained by a long day at the office. Hopping out of bed at five in the morning and hitting the weights is not for everyone. Most people find that they need a few hours just to wake up, and that maximum energy and alertness levels take longer to achieve. Peak efficiency is reached somewhere between 3 and 6 p.m.

An Olympian physique like Dorian Yates's can't be built without regular and consistent training.

One of female bodybuilding's greatest – Marjo Selin.

"As you know, I do less volume of training than many bodybuilders. You won't find me in the gym seven days a week, several hours a day on a double split. I train two on and one off during the off-season, and then three on and one off during precontest training. This schedule works for me because it gives sufficient time for the muscles to rest and grow." — **Lee Labrada**
Mr. Olympia runner-up

There are endless routine combinations for working out, and the following are among the most popular. These are based on intensity, available time, and purpose (off-season mass-building, or precontest shaping and defining). We have designed this text to take you from novice to the competitive level of bodybuilding. If you are new to bodybuilding, don't make the mistake of skipping the beginning routines and following a more advanced training schedule. As a beginner you would be wasting your time following a six-day-per-week routine. Three or four times per week is ample. (In fact, many top professionals follow a four-day routine during the off-season.) The following are among the most popular bodybuilding routines. Later in the book we will go into each plan in more detail, giving advice as to when to graduate to each level.

THREE TIMES A WEEK – THE WHOLE BODY

The most common beginning routine is performed on three alternate days (e.g. Monday, Wednesday, Friday). The whole body is worked each time, 3 to 5 sets performed per bodypart. By skipping a day between workouts, the body's recovery system is given sufficient time to do its job. Also a three-day routine leaves you four days for other aspects of life (family, classes, work).

One disadvantage to this routine is that you'll only have sufficient energy to perform 4 or 5 good sets per muscle group. Working the whole body with additional sets would leave you overtrained. Besides, doing 10 to 20 sets per bodypart would take about three to four hours.

THREE TIMES A WEEK – ALTERNATE WORKOUTS

This is a variation on the standard three-day-a-week routine. You divide your training into two programs, performing half on Monday and Friday and the remaining half on Wednesday. The following week you switch. Perform Wednesday's routine on Monday and Friday, and the Monday/Friday routine on Wednesday. This approach enables you to work each bodypart three times in a two-week period. Confused? Here's an example:

Week 1:
Monday – chest, back, biceps
Wednesday – legs, shoulders, triceps
Friday – chest, back, biceps

Week 2:
Monday – legs, shoulders, triceps
Wednesday – chest, back, biceps
Friday – legs, shoulders, triceps

Because you exercise half the body per workout, you can perform additional sets for each muscle group. Taking a day off between workouts allows adequate time for recovery. Many bodybuilders who have adopted this routine, after following a more intense program, find they have energy to spare.

FOUR-DAY-A-WEEK SPLIT

Moving up in intensity, the Monday-Tuesday-Thursday-Friday split is the most common. Half the muscles are worked on Monday and Thursday, the other half on Tuesday and Friday. Two workouts are followed by a day of rest (Wednesday), and then the cycle repeats. Even though you work out four times a week, the same muscles are hit only twice a week.

If there's a disadvantage, it may be the back-to-back exercising. Some individuals find working out on consecutive days too taxing. Others, however, will start losing size if they work out less.

SIX DAYS A WEEK

The next progression is the six-day-a-week plan. In most cases three different routines are followed for three successive days. After a day off the cycle repeats for three additional days. A variation is to train the full six days, then take the seventh off.

Former Mr. Universe Vic Downs was very successful with the one-muscle-a-day routine in the '60s.

This is a very intense training cycle, and should be followed only by advanced bodybuilders. If you are exercising six days a week, your calorie requirements are enormous. As well, you will need to get ample sleep to recover from each workout. Experience has shown that only the most genetically gifted bodybuilders can handle such a training schedule. Even then, many of the top bodybuilders reserve such a routine for their precontest cycle. At this stage their focus is on refining and preparing for competition.

DOUBLE-SPLIT ROUTINES

Another variation is the split routine. Here the bodybuilder will work out twice a day, training only one or two bodyparts – usually a large one such as legs and a smaller one such as biceps. By hitting the gym twice a day you can devote all of your energy to training one muscle group per workout. Your energy level remains high as your workouts do not exceed 30 to 45 minutes. The split routine can be modified from any of the above routines, although the six-day split is the most common.

The biggest disadvantage of split routines is that they have little respect for a standard North American day. If you're a full-time student or hold a full-time job,

finding time to train more than once a day will be difficult. Some get around this by using their lunch break for training. This is fine if you have a long (60 minutes or more) lunch break or if you work close to a gym. (You have it made if you work *at* the gym!) But for most a split routine is just not feasible.

HOW ABOUT ONE MUSCLE A DAY!

Although it would seem that this approach should be placed first in our list of training schedules, we have left it till last as it is not a very popular training strategy. There are, however, a number of good reasons why it should be.

It's safe to say that the biggest impediment to gaining muscular body mass is overtraining. With so many techniques available to blast muscles, to what were once unheard-of degrees, modern bodybuilders are often their own worst enemies. For most people training more than two or three times per week is counterproductive. There is no way a natural bodybuilder can train two or three muscle groups a day, four to six times a week. But how about training just one muscle group a day? Could this be the answer to all your overtraining worries?

The one-muscle-a-day routine is not new – former Mr. Universe Vic Downs followed it back in the '60s. This plan allows train-aholics six workouts a week, but at the same time training one muscle a day reduces the drain on the body's recovery system. A typical one-muscle-a-day routine would be as follows:

> Monday – legs
> Tuesday – chest
> Wednesday – back
> Thursday – shoulders
> Friday – triceps
> Saturday – biceps

(Such a routine means fitting abdominals and forearms in where convenient.)

Working one muscle a day has another advantage. You can really blast the muscle without having to save energy for another muscle group. Instead of doing 10 to 12 sets you can go up to 15 or 20. This way you can hit the muscle from almost every conceivable angle – something too draining to try while on a multi-muscle-a-day routine. When finished you simply leave the gym – in and out in an hour.

We caution you, however, not to take this idea to the extreme. Spending two hours in the gym, six days a week, whether training one muscle or three, still adds up to two recovery-draining hours. Limit your workouts to 12 to 15 total sets and get out of there.

If you suspect that you're in a state of overtraining (see the chapter later in the book on overtraining), you might want to give the one-muscle-a-day routine a try. We won't guarantee the Mr. Olympia crown in two months, but we're confident that it will make your workouts much more productive.

**Charles
Clairmonte**

high-intensity theory, your workouts will last 30 to 45 minutes, whereas a typical 20-set-per-bodypart routine could take you two hours. On average the typical bodybuilder spends about 90 minutes in the gym. Of course, if you alternate sets with conversation, you could easily spend two to three hours working out.

The topic of workout duration has been widely debated. Some suggest that keeping energy levels high for two hours or more is virtually impossible. Others add that a two-hour workout places undue stress on the body's recovery system. Advocates of long workouts counter that they are unable to get the required stimulation from a 45-minute routine. Also, a long workout improves the body's cardiovascular system. If you like the high-set system, budget 90 to 120 minutes for your workouts. On the other hand, a 45-to-60-minute routine might be best for your particular lifestyle or genetics.

MISSING WORKOUTS

No matter how hard you try to train regularly, sooner or later you will miss the occasional workout. Don't worry about it. Most bodybuilders train too much, and the day or two off will only help, not hinder, progress. If you find yourself making excuses to miss workouts, perhaps you should reevaluate your overall training philosophy.

Numerous legitimate reasons exist for missing workouts. If you're a full-time student, exams should take priority over training. A chapter test may not affect your training, but final exams will. Take two or three weeks off for study. You won't lose size – any such perception will be psychological – and good marks will have more of an impact on your life than a couple of workouts.

Your job will periodically cause you to miss a workout. Staff meetings, new proposals, extra paper work – all may interfere with your gym schedule. Many jobs require extensive travel. No problem here – most cities and large towns have weight-training facilities. You may have to search through the Yellow Pages to find them. Before doing this, check the hotel where you are staying. Many of the larger hotel chains have fitness centers. Your daily workout may be just an elevator trip away, but the results are worth it. Working out in strange gyms can be enjoyable. Besides variety, you will meet some interesting characters on the road. Bodybuilders are the same the world over. Business person or mechanic, doctor or construction worker, most drop their social standing when they enter a gym. If you are constantly traveling, check out "Bodybuilding on the Road" later in this book.

WHICH ONE FOR ME?

"Don't just blindly follow others. If an exercise or a certain strategy doesn't feel right, don't do it."
– Charles Clairmonte
IFBB Professional Bodybuilder

We have described for you the most common routines followed by bodybuilders. A number of factors will determine which routine you follow. Among these are time considerations, goals, and personal preference. We strongly suggest following the routines as arranged in this text. They have been grouped in ascending order of difficulty. Don't make the mistake of jumping into a split routine with only three weeks' training under your belt.

WORKOUT DURATION

The length of a workout ultimately depends on the type of program being followed. If you follow the low-set,

Aaron Baker

Lack of transportation may prevent your workout. Most of us get around by car, but these wonderful machines (a concept easily debated) are notorious for refusing to start at the most inconvenient times. If you drive an old clunker, you may spend as much time curling a wrench as you do a dumbell. At times like this you'd better be acquainted with the bus schedule. Buses are inexpensive, comfortable, and usually very punctual. Taxis can be expensive, but you have to balance the cost with your eagarness to train.

The most extreme impediment to working out is a lack of training facilities, but even this difficulty can be circumvented. You may not have access to a gym, or your basement may be free of weights, but there is no such thing as "no training facilities". Just think of all the exercises you did in high school gym class. How many involved specialized equipment? Very few, right? With a little improvising you can use everyday items to keep in shape. Such exercises as situps, pushups, dips between chairs, and no-weight squats are all excellent ways to maintain – if not stimulate – muscle growth.

If you are handy with a blowtorch, an unlimited number of exercises can be at your disposal. Some of the biggest bodybuilders around got started in garages outfitted with homemade equipment. Often the source of metal was a scrapped car.

If mechanics is not your trade, various isometric movements will keep your muscles firm and toned. Try pushing against a wall or support beam. With a rolled or twisted towel (a thick one) you can do all sorts of upper-body exercises, and the beauty is you can do them just about anywhere – hotel room, college dorm, your own bedroom, etc.

The bottom line is, no matter where you are or how limited the equipment, you can always find some means of exercising. Granted, it's nice to have proper facilities, but don't make excuses.

The final reason to miss a workout is that we highly recommend it! Repeatedly subjecting the body to heavy weights – even with good exercise style – can play havoc with the body's joints and connective tissues (muscles, ligaments, tendons). Most bodybuilders have minor aches and pains which they ignore and train around. Combine these conditions with the occasional bout of tendonitis, and the importance of taking an occasional break from training becomes obvious.

Many bodybuilders are afraid to take time off because they fear losing size or strength. This is a misconception as a few days off will make no difference to muscle size or strength. In fact, taking a few days (or even weeks) off allows your recovery system to catch its breath, giving minor injuries time to heal. After a few days' rest you will feel mentally and physically refreshed. Your enthusiasm level will be much higher, and all those little aches and pains will have disappeared.

Family responsibilities (e.g. a child's school play, a sick spouse) can mean skipping a workout. Once again it's a matter of priorities. Your family should always take precedence over your training.

There are a number of personal reasons for putting your training on hold. The common cold, while not life threatening, should be attended to. The flu virus weakens the body, and intense training will only impede the body's immune response. We're sure other gym members will be appreciative when you refrain from spreading the flu around, so take a few days off and rest.

If you live in Canada or northern states of the USA, Mother Nature may rear her ugly head. Although gyms try to stay open even in the most inclement weather, a winter snowstorm may shut facilities down for a day or so. Even if the gym stays open, you might want to decide whether your workout is worth a dangerous drive. Working out at home might be safer. You will get virtually the same benefit without having to worry about hazardous road conditions.

Ronnie Coleman's arms are among the best in the business.

Chapter Five

THE EQUIPMENT

The very first Mr.Olympia, Larry Scott, and "The Golden Eagle," Tom Platz, show off their fancy footwear.

PERSONAL EQUIPMENT

Although the gym is not the local nightclub (more on this later), there are a few things to keep in mind before you go for that first workout. For starters, even if you *wanted* to go half-naked, most gyms have a dress code. At the minimum this means shorts and a T-shirt. Few gyms allow members to go topless. Nothing is as annoying as having to wipe someone's sweat off a bench before you sit or lie on it. Depending on the temperature in the gym, you might want to skip the T-shirt and wear a sweatshirt. This helps keep the muscles warm, insulates you from the sweat of others, and keeps them guessing as to what physical condition you're really in. (Don't laugh – many competitive bodybuilders refuse to show their physiques in the weeks leading up to a contest. They say it keeps their opponents guessing.) The same approach can be taken with the lower body, trading the shorts for sweat pants. Of course, in summer when the temperature is much higher, you might want to revert to lighter clothing. Basically, choose something you find comfortable to wear for training.

If you want to check out the latest gym fashion, just flip through a recent copy of *MuscleMag International.* Many of the bodybuilding superstars, including Mike Quinn, Gary Strydom and Mike Christian, offer their own line of stylish workout wear. Combining the latest in design and fabric, these clothes will make you the envy of any gym.

With regard to footwear, nothing beats the good old sneaker. You can spend hundreds of dollars for the latest version of Nike or Adidas, or you can head for Wal-Mart and buy a pair of $20 specials – there really isn't much difference. If you can swing it financially, though, buy the expensive variety as they offer better ankle support, a must when performing such exercises as squats and leg presses.

Occasionally you might want to go barefoot, but first check your gym's policy on this. Many establishments have strict rules concerning hygiene and safety, and barefoot is usually a no-no. If allowed, try a few chinups without footwear. While the difference in weight is only a pound or two, the perception of freedom will give a few extra reps. Another exercise that lends itself to bare feet is the standing calf raise. Athletic shoes reduce the range of movement at the top and bottom of this exercise. Barefoot, you can get those few extra degrees of movement. If you have weak ankles, we suggest barefoot calf raises on light, high-rep days only. You will need the ankle support of sneakers on the heavy days.

Many bodybuilders find that during an intense workout sweat irritates their eyes. One solution is to wear a headband (sweatband) – a piece of material an inch to one and a half inches wide that soaks up perspiration. You can buy a fancy sweatband for $10 to $20, or you can go to the nearest fabric store and invest $2 or $3 which will get you enough material to make 10 or more sweatbands. All you need is a few minutes with scissors and thread. Who knows? Others in the gym may come up to you and ask about your head-wear. The road to your own personal clothing line could start right there!

ANTIGRAVITY BOOTS

Antigravity boots are specialized footwear that allow you to hang upside down from an overhead bar. The theory behind the boots is that gravity continuously compresses the spine and over time pulls the internal organs downward. Proponents of antigravity boots suggest that hanging upside down relaxes you and relieves tension on the spine.

As hanging upside down has little benefit in terms of gaining muscle mass, you probably don't need to invest money in buying a pair. If you do give them a try, start out by hanging for only short durations. You need time to get used to the buildup of pressure in the head.

GLOVES

If you've done no previous weight training at all, your first workouts will likely lead to hand blisters. After a few weeks these blisters will be replaced by calluses, which are a buildup of dead skin cells. Skin is the body's first line of defense against germs. Calluses prevent the skin from breaking and allowing harmful organisms in. If you have sensitive skin, if soft hands are necessary in your profession, or if you just hate the look of calluses, there is a protective measure. For $15 to $20 you can buy a pair of specially designed gloves that protect the hands from the rough barbell. They often have the fingers cut away to allow a better grip while protecting the sensitive area at the base of the fingers.

Some bodybuilders substitute golf gloves. While not as thick as the bodybuilding variety, they do provide some protection. If gloves are not your style, try holding a sponge or a piece of rubber between your hands and the bar. This may seem awkward at first but with practice you won't even know the sponge is there.

A final suggestion for gloves – unless you *must* wear them for one of the above reasons, *don't!* After your first few weeks of training, your hands will become thickened and desensitized. You'll have a better grip, and you won't have to worry about developing blisters from any type of manual labor.

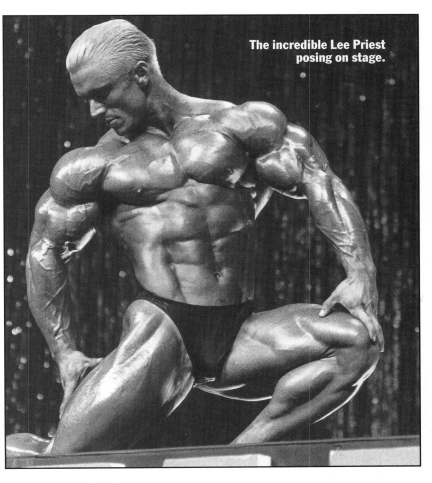

The incredible Lee Priest posing on stage.

WRAPS

You'll soon notice in the gym that some bodybuilders are wrapped up like Egyptian mummies. They have all the major joint areas (wrists, elbows, knees) bound with seemingly yards of bandages. For some this is preventive medicine; for others it's protecting an injury. As you progress in your workout poundages your joints may begin to give you trouble. No matter how much you warm up or perform the exercises in strict style, you will experience joint problems sooner or later. Most will be minor irritations that you can train around. A few, however, will need attention.

If you develop sore joints (more on injuries later in the book), try wrapping the area with an elastic bandage. Most drug stores sell these for a few dollars. The larger chains have entire sections devoted to athletic supplies. A bandage will keep the area warm and secure, giving it a chance to heal.

Some bodybuilders abuse this procedure as they do many practices. Instead of wrapping only the injured area, they cover every possible joint. Not only are they limiting their range of movement and cutting off circulation (as a tightly wrapped bandage does), but they are causing the joint to be dependent on the binding. Except for injuries, you shouldn't need bandages early in your training career. Only later, as your workout poundages increase, might wrapping a joint be

CHAPTER FIVE – THE EQUIPMENT

necessary, and even then only during heavy exercises like squats and bench presses.

THE WEIGHTLIFTING BELT

"I always use a weightlifting belt. I don't agree with those who say that continued use of a belt promotes dependency upon it and detracts from fully developing your own body. I believe that a belt stabilizes you, holds in the abdominal wall, and helps keep your waist small and tight. I think you need to wear a belt."

– Lee Labrada, IFBB Professional Bodybuilder

The weightlifting belt has always been one of the essentials, and no serious bodybuilder would be complete without one. In the old days lifting belts were used only when performing shoulder presses of one kind or another. Before long, squats and deadlifts would not be attempted without a belt. The practice has now reached the point where some bodybuilders put their belt on at the beginning of a workout and remove it only when finished. Maybe, just maybe, they'll take it off to work abdominals.

The purpose of a belt is to provide protection when performing exercises that place unwanted stress on the lower back. The muscles and bones of the lower back were not designed to handle the very heavy poundages that some bodybuilders use. The average human did not evolve to execute 500-pound squats or 600-pound deadlifts. Such movements place tremendous stress on the lower back's spinal erectors and lumbar disks.

Besides the spinal erectors, the spine is held upright by another force – internal pressure. This pressure takes two forms, intra-abdominal (IAP) which is below the diaphragm, and intra-thoracic (ITP) which is above the diaphragm. Both pressures are caused by a forceful contraction of the abdominals against the body's internal organs. Some researchers estimate that these pressures increase by a factor of 10 when lifting without a belt. A weightlifting belt gives the abdominals something to push against, thus increasing internal pressure. Finally, as with wraps, you should wear a belt only when absolutely necessary, because you can become too dependent on it. Relying totally on a belt may also cause a weakening of the muscles in the abdominal region. As a general guide, you should wear a belt on the following exercises:

- squats
- deadlifts
- bent-over rows
- T-bar rows
- shoulder presses
- shrugs

If you had a serious back injury in the past, you may want to wear a belt for the entire workout. Let's face it – even hoisting 25-pound plates can put unwanted stress on the lower back.

Because of the increased popularity of bodybuilding, many leather goods stores carry weightlifting belts. They average in price from $25 to $100-plus. If money is no object, have one tailor-made by a leather crafter. It will set you back a few extra dollars, but the finished product will be designed to fit your unique contours.

Belts come in several styles. They generally range in width from four to six inches. (For those competitive powerlifters among you, regulations state that a belt must not exceed 10 cm or four inches in width.) Weightlifting belts are secured around the waist in much the same manner as dress-pants belts. Usually there's a one- or two-prong buckle, but some of the heavier belts have three or four prongs. The fashion conscious can purchase a velcro-fastening belt.

Here's a list of tips to follow when using a belt:

1. Make sure your belt fits properly. It must be tight enough to provide support, but not tight enough to damage internal organs. Most bodybuilders use the word *snug* when describing the way a good belt should fit.

2. Make sure the belt is of good quality. Often the cheap belts ($25 or less) lack the thickness that provides the necessary support. Granted, many cannot afford a $100 to $150 custom-made belt, but, if at all possible, buy a belt that is of good quality. You have our assurances that your back will thank you for doing so!

3. Always wear a belt during heavy lifts such as those listed above. If an exercise puts uncomfortable stress (you will have to judge this for yourself) on the lower back, avoid that exercise. If more than one exercise causes discomfort, see your physician.

4. Perform all your warmups without a belt to help stimulate the muscles supporting the lower back region. Doing ab exercises wearing a belt is extremely uncomfortable. A belt tends to chafe the skin during crunches. It also limits the range of movement. (That's what it is designed to do – keep the back straight.)

5. If you have a minor back injury or if the muscles in the lower back are unusually tired one day, a good idea might be to wear the belt during the entire workout. Once you're back to normal, wear the belt only on heavy movements. Use your best judgment.

WRIST STRAPS

Debate continues on the merits of straps. In the past powerlifters used them to increase their poundages on deadlifts and pullups. The glossy magazines of the '50s were filled with tales of Paul Anderson deadlifting 1,000 pounds with the aid of straps and, although their use quickly spread among powerlifters, bodybuilders took longer to accept the potential benefits.

Wrist straps are short, narrow pieces of strong material (usually less than two feet long, an inch to an inch and a half wide), which are wrapped around the wrist and around the bar being gripped. Wrap in the direction that makes the straps tighten as you pull on the bar. This support gives you a stronger grip. Straps are most commonly used when performing deadlifts, shrugs and chins (i.e. when your forearm strength is the weak link in the chain). Wrist straps enable the lifter to use more weight than could normally be gripped. In short, they prevent a weak grip from limiting your workout poundages.

Straps have a number of disadvantages, one of which is dependence. If you regularly use straps, your forearms will never develop gripping strength. Using them for a few selected exercises (shrugs being the most common) is acceptable, but do not go overboard.

A second disadvantage concerns improper use. Many bodybuilders experience wrist pain during or shortly after the days on which they perform shrugs and various back exercises. This pain is usually attributed to the poundages used, but the real culprit is often the position of the straps on the hands. To fully understand the problem, we have to look at wrist physiology in more detail.

The wrist is a meeting point between the forearm and hand bones. The forearm bones, called the radius and ulna, connect to the small wrist bones, called carpels. Both the radius and ulna terminate at the wrist by way of a bony extrusion (bump). You can see one of these bumps by turning the hand palm down. Notice the bump on the outside (away from the body) of the wrist? These bumps play an important role in strap usage.

Many bodybuilders place the straps directly over the bumps. This is a bad idea, and here's why. As soon as the weight (often 300 to 500-plus pounds) is placed on the straps, the force is transferred to the small wrist bones and ligaments by way of the bony prominences. The result – stretched ligaments, pain and future wrist instability. The small bones and ligaments in your wrist were not meant to have 500 pounds of force placed on them.

Another reason to avoid placing the straps over the wrist concerns one of the functions of the carpels.

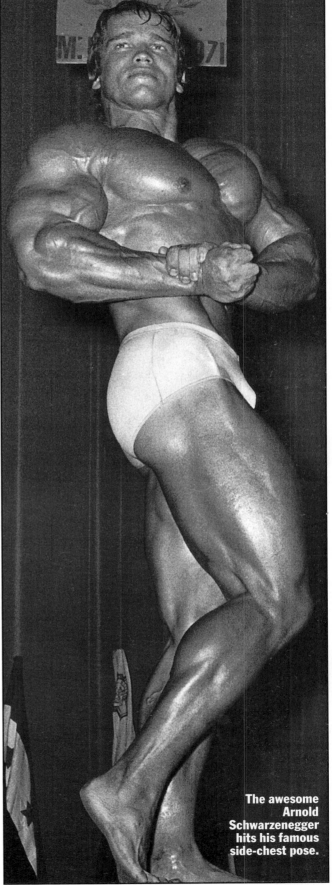

The awesome Arnold Schwarzenegger hits his famous side-chest pose.

Besides providing support, these small bones also form a housing or tunnel which permits the hand nerves to pass through. Wearing straps may cause a stretching of the connecting ligaments, leading to carpel instability. In other words, you would be interfering with proper nerve functioning.

The solution is to place the straps *above* the bony prominences of the wrist. Not only will you be protecting the bones, ligaments and nerves of the wrist, but the bony protrusions also help prevent the straps from sliding down the forearms. When the straps are in the correct position, the wrist should be completely visible. If the wrists or any part of the hands are covered, the straps are too low.

If you have experienced wrist pain in the past (or want to prevent it in the future) we suggest you follow these directions. Usually all that is required is a repositioning of the straps.

TYPES OF STRAPS

Straps are either commercially manufactured or homemade. Although prices vary, on average you will pay about $15 to $20 for a good pair. If you're on the creative side, you can make your own.

There are two general types of wrist straps – straight pieces of material about 25 to 30 inches long, or straight with a loop on the end. Most bodybuilders prefer the looped variety for lighter exercises and the straight version for the heavier movements like deadlifts and shrugs.

Because of the simplistic nature of straps, they are cheap and easy to make. Go to a fabric store and pick up a few feet of tough, stout webbing or nylon material. (This will give you enough fabric to make a couple of pairs.) Cut the material into straps 20 to 30 inches long and 1.5 to 2.5 inches wide. Don't make them less than 1.5 inches wide as they will cut into your skin. (Some straps have a sponge glued on at the point where the strap rests against the wrist, preventing tearing of the skin.)

For extra strength and protection against wrist cuts, double the material – that is, cut the strips four to five inches wide, fold down the middle, and then stitch. By positioning the folded side against your wrist, you have less chance of it cutting.

If you intend to make the looped version, allow enough material to make a loop large enough to fit your hand through, but not so big that the hand slips out. As the strap will be taking an enormous amount of weight, make sure you use heavy thread or double stitches when attaching the loop.

If sponge pads are required, obtain a good piece of foam of suitable thickness and density. Cut out two equal-sized pieces about six inches long, and stitch or glue them in the correct position.

A final source from which to attain a good pair of straps is an old martial arts belt. The belt material from judo or karate suits makes excellent straps. Because the material is so thick, you don't have to worry about it breaking or cutting into your wrists. (For that extra bit of

Flex Wheeler, Charles Clairmonte and Michael Francois

The phenomenal physique of Roland Cziurlok. Muscle like this can only come from hard and heavy training!

the end. Most bodybuilders will have no problem developing neck size and strength indirectly from the various exercises they perform. A few, however, will need direct neck-training. Head straps allow the user to work the muscles that support the head directly. Some of the older Universal machines have a neck harness attached to the leg curl. Instead of using free weight, you simply select the weight from the stack.

Many bodybuilders and football players have that "My God, he has no neck!" look. This appearance is caused by massive development of the neck muscles, which creates the impression that the man's shoulders run directly to his head.

The advantages of a strong neck are numerous. Certainly in such sports as wrestling, judo or football a strong neck is a must. If you plan to compete in bodybuilding contests, your neck muscles must be in proportion to the rest of your physique. If you notice your neck development lagging behind, invest in a neck harness and perform a few extra sets.

CHALK

Bodybuilders often find that after a few sets their palms begin to sweat to the extent that holding onto a bar becomes difficult, if not dangerous. Taking a cue from powerlifters, Olympic lifters and gymnasts, some bodybuilders like to *dry* their hands with chalk. Chalk is made from the shells of dead marine organisms, and can be bought in most sports stores. It may be advertised as gymnastics chalk, but don't worry. It's the same stuff. It comes in small blocks. Here is a word of caution, however. Many gyms that are very conscious of their appearance don't want white chalk (or any other color for that matter) all over the floor. When using chalk try to keep it on your hands and the bar, not on the floor. If an excessive amount gets on the floor, common courtesy would be to clean it up. Finally, some gyms prohibit chalk entirely, so before investing money, check your gym's policy.

THE GYM

"Beginners are frequently puzzled by all the exotic types of apparatus they see in gyms or read about. Having tried them all myself, even the glamorous, multipurpose units now in vogue with pro football teams and other athletes, I'm convinced that no machine compares with pure free weight training."
– Dr. Franco Columbu, Two-time Mr. Olympia
IFBB Professional Bodybuilder

When you first enter a modern weight-training gym, you will be amazed at the assortment of equipment available. Gone are the days when a few iron weights and benches were haphazardly strewn about. You may feel that much of the equipment is reminiscent of machines found in the dungeons of a medieval castle. You're partially right, as improper use of the equipment can lead to the same outcome – torture!

attention, dye the belt black and say you took it from the previous owner. That way no one will steal your straps from you!)

HEAD STRAPS

These are nothing more than leather harnesses that fit around the head and have an attachment for weight at

Mauro Sarni

Bodybuilding equipment can be divided into two main categories – free weights and machines. We'll look at free weight first.

FREE WEIGHT

No, it's not *free,* and with time you'll begin to question why you even paid to use it in the first place! Seriously, free weight is the term given to barbells and dumbells. By *free* we mean there are no attached pulleys, cables, pins or weight stacks, etc. Free weight is the most basic form of bodybuilding equipment, and for some the only type.

THE BARBELL

The standard piece of free weight is the barbell, a long iron bar (four to seven feet) on which stacks of circular weight plates are placed. At one end of the spectrum there are Olympic bars. These are specially machined, seven-foot bars standardized to 45 pounds (20 kg). The next time you watch an Olympic weightlifter throw 400 pounds above his head, you can be sure he is using an Olympic bar. Because of their special construction,these bars can be loaded with hundreds of pounds of weight (800 to 1000-plus pounds). Their large size makes them awkward for arm exercises, so most bodybuilders use them only for the basics like squats, deadlifts and bench presses.

Besides Olympic bars, most gyms have shorter bars available (four to six feet). Many versions have a hollow tube called a *sleeve,* surrounding their center.

The assortment of equipment available today is amazing.

The sleeve has rough grooves that provide a better grip than the underlying smooth bar. Also, the sleeve allows the bar and plates to rotate in the user's hands, reducing wrist strain and making the exercises more comfortable.

To keep the plates from sliding on the bar, two sets of collars are utilized. Inside collars prevent the plates from sliding towards the center, and may be either welded in place or adjustable. Outside collars prevent the plates from sliding off the bar's ends. Some gyms have a rack of fixed bars. In this case both sets of collars are welded in place, and the weight cannot be adjusted. You simply choose the bar with the correct poundage. The bar's weight is usually marked on the outside plate. For both appearance and more importantly, safety, gyms require you to return the bar to the rack when you're finished.

Plates range from 2.5 to 100 pounds, and may be iron or plastic. Plastic plates are hollow coverings filled with sand or cement. Many bodybuilders experienced their first workout using a plastic York barbell set. These plates are ideal for home training, as the smooth plastic is friendly to carpets. The chief disadvantage is plate size – their thickness limiting the number that can be placed on a bar. Still, they're ideal for a home gym.

The plates of choice found in commercial gyms are made of iron, and may be measured in kilograms or

Lenda Murray, Sharon Bruneau and Laura Creavalle

pounds. With the majority of major manufacturers located in the US, most North American gyms use the imperial system (pounds) for their equipment. If you want to convert metric weight to pounds, you need to know that 1 kilogram equals 2.2 pounds. For example, a 20-kilogram plate is approximately equal to a 45-pound plate (20 kg x 2.2 = 44 pounds).

THE EZ-CURL BAR

Gyms commonly carry a derivative of the barbell called the EZ-curl bar. Being shorter (about three feet in length), EZ-curl bars were specifically designed to train the arms. With their double S shape and lighter weight – most are 25 pounds – these bars allow the user to train the biceps and triceps without the awkwardness of the standard barbell. The bar's S shape enables the biceps and triceps to be hit from different angles. In the case of the biceps there is also the added benefit of reducing the stress that a straight bar places on the wrists.

DUMBELLS

The word *dumbell* has taken on a multitude of meanings over the years. In bodybuilding it refers to the short bars (10 to 15 inches) that supplement barbells. Unlike barbell exercises, those with dumbells are usually performed with a dumbell in each hand. For convenience most gyms have the dumbell plates welded in place. They may range from 5 pounds up to 150 pounds. Dumbells can be found on a special rack, usually next to a mirror. As you will do most of your dumbell exercises with two arms, the mirror helps you to maintain exercise coordination.

A few of the larger gyms have adjustable dumbells. They operate in the same manner as a barbell, and you add the required plates and adjust the collars. A few of

the larger bodybuilders perform their dumbell presses with 180 to 200 pounds – a feat you have to see to believe!

The chief advantage of dumbells is that they allow a much greater range of movement than a barbell. On many barbell exercises the bar touches the chest or shoulders, depriving the user of the last 10 to 20 degrees of movement. Because they are shorter and held in each hand, dumbells allow the muscle to be worked through its full range of movement.

BENCHES

Benches are probably the most commonly used piece of nonweight gym apparatus. You will perform many, if not most, exercises on one of these three angled benches – flat, incline and decline.

FLAT BENCH

As the name implies, flat benches are horizontal. There are no attached weights, cables or pulleys – just a simple, four-legged upholstered bench. You can use a flat bench to sit on while doing one-arm dumbell triceps extensions or to brace yourself when performing various exercises (e.g. one-arm dumbell rows).

INCLINE BENCH

To work the upper chest, your body must be angled with respect to the horizontal (floor). Generally incline angles are from 30 to 45 degrees. Most bodybuilders find that as they approach 45 degrees or more, the strain shifts from the upper chest to the front deltoids (front shoulders). Biceps and triceps exercises can be performed on an incline bench too.

DECLINE BENCH

Decline benches can be considered the opposite of inclines. They enable the user to work the lower outer chest region. Many bodybuilders substitute decline presses for flat bench presses, finding the decline keeps the stress on the chest, not the triceps and front deltoids.

Incline and decline benches may be either fixed or adjustable with respect to their angle. If you have access to an adjustable bench, experiment with the angle. Just because another bodybuilder finds 30 degrees best for his upper chest doesn't mean you have to use the same angle. You may find that 40 to 45 degrees is most efficient and 30 degrees is just not high enough. Remember, everyone is different. What works for one may not work for another.

The words *incline* and *decline* relate to the position of the body with respect to the floor. The angle may be the same (e.g. 45 degrees) but the position of the head and feet determines whether the bench is inclined or declined. If the head is *above* horizontal and the feet *below*, you are inclined. If the reverse is true (feet above, head below) you are declined. Many bodybuilders find the fixed decline bench (about 25 to 30 degrees) just right for performing inclines, provided the head and feet are aligned properly. These terms will become clearer once you begin the exercises.

"The Real Deal" Chris Cormier displays one of the world's top physiques.

Legendary bodybuilder Lee Labrada performs biceps barbell curls with an EZ-curl bar.

Start

Finish

CHAPTER FIVE – THE EQUIPMENT

Start

Bodybuilding's first Mr. Olympia, Larry Scott, builds his amazing biceps with barbell preacher curls.

PREACHER/SCOTT BENCH

This apparatus was originally called the preacher bench. After bodybuilding's first Mr. Olympia, Larry Scott, revealed that he had used one extensively in his training, the name *Scott bench* was adopted. The Scott bench allows the user to almost totally isolate the biceps. Its wedge-shaped pad prevents swinging, thus making the exercise more effective.

The angle of the bench places most of the stress on the lower biceps. This emphasis gives the muscles a longer, fuller appearance. Keep in mind that biceps length is primarily genetic, and Scott curls can't change this. Still, you should be incorporating them into your training program because Scott curls are one of the best biceps exercises.

ABDOMINAL BENCH

This is nothing more than a long bench with a set of round pads (often called rollers) at one end. In addition there is a short handle sticking up from the board. The bench has a set of hooks that insert into a vertical board, allowing the user to change the angle of the bench.

By placing the feet under the rollers, you can perform situps. This movement primarily works the upper abdominals. By flipping over and grabbing the straight handle you can do leg raises, which work the lower abdominals. By increasing the angle of the bench, you can make both movements more difficult.

DIPPING BARS

Although simple in appearance, dipping bars are among the most effective pieces of apparatus for working the lower and outer pectorals and triceps. One of bodybuilding's most notable characters, Vince Gironda (the Iron Guru), swears that dips are more effective than flat bench presses. While the debate rages on, few disagree that the movement is one of the most basic and effective of bodybuilding exercises.

Dipping bars may be parallel, like gymnastics bars, or they may be V-shaped. By performing the movement with the body held vertical, you place most of the stress on the triceps. Touching the chin on the chest and leaning forward shifts the stress to the lower chest muscles.

CHINUP BAR

Chinups are one of the first exercises people learn. You may have fond (or perhaps not so fond) memories of gym class in school. A high school fitness test may have required you to perform a certain number of chinups. At the time the maneuver may have been nothing more than an annoyance, but now that your bodybuilding career has started, let us be the first to inform you that chins are one of the best – if not *the* best – back exercises. You were not wasting time in gym class after all.

The chinup bar is a long (four to six feet) iron bar bolted either to the gym wall or to part of the Universal multistation. Various attachments are available (e.g. V-shaped handles) that allow a wide range of back

Finish

exercises to be performed. You can also work the biceps by doing chinups with a narrow (10- to 12-inch) grip.

PULLEYS

Most gyms have an assortment of cable and pulley machines. Usually the weight stack is connected to a long cable that terminates in a small handle. The most common pulley exercise is cable crossovers. This exercise primarily works the inner chest muscles. With a bit of creativity a bodybuilder can work all the muscles of the body using cables and pulleys, and they play a major role in precompetition training.

RACKS

Besides benches, gyms have a variety of upright structures called racks. Racks may be used for storing equipment, such as barbells and dumbells, or integrated into specific exercises. For example, most people will quickly reach the point on squats where they need the weight suspended on a rack. Lifting the bar from the floor and placing it on the shoulders would be out of the question. Also chest and shoulder barbell exercises often require some sort of stationary rack. Because of the amount of weight supported, racks are usually constructed of iron.

A specialized rack structure is the Smith machine, which is really a combination of barbell, machine and rack. The bar is loaded just like a standard barbell, but both ends slide up and down on two upright steel rods. Smith machines provide the benefits of free weights (full range of movement) with the safety of a rack. Catching pins or latches prevent the bar from dropping

to the floor. Many bodybuilders like to perform half- or quarter-movements with Smith machines, which provides the safety necessary for using large poundages in these exercises.

THE ARM-BLASTER

First popularized by Arnold Schwarzenegger and Franco Columbu, these small training aids will add variety to your biceps workouts. An arm-blaster is a two-foot long, half-foot wide, flat, curved metal bar (usually aluminum). It fits around the waist and is supported by a strap behind the neck. Used properly, the arm-blaster eliminates much of the cheating that many bodybuilders employ when executing biceps curls. With the elbows locked against the bar, swinging the weight up is virtually impossible.

MACHINES

The second major type of equipment found in gyms are machines. The oldest and most common are Universal Gym machines. During the last 20 years or so other manufacturers such as Nautilus and Polaris have exploded onto the bodybuilding scene. Some machines are designed for working individual muscles. Others may consist of one multistation that works the whole body. The Universal multistation machine, often called a *Gladiator,* is probably the most popular exercise assembly in the world. Because of its compact size and the variety of exercises that can be done with it, this unit is found in virtually all gyms – especially on school and college campuses. Although outdated by most of its younger rivals, the dependable Universal still finds its share of supporters.

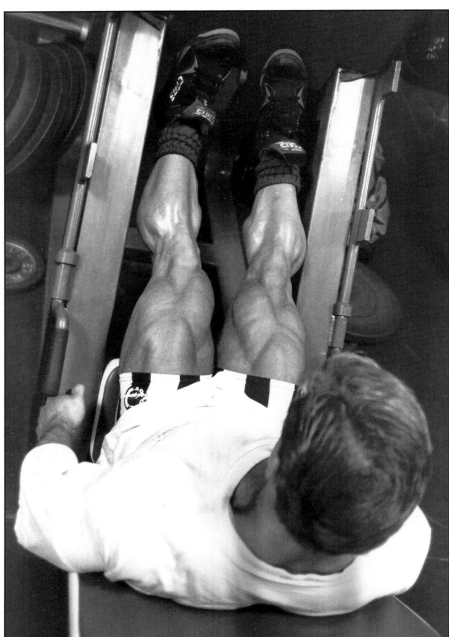

Lee Priest trains his massive quads on the leg press machine.

LEG MACHINES

While the barbell squat is considered the best leg exercise, there are a number of machine exercises that effectively work the legs. Many trainers find squats too painful on the lower back and knees. Others find squatting does nothing more than develop a large set of glutes (big ass!). Even if you make squats the mainstay of your leg training, you will still need to use other exercises to get maximum thigh development. Let's take a look at a few of the machines designed for leg work.

LEG-PRESS MACHINE

If the squat is the best thigh exercise, the leg press runs a close second. Most early leg presses required you to lie down on the floor and push the weight stack straight up, but, as mentioned in the safety section, this position is dangerous. It creates an enormous pressure buildup in the head. If you have high blood pressure or a high incidence of stroke in your family, *avoid this type of leg press!* Although most leg presses nowadays are set on a 45-degree angle to reduce pressure, you should still be aware of your family's medical history.

Leg presses have two main advantages over squats. First, you can load up the machine with plates. Before long you will have 500 to 1000 pounds on the machine. As you're seated, you don't have to worry about slipping or falling. Also, leg presses place less stress on the buttocks and lower back, and by adjusting your foot position you can reduce or even eliminate knee stress.

HACK MACHINE

Once you have a good thigh foundation developed by leg presses and/or squats, the next course of action is to start refining the area. Hack squats give that outer sweep to the thighs. Hacks (as they are affectionately called) are performed by lying against an angled platform with the weight attached to the rear or sides.

LEG EXTENSIONS AND LEG CURLS

This is really a two-in-one machine. The machine consists of a stack of weights attached to a long cable, a long flat bench, and an attachment with four round pads. By sitting on the end of the bench, he or she can work the lower quadriceps, particularly the muscles around the knee. By lying face down, the user can work the leg biceps (hamstrings). Your gym may have separate machines for leg extensions and leg curls.

CALF MACHINES

There are two types of calf machines – standing and seated. The standing calf machine works the upper calf muscles (gastrocnemius). It consists of a weight stack attached by a cable or iron bar to two shoulder pads. The user places the pads on the shoulders, and with the legs kept straight, flexes up and down on the toes.

The seated calf machine consists of a weight stack attached to a set of round pads, and a bench or chair to sit on. Instead of placing the pads on the shoulders, you place them on your knees. The seated calf machine works the lower calves (called the soleus).

LAT-PULLDOWN MACHINE

Like the chinup bar, the lat machine may stand on its own or be part of the Universal multistation. The word *lat* comes from *latissimus dorsi*, the large back muscles. Although chins are considered the best back exercise, they have one limitation. The user is restricted to using bodyweight only. Many people have difficulty performing more than 2 or 3 reps on the chinup bar.

The lat machine was developed to address this problem. Instead of pulling the bodyweight up, the user pulls down a bar, which is connected to a weight stack. This arrangement allows users to adjust the weight to suit their own needs.

Big Mike Francois sculpts his freaky calves on the standing calf machine.

Start

Finish

Start

Finish

TO USE OR NOT TO USE

The general consensus regarding machines is that you either love them or hate them. They have their advantages and disadvantages. On the plus side, you don't have to keep changing plates – simply move the selector pin. Unlike barbell and dumbell exercises, machine exercises do not present the problem of balancing the weight. You don't have to fight to keep the bar on an even keel. Simply push it up – it's balanced for you. This advantage is also the chief disadvantage of machines. The muscles you would use to stabilize and balance a barbell or dumbells are left out of the action with most machine exercises. Also, if one side of your body lags behind the other in terms of development, the imbalance can never be corrected by using machines.

The gorgeous Ericca Kern shapes her lats with lat pulldowns to the rear – one of the best back exercises.

Of course, there are other benefits to using machines. Some exercises are not possible with barbells. The pulldown is a good example. Most people have trouble lifting their bodyweight; therefore, one of the best back exercises, the chinup, is all but eliminated. The pulldown nearly duplicates the same movement, with the added benefit that you're able to adjust the weight. As well, there are many cable exercises that cannot be duplicated by free weights. Most bodybuilders incorporate a combination of machines and free weights into their workouts. You should do the same.

Posing between sets during your workout can be very beneficial to muscle stimulation and growth. — Mike Matarazzo and Ericca Kern.

Jason Arntz

Getting Started

Chapter Six

KNOWING WHAT YOU'RE MADE OF

BODYBUILDING BIOLOGY

A number of years ago the National Geographic Society released a book entitled *The Incredible Machine.* They were not referring to the latest jet fighter or to the newest supercomputer – their incredible machine was the human body!

In many respects the human body parallels a motor engine. Both take in fuel, both give off waste products, both have breakdowns, and perhaps most importantly, both need to be well maintained to run efficiently. While bodybuilding is primarily concerned with exercising the muscles, other systems of the body are also stimulated when you train. This chapter is an introductory lesson in human anatomy and physiology. We have placed special emphasis on those systems that are kept in good running order by bodybuilding.

MUSCLES

The skeleton is covered by approximately 650 muscles which create distinct contours and shape of the human body. Anatomists disagree as to the exact number of muscles. The main area of controversy concerns whether particular muscles are one unit or two units working together. (Clearly we did not evolve to please anatomists.) It is generally accepted that there are over 600 muscles in the human body. By contracting and relaxing, muscles produce movement. As anyone who has tried to walk down an icy sidewalk can verify, life would be much less exciting without them.

Although bodybuilding helps strengthen bones, ligaments and tendons, it is the muscles that receive the greatest benefit from this sport. The words *bodybuilding* and *muscles* go hand in hand. Muscles show the results of your labor. You don't ask a person to show you his Achilles tendon – you ask to see his biceps. Muscles are the symbol of strength even though pure strength relies on tendon power and leverage as much as muscle power. The associated ligaments and tendons are forgotten in the excitement – until you pull one.

There are three types of muscle tissue – cardiac, smooth and skeletal. From a bodybuilding standpoint we are concerned with the third type, so we will be brief when describing the first two.

Cardiac muscle is found only in the heart. Its main function is to force blood throughout the body's arteries, veins and capillaries. Smooth muscle makes up the

walls of such internal hollow organs as the small and large intestines, respiratory tract, and most of the reproductive system.

One of modern bodybuilding's greatest physiques belongs to Texas police officer Ronnie Coleman.

Skeletal muscle acquired its name because most is attached to the body's skeleton. This type of muscle is often said to be striated because of the alternating dark and light areas. (Smooth muscle is nonstriated, while cardiac is finely striated.) Unlike smooth and cardiac muscle which contracts involuntarily (i.e. you have no direct control over it), skeletal muscle contracts mainly voluntarily. This means you can contract it whenever you want.

Skeletal muscles are covered and held together by fibrous connective tissue called fascia. Fascia can be divided into two types – superficial and deep. Deep fascia is composed of layers of dense connective tissue and is found between individual muscles and between groups of muscles. As does superficial fascia, deep fascia contains an assortment of nerves, blood vessels and lymph vessels.

FUNCTION

Skeletal muscle has three main functions – movement, heat production and posture. In normal day-to-day activities (standing, walking, sitting, etc.) the contracting and relaxing of muscles produces much of the heat responsible for maintaining the body's internal temperature (average of 98.6 degrees Fahrenheit, 37 degrees Celsius). Even holding normal posture is a function of skeletal muscle. This is most obvious in people with lower-back injuries. The muscles of the lower back, called spinal erectors, help keep the body in an upright

position. If they become injured or even just tired, the person will have great difficulty sitting or standing upright.

STRUCTURE

Skeletal muscle is composed of long muscle cells called muscle fibers. These fibers give skeletal muscle its striated look. Muscle fibers are composed of smaller fibers called myofibrils, which in turn can be broken down into myofilaments.

The muscle fibers are supplied with blood by a network of capillaries, small blood vessels that branch off from larger arteries. Capillaries serve two main functions: They bring oxygen and nutrient-rich blood to the muscles, and at the same time they remove the waste products of metabolism.

Muscle contraction is under the control of the central nervous system, and follows an all-or-none principle. As this book is not a biophysiology text, we will not go into great detail here. Suffice it to say that, for a muscle fiber to contract, it needs a certain amount of stimulus. When this stimulus is received, the muscle fiber in question *fires* (neurophysiological jargon for *contracts*) to its full extent. A smaller stimulus does not produce a smaller contraction of a given muscle fiber. Once the minimum stimulus needed is received, the particular muscle fiber contracts fully.

Kevin Levrone winning the 1994 Arnold Schwarzenegger Classic.

Big Jim Quinn in a most-muscular pose between sets.

If the stimulus is spread over a large area (i.e. the whole muscle), all the muscle fibers involved will contract. The *amount* of muscle contraction is based on the number of fibers contracting, not the intensity of each fiber. Lifting a 20-pound dumbell will cause more fibers to contract than lifting a 10-pound dumbell. The individual muscle fibers, however, are contracting with the same intensity.

MUSCLE CONTRACTION

Most people know that muscles can become shorter by contracting, and then lengthen by relaxing. This action enables us to lift and hold objects, walk, breathe, and perform many other activities which involve movement. While most are aware of this concept, few understand the actual mechanisms involved.

Scientists explain the shortening of muscles with the sliding filament theory. Basically the theory states that muscle fibers contain two major proteins called actin and myosin, which are arranged in cylindrical

bundles. When a muscle contracts, the ends of the myosin attach to the actin molecules of adjacent fibers. The myosin then undergoes a conformational change which results in the end of the fiber bending, and thereby pulling the actin fiber. Once the myosin filament completes this change, it detaches itself from the actin fiber and straightens out. The whole process then repeats in a kind of "leap frog" manner, with adjacent fibers sliding past one another.

In order for this process to work most effectively, sufficient quantities of substances such as calcium, sodium and tropomyosin must be present. Most of these are supplied in the diet, so it's obvious why nutrition plays such an integral part in muscle contraction and growth.

ISOTONIC VERSUS ISOMETRIC

Muscle contraction falls into two broad categories. The first, isotonic, is what comes to mind when we think of muscle contraction. It involves a shortening and thickening of the muscle. Just about all bodybuilding exercises involve isotonic contractions.

The second type of contraction is called isometric. Readers familiar with bodybuilding history may remember Charles Atlas's training courses from the 1940s and 1950s. These exercises were based heavily on isometric contraction. Unlike isotonic contractions, isometric contractions don't involve a shortening of the muscle. As an example, forcefully push the heels of your hands together. While the muscles are tight and tense, they are not changing in size. You can get the same effect holding a barbell. Grab a bar and prepare to do a standing barbell curl. Before the bar moves up, the muscles are contracted but have not changed length. This is an isometric contraction. As soon as you start moving the bar, the biceps muscles begin to shorten and bunch up (get thicker). This is an isotonic contraction. Both types of contraction require energy and produce heat. Most body movements are a combination of the two, although some are predominantly one or the other. Walking is mainly isotonic, whereas standing is primarily isometric.

From a bodybuilding viewpoint it is generally accepted that isotonic movements are, by far, the more effective. There is a limit to what isometrics can accomplish. They are probably useful only when access to weights is impossible such as when you're on the road or staying in a hotel room. Some bodybuilders find that isometric (often called isotension) exercises add that extra bit of hardness when they're preparing for a contest, but from a mass-gaining point of view, sticking with basic isotonic exercises is advisable.

FIBER TYPES

Muscle fibers can be divided into two broad categories – fast twitch and slow twitch. The ratio of slow- to fast-twitch muscle fibers is determined by genetics, and doesn't change much over a lifetime. (We say *much* because recent research suggests that it might be possible to transform one into the other.)

FAST-TWITCH MUSCLE FIBER

Fast-twitch muscle fibers are adapted for rapid short-duration contraction. For example, the small muscles controlling the eyes and fingers are adapted for very quick movements, but they have a very short duration. Try blinking your eyes very fast for a sustained period of time. You'll find that after a minute or so (maybe less), they tire to the point that you can hardly move them. The reason? These muscles have a reduced amount of myoglobin, an oxygen-binding protein that speeds the rate of oxygen movement into a muscle

Anja Langer hits a front double-biceps pose onstage.

fiber. Fast-twitch muscle also has a smaller number of capillaries than slow-twitch muscle. This means a slower rate of nutrient replenishment.

The shortage of capillaries and myoglobin means a reduced number of red blood cells, giving the muscle a pale color. Such muscles are called white muscles.

SLOW-TWITCH MUSCLE FIBER

"Through intense endurance training you actually decrease your fast-twitch fibers while increasing your slow-twitch fibers. A transformation also takes place. Properties of slow-twitch fibers become those of some fast-twitch fibers, making them endurance oriented. With this in mind, you can see why endurance training can leave you with reductions in strength/power, size and density." **– Anja Langer, Pro Bodybuilder**

Areas of the body that need prolonged steady contractions are controlled by slow-twitch muscle fiber. Slow-twitch muscle fibers don't tire as easily as fast-twitch. For example, the spinal erectors of the back, which keep us upright all day, are primarily composed of slow-twitch muscle fibers. Unlike fast-twitch, slow-twitch muscle fibers have a large capillary network and increased amounts of myoglobin. The increased myoglobin gives the muscle a reddish color. The most easily visible examples of red and white muscle tissue are in poultry (chicken, turkey, duck, etc.). What we refer to as white meat and dark meat is in reality fast-twitch and slow-twitch muscle fiber.

What does this distinction mean for bodybuilding? For starters, most of the body's main muscle groups are predominantly fast- or slow-twitch. This means that each muscle group will respond differently to varied rep ranges. Calves and forearms respond best to high reps (20 plus), whereas other muscles such as those of the chest and back seem to require lower reps (8 to 10). Of course, these are generalizations. Some bodybuilders find heavy weight and low reps (6 to 8) to be the most effective combination for the calves.

An individual who has a predominance of slow-twitch muscle fibers would need to include a high number of sets and reps to adequately stimulate his or her muscles. Conversely, someone with a proportionately high number of fast-twitch muscle fibers would probably respond better to heavier weights and lower reps.

The latest research suggests that fast-twitch muscle fibers contract twice as quickly (it takes about one millisecond for a muscle fiber to contract) and are 10 times stronger than slow-twitch muscle fibers. They respond best to workouts involving 2 to 6 sets of 4 to 6 reps. The sets should be performed with the maximum amount of weight that can be handled for the given number of reps, the sixth rep being the last that could be completed. Slow-twitch muscle fibers were found to respond most effectively to a high-set (8 to 10), high-rep (12 to 20) routine.

CHAPTER SIX – KNOWING WHAT YOU'RE MADE OF

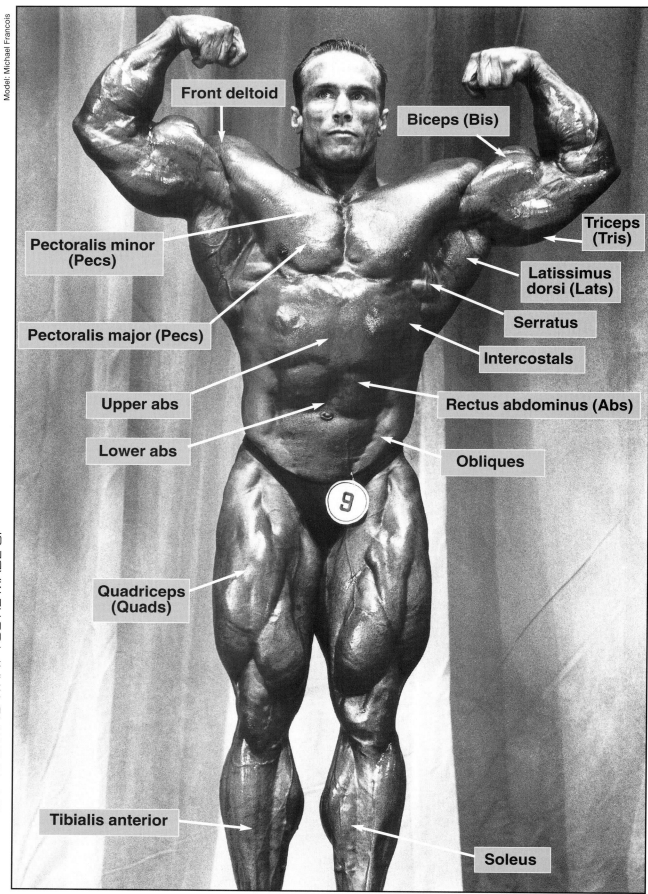

Front deltoid

Biceps (Bis)

Triceps (Tris)

Pectoralis minor (Pecs)

Latissimus dorsi (Lats)

Serratus

Pectoralis major (Pecs)

Intercostals

Rectus abdominus (Abs)

Upper abs

Lower abs

Obliques

Quadriceps (Quads)

Tibialis anterior

Soleus

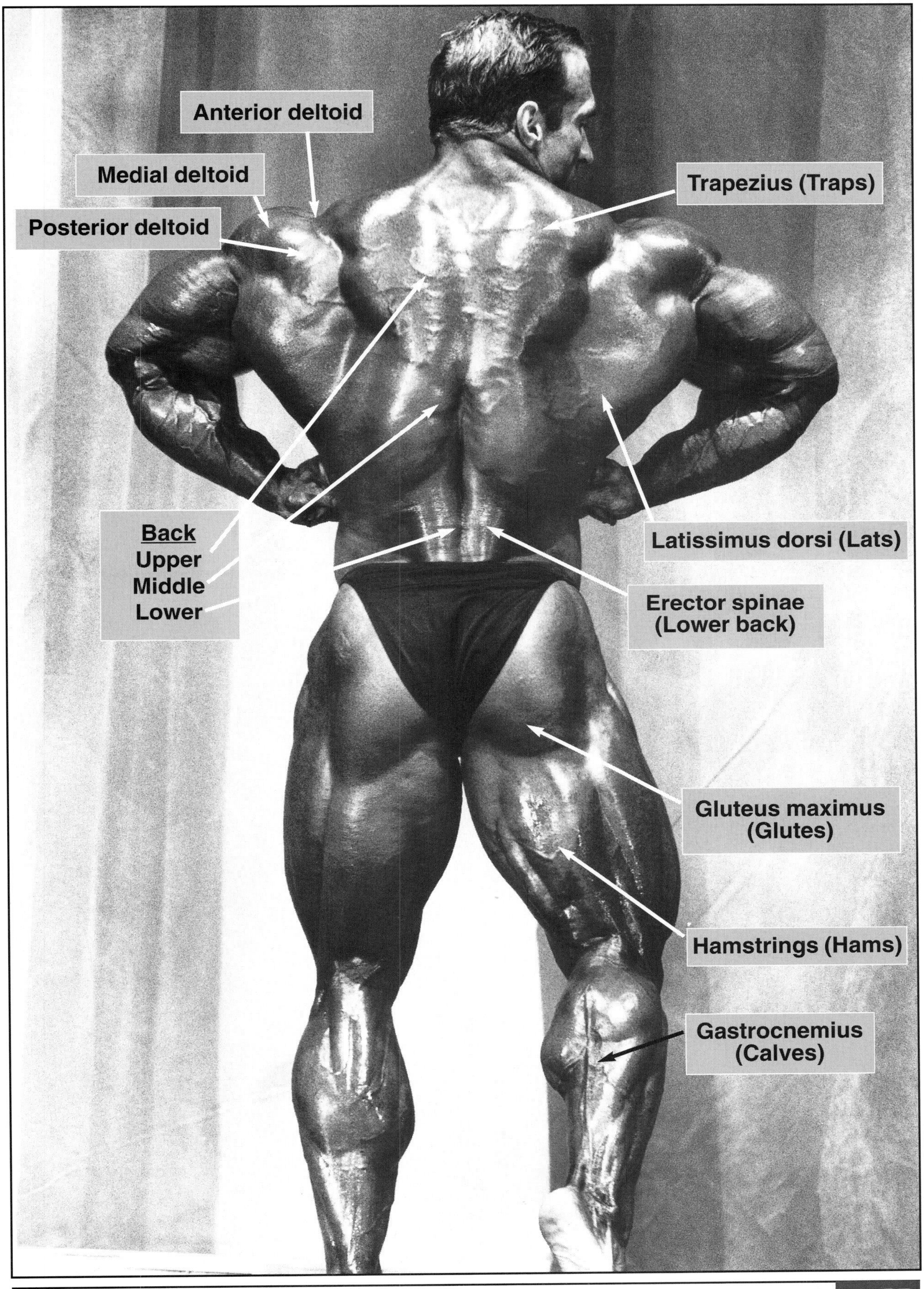

Anterior deltoid

Medial deltoid

Posterior deltoid

Trapezius (Traps)

<u>Back</u>
Upper
Middle
Lower

Latissimus dorsi (Lats)

Erector spinae (Lower back)

Gluteus maximus (Glutes)

Hamstrings (Hams)

Gastrocnemius (Calves)

CHAPTER SIX – KNOWING WHAT YOU'RE MADE OF

One of bodybuilding's fittest couples – Sue Price and Dave Fisher.

The average untrained person has muscles with a 50:50 fast-twitch to slow-twitch ratio. For top athletes, however, we find a different ratio. This is because their muscles respond to the specialized demands placed on them. In simple terms the body adapts to the type of stress endured – e.g. running versus weight training. The ratio of the two contributes to success in the athlete's chosen sport. Muscle biopsies on marathon runners reveal muscles with as high as 90 percent slow-twitch muscle fiber. For bodybuilders the ratio is reversed – red muscle fibers account for 80 percent of the muscle. The high percentage of red fibers can be explained by the type of workouts performed. Slow and continuous exercises with moderate to heavy weights (average rep range of 8 to 12) stimulate the production of red muscle fiber.

As for the white muscle fiber, recent studies suggest that white muscle fiber can be converted into red muscle fiber. This change results from slow and steady contractions over time. It's believed that the type of nerve impulse determines the ratio of fast-twitch to slow-twitch (white to red) muscle fiber.

Even among the top bodybuilders there is much variation. Some have ratios in favor of fast-twitch, others in favor of slow-twitch. Through trial and error each group has determined which type of training works best for them. Unless your ratio is extreme – a rare phenomenon for the average person – you can make great progress no matter which type of muscle fiber predominates.

For all of the above reasons bodybuilders generally alternate rep ranges (6 to 8 versus 12 to 15). This way, no matter what the individual fiber ratio, you can be sure that the muscles are being fully stimulated.

MUSCLES – HOW THEY WORK

Skeletal muscles produce movements by pulling on tendons which in turn pull on the connecting bone. Most muscles pass across a joint and are attached to the bones that form the joint. When a muscle contracts, one of the attached bones remains stationary while the other moves along with the contraction. For convenience we say that the muscle section attached to the stationary bone is called the origin, and the point of muscle attachment on the moving bone is called the insertion. Keep in mind that origin and insertion are relative terms, and can be reversed depending on the action involved.

Contrary to popular belief, muscles can only pull, not push. Even though many exercises are considered pushing movements, the muscle being worked is actually pulling the associated bone. When you're performing triceps extensions, the triceps muscle is contracting and *pulling* the forearm to an extended position, yet most bodybuilders refer to triceps extensions (as well as any other triceps exercise for that matter) as a pushing movement. Similarly the bench press, while commonly called a pushing exercise, causes the chest muscles to contract, pulling the arms toward the center of the body.

The human body evolved so that many of the major muscle groups work in opposing pairs. Triceps and biceps provide a classic example. Contraction of the biceps draws the forearm towards the body, whereas the triceps extends the forearm away from the body and back to its original extended position.

To further enhance your bodybuilding biology vocabulary, the muscle that contracts to produce a desired movement is called the agonist. The muscle that produces the opposite movement is called the antagonist. English majors will recognize the terms from studying novels, the protagonist being the central character, while his or her opponent is the antagonist. When the agonist (e.g. biceps) is contracting, the antagonist (triceps) is relaxed. As with insertions and origins, an agonist in one movement may be an antagonist in another.

Bodybuilders often replace the words *agonist* and *antagonist* with *flexor* and *extensor.* Contraction of the biceps brings the lower and upper arm bones closer together. Conversely, flexing the triceps (bodybuilders rarely say they are flexing the triceps; instead they use the word *extending)* draws the bones away from one another, increasing the angle. You flex the biceps and extend the triceps.

Most complex exercise movements are the result of many muscles working together. For example, the bench press is considered to be primarily a chest exercise, but the shoulders and triceps also receive a great deal of stimulation. In fact, some trainers find the bench press a poor exercise for chest – all they get is a well-developed set of front deltoids or triceps. There is nothing wrong with this. It just means you have to start doing other exercises to work your chest.

In the bench press the chest muscles (pectorals) are called the primary movers, and the deltoids and triceps are referred to as secondary movers. Besides secondary movers, there are other muscles that assist the primary movers. The back muscles (latissimus dorsi) help stabilize the body. Even though they are not directly involved in moving the weight, they nevertheless assist the primary movers.

Aaron Baker checks out his incredible physique after another grueling training session.

CHAPTER SIX – KNOWING WHAT YOU'RE MADE OF

The amazing Kevin Levrone.

NAMING

The name of a muscle typically tells us something about its structure, location, size or function. Shape is described in such muscles as the trapezius, deltoid or gracilis. The corresponding shapes are trapezoidal, triangular and slender, respectively. Gluteus maximus and gluteus minimus, the muscles that make up the buttocks region, are two names that indicate relative sizes.

Such terms as supraspinatus and infraspinatus indicate relative position – *supra* indicating above the spine of the scapula, and *infra* below the spine of the scapula. Familiar to most bodybuilders are the latissimus dorsi. They are named as such to indicate they are found laterally on the body towards the dorsal or back region. (Just remember where a shark's dorsal fin is located.) Likewise the rectus abdominus are located in the abdominal region.

Some muscles are named according to the number of their heads. The head is defined as the expanded, rounded surface or *belly* of a muscle. The biceps muscle has two heads, hence the prefix *bi.* The triceps has three heads, and the thighs, called quadriceps, have four heads.

Muscles can also be named according to the direction of their fibers – transverse (across) and obliques (slanted). They indicate the direction of the muscle fibers with respect to the structures to which they are attached.

Most muscle groups are named by a combination of two or more of the previous examples. For simplicity, bodybuilders divide the body into eight to 10 muscle groups – chest, back, thighs, hamstrings, shoulders, biceps, triceps, calves, forearms and abdominals.

Keep in mind that these names refer to muscle groups, not individual muscles. Later in the text we will start designing exercise programs based on the muscle groups. The following table lists the major muscle groups that will become familiar as you progress in your bodybuilding. The authors have no intention of listing the 650 or more individual muscles of the body!

NAME OF MUSCLE	COMMON NAME	FUNCTION
Trapezius	Traps	To elevate, rotate and retract the scapulas (shoulder blades).
Pectorals (major and minor)	Pecs	To draw the arms forward toward the center of the body.
Deltoids	Delts (shoulder)	To elevate and rotate the arms.
Latissimus dorsi	Lats (back)	To draw the arms back toward the dorsal region.
Biceps	Bis	To flex (curl) the forearm at the elbow joint.
Triceps	Tris	To extend the forearm at the elbow joint.
Quadriceps	Quads (thigh)	To extend the lower leg at the knee joint.
Leg biceps	Hamstrings	To flex (curl) the lower leg at the knee joint.
Soleus	Calves	To flex the foot at the ankle joint (primarily when the leg is bent).
Gastrocnemius	Calves	To flex the foot at the ankle joint (primarily when the leg is straight)
Abdominals	Abs	To bend the body at the waist and stabilize it when walking and sitting.

THE PUMP

"Ve vant to pump you up!"
**– Hans and Franz, those endearing characters
with that familiar Austrian accent, from SNL**

Before we leave muscles, we should mention a unique bodybuilding term – *the pump*. Considered by some athletes to be almost sexual in nature, the pump is conceivably the most desired sensation of hard-training body-builders. After a couple of sets of an exercise the muscle becomes engorged with blood. It swells, the veins stand out, and the owner begins to think that on any day of the week he could match physiques with Arnold Schwarzenegger!

The pump is caused by blood rushing into the muscle faster than the circulatory system can remove it. Most bodybuilders assess the quality of the workout by the level of pump. If the worked muscle does not pump to any degree, the individual often feels the workout was wasted.

The level of pump varies among individuals and also within individuals. One set may produce an incredible pump one day, while on another day no amount of exercise will bring on the desired feeling. In addition, it's possible to fully pump the muscle, only to lose the pump with continued exercising. When you begin to lose the pump, stop exercising that particular muscle. The idea is to become so in tune with your body that you know exactly the maximum number of sets to perform without losing the pump.

Is a good pump necessary? Although it's not a prerequisite for growth to occur, the general consensus is that the better the pump the greater the development. For one thing, a good pump signifies that the muscle in question is receiving a good blood supply. Also, the speed at which a muscle pumps is indicative of its neuromuscular pathway. There is a definite relationship among blood supply, nerve transmission and muscle growth. In short, the better the blood supply to a muscle, the better it pumps, and the faster it grows.

More pump normally means more growth because of the increased blood supply. It's not so much the blood that's important as what it carries. As the body's chief transport medium, blood brings to the muscles all the nutrients and oxygen needed for growth and repair. At the same time blood removes such metabolic wastes as carbon dioxide and lactic acid. An increased

Christa Bauch monitors her progress in the gym mirror between sets.

blood supply also means the establishment of more blood vessels.

If you need more convincing, ask yourself this question: "What are my best bodyparts?" Chances are your best muscle groups are those which pump up the fastest and to the greatest extent. On the other side of the coin, we bet those muscles that lag behind probably pump little or not at all.

Achieving a proper pump requires intense, heavy training, not endless sets of reps using light weight.

Top Canadian pro Joe Spinello.

thighs, and marathon runners have long slender thighs? Sprinters concentrate on doing the maximum amount of work in the shortest time. Marathon runners, on the other hand, expend so much energy over such a long time that their systems (particularly their muscles) never get a chance to totally recover. The same principle holds true for bodybuilders. Spend hours on the stationary bike or performing endless high-rep sets, and the muscles cannot help but take on a stringy appearance. There is a fine line between too much and not enough.

If you're eating properly and not overtraining, the lack of a pump is due to some other cause. How long do you rest between sets? Anything over two minutes is way too much. Most bodybuilders find 45 seconds to a minute to be the best rest interval. If you can operate on less rest – say, 30 seconds or so – you most certainly will achieve a pump as long as you're getting 6 reps per set.

Other training techniques that almost certainly guarantee a pump are supersets, trisets and giant sets. All of these training practices ensure much work being done in a short time – the perfect conditions for a great pump.

While achieving a pump is not an absolute necessity, it is one of the most frequently used benchmarks for measuring the adequacy of a workout. Make a habit of leaving the gym with a muscle-busting pump, and there can be but one outcome – growth.

EXERCISE AND ADAPTATION

Unlike a machine which cannot repair itself, the human body is continuously modifying its physiology. If a harmful organism invades, antibodies and white blood cells rush to the defense. A small skin abrasion is repaired in a few days, and muscle growth follows a similar pattern.

Many people refer to bodybuilding as progressive resistance training. This is an adequate description as your goal is to gradually increase the amount of weight lifted in each exercise. Muscles do not grow during training. Think of exercise as a type of message. By working out you are ordering your muscles to get bigger and stronger. With time you have to send stronger messages (heavier weight) to get the same effect.

Adaptation is defined as a change in response to a stimulus. Let's see how this definition applies to bodybuilding. When you perform an intense set of curls, after a given number of reps the biceps will become fatigued. Over the next couple of days the body repairs the damage. (This is a relative term and does not imply that the muscle has been injured, only that some muscle tissue has been broken down.) Repair involves the use of building blocks called amino acids (more on these in the nutrition chapter). The body combines the amino acids into protein which is then integrated into muscle tissue.

Such training strategies as Vince Gironda's 6 sets of 6 reps with 30 seconds between sets, and Dorian Yates's high-intensity training (a modification of Mike Mentzer's heavy-duty system) are great ways to achieve the maximum pump in the shortest time.

What happens if you fail to achieve a pump or it's much smaller than usual? Such a failure is caused by one of several factors. Perhaps you're not eating enough carbs to maintain muscle glycogen levels. All the training in the world will not produce a pump if there is no glycogen in your muscles. A flat look to the muscles and a failure to achieve a pump are caused by insufficient glycogen storage. You haven't consumed enough carbohydrate in your diet. If you notice a failure to get a pump, recheck your diet to see if it contained sufficient carbohydrate. Such foods as oatmeal and potatoes are great in this respect.

Another reason for a less than adequate pump is overtraining. Doing 20 sets per bodypart is the surest way to hold back and in many cases reverse your progress. There is no way your recovery system can restock the body's muscles with glycogen by following such a routine. Why do sprinters have huge muscular

An interesting fact about the recuperation process is that the body doesn't repair the muscle as it was. Instead it goes a step further, making the muscle slightly larger and stronger. Over time – a few months to a few years, depending on the individual – the muscle becomes noticeably larger and stronger. To keep the muscle growing, the amount of weight lifted must be gradually *(gradually!)* increased.

The number of skeletal muscle cells in the body does not increase as a result of strenuous exercise – only their diameter increases. In addition, the muscles' blood supply and number of mitochondria (energy-producing organelles) is increased. This whole process is called hypertrophy. The opposite may also occur. If a muscle is not regularly exercised, or there has been some sort of nerve damage, it begins to shrink. This process is called muscular atrophy. A good example of atrophy can be seen in astronauts who spend long periods of time in orbit. The reduced gravity means their muscles don't have to work as hard and they lose muscle mass.

Dave Fisher hits a twisting back double-biceps pose.

ASSOCIATED STRUCTURES

TENDONS

Muscles are not attached directly to bones or other muscles. They are connected by a tough cord of connective tissue called a tendon. A tendon may connect a muscle to another muscle, or a muscle to a bone. The thickest tendon in the human body is the Achilles tendon. It attaches the calf muscle to the heel bone. From a bodybuilding perspective, the biceps tendon, which connects the biceps to the radius bone of the forearm, is probably the most familiar. Tendons add length and thickness to muscles and are especially important in reducing muscle strain.

LIGAMENTS

Bones are not attached directly to one another, but are joined by fibrous connective tissue called ligaments. Varying in shape and even strength depending on their location and function, most ligaments are considered *inelastic,* yet they are pliable to permit movement. Ligaments tend to tear rather than stretch, but because

The superb physique of Paul DeMayo.

One of the most frequent sports injuries is torn knee cartilage. When this happens the cartilage may become lodged between the upper (femur) and lower (tibia) leg bones, causing the joint to lock. The patient of 20 years ago could look forward to months of therapy and pain. Recent advances in arthroscopic surgery have cut the recovery time in half. Using microscopic tools, surgeons can repair the damaged cartilage, thus preventing the surrounding muscles from atrophying.

As with other sports, the most common bodybuilding injuries involving cartilage concern the knee region. Bouncing at the bottom of the squat does not make for a great set of thighs. Neither does forcefully locking out in the leg extension. Remember, perform the movements in a nice, slow manner.

BURSAE AND TENDON SHEATHS

Two other structures associated with muscles and joints are bursae and tendon sheaths. Bursae are flattened sacs that are filled with synovial fluid. They are found wherever it is necessary to eliminate the friction that occurs when a muscle or tendon rubs against another muscle, tendon or bone. Bursae also cushion certain muscles and facilitate the movement of muscles over bony surfaces.

A modification of bursae is tendon sheaths – long cylindrical sacs filled with synovial fluid that surround long tendons. Tendon sheaths allow tendons to slide easily. They are found in areas where the tendons are under constant movement and friction such as wrists, fingers and palms.

of their strength they can withstand a great amount of stress. When they do tear, the condition is marked by intense pain and swelling. Often surgery is needed to correct the problem.

CARTILAGE

Closely associated with ligaments is cartilage. This specialized type of connective tissue can be called the shock absorbers of the body. Its main function is to prevent the bones from rubbing against one another at joints. With time, disease or injury, cartilage tissue may become damaged, resulting in reduced movement and pain.

CARDIOVASCULAR SYSTEM
HEART

The cardiovascular system is composed of the heart, blood vessels and blood. The heart is shaped like a blunt cone and is about the size of a clenched fist. In males it weighs about 300 grams, in females about 250 grams. Because of its importance the heart is one of the first organs to begin functioning in a developing embryo about four weeks after conception.

The heart is divided into four chambers – two entering chambers called atria and two pumping chambers called ventricles. Because of this unique arrangement, the heart can be considered a double pump. The oxygen-depleted blood from the body's tissues returns to the right atrium and is then pumped by the right ventricle into the lungs where oxygen and carbon dioxide are exchanged. The newly oxygenated blood returns to the heart at the left atrium. From here it is pumped by the powerful left ventricle to the rest of the body.

BLOOD VESSELS

Although the heart is the centre of the cardiovascular system, it's the affiliated blood vessels that carry the blood throughout the body. There are three types of blood vessels – arteries, veins and capillaries. While all three carry blood, each has a different task.

Arteries carry blood away from the heart. Because of this function arterial walls are very elastic and can expand in relation to the blood being pushed by the contracting ventricles. You can feel this sensation the next time you perform a heavy set of squats. Place your fingers on your wrist and notice the pulsations just below the skin surface. Each pulse corresponds to one beat of the heart. We commonly refer to it as pulse rate, though in fact we are measuring heart rate.

Veins return blood to the heart. They are more flexible than arteries because of their thinner walls, and will collapse if blood pressure is not maintained. The speed of blood traveling through veins is much slower than through arteries.

Capillaries are microscopic blood vessels which serve as exchange points among arteries, veins, and the body's tissues. Their small size and large numbers supply an enormous amount of surface area for the exchange of gases, nutrients and waste products. To give an idea of the amount of surface area involved, if the capillaries of the body were connected end to end, the resulting chain would stretch 100,000 kilometers. Perhaps more revealing is the fact that for every pound of fat lost, the heart has 1700 fewer kilometers to pump blood through.

BLOOD

The main purpose of all this plumbing is to provide a highway for the body's blood supply. As blood circulates throughout the body, tissues are continuously adding their waste products, secretions and metabolites. Simultaneously the body's tissues remove vital nutrients, oxygen, hormones and other important substances from the blood.

In summary, blood serves the following functions:
1. Transports oxygen from the lungs to the body tissues and transports the resulting waste products of cellular metabolism from the body's tissues to the various filtration organs. These include the liver, kidneys and sweat glands.
2. Regulates blood-clotting to stop bleeding, body temperature by increasing or decreasing blood flow to the

Kevin Levrone and Vince Taylor flex their flawless abs.

skin, acid-base balance (PH) through the distribution of buffers, and the amount of water and electrolytes in body fluids.

3. Protects against harmful microorganisms and other dangerous substances by transporting white blood cells, proteins and antibodies to the site or sites of infection.

Blood makes up about eight percent of the bodyweight of an average male, translating into a volume of about five to six liters. It consists of a liquid part, called plasma, and a solid part called formed elements. The formed elements include red blood cells, white blood cells and platelets.

THE COMPONENTS OF BLOOD

Plasma – the liquid part of blood which is composed of 90 percent water, seven percent proteins, and three percent dissolved substances such as amino acids, glucose, enzymes, hormones, electrolytes, wastes and nutrients.

Red blood cells (RBCs) – make up half the volume of the blood. They are shaped like a flat donut without the hole in the middle. There are about 25 trillion RBCs in the human body at a density of six million for every cubic millimeter of blood. Virtually the entire weight of the RBC is composed of an oxygen-attracting globular protein called haemoglobin. Since part of the haemoglobin molecule contains iron, the RBC has a reddish color – hence the name red blood cell. The main function of RBCs is to transport oxygen from the lungs to the body's tissues. At the same time waste gases such as carbon dioxide are transported to the lungs where they are exhaled.

White blood cells (WBCs) – serve as scavengers that destroy microorganisms at infection sites, help remove foreign molecules, and remove debris that results from dead or injured tissue cells. In adults there are between 4000 and 11,000 WBCs per cubic millimeter of blood. This number may increase to 25,000 or more in times of infection.

Platelets – are disk-shaped blood cells whose main function is to start the intricate process of blood-clotting. Roughly 200 billion platelets are produced by the body every day, each with a life span of only seven to eight days. When a blood vessel is injured, platelets immediately move to the injured area and begin to clump together. In so doing, they release a chemical called serotonin, a blood-vessel constriction. If the cut is small, the platelet plug and associated constricting will prevent blood loss. If the cut is considerable, platelets begin the process of blood-clotting. This mechanism will not be looked at in detail here. Suffice it to say that it involves numerous steps with the end result a fibrous net which entangles escaping blood cells, forming a clot. After a few hours the clot begins to dry out, and a solid barrier is left. After a few days the dried-out clot (commonly called a scab) falls off, exposing the repaired, underlying tissue.

LYMPH SYSTEM

In addition to the blood circulatory system, there is a subsystem called the lymphatic system. Its three main functions are:

1. collection and return of interstitial fluid to the blood.
2. contribution to the immune system's fight against invading organisms.
3. absorption of lipids from the digestive tract.

The awesome mass of Lee Priest.

The lymphatic system is similar to the cardiovascular system in that it has a network of transport vessels and associated fluid. The fluid, called lymph, is a clear liquid that serves as the system's transport medium. At regular intervals lymph vessels are organized into small masses of tissue called lymph nodules (nodes). Your tonsils (if you still have them) and adenoids are two such examples. The thymus gland and spleen are also part of the lymph system. You're probably aware that it's possible to survive without parts of the lymph system (spleen and tonsils). If these become infected and have to be removed, other parts of the body take over and perform the same functions.

HOW IT WORKS

As with the cardiovascular system, the lymph vessels terminate at the body's tissues with a network of capillaries. Interstitial fluid enters the capillaries and is passed on to larger vessels called lymphatics. This fluid is then carried by way of the lymphatics to the various lymph nodes, the most prominent being found in the neck, armpits and groin. Here it is filtered to remove bacteria and other harmful matter. Afterwards the fluid reenters the circulatory system by way of the subclavian veins found in the shoulder region.

Unlike the cardiovascular system, the lymph system does not have a pumping muscle analogous to the heart. Instead, the walls of the lymph vessels pulsate, pushing the fluid along. Valves within the vessels prevent the lymph from flowing backward. The rate of flow is increased when anything compresses body tissue. When muscles contract or arteries pulsate, the increased pressure on the lymph vessels enhances the flow of lymph fluid.

Bodybuilders and other hard-training athletes may periodically notice a swelling of the lymph nodes, particularly in the neck and armpit regions. This is usually a sign of overtraining. The increased stress placed on the body taxes the lymph system to the limit. The swelling is the result of a buildup of fluid containing the byproducts of exercise. The lymph system will cleanse itself of such metabolic debris after a few days, and the swelling will go down. Of course, if you keep overstressing the body with a twice-a-day, six-day-a-week program, this process will be impeded. We will take a more detailed look at overtraining later in the book.

SKIN – THE FIRST LINE OF DEFENSE

What's the largest organ in the human body? No, it's not the liver. Nor is it the heart or brain. Give up? The body's largest organ is the skin. Most people don't think of it as an organ because it's neither internal nor fixed in its shape – i.e. it's not a neat little package like a kidney. It measures 20 square feet in surface area and has an average thickness of 2 mm. Because of its importance to the body, the skin receives roughly one-third of all circulated blood.

The skin is the body's first line of defense against invading organisms. Long before the immune system comes into play, harmful pathogens have to contend with this protective outer covering. Germs make their way into the body at breaks or tears. This can be seen the next time you receive a small cut. The area first takes on a reddish color, and soon white blood cells (commonly called pus) rush to the area and engage the invaders. In all but the most extreme cases the condition clears up within a few days.

Kim Chizevsky hits an abdominal-and-thigh pose.

Besides protecting, the skin helps regulate body temperature. On hot summer days millions of sweat glands release water, the evaporation of which cools the body. Make sure you consume sufficient water during long, hot training sessions. Failure to do so could lead to heat exhaustion or heat stroke.

Two skin characteristics make it important to bodybuilders – color and thickness. The darker-tanned competitor will have an advantage over his lighter opponent. For this reason bodybuilders will spend many hours prior to a contest working on their tan. (For the full treatment of this topic see the section on competition.)

Diana Dennis displays her beautiful physique onstage.

Your nervous system can be called the "first and last" system of the body. It is the first system to develop in an embryo, and the last system to shut down (not counting a sudden tragic death) when you die.

The nervous system can be subdivided into the central, autonomic and the peripheral nervous systems. The central nervous system (CNS) consists of the brain and spinal cord, which are protected by the skull and vertebral column. The CNS may be thought of as the body's principal control center. Here messages are received, sorted, interpreted and relayed to and from all parts of the body.

The peripheral nervous system (PNS) consists of nerve cells and their associated fibers, emerging from and going to the CNS. The PNS serves as an intermediary between the body's muscles and organs and the CNS.

The autonomic nervous system controls the body's smooth muscles, glands and organs. As the name implies, the autonomic system controls the involuntary target organs – organs you have no direct control over. You have no authority over your digestion rate – except through drug use – and although you can change your heart rate, this is an indirect action.

The nervous system conducts messages with nerve impulses. These are electro-chemical changes set up between adjacent nerve cells. These chemical changes are under the control of specific ions (charged atoms), the most common being sodium, potassium and calcium. The presence or absence of one or more of these ions sets up different electrical charges between adjacent nerve cells. These electrical differences (called potential gradients) cause the nerve cell to "fire," the result being a nerve impulse.

Another name for these ions is *electrolytes.* Many bodybuilders consume electrolyte drinks to replenish their supply of these important substances which are lost in sweat during an intense workout. For proper biochemical functioning, electrolyte levels must be in balance. Too much sodium, for example, causes the body to dehydrate as it tries to flush the sodium out with water. Too little interferes with the nervous and muscular systems. The muscle cramps experienced by some bodybuilders during a contest are often caused by an improper electrolytic balance, frequently brought on by diuretics (more on this in the competition and nutrition sections).

From a bodybuilding perspective, it's probably the spinal cord that causes the most problems. Even with good form and proper warmups, sooner or later many bodybuilders develop a bad back. Most injuries are minor and consist of slight muscle strains to the spinal erectors. Reducing the weight or changing exercises is all that is necessary to address the problem. In a few cases, however, the underlying problem is within the spinal column itself. This is a much more serious situa-

Skin thickness also plays an important role in the success of a bodybuilder. Thick skin obscures muscle separation and striations. Tanning tightens the skin, making it hug the body's contours. Rapid weight fluctuations (bulking up) can lead to baggy skin or stretch marks, both of which detract from the final product – a contest-winning physique.

Unlike a best-selling book, a great physique *is* judged by its cover. Proper skin care is an integral part of modern bodybuilding. Don't make the mistake of neglecting your cover!

THE NERVOUS SYSTEM

In order to maintain homeostasis (a fancy term that means internal balance with respect to outside factors), the body is constantly reacting and adjusting to the external environment. Such changes are detected and conveyed via nerves to the spinal cord and brain. Here the messages are analyzed, combined, compared and coordinated by a process called integration. After being sorted out, messages are conveyed by nerves to the body's various target organs, of which glands and muscles are two of the most prominent. Once stimulated, muscles contract or relax, and glands release their products (called hormones).

tion so at the slightest sign of such an injury, stop your training and see your physician. To give some idea of why back injuries are among the most common, let's take a closer look at the back's structure.

THE VERTEBRAL COLUMN

There are 31 pairs of spinal nerves exiting the spinal cord through the associated spinal bones called vertebrae. The great number of vertebrae gives the spine tremendous flexibility. If the spine consisted of only one or two bones, such simple movements as bending over or sitting down would be almost impossible. Evolution has tackled this problem by fitting the human spine with 31 articulating vertebrae. Many individuals have healthy spines but reduced flexibility. In this case the lack of flexibility can be traced to the associated muscles and connective tissue. Regular stretching exercises will greatly enhance the spine's flexibility. The vertebrae allow ranges of movement that otherwise could not be accomplished with a lesser number of bones.

Each vertebra has a pencil-sized hole in the middle which houses and protects the spinal cord. Unfortunately, with improper exercise technique or too much weight, damage is often done to the spinal area, particularly the lower spinal region.

Tom Platz blasts his chest on the pec-dek.

CHAPTER SIX - KNOWING WHAT YOU'RE MADE OF

The beautiful Tonya Knight.

Of all the exercises that may injure the lower back, perhaps none contributes mishaps more frequently than squats. The human spine was not designed to support hundreds of pounds of weight. Some medical experts argue that it does a poor job of supporting bodyweight, given the number of bad backs diagnosed each year. One of the arguments put forward for the large number of bad backs is the theory that human brains outstripped human physiology. In short, humans stood up too quickly. We are walking around with a spinal design that would probably be more suited to walking on all fours. Whether you agree with this theory or not, few would argue that spinal injuries are to be avoided at all cost. Later in the text we will look at injuries in more detail, and what you can do to avoid or treat them.

THE ENDOCRINE SYSTEM

The endocrine system works with the nervous system to maintain the body's internal balance. It is, in other words, a regulatory system. Regulation can take two forms – monitoring and adjusting internal physiological mechanisms, and adapting the body to external stimuli. The endocrine system carries out these important functions by use of chemical messengers called hormones. By definition a hormone is a chemical substance that is produced in one part of the body and travels by way of the bloodstream to another area where it carries out its action. Bodybuilders will be interested to know that hormones are either protein or steroid in nature.

Hormone production and release are controlled by various parts of the brain. Among these areas are the hypothalamus, and anterior and posterior pituitaries. These activation centers stimulate the various endocrine glands that are located throughout the body. Everything from excretion to digestion to sleep and sex drive is controlled by hormones. For the purposes of this book it's not necessary to go into great detail. To give the reader a basic understanding of endocrinology (the study of hormones), we shall look at one hormone, testosterone, and its implications for bodybuilders.

Testosterone is produced by the testes of sexually mature males. It's often called "the male hormone," but this term is misleading as females also have testosterone circulating in their bodies. Conversely the hormone estrogen, often referred to as "the female hormone," is found in males. It's the relative concentrations of both that have given rise to the descriptions *male* and *female.*

Through a number of intermediate steps, testosterone is produced from the precursor, cholesterol. (Yes, there is a use for it after all, but don't consciously try to include it in your diet as you will get all you need, even if you cut down on high-cholesterol food.)

Testosterone has numerous functions, among which are deepening of the voice, growth of pubic hair, increased muscle size and strength, and sperm production. This is the hormone that causes males to be, on average, larger and stronger than females. Even among males there is much variation. Ectomorphs tend to have low levels, and are usually underweight, timid and nervous. Nervousness could possibly reduce testosterone levels, so it's difficult to say which is the cause and which is the effect.

Mesomorphs have bloodstreams loaded with testosterone. The result – low bodyfat level, a skeleton covered with muscle (or great potential for it), and a tendency towards increased aggression. The high levels of circulating hormone produce rapid muscular weight gains, and at the same time keep bodyfat percentage to a minimum.

Endomorphs fall somewhere in between. They have good muscle size but they are also inclined to carry excess fat.

The most recent research suggests that regular exercise (including bodybuilding) increases production of testosterone. Naturally there is an upper limit. Train too hard for too long and you'll overtax the body's recovery system. To combat stress, the body reduces testosterone production and increases cortisol production. Cortisol has the opposite effect of testosterone, as it reduces muscle mass. This is why we keep stressing the perils of overtraining throughout the book.

The great Ronnie Coleman.

Chapter Seven

WARMING UP AND RECORD KEEPING

The flawless physique of Bob Paris.

"I make it a point to spend at least 10 to 15 minutes warming up before training a particular bodypart. Warming up can be accomplished by many means, such as stationary cycling, walking the treadmill, using a stair machine, performing several light sets of a given exercise that stresses the same muscles as you'll be training, etc."
– Bob Paris
IFBB Professional Bodybuilder

THE WARMUP

Before plunging headfirst into training, it's essential that you adequately prepare the body. This, of course, means warming up, and although often neglected, the warmup should be an integral part of any workout. In their quest to attack the weights, many bodybuilders ignore one of the most basic athletic fundamentals – exercise preparation.

The following are the benefits of a proper warmup:

1. A proper warmup helps prevent injuries to muscles.
2. Warming up increases the removal of lactic acid accumulated during previous workouts.
3. Warming up increases the efficiency of contracting muscles.
4. Research suggests neuromuscular coordination is enhanced by warming up.
5. A proper warmup improves the coordination of individual exercises.
6. A good warmup increases heart rate and speeds blood circulation.
7. A good warmup brings greater oxygen reserves to the muscles.

There is a fine line between a warmup that prepares the body for intense exercise and one that infringes on the

Bob Paris knows the importance of warming up before each workout.

workout. If the warmup is not adequate, you run the risk of injury. Too intense a warmup will deplete energy reserves. As a general rule, a good warmup should raise the heart rate, produce light sweat, and cause an increase in body temperature. Here are some guidelines:

1. Tailor your warmup so that it increases body temperature and produces sweat, but at the same time does not produce fatigue.

2. A good warmup should include stretching exercises to loosen the muscles.

3. Include movements that are common to the exercises you will be doing in your workout. This prepares specific muscles for intense exercise.

4. End the warmup far enough in advance so it does not impede performance, but don't wait so long that the effects of the warmup wear off.

Warmups can be divided into three broad categories, and we'll look at all three in detail.

PHASE ONE

The first phase can be considered a whole-body warmup. You may call it "chest day" or "leg day," but keep in mind that the heart and lungs are an integral part as well. Like your muscles, they need to be working efficiently for an optimum workout.

For most bodybuilders a stationary bike can accomplish this goal. Five to ten minutes of light to moderate pedaling is sufficient. There's no need to run the *tour de France!* A few minutes on the bike will get the heart and lungs pumping. Doing so ensures full circulation when you hit the weights. If a bike is not available (or you still have a childhood aversion to bikes), try a treadmill. Many bodybuilders find this an adequate apparatus for warming up. The seated rowing machine can also be used (light tension, short duration). Other exercises to warm up the whole body include a 5- to 10-minute run, jumping rope, or running in place. Any of these exercises will prepare the body's circulatory and respiratory systems for an intense workout.

One of Australia's greatest – Sonny Schmidt.

Never underestimate the importance of stretching.

PHASE TWO

The second phase of warming up should focus on the body's muscles for both injury prevention and efficient functioning. The best exercises for this phase are various stretching movements. In fact, stretching is one of the most underrated forms of exercise.

"I like to stretch before I train shoulders and in between shoulder exercises. Stretching feels good, helps me work through the fullest possible range of motion and helps prevent injury." – **Sonny Schmidt**
IFBB Professional Bodybuilder
1995 Masters Olympia champion

Stretching is one of the most basic of physical acts. For most people the first form of physical activity upon waking in the morning is stretching. How many of you have stimulated your body to alertness by that first vigorous arms-straight-out stretch? It feels good while we're doing it, and even better when we stop. Stretching helps loosen, relax and reduce early morning tension. Surely any activity that has such positive attributes would be a regular part of a bodybuilder's daily routine. But unfortunately this is not the case, and few bodybuilders take the time to stretch their muscles.

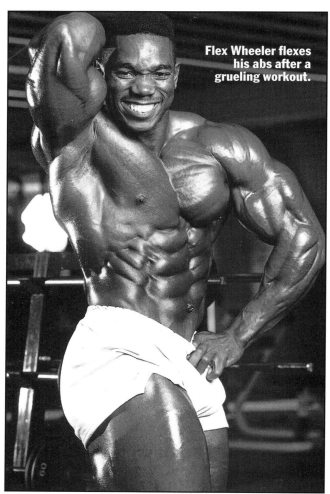

Flex Wheeler flexes his abs after a grueling workout.

For bodybuilders trying to add size and prevent injuries while doing so, there are two types of tissue that should be stretched, the fascia and the tendons and ligaments. Both are connective tissue, but the fascia are more elastic in nature, and consequently should receive the lion's share of attention. Conversely, overstretch the tendons and ligaments, and you may weaken their attachment points, thus increasing the risk of injury.

In spite of the risk of injury it's essential that you stretch the tendons and ligaments because of their relationship to the Golgi tendon organs (GTIs) – stretch receptors located in the ends of the tendons near the muscle attachments. GTIs act as safety switches in the event of overstretching. In short, if the muscle stretches beyond a certain point, or if the muscular contraction exceeds the GTIs' reflex setting, the GTI shuts down muscular contraction. As a result the muscle relaxes and the excessive stretch or tension is eliminated, thus saving the muscle from injury (provided damage has not already occurred). If GTIs didn't exist, the muscle or tendon could be torn off its attachments.

You have probably experienced this shutting-down phenomenon while training in the gym. Besides having the muscle fail because of muscular fatigue, the GTIs kick in and shut the muscle down. Notice how after 9 or 10 reps on the Scott curl, your biceps begin to wobble and go to rubber? Despite your best efforts the bar won't budge. What has happened is that your GTIs have said, "All right, buster, if you're not going to stop, we'll do it for you!" They think you're about to injure yourself so they kick in and terminate muscular contraction.

By regularly stretching, it's possible to increase the GTIs' "switch" setting. GTIs have evolved to fire or "kick in" at a given reflex setting. Regular stretching can increase this threshold, thus allowing the bodybuilder to use heavier weights for the same reps. Also with an increased GTI threshold, muscular contractions are harder, promoting greater muscle growth. One of the primary reasons why advanced bodybuilders can lift heavier weights for more reps is that their GTI thresholds are higher.

The exact physiological mechanism behind the stretching/GTI threshold relationship is not fully understood. Current research suggests that repeatedly stretching and forcing the GTIs to fire makes it less likely for them to fire in the future. In short, you desensitize them by raising their threshold for firing. A raised threshold means a stronger tendon and less chance the muscle will shut down.

Besides the GTI relationship to stretching, we have the fascia to consider. Fascia is the protective sheath of connective tissue that surrounds the muscle. With time the soft texture of the fascia gives rise to a toughened outer shell, to the point that it may even restrict muscle growth. Stretching helps alleviate this condition, turning large flat muscles into highly separated entities.

The analogy of blowing up a balloon can be used to illustrate the relationship between fascia and muscle growth. The first time you try to blow up the balloon it's difficult because of the toughness of the rubber. After repeated inflations, however, the rubber softens, making it easier to blow up.

Exercise kinesiologists suggest the best time to stretch the fascia is after your muscles have been pumped to the maximum. In fact, it's highly recommended to stretch after every set. Of course, this stretching concerns only the fascia. For overall effect you should spend 10 to 15 minutes stretching before starting your workout, and then include stretching between sets. If this plan is not to your liking, try stretching after finishing squats, before you start leg extensions. At the very least, stretch after individual muscle groups. Finish legs, stretch, and then start shoulders (or any muscle of your choice).

If you are not convinced yet of the value of stretching, take the advice of bodybuilding superstar Flex Wheeler:

"I stretch to the max because I know how valuable stretching is, and I think you should incorporate some into your routine too. After all, anything that helps you be better than the next guy is valuable!"

The following stretching exercises can be performed before, during or after a workout. In addition to these, there are hundreds of stretching exercises that can be done for each individual muscle group. Pick a few favorites and stretch to success!

Bodybuilders aren't flexible? Flex Wheeler proves otherwise.

1. Standing Hamstring Stretch – This is perhaps the grandfather of all stretching movements. With one leg locked out, place the other on an upright object. Now with your hands, slowly try to touch the toes of the elevated foot without rounding your back. Hold the position for a few seconds, and return to upright. Take a breath or two, and then bend down for another stretch. Notice the stretch in the back of your leg. Don't bounce during the movement in an attempt to reach farther. Such a motion places unwanted stress on the lower back. (It also causes a muscle-nerve reflex which defeats the exercise's purpose.) At first you'll probably only reach your ankles. The less flexible may only reach their knees! Fine, don't worry about it. With time you'll be touching your toes. Perform 10 to 12 reps in this manner (one rep being one full movement from the upright starting position, down to the toes, and back to the starting position again) and then switch legs.

2. Seated Hamstring Stretch – This exercise is similar to the above but rather than standing, you are seated on the floor. With one leg bent behind you, lock the other straight out in front. Once again try to touch your toes in a slow and controlled manner. Alternate the legs and perform 10 reps per side.

3. Standing Wall Stretches – No, you are not stretching the wall! You use one, however, to brace against as you stretch your upper and lower body. Stand facing a wall with one leg in front of the other. The front leg should be slightly bent while the rear leg is kept straight. Place both hands on the wall (arms locked straight) and slowly push your head down between your arms. You will feel the stretch in your triceps, lats and hamstrings. A variation of this movement is to release one hand and lean down and touch the toes.

4. Regular Splits – The old standby from gym class. With the upper body kept erect (perpendicular to the floor), slowly lower, trying to touch the glutes to the floor. Many will need months – if not years – to accomplish this feat. A few will never be able to do a full split because of their unique tendon attachments. No matter how far down you go, try to maintain that position for 10 seconds or so. Each time you do the movement you should be able to go a little farther down.

5. Alternate Lying Leg Raises – With your back flat on the floor, raise one leg as high as possible, and then have a partner push the leg backward. Alternate both legs and hold for eight to 10 seconds in the full stretch position.

6. Pushups – No need to go into great detail here. Pushups are one of the most effective upper-body exercises. With the hands and toes resting on the floor, push up to a locked-arm position. From here, lower back down until your chest touches the floor. Don't stop at the bottom and lie down! The exercise should be done in a touch-and-go manner. If you lack the strength to lift your bodyweight, rest your knees on the floor. This technique will remove the weight of your legs (about half your bodyweight) from the exercise. The stronger among you can perform pushups between chairs or benches. But don't go too far, as you are not trying to duplicate dips (a mass-building exercise). You are merely warming up.

7. Crunches – Although crunches are a mainstay of an abdominal workout, they also make a great warmup exercise. Lie down on your back with the legs resting on a bench. Move close enough to the bench so that your upper legs are perpendicular to the floor. Now bend forward and try to touch your legs. No need to do a full abdominal workout. 1 or 2 sets of 15 to 20 reps is adequate.

8. Free-Weight Squats – As the legs compose about 50 percent of your body's muscle mass, exercising them is a great overall warmup. You can do free-weight squats in two ways. First, place both hands on the hips

and bend down to a full squat position. Now straighten the legs and return to a standing position. If keeping balance is a problem, try holding an upright for support (squat rack, shoulder-press bench, Smith machine, etc.). Perform the exercise in the same manner as regular squats. You might want to switch your holding arm for variety.

9. Hanging Leg Raises – While this movement is great for the lower abdominals, it also stretches the entire upper body. Holding onto the bar stretches the arms, shoulders, back and chest. A less obvious benefit is the reduced spinal tension. To perform the movement, grab a chinup bar with the palms facing forward. With legs slightly bent (straight-leg leg raises place stress on the lower back), lift them up until they are parallel with the floor. Pause for a second and return to the starting position. Do not swing the legs as this defeats the purpose of the movement by involving momentum.

PHASE THREE

The third phase of warming up entails doing a few light sets of a specific exercise before using your top poundages. If you work up to 150 pounds on the shoulder press, start with a set of 20 reps with 50 pounds. Next do 12 to 15 reps with 90 to 100 pounds. You might even want to throw in a third warmup set. Don't jump to your top poundages until at least the third set. Even then this progression might be too quick. If you're working up to

400 pounds in the bench press, it's a good idea to do four or five warmup sets. Jumping to 400 pounds after only one or two light sets is just too dangerous. No doubt some of you reading this have been following such a procedure for years, so far without injury, but the odds are one day an accident will occur. You will be going along fine until rr-ii-pp – an injury that requires six months of recovery. Please take our advice: Put the ego on hold and warm up properly!

WARMUP CONCLUSION

Your cardiovascular and general body workout should last no longer than 20 minutes. This is a small investment to make in bringing the body up to peak operating efficiency. As for specific muscles, all bodybuilders, no matter what level, should do some sort of warmup. Contrary to popular belief, the more advanced you are in your training, the greater the need for a warmup. Let's face it – an advanced bodybuilder will be using hundreds of pounds for most of the exercises. It's foolhardy to start benching 300 to 400 pounds without first warming up. While a beginner using 75 to 100 pounds might (we say *might*, but assume otherwise and warm up) get away with it, our advanced friend will not. You may save time by skipping the warmup, but how much time will be wasted if you tear a pectoral muscle or injure your lower back? A lot longer, we assure you.

EVALUATION

One of the most basic rules of bodybuilding is to keep following a routine as long as it works, and to discard it when it ceases to be effective. In short, never throw away a winning hand, but don't stick to a plan that doesn't bring results.

If you're training hard, eating well, and allowing enough time for recovery, and still not gaining, then something is amiss. It's your job to find out what. Don't continue training, thinking the problem will solve itself. On a few occasions it might, but the odds are it won't. You have to sit down and evaluate your whole training philosophy.

For a proper evaluation you need records to refer to. Such records give answers to questions like "Am I receiving enough protein?", "Is my calorie intake sufficient to meet my energy demands?" or "Am I adding enough variety to my routine?" It's extremely difficult to answer such questions without referring to notes. Only by carefully reviewing all aspects of your training can you objectively make the changes needed for continued growth.

There are three basic types of records used by bodybuilders during their careers – written logs, photographs and tape measurements. You might want to use one or all three to keep track of your progress. Let's take a closer look at them.

TRAINING JOURNAL

"Forget about training logbooks. When the energy is there, why wait? Use it now!" – *Dr. Franco Columbu*
Two-time Mr. Olympia

Contrary to Franco's comment, most athletes keep some sort of training log, so why should bodybuilders be any different? Many of the top bodybuilders keep a daily record of their progress. This enables them to compare workouts on a monthly or yearly basis. By examining such records they see what works and what doesn't. Some muscles respond well to training; others need to receive additional attention.

There are different methods for keeping a diary or training log. At the very least, record the date (year, month, day), exercises, weights, and the number of sets and reps. No need to get fancy with expensive record books. An inexpensive spiral-bound exercise book will do just fine. Some bodybuilders use loose-leaf binders, but you run the risk of losing pages this way. Of course, if money is no object, you can buy commercially made record books at many book stores. Also, many of the better muscle magazines carry advertisements for such journals.

The legendary Franco Columbu.

Like most professions, bodybuilding has a form of shorthand. The general format is to list (from left to right) the exercise name, weight and number of reps. Here's a typical example:

Flat bench press – 200 x 10, 200 x 8, 200 x 6

Here the bench press was performed for 3 sets using 200 pounds. We can see that the number of reps decreased with each successive set. If you use the same weight for the same number of reps, you abbreviate the entry this way:

Flat bench press – 200 x 8 x 8 x 8

...or even simpler:

Flat bench press – 200 x 8 x 3

In this case the person performed 3 sets of 8 reps using 200 pounds.

It's a good idea to put the date somewhere on the top of the page. This way you can flip through your journal and quickly find any specific day. List the exercises down the page in the order you performed them.

Many bodybuilders like to record everything that is applicable to a workout. Such details as meals and supplements are included. This approach is especially useful during the competitive season when you are dieting and need to keep track of calories.

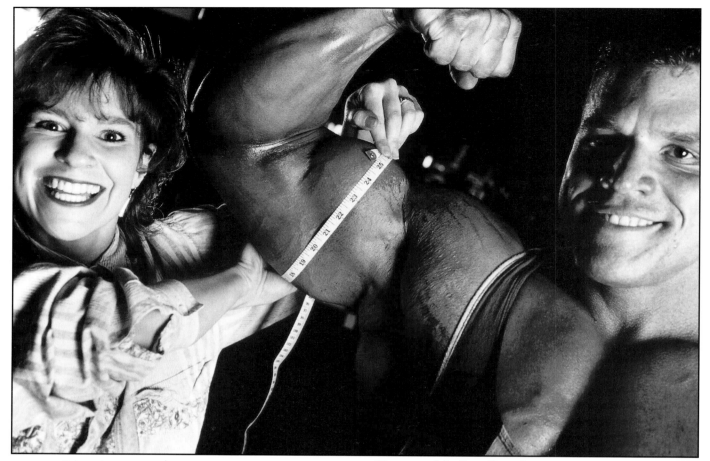

Man-mountain Greg Kovac's arms are among the biggest in bodybuilding.

Other data to record include energy levels, moods, emotions, and even how well the workout went. If you want, record your day-to-day activities. Perhaps there is a connection between your daily life and how well your workout went. For example, you may notice Wednesday's workouts are sluggish. Your training diary may give you a hint as to what factors are contributing to this lethargy.

PHOTOGRAPHS

We should warn you that the first set of photographs you take will probably depress you! And if you compare them to the pictures in *MuscleMag International*, you'll start contemplating retirement. Please don't despair. The bodybuilders in *MuscleMag* probably felt the same way early in their careers. If you easily get depressed, put the pictures away and don't look at them for a few months. By then you will have additional pictures for comparison and will be able to see your progress.

There are a number of reasons for taking pictures. First, they show your progress over time. Pictures taken three months apart will give you a much better idea of progress than looking in the mirror daily. Second, they reveal your weaknesses. Pictures rarely lie. Your girlfriend may flatter, a gym buddy may say you're Dorian Yates incarnate, but the 4 x 6 black and white will quickly set you straight. You may be familiar with the front of your physique, but your lats may lack

thickness. A series of good pictures will show such weaknesses. You can then alter your training, giving more attention to the lagging muscle groups. We discuss photography in more detail in the competition section.

TAKING MEASUREMENTS

"The tape measure is of little importance in measuring leg development. After a bodybuilder has been training his legs, and they show signs of development, he should put the tape measure away. It's the visual concepts of leg development that are most important. In other words it's how they look."   *– Frank Zane*
Three-time Mr. Olympia

Opinion is split on measurement-taking. Unless you are one of the genetically gifted members of the sport, you won't notice an appreciable increase in muscle size on a monthly basis. If you decide to take measurements, do so only every four to six months. Even then there might not be much change. Realistically you can expect to gain 10 to 20 pounds in your first year of training. As this will be spread over your entire body, the individual muscle measurements will not change significantly. An inch on the arms and a couple of inches around the chest would be considered

MuscleMag writer and photographer Jason Mathas snaps some pix of Darin Lannaghan in Gold's Gym, Venice.

than quantity that changes. Advanced bodybuilders are more concerned with hardness, shape and definition than with size. Still, bodybuilders love to compare muscle statistics, especially arm and chest measurements, so here's how you do it.

Wrap a tailor's tape around the flexed muscle at its thickest point. Take the measurement before a workout as afterwards the muscle will be gorged with blood, thus giving an artificial measurement. The most common measurements are biceps (arms), chest, waist, thighs, calves and neck.

There is a final, less obvious reason for keeping a detailed training record. If you become a champion bodybuilder, Robert Kennedy will want to interview you for the pages of *MuscleMag International!* Look at it this way: Every superstar started in the same way, and you're no different. A record of your early training programs makes great reading (and a series of pictures greatly enhances such articles) and at the same time provides tips for the next generation of bodybuilding superstars. So get out the pen, paper and camera, and start recording!

average. An inch a year does not sound like much, but it means that over a five-year period a 15-inch arm becomes a 20-inch arm! As the years advance, there'll be even less change in overall muscle size. This is because, on average, bodybuilders gain about 90 percent of their total muscle mass in the first five years of training. (As we said earlier, there are exceptions to this generalization.) Beyond this point it's more quality

Top physique photographer Jim Amentler in action.

THE BEGINNER'S LEVEL

"It is suggested that as a beginning bodybuilder you train three times a week. Mondays, Wednesdays and Fridays are ideal because your weekends will be free. Train your whole body on each of the three days. Perform your exercises in good, strict style. Never bounce or heave the weight."

– Ben Weider, IFBB President

Congratulations, and welcome to the first phase of your bodybuilding career. This morning you may have looked in the mirror and, after hitting one most-muscular, decided that Lou Ferrigno was safe for now. That 110-pound barbell set in the basement doesn't cut it any more. It's time to get serious, and this means only one thing – going to a hardcore training establishment.

Now before you load up the barbell with Yates-sized poundages, stop for a moment and take heed of the following advice. It's meant neither to dampen your spirit nor insult your intelligence, but merely to set you straight on the road to the Olympia. Follow it and Joe Weider's Sandow statue could be yours. Ignore it and the local paramedics will work overtime. The choice is yours.

A building is said to be only as good as its foundation, and the same can be said for bodybuilding. Without first learning the basics, you can never hope to achieve success. Further, the bodybuilder who skips the basics is setting himself or herself up for injury down the road. Of all the training levels described in this book, the beginning stage is by far the most important. Abuse or ignore the fundamentals and you'll probably never reach the more advanced rungs of the bodybuilding ladder.

If beginning bodybuilders have one characteristic in common, it's confusion. Among the more conflicting views are the following:

- Free weights vs. machines
- High reps vs. low reps
- Many sets vs. few sets
- Split routines vs. training the body every day
- A few large meals vs. many small meals
- To take supplements or not
- To bulk up or stay lean

... etc., etc., etc.

What's even more confusing is the fact that one magazine may feature proponents of both ends of the bodybuilding spectrum. Some bodybuilders advise

Posedown! (From left to right) – Chris Cormier, David Dearth, Aaron Baker, Vince Taylor and Lee Priest.

doing a few high intense sets, while others suggest using moderate weight for many sets. What's a person to do?

"I'll never forget this: John told me there were three things I needed to do if I was gonna be good in bodybuilding. Train big, eat big, sleep big. I went home that night, about an hour later, and started eating."
– Vince Taylor, top Pro Bodybuilder
1996 Masters Olympia champion
(reminiscing about advice he received
from former Mr. Universe John Brown)

One of the sport's all-time greats, Vince Taylor.

While there are no hard rules in bodybuilding, there are definite do's and don'ts. Establishing these guidelines was the main purpose behind the compilation of this book. Unfortunately many beginners, wanting to make the fastest gains possible, ignore the advice given to them, or else follow advice which should have been ignored in the first place. Instead of making rapid progress, they see their training come to a halt, and often there are associated injuries.

As a beginner, you should first have a medical checkup. If you are a teenager who has been actively involved in high school sports, the odds are good to excellent that you're already in healthy condition. If on the other hand you have been living a sedentary lifestyle for the past 10 years (i.e. the most exercise you've done is push the TV remote!), make an appointment with your physician. Only he/she knows for sure whether or not you need a stress test. If you are over the age of 40, you should request a stress test. (There are exceptions. If there is a history of heart disease or stroke in your family, you should get a stress test regardless of your age.) Don't worry – it sounds worse than it is. You will be asked to spend a short time on a treadmill or stationary bike. A few measurements will be taken and any abnormalities (irregular heart beat, etc.) will be detected. It's better to discover the problem in the doctor's office than under a barbell.

The next piece of advice is to look at your lifestyle. If you smoke or are a heavy drinker, stop right now! Nothing destroys physical health like cigarette smoke. The nicotine and other associated chemicals play havoc with your system. At the least these chemicals will slow down your recovery. Often they lead to lung cancer and heart disease. Enough said.

With regard to alcohol, keep consumption low or moderate. Don't expect to go on a typical Friday-to-Sunday drinking binge and then stroll into the gym on Monday, bursting with energy. The human body requires a couple of days to get rid of the alcohol. One or two beers a night will probably not hurt, and a glass or two of wine with your meals is fine, but please don't abuse the bottle. You may argue that recent studies suggest that moderate drinking is beneficial. The key word here is *moderate*, and even then there is much debate. Most of the studies involve comparing the health of wine drinkers. While a few glasses of wine may help keep the arteries open, research is not conclusive enough that we recommend you start drinking if you are not presently doing so.

BEGINNING-LEVEL GOALS

Perhaps the first question to ask is "Why did I begin training in the first place?" For many the goal is simply to firm and tone the muscles. Obtaining a Mr. Olympia physique is the furthest idea from your mind. You will be happy if you can take a few inches from your waist and add them to your chest. (Many pros started this way, and a few inches became many inches. Once you obtain a 45-inch chest you will shoot for 46, 47, and so on. Few trainers reach a level where they are completely satisfied.) Great! This is what makes bodybuilding such an exciting sport. You can tailor your workouts to suit your goals.

Tom Platz, without question, has the greatest legs bodybuilding has ever seen.

For others among you, nothing short of elbowing Dorian Yates off the competitive stage will suffice. A 40-inch chest just doesn't cut it with you. Yours has to be 55 inches of ripped, striated muscle. Fine, go for it! But keep in mind that whether you are training for overall fitness or have plans to become a competitive bodybuilder, you first have to introduce the body to weight training. You don't learn how to ride a bike by hopping on a Harley-Davidson motorcycle. The same principle applies in bodybuilding. First you learn how to do straight sets, and then you can think about such advanced training techniques as giant sets or pre-exhaustion.

GETTING STARTED

"My mass-building maxim is 'Think mass, eat mass, train mass.' I'd even suggest that you print up a sign with this maxim and place it over your posing mirror so you'll be constantly reminded of its importance."
— **Tom Platz, Mr. Universe**

The primary goal of a beginning-level bodybuilder is to lay down an adequate foundation – nothing fancy, just basic exercises. For the next few months you will gradually prepare the body for more advanced routines. Before we go any further, we must stress that you follow the advice as laid out in this chapter. Don't go adding sets or exercises, and more important, don't skip over this section. No doubt many of you think that jumping right to Vince Taylor's arm routine is the way to go. Nothing could be further from the truth. Vince and

other bodybuilding stars didn't start out by following their current training routines. Nor do they follow such routines year round. For the most part the programs you see in the various muscle magazines are precontest routines. Such intensity cannot be maintained for more than a few weeks, even by the top stars. The pros began their careers by following the basic exercises and gradually worked up the intensity ladder. You must do the same.

Your beginning bodybuilding program should be performed three times a week on alternate days. For most Monday-Wednesday-Friday is the desired schedule. This allows a day of rest after each workout, and gives you the weekends off. Of course, you can vary the program and work out on any three nonconsecutive days (Tuesday-Thursday-Saturday, Thursday-Saturday-Monday, etc.). The bottom line is three workout days with one day of rest after each.

You will train the whole body each workout, performing one exercise per muscle group. Each exercise will be performed for 3 sets of 8 to 12 repetitions. As your workouts progress, the weight will begin to feel lighter. This means your muscles are adapting to the increased resistance. You have grown stronger. Congratulations! You're well on your way. Now add five pounds to the bar. After a few workouts this too will seem light. Add still more weight. Keep this pattern up as long as you make progress. Granted you'll have periods of little strength gain, but overall you should be adding weight to the bar every 8 to 10 days. Now you

The "Lion of Lebanon" Samir Bannout.

BULKING UP

"I don't believe in bulking up. For most bodybuilders bulking up is simply an excuse to eat like a pig for three or four months. Even in the off-season my body has grown to crave high-quality foods rather than pizza, cake, cookies, chocolate, and all of the other goodies that used to be so important to me."

– Samir Bannout, 1983 Mr. Olympia

The term *bulking up* is seldom heard in gyms these days. It refers to the practice of gaining 20, 30 or more pounds of bodyweight in the off-season. If the bodybuilder wanted to compete at, say, 200 pounds, he would bulk up to 230 or 240. About three months before the contest the excess fat would be dieted off.

"Staying lean as you train makes it easier to hold onto your gains while you're training and dieting for competition." **– Shawn Ray, top Pro Bodybuilder**

The theory behind bulking up was overkill. By eating enormous quantities of food, the bodybuilder could train very heavy. This led to maximum gains in bodyweight. Unfortunately much of this weight was fat that had to be removed before a contest. Not only was this reduction difficult, but the rapid weight gain also left the skin stretched and saggy.

see why weightlifting is often called "progressive resistance training."

The exercises we have chosen are considered the most productive for the beginning-level bodybuilder. They are called compound movements because they work more than one muscle group. For example, even though the bench press is considered a chest exercise, it also stimulates the shoulders and triceps. At this stage of your training you will not be doing any isolation or shaping movements. By following our routine you'll work all the body's major muscle groups. The emphasis will be more on developing size and strength than on targeting individual muscle groups.

Your workout should last no longer than 45 to 60 minutes. If you must have a chat, fine, but try to limit it to before or after your workout. Don't get us wrong. We are not suggesting you go into the gym and ignore everyone else. In fact, much of what you learn will be from conversing with other trainers. We encourage you to strike up conversations with more advanced bodybuilders. Often they will have experienced the same problems that you may encounter. Instead of spending months or years discovering the solution yourself, you may find the answer in a five-minute conversation. All we're suggesting is to keep your attention focused on the exercises.

Shawn Ray

CHAPTER EIGHT – THE BEGINNER'S LEVEL

Bulking up was popular in the 1950s, 1960s and early '70s. In the late '70s the "ripped" look began to predominate in bodybuilding contests. Obtaining this new look was virtually impossible after gaining 25 to 30 pounds during the off-season. Nowadays bodybuilders try to keep their bodyweight within 10 to 15 pounds of their contest weights. In doing so, they eliminate the energy drain associated with intense dieting and they look good year round.

Jason Arntz possesses one of the most aesthetically pleasing physiques in bodybuilding.

Does bulking up have its place? Well, that depends on the bodybuilder's somatotype. Endomorphs should avoid the practice. They already tend to carry too much weight. Gaining 20 to 30 pounds will only compound the problem. Mesomorphs may benefit by gaining 15 to 20 pounds, but keep in mind it all has to come off if you plan to compete. It probably won't hurt during your first few years' training, but later on you should adopt the practice of keeping your off-season weight within 10 to 15 pounds of your competitive weight.

The only group to whom we could possibly (with the emphasis on the word *possibly*) recommend bulking up are the ectomorphs. These people gain weight slowly to begin with so they might benefit from a bulking-up approach. By eating large meals combined with one or two protein shakes, they would be assured of receiving adequate nutrition. As staying lean is no problem for them, most of the weight gained would be muscle. They don't have to worry about excess baggage around the waist.

Ultimately the decision to bulk up is yours. If you are predominantly ectomorphic in body type, go for it. If endomorphic, don't even think about it. As for mesomorphs, you may experiment, but don't go overboard. The extra size may look good in clothes, but if much of it is fat, forget about competition. The winners these days are the most ripped competitors onstage. The large smooth look is definitely a thing of the past.

RIB-CAGE EXPANSION

"I believe that half the battle in acquiring a fully developed chest is in correct stretching of the rib cage. By super-setting the squat with cross-bench dumbell pullovers in the right way, you can slowly stretch the length of the cartilages that attach the ribs to the sternum. I feel that you can add up to six inches to your chest measurement within six months of stretching regardless of your age."
– Dennis Tinerino, former Mr. Universe

There are two procedures that you can follow to develop a huge chest measurement: increase the size of your pectoral muscles, and expand your rib cage. We will be looking at pectoral development in the training section. Our purpose here is to outline a few techniques that will give you an impressive foundation to develop your pectorals on. Keep in mind that the following exercises will not stretch an ectomorph's 40-inch chest into a mesomorph's 60-inch chest. Genetics dictates the upper limit. Still, by regularly using the following routine, you can be assured of maximizing your potential. Every little bit counts, and this program takes only five to 10 minutes.

We should point out first (and we hate to break it to you this way) that, if you are over the age of 20 to 21, you will experience less success with this routine than someone 15 to 16 years old. The underlying basis for rib-cage expansion is stretching the cartilages that connect the ribs to the sternum (center rib-cage bone). By your early 20s these cartilages have begun to harden and lose their pliability. This means stretching and lengthening them is much more difficult. It doesn't mean a 30- or 40-year-old can't expand his rib cage. He can. It's just that the teenage years are the most productive for stretching the rib cage. Once you reach your mid to late 20s, rib-cage expansion is much more difficult.

To effectively stretch the rib-cage cartilage, we must attack it from two different angles. The first approach is from the inside out. Every time you inhale, you are in effect stretching the rib-cage cartilage. We take advantage of this fact by performing what are commonly called breathing squats. Breathing squats are performed like regular squats, but with the emphasis on breathing rather than thigh development. Because the movements are so similar, we suggest you perform breathing squats on the same day as your leg workouts. Instead of heavy weight for 10 to 12 reps, we suggest 25 to 30 reps with a light weight. Inhale as deeply as you can, and then exhale as fully as possible. Follow a set of breathing squats with a set of dumbell pullovers, lying across a bench. Some books suggest lying lengthwise on a bench and using a barbell, but performing pullovers in this manner limits the range of movement. By lying across a bench you can fully arch and stretch the rib cage. Using a barbell will put most of the stress on the back and triceps muscles. A dumbell can be held in a manner that eliminates much of this strain.

As with breathing squats, the emphasis is on breathing, not the amount of weight used. (For a full description of squats and pullovers, see the training sections in this text.) We recommend performing 2 or 3 sets. Although it's personal preference, most bodybuilders like to perform the exercises at the end of their workouts.

Now that we have outlined a technique to improve your rib cage, the next order of business is to explain why. The first and most obvious reason is cosmetic. A large rib cage gives you a larger chest measurement. All things being equal (i.e. similar pectoral development), the bodybuilder with the larger rib cage will look far more impressive in a side chest shot. You may be limited by genetics in developing large pectoral muscles, but you can compensate by displaying your moderate chest muscles on a large rib box.

There is another reason for developing a large rib cage. If you have the potential for developing thick pectorals, a solid foundation is a necessity. No matter how large your chest muscles, they will never have that full appearance unless they are displayed on a well-developed platform.

A final reason for rib-cage expansion is health. Regular breathing squats give the heart and lungs a terrific workout. As well, a large rib cage provides greater protection for the body's internal organs – its main function after all.

BEGINNING-LEVEL ROUTINES

"I seldom missed doing squats in my own thigh workouts and have squatted as consistently heavy as I could since my first days as a bodybuilder. With heavy squats you'll make better muscle gains all over your body, not just your legs." **– Lee Haney, Eight-time Mr. Olympia**

Now that we've discussed such topics as record-keeping, rib-cage expansion, and warming up, it's time for you to start "pumping iron." What follows are our recommended beginning training programs. At first you may consider them elementary, and you're correct – they *are* rather rudimentary and basic. But they've been designed that way for a purpose. If you think such simplicity is a waste of time, you should be aware that there are a couple of top bodybuilders who advocate such routines for gaining muscle mass, no matter what the level of experience.

"Mr. Heavy Duty" Mike Mentzer.

"When you first start bodybuilding, almost anything you do in the weight room results in gains. You really can get bigger and stronger just by putting the weights away for other people!" **– Mike Mentzer esteemed writer and former Mr. Universe**

ROUTINE 1

EXERCISE	# SETS	REPS
Crunches	2	20-30
Squats	3	12-15
Leg curls	3	12-15
Flat-bench presses	3	10-12
Chinups	3	10-12
Presses behind the neck	3	12-15
Triceps pushdowns	3	10-12
Barbell curls	3	10-12
Standing calf raises	3	15-20

ROUTINE 2

EXERCISE	# SETS	REPS
Bent-leg leg raises	2	15-20
Leg presses	3	12-15
Leg curls	3	12-15
Incline bench presses	3	10-12
Lat pulldowns	3	10-12
Front military presses	3	12-15
Lying triceps extensions	3	10-12
Standing dumbell curls	3	10-12
Standing calf raises	3	15-20

ROUTINE 3

EXERCISE	# SETS	REPS
Crunches	2	20-30
Squats	3	12-15
Leg curls	3	12-15
Flat dumbell presses	3	10-12
Seated pulley rows	3	10-12
Dumbell shoulder presses	3	12-15
One-arm dumbell extensions	3	10-12
Seated dumbell curls	3	10-12
Calf flexes on leg press machine	3	15-20

ROUTINE 4

EXERCISE	# SETS	REPS
Crunches	2	20-30
Leg presses	3	12-15
Leg curls	3	12-15
Dips	3	10-12
One-arm dumbell rows	3	10-12
Presses behind neck	3	12-15
Triceps pushdowns	3	10-12
Incline curls	3	10-12
Standing calf raises	3	15-20

ROUTINE 5

EXERCISE	# SETS	REPS
Bent-leg leg raises	2	15-20
Squats	3	12-15
Flat dumbell presses	3	10-12
Barbell rows	3	10-12
Dumbell presses	3	12-15
Upright dips	3	10-12
Preacher curls	3	10-12
Standing calf raises	3	15-20

You'll notice that we recommend higher rep ranges (10+) on most of these exercises. This is done for two reasons. First, higher reps will prepare the muscles for more intense programs later on. Second, higher reps necessitate using lighter weight, thus reducing the risk of incurring an injury. When you have a couple of months' training under your belt, you may want to drop the rep ranges slightly, say, from 12 to 15 down to 8 to 10. Save the 4- to 6-rep stuff for later when your muscles and tendons have had a chance to strengthen. We can't stress enough the importance of training the muscles and not the ego!

EXERCISE DESCRIPTIONS

Following are descriptions of all the exercises listed above. Although we have tried to be as clear as possible, you may occasionally need to check with a more advanced bodybuilder. Have him or her observe you for a couple of sets. Any mistakes can be quickly corrected. Finally, never perform an exercise if you are unsure of the proper technique. Check its description in this book, a bodybuilding magazine, or with someone at the gym.

ABDOMINALS

Crunches – You will need a flat bench or chair to perform this exercise. Lie down on the floor and rest your calves on the bench. Adjust your distance from the bench so that your thighs are perpendicular with the floor. Now bend forward and try to touch your thighs.

England's amazing Charles Clairmonte hits a front double-biceps pose onstage.

Comments – Most bodybuilders consider crunches one of the best abdominal-builders. At first you may want to perform the movement with your hands by your sides. As you get stronger, place your hands to the side of the head. Doing so adds the weight of the arms to your upper body, thus making the exercise more difficult.

Muscles Worked – Crunches primarily work the upper abs, but there is some lower-ab stimulation too. The exercise also brings the hip abductors into play, although to a much lesser extent than situps.

Bent-Leg Leg Raises – You can use the chinup bar on the Universal multistation or a free-standing version. Jump up and grab the bar with both hands. With the legs slightly bent, lift them up to the horizontal position. Lower them slowly until they are once again in line with the upper body.

Comments – Some bodybuilders perform this movement with the legs straight. This technique is not recommended as straight-leg leg raises place unwanted stress on the lower back. While perhaps not noticeable now, it may lead to problems down the road.

Don't swing the legs up and down as this momentum only defeats the purpose of the exercise. You want to lift the lower body using abdominal power, not momentum.

Muscles Worked – This exercise mainly works the lower abdominals, but there is some upper-abdominal and hip-abductor stimulation.

Lying leg raises – Lie down on the abdominal board with your hands holding the hand-grip behind your head (i.e. your head is towards the hand-grip/foot rest, unlike situps where your feet are closest to the hand-grip/foot rest). With your legs slightly bent, raise them to the vertical (or just short of the vertical) position. Pause a second and then slowly lower them. Try not to touch the board at the bottom. This control will keep tension on the abdominals throughout the exercise.

Comments – Once again, don't perform the movement with straight legs. Also, resist the urge to use your upper body to pull your legs up. Use only abdominal strength. Start with the abdominal board placed in the lowest position. As you get stronger you can increase the angle of the board, thus making the exercise more difficult.

Muscles Worked – Lying leg raises work the lower abdominals, but the upper abs and hip abductors also come into play.

LEGS (THIGHS)

Squats – Place the barbell on the squat rack about shoulder height. Step under the bar and rest it across your traps and shoulders. Step back, away from the rack, and place your feet slightly less than shoulder width apart. Now in a slow and controlled manner bend your knees and descend toward the floor. Stop when your thighs are approximately parallel with the floor. Pause for a second and then return to the starting upright position.

Comments – Most consider squats to be the king of the thigh-builders. If done properly they will build you a phenomenal set of thighs (quadriceps). Done improperly they may put you in traction. Try to use a squat rack with "catchers". These are pins which will stop the weight if you get into trouble. If none are available, make sure you have one or two spotters watching you. Besides the safety feature, spotters can tell if you are performing the exercise properly.

Always wear a belt when performing squats. Do not bounce at the top or bottom of the exercise. Remember, you have a loaded barbell on your shoulders which is putting a lot of stress on your spine. Keep control of the weight throughout the movement.

Make sure you rest the bar across your shoulders and traps, not on the bony protrusion at the base of

Mighty Mike Francois hammers out barbell squats in the power rack.

Start

Finish

Finish

Start

Shawn Ray blasts his quads on the leg-press machine.

your skull. Do so and you will need regular chiropractic treatments.

To put most of the stress on the thighs, try resting the heels on a two-inch block of wood. If you perform squats flatfooted, much of the lifting will be done by your glutes. In addition, keep your stance shoulder width or less. The wider the stance the more glute involvement. (This is why powerlifters use a fairly wide stance. They need the tremendous power of the glutes to help in lifting their huge poundages.)

Muscles Worked – While principally a thigh-builder, squats will stimulate the whole leg region. Even with a narrow stance the glutes will come into play. Also, the calves and hamstrings are used in stabilizing the legs as you move up and down.

Much less obvious, the spinal erectors (lower-back muscles) are needed to keep the body upright. They are often the weak link in the chain. Most injuries sustained while doing squats center around the lower-back region. This is why you must concentrate when performing this exercise.

Leg Press – You will need to use the leg-press machine to perform this exercise. Sit in the seat and place your feet on the pressing board about shoulder width apart. The spacing can be varied to work different parts of the thigh. Extend your legs to the locked-out position, pause, then bring them down until your knees touch the chest. Perform the movement in a slow, controlled manner.

Comments – Although leg presses don't give the same degree of thigh development as squats, they are a close second. And if you have knee or back problems, the leg press will adequately work the thighs without aggravating these areas.

As with squats, the wider the foot position, the more glute involvement. By making a V with the feet (heels together, toes apart) you can do wonders with the inner thigh region (vastus medialis).

Perhaps the greatest advantage of leg presses is the amount of weight you can use. Unlike squats, where the lower back is a limiting factor, the leg press allows you to pile on hundreds of pounds of plates. Before long you will have six to eight (or more) 45-pound plates on each side. Provided you do the exercise in good style, you can really let the ego go wild on this exercise. The lower back is virtually eliminated, and even the knees don't have the same stress placed on them.

A word of caution concerns hyperextending the legs. If you place the feet low on the pressing board, you risk locking the legs and forcing them into a hyperextended position at the knee joint. When performing the exercise, don't forcefully lock out the legs, as this may damage the knees' supporting connective tissues (ligaments, tendons and cartilage).

Muscles Worked – The design of the leg press means that most of the stress is placed on the thighs. There is very little glute involvement, and the spinal erectors are

Start

Finish

**Standing leg curls are a great movement for the leg biceps (hamstrings).
– Mike Francois**

all but eliminated from the exercise. The calves and hamstrings play only a small role in stabilizing the legs during the exercise.

Milos Sarcev and Porter Cottrell

LEGS (HAMSTRINGS)

Leg Curl – Lie face down on the leg-curl machine with your feet placed under the round foot supports (often called rollers). Pretend you are doing biceps curls (in fact the hamstrings are leg biceps) and curl the legs towards your butt. Pause at the top, and slowly lower the legs back to the starting position.

Comments – Some gyms have three variations of the leg-curl machine. Two of them force you to lie face down on a bench. The bench may be either level or partly angled. The angled bench forces you to do the exercise more strictly. It keeps you from swinging the legs up. A third type of leg-curl machine allows you to stand up and work one leg at a time. The movement is similar to one-arm concentration curls for the biceps.

Just as you wouldn't do biceps curls in an awkward manner, so too must leg curls be performed in a slow, rhythmic style: no jerking or bouncing the weight, and try to avoid lifting your pelvis off the bench. If you have to raise your glutes, you're probably using too much weight.

Muscles Worked – Leg curls primarily work the hamstrings although there is some calf involvement. The glutes and thighs come into play only to stabilize the legs during the exercise.

CHEST EXERCISES

Flat-Bench Barbell Press – Lie on your back and take the barbell from the supports, using a grip that is six to eight inches wider than shoulder width. Lower the bar slowly to the nipple region, and then press it back to the locked-out position.

Comments – King of the chest exercises, bench presses are performed by virtually every top bodybuilder. A few points need to be stressed. Don't drop the bar and bounce it off the chest. Yes, you can lift more weight this way, but you are robbing the exercise of its effectiveness. You also run the risk of breaking ribs or splitting your sternum. Then there is the pec-delt tie-in to worry about. Dropping the bar in a loose fashion increases the risk of tearing the area where your chest muscles connect to your shoulder muscles. To avoid such nasties, lower the weight in a slow, controlled manner, and then push it back to arms' length.

Whether you lock the arms out or not is your personal preference. Some bodybuilders find stopping just short of lockout keeps tension on the muscles throughout the movement. Others find locking out feels more comfortable. As the split is about 50-50 on the issue, try both methods and choose one. (This principle of choice applies to virtually all the exercises.)

Don't arch your back off the bench. You may increase your lift by a few pounds, but at what cost? Arching decreases the amount of pectoral stimulation, and it certainly is no benefit to your lower back.

If you have trouble keeping your back on the bench, perform the movement with your legs up in the air. You will not be able to use as much weight, but there is no way you can arch your back when in this position.

Muscles Worked – Flat bench presses mainly work the lower chest region, but the whole pectoral-deltoid area is stimulated. You will also find your triceps receiving a great deal of stimulation. The muscles of the back and forearms are indirectly used for stabilizing the upper body during the exercise.

Incline Barbell Press – If using an adjustable bench, set the bench to an angle of about 25 to 30 degrees. Incline-bench presses are performed in the same manner as flat benches, the only difference being that, instead of lowering the bar to the nipple region, you bring it down to the center of the chest, just under the chin.

Comments – Most bodybuilders find angles above 30 degrees place too much stress on the front delts, and not on the upper pectorals. Of course, your bone structure may dictate the opposite. You may have to play around with the angle of the bench to see what's best for you. If you don't have access to an adjustable bench, make do with the fixed version. In many cases these fixed benches are angled at about 45 degrees which is too steep for working the upper pecs. You may find that slightly arching the back can shift most of the stress from the shoulders to the chest, but be careful as the lower back was not meant to be arched to any degree. A better solution is to raise one end of a flat bench. You can use a couple of pieces of wood, another bench, or a specially constructed wooden block (most gyms have these for performing bent-over rows) to prop up the flat bench.

Muscles Worked – The incline barbell press works the upper chest. It also stresses the front delts and triceps. Most bodybuilders find inclines excellent for the pec-delt tie-ins. Remember, as you increase the angle, the stress shifts from the upper chest to the shoulders.

Flat Dumbell Press – This exercise is similar to the barbell version, but you use two dumbells instead. Start by sitting on a flat bench and cleaning (lifting) a pair of dumbells to your knees. Lie back on the bench, and with the dumbells pointing end to end (i.e. they form a straight line across your chest like a barbell) lower them to your sides. Pause at the bottom, and then press to arms' length.

Comments – The advantage of using dumbells is the greater range of movement. A barbell can be lowered

"The Real Deal" Chris Cormier shows off his flawless physique.

only to the rib cage, whereas the dumbells can be dropped below the rib cage. This lower position gives the chest muscles a greater stretch. But be careful as the lower part of the movement is the most dangerous, and if you drop the dumbells in an uncontrolled manner, you run the risk of tearing the pec-delt tie-ins. Although there is much personal preference, most bodybuilders find a dumbell spacing about six to eight inches wider than the shoulders to be the most effective.

Muscles Worked – Dumbell presses are great for developing the pec-delt tie-ins. If you squeeze them together at the top, the inner pecs are also worked. And no matter how much you try to eliminate them, the triceps and shoulders will be involved. This is fine, as at the beginning stage you want to work as many muscles as possible.

Incline Dumbell Press – This is the inclined version of the flat dumbell press. With the exception of the angle, the exercise is performed in the same manner.

Comments – Because you have to hoist the dumbells up higher to get them into starting position, it might be a good idea to obtain the help of a spotter. Most body-builders lift one of the dumbells up, and have a partner pass the other one. If two helpers are available, have both dumbells passed to you. Lower the dumbells slowly, going for a full but controlled stretch at the bottom.

Muscles Worked – Incline dumbell presses are an excellent exercise for developing the upper chest. Because of the increased angle they also hit the front deltoids. As with most chest exercises, there is some secondary triceps involvement. If your shoulders are taking too much of the weight, drop the angle of the bench a few degrees.

Dips – One of the simplest but most effective of chest exercises is dips. Most gyms have a set of parallel bars for doing dips. If your gym doesn't, you can substitute the Universal shoulder press. Start the exercise with your arms in a locked-out position. Holding the chin on the chest, lower your body between the bars, pause, and push yourself back to arms' length.

Comments – Dips are considered by many to be one of the best chest exercises – and *the* best by Vince Gironda. To keep the stress on the chest, lean forward and flare your elbows out to the sides. If you keep vertical and have your elbows in tight, the exercise is more of a triceps-builder. As with other chest exercises, don't bounce at the bottom. Doing so places much of the stress on the pec-delt tie-ins.

Muscles Worked – Dips work the lower, outer chest. They produce that clean line under the pecs. They also stimulate the front delts and triceps, so for this reason dips are an excellent beginning exercise.

BACK EXERCISES

Chinups – You will need access to an overhead bar to perform this exercise. Most Universal multistations have one attached but a wall-mounted version is just

Start

Finish

Bob Paris performs dips, one of the best chest exercises, on the parallel bars.

Ericca Kern shapes her back with lat pulldowns. Start

Finish

as good. Jump up and grab the bar with a grip that is about twice your shoulder width. Now pull yourself up and try to touch your chest to the bar. Lower back down to the starting position in a controlled manner.

Comments – Chins are considered to be the best back exercise. Most bodybuilders of all levels make them the mainstay of their back routines. They give that great V-shape. When doing the movement, try to pull with the large back muscles (latissimus dorsi), not the biceps and forearms. Don't drop back to the starting position in such a manner that you risk yanking your arms out of the shoulder sockets. Do the exercise nice and slow.

At first you will find chinups to the front easier. As you get stronger you can pull up so that the bar is behind your head. There is little difference between the two styles. When you can do 12 to 15 easy reps, attach a weight around your waist or hold a dumbell between your legs. This added weight increases the resistance and keeps the muscles growing.

Muscles Worked – Chins work the large latissimus muscles (lats). Additionally they stress the smaller back muscles like the teres. Rear delts and biceps are also brought into play.

You will find that by pulling to the front, the lower parts of the lats are worked the most. Conversely, pulling behind the head stresses the upper section. Keep in mind that these divisions are not carved in stone, and at the beginning level either method is adequate. If you have the strength, you might alternate the two on the same day or alternate days.

Lat Pulldowns – Although not quite as effective as chins, pulldowns enable you to adjust the amount of weight. Chins force you to use your bodyweight, whereas the lat machine allows the user to select the desired poundage. Instead of pulling yourself up to an overhead bar, you pull the bar down to you. Take a wide grip (about twice shoulder width) and sit on the attached seat, or kneel down on the floor. Now pull the bar down, either behind your head, or to the front to touch your chest. Pause at the bottom and squeeze your shoulder blades together. Return to the outstretched-arms position.

Comments – Whether you pull to the front or to the back is a personal decision. There is little difference between the two styles. Either version will add tremendously to back width, giving that much coveted V-shape. Generally speaking, when you pull to the front, you hit more of the lower part of the upper back (i.e. the lower insertions of your lats). Pulling behind the head works the upper regions of the lats and the rear delts. There is so much overlap between the two movements, however, that at the beginning level either movement is sufficient. You might want to rotate both movements, either on the same day or on alternate back days.

Keep your grip fairly wide as narrow-grip pulldowns place much of the stress on the biceps. Many bodybuilders perform narrow-grip chins and pulldowns as biceps exercises.

Because you have to grip the bar, the muscles of the forearms get a good workout. They may be the weak link in the chain.

Muscles Worked – Lat pulldowns work the whole back region, from the large latissimus muscles to the smaller teres, rhomboids and rear deltoids. They also stress the biceps and forearms.

Bent-Over Barbell Rows – Bend over at the waist so that your upper body is almost parallel with the floor. Grab a standard barbell, and using a wide grip, pull it up to the abdomen. Lower slowly and then repeat. Concentrate on using the upper back muscles (lats) and not your spinal erectors.

Comments – You must be especially careful on this exercise. Any sudden bouncing or jerking will put great stress on your lower back. If you have to "throw your lower back into it" you are using far too much weight. Take off a few plates and do it more strictly. The only part of the body that should move is the arms. Your upper body and legs should remain stationary. To get a full stretch, stand on some sort of low platform. Most gyms have specially constructed boxes to stand on while performing bent-over rows. The extra 10 to 12 inches of stretch will add greatly to the effectiveness of the exercise. Bending your knees slightly will help reduce stress on your lower back.

Muscles Worked – This exercise is considered by most to be one of the best back-builders. It's particularly effective in producing thickness in the back. Besides the back muscles, bent-over rows stress the biceps and forearms. Because of the bent-over position the exercise stretches the hamstrings and spinal erectors also.

T-Bar Rows – Many gyms have a long bar with one end bolted to the floor. By placing plates on the free end and grabbing the short crossbar, you can perform a variation of the barbell row. Called T-bar rows because of the shape of the bar, they are an effective substitute for the barbell version. Holding the crossbar, pull the plates up to the chest/abdominal region. Squeeze at the top and then lower back to the floor. Don't touch the plates to the floor, but stop a few inches from it.

Comments – Don't bounce or jerk the weight up. Like barbell rows, T-bar rows place a great deal of stress on the lower back. Keep your upper body stationary, and lift the plates with your back muscles and arms only. If your gym does not have a specially designed T-bar, you can do the same movement with one end of a regular Olympic bar pinned in a corner. Check with the gym's management first, however. Rotating an Olympic bar on one end may damage its sleeve/ball-bearing mechanism. If you are allowed to do the exercise, try to use an old bar. Your gym may even have an old bar set aside just for this purpose.

Bent-over barbell rows are one of the best lat exercises. – Chris Duffy

Muscles Worked – T-bar rows work the same muscles as the regular barbell row. The lats, teres, rhomboids, rear delts, biceps, forearms and lower back all come into play. Because of the assortment of muscles worked, both types of rows are excellent mass-builders.

Note – If you have lower-back problems, you might want to avoid these exercises. If you must do them, start by using light weight. Gradually build up the poundage. Don't make the mistake of slapping on 45-pound plates from day one. This will come with time. Keep in mind that lower-back injuries often don't heal. You may have them for life. Therefore the emphasis should be on preventing them. In a manner of speaking, rows can be a double-edged sword. Done properly they will help strengthen the lower back, thus reducing the chances of future injuries. Done improperly they may be the cause of the injury. So pay strict attention to your exercise style. Don't get carried away with the weight, and don't lift with the lower back.

Seated Pulley Rows – You will need a cable machine to do this exercise. Grab the V-shaped pulley attachment, and sit down on the floor or a convenient surface. With the legs slightly bent, pull the hands into the lower chest/upper abdomen region. Pause for a second and squeeze the shoulder blades together. Now bend forward and stretch the arms out fully.

Comments – You can perform this exercise with a number of different pulley attachments. The most frequently used is the V-shaped double-handle bar. Some bodybuilders like to use a straight pulldown bar. Still others use two separate hand grips. Our advice is to experiment with the different attachments and select the one that feels the most comfortable. Cable rows can also be performed on the lat pulldown machine. To get the full effect, lean back and pull the hands to the lower chest. The direction of force should be about 90 degrees to the body.

Remember, when doing the seated version, to keep the legs slightly bent. Performing the exercise with straight legs won't do your lower back any good.

Muscles Worked – Seated pulley rows are another exercise that works the whole back region. They are more of a thickness movement than a width-builder. Like other rowing exercises, seated pulley rows work all the major muscles of the back. They also stimulate the biceps and forearms.

One-Arm Dumbell Rows – Instead of using a barbell or cable, you can do your rows using a dumbell. Bend over and hold a bench for support. Place one leg behind the other in a running-type stance. Grab a dumbell with the arm that is farthest from the bench (the bracing arm is closest to the bench) and stretch it down and slightly forward. Pause at the bottom and then pull the dumbell up until the arm is fully bent. The movement is comparable to that of sawing wood.

Comments – One-arm rows are great because they allow you to brace your upper body. This support is essential if you have a lower-back injury. Even though your biceps will be involved in the exercise, try to concentrate on using just your back muscles. Once again, no bouncing or jerking the weight. If you have to contort the body to lift the weight, the dumbell is too heavy.

SHOULDER EXERCISES

Behind-the-Head Shoulder Press – With a grip that is about six to eight inches greater than shoulder width, take a barbell from the rack. Lower the bar behind your head, stopping just short of your traps. Push the bar to arms' length and then repeat.

Tonya Knight sculpts her upper back with one-arm dumbell rows.

Finish

Start

Mike Ashley shapes his phenomenal shoulders with seated dumbell presses.

Start

Finish

Comments – Don't bounce the bar off your neck. If you strike either of the top vertebrae (atlas and axis) you run the risk of nerve damage. Perform the exercise in a slow and controlled manner. You don't need a rack to position the bar, but cleaning a loaded bar to your shoulders, doing your reps, and then having to lower it back to the floor is very energy-consuming. After a few months it will be impossible. Use either the squat rack or, even better, the shoulder-press rack. Most gyms have a special seat with a vertical back support. Two long supports enable the user to position the bar behind the head. All you have to do is reach back and lift the bar from the racks. Once your reps are finished, you simply lay the bar behind your head.

Muscles Worked – Behind-the-head presses work the entire shoulder region, particularly the front and side delts. They also stress, to a lesser degree, the rear delts and traps. As with most pressing movements, the triceps are brought into play.

Front Military Press – This exercise is performed in the same manner as the previous movement, except that instead of lowering the bar behind the head, you lower it to the front. Bring the bar down until it just touches the upper chest. Once again, no bouncing – just smooth controlled reps.

Comments – Most bodybuilders find the front press more comfortable. It also eliminates the risk of striking the head or neck. There is a tendency to arch when doing the exercise, so be careful. A slight arch to bring the bar to the upper chest is fine, but you should avoid excessive bending.

Muscles Worked – Front presses put most of the stress on the front and side delts. The rear delts and traps receive some stimulation, but not to the extent they do from rear presses. The upper pectorals are worked if you lean back when doing the exercise.

Dumbell Press – Instead of performing your pressing movements with a barbell, hoist two dumbells to shoulder level. You can stand or sit when pressing the dumbells, but if standing, be careful not to excessively arch the lower back.

Comments – You can press both dumbells at the same time or in an alternating fashion. As with the barbell version, be careful of the lower back. Try not to arch excessively, and don't drop the dumbells into the starting position.

Muscles Worked – This exercise stresses the whole deltoid region. Particular emphasis is placed on the front and side deltoids. There is also some secondary trap and rear-deltoid involvement.

TRICEPS EXERCISES

Triceps Pushdowns – You will need to use the lat-pulldown machine for this exercise. Hold the bar with a narrow grip, anywhere from two to eight inches. Keeping your elbows tight to your sides, press the bar down to a locked-out position. Pause and flex the triceps at the bottom, and then return the bar to about chest level.

Lee Priest flexes his superfreaky triceps.

Comments – Use a false (thumbs above the bar) grip when performing triceps pushdowns, and resist the urge to flare the elbows out to the sides. If you have to swing to push the bar down, you're probably using too much weight.

Muscles Worked – Triceps pushdowns work the entire triceps region, especially the outer head.

One-arm Dumbell Extensions – Grasp a dumbell and extend it above your head. Keeping the upper arm stationary, lower the dumbell behind the head. Try to perform the movement in a slow, rhythmic manner.

Comments – It's possible to work up to 75-plus-pound dumbells, but keep in mind that the elbow joint and associated tissues (ligaments, cartilage and tendons) were not designed to support huge poundages. Never bounce the dumbell at the bottom (arm in the bent position) of the exercise. Try to place the emphasis on style rather than weight.

Muscles Worked – Although it works the whole triceps region, this exercise is great for the lower triceps.

Lying Triceps Extensions – Place an EZ-curl bar on the end of a bench. Lie down on the bench so that the bar is above your head. Now reach back, grab the bar, and hoist it to arms' length. Keeping your elbows in, lower the bar to your forehead. Extend the bar back to arms' length.

Comments – If you are apprehensive about lowering the bar to your head, lower it behind your head and lightly touch the bench. Don't bounce the bar off the bench, but merely pause and then extend the arms again. Try to keep the elbows in.

Muscles Worked – This is one of the main triceps mass-builders. It stresses the whole triceps, particularly the long rear head of the muscle. Lowering the bar behind your head brings the lower lats and upper chest into play. The exercise also works the intercostals, located just below the rib cage.

Upright Dips – For this exercise you use the same apparatus as when performing dips for the chest. With a few minor modifications you can shift the strain from the chest to the triceps. For starters keep the elbows tight against the body. Flaring them to the sides will work the chest. Also, unlike dips for the chest, (in which you bend forward), keep your body as vertical as possible. Some bodybuilders lean back slightly to get that extra degree of triceps stimulation.

Comments – As with most exercises that rely on lifting your bodyweight, you will eventually reach a point where you can bang out 12 to 15 reps with ease. To increase resistance, hold a dumbell between your legs, or attach a plate to a special dipping chain on your belt. Before you know it you will be dipping with 50 to 100 pounds.

With regard to safety, be careful at the bottom of the movement. Although dips are an excellent triceps exercise, they also place much stress on the front delts, particularly the pec-delt tie-in. Don't bounce at the bottom. Perform the exercise in a slow and controlled manner. (You might want to write out the phrase "in a slow and controlled manner" in large black letters and post it on your bedroom wall! It's perhaps the most important piece of advice we can give, and this is why it's emphasized so much.)

Muscles Worked – Performed in an upright manner, dips place most of the strain on the long rear head of the triceps. Because of the weight used (minimum of your bodyweight) they also work the other two heads quite nicely. And even though you may attempt to eliminate other muscles from the exercise, the front delts and chest will take some of the strain. This is fine at the beginning level where the goal is to add overall muscle mass.

Start

Finish

Standing barbell curls are one of the greatest biceps-builders around. – Michael Francois

BICEPS EXERCISES

Standing Barbell Curl – This is perhaps the most used (and abused) exercise performed by bodybuilders. You can use the standard Olympic bar, a smaller straight bar, or an EZ-curl bar. Grip the bar slightly wider than shoulder width and curl it up until the biceps are fully flexed. Try to keep your elbows close to your sides, and don't swing the weight up with your lower back. Lower the weight back to the starting position in good style. Don't simply let the thing drop! Not only are you losing half the movement, but you also run the risk of tearing your biceps tendon. (You can ask Dorian Yates, Lou Ferrigno or Tom Platz what this feels like.)

Comments – Barbell curls are considered the ultimate in biceps exercises. Many bodybuilders forget that the negative (lowering) part of the movement is just as important as the positive (hoisting) section. Try to lower the bar with about the same speed as you curl it up.

Keep your back straight and avoid swinging. If you want to employ the "cheating" technique, save it for the last couple of reps. For example, perform 8 to 10 reps in good style and then cheat one or two more. Don't abuse a good thing, however. One or two cheat reps is fine, but cheating from the start is counterproductive. At your level of development you'll get all the stimulation you want from strict reps.

If you have weak wrists or forearms, you might want to give the EZ-curl bar a try. The bent shape of this bar allows you to rotate the forearms slightly, thus reducing the tension on the wrists and forearms. Most bodybuilders use a straight bar, but you can play it by ear. Give both types a try and pick the one that is the most comfortable and produces the greatest biceps stimulation.

Muscles Worked – The barbell biceps curl works the entire biceps muscle. Also, because you have to forcibly grip the bar, the exercise will give you a great set of forearms. The front delts and lower back come into play for stabilizing purposes.

Standing Dumbell Curls – Instead of using a barbell, select a pair of dumbells. Although raising both dumbells simultaneously is possible, most bodybuilders do what are called alternate dumbell curls. As the name implies, you curl the dumbells one at a time. Start the dumbells by your sides with the ends pointing to the front and back (i.e. the dumbells are parallel to each other). As you curl, rotate your palms from the facing-in position to a facing-up position. This twisting motion is called supination. Many bodybuilders are not aware that the biceps has two main functions. Besides the better-known curling movement, the biceps also rotate the forearms. You can see this function if you hold your arm by your side and rotate the hand back and forth. Notice the biceps flexing as the hand approaches the palm-up position. By using dumbells, you can take advantage of this physiological trait. You would have to use a very heavy dumbell (more than you could curl) to

Milos Sarcev and Sonny Schmidt shown during a comparison round onstage.

get the full effect of supination. Still every bit helps, so give it a try.

Comments – Limit any swinging to the last one or two reps. Even then it's probably not necessary at this stage of your development. Try to put total concentration into each and every rep.

Besides the psychological aspect of curling one dumbell at a time, there may be a physiological basis. Neurologists suggest that when two arms are used simultaneously the brain has to split the nerve impulses, whereas by alternating the dumbells you get full nerve transmission to each biceps. How much is fact and how much theory is open to debate. Although you have no control over nerve impulses, you do have control over exercise performance, so choose the version that feels most productive. As a final comment, Arnold favored the alternating version. Need we say more?

Muscles Worked – Dumbell curls are great for working the belly of the biceps. They also reduce stress on the wrists and forearms. Many bodybuilders suggest starting your biceps workout with dumbells so as not to overstress the weaker areas. (This advice applies only to intermediate and advanced bodybuilders who are performing more than one exercise for their muscles.)

Preacher Curls – Also called Scott curls, this exercise is great for working the lower biceps region. Start by sitting on the stool or bench connected to the preacher board. Adjust yourself so that the padded board fits snugly under your armpits. Take the barbell (straight or EZ-curl bar) from the supports and curl it until the biceps are fully flexed. Lower to the starting position and repeat.

Comments – Although biceps length is genetic, you can create the illusion of length by building the lower regions. Some Scott benches require you to stand up when doing the movement. If your gym has both types, give both a try and pick the one that suits you.

Of all the biceps exercises this one is the most dangerous if not performed in good style. Under no circumstances should you drop the barbell to the bottom position. You can easily rip the biceps tendon from where it inserts on the forearm bone. The only option open to you then is surgery and many months of inactivity. With a little attention paid to good style, you can avoid the aggravation.

Muscles Worked – Although they work the whole biceps muscle, Scott curls are primarily a lower-biceps exercise. Because you are braced by the padded board, it's virtually impossible to cheat and bring your lower back into the movement. You will notice a great deal of forearm stimulation. This is fine as you will need a strong grip for many of the other exercises.

Incline Curls – You will need an incline bench to perform this exercise. Unlike incline presses for your chest, incline curls require a bench with an angle of at least 45 degrees. Anything less will place too much strain on your front delts. Lie back on the bench holding two dumbbells. Curl the dumbbells up until the biceps are fully flexed. All the tips suggested for standing dumbell curls apply here as well: Rotate the hands from a facing-in to a facing-up position, don't swing the weight up, etc.

Comments – Once again you have the option of curling the dumbbells simultaneously or alternately. When you lower the dumbbells, be careful not to hit the side of the incline bench. This is another reason for starting the dumbbells in a forward-pointed position. If they were in the standard end-to-end position, they would have less clearance with the bench.

The advantage of using the incline bench is that it limits the amount of cheating you can do. You can't swing very much if you have your back braced against a rigid board.

Muscles Worked – Incline curls work the whole biceps region. Many bodybuilders find that they are great for bringing out the biceps peak although peak is more genetic than anything else. The exercise does provide some forearm stimulation, but not to the same extent as the various barbell curls.

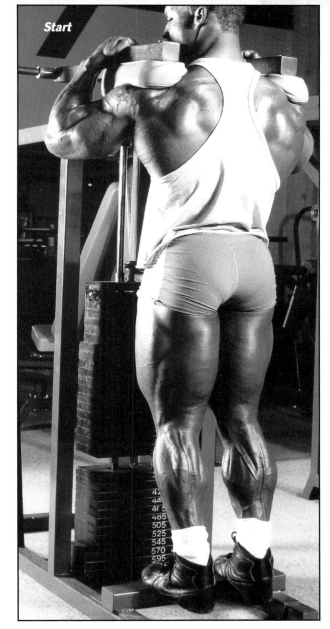

Start

Shawn Ray sculpts his superb calves with standing calf raises.

Finish

42
44
46
485
505
525
545
570
595

CALF EXERCISES

Standing Calf Raise – You will need access to the appropriate machine to do this exercise. Position your toes on the attached block of wood, and rest the pads on your shoulders. From here the exercise is straightforward. With your legs locked, move up and down on your toes. Stretch all the way down and flex up on your toes as far as possible. Go for that intense burn!

Comments – Even though this is chiefly a stretching exercise, don't be afraid to load the machine with hundreds of pounds of weight. Keep your back and legs straight. The only movement is at the ankle joint. Calf injuries are extremely rare (the calf muscle is composed of very dense muscle fiber which makes tearing very difficult), but you still shouldn't bounce at the bottom of the movement as you might strain the Achilles tendon.

Muscles Worked – Standing calf raises work the entire calf muscle, with the primary focus on the upper (gastrocnemius) calf region.

Calf Flexes on Leg-Press Machine – This is another example of using a machine for an exercise it was not designed for. Instead of pressing the weight with your thighs, you "flex" the weight platform using only your feet. As with the standing version, go for the maximum amount of stretch at the top and bottom.

Comments – The advantage of this exercise is that you don't have the entire weight pushing down on your spine. The disadvantage is that it will take a bit of practice to get the foot positioning correct. Still, the exercise is an adequate substitute if you don't have access to a standing calf machine.

Muscles Worked – Most of the stress is placed on the lower calf, but the upper calves are also worked. If you really want to get that extra burn in the lower calf, use less weight and bend your legs slightly. This adjustment will shift all the stress to the lower calf. After one set of these babies your calves will be burning like crazy!

Thierry Pastel

BOOK THREE

Eating for Success

BODYBUILDING NUTRITION

"If you see the Golden Arches, you're probably on your way to the Pearly Gates." **– Quote from a heart specialist with the Framingham Heart Study**

"Diets are like political manifestos; everyone believes in them until they're put into practice."
– Dr. Michael Rabinowitz, psychologist (commenting on why people find it hard to stick to their diets)

Lee Priest

Food is more than just a necessity of life. It is a part of our culture. We celebrate birthdays and weddings with food, we propose over candle-lit dinners, and feast our way through the holidays. Cooking is an art form, and the kitchen a studio where every person can demonstrate the genius that titillates the taste buds. Food is our friend, a source of pleasure, and a communal way of celebrating our existence. For bodybuilders, food is as essential as the weights we lift. And food kills. Of the 4,000 heart attacks that occur every day in the USA, only 10 percent would happen if people stopped eating junk food. Tobacco use is responsible for 35 percent of cancers, but poor diet is responsible for 65 percent of cancers. Diets high in animal fats lead to heart disease. Diets with a high vegetarian content lead to a drop in mortality rates and a reversal of heart disease symptoms. Bodybuilders leave very attractive corpses. It's not enough to eat for mass because putting on mass takes time. To be a successful bodybuilder, you've also got to eat for time and most importantly – health!

In this chapter we begin with what food is, generally and specifically: fats, proteins, carbohydrates, fiber, water, vitamins and minerals. The digestive and metabolic processes are reviewed, followed by food preparation and storage. Bodybuilding recipes, supplements, and sample menus conclude this section.

THE BASIC FOOD GROUPS

"Yeah, I do my own cooking... and if I want to add taste, I just burn it!" **– Australia's Lee Priest**

For the purposes of this chapter we have classified foods according to the nutrients they share, and have come up with the six basic food groups:

Dairy Products Group – This group contains sour cream, cheese, ice cream, cottage cheese, yogurt, buttermilk and milk. Each of these foods provides the following nutrients: vitamins A and D, riboflavin, calcium, phosphorus, fats and proteins.

Vegetable-Fruit Group – This group contains all the fruits and vegetables. In fact, some vegetables are really fruits. Fruit is the fleshy part that surrounds the seeds. Therefore tomatoes, eggplants, peppers and cucumbers are fruits. Despite the confusion in definition, fruits and vegetables all provide the following nutrients: B vitamins, vitamins A and C, iron, phosphorus, calcium and fiber.

Protein Group – This group contains meats, poultry, eggs, fish, shellfish, beans and nuts. These foods are the richest nutrient sources of proteins, B vitamins and iron.

Bread-Cereal Group – This group contains enriched bread, whole-grain cereals, flour, pasta, corn meal, oatmeal and all other grain products. The nutrients provided are the B vitamins, iron and carbohydrates.

Oils-Fats Group – This group contains all the edible animal and vegetable oils, butter, margarine and honey. The nutrients provided are simple carbohydrates and fats.

Utter-Crap Group – This group contains all the "foods" that can derail any bodybuilder's dreams of success. They include table salt, potato chips, refined sugar (in excessive amounts), candy, processed meats, donuts, cakes, prepackaged pastries, soft drinks, and just about everything from a fast-food restaurant. The more nutrients a food contains in relation to the number of calories, the higher the nutrient density. The foods in this group are utter crap because of their low-nutrient density. Remember, you are what you eat.

BASICS OF NUTRITION

Food is composed of proteins, carbohydrates, fats, vitamins, fiber, minerals and water. Though the majority of foods contain several of the basic nutrients, no single food has them all (with the exception of breast milk). Thus to satisfy the body's needs, we must consume a wide assortment of foods. With eating, variety is the spice of life!

PROTEIN – THE BODY-BUILDER

"Many years ago I quizzed a doctor on the subject of getting too much protein, and he told me that as long as plenty of water was taken every day plus fruits and vegetables, there was really no danger in a high-protein diet."
– The late Bruce Page, nutrition consultant

Protein is formed from smaller subunits called polypeptide chains. These chains can be further broken down into subunits called amino acids (the building blocks of life). There are 20 amino acids, 11 of which the human body can manufacture. The other nine, called essential amino acids, cannot be manufactured and must be consumed in the diet. Not all forms of protein are the same. Animal protein (beef, chicken, eggs, milk, cheeses and fish) contains all the essential amino acids, whereas no single plant source does. For this reason a wide range of plant protein (vegetables, nuts and fruits) would have to be consumed to get the same benefit as one large beef steak. This generalization applies only to protein. Vegetables, nuts and fruits have nutritional benefits to offer that meat does not. In the time of the Roman Empire gladiators were fed a diet heavy in barley. It was considered the best and cheapest muscle-building food around.

Protein is involved in the production of healthy red blood cells, antibodies that prevent diseases, and hormones that regulate body functions. With so much to do, protein supplies are quickly used up and need to

Dorian Yates

be replenished frequently. Sedentary adults require about 65 grams of protein daily. Most of the body's energy comes from fats and carbohydrates, but when they aren't sufficient, protein can be used to supply energy. Excess protein in the diet is converted to bodyfat.

Plant forms of protein can be combined with high-quality sources to make them nutritionally valuable. A good example is macaroni and cheese because plant and animal proteins (pasta, cheese and milk) are combined.

PROTEIN REQUIREMENTS IN BODYBUILDERS

"How much protein is enough? It depends since everyone varies in needs and abilities, but I'd say a minimum of one gram of protein per pound of bodyweight, divided equally into five or six servings throughout the day, since your body can absorb only so much at one time. I generally try to eat every three hours throughout the day." **– Dorian Yates, Five-time Mr. Olympia**

For a hard-training bodybuilder to make the desired gains in muscular size and strength, an adequate amount of high-quality food must be ingested daily. A high proportion of the food must be composed of protein. The Recommended Daily Allowance (RDA) for the average individual is 0.8 to 0.9 grams/kg of body-weight. It must be added that the RDA was developed by studying essentially sedentary (nonactive) subjects. Although some subjects exercised, the exercise was minimal and certainly nothing like that undertaken by a bodybuilder in heavy training.

One study found that the top-ranked bodybuilders engaged in intensive training routines required from 1.12 to 1.67 times more protein than did sedentary controls. Another study found that football players were consuming two grams of protein per kilogram of body-weight. In a study carried out in Romania, Olympic weightlifters who normally ingested 2.25 times the RDA were given 4.4 times the RDA. The results showed impressive gains in muscle size and strength.

IS TOO MUCH PROTEIN DANGEROUS?

"I have 300 to 400 grams (of protein) a day. The guy who made up the one-gram-to-one-pound-of-body-weight rule was only this big! You have to overload with protein. I've eaten 15 cans of tuna a day – mixed in the blender with apple juice." – Mike Matarazzo, IFBB Pro

Exercise and nutrition researchers are concerned that bodybuilders using too much protein are aggravating other problems they might have. For example, bodybuilders tend to be dehydrated from not drinking enough liquids during and after a hard training session. If a high-protein diet is being followed, additional water is needed to help digest the protein and speed up excretion. High-protein diets also place a tremendous strain on the liver and kidneys, which have to process and remove the waste products generated by protein metabolism. Is it possible that bodybuilders are taking needless risks? Researchers have suggested that many bodybuilders are driven by the placebo effect. The placebo effect involves the belief by bodybuilders that supplements will speed up the rate at which they gain muscle mass. The increased strength and size are not caused by any biochemical benefit from the supplements, but by the bodybuilder's *belief* that these substances are beneficial.

While some research has indicated that a high-protein diet is not necessary, and possibly even dangerous, other studies suggest the opposite – that hard-training athletes need above average RDA amounts of protein. The bottom line may be determined with statistics. Millions of bodybuilders have been using protein supplements, in addition to their already high-protein meals, for the past 30 to 40 years, yet how many have suffered medical problems that could be directly attributed to their excessive protein intake? Some argue for a placebo effect while others say that high protein works. The debate continues.

FATS – CONCENTRATED ENERGY

"Let me have men about me that are fat, sleek headed men, and such as sleep o' nights. Yon Cassius hath a lean and hungry look; he thinks too much; such men are dangerous." – **Julius Caesar, from William Shakespeare's play of the same name.**

It's hard to think of fats as being an essential part of a well-balanced diet, especially if you are trying to lose weight. Yet they are just as important as carbohydrates and protein.

Fats are highly concentrated forms of energy. They provide nine calories per gram compared to four calories per gram of protein and carbohydrate.

Fats transport vitamins A, D, E and K into the body where they can be absorbed. A certain amount of fat makes food taste good, and because fats are digested slowly, they keep you from feeling hungry longer than do proteins and carbohydrates.

As you might expect, fat is a natural insulator and helps your body maintain its normal temperature. The most common sources of fat in your diet probably are

Boston's Mike Matarazzo

oils, butter, margarine, shortenings and meat, but there are hidden sources of fats, too – e.g. baked products, fried foods, dressings, nuts, eggs, some milk products, and even lean meat.

Fats that are solid at room temperature are called saturated fats. Unsaturated fats are usually liquid. Polyunsaturated fats (such as safflower, corn, peanut, and soybean oils) are a chemical variation of unsaturated fats and contain essential elements that the body can't manufacture.

Medical authorities believe that saturated fats tend to increase blood cholesterol levels. Researchers say that high dietary cholesterol plays an important role in heart disease.

Each species of animal stores fat, which contains varying proportions of the different fatty acids. Beef fat, when eaten, must be converted by the liver into the type of fat characteristic of humans. Stored fat, besides being a source of energy, serves as a supporting cushion for certain internal organs, and as an insulating layer under the skin, preventing rapid heat loss.

Fats are also a source of energy. If your body has no pressing energy needs, the fat is stored in adipose tissue for a rainy day – 50 percent of fat is placed in subcutaneous tissue, 20 percent in genital areas, 10 to 15 percent around the omenta (adipose tissue found in the abdominal cavity), 12 percent around the kidneys and 5 to 8 percent between the muscles. While fat people may be inactive, their fat reserves are not. Fat is continually released from storage, transported by the blood, and stored in other adipose tissues. It is believed that up to 50 percent of the body's fat reserves change position daily. Perhaps one day obese people will be cured using dialysis machines that can filter out fats.

CARBOHYDRATES

"In fact, there are far more nutrients in a Snicker's bar or in Twinkies than you find in an apple or an orange – plus of course, a lot more calories. If you ask me what's in a diet cola, I say it's one of the best sources of water you can get simply because it's clean."
– Paul Saltman, California nutrition researcher (commenting on junk food)

"Nobody in his right mind would attempt to compare the nutritional value of chocolate cake with that of a fresh, raw vegetable salad, so why compare apples and oranges, or in this case, Twinkies and oranges?"
– Bernard Centrella, nutrition expert (commenting on Saltman's views)

Carbohydrates are compounds containing only carbon (C), hydrogen (H) and oxygen (O) in the ratio of C:2H:O. Some examples of carbohydrates are sugars, starches and cellulose.

Glucose is the only sugar found in any quantity in the human body. The other carbohydrates consumed are converted by the liver into glucose. Glucose is an

The amazing Laura Creavalle

indispensable component of blood. No particular harm results from a simple increase in the amount of glucose in the body, but a reduced concentration leads to increased irritability of certain brain cells, so that they respond to very slight stimuli. Impulses from these cells may cause twitches, convulsions, unconsciousness and even death. An extremely complex mechanism involving the nervous system, liver, pancreas, pituitary and adrenal glands maintains the proper concentration of glucose in the blood.

The largest carbohydrate molecules are starches and cellulose. They are composed of large numbers of single sugars joined together in a chain or branched-chain type of arrangement. Starches vary in the number and kind of molecules present, and are common constituents in plant and animal cells. Carbohydrates are stored as glycogen in the liver and muscles of animals, and are stored in plants as starches. Most plants have a strong supporting outer wall of cellulose, an insoluble complex sugar resembling starch in that it is made of many glucose molecules. Because the chemical bonds between the glucose molecules of cellulose are of a different type from those found in starch or glycogen, the enzymes that digest starch will not digest cellulose. Carbohydrates primarily serve as a readily available fuel to supply energy for metabolic processes in the

Pro champion Michael Francois

ing carbohydrates, they create a rebound effect. This effect, an increased storage of glycogen exceeding normal levels, ensures the athletes a more than adequate energy supply at competition time. For a competitive bodybuilder the extra glycogen means larger muscles because of the extra water held by the glycogen (more on this in the chapter on competitive bodybuilding).

FATS VERSUS CARBOHYDRATES

"We have our top ice-cream investigators on top of this one, and we are looking for some fat, contented kids."
– Sgt. Norm Miles, York Regional Police (commenting on the disappearance of 5,600 ice cream cones and bars)

Fats are important as fuels and structural components of the body, while carbohydrates serve as short-term sources of energy. Fats yield more than twice as much energy per gram as carbohydrates, and thus are a more economical form for local storage for food energy reserves. Carbohydrates can be transformed into fats and stored. The reverse may also occur: Parts of the fat molecule may be converted into glucose and other carbohydrates.

VITAMINS

"Even though vitamin supplementation has been, and continues to be, widely practiced by athletes, there are few research data to support its effectiveness in the well-nourished athlete. A variety of studies have been conducted over the past 40 years involving vitamin supplementation and physical performance, particularly with vitamins C, E and the B-complex, and, with a few exceptions, they have not revealed any beneficial effects."
– Dr. Melvin Williams, director of the Human Performance Laboratory, Old Dominion University, Virginia.

Until the early 1900s, it was believed that only carbohydrates, protein, some minerals, water and fat were needed to maintain health. We know now that such a diet will not sustain life, and that other nutritional components of food are essential. These nutritional components were named vitamins.

Casimir Funk, a Polish biochemist working in London, studied the effects of beriberi, a disease caused by malnutrition. He prepared a potent antiberiberi substance from rice. Since biochemically it was an amine (a nitrogen containing organic compound) and it was vital for life, he coined the name "vitamine". As other "vitamines" were discovered, only a few were found to be amine in nature; hence the final *e* was dropped, giving the present term *vitamin*.

Vitamins can be defined as chemical compounds which are necessary for growth, health and normal metabolism. They may be essential parts of enzymes (organic compounds that control the rate of chemical

body. If carbohydrates are in short supply, the body will use proteins as an energy source.

CARBOHYDRATE LOADING

"As far as carb-loading and depletion are concerned, I'll deplete for three days, cutting my carb intake by about 50 percent, going from 400 down to 200 calories from carbs. To replace these calories, which is important, I'll increase the protein. Some people make the mistake of cutting the carbs but then not replacing calories, so then they burn muscle tissue. I never go to zero carbs."
– Dorian Yates, Five-time Mr. Olympia

The practice of depleting muscle glycogen through diet and exercise, and then loading muscle glycogen by a high intake of carbohydrate, is widely utilized by many athletes prior to an endurance competition. By depleting the body's glycogen reserves, then consum-

Lee Priest's development is even more impressive when one considers his youth.

reactions), or may be essential parts of hormones (chemical messengers of the body).

"If people eat normally they don't need to take vitamins – they're inescapable in foods." **– Dr. Stephen Barret Pennsylvania psychiatrist who fights nutrition quackery.**

Traditionally vitamins are divided into two categories: fat-soluble and water-soluble.

FAT-SOLUBLE VITAMINS:

"This is one hormone people should avoid consuming unless there is a clear medical reason for its use."
– Professor James Moon (commenting on vitamin D)

These vitamins are called fat-soluble because they can be stored in bodyfat. Excessive amounts of fat-soluble vitamins in the diet accumulate and are stored for use at a later time. If these amounts become too excessive, they can become toxic (harmful) to areas

of storage such as the liver. Too much vitamin D, for example, can lead to heart disease, kidney stones and other ailments.

The principal fat-soluble vitamins are:

FAT-SOLUBLES:	SOME NATURAL SOURCES:
Vitamin A (retinol)	Carrots, yellow and green vegetables, fish, liver, milk and butter.
Vitamin D (cholecalciferol)	Cod-liver oil, egg yolk, fortified milk.
Vitamin E (alpha-tocopherol)	Corn oil, green leafy vegetables, fresh nuts and wheat germ.
Vitamin K (Menadiol) *	Cheddar cheese, spinach, cauliflower, cabbage, liver.

A different form, Menadiol sodium diphosphate, is water-soluble.

WATER-SOLUBLE VITAMINS:

Water-soluble vitamins cannot be stored in the body to any great extent. The daily amount needed must be provided in the diet. Under some circumstances it may be difficult or impossible for an individual to obtain enough vitamins simply by eating his/her normal diet. The amount of vitamins a person needs during heavy training and excessive water consumption may be increased. A vitamin supplement may be necessary for these people.

The principal water-soluble vitamins are:

WATER-SOLUBLES	SOME NATURAL SOURCES:
Vitamin B-1 (thiamine)	Yeast, whole-grain cereals, nuts, eggs, pork, liver.
Vitamin B-2 (riboflavin)	Yeast, whole-wheat products, peanuts, peas, asparagus, beets, eggs, lamb, veal, beef, liver.
Vitamin B-3 (niacin)	Yeast, whole-grain breads and cereals, nuts, beans, peas, fish, meats, liver.
Vitamin B-5 (pantothenic acid)	Whole-grain products, yeast, green vegetables, cereal, eggs, kidney, liver, lobster.
Vitamin B-6 (pyridoxine)	Yeast, whole-grain cereals, spinach, tomatoes, yellow corn, yogurt, salmon.
Vitamin B-9 (folic acid)	Wheat, wheat germ, barley, fruits, rice, soybeans, green leafy vegetables, liver.
Vitamin B-12 (cyanocobalamin)	Clams, meat, liver, kidney, cheese, eggs, milk.
Vitamin H (biotin)	Chicken, yeast, liver, egg yolk, kidneys, tuna, walnuts.
Vitamin C (ascorbic acid)	Citrus fruits, green leafy vegetables, potatoes, tomatoes.

FIBER

Dietary fiber is a catch-all phrase for a number of non-nutritive plant substances that can't be digested well by the body. Most fiber comes from the structural parts of plants – the leaves, flowers, seeds, fruits, stems and roots. The most common fiber is cellulose, found in the cell walls of vegetables. You can increase the amount of fiber in your diet by eating more foods made with

The majority of people in modern society ingest far too much salt.

appear in combination with each other, or in combination with organic compounds. Minerals constitute about four percent of the body's total weight, and they are concentrated most heavily in the skeleton. Some elements are known to be as essential as mineral salts in the diet and must be consumed frequently. Others are needed only in trace amounts.

MINERAL:	FUNCTION:
Calcium	Essential for blood clotting, muscle and nerve activity, bone and teeth formation.
Chlorine	Maintains water balance, Ph balance of the blood, and forms HCL in the stomach.
Magnesium	Part of many coenzymes, essential for muscle and nerve activity, involved in bone formation.
Phosphorus	Involved in the transfer and storage of ATP, buffer system for the blood, essential for muscle contraction and nerve activity, component of DNA and RNA, involved in bone and teeth formation.
Sodium	Part of the bicarbonate buffer system, strongly affects distribution of water in the extracellular fluid.
Sulphur	Part of many proteins and hormones (including insulin) and some vitamins (including biotin and thiamine). Thus it helps regulate bodily activities.

TRACE ELEMENT:	FUNCTION:
Cobalt	Component of B12, needed for the stimulation of erythropoiesis (the production of red blood cells).
Copper	Part of an enzyme required for melanin pigment formation, essential for the synthesis of haemoglobin.
Iodine	Needed by the thyroid gland to form two hormones that regulate metabolic rate: triiodothyronine and thyroxin.
Iron	Part of the coenzymes that form ATP from catabolism, part of haemoglobin that carries oxygen to the cells.
Zinc	Part of enzymes involved in growth.
Chromium	Enhances effect of insulin in glucose utilization, helps transport of amino acids to heart and liver cells.
Manganese	Necessary for growth, reproduction, lactation, haemoglobin synthesis, and essential for the activation of several enzymes.

whole grain (such as breads and cereals), bran, dried peas and dried beans, nuts and fruits. Fruits and vegetables that have edible seeds, or which can be eaten unpeeled, are among the best sources of fiber.

SALT

Salt is a mineral combination of two elements, sodium (Na) and Chlorine (Cl). Salt is vital for nerve conduction and the overall metabolic activities of the body, but as meat eaters we tend to ingest far more salt than we need. Salt is present in almost every food we eat, especially processed foods. For example, there's enough salt in two slices of bread to meet the body's daily requirement for salt. Excess salt causes fluid retention, and is linked to high blood pressure, kidney failure and other diseases.

MINERALS

Minerals play a crucial role even though they occur in the body in minute quantities.

"Manganese can strengthen connective tissues, prevent injuries and decrease fatigue."

– The late Bruce Page, nutrition consultant

There is a clear and important distinction between the terms mineral and trace element. If the body requires more than 100 mg of an element each day the substance is called a mineral; if the body requires less than that amount, the element is called a trace element.

Minerals (elements such as iron and magnesium) can be defined as inorganic substances. They may

Minerals are required for growth, maintenance and repair of the body. In addition, minerals participate in the proper functioning of the nervous and muscular systems. A diet that contains no minerals is rapidly more fatal than total starvation. This is because when the body excretes wastes, it must in the process also

Water is an essential component of every cell, and makes up two-thirds or more of the mass of the human body. It is the fluid part of the blood, the medium in which all chemical reactions occur, and is essential for digestion. Water dissolves metabolic wastes, distributes and regulates body heat, and in the form of perspiration cools the body's surface. The amount of water lost daily averages about two liters, although this figure varies with individual activities and the climate. Humans can live for weeks without food, but only a few days without water. For these reasons hard-training athletes should replenish the water lost during physical exercise by consuming adequate amounts of fluids during and after training. Intensive training without replenishment of lost fluids can result – and has resulted – in dehydration leading to kidney failure. In some cases this has led to permanent kidney damage, and even death.

Our advice is to drink at least seven glasses of water a day, and two to four liters during a heavy workout. During the workout swallow a mouthful of room-temperature water after every set. Your muscles can't grow if the liquid medium for growth is in short supply.

excrete a certain amount of salt. It is important to eat a well-balanced diet, so that the approximately 30 g of mineral salts lost daily through excretion are replaced. Because most minerals are widely distributed in foods, severe mineral deficiencies in the general population are unusual in developed countries, although they are seen in specific groups. The following are the principal minerals and trace elements and some of their natural sources:

MINERAL	SOME NATURAL SOURCES OF:
Calcium	Green leafy vegetables, shellfish, egg yolk and milk.
Chlorine	Meat, fish and table salt.
Magnesium	Wheat germ, soybeans, green leafy vegetables, nuts, sunflower seeds and fish.
Phosphorus	Nuts, dairy products, fish, poultry and meat.
Sodium	Meat, fish and table salt.
Sulphur	Beans, eggs, cheese, fish, poultry, lamb, beef and liver.

TRACE ELEMENT:	SOME NATURAL SOURCES OF:
Cobalt	Clams, meat, liver, kidney, cheese, eggs and milk.
Copper	Barley, mushrooms, oats, whole-wheat flour, beans, asparagus, spinach, beets, eggs, fish and liver.
Iodine	Cod-liver oil, iodized table salt, seafood and sunflower seeds.
Iron	Whole-grain products, cashews, beans, dried fruits, cheddar cheese, egg yolk, shellfish, caviar, meat and liver.
Zinc	Yeast, whole-grain products, soybeans, sunflower seeds, fish, poultry and meat.
Chromium	Whole-grain products, fresh fruit, potato skins, seafood, poultry and meat.
Manganese	Barley, bran, buckwheat, ginger, coffee, spinach, peas and peanuts.

WATER

"It's very hard. You have to be very, very careful, especially with diuretics. I start cutting down two nights before the contest, and the night before the contest I sip on ice cubes. I was in hospital eight days after the Arnold Classic last year. Never again."

– Mike Matarazzo, answering the question, "How much do you limit water intake before a competition?"

Very rarely can you drink too much water.
– Debbie Kruck

DIGESTION

"Learn to chew and spend more time masticating your food. You cannot expect to zoom through a 30-minute meal in just eight minutes! Body processes cannot be rushed." **– MuscleMag International** *founder and publisher,* **Robert Kennedy**

Bodybuilders are often knowledgeable about carbohydrates, fats and proteins; but you need to understand also what happens to food after it has entered your digestive system. Because the vast majority of foods are too large to be absorbed across the plasma membranes of the cells, the food must be broken down first, both chemically and mechanically. This process is called digestion.

What follows is a very technical discussion of digestion and metabolism. Outside of a biology or medical text book one would not normally encounter such detail. Our logic in adopting this approach was to ensure that you, the bodybuilder, would be fully informed as to how your digestive system works. Understanding this process empowers you to make better decisions regarding diet and the use or nonuse of supplements.

Mechanical digestion consists of various movements that aid chemical digestion. Food must be broken down by the teeth before it can be swallowed. Then the smooth muscles of the stomach and small intestine churn the food so that it is thoroughly mixed with the enzymes that catalyze the reactions.

Chemical digestion is a series of catabolic (decomposition) reactions that break down the large carbohydrate, lipid and protein molecules of food into smaller molecules. These products of digestion are small enough to pass through the walls of the digestive organs, into the blood and lymph capillaries, and finally into the body's cells.

The digestive system is divided into two main sections: the gastrointestinal tract (GI), also referred to as the alimentary canal, and the accessory organs.

John Terilli

CHAPTER NINE – BODYBUILDING NUTRITION

The GI is made up of the mouth, pharynx, esophagus, stomach, small intestine and large intestine. The GI tract holds the food from the time it is eaten until it is prepared for excretion. Muscular contractions in the walls of the GI tract break down the food physically by churning it. Secretions produced by cells along the GI tract break down the food chemically.

The accessory organs include the teeth, tongue, salivary glands, liver, gallbladder, pancreas and appendix. Teeth protrude into the GI tract and aid in the physical breakdown of food. With the exception of the tongue, the accessory organs lie outside the GI tract, and produce or store secretions that aid the chemical breakdown of food. These secretions are released into the tract through ducts.

DIGESTION - BY LOCATION

THE MOUTH:

Digestion in the mouth is for the most part done by the salivary glands, teeth and tongue. The salivary glands produce most of the saliva, with the buccal glands of the mucous membranes that line the mouth producing the remainder. Saliva is a fluid that is continuously secreted by glands in or near the mouth. Saliva is secreted to keep the mucous membranes of the mouth moist. When food enters the mouth, secretion increases so that saliva can lubricate, dissolve and chemically break down the food. Through chewing, the teeth tear the food apart and mix it with saliva. Saliva is 99.5 percent water and 0.5 percent solutes. These include salts – chlorides, bicarbonates, and phosphates of sodium and potassium. Also found are mucin, the bacteriolytic enzyme lysozyme, and the digestive enzyme amylase.

The water in saliva provides a medium for dissolving foods so that they can be tasted and digestive reactions can be carried out. The chlorides in the saliva activate the amylase. The bicarbonates and phosphates buffer chemicals that enter the mouth and keep the saliva at a slightly acidic Ph of 6.35 to 6.85. Mucin is a protein that forms mucus when dissolved in water. Mucus lubricates the food so that it can be easily turned in the mouth, formed into a ball or bolus, and swallowed. The enzyme lysozyme destroys bacteria, thereby protecting the mucous membrane from infection and the teeth from decay. The enzyme salivary amylase initiates the breakdown of polysaccharides (carbohydrates); this is the only chemical digestion that occurs in the mouth. The function of salivary amylase is to break the chemical bonds between some of the monosaccharides that make up the polysaccharides called dextrins. In time the enzyme can further break down the dextrins into disaccharide maltose, but the food is usually swallowed so quickly that only three to five percent of the dextrins are broken down in the mouth. The salivary amylase continues to act on the polysaccharides in the stomach for another 15 to 30 minutes until stomach acids inactivate the enzyme.

Before we go any further, consider what you've just read. When bodybuilding contests became popular decades ago, judges used to inspect the contestants' teeth! Perhaps it wasn't such a silly concept after all. What's the point of buying expensive foods and supplements if you can't digest them properly? Just as an army marches on its stomach, the most important muscles in bodybuilding are found in the digestive tract. Before you work them out, see your dentist.

Melissa Coates

One of the best ever, Shawn Ray.

After being chewed, food is swallowed (deglutition) and travels down the esophagus (a muscular, collapsible tube located behind the trachea). The food is pushed down by muscular contractions in a process called peristalsis. It then passes through the inferior part of the esophagus called the gastroesophageal sphincter (a sphincter is an opening that has a thick circle of muscle around it) into the stomach.

THE STOMACH:
A few minutes after food enters the stomach, peristaltic movements ripple across the stomach every 15 to 25 seconds except for a part of the stomach called the fundus, which acts as a storage area. Here foods may sit for an hour or more with only salivary digestion continuing. In the rest of the stomach the movements, or mixing waves, churn the food with the gastric secretions, producing a thin liquid called chyme.

The main chemical activity of the stomach is to begin the breakdown of proteins. This is accomplished by the gastric juice, which is made up by the enzymes pepsin and rennin, and hydrochloric acid (HCl). Pepsin breaks certain peptide bonds between the amino acids that make up proteins. Hence a protein chain of many amino acids is broken down into fragments of amino acids. Long fragments are called proteoses and short fragments are called peptones.

Rennin solidifies casein, a milk protein. Thus it can be held in the stomach long enough for pepsin to break it down. Pepsin is most effective in the acidic environment of the stomach (Ph of 1). The HCl in the gastric juice ensures an acidic medium.

A less important enzyme is gastric lipase. This enzyme breaks down the butterfat molecules in milk. Because this enzyme works best at a Ph of 5-6, adults rely on an enzyme in the small intestine to digest fats.

The stomach releases its contents into the duodenum two to six hours after ingestion. Food rich in carbohydrates leaves the stomach after only a few hours. Protein-rich foods are slower, and fatty foods are the slowest of all to be emptied out. The stomach is impermeable to the passage of most materials into the blood (with the exception of some water, salts, certain drugs and alcohol), so most substances are not absorbed until they reach the small intestine.

THE SMALL INTESTINE:
Chemical digestion in the small intestine depends not only on its own secretions but also on the activities of three organs outside the GI tract: the liver, gallbladder and pancreas.

Carbohydrates in the form of dextrins are reduced to disaccharide maltose by the enzyme pancreatic amylase. Two other disaccharides, sucrose and lactose, are also reduced. The enzyme sucrase splits sucrose into a molecule of fructose and a molecule of glucose. Lactose is reduced to a molecule of glucose and a molecule of galactose by the enzyme lactase. And the enzyme maltase splits maltose into two molecules of glucose.

Proteins that may have escaped reduction in the stomach are dealt with in the small intestine. The pancreatic enzymes trypsin and chymotrypsin digest any intact proteins into proteoses and peptones, break them into dipeptides (containing only two amino acids), and divide some of the dipeptides into single amino acids. The enzyme carboxypeptidase reduces whole or partly digested proteins to amino acids. Any remaining dipeptides are reduced to single amino acids by a group of enzymes given the collective name erepsin.

Fats are digested in the small intestine. Bile salts break down the globules of fat into droplets (emulsification) so that the fat-splitting enzyme can attack the fat molecules. Then the enzyme pancreatic lipase hydrolyzes each fat molecule into fatty acids, glycerol and glycerides.

Mechanical digestion consists of three distinct peristaltic movements which serve to mix the chyme with the digestive juices and move the entire mixture further down the G.I. tract.

The products of digestion are now ready for absorption. The monosaccharides and amino acids are absorbed into the blood capillaries of the villi and transported via the bloodstream to the liver. Fatty acids, glycerol and glycerides are surrounded by bile salts to form water-soluble particles called micelles, which are then absorbed into the intestinal epithelial cells. The fat molecules are resynthesized. These molecules, together with small amounts of cholesterol and phospholipids, are organized into protein-coated fat droplets called chylomicrons. The protein coat prevents the chylomicrons from sticking to each other and the walls of the lymphatic and circulatory system. Transported by these two systems, the chylomicrons reach the liver.

THE LARGE INTESTINE:
Digestion is almost complete by the time the chyme reaches the large intestine. Bacterial action results in the synthesis of vitamin K and some of the B vitamins. Any remaining proteins and amino acids are broken down by bacteria into simpler substances: fatty acids, hydrogen sulfide, skatole and indole. Together with intestinal water, some of it is absorbed. What is left is passed out of the body.

METABOLISM
Growth is an adaptively regulated process in which anabolism predominates over catabolism. For bodybuilding this means the building up of protein into the permanent muscle mass of the bodybuilder. The passing of digestive products from the GI tract to the circulatory and lymphatic systems makes these products available to be incorporated into the living tissues of the body. But these products will also be used for maintenance, or stored as energy reserves, or burned off immediately to satisfy present energy demands. A simple meal initiates a complex sequence of events that are all compounded by the body's need to maintain an internal balance, called homeostasis. Life depends on the composition of body fluids remaining within very narrow boundaries. The flood of lymph and blood with the products of digestion runs counter to this principle. Thus the body uses hormones like insulin and human growth hormone (HGH) to restore normality.

The point here is that just because you consume a high-quality supplement does not mean you will see a corresponding increase in muscle mass. The body has its own agenda. Those multivitamins and carbohydrates will have their fates decided at the cellular level. The only certainty is that we can artificially shift the odds in favor of greater muscle mass by consuming high-quality foods and supplements while creating a metabolic demand through heavy exercise.

METABOLISM OF FAT
The metabolism of fats is controlled partly by hormones from the pituitary and adrenal glands, and partially by sex hormones. Any severe disturbance of liver function results in the almost complete absence of fat from the usual adipose tissues. This lack indicates that the fat must be acted upon in some way by the liver before it can be stored or metabolized.

Rich Gaspari almost took the Olympia title away from Lee Haney three times in the late '80s.

GLUCONEOGENESIS:
Current research has demonstrated that in addition to carbohydrates and fats, amino acids can contribute to energy metabolism. During periods of exercise hormones called glucocorticoids are released from the adrenal glands located on top of the kidneys. These hormones cause the body to remove amino acids from muscle tissue.

Glucocorticoids work with other hormones in promoting normal metabolism. Their role is to make sure that enough energy is provided. They increase the rate at which amino acids are removed from cells and transported to the liver. These amino acids may be synthesized into new proteins, such as the enzymes needed for metabolic reactions. If the body's reserves of glycogen or fat are low, the liver may convert amino acids to glucose. This process is called gluconeogenesis.

THE DEHYDRATION AND HYDRATION CONTROVERSY
"Do you really believe that bodybuilders eat only 1000 to 1500 calories the day before a contest? I can't maintain my right leg on that many calories!"
— *Gary Strydom, IFBB Pro*

Former WBF champion Gary Strydom

Although you would think the opposite, perhaps the most dangerous time for a competitive bodybuilder is the few weeks before the contest. It is a common practice in the weeks leading up to a competition for bodybuilders to drastically increase their protein intake, while dropping their daily carbohydrate intake to 30 grams for three to four days. Then they carb-load for the remainder of the week before the show. Of course, timing is critical. A competitor can look terrible at the contest, and look incredible the following day.

During the carb-loading phase, many competitors drink a gallon or more every day of distilled water. Thus there are no mineral salts ingested. For the three to four days prior to competition the competitor will drink as little as one quart a day for two or three days. This is done to dehydrate the body, causing water (theoretically) to be drawn into the muscle through the carb-loading phase. The result is a full muscle with well-defined vascularity.

"I don't really believe in dehydrating. There have been a lot of problems with competing dehydrated. I don't think it's really necessary to take things to that extent. I realize that you've got to be a pretty driven personality to get to the top of any sport, but then some people think that they've got to do drastic stuff."
– Dorian Yates, Britain's first Mr. Olympia

This sounds great in theory, but in actuality the practice is extremely dangerous. What's worse, the sport's new standards demand competitors compete in such dehydrated states. Faced with this reality, many competitors use diuretic drugs and creams to flush as much water as possible from the body. In most cases they succeed and end up onstage ripped to shreds. In a few cases, however, too much water is excreted, leaving the bodybuilder in a precarious state of health.

All life began in the sea. Our blood has the same salt content as seawater. Our bodies need water to carry out normal metabolic activities. Depriving the body of water is like depriving it of oxygen. There is a serious risk of permanent damage and/or death. If you have followed the dietary tips given in this chapter, you will not need to dehydrate yourself. Always drink lots of water before, during and after a competition. No competition is worth being dead or left on a kidney-dialysis machine for the rest of your life.

We can provide you with a much safer alternative, using two legal drugs, ephedrine and caffeine. In a study done at the University of Copenhagen in Denmark, obese women were given 20 mg of ephedrine with 200 mg of caffeine three times a day while being kept on a low-calorie, low-fat diet. Ephedrine is an ergogenic that enhances endurance, energy and strength. It is also a lipolytic that promotes fat loss while sparing lean muscle mass. Both caffeine and aspirin increase ephedrine's activity. The results of the study were amazing. The diet-only group lost 8.6 pounds of muscle and 9.9 pounds of fat. The ephedrine group only lost 2.4 pounds of muscle while losing 19.8 pounds of fat!

If taking tablets of legal drugs offends you, you can obtain your ephedrine by drinking a tea made from the Chinese herb mahuang (pronounced mow wang), followed by a spoonful of willow bark extract, an aspirin, or a cup of strong coffee. This ephedrine/caffeine/aspirin stack is a strong fat-burning formula. The recommended cycle is six days a week for 12 weeks, then two to three weeks off the stack. Because increased metabolism results in an increase in free radicals being produced, it would be wise to include an antioxidant in your diet. Be sure to take mineral supplements with this stack, as it can put a strain on the adrenal glands and the thyroid.

WARNING! Do not take ephedrine in tablet or herbal form if you have underlying cerebral vascular or cardio-vascular disease, high blood pressure, diabetes or hypothyroidism. Always check with your doctor before beginning a regimen of legal drugs, herbal extracts or supplements. What you don't know *can* hurt you.

DIET-INDUCED THERMOGENESIS

Many people claim that they gain weight just looking at food. These same people would probably be surprised to learn that breathing might be the key to losing fat.

Many bodybuilders wrestle with trying to maintain muscle gains while keeping bodyfat to a minimum. While genetics are a factor in bodybuilding success, they are also a factor in obesity. Using recently available technology, respiration may be the key to correcting this problem.

We have special cells that act as furnaces. We burn energy to produce heat. The person who can't burn the energy as efficiently becomes fat. Heat output is the crucial factor. In tests conducted at Queen Elizabeth College in England, some people when overfed took in more oxygen to burn off the excess. Thus metabolic factors may control obesity. It is a false argument to suggest that obesity is a simple result of overeating.

The University of Vermont carried out an experiment with prisoners from the state prison who had no history of family obesity. These volunteers ate 3000 extra calories every day. Their exercise programs were kept the same as before the experiment began. Some subjects could eat this excess without any weight gain. How did they get rid of the excess? The only explanation was that their bodies increased their metabolic rates and the excess was burned off through heat production. This theory is very difficult to measure

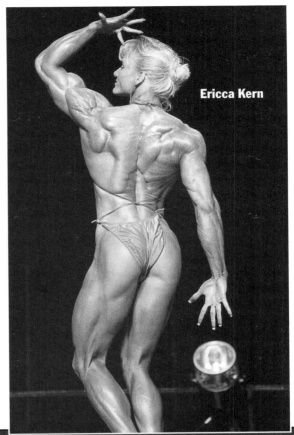

Ericca Kern

A true ultrafreak – Paul Dillett.

Alq Gurley

normal bodyweights had the same poor energy production as the currently obese subjects, which was one-half the heat production of the lean participants.

Obesity has a genetic link. Animal studies have shown that genetically obese mice are unable to maintain their body temperatures in cold conditions, whereas genetically lean mice have no problem. This observation is surprising given the fact that an obese animal has an insulating layer of fat. Clearly there is a relationship between the storage of fat and temperature regulation. At the National Research Council (NRC) in Ottawa, Canada, scientists Foster and Freedman did pioneering work which explained this relationship. They found that cold-adapted animals, when placed in a cold chamber, sent one-quarter of their cardiac output to the IBAT (interscapular brown adipose tissue, or brown fat between the shoulder blades). They also increased their oxygen intake. These rats were burning fat to regulate their body temperatures.

Brown fat cells contain droplets of fat which are burned for energy when stimulated by the neurotransmitter hormone noradrenaline. They are brown because they are blocked with mitochondria, the cellular organ that burns fat molecules. The BFC mitochondria are larger and more numerous in lean animals than in fat animals.

During World War I women working with an explosive called melanite were exposed to a chemical component called dinitrophenol. The symptoms were high fevers and weight loss, and though most survived there were 27 fatalities. This particular phenol causes the mitochondria to go into overdrive, sending metabolic rates through the roof. It was tried as a reducing agent in the '30s with horrendous side effects.

AN OXYGEN ALTERNATIVE?

There may be an alternative to thermogenic drugs. When people increase their metabolism of fat they take in more oxygen. Conversely, artificially increasing oxygen intake should result in increased fat metabolism. The use of a hyperbaric chamber would appear to be the answer. At the moment they are still expensive, and primarily used by professional sports teams to speed injury recovery. As they become more accessible we urge bodybuilders to take advantage of this new technology. It is safe and drug-free.

CALORIES – WHO REALLY CARES?

"I'm good enough, I'm smart enough, and gosh darn it, people like me!" — **Self-affirmation from Stewart Smiley (comedian Al Franken), SNL character, who, while not a licensed therapist, is a member of several 12-step programs. One thing is for sure – he really cares.**

and prove in people because many of the foods we enjoy are difficult to burn and measure. Subsequent rat studies at Cambridge University in England were used to verify this explanation.

Rats were induced to overeat. They were then humanely killed and their carcasses burned. The amount of energy released in the burning was measured and subtracted from the amount of energy taken in the form of food during the rat's life. Any remainder would have been lost through wastes (which were also measured) and metabolism. Indeed, there were rats that did not become obese, but had increased their metabolisms to burn off the excess calories.

During the experiment rats were placed in special temperature-controlled chambers. The amount of oxygen provided was measured. Researchers found that the animals that kept the weight off had an increased percentage of oxygen use.

Understanding how energy excess is controlled in the lean individual allows us to comprehend what has gone wrong in the obese person. Some might argue that the difference in heat output is simply a result of the fat itself, and not a cause, but they would be wrong. Using human calorimeters (chambers where subjects live and in which all metabolic output can be measured) it was found that obese people who had dieted down to

A calorie is a measure of the heat produced by a substance when it is burned. Food is metabolically combined with oxygen (oxidation), and the energy released is used as heat, power for metabolic functions, or stored as fat. One gram of protein or carbohydrate will produce four calories, while one gram of fat will produce nine calories. Therefore we can calculate the calories we're taking in every day and plan our meals accordingly, right? Possibly.

Carrying little books with cards and calculators to figure out calories is ultimately bewildering and a complete waste of time. Bodybuilders do not need to concern themselves with trivial details like the number of calories in one slice of whole-grain bread. They just have to eat five or six small, nutritious meals that include proteins, minerals, fats, vitamins and carbohydrates. Your own progress and natural sense of hunger will reliably tell you if you're eating enough.

"7,000 to 9,000 a day. You have to eat big to get big. At 19 I was nothing pretty to look at – fat face, fat fingers, fat ass – but I had 21-inch arms."
– Mike Matarazzo (describing the number of calories he consumes in the off-season)

One of the first changes in your diet is the drastic reduction in the percentage of animal protein consumed. A healthy bodybuilder should be eating a diet of which 17 percent is meat or fish. This does not mean that you must stare glumly at a tiny fleshy glob that is dwarfed by its baked potato neighbors. Rather, you must learn to prepare your food differently so that the meat becomes more of a flavoring component to your meals. You may prefer to have a large steak that dominates your plate and leaves little room for the frightened clump of coleslaw clinging to the edge, but this preference is cultural, which means it was learned. And anything that is learned can be unlearned.

The most effective way to stretch that flavor value is to combine the meat with other foods in the form of soups, stews and miscellaneous meat-vegetable combinations. What's that you say? You don't like veggies? We bet you don't like doing squats either, but you can learn to like them (the veggies). We have a series of recipes that will bulge your biceps and blow away your taste buds, so put down that barbell, and let's do some serious bodybuilding in the kitchen!

OUTFITTING THE KITCHEN

"I eat six meals a day – three to four pounds of red meat every day. (I have a steer farm at the back of my apartment!) I load up my freezer with chicken and beef." **– Mike Matarazzo**

This section is primarily aimed at those who are just setting up their own house or apartment. Some of it may seem redundant, but let's face it – eating properly is as much an art as training or posing, so you might as well learn to do it right from the beginning.

You'll need some big ticket-items if you are seriously into bodybuilding. Among these are a stove, fridge, freezer, breadmaker, deep fryer and microwave.

The ingredients are stored in the fridge. The culinary delights are stored (labeled and dated) in the freezer. Don't just pile things in; organize it like a filing cabinet. Divide your freezer into sections: bread, sandwiches, soups, stews, meats, fish and daily mini-meals. Good eating means being organized. When freezing foods remember the following:

1. Remove as much air as possible from airtight containers like freezer bags. Otherwise the trapped air will absorb flavor from the food and will form a frost. If the bag loses its airtight quality, that frost will give off odors that can be picked up by other foods in the freezer.

Ofer Samra

Debbie Kruck and Lee Apperson

The breadmaker allows you to make fresh bread that is delicious, nutritious and of high quality. The deep fryer allows you to fry foods without risking a fire. (Many house fires are caused by deep frying in an open pot.)

Your best friend will be your microwave. Its job is to heat your food. But like all friends, it can be hard to get along with if you don't understand it. This next paragraph is technical, but necessary.

Your microwave oven works in the following way. Electricity is converted into microwave energy by a part of the oven called the magnetron. These microwaves are directed at the food inside the oven. Water molecules inside the food absorb the microwave energy and display it as kinetic energy. The kinetic energy is released in the form of vibrations – approximately 2,450,000,000 vibrations per second! This vibration causes friction inside the food, which generates heat. It is this heat which cooks the food.

Why not cook with the microwave? Because cooking large amounts is easier with a conventional stove. It takes longer, but that extra time reduces the likelihood that you're going to ruin your food. Cooking with a microwave isn't difficult, but cooking well is. Everything from the temperature of the ingredients to the power drain of other appliances can affect cooking times. Keep life simple. Follow the recipes and warm the results in the microwave.

What can you put into the microwave? Food, microwaveable dishes, cups and bottles – nothing else! Anything with metal will cause an electrical storm in your oven. Some glassware will crack. One enterprising lady caused a small fire when she tried to dry her panties in the microwave! Make sure that you have removed the food from its freezer bag or other container beforehand, unless the container is certified as being microwaveable. Never cook whole eggs in their shells in the microwave! They can explode, and have caused burns and eye injuries! Always remove the egg from the shell before cooking.

What power setting, and for how long, depends on what, and for how much. For most frozen stews and soups a frozen single serving or mini-meal requires a power setting of eight for three minutes. But this setting will vary. At least you will know that the food was thoroughly cooked before it went into the microwave, and you only have to heat the meal until it suits your needs.

WHAT OILS TO COOK WITH?

"…At the national level it's tough. I tell you, when I'm getting ready for a show, I'm dieting just as strictly and training just as hard as a bodybuilder. In many ways it's

2. Prevent freezer burn by properly sealing your containers or bags. The air in the package can absorb moisture from the food, causing a greyish-white discoloration on the food surface. If you are using plastic containers, seal them with freezer tape no matter how airtight they appear.

3. Do not put too much into your freezer at once. As packages are put in, space them so that the air can circulate around them. In this way the food will be solidly frozen.

4. Wash your hands and always use clean equipment when putting your food into containers for freezing. Freezing will not kill the bacteria. It will merely hold them in check.

5. Never use metal to wrap acidic foods.

6. Make sure all containers are labeled and dated.

FOOD	TIME POSSIBLE IN FREEZER
Stews	6 months
Meat and poultry	1 to 3 months
Soups	6 months
Fish	3 to 6 months
Sandwiches	1 month

powerfully to protect butter from oxidation. And what about the artery-clogging effects of the saturated fats in butter? Well, margarine is only slightly better. Margarine is made from polyunsaturated fats that have undergone hydrogenation, a process that turns an oil into a solid. The byproducts of this process are transfatty acids (TFAs), which are also remarkably efficient at blocking blood vessels.

Once the oil is removed from the plant material, it seems to become susceptible to a host of destructive influences. As long as the vegetable oil remains part of the whole food, it is apparently healthful, assuming a balanced diet. So what oil should a bodybuilder cook with? It's a lifestyle choice based on risk. What are you at greater risk for, heart disease or cancer? If you have high cholesterol or a history of heart disease in your family, you might want to use polyunsaturated oils. If you have or have had cancer, or cancer has occurred in your family, you might opt for saturated fats. Your best step is to limit your fat intake. Drain the oil from your food after cooking, and only use the absolute minimum to cook with.

harder because I don't have the benefit of drugs to help get rid of bodyfat. The natural athlete has to work much harder to get into condition than the drug user. I work just as hard, if differently, as I did when I was doing bodybuilding shows…"
**— Amy Fadhli,
fitness competitor**

This is not an easy question. All of the oils used for human consumption are different forms of fat. Until recently researchers condemned all saturated fats of animal origin as "bad fats". "Good fats" were polyunsaturated and of vegetable origin. This idea has since been exposed as a vegan myth.

When polyunsaturated oils are heated, the fat molecules undergo oxidation. The fat is altered and new compounds result. Some compounds are less useful and others are possibly harmful. The byproducts of this oxidation – free radicals and reactive oxygen – will readily jump over to other molecules such as vitamins, oxidizing them and changing their structure so that they are no longer biologically useful.

Consumption of large quantities of vegetable oils accelerates the aging process in the skin because of the presence of the free radicals, and the result is increased wrinkling about the face. Polyunsaturated oils can also cause chromosome damage. The latest statistical information shows that while large numbers of people switched from saturated fats to vegetable oils, deaths from heart disease decreased, but overall mortality rates remained the same. The decrease in heart disease was matched by the increase in deaths from cancer. Research has shown that a high intake of polyunsaturated oils increases your risk for cancer.

And the "bad fats" aren't all bad. Compounds which prevent free radicals from causing damage are called antioxidants. These are found in butterfat and work

Amy Fadhli

Dorian Yates and
Shawn Ray

FOOD PREPARATION

"I eat it with steamed vegetables, rice or digestive enzymes (papaya). Sometimes I grind up the sirloin in a salad. My food bill is $300 to $400 a week. (It was great when I was living at home!)" **– Mike Matarazzo, describing what he likes to eat with red meat.**

While most bodybuilding magazines are a rich source of information, there is the occasional article that is just out to lunch. All too often one will find an article on diet that extols the virtues of raw meat and fish. It is true that cooking meat and fish will reduce their nutritional value, including the percentage of digestible proteins, but the purpose of cooking is not just to make the meat and fish more palatable. It is to prevent these rich protein sources from killing us!

The Canadian Arctic provides an interesting case. The native people, the Inuit, live on a diet largely composed of raw caribou and raw fish called Arctic char. They are a healthy people. The men are generally muscular and strong. Their exercise comes from lengthy hunting trips on the land.

But one must remember that the caribou live on the barrens, a treeless land that is generally clean and unspoiled. Further, freezing the meat kills the trichinosis parasite. Although the Inuit will eat frozen caribou, they will eat polar bear flesh only if it is thoroughly cooked. Cooking was once difficult in a treeless land where they burned seal oil. Now they have stoves and microwave ovens.

The cattle, pigs and poultry that provide meat for the North American market are raised commercially in large groups. Parasites and bacteria have established themselves in these populations. Once the animals have been slaughtered, the meat remains contaminated. Only by thorough cooking can these harmful agents be killed. Some people have died as a result of eating undercooked hamburgers from fast-food restaurants. Others have suffered tapeworm infestations after eating raw fish. The single biggest development in the history of medicine was the invention of fire because it made meat safe to eat. Always thoroughly cook meat, fish and eggs. Remember one additional truth: Your body cannot absorb all the nutritional value in one meal. It will use what amino acids it needs, and some will be converted to fats. The rest will be excreted.

CHOLESTEROL, EGGS AND WHOLE MILK

"It's not the cholesterol intake that hurts the heart. It's letting the cholesterol build up. This can be prevented with physical exercise." **– Dr. Frederick Stare, former head of Harvard's Nutritional Department.**

"My family has such high cholesterol levels that they've been written up in medical journals. I had a nine-year-old cousin who dropped dead from a heart attack. My 36-year-old uncle is on permanent disability because of his heart condition. He can't even walk down the street.

He has to drive. My brother is on all kinds of anti-cholesterol medications. Me, I won't take any. I smoke, I drink, I eat fatty foods, and I'm slightly overweight. See, half of my family has died from heart disease, and everyone else has died from Alzheimer's. Even if I make it I'll never know it." – Anonymous, explaining the reasons behind his poor dietary habits.

Cholesterol is a naturally occurring steroid that is necessary for good health. It is a structural component of body tissues, particularly the cardiovascular and nervous systems. Cholesterol is one of the building blocks of the sex and adrenal hormones, bile and vitamin D.

Cholesterol comes in two forms – high-density lipoproteins (HDLs or the good guys) and low-density lipoproteins (LDLs or the bad guys). LDLs target the cells, especially those in the artery walls. When the body attempts to dispose of the excess through the circulatory system, the LDLs' sticky nature causes them to accumulate, forming blockages that can clog the arteries.

HDLs carry away LDLs before they can form hardened plaques inside the blood vessels. These good guys also carry extra cholesterol to the liver, where it can be filtered out and excreted in the form of bile salts.

Risk factors for LDLs are too much sugar, fats (chiefly animal fats), carbohydrates, stress, smoking, excessive drinking, diabetes, obesity and genetics. Most of these factors can be controlled. Quit smoking, quit drinking or drink in moderation, eliminate refined sugar from the diet, reduce fat intake, reduce consumption of meat, lose weight and learn to relax.

"...most informed people believe that daily exercise contributes more to soldiers' health than do doctors." – Judgment made by Begetius, a fourth-century writer in the time of the Roman Empire.

The role of dietary fat in heart disease is supported by the examples of Albania and Hungary. Albania is by far the poorest country in Europe. Life expectancy is a respectable 70 for men and 76 for women, the third highest in Eastern Europe. The incidence of cancer and heart disease is relatively low. Albanians under Communism didn't eat much meat, and they can't afford to now. It makes up only 17 percent of the diet, less than half the West European average. The unavoidable daily exercise of walking in a basically carless society also provides significant health benefits. Compare this situation to that of Hungary.

Hungary is one of the wealthiest nations in Eastern Europe, but Hungarians also have one of the highest rates of heart disease of all Eastern Europe. In Hungary 60 percent of adult males smoke, and 15 percent of the entire population suffer from alcohol-related ailments. While one must consider the stress from a difficult economic change, the amount of fat consumed in the diet is a key factor. The fat level in the Hungarian diet rose from 30 percent in 1970 to 38 percent in 1994. At the same time the death rate from heart disease rose proportionately, from 5.7 to 8.5 per 1000.

Taking into account these risk factors, the two best natural foods for bodybuilders are still eggs and 2 percent milk. Yes, they both have cholesterol, but they also contain nutrients that are indispensable for bodybuilding. Further, eggs by themselves won't elevate serum cholesterol levels because eggs contain choline and lecithin. Choline is a precursor of the neurotransmitter acetylcholine; lecithin is a phospholipid composed of saturated, unsaturated and polyunsaturated fatty acids. It also contains phosphorus, glycerin and choline. Both choline and lecithin keep the cholesterol in the egg emulsified, and the cholesterol in

the bloodstream moving. The cholesterol in 2 percent milk is one of the building blocks of nerve fibers and myelin sheaths, and the fats present can be compensated for by eliminating fat from other food sources. Referring to our Albanian example, Albanians drink whole milk and get their protein from eggs, and they're grateful.

Dietary cholesterol is only one factor in heart disease. As a general rule, the incidence of heart disease increases with the amount of cholesterol in the diet. And yet there are vegetarians who get heart disease, and people who eat almost nothing but animal fats who appear immune to heart disease. Such cases result from heredity; our bodies are genetically programmed to produce a certain amount of cholesterol. The ratio of LDLs to HDLs is also genetically influenced. If our bodies cannot obtain enough cholesterol from the diet, the body will synthesize its own cholesterol to make up for the shortfall.

What should you do? Go to your doctor, and get a cholesterol profile done. It's more expensive than a regular cholesterol test, but it will tell you what kind of ratio of LDLs to HDLs you have. If the HDLs are in the majority, you're already ahead of the game. If the LDLs are in the majority, your doctor may want you to go on anticholesterol medications. You should also be taking lecithin supplements. (Just remember not to take them with vitamin B3, an antagonist.) Since your body is having a hard time dealing with cholesterol, lay off the eggs and milk until the ratio has been corrected just to be on the safe side. In either case include aerobic training as part of your workout. This is a proven method of reducing LDLs. Reducing or eliminating animal fats from your diet, as demonstrated by our European examples, will also give your body time to repair itself

and maintain a healthy ratio. Fruit pectin supplements and increased fiber are well-known ways of correcting and maintaining the cholesterol ratio.

Once your cholesterol ratio of good guys outnumbers the bad guys, you can start having an egg and one glass of 2 percent milk *with* each mini-meal. If you are going for the ripped look instead of mass, drink skim milk. If you are pursuing a pre-contest diet, then drink water (and lots of it). You can still eat the egg (but it *is* the mini-meal). Therefore, we are talking a daily intake of five or six eggs and five or six glasses of 2 percent milk on top of the nutritious mini-meals that we have described in this chapter. You should also continue taking the lecithin supplements. WARNING! Discontinue lecithin if you develop the possible side effects of "fishy" body odor, nausea, dizziness or vomiting, and see a doctor right away. Not every supplement is for everyone.

Remember to get a cholesterol profile done every six months. It may seem trivial, but your muscles won't stay big if you destroy your heart in the process.

BUYING, STORING AND COOKING VEGETABLES

"Oh how I once loved tuna salad,
Pork and lobsters, lamb chops too,
Till I learned to look at dinner
From the dinner's point of view."

– From the poem
"Point of View" by Shel Silverstein.

Gradually change your diet so that vegetables, fruits and carbohydrates make up over 80 percent of it. Don't do this overnight. Otherwise the balance of power between the bacterial groups in your intestines will be upset, and your bowels will bear witness to a digestive "ethnic cleansing". We do not recommend that bodybuilders go totally vegetarian. It is very difficult to make the transition to a totally vegan diet, though it can be done. The richest source of plant protein is found in legumes (seeds that grow in a pod), such as peanuts, peas, lentils and beans. No single plant has all the essential amino acids, but when legumes are combined with seeds, nuts and grains all of the amino acids are obtained. Such combinations as rice and beans, baked beans with brown bread, and whole-grain bread with peanut butter can provide complete protein – a concept called protein complementary. If you do decide to go the vegan route, just remember to take vitamin B-12 supplements, as plants are generally poor sources. If you also decide to drive a Volkswagen Bug, wear love beads, become an expert on socialist economics, and you might want to pick up the odd burger to touch in with reality.

Buying Fresh Vegetables

1. Buy only ripe vegetables. Unlike fruits, unripe vegetables will not ripen in storage, and the taste will be poor.
2. Buy only vegetables that are in good condition. Bruised and damaged vegetables may be cheaper, but they are lacking in nutrients and will not last long.
3. Look for green and yellow vegetables with deep colors. The deeper the color, the more nutrients inside.
4. Squeeze your veggies. (Make sure the store clerk isn't looking.) Vegetables should be firm; if they are soft and mushy before you cook them, just imagine what they'll be like after cooking!
5. When buying root vegetables like onions or potatoes, don't buy the ones that have sprouted. Never buy green potatoes; the green and sprouted parts contain a poisonous chemical called solanine. If this has happened during storage, cut away all green or sprouted parts before cooking.

Storing Fresh Vegetables

1. Do not refrigerate onions or potatoes. The humidity in the refrigerator can cause mold, and the cold temperature in the fridge will change potato starch into sugar. Not only will the taste and texture of the potatoes change, but they will also darken in color when cooked. Store onions and potatoes in a dark, dry, cool place.
2. Never store onions and potatoes together. The potatoes will sprout faster if stored with onions. The onions will absorb moisture from the potatoes and become moldy. These two vegetables should be combined only at mealtime.
3. Potatoes should be stored in paper bags. Air can then circulate, and the paper prevents light from causing the potatoes to turn green. Onions should be stored in a loose net bag so that air can circulate. (Yes, you can use fishnet stockings, but wash them first.)
4. Wash flower vegetables (cauliflower and broccoli), leaf vegetables (greens, cabbage, lettuce, spinach), and stem vegetables (celery and asparagus) with

water. Shake off the excess water, put the vegetables into plastic bags and refrigerate immediately. The veggies will stay fresh and crisp.

Fresh vegetables should be consumed or cooked within two to three days. Potatoes and onions can be kept for several weeks.

Buying Dried Vegetables

1. Buy in bulk for cheaper shopping.
2. Inspect for insect holes, foreign material, and cracked coats in legumes. Don't buy if you find any. These are all alarm signals of a bad product on sale. Speak to the manager.
3. Legumes should be bought in uniform size. Small beans cook faster than big beans, and that can ruin your meal.
4. Look for legumes with bright, uniform color. A lack of color can mean longer cooking time because the legumes are stale.

Storing Dried Vegetables

1. Store in sealed bags in a dry, cool place.
2. Once a bag is opened, the contents should be stored in a glass or plastic container with an airtight lid. This will prevent any insect problems.

from the parmesan cheese. (Use a cheese shaver. If you're not sure what it looks like, ask someone in the store.) Crumble the slices and sprinkle them over the asparagus. Serve with sliced cucumber and tomato and a sprig of parsley. Everyone will be back for seconds!

BUYING AND STORING GRAIN PRODUCTS

"I eat as much as I need. Because of my job I have gone days without eating much food and don't lose any weight. This has shown me that power eating huge calories is not necessary for me to grow. I feel it is the protein quantity in the diet that is most important, not the calorie content. I grow the muscle I need from the protein, and keep my bodyfat low from the low-fat and moderate calories."
– Fred Bigo, accomplished bodybuilder and businessman, and he's only 22!

Grain products are made from the seeds of cereal grasses, such as barley, oats, rye, corn, rice and wheat. The seed itself consists of three parts. The outer covering is called bran and is rich in fiber and the B vitamins. Most of the meat of the seed is made up by the endosperm, which is rich in proteins and starch. The sprouting section inside the seed is called the germ, and it is rich in oil, fats, the B vitamins and minerals. When whole grains are processed, the germ and bran are removed so that most of the nutrients are lost. That is why processed flour is artificially enriched, and even fortified with additional nutrients. The whole-grain products that you purchase in stores may also have nutrients added, even though they have not been processed. Bodybuilders are better off using whole-grain products, particularly barley, because they have a proven track record in building muscle and maintaining good health.

When buying and storing grain products, follow the same directions given for buying dried vegetables. The only difference when keeping whole-grain products is that refrigeration is required for long-term storage. Their natural oils will eventually turn rancid at room temperature.

Pasta is a generic term used to describe all noodle and macaroni products. It is a processed food generally made from durum wheat flour, egg solids and water. Pasta is a nutritious source of carbohydrates, but be careful about the amount of fats in the sauce you add to it. Most bodybuilders use pasta for glycogen loading before a competition.

Breakfast cereals come in a variety of forms. You should check the labels and make sure you are purchasing whole-grain cereal that is fortified, rich in fiber, and does not have any sugar or salt added. Stay away from the sugary garbage (like Captain Crunch – he should have been keelhauled) that belongs in the nutritional hall of shame.

Dried vegetables will last for months.

Canned and frozen vegetables are self-explanatory. Just remember a warning about home-canned vegetables. If the can starts to bubble when being opened, throw it out, and make sure to rinse the opener with scalding hot water. Always boil home-canned vegetables for 20 minutes to kill any microorganisms that might have gotten in.

To properly microwave vegetables, you first have to cut them so that they're in small pieces of uniform size. When cooking whole washed potatoes, cut the skins so that they won't burst, and cook on high for two minutes. Then place them in the oven and broil for a few minutes. The result will be a plate of crisp, well-cooked potatoes. When cooking a vegetable such as broccoli, lay the pieces in a circle with the buds in the center. Thus the stalks will be more intensely cooked. After you have microwaved the vegetables, let them sit in the microwave. Their stored heat will finish the cooking process.

Many people don't like vegetables because they are bland and squishy. That is only because they have been overcooked. Once you have peeled and washed your vegetables, you'll be surprised how delicious they are raw. Or you can experiment with different cooking times. Try the following recipe for asparagus:

Ingredients: *500 g asparagus*
extra virgin olive oil
red wine vinegar
parmesan cheese
black pepper

Fill a pot with filtered water and bring to a boil. Add the asparagus and cook for three minutes (al dente for cooking specialists). Remove and submerge in cold water. Then pat dry with paper towels and chill. Before serving, drizzle a small amount of extra virgin oil and red wine vinegar over the asparagus. Shave thin slices

BUYING AND STORING MEAT

Meat is primarily the muscle portion of the animal. To a lesser degree it also contains fat, connective tissue and bone. Beef, lamb and veal are graded in both the US and Canada. The stamp itself is a harmless vegetable dye, so you don't need to remove it before cooking. The top grades of meat have the most marbling. Marbling gives meat juiciness and flavor. It means that there is a lot of fat strewn throughout the meat. The three grades used, from top to bottom are prime, choice and select. In terms of health they should be the other way around. The select cuts are the leanest forms. They are the grade that bodybuilders should purchase. Animal fats may give flavor, but they also cause heart disease.

Pork comes from young hogs, and is so uniform that it is not sold in grades. Once the fat has been trimmed, pork is an excellent source of animal protein.

A protein available to Canadian bodybuilders is seal meat. It can be bought in canned form from commercial stores in Newfoundland. It has all the benefits of fish oil, plus the animal proteins. Seal oil has recently been shown to have beneficial effects on the cardiovascular system, and may be of benefit to AIDS patients because it can help boost the immune system. The Inuit consume a large amount of seal meat, and their muscular development is extraordinary. American bodybuilders cannot order seal meat because importation of products made from marine mammals is illegal in the US.

The term organ meats refers to animal organs sold for human consumption. Bodybuilders should have one mini-meal a day that includes liver. Liver is the best cut of meat in terms of minerals, vitamins and proteins. You don't like liver? Did you know that it is still one of the cheapest cuts of meat that you can purchase? If you want to build muscle, eat liver. Go on, be brave!

When buying beef, you may occasionally notice a blue discoloration on the inside. The meat is fine. The discoloration is caused by the blood present. When it is exposed to oxygen, it turns red.

Storing Meat

1. Fresh meat should be used within two days.
2. Store it in the coldest part of your refrigerator.
3. If it is prepackaged, store as is.
4. If it is wrapped in butcher paper, rinse the meat and rewrap in plastic or foil.
5. Label and date the meat as you put it into the fridge.
6. To freeze the meat, rewrap it in freezer wrap (even if prepackaged) and seal it with freezer tape. Don't forget to label and date.
7. When defrosting the meat, do so in the fridge or the microwave, but *never* at room temperature. The outside can defrost first and spoil before the inside has finished thawing.
8. Occasionally uncooked meat can go off. It will

Lee and Debbie make healthful food choices when shopping.

develop an off odor, and the color will change to a dull greyish brown. If the package is unopened, the surface of the meat may have a slippery feel. If you have any doubts at all, just chuck it out.

BUYING AND STORING POULTRY

Poultry generally includes meat from chickens, turkeys, geese and ducks. For bodybuilders geese and ducks have too much fat and should be avoided. Chickens and turkeys are graded A or B. Grade A is the top, and refers to a meaty bird. Bodybuilders should buy only grade A. Poultry is also classified – from youngest to oldest – as broiler or fryer, roaster, capon and stewing fowl. Stewing fowl, the meatiest but the least tender, is the class that bodybuilders should buy. If the chicken is well cooked, it will be tender enough. Using the mini-meals provided, the meat is meant to be a flavoring component, and not the main course.

When buying turkey or chicken, it is more economical to buy large birds. You will get more servings because there is more meat in proportion to fat and bone. For storing poultry follow the same guidelines given for meat.

Store eggs in the original carton; otherwise, they will absorb odors from other foods.

BUYING AND STORING FISH AND SHELLFISH

These foods are low in calories, good sources of unsaturated fats, and high in nutrients and proteins. Fatty fish include lake trout, salmon, mackerel, shad and herring. These are good fats, however, and the fish are still leaner than any meat or poultry. Lean fish include tuna, cod, flounder, mullet, carp, pollock, turbot, whiting, haddock and ocean perch.

Buying Fresh Fish

1. Squeeze the fish to make sure the flesh is firm.
2. The eyes should appear to be clear, bright, bulging.
3. The skin should be bright and shiny.
4. The gills should be red and slime-free.
5. Smell the fish; it should have a mild, fresh scent.
6. If the fish has not already been been cleaned, have them do it at the store or do it at home.
7. Rinse, wrap in plastic, refrigerate immediately and use within two days.
8. If you are going to keep uncooked fish longer than two days, wrap in an airtight container and freeze.

Some people don't like cooking fish because of the strong smell. Adding lemon will take care of that problem. You can also wash your hands in vinegar to remove the fish scent.

Buying Frozen Fish

1. The fish should be wrapped airtight.

2. There should be no smell detectable, or if detectable it should be very mild.

3. The fish should be a uniform color.

When buying canned fish such as tuna or salmon, always look for fish packed in water. Avoid fish packed in oils or sauces, as they tend to be high in fats and added salt. Rinse the top of the can with boiling water before opening. That way if the top falls in while you're opening, it won't contaminate the fish. Transfer it to a covered container and refrigerate. Like cooked fish, canned fish should be consumed within three to four days.

Do not buy fish or shellfish in a pickled state. They are too high in salt.

Shellfish fall into two groups: mollusks, which have a rigid outer shell, and crustaceans, which have a segmented outer covering and basically look like big bugs.

One of the few foods eaten live in the US and Canada is the oyster. People have become seriously ill from this practice. Oysters belong to a group of animals that biologists refer to as the "snot-feeders." They secrete mucus to catch particles of whatever happens to be floating by, and swallow it in a ball. If an oyster bed happens to be near a sewage outlet, these filter-feeders tend to accumulate a host of infectious agents. How anyone can consider a snot-feeder to be an aphrodisiac is beyond us. *Never eat raw oysters!* The restaurant might assure you that they came from a safe area, but you've still got the problem of a variety of marine parasites, including tape worms.

Buying Fresh Shellfish

1. If sold live, clams and oysters should have their shells tightly closed.

2. Pick up a live lobster by its head. If the tail curls under, it's healthy. If the tail hangs down, then it's sick or dying. Buy the healthy one.

3. Fresh scallops should have a slightly sweet smell and be a creamy-pink color.

4. Live crabs should be very active.

5. Fresh shrimp should have little or no odor, and be firm to the touch.

6. Shucked (shell removed) clams should be plump and free of any foreign material.

When storing shellfish follow the same guidelines for fresh fish (where applicable). If you are going to keep uncooked shellfish longer than one day, wrap in an airtight container and freeze.

BUYING AND STORING FRUIT

Fruit can be purchased fresh, frozen, canned or dried. The quality of fresh fruits depends on how mature and ripe they are. Ripe means they are ready to eat. Mature means they have reached their full size. Most fruits are picked when they are mature but not yet ripe. Immature fruits have poor color and texture, and are smaller than normal. They will never ripen and are a complete waste of money.

Citrus fruits and grapes are the only fruits that are picked after they are fully ripe. You may occasionally see green oranges in the store. During warm weather or because of bright lights in the produce department, the chlorophyll returns to the orange skins. This process is called regreening. These oranges are fine to eat and are just as fully ripe as their orange neighbors.

Sometimes the store will have a sale on overripe, damaged or immature fruit. Don't waste your money. The texture, flavor and nutrient value will all be poor, and the fruit will not keep long.

Buying Fresh Fruit

1. Squeeze the fruit gently. If it gives slightly, it is ripe enough to eat.

2. Select fruits that are firm and plump. Don't buy fruits that are dry, very hard, very soft or appear withered.

3. Look for good shape Fruits have characteristic shapes. Deformed fruits often have poor texture or flavor.

4. Consider weight. Fruits that are heavy for their size are full of juice.

5. Smell. Ripe fruit gives off a pleasant scent.

Storing Fresh Fruit

1. Fresh fruit should be consumed within a few days.

2. Citrus fruits can be stored at room temperature, but use the refrigerator if you want to keep them for a longer period.

3. Fruit that is not yet ripe can be allowed to ripen at room temperature. You can speed ripening by putting fruit in a brown paper bag.

4. Grapes, berries and cherries do not last long. Wash them and remove any decayed or damaged fruit, seal in an airtight container, and place in the refrigerator. Wash them again before serving.

5. Pineapples and melons have very aggressive scents that will flavor other foods stored in the fridge. Wrap them in foil or plastic to keep these pleasant stinkers under control.

6. Fruit that has already been cut should be sprinkled with lemon juice (to keep it from turning brown), wrapped in plastic or foil or placed in an airtight container, and refrigerated.

7. Bananas can be stored at room temperature until they ripen. After they ripen you can refrigerate them.

The bananas are still nutritious, though the increase in natural sugars increases the number of calories.

Always wash bananas! They were picked in Third World countries where hepatitis is rampant, and washroom facilities in the field nonexistent. The person who picked your bananas may not have washed their hands. And tropical places have varied insect populations which happily reproduce using egg-sacks attached to bananas. Never assume the store has washed them. Produce workers have been bitten and stung by tarantulas and scorpions that hitched a ride. Look over the bananas before you take them home, and then wash them right away.

8. All other fruits should be rinsed well, dried with paper towels, loosely wrapped with plastic or foil, and refrigerated.

One of the best bodybuilding fruits is the kiwi. It gives you the most nutritional bang for your buck. Gram for gram the Kiwi provides more vitamin C, riboflavin, iron, magnesium, phosphorus, potassium and fiber than apples, peaches, oranges and pears. Kiwis can be stored in the fridge for a few weeks.

WARNING! If you have any food allergies to nuts, do not eat kiwis. They are originally descended from a wild Chinese berry called the mihoutao (monkey peach). For some reason these berries are able to trigger allergic responses in people allergic to nuts, especially walnuts and peanuts. People have died from merely biting into the wrong foods. Consult your allergy specialist first. You can still bodybuild without kiwis.

When buying canned fruit, look for fruits packed in water or their own juices. That way you know no sugar has been added and they have the same number of calories as fresh fruit. When buying fruit juices, look for containers labeled "100% fruit juice" to avoid added sugar.

Frozen fruit is very convenient for stocking up, as fresh fruit has a short shelf life. But not all fruits freeze well (berries do the best), so you shouldn't completely thaw them before eating. Otherwise you'll end up serving fruit slime to your friends. Fruits have a high water content and often a fragile cell structure. During freezing, water turns into ice crystals and expands. These growing crystals rupture the cell walls. Once the fruit begins to thaw, all the cells leak, and the overall structure collapses. Therefore, serve that fruit salad chilled.

Buying Frozen Fruit

1. The package should be frozen solid.
2. Don't buy if there is an ice coating on the package; it indicates that it has been thawed and refrozen. The fruit will now be of poor quality.
3. Don't buy if the package is dirty or has any openings or damage. Never pay good money for food that has not been looked after.
4. You can also buy fresh fruit, following the directions already given, and freeze it. Just remember to use airtight containers, and label and date the fruit.

Dried fruits have become very popular in recent years. They are usually dried in the sun (raisins for example) or by a mechanical process. Food dehydrators have come down in price, and many bodybuilders find they can save money from their food bill by buying fruit in bulk when it is in season (and thus at its cheapest) and drying it for use throughout the year. Four to five pounds of fresh fruit is required to make one pound of dried fruit. The only drawback is that, though it is still nutritious, the natural sugars have become concentrated, increasing the number of calories present. Therefore eat sparingly, and brush your teeth afterward. Even natural sugars can cause cavities.

Amy Lynn

Buying Dried Fruit

1. Don't buy if there is foreign material present or evidence of insect holes. Speak to the manager.
2. The fruit should be of uniform color.
3. The fruit should still be soft and pliable. Don't buy if it is completely dry.

Storing Dried Fruit

1. Keep it in a cool, dry place.
2. Once opened, keep it in an airtight container in the refrigerator.

HONEY

Honey is a natural sweetener made by bees. The bees gather flower nectar, which is a thin syrup of sucrose. The insects add an enzyme which changes the syrup into a 50:50 mixture of fructose and glucose. It is stored in the hive, in an aggregate of hexagonal cells called a honeycomb, where the combined effect of hundreds of bees fanning their wings causes air to blow over the syrup. This air removes moisture from the syrup, making it into the thick, sticky substance

Don't waste your money on overripe or damaged fruit. The texture, flavor and nutrient value will be poor.

we call honey. When the honey is commercially harvested, it is pasteurized (cleaned and boiled) before being poured into jars.

After honey has been stored for a while, it may begin to have a murky appearance, with a hardened crust that is crumbly in texture. It is still okay to eat. Honey is in reality a supersaturated sugar solution that is only 17 percent water. This makes the solution unstable, with the result that glucose will precipitate out of the solution and form crystals. To correct this situation, simply warm the jar in a pan of water. The glucose will redissolve into the solution, and your jar of honey will be as good as new.

Don't worry if you have an allergy to honey. You can still use very small amounts of refined sugar instead. We recommend the honey because it possesses additional vitamins so it is mildly superior to refined sugar. Just remember, go easy on the sweeteners.

HYGIENE IN THE KITCHEN

Which room in the average home has the highest bacteria levels? Most people would answer the bathroom. They would be wrong; the most infectious room is the kitchen!

While bodybuilders are often experts on nutrition, some may pay little attention to cleanliness during food preparation. No matter how big and tough you are, those little germs can give you a severe case of food poisoning. Here's how to prevent that problem.

Scrub your sink with Javex every day. Use kitchen cleaners that have antibacterial action, and wipe down your stove top, counters and table after every meal. Use disposable paper towels. If you're going to use wash cloths, make sure you wash them with a Javex solution; otherwise, you're just moving the bacteria around.

Have separate cutting boards for meat, fruit, vegetables and bread. Wash the boards with dish-washing soap and water after use. If you don't take proper care of your cutting boards they can become condominiums for nasty bacteria.

Wash your hands with soap and hot water before eating. Clean your fridge at least once a week. If you're not sure how long something's been there, chuck it out.

Don't put the mail or the newspaper on the kitchen table. How many people handled it before you did? Did they wash their hands?

When freezing foods, label them and record the date. Unlike wine, food does not improve with age.

RECIPES FOR BODYBUILDING HEALTH

We have provided a list of recipes that are simple to follow and will provide the maximum amount of nutrients with the minimum of calories. After you have made some of them, you will soon see a pattern. No salt is added. Meat is always limited to a maximum of 200 g.

The foods are prepared on a stove. They can then be stored in plastic containers and ziplock bags for reheating in the microwave as one of your five or six mini-meals throughout the day. You should buy yourself a cookbook (there is an endless variety, and they are inexpensive), and redo the recipes, dropping the salt, substituting whole-wheat flour for white flour, and adding barley to soups and stews. Avoid adding refined sugar. Use very small amounts of honey. Have at least one slice of home-baked bread with each mini-meal. You need the carbohydrates. Drink 2 percent milk unless you're dieting down for a contest. By eating well-balanced, nutritious meals, you are halfway there to building the body you have always wanted.

A brief note for our hillbilly bodybuilders and Rocky Mountain weightlifters: Most recipes have been developed for low-altitude cooking. As altitude increases, the air becomes thinner, making the air pressure lower. As a result water boils at a lower temperature. Up to 915 m (3000 ft.) above sea level this is not a problem. But for every increase of 153 m (500 ft.) above this point the boiling point of water drops 0.5 degrees C (1 degree F). Even though foods may appear to be boiling, in reality they are cooking at a lower temperature. Thus a longer cooking time is needed. To take this variance into account we have provided recipes that call for long cooking times, regardless of altitude. Therefore you do not need to vary your cooking times.

BREAKFAST:

"Yeah, training hard and training intensely are real important for lifters. Maybe not everyone can come in here and train with the consistency that it takes, but if you look around, you see there are a lot of people who come in regularly but aren't ever going to be able to compete because they can't handle the diet. Just about everybody who's motivated enough can train hard – you can even go on the sauce and get bigger – but dieting is special. It takes a special kind of person to be able to do the diet. Not just anybody can do that. It's like a hatchet; some people just can't give up that food."

– Quote from a female bodybuilder to Anne Bolin, researcher, writer and, competitive bodybuilder.

Breakfast is not just an important meal. It is *the* meal! The word itself is self-explanatory: *break-fast*, the breaking of the fast. While you slept you did not eat. Your body has not taken in any nutrients. When you wake, you must end your fast promptly. If your body does not have enough amino acids in reserve, it will start breaking down proteins to meet those immediate needs. This is the time to take amino acid or protein supplements. Wash them down with juice or milk. Give your stomach 10 or 15 minutes to settle. A lot of people have trouble eating breakfast. Usually this is because they get up too late to have the time to enjoy their

Shawn Ray, Dorian Yates, Lee Haney and Vince Taylor

Charles Clairmonte

Even with the right amount, it will still be pretty bad going down. Make it taste better the right way. For example, if you're using milk – and we recommend you do unless you're lactose intolerant – add lots of sliced banana (don't skimp) and 30 grams of bran cereal. (Don't add citrus fruits or kiwis to milk. It will curdle.) Then blend away. Now you've got a drink swimming with essential amino acids, calcium and milk fats (you need some fats), potassium from the bananas (which will not only help lower your blood cholesterol, but will also help prevent strokes), and lots of fiber (to keep your digestive system healthy). And you still haven't eaten breakfast.

Milk may not be the best idea for our older bodybuilders. As we age, we stop producing rennin and we are no longer able to fully digest milk. And if you are prone to indigestion, a citrus-based fruit drink may only add to your misery. Ask your doctor or pharmacist about enzyme products that can help you consume milk. If you find that these don't help, we suggest yogurt as an alternative.

Yes, yogurt is made from milk. It is also readily tolerated by people who cannot tolerate milk. The reason is that the yogurt bacteria break down some of the problem-causing lactose. One type of these bacteria, *Lactobacillus acidophilus*, implants itself in the intestine, producing the B vitamins. (You will still need B-12 supplements as our digestive bacteria cannot produce enough for our own needs.) Most commercial yogurts do not have this particular bacteria, so pick up a culture from a nearby health-food store.

You should make your own yogurt. You'll get better quality, and it's cheaper. All you have to do is get a yogurt-maker (they're very cheap), and mix two liters of milk with the yogurt culture. The yogurt-maker will keep the blend at 110 degrees F until it turns into what we consider yogurt after about four hours. You can then cool the yogurt in the fridge, and later blend the chilled yogurt with the protein powder, sliced banana and cereal bran.

Yogurt is an amazing food. It lowers cholesterol, inhibits tumor growth, and high consumption is associated with longevity. So grab your bowl of protein-enriched yogurt, and chow down!

If you're going to have coffee, take an iron supplement with it. The iron will bind to the caffeine and will be excreted. Caffeine removes iron from the blood and causes a loss of calcium. Since some people are addicted to coffee, we simply recommend that you restrict your coffee intake to one or two cups per day. If you are borderline anemic, or anemic, or dieting down for a competition, or a female bodybuilder, then drink only decaffeinated coffee.

Porridge is an excellent start for your day. It is easy to make. Buy cornmeal, oats, barley and other cereals in bulk. This is a lot cheaper than prepared porridge, and does not contain the added salt and sugar. One

morning meal. Give yourself time for your digestive system to warm up on the milk or juice.

Mixing protein drinks should be the simplest thing to do, but you would be amazed at the number of people who screw it up. First, we're building muscle, not mass. If you want mass, throw away this book and go to a donut shop. That kind of mass is called fat, and we're trying to persuade bodybuilders to stop dying of heart disease. Check the ingredients in your protein powder. Don't buy the sugar stuff. Yes, it tastes sweet but you're taking in a lot of extra calories that you don't need.

Buy a blender. You found the money to buy this book, so you'll find the money to buy a blender. If you try to mix these drinks by hand with a spoon, you'll find yourself alternately drinking and eating protein sludge. Read the instructions that go with the blender. Test it out with plain water. Wash it thoroughly. Then take the recommended amount of protein powder, which will vary depending on the supplement you're using. Don't be stupid and take more than they recommend. The people who make the stuff know that any excess will just be converted to fat, but more importantly, much of this stuff tastes gross, and too much will overpower the milk or juice you're mixing it with.

simple concoction is a cornmeal porridge – called "grits" in the US and "bidia" in West Africa. Place equal amounts of milk and cornmeal in a microwaveable bowl. Stir the mixture, cover with another microwaveable dish, and microwave on high for one minute. If it's not fluffy enough for your liking, microwave it at one minute intervals until it's suitable. If milk is a problem for you, substitute filtered water.

It's the same story for the other cereals. You can add raisins, strawberries, dates, nuts and a dash of cinnamon to make a really tasty meal. You can also make Russian kasha (which is coarsely ground buckwheat kernels with the bran removed) the same way as grits. The difference is that kasha can be eaten with meat.

Let's not forget the toast. But before we make the toast, we have to make the bread, so buy a bread maker. Store-bought bread was not designed for bodybuilders. (Two slices of regular white bread will provide your daily salt requirement!) All you have to do is pour in the ingredients. You can reduce the salt and sugar added, and replace the white flour with barley flour, which is a prime bodybuilding food. The Romans used barley to bulk up their gladiators – a group of guys who only saw a piece of meat when it was cut off an opponent in the arena! That vegetable protein will build muscle, so bake some barley bread and chow down on a couple of thick slices that have been coated with low-fat margarine and peanut butter. Go for brands that are low in sugar and salt. We don't recommend the natural peanut butter you get in health-food stores because it tastes awful and is so sticky there's a good chance you'll choke! When you do put peanut butter on your bread, begin with a thin layer of margarine. The margarine will lubricate the peanut butter and help it slide down.

Wash it all down with a glass of barley water. This is a traditional drink in Ireland and England. Barley water is believed to flush out the kidneys and keep them free of infection. Add barley concentrate (available from a health-food store) to a glass of filtered water with a lemon wedge and a teaspoon of honey. Drink with pinky extended. You might also want to fire one of the servants.

Now brush your teeth, and go to (school, work, the gym) ready for the day. You are now energized after a protein drink, a bowl of porridge, two slices of toast, one cup of coffee and a glass of barley water. That is not a large meal, but it is a nutritious meal. It is certainly a delicious meal. The muscles may be trained in the gym, but every workout begins in the kitchen.

One of the problems you may encounter with a high-fiber diet is flatulence. This will become particularly evident if you're doing squats in a crowded gym. Brewer's yeast was once a very popular supplement among bodybuilders, but it often had an explosive side effect which made it socially unacceptable. Solutions exist however. There are some over-the-counter food additives, such as Beano, that with only a few drops eliminate the later chorus of rumblings. The additives break down the indigestible sugars, eliminating most of the flatulence. If you're into bean salads, you should soak the beans for three hours, then boil for 30 minutes. This will remove the gaseous qualities. Pour out the water and the beans are ready for eating. Some stores sell precooked beans. Stay away from canned bean preparations as the sugar, salt and fat content can be high.

If you became a professional bodybuilder, where would you live? Maybe you'd want to continue working (old habits are so hard to break) – perhaps a TV contract, hosting an early-morning workout show. Naturally you'd want a tropical locale. If you chose the Caribbean, the place where beans have been given a special place in the diet, try out the following Island delicacy.

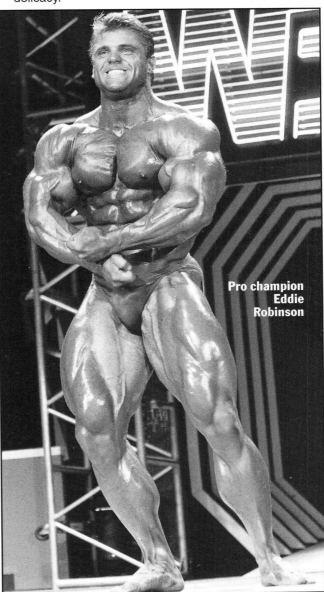

Pro champion
Eddie
Robinson

Black Bean Soup

Ingredients:
- 3 cups black beans
- 1 hambone
- 2 bay leaves
- 1 tablespoon vinegar
- 1/2 teaspoon pepper
- 2 cloves garlic
- 2 large onions

Prepare the beans as previously directed. Place the beans in a large pot, and add 8 cups of filtered water. Grate the onions and garlic, and add them to the pot. Add the bay leaves and pepper, and bring to a boil. Then reduce the heat and let the soup simmer for 2 hours. Remove the bay leaves and hambone, cut off the meat and throw away the bone. Finely chop 200 g of meat (freeze the rest) and add it and the vinegar to the pot. Continue cooking and stirring for an additional 5 minutes. Serve with black Jamaican coffee (decaf) sweetened with honey, barley bread with margarine, and chunks of fresh pineapple.

Samir Bannout, 1983 Mr. Olympia

Chicken and Vegetable Soup

Ingredients:
- 200 g chicken
- 1 large onion
- 1/2 cup barley flour
- 2 cups frozen mixed vegetables
- 1/4 teaspoon thyme
- 1/2 teaspoon pepper
- 1 teaspoon dry mustard
- 2 tablespoons margarine
- 2 cups 2 % milk

Chop the onions into cubes. Melt the margarine in a large pot, and add the onion, cooking until tender. Pour in the milk, and then while stirring, add thyme, pepper, mustard and barley flour. Cook at medium, and stir until thickened. Remove the skin and any fat from the chicken. Finely chop and add it to the soup. Add the mixed vegetables. Cook and stir for an additional 10 minutes.

Not surprisingly, the oldest civilizations have the most to teach. India has foods that dazzle the palate in both variety and taste. The following recipe is merely a sample of the eastern delights that await.

Lamb Curry

Ingredients:
- 2 large onions
- 1 clove garlic
- 8 medium-sized tomatoes
- 3 large potatoes
- 2 medium green peppers
- 4 tablespoons barley
- 3 tablespoons whole-wheat flour
- 200 g lamb
- 1 tablespoon Madras curry powder
- 1/2 teaspoon ground ginger
- pinch of cinnamon (what you can pick up between thumb and forefinger)

Finely chop lamb until you have 200 g measured out. Using a Teflon frying pan, brown the lamb, then remove and place into a large pot. Chop the onions into small cubes, and put them into a mixing bowl. Add the ginger, curry and cinnamon. Mince the garlic and add it to the mixture. Stir thoroughly, and then pour the mixture into the frying pan. Cook the onions in the same skillet that the lamb was done in. Once the onions are tender, transfer them from the pan to the pot with the lamb. Slice the tomatoes and add them to the pot. Add 3/4 cup of filtered water, cover the pot and let it simmer for an hour. Peel the potatoes and cut them into small cubes. Cut the peppers into very thin slices. Add the potatoes, peppers and barley to the pot. Cook for an additional 40 minutes. Add 3/4 cup of filtered water and the whole-wheat flour. Continue stirring and cook until thickened. Keep cooking and stirring for another 5 minutes.

This meal is nicely complemented by camomile tea with lemon, and fresh-baked oatbran bread topped with apple slices coated with a pinch of cinnamon and a drop of honey.

In many parts of the world the eating of meat is usually part of a celebration because it is such an expensive protein source. West Africa is no exception. This wonderful Nigerian dish is a bodybuilder must because it is an incredible combination of animal protein, fiber, carbohydrates and vitamins.

Jollof Rice

Ingredients:

200 g chicken
200 g lean beef
1 large eggplant
4 medium onions
2 large tomatoes
3 cloves garlic
1/2 small cabbage
500 g white rice
250 g carrots
pepper
cayenne pepper
1/2 liter groundnut oil
1 1/4 liters water

Rinse the beef and chicken. Remove and discard the skin and fat. Cut the meat into small cubes. Mix with a teaspoon of pepper and 3 cloves of crushed garlic. Refrigerate the mix for an hour. Then place the mix into a deepfryer, and fry in the groundnut oil until the beef is brown and the chicken a nice golden color. Remove the beef and chicken and drain off the oil. Next slice the onions and deep fry them in the deepfryer. Once they are golden, remove and drain off the oil. Allow the groundnut oil to cool, and then transfer it to a large saucepan. Add the water. Slice and peel the tomatoes and put them into the saucepan. Pour in one can of

Nasser El Sonbaty, Ronnie Coleman and Vince Taylor

tomato sauce. You can also purée 3 large tomatoes if the tomato sauce has a high salt content. Bring the mixture to a boil. You may wish to add chicken stock for flavor. Then add all the previously fried chicken, beef and onions. Chop up a small cabbage and add it to the stew. Dice the eggplant and add it. Follow with finely sliced carrots. Allow it all to simmer for what will seem like an eternity – actually 40 minutes. While you're waiting, boil the rice, and once done strain and spread it across a large serving plate. Try not to salivate as you strain the beef, chicken and vegetables from the saucepan, and lay them lovingly on the warm bed of white rice. You might consider a dash of dill and garnish of parsley. The Lion King never had it so good!

One of the best ways of stretching that food dollar is to make soup. And what better recipe could we choose than an old Canadian favorite:

Pea Soup – Bodybuilder Style

Ingredients:

1 hambone
200 g ham
600 g split peas
2 onions
6 carrots
1 celery stock
2 bay leaves
6 peppercorns
6 bouillon cubes (low-salt)
4 liters water

CHAPTER NINE – BODYBUILDING NUTRITION

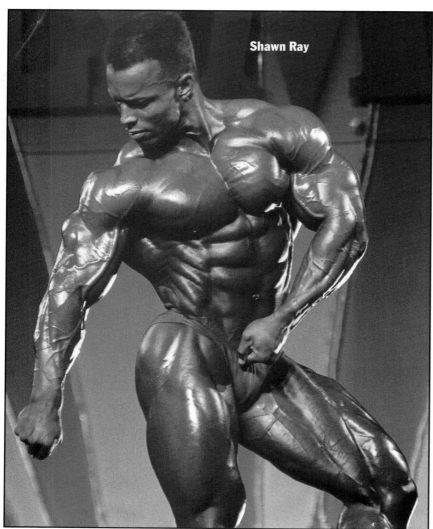

Shawn Ray

Yam Balls
Ingredients:

1 kg yams
2 cups barley flour
2 medium-sized onions
2 large tomatoes
3 eggs
200 g lean beef
2 teaspoons cayenne pepper
1 liter groundnut oil

Peel the onions, yams and tomatoes. Dice the onions and tomatoes, and separate them into two equal amounts. Pour some groundnut oil into a large frying pan, and gently fry one half of the tomatoes and onions until soft. Remove and drain off the oil. Save the oil and fry up the beef, which should also be diced. Next boil the yams in water until they are soft. Mash the yams, and mix them with all of the beef, onions and tomatoes. Beat the 3 eggs separately and mix them into the mash. Sprinkle some flour onto a cutting board, and using a handful of mash, roll it on the board into the form of a ball. Do this until you run out of mash. Using a deep fryer, deep fry the yam balls in groundnut oil until they are a rich golden brown.

You can substitute chicken or pork for the beef. Just remember to remove the chicken skin and trim any fat off the pork. This meal is complemented by boiled broccoli with cheddar-cheese sauce and a crisp, fresh salad. Use a light vinegar/oil dressing, as a heavy dressing will spoil your enjoyment of the yam balls. A sparkling fruit-flavored mineral water will quench the thirst of your dining partner, who will only be able to marvel at your culinary genius. Follow this meal with a homemade fruit salad and Earl Grey tea. After all, not all bodybuilders are barbarians.

And what of those days when you find yourself daydreaming about southern California? If you can't train with the stars, you can still eat like them. Try this Mexican-American favorite:

California Chili
Ingredients:

200 g pork
2 large onions
2 large green peppers
1 clove garlic
8 large tomatoes
1 can tomato paste
(no salt or sugar added)
2 jalapeño peppers
2 dried red chili peppers
2 tablespoons chili powder
1 tablespoon brewer's yeast
1/4 teaspoon oregano
1 kg kidney beans

Pour the water into a large pot. Add the hambone, the bay leaves and the peppercorns. Finely dice the onions and add them to the soup. Bring the soup to a boil and let it simmer 4 to 5 hours.

Remove the bone, bay leaves and peppercorns. Let the bone cool, and then cut the meat from the bone. Dispose of the bone, bay leaves and peppercorns. Finely chop the meat, and add 200 grams to the soup. Put the rest in a ziplock plastic bag and freeze it for another time. Add the bouillon cubes and the peas, and let the soup cook for another 2 hours or until thick. Then finely dice the carrots and celery and add them to the soup. Cook for an additional 30 minutes, and your soup is ready to serve.

This soup is nicely complemented by a glass of ice-cool barley water with a slice of lemon, and slices of dark whole-grain bread with margarine. Dessert should be fresh sliced kiwi fruit with apple tea, served in front of a warm fire.

As we proceed in reducing our meat content, we return to West Africa for another charming health-food treat. And best of all, this nutritious meal is deep-fried!

Prepare the beans as directed on package. Finely chop the pork and cook in a skillet. Then place the pork in a large pot. Add the beans, chili powder, oregano and tomato paste. Finely chop the tomatoes, onions, jalapeño peppers, chili peppers and garlic, and add to the pot. Add 3 cups of filtered water. Stirring all the time, bring the chili to a boil. You may add additional water as desired. Then cover and let simmer for 30 minutes with occasional stirring.

The British bodybuilders are getting beefier every year. Rumor has it that an ancient Roman manuscript was dug up near Hadrian's Wall, and that it was a record of recipes for the Imperial Roman Army. These recipes have since been translated and secretly circulated among top British athletes, including the bodybuilding elite. No one knows for sure, but this recipe might have come from that lost piece of history.

Beef and Barley Soup

Ingredients: 200 g lean beef
8 large tomatoes
1 clove garlic
1 can tomato sauce
1 cup dry red wine
4 stalks celery
500 g carrots
1 cup barley
1 bay leaf
1/4 cup fresh parsley
1 teaspoon thyme
1/2 teaspoon pepper

Finely chop the beef and brown in a skillet. In a large pot combine the beef, tomato sauce, bay leaf, wine, thyme, 6 cups of filtered water and pepper. Finely chop tomatoes and add them to the pot. Bring to boil, cover, and let simmer for 1 hour. Peel and finely chop the carrots and celery and add to the soup. Add barley to the soup and let simmer for an additional hour. Stir occasionally. Remove bay leaf and stir in parsley just before serving.

To see really powerful men, one needs to attend the Highland Games in Scotland. There you'll see legs as thick as the cabers that are tossed! Obviously they train hard, but they also eat traditional foods, like this recipe for **Beef Stew.**

Ingredients: 200 g lean beef
4 tablespoons whole-wheat flour
4 medium tomatoes
4 large potatoes
4 carrots
2 large onions
4 stalks celery
1 can green peas
1 cup Burgundy
1/2 cup barley
1 teaspoon pepper

Finely chop the beef and roll it in flour. Lay the beef on the bottom of a large pot. Finely chop tomatoes and

onions and add to the pot. Peel the carrots and potatoes, and cut into large chunks. Add to the pot. Finely chop the celery and add it with the barley to the stew. Drain the peas and add them too. Add the pepper, Burgundy and 1 cup of filtered water to the stew. Cover the pot, put it in the oven, and bake at 400 degrees F for 2 hours.

But now, dear reader, let us leave the cold Scottish Highlands for the refreshing breezes from the Gulf of

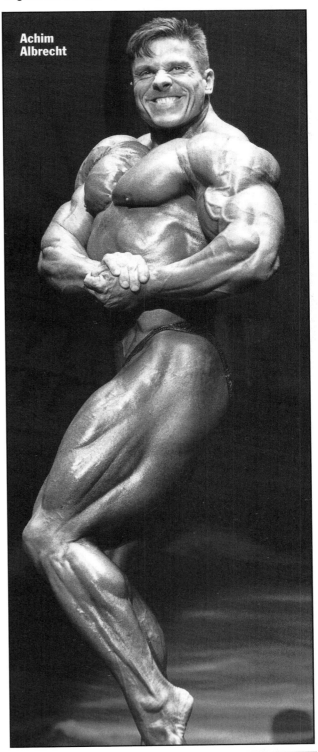

Achim Albrecht

Lee Labrada

20 minutes. Drain and finely chop the tuna, shred the lemon peel, and add both with the flour to the skillet. Add the sour cream. Stir until thickened.

Getting homesick? Got a craving for old-fashioned cheddar cheese? Well, you can't have it! Too much fat! However, you can have low-fat cheddar cheese, but only if you spoil yourself with this recipe.

Cheese-on-the-Beer Soup

Ingredients: 200 g low-fat cheddar cheese
1/2 cup beer (lite)
3 cups 2% milk
1/4 cup low-fat margarine
1 small onion
1 large carrot
1/4 teaspoon dry mustard
1/8 teaspoon ginger
1/2 teaspoon pepper
1 cube chicken bouillon (low-salt)
2 tablespoons whole-wheat flour
1 tablespoon brewer's yeast

In a deep skillet melt the margarine. Peel and shred the carrot and onion, and cook in the skillet until tender. Pour in milk, and then stir in dry mustard, ginger, pepper, whole-wheat flour and a bouillon cube. Cook at medium heat and stir until thickened. Reduce heat and add the beer and cheese. Continue cooking at low heat. Stir until cheese is melted.

Perhaps our female readers can answer a question. Is the man in your life taking you for granted? Get his attention by telling him to be at your place this evening for some T & A! To be more specific, T & A Stir Fry. (Actually, the T & A stands for tomatoes and asparagus.)

T&A Stir Fry

Ingredients: 3 large onions
2 cups canned mushrooms
2 large tomatoes
500 g frozen cut asparagus
1 tablespoon vegetable oil
1 teaspoon cornstarch
1/2 teaspoon soya sauce (low-salt)

Pour 2 tablespoons of filtered water into a skillet. Mix with soya sauce and cornstarch. Add vegetable oil and asparagus. Cook at high heat until asparagus is tender. Stir frequently. Peel and grate the onions and add them and the mushrooms to the skillet. Chop the tomatoes into thick slices and add them to the skillet. Reduce the heat to medium and stir frequently. Once all the vegetables are tender and the stir fry has thickened, it is ready to be served.

Some of the strongest Americans have their roots among the hillbillies of Tennessee and West Virginia. These folk lived life on their own terms. They were poor, but they made do with what they had. Nothing was wasted, and children grew big and healthy on leftovers thrown together. We've altered the recipe to lower its fat content.

Siam, on the coast of Thailand. In this bustling land where East meets West, the ancient delights of Thai cooking can now be shared. Try this recipe.

Curried Tuna Soup

Ingredients: 1 can tuna (packed in fresh water)
1 large apple
1 large onion
4 cups chicken broth
1/2 cup sour cream (lite)
1/4 cup margarine
1/4 cup long-grain rice
1 teaspoon Madras curry powder
1 teaspoon Calcutta curry powder
1/2 teaspoon lemon peel
2 tablespoons whole-wheat flour
2 tablespoons barley

Peel and finely chop the onion and apple (core it first). In a deep skillet combine the onion, apple and curry powder, and cook until the onion is tender. Add the broth and bring to a boil. Stir in the rice and barley, reduce the heat, cover and allow it to simmer for 15 to

Turkey Soup

Ingredients:	200g turkey (skin and fat removed)
	100g cheddar cheese (lite)
	1 small onion
	3 cups 2% milk
	500g frozen cut asparagus
	1/2 cup barley
	2 large potatoes
	2 tablespoons margarine
	1 tablespoon whole-wheat flour
	1/2 teaspoon pepper
	1 teaspoon dry mustard

Finely chop the turkey and place in a large pot. Grate the cheese, finely chop the onion, peel and slice the potatoes and add them all to the pot. Add the margarine, flour, mustard, barley, asparagus and milk. Stir and bring to a boil. Cover and let simmer for 30 minutes, with occasional stirring.

SUPPLEMENTS

"I take more amino acids prior to a contest and I take more L-carnitine prior to a contest. I may increase my intake of B vitamins and also vitamin C."
– Kathy Unger, world amateur champion

With the development of specialized supplements, and a better understanding of the biochemistry of exercise and its relationship to nutrition, modern body-

Christa Bauch

builders have a host of anabolic boosters to choose from. What should the bodybuilder take? This is a very individual matter. What does wonders for one person may have absolutely no effect on another.

There is a wide range of products to choose from. Nature's Best, Cybergenics, MET-Rx, Ultimate Nutrition, Gorilla and Twinlab all offer quality products. And new companies with new products come on line almost every month.

Often a person will take a supplement, and find that it does nothing. Remember that these supplements were designed to be used by individuals who are not only training hard, but are also following strict body-builder diets as outlined in this chapter. It doesn't matter how high the octane rating is on the fuel you put into your car; if you put sugar in the motor, it won't run. That principle works biochemically as well. Throw junk food into the mixture, and no matter what supplement you're using – it could have been designed for you alone – it won't work. Supplement use *must* be accompanied by careful attention to diet.

"I also take a huge amount of supplements – 30 or 40 at a time. My body can process them because of all the energy I put out." **– Strongman Anthony Clark (who weighs a formidable 330 pounds and holds several strength records)**

WARNING!... Supplements can change the internal physiology of the body and exert a biological effect while present. This is also the definition of a drug. While the supplements presented here are generally safe if used properly, individual reactions may vary, and unexpected side effects might occur from supplement interactions. Before taking any of the supplements mentioned in this chapter, get a physical including a cholesterol profile. Then discuss your diet, the supplements you plan to use, and the dosages you want to take with your physician. It would also be wise to check with a dietitian. To be even safer, get a second opinion from both professionals. Speak to your local pharmacist. The advice usually won't cost you anything, and pharmacists know their drugs. Until you've done all this, don't take any supplements. Only a fool takes a drug without medical supervision.

PROTEIN SUPPLEMENTS:

"A dozen every morning. When I was working 12-hour days on heavy machinery, I used to brown-bag four bags of food to work. I believe in eggs. My grandfather lived to 103, and he had four eggs every morning."
– Mike Matarazzo (commenting on eggs)

Protein supplements are usually composed of powders that are mixed with a beverage, such as milk or juice. Supplements must be of high biological value, the quality of which depends on the proportions of amino acids present and their digestibility. Correctly used, milk-and-egg protein powders are excellent forms of

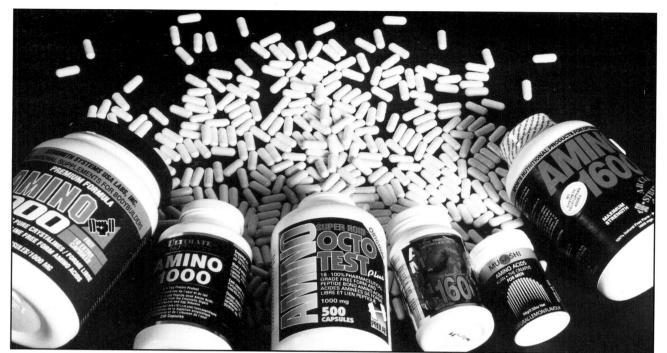

supplementary protein. Protein drinks are convenient and offer rapid assimilation. When mixed with water, these powders contain 25 to 35 grams of protein with 110 to 125 calories. Bodybuilders who are dieting for a contest may be consuming only 1000 to 1500 calories a day. A supplement will provide enough protein to maintain muscle size while bodyfat can be reduced by low-calorie dieting. While supplements in the form of protein powders are still used in great quantities, science has now offered the bodybuilder an alternative – the amino acids themselves.

AMINO ACIDS:

"In order of importance: amino acids (loads of 'em); vitamin C around 3 to 4 grams per day; vitamin B complex 2 per day. Protein powders are good, depending on the diet that you are on at the time."

– British bodybuilding guru and writer Mick Hart (describing the supplements that he would recommend)

All amino acids consist of an amino group at one end and an acid group at the other, both connected to a central carbon atom. The distinguishing characteristic separating one amino acid from another is the attachment of a third side group, which is different in all amino acids.

$$
\begin{array}{c}
H \\
| \\
| \\
Amino - > NH - C - COOH < - \text{Acid Group} \\
| \\
| \\
R \\
\text{Third Group}
\end{array}
$$

Kathy Unger

not. If one aspirin will kill your headache, will 100 aspirin make you better faster? No, but they will end your headache problem permanently by killing you. Your body has been designed by evolution to remove the amino acids it needs from food and process them accordingly. Jumping the first stages of digestion does not necessarily lead to an improvement in health. It may overload the system and throw off your internal balance. There is a logical reason for our body's breaking down food in the first place – to selectively remove what is needed at a rate at which it can be safely absorbed. Putting in too much may cause the body to shift gears in an effort to remove the excess. For example, one prune a day will help regulate your bowel movements; a large bag of prunes will result in a bowel movement that lasts all day. Your body needs fiber, but too much will give you severe diarrhea. Moderation would appear to be the key.

Another school of thought says that enough research has been done to show that one can safely supplement, using pure amino acids. Understand that amino acids are important in maintaining the body's nitrogen balance. The amount of nitrogen being taken in from protein and amino-acid sources should be greater than the amount being excreted as nitrogenous wastes. This positive nitrogen balance means that muscle growth is occurring. To achieve such a balance, a hard-training bodybuilder must take in more protein to build up the components of growing muscle tissue. While a diet of high-protein mini-meals every two to three hours should provide enough protein, supplements and amino acids can be used to ensure a positive nitrogen balance.

Some researchers are convinced that when certain amino acids are taken in dosages of 2 to 3 grams, beneficial biochemical results are obtained. The following list shows a few amino acids and their potential effects:

AMINO ACID	EFFECT
serine	energy
alanine	improves glycogen storage
arginine	growth hormone release
proline	tissue repair
histidine	protein synthesis

How the amino acids should be used is perhaps the greatest source of controversy among bodybuilding researchers. The use of single amino acids has generally dropped out of favor. When single amino acids surge into the bloodstream, the body will maintain its internal balance by excreting the excess. Even if there is a demand for that particular amino acid, the body may be unable to use it because another amino acid is in short supply (the limiting amino factor).

There are some nutritional specialists who believe

Amino Acids:

alanine	asparagine
arginine	aspartic acid
cysteine	glutamine
glutamic acid	glycine
histidine*	isoleucine*
leucine*	lysine*
methionine*	phenylalanine*
proline	serine
threonine*	tryptophan*
tyrosine	valine*

essential amino acids

At first glance consuming amino-acid supplements is attractive. You can consume the amino acids in their pure form, rather than large amounts of protein. Amino acids eliminate the increased strain that is placed on the liver and kidneys by having to break down excessive amounts of protein in the diet. The amino acids can be directly absorbed into the bloodstream, bypassing this process.

But as we look closer, we see that certain problems arise. First, scientists do not know in what proportions the amino acids should be taken. Second, as there are 20 different amino acids, an athlete would have to consume 20 different supplements. Third, amino acids tend to be more expensive than less refined protein supplements. And most serious of all, large amounts of single amino acids can be harmful, either by themselves or through interactions with other amino acids or medications.

There are two schools of thought on this issue. One is that, if you eat the daily minimal amounts of animal meat or fish (one gram for every kilogram of mass that you carry), amino-acid supplements are not necessary. People have this attitude that more is better, and it's

that the key to successful muscle growth can be found among three amino acids: leucine, isoleucine and valine. All three are essential amino acids that have side chains attached to their basic structure. Thus they are called branched-chain amino acids, or BCAA. According to Dr. Fred Hatfield, BCAAs are the most rapidly absorbed amino acids. He states that 70 percent of the amino acids processed by the liver and then released into the bloodstream are BCAAs. Within three hours of a meal, 50 to 90 percent of amino-acid uptake into muscle tissue consists of BCAAs. This is because BCAAs are metabolized in the muscle. Scientists believe that if an excess of BCAAs are taken in, the muscles will absorb more amino acids to balance them out. Leucine stimulates the production of insulin. As a result blood glucose is taken up by muscle cells and can be used as an energy source. Insulin and the BCAAs act together to cause other amino acids to be utilized for building muscle tissue. The result is an anabolic effect.

Marjo Selin

Dr. Hatfield suggests that 1 to 4 g of each BCAA should be taken 60 to 90 minutes after a workout. To ensure that the BCAAs can do what they're supposed to do, also take 50 to 100 mg of vitamin B6 daily. The only fly in the ointment is that the BCAAs actively compete with tryptophan and tyrosine. Therefore, if you are also consuming these amino acids, you should take them at different times.

Other specialists, such as the people at L & S Research, believe that it is not the form of the amino acid that is crucial, but the proportions in which the amino acids reach the muscles. This compensation is claimed to be necessary because intensive resistance training creates specific metabolic demands. These needs result in the disproportionate consumption of certain amino acids for energy production and other nonanabolic needs. Our bodies use amino acids in precise proportions. By providing amino acids that are in the same proportions as they would be found in high-protein foods, we can exploit the ability of the body to absorb and utilize amino acids to produce an anabolic effect.

MCT OIL SUPPLEMENT:

"This CapTri is fantastic stuff. I don't know what it is, but it really works. It's especially great the last six to eight weeks before a contest as it helps to maintain muscle mass while you diet down for a show. In the past I always lost too much size as I dieted down, but this time, using the CapTri, I was still able to train heavy right up until the show, and in fact, I actually put size on while I was dieting down and losing fat. I never felt hungry. I never got that grouchy, irritable, low-carb feeling. I never felt better. I'm telling you this stuff is great."

– Rita Boehm, 1990 overall Canadian bodybuilding champion (commenting on CapTri, an MCT oil supplement)

Medium-chain triglycerides are the latest rage in bodybuilding. Almost all the pros admit to using them. It is claimed that they are fats that act like carbohydrates, capable of supplying energy to the body without being stored as fat. The MCTs speed up the metabolic rate, causing bodyfat to be consumed faster, resulting in enhanced muscular development and a more "ripped" appearance. MCTs produce a large amount of ketones, the byproduct of fat metabolism, which in turn can be used as an energy source. Ketones help bodybuilders on a precontest diet by suppressing appetite. MCTs also reduce serum cholesterol.

John Parrillo, who manufactures CapTri, an MCT oil product, recommends that bodybuilders start at half a tablespoon per meal for the first three days, slowly increasing the dosage as it is tolerated. Always take CapTri with food. An excess of oil can cause nausea, diarrhea, stomach cramps and even vomiting. Tolerance builds up with time. Some bodybuilders have worked up to taking 20 tablespoons a day before their contests.

On the down side MCTs in large amounts can interfere with the absorption of fat-soluble vitamins A, D, E and K. Therefore these vitamins must be supplemented. MCTs are not for diabetics because diabetics already produce too many ketones as part of their disease. MCT use would increase already high ketone levels, possibly leading to acidosis, a condition which causes more acid in the body than normal.

NUCLEIC ACID SUPPLEMENTS:
Nucleic acids (inosine for example) taken orally are destroyed in the intestinal tract before they can have a biological effect. Don't waste your money on them.

LACTATE SUPPLEMENT:
An athlete burns off enormous amounts of glycogen during a typical training session. It is now known that ingesting enormous amounts of carbohydrates does not sufficiently replenish glycogen levels if the body is under physical stress. Studies have shown that lactic acid, which was once thought to be a waste product, is absorbed by the liver and used to replenish glycogen supplies. The human body does not produce enough lactic acid to meet the liver's glycogen demands. Researchers have modified lactic acid by removing a single hydrogen atom, resulting in a version of lactic acid known as lactate. According to research by Dr. Douglas Crist, the presence of lactic acid in the muscles during exercise may be the stimulus for growth-hormone release. Theoretically the consumption of lactate during a workout might produce an enhanced release of growth hormone.

The increase of natural growth-hormone levels through diet is a two-edged sword. GH will promote protein anabolism and increased fat oxidation, but GH also decreases the uptake of glucose by muscular tissues, causing a rise in blood-sugar levels. Thus a diabetes-like situation is created. Many people are borderline diabetics. Before taking a supplement, speak to your physician, and get checked for diabetes just to be on the safe side.

CHROMIUM PICOLINATE SUPPLEMENTS:
Chromium picolinate is the most biologically available form of chromium, an essential mineral. Chromium is essential for the normal functioning of insulin. This hormone carries amino acids from the blood to the cells, as well as being involved in fat and carbohydrate metabolism. Hard-training bodybuilders lose a great deal of chromium during exercise, and thus are low on chromium when they need it most. Replacing the lost

Dorian wins his 1993 Olympia crown.

chromium should restore the normal action of insulin and help the body reach its anabolic potential.

Buyer beware! Remember that chromium picolinate is only about 12 percent chromium. If you take 100 micrograms of chromium picolinate, you are consuming only 12 micrograms of chromium. Since you need a minimum of 400 micrograms a day, you would have to consume 4,800 micrograms of chromium picolinate. To get the most bang for your buck, check the label for the elemental value (the actual amount) of chromium in each tablet.

CARNITINE SUPPLEMENTS:
Research has shown that carnitine speeds up the rate of fat oxidation. It does this by accelerating the binding

Nasser El Sonbaty

of fatty acids with special enzymes called CAT1 and CAT2, thus easing the entry of the fatty acid-enzyme complex into the mitochondria where it is oxidized. The result is a prolonged source of energy and a lower bodyfat level. Its most important biochemical benefit to athletes is its ability to speed up the intake of oxygen into the body's cells. The result is greater availability of oxygen for the cells in times of strenuous physical activity.

As with chromium picolinate, check the elemental value for carnitine. L-carnitine is 67 percent carnitine.

GAMMA ORYZANOL SUPPLEMENT:
Some bodybuilders claim that taking gamma oryzanol builds size and strength. Its mechanism of action is not fully understood and bodybuilders find that to get the most benefit from this supplement, they must take up to 1000 mg a day.

CREATINE:
Creatine (the supplement is called creatine monohydrate) is a substance that readily binds to phosphate, creating a high energy bond. This phosphate will later be used to rebuild adenosine triphosphate (ATP), which is used to power all of the energy-requiring reactions of cellular metabolism. When glucose is oxidized, energy is released and can be used to add inorganic phosphate (P_i) to adenosine diphosphate (ADP), forming ATP. This energy reserve is found in minute amounts in every cell. The hydrolysis of ATP to ADP + P_i releases energy that can power the needs of the cell.

Muscle cells require more energy during contraction, and may use up all the available ATP. To compensate for this shortage, muscle cells maintain a reserve of creatine phosphate. When needed, the creatine will donate a high-energy phosphate to ADP, forming ATP.

Creatine supplementation has been shown to decrease fatigue and increase the number of reps possible during a workout. Since creatine in the muscle takes at least five minutes to recharge with high-energy phosphate, resting periods between sets should reflect this fact.

Brian Rowley, a graduate student in the pharmacology department at the University of British Columbia, recommends that creatine be taken in warm fruit juice (not hot, which will break down the creatine, and not cold, because it will not dissolve) four times a day. The total daily dosage should be 0.14 gram per pound for the first six days. The muscles will become saturated. Then the dosage can be reduced to 0.014 gram per pound to maintain optimum creatine levels.

Diabetic bodybuilders should take their creatine after an insulin injection, because insulin promotes creatine uptake. *(WARNING!* Check this with your doctor first! It may not just be creatine in your supplement!) If you are not diabetic, take the creatine after consuming a mini-meal. The carbohydrates in the main course and in the bread will stimulate insulin secretion. A low-dose vitamin E tablet will also help creatine absorption.

Another benefit from creatine is that you can target muscle groups. Your calves won't grow? You find that squats are sheer agony? Follow your exercise program with a mini-meal and creatine. Exercised muscles have an affinity for creatine. Those stubborn muscles will start giving you more reps once you've got their creatine levels to the max.

The disadvantage of creatine is that it causes water retention. Stop taking creatine at least two weeks prior to a contest.

GINSENG:

This herbal (Panax quinquelfolium) supplement is an ancient Chinese remedy for a multitude of ailments. Ginseng can decrease blood-sugar levels and stimulate the blood vessels. It is claimed to be a medicine for any physical stress – bodybuilding for example. It is a safe herb provided it is taken in small doses for two weeks or less. Check with your doctor before using, and discontinue if any of the following side effects occur: vomiting, nervousness, insomnia, nausea or diarrhea.

SIBERIAN GINSENG:

The best Soviet "secret" to escape during the days of the Iron Curtain is claimed to be Siberian ginseng (Eleuthrococcus senticosis). A group of natural compounds called adaptogens have been used by East European bodybuilders to speed gains and recovery. According to Dr. Moris Silber, in order to be classified as an adaptogen, a compound must meet the following criteria:

1. The substance should cause minimal disruption to the physiological processes of the body.
2. The action of the substance should be nonspecific – i.e. should increase resistance to adverse influences from a wide range of physical, chemical and biological factors.
3. The substance may possess a normalizing action (bringing the body back into balance) irrespective of the foregoing pathological changes.

Siberian ginseng's compounds show a wide spectrum of pharmacological activity including positive tonic effects on performance, energy metabolism, memory, immune stimulation and the cardiovascular system. This result is believed to be accomplished through several biochemical processes occurring at the cellular level. These processes include antioxidant action, the stimulation of RNA and proteins, and a general bio-resistance to stress. Researchers claim that the greater the physical stress, the greater the benefits from Siberian Ginseng.

Dr. Silber recommends that this herb be taken from a pure standardized extract of 8:1 or 10:1 in capsule or tablet form. The dosages for a recovery effect from hard training should be 400 mg, two or three times daily. For a biostimulant effect, three or four tablets (1,200 to 1,600 mg) should be taken before a workout. Before a competition bodybuilders might take double the previous amount. There is a wide variety of response to this herb, and the user may need to vary the dosage. As with any herb, always check with your physician before taking, and discontinue if you have any side effects.

ENZYMES:

Among the latest supplements to appear are enzyme preparations. Lactose-intolerant people can be helped by taking the enzyme lactase. Researchers now offer the bodybuilder a variety of enzymes that can be taken to help break down other foods in the system, the logic being that more nutritional value can be realized if the body can increase its digestive efficiency.

There are a couple of problems with this concept. Lactase works as desired because it replaces an enzyme that is already deficient or perhaps absent. Throwing extra enzymes into the digestive tract, adding to the same kind of enzymes already present, may produce the opposite effect from the one desired. The body must maintain an internal balance that has very narrow boundaries. If the body detects an excess, the system shifts gears to correct the balance. Thus adding an enzyme that breaks down proteins might cause a flooding of amino acids into the system. Despite a

Nikki Fuller

metabolic demand for aminos in the muscle cells, the body must protect itself by removing the excess aminos as quickly as possible. The net result might be that less aminos are utilized than if the digestive system had been left alone to do its job. Think about it. If it's not broke, why fix it?

Further, enzymes work at different points in the gastrointestinal tract. They can be denatured or rendered inactive along the way before they can get to the site where they are supposed to work.

Before using any enzyme preparation, see your doctor. He or she can advise you on whether it's worth taking.

VITAMIN SUPPLEMENTS:

Vitamin supplements do not take the place of good nutrition. The body needs other substances such as carbohydrates, fats, proteins and minerals for adequate nutrition. And yet the North American diet has resulted in bodybuilders who are overfed and undernourished. A balanced diet cannot be achieved by just eating from the main food groups.

Considerable misinformation and exaggeration exist regarding the relationship between vitamins and exercise. Vitamins are not a source of energy. Coaches, magazines, fitness journals and even the media send the message that high levels of vitamins are needed by hard-training athletes. Does vitamin supplementation improve athletic performance?

One study examined the effect of large doses of vitamin supplements on endurance and performance. The researchers concluded that no single vitamin or combination of vitamins had any effect on performance. After 40 years of research there is no conclusive evidence to suggest that vitamin supplementation improves performance in individuals whose diets are nutritionally adequate.

In recent times researchers have focused on the role of specific vitamins and their effect on exercise. Particularly popular subjects for research were the vitamins B-3, C and E. Once again the researchers concluded that these vitamins, used as supplements, were of no benefit in improving athletic performance if the athlete receiving the supplement was following a balanced diet.

These same researchers made one strategic error. They administered vitamins in a single large dose, or more than one large dose daily. If a large dose is taken at one time, the result is decreased absorption and increased excretion. For example, if vitamin C is taken at doses of 100 mg or more, less will be absorbed than if a dosage of 50 mg were taken. Therefore, vitamin supplements should be taken at low dosages several times a day.

If vitamins do not affect exercise (under certain conditions), does exercise affect vitamin requirements? There is evidence to suggest exercise may indeed increase the body's need for certain vitamins such as C, B-2 and B-6.

Each of the principal vitamins required by our bodies performs a specific function that no other nutrient can. Vitamins trigger the release of energy in the body, and manage the way the body assembles tissues and uses food.

Kevin Levrone, Achim Albrecht, Porter Cottrell, Vince Taylor, Sonny Schmidt, Paul Dillett and Chris Cormier

Here's a list of the important vitamin functions:

•Vitamin A aids night vision and helps prevent eye disease, promotes bone growth in infants and children, and helps maintain the mucous membranes in the ears, nose and intestinal lining.

•Thiamine helps regulate your appetite, maintain a responsive nervous system (necessary for the synthesis of acetylcholine, a neurotransmitter), and release energy from carbohydrates (acts as a coenzyme for 24 different enzymes involved in the carbohydrate metabolism of pyruvic acid to CO_2 and H_2O).

•Riboflavin aids food metabolism (component of certain coenzymes involved with carbohydrate and protein metabolism), promotes healthy skin, and helps the body use oxygen.

•Niacin is involved in fat metabolism (during lipid metabolism inhibits the production of cholesterol and aids in fat breakdown), tissue respiration, and the conversion of sugars to energy (essential coenzyme concerned with energy releasing reactions).

•Pantothenic acid is a part of coenzyme A, which is essential for the transfer of pyruvic acid into the Kreb's cycle during protein metabolism. It is also involved in the transformation of amino acids and fats into glucose and the formation of cholesterol and steroid hormones.

•Pyridoxine is an essential coenzyme for amino-acid metabolism and may function as a coenzyme in fat metabolism. It assists in the production of circulating antibodies.

•Folic acid is part of the enzyme systems that synthesize the purines and pyrimidines built into RNA and DNA. This vitamin is necessary for normal production of red and white blood cells.

•Vitamin B-12 is a coenzyme necessary for formation of red blood cells and the manufacture of the amino acid methionine and the neurotransmitter precursor choline. It is also responsible for the entrance of some amino acids into the Kreb's cycle during the metabolism of proteins.

•Vitamin D is vital for absorption and utilization of the minerals calcium and phosphorus from the GI tract. This vitamin may work with the parathyroid hormone that regulates calcium metabolism.

•Vitamin E is involved in the manufacture of RNA, DNA and red blood cells. It behaves as a cofactor in several enzyme systems. Vitamin E works as an antioxidant, prevents the enzyme action of peroxidase on the unsaturated bonds of cell membranes, and protects red blood cells from dissolving.

Pro champion Sue Price

•Biotin is a vital coenzyme for the conversion of pyruvic acid to oxalocetic acid and the manufacture of purines and fatty acids.

•Ascorbic acid (vitamin C) helps form collagen, the substance that binds body cells together. This acid promotes many metabolic reactions, particularly protein metabolism. It is essential to the growth and repair of teeth, gums, blood vessels and specialized cells in the bones. This vitamin works with antibodies, and as a coenzyme may bind with poisons, rendering them harmless.

While all bodybuilders should ingest low-dose multivitamins throughout the day, it is critical that they take ascorbic acid. Russian bodybuilders have long used vitamin C as an anabolic agent. This vitamin is rapidly depleted by physical stress and increased water consumption which are characteristic of a bodybuilding workout.

An individual normally possesses 5,000 mg of ascorbic acid: 200 mg in the extracellular fluids, 30 mg

Anja Schreiner

in the adrenal glands, and the remainder distributed throughout the body. This vitamin is essential to the formation of adrenaline, and is rapidly depleted. The RDA for an adult is 60 mg; a stressed adult can add 20 mg to that dose. Consult your doctor about the dosage you wish to take.

Recently, megadoses of ascorbic acid (1,000 mg or more daily) have come into vogue. *This is dangerous!* It can lead to kidney stones, gout and/or anemia. Symptoms of vitamin C overdose include nausea, cramps, diarrhea, headache, flushed face and increased urination. If these signs occur, discontinue use immediately and contact medical help.

MINERAL AND TRACE ELEMENT SUPPLEMENTS:
Evidence exists to show that highly trained athletes have a deficiency in the trace element iron. One study that investigated iron-deficiency in Olympic athletes found that five percent of the female and two percent of the male athletes had iron deficiency anemia (a decrease in certain elements of the blood). Another study involving 18 adolescent female cross-country runners found that 50 percent had either iron deficiency or iron-deficiency anemia. Researchers suggested that irregular and unbalanced diets followed by the athletes may have contributed to the condition. Another explanation offered was that athletes lose more than a normal amount of iron through the feces, urine, sweat and menses. Runners were found to lose more iron through sweating than the average person.

Exercise may also cause large increases in excretion of chromium, zinc and copper. Without proper amounts of these trace elements many metabolic processes are altered, possibly affecting athletic performance. There is no evidence to indicate that taking large doses of these trace elements will improve health or athletic performance.

Heavy training, high water consumption, and the use of a variety of supplements may cause a loss of minerals or trace elements. The bodybuilder should take low-dose mineral/trace-element supplements. As in the case with vitamins, the body better absorbs lower doses than higher ones.

ADDITIONAL SUPPLEMENTS:

"Theoretically, you might be able to prevent adult diabetes." **– Dr. Richard Anderson, a scientist with the Human Nutrition Research Center of the United States Department of Agriculture (commenting on the benefits of cinnamon)**

• Cinnamon – Researchers have found that the spice found in our kitchens can increase the ability of insulin to metabolize blood glucose by up to ninefold. While an exact therapeutic dosage has not been determined, some diabetics report normal glucose levels while eating 1/4 teaspoon of cinnamon a day.

Cinnamon is known to interfere with the absorption of iron and other minerals. It is generally safe to take in very small doses for a short period of time. Too much of a good thing can be dangerous though. A dose of 0.5 mg/kg of bodyweight is enough to cause kidney damage or even death! Cinnamon can also produce a wide range of side effects including vomiting, nausea, hallucinations, convulsions and dizziness. If any of these side effects occur, discontinue use and seek medical attention. As with all herbs, consult your doctor before using.

•Desiccated liver tablets – a good source of protein, minerals and vitamins. Liver is a very healthful food. In fact it's so nutritious it should be in a food group all by itself. Desiccated liver tablets were the first convenient form of protein supplement widely marketed in the USA. Bodybuilders tend to be brand-loyal, and many of today's bodybuilding gurus trained with these tablets. The idea behind their use was that the body must maintain a positive nitrogen balance in order to promote protein synthesis. The frequent consumption of tablets provided a ready pool of nitrogen.

Others argue that if a healthful diet is followed, the tablets are unnecessary. If you include liver as one of your mini-meals, you don't need the tablets. You'll be getting plenty of protein with the menu provided.

•Brewer's yeast – an excellent source of nutrients, protein, minerals, the B vitamins and fiber. It is a very inexpensive source of chromium. Take a maximum of one tablespoon of yeast a day. Make sure that you add a few drops of Beano to decrease the flatulence that can occur. WARNING! If you develop diarrhea or vomiting, discontinue use and seek medical help.

•Licorice – a way to grow testosterone receptors through diet: In larger gyms one may find some body-builders who use low doses of one anabolic steroid to be just as big as the trainers stacking five to seven different anabolic steroids. Why? The answer is both diet and genetics. Going on the juice will not compensate for poor diet or a lack of testos-terone receptors. Some people are naturally muscular because they have been blessed, not with higher testosterone levels, but with more receptors that their testosterone can interact with. The latest research has been directed at manipulating endogenous hormones through diet. A simpler approach would be to increase the number of receptors. This can be done using licorice – not the candy, but the herbal root *Glycyrrhiza glabre*.

Licorice possesses compounds that resemble estrogen and can survive the digestive process to exert an estrogenic effect. Estrogen has the remarkable property of inducing the production of testosterone receptors. By including this food in your daily diet, you can experience an enhanced anabolic effect from your own natural testosterone.

Now before you start consuming vast quantities of licorice, please be warned that excessive amounts can cause hypertension and cardiac dysfunction. Check with your doctor before you add licorice to your daily diet. Consume only small amounts and do not use licorice on a daily basis for more than four weeks. If you suddenly experience headaches, nausea, weakness or irregular heartbeat, discontinue use immediately and seek medical attention.

•Soya – an anabolic steroid? Soya is that versatile plant protein which is capable of imitating hamburgers or hotdogs in various vegetarian concoctions. It is often used as the base protein for protein-powder supple-ments. What you might not know is that soya may contain a natural anabolic steroid. Allow us to explain with a slight amount of organic chemistry.

Soya contains progesterone, which survives the digestive tract and can be absorbed. Progesterone is one of the building blocks of the sex hormones. Hydroxylation of progesterone at C-17 begins the synthesis of the androgens (male hormones, all con-taining 19 carbon atoms). C-20 and C-21, which form a side chain, are cleaved off to produce androstenedione, an androgen. A further reduction of androstenedione's 17-keto group yields testosterone.

With the addition of NADPH and O2, estrogens can be formed from androgens by the removal of the C-19 angular methyl group and the formation of an aromatic A ring. Thus, estradiol is formed from testosterone and estrone is formed from androstenedione.

Edgar Fletcher

Ericca Kern and
Susan Kaminga

In other words, when you consume soya, you add progesterone to your system (in tiny amounts, admittedly). Your body will convert progesterone to an androgen or an estrogen. Since both have anabolic properties, you can't lose!

Pro champion
Flex Wheeler

SAMPLE MENUS

"I only ate the biceps."
– Jeffery Dahmer,
not really helping his case.

Successful dieting is like financial budgeting – both require planning and organization. Don't just plan what you're going to put into your meals. Write down what you're going to eat and when you're going to eat it. To get you started, we've provided a sample menu:

Breakfast:

 1 protein drink
 1 bowl porridge
 1 hard-boiled egg
 1 glass 2 % milk
 1 slice barley bread with margarine and lite peanut butter
 1 low-mg multivitamin (LMV) and low-mg multimineral (LMM)
 1 cup coffee with honey and milk
 1 iron supplement
 2 glasses of water
 1 glass barley water

Midmorning: 1 glass barley water
 1 bowl Canadian pea soup
 1 slice whole-wheat bread with butter or margarine
 1 hard-boiled egg
 1 glass 2 % milk
 1 kiwi
 1 LMV and LMM
 1 dose creatine
 1 dose lecithin
 1 dose pectin
 2 glasses water
 1 tablespoon brewer's yeast with two drops Beano

Lunch: 1 protein drink
 1 bowl beef stew
 1 slice barley bread with margarine and lite peanut butter
 1 hard-boiled egg
 1 glass 2% milk
 1 apple
 1 LMV and LMM
 1 dose creatine
 1 dose pectin
 2 glasses water

Mid-Afternoon: 1 yam ball
 1 slice oatbran bread with lite jam
 1 hard-boiled egg
 1 glass 2 % milk
 1 orange
 1 dose chromium picolinate
 1 dose creatine
 1 LMV and LMM
 2 glasses water

Supper: 1 protein drink
 1 bowl California chili
 1 slice bran bread with margarine or butter
 1 hard-boiled egg
 1 glass 2 % milk
 1 prune
 1 dose creatine
 1 LMV and LMM
 1 dose lactate
 2 glasses water

Craig Titus

Midmorning:
1 plate T & A stir fry
1 spoon MCT
1 LVM and LMM
20 mg ephedrine
200 mg caffeine
1 kiwi
3 glasses water

Lunch:
1 hard-boiled egg
1 spoon MCT
1 LVM and LMM
1 kiwi
3 glasses water

Midafternoon:
1 bowl black bean soup
1 spoon MCT
1 LVM and LMM
20 mg ephedrine
200 mg caffeine
1 peach
3 glasses water

Supper:
1 hard-boiled egg
1 spoon MCT
1 LVM and LMM
1 dose carnitine
1 pomegranate
3 glasses water

Midevening:
1 serving Jollof rice
1 spoon MCT
1 LVM and LMM
20 mg ephedrine
200 mg caffeine
1 prune
3 glasses water

Evening:
1 plate lamb curry
1 slice barley bread with margarine and lite peanut butter
1 hard-boiled egg
1 glass 2 % milk
1 LMV and LMM
1 dose carnitine
2 glasses water

Follow this type of menu while working out hard and regular, and you won't need to diet down for any contest. If you want to lose what little fat you've gained, eliminate the whole milk and bread from your menu, and remember to stop the creatine two weeks before the contest. Try this precontest sample menu:

Breakfast:
1 hard-boiled egg
1 orange
1 spoon MCT
1 LVM and LMM
1 cup tea
3 glasses water
1 dose chromium picolinate
1 iron supplement

CONCLUSION

"Praise no day until evening, no wife before her cremation, no sword till tested, no maid before marriage, no ice till crossed, no ale till it's drunk."

– Quotation from the Nordic Havamal, the ancient sayings of Odin. Apparently Odin wasn't big on small talk.

How do you know if you're eating enough? Simple – you'll lose bodyfat and gain mass. What if you find that you're hungry all the time? Then slightly increase the size of your portions. If you start gaining bodyfat, you know you're eating too much. If all this sounds vague, there is a reason. We don't know your bodyfat levels, or your workout level, or your metabolic rate. We could include impressive charts and tables, but they would only confuse, and such information is speculative at best. It is your body. Only you can know whether you're getting enough or too much to eat. In this chapter we have provided facts, guidelines and suggestions. The rest is up to you.

Dennis Newman

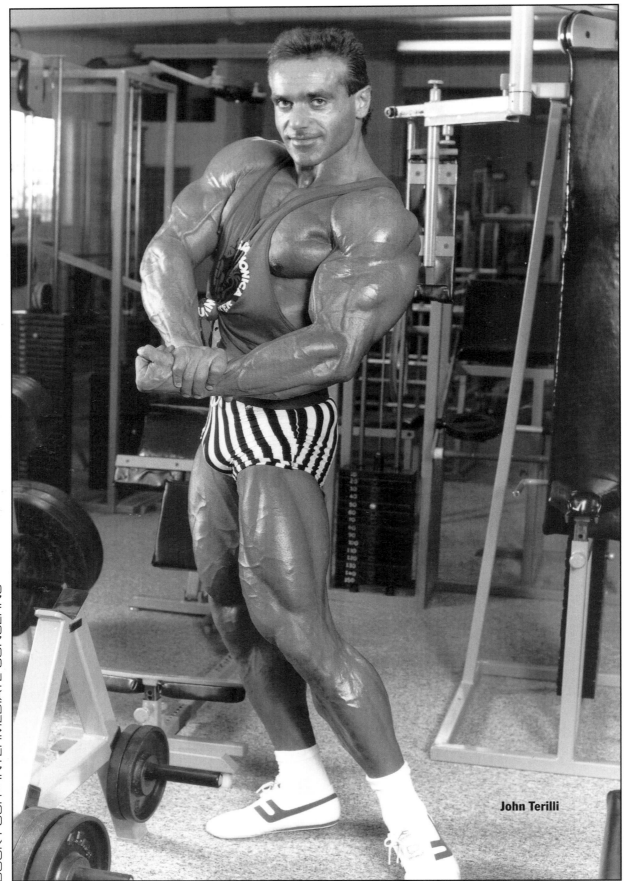

John Terilli

BOOK FOUR

Intermediate Concerns

4

SYMMETRY & PROPORTION

WHICH COMES FIRST – SIZE OR SHAPE?

"You cannot build a good physique using just a few basic movements. It is impossible. Just think for a moment. How can an individual build a balanced physique when typically his workout routine includes 15 sets of bench presses, 10 sets of squats, only 5 sets of shoulder presses, even fewer back movements, and probably no forearm, calf and abdominal work at all?"
– Vince Gironda, the "Iron Guru"

Francis Benfatto

If you're a regular reader of bodybuilding magazines, you're aware that one of the main themes consistently thrown at you is the issue of size and shape. The general feeling is that one should first concentrate on building size, and worry about shaping later on. Such statements as "You can't shape what you don't have" echo around the locker rooms of bodybuilding gyms. But is this good advice? Probably not, and here's why.

There really should not be a size/shape debate at all as the two are interrelated. You can't have one without the other. Look at it this way. If you gain a tremendous amount of mass, you automatically change the body's shape, and shape is determined by where you add the muscle mass.

Of course, you need some size in the first place for the muscles to have shape, but you don't build size first, and then shape it. The desired physique should be created by adding and redistributing muscle size over the entire body.

"Where Haney stands alone is in his quality of muscle. He had no peers in rounded, full, deep, healthy contours, with separations emphasized by the balance of all bodyparts." **– Muscle and Fitness *writer* Julian Schmidt**

When we say a bodybuilder has good lines – say, along the lines (no pun intended) of a Frank Zane, Lee Labrada or Shawn Ray – we are really commenting on how these bodybuilders have gained mass in the right places. List the top bodybuilders in history and you'll see what we mean. Arnold, Lou Ferrigno, Lee Haney, Sergio Oliva, Frank Zane, Shawn Ray, Paul Dillett, Larry Scott, Robby Robinson, and yes, even Dorian Yates, all have physiques with muscle mass distributed evenly over their bodies. Some writers have criticized Dorian for having a "blocky" physique. Nothing could be further from the truth. Take a look at those broad shoulders, perfectly balanced legs, and that wide flaring back. Maybe he doesn't have a 28-inch waist, but what's there is rock-hard muscle, slightly thicker than average size, and offset by his large torso and leg muscles. No, it's not an exaggeration to say that bodybuilding's first British-born Mr. Olympia has a well-proportioned body.

Thierry Pastel

and shape. Not only will you be as large as those who stuck to basic exercises, but you'll also have the symmetry to go with the mass.

Cory Everson and Marjo Selin

"Proportion is largely a genetic factor, but it can also be attained through training. In bodybuilding it's called balance and it can be achieved by really concentrating on the muscle you're training." — *Thierry Pastel* **IFBB Pro Bodybuilder**

If your goal is competitive bodybuilding, you should concentrate on shaping your body from the beginning. This doesn't mean using isolation exercises to shape in the traditional sense. It means putting mass where it belongs. You still use basic exercises, but your primary concern is keeping one muscle group in proportion with the next. Why invest all that time and energy, only to end up looking like a blob (with all due respect to the blobs among you). By using a bit of intelligence, you can do wonders with your physique. A couple of years down the road people will comment on both your size

How does all this affect your training? Remember, every exercise is a mass-builder. No exceptions. The old "this exercise is for shape, and that one for shaping" just doesn't hold much water. Granted some exercises are better mass-builders (bench press, squat, shoulder press), but even the so-called "shaping" movements like lateral raises and cable crossovers will develop mass, albeit over a smaller area of the body. The shape comes from where the size is laid down. Laterals for example "shape" the shoulders by building the side deltoid. Likewise, cable crossovers build up the center pectoral region. To really emphasize the point, let's look at that most basic of all chest exercises – the bench press.

One of the greatest bodybuilders of all time was (and still is) Serge Nubret. Remember Serge popping up from nowhere to place second to Arnold at the 1975 Mr. Olympia? (That's one of the subjects of the classic bodybuilding documentary, *Pumping Iron.*) Even

CHAPTER TEN – SYMMETRY AND PROPORTION

Shawn Ray

still plugging away on the flat bench, expecting some miracle in chest development. In most cases, however, it never comes.

Please don't become set in your ways and fall into this trap. It's fine to "go by the book" initially, but there comes a point in time when you have to burn the book. (Not this one we hope!) If a certain exercise is not giving the size (and consequently the shape) you desire, discard it and try something new. Frank Zane was fond of saying that he would never do an exercise if it didn't enhance and improve his physique.

The notion of training for shape applies to the entire physique. Just as an engineer needs a blueprint to build a dam, so too does a bodybuilder need a set of guidelines to develop his body. To be sure, there are a few genetically gifted individuals who end up looking great, no matter what they do, but for these people, all roads lead to Rome. For the most part, bodybuilders who train in an unguided, haphazard manner will end up looking like a house built without plans. None of the pieces fit.

Your first step on the road to proportionality should be a trip to the library or book store. Read as many books as possible on anatomy and physiology. A friend's kinesiology texts will also guide you in the right direction. There is no such thing as too much knowledge.

The next step is listening to your body. Often called instinctive training, the ability to experiment and make an unbiased self-judgment is truly a bodybuilding art form. Those who master it seldom place out of the winner's circle. At its simplest, instinctive training means not becoming a conformist. Just because the bench press works for most, that doesn't mean you have to follow it for the rest of your bodybuilding career. Sure, give it a go, but don't let peer pressure camouflage weak pec development.

TRAINING GUIDELINES FOR SHAPE AND PROPORTIONS

"My bodybuilding philosophy is that you're never good enough – you always have room to improve. Nobody is perfect. When I look in the mirror, I can see what's good about my physique, but I can see my weak points as well." **– Shawn Ray, IFBB Pro Bodybuilder**
Arnold Classic winner
1994 Mr. Olympia runner-up

As long as you keep in mind that bodybuilding is about building not the largest but the most perfect body, you're on the right track. You can't just slap on muscle aimlessly and haphazardly, and hope to end up with a proportioned body. You must focus your training on which exercises you do, why you do them, and where you're building muscle. This is the only way to shape the body as Michelangelo sculpted a statue.

Try to emphasize your slowest-growing or least-developed muscles in your training more than your fastest-growing or best-developed. As soon as you

when compared to today's massive Yates and Dillett standards, Serge's chest is considered by many to be the greatest of all time. Competitors commonly stood back in awe when first confronted by those awesome pectorals.

Perhaps even more amazing than those pecs was Serge's method for building them. To all intents and purposes, he relied solely on flat bench presses. Years of multiple sets of 20 reps produced a chest that was both huge and perfectly proportioned. Now, isn't the bench press a basic, mass-building exercise? Did you ever hear a bodybuilding "authority" call the bench press a shaping exercise? No, of course not. But it's a perfect example of what we mean when we say that size and shape are interrelated. With the right combination of genetics, leverages and style, Serge could use the bench press to target all his pectoral muscle fibers. The end result – both size and shape!

Serge is probably in the minority when it comes to chest development. Most bodybuilders find the bench press good for building the lower chest, but need other exercises to bring up the upper pecs. Unfortunately many stick with the bench press, having been warned to stay with the basics. Years down the road these people are

notice weak points (or some trustworthy individual points them out to you), give them priority in your training. Train them first when your energy reserves are highest. Don't be afraid to perform extra exercises and sets for these lagging muscles either. In order to develop a symmetrical physique, it's sometimes necessary to hold back the progress of fast-growing muscles to allow slow-growing muscles time to catch up. For example, if your upper pecs lag behind your lower pecs, reduce the number of sets of lower-chest work and increase the work for the upper chest. The same logic can be applied to the legs. You may have to do less quad work and more hamstring work. If this means eliminating squats or leg presses until your hamstrings catch up, so be it.

Closely related is the issue of muscle size. You should never try to develop all muscles to their maximum if it means ruining your proportions. Such muscles as the front delts, lower chest and upper thighs grow too fast and easily. On the other hand the calves, serratus and rear delts take their time in responding to regular exercise. As these muscles can never really be overdeveloped (did you ever hear of a bodybuilder losing because his calves were too big?), you should train them for maximum size. Don't let one muscle group overpower another muscle group.

The key to great proportions is striking a balance between your "uppers" and "lowers" – upper and lower pecs, upper and lower biceps, and upper and lower thighs. Often to achieve the desired balance, you need to emphasize one over the other. For instance, most bodybuilders find their lower chest outgrowing their upper chest. The problem usually lies in sticking with the barbell bench press for too long. To correct the situation, gradually phase out barbell bench presses and include more incline presses and flyes.

The legs often present the reverse predicament. Years of squats will build great upper thighs and hips, but there is often a lack of muscle in the lower thigh area. A greater emphasis on such exercises as hack squats and leg extensions will remedy the problem.

Another point to keep in mind is that muscles have two main parts: the large muscle belly, and the origins and insertions. Whem training biceps, standing barbell curls are great for the central muscle belly, but they do little for the lower biceps where the muscle connects to the forearm. For full, long biceps you need to include Scott (preacher) curls in your training. If you rely on basic exercises you'll end up with decent muscle mass, but the muscles often have a bunched-up appearance. For a nicer shape use isolation exercises to develop the origins and insertions.

ILLUSION – NOT JUST FOR HOUDINI

By now you should realize that muscle size, shape and symmetry are not purely the result of genetics. How you train is a major factor. Intelligent training allows you to improve your symmetry by overemphasizing weak areas, and de-emphasizing fast-growing areas. Even with limited genetic ability you can turn mediocrity into greatness. You may never carry the Olympian muscle mass of a Lee Haney or Dorian Yates, but obtaining an eyecatching physique is within your reach.

If you fall at the lower end of the bodybuilding spectrum, don't despair. Many of the sport's greatest champions were not first in line when genetics were handed out. Franco Columbu won all the major titles

Frank Zane

CHAPTER TEN – SYMMETRY AND PROPORTION

Joe Weider and Arnold congratulate a triumphant Vince Taylor.

while being less than genetically blessed. By using that great intelligence of his, Franco transformed his physique from average to Olympian standards.

Frank Zane never had the mass of a Mike Mentzer or Casey Viator, but he won three Mr. Olympia titles. In fact, to this day many consider Frank to be the epitome of bodybuilding excellence.

Today such superstars as Lee Labrada and Shawn Ray regularly beat guys outweighing them by 50 pounds. Both have taken the sport to new heights by emphasizing symmetry and proportions. Until you see them step on a scale, you'd swear they weighed much more. Their outstanding physical proportions make them appear 30 to 40 pounds heavier.

At this point you are probably saying, "What's Shawn Ray or Lee Labrada got to do with me?" Well, if you're like most bodybuilders, chances are you have weaknesses. Maybe gaining mass is a problem, or perhaps your bone structure is less than ideal. Whatever the problem, you can work around it by training intelligently, and at the center of this is the art of illusion.

For thousands of years magicians and sorcerers used illusion to make people see what wasn't there. In modern times such illusionists as David Copperfield and Doug Henning have used illusions to entertain millions. From a bodybuilding perspective illusion can be a genetically challenged competitor's best friend.

While we will be the first to admit that structural weaknesses cannot be totally hidden or altered, they can be minimized or disguised. That's what creating an illusion is all about. You attack the weakness on two fronts, building up the weak point, and reducing the nearby strong point that emphasizes the weak point.

The best example of bodybuilding illusion involves "creating" width on someone who is naturally narrow shouldered and has a wide waist and hips. Such people have little or no V-taper, and on first glance would not seem destined for the bodybuilding stage. Yet with a bit of creativity our narrow shouldered friend, can appear to be inches wider. Here's how it's done.

Using the two-front approach, we start by emphasizing the side deltoids. Add one inch to each delt and the shoulders appear two inches wider. At the same time a combination of diet and exercise reduces the waist and hips by two to three inches or more. The net result is a pair of shoulders that appear four to five inches wider.

Notice we have not changed the actual width of the shoulder structure (this is determined by genetics), but merely added the illusion of width. Besides the obvious difference in shoulder appearance, the individual's V-taper improves dramatically as well. Still think this person has no bodybuilding future? Read on.

Let's continue by transforming those legs of his.

We'll take an inch or so off the upper thighs and place it on the lower thigh (fewer squats and more leg extensions and hack squats). Short calves? No problem. Add a few extra sets of seated calf raises and we bring out the lower calf. While Mike Matarazzo probably won't lose any sleep, our previously high-calved friend now appears to have lengthened his.

Moving up the body we can make improvements all over the place. Take the chest. Nothing adds impressiveness to the pecs like dips and decline presses. By emphasizing the lower and outer pecs we can create the illusion of width. This is essential for someone with naturally narrow shoulders.

Finally we come to the arms. Put in a special order for lateral triceps development and the arms take on a totally new look. Instead of two rods hanging by the sides, they resemble two sides of ham protruding from the rolled-up sleeves.

Having made these improvements, our less-than-gifted friend now begins to look like a bodybuilder. Another year or so of adding mass might put him in his first bodybuilding contest. The odds are he'll never make it past the local or regional level, but then again, who knows? Some of the sport's greatest stars looked rather pathetic early in their careers.

EXERCISES FOR SHAPE AND ILLUSION

"I thought I was doing pretty good until one day my boss told me I had good arms and calves, but nothing in the middle to connect those two bodyparts. It didn't burst my bubble, but it let me know what I needed to do and what I had to work with. That's when I decided it was time to get serious."
– Vince Taylor
IFBB Pro Bodybuilder
Night of Champions winner

Now that you know where to build muscle and the importance of doing so, let's look at some of the best exercises for developing symmetry, proportion and illusion.

Upper Chest – The best exercises are incline presses done with barbells, dumbells and a Smith machine. Dumbell flyes also stress the upper pecs. For the illusion of width perform the barbell inclines with a wide grip. To isolate the upper pecs, pull the elbows back in line with the shoulders, and at the same time lower the shoulders and arch the rib cage. To emphasize the outer pecs while using dumbells, stop the bells about 12 to 15 inches from the top. Bringing them together stresses the inner chest.

Outer Pecs – We can hear Vince Gironda describing this one! With the elbows held wide, chin tucked on the chest, the body leaning forward, perform three-quarter reps of wide dips – that is, come up only about three-quarters of the way. When you lock the arms, the triceps and inner chest come into play. Flyes and wide-

grip variations of dumbell and barbell presses also work the outer chest.

Lateral Head of the Triceps – To hit the lateral or side head of the triceps, try triceps pushdowns with the elbows held wide. Also, turn the wrists out at the contracted position. Another good exercise is lying dumbell extensions. Instead of lowering the dumbells to the side of the head, bring them across the face. This shifts the strain from the rear to the side triceps head.

The fabulous Serge Nubret

Ron Love

Side Deltoids – By far the best way to widen the shoulders (at least in terms of muscle mass) is to put a cap of muscle on the side deltoids. It's almost universally accepted that the dumbell lateral raise is the number one exercise in this regard. You can use one arm or two arms at the same time. For variety try lateral raises with a cable. Other great side-delt exercises are medium-grip upright rows, dumbell upright rows, Nautilus-machine side laterals, and behind-the-neck presses done after side laterals.

Rear Delts – Nothing adds impressiveness to back shots like a well-developed set of rear delts. Take a look at Flex Wheeler or Paul Dillett next time they hit a rear double-biceps pose. Incredible, isn't it? And here's how to develop them.

Grab two dumbells and with your head braced on a medium-high bench or chair, perform lateral raises. Being in the bent-over position shifts most of the stress from the side to the rear deltoids. Another great exercise, if you have access, is the rear-delt machine. You can also perform rear-delt exercises on some pec-dek machines by turning around and facing the upright back rest. Your rear delts get a good blast every time you train back, especially on such movements as bent-over rows and seated cable rows.

Lower Lats – If you have the right genetics, your lats will attach way down around your waist. (Check out Franco Columbu and Dorian Yates.) Less fortunates like Paul Dillett and Gary Strydom have what are called "high lats," in which the attachments are higher up the torso. If you fall into this category, try the following exercises.

Instead of performing pulldowns with a wide, standard grip (palms facing forward), do them narrow with a reverse grip. If you have the strength, try the same variation with chins. Barbell rows can be performed in the same manner, but we don't recommend using 450 pounds like Dorian Yates. When doing one-arm dumbell rows, pull the dumbell slightly to the rear and emphasize the stretch at the bottom. Between sets try stretching the lats by grabbing an upright and pulling downward with the arms. Although it's impossible to move the lat attachment points, by thickening the lower lats you can create the illusion of such.

Lower Triceps – If the triceps are short, you can create the illusion of length by stressing the lower ends of the muscle. Lying EZ-curl bar extensions with the elbows flared wide are good for doing this. Also, one-arm cable pushdowns will hit the lower end of the rear triceps head.

Lower Biceps – The number one exercise for lower biceps is the Scott curl. You can use an EZ-curl or straight bar. For variety try the exercise with dumbells. To fill in the gap between the forearm and lower biceps, perform Zottman curls and reverse barbell curls.

Serratus – For that Robby Robinson look try dumbell pullovers across a bench. Also, narrow-grip chins and pulldowns affect the serratus to a degree. Straight-arm pushdowns will tie the serratus and lower lats together. Don't forget the diet either. A layer of fat covering your midsection will blur any serratus development.

Upper Thighs or "Thigh Rods" – These are the chords of muscle located at the top of the thighs. When properly developed, they go right in under your posing trunks. The best exercises to bring them out is the lying leg extension. If your gym doesn't have a leg-extension machine that allows lying down, try sissy squats and lunges. Practice flexing your upper thighs between sets.

Lower Thighs – The best lower-thigh exercise is the leg extension performed in a sitting position. Make sure you lock out completely, and try pausing for one or two seconds. Other great lower-thigh builders are hack squats, Smith-machine squats with the feet placed slightly back, and front squats. Try regular squats for partial reps, emphasizing the locking-out phase of the exercise.

Lower Calves – Most people with poor calves have what are called "high calves". The solution is to emphasize the lower soleus muscle. Although the seated calf-raise machine is the best, try toe presses on the leg-press machine with the legs slightly bent. If your gym doesn't have a seated-calf machine, try placing a few plates (or a heavy dumbell) on your knees and stretching the calves on a high block of wood. You can emphasize the different heads of the calf by pointing your toes in different directions.

Albert Beckles

CHAPTER TEN - SYMMETRY AND PROPORTION

CHAPTER ELEVEN

THE INTERMEDIATE

INTERMEDIATE TRAINING

"There's nothing more important in my life than the concept of improvement. Whenever I hit the gym, I do so with a predetermined purpose to improve."
– Paul Dillett, top IFBB Pro Bodybuilder

A pre-pro Paul Dillett.

Now that you have three to six months' experience, it's time to graduate to the intermediate level of bodybuilding. Initially one set per bodypart is adequate, but by now your muscles have the strength and endurance to handle more intense workouts. You'll continue to perform basic, mass-building exercises, but you'll also add some isolation exercises. A basic movement will be performed first, followed by an isolation movement.

The additional exercises require you to split your workouts into halves. The most common split is a Monday/Thursday and Tuesday/Friday schedule. Half the body will be exercised on Monday and Thursday, the other half on Tuesday and Friday. Of course, you can incorporate Wednesdays and weekend days into the routine if your weekly schedule dictates.

"For intermediate bodybuilders trying to pack it on, I would suggest three-on/two-off, or possibly an every-other-day routine could do the trick to get them growing. They should also keep the sets on the low side."
– Mike Francois
IFBB Pro Bodybuilder
Arnold Classic winner

INTERMEDIATE SPLIT ROUTINES

The four-times-a-week split is by far the most common intermediate exercise routine. Training four times a week allows three days of rest and means that each muscle is worked twice a week. Most of your muscle mass will be developed using a four-day split routine, and even if you go to a six-day-a-week split, you'll probably find that dropping back to a four-day routine produces the greatest gains.

A variation of the four-day split routine has become popular in recent years. Called the every-other-day split, the routine involves dividing the workout into two sections, and training on nonconsecutive days. The advantage of such a routine is that the body receives 48 hours of rest between workouts. For many people, working out on consecutive days is still too taxing on the recovery system – even if different muscle groups are targeted.

The following routines are divided into three- and four-day splits. If you find four days a week too draining, give the three-day routine a try.

THE ROUTINES

FOUR-DAY SPLITS...

ROUTINE 1:

MON.-THURS.

Flat bench presses – *3 x 10-12*
Incline flyes – *3 x 10-12*
Chins – *3 x 10-12*
One-arm rows – *3 x 10-12*
Standing barbell curls – *3 x 10-12*
Concentration curls – *3 x 10-12*
Crunches – *3 x 20-30*
Leg raises – *3 x 15-20*

TUES.-FRI.

Squats – *3 x 12-15*
Leg extensions – *3 x 12-15*
Lying leg curls – *3 x 15-20*
Standing calf raises – *3 x 15-20*
Seated calf raises – *3 x 15-20*
Shoulder presses – *3 x 12-15*
Lateral raises – *3 x 12-15*
Dumbell shrugs – *3 x 12-15*
Triceps pushdowns – *3 x 10-12*
One-arm cable pushdowns – *3 x 10-12*

ROUTINE 2:

MON.-THURS.

Incline bench presses – *3 x 10-12*
Flat flyes – *3 x 10-12*
Bent-over rows – *3 x 10-12*
Pulldowns – *3 x 10-12*
Preacher curls – *3 x 10-12*
Standing dumbell curls – *3 x 10-12*
Crunches – *3 x 20-30*
Lying leg raises – *3 x 15-20*

TUES.-FRI.

Leg presses – *3 x 12-15*
Hack squats – *3 x 12-15*
Lying leg curls – *3 x 15-20*
Leg-press toe raises – *3 x 15-20*
Seated calf raises – *3 x 15-20*
Front military presses – *3 x 12-15*
Bent-over lateral raises – *3 x 12-15*
Barbell shrugs – *3 x 12-15*
Lying triceps extensions – *3 x 10-12*
Dumbell extensions – *3 x 10-12*

ROUTINE 3:

MON.-THURS.

Flat bench presses – *3 x 10-12*
Incline dumbell flyes – *3 x 10-12*
Dumbell presses – *3 x 12-15*

Lateral raises – *3 x 12-15*
Upright rows – *3 x 12-15*
Upright dips – *3 x 10-12*
One-arm pushdowns – *3 x 10-12*
Crunches – *3 x 20-30*
Hanging leg raises – *3 x 15-20*

TUES.-FRI.

Squats – *3 x 12-15*
Hack squats – *3 x 12-15*
Lying leg curls – *3 x 15-20*
Standing calf raises – *3 x 15-20*
Seated calf raises – *3 x 15-20*
T-bar rows – *3 x 10-12*
Seated cable rows – *3 x 10-12*
Barbell curls – *3 x 10-12*
Alternate dumbell curls – *3 x 10-12*

ROUTINE 4:

MON.-THURS.

Dips – *3 x 10-12*
Incline dumbell presses – *3 x 10-12*
Behind-the-head shoulder presses – *3 x 12-15*
Lateral raises – *3 x 12-15*
Dumbell shrugs – *3 x 12-15*
Triceps pushdowns – *3 x 10-12*
Triceps kickbacks – *3 x 10-12*
Roman-chair situps – *3 x 20-30*
Lying leg raises – *3 x 15-20*

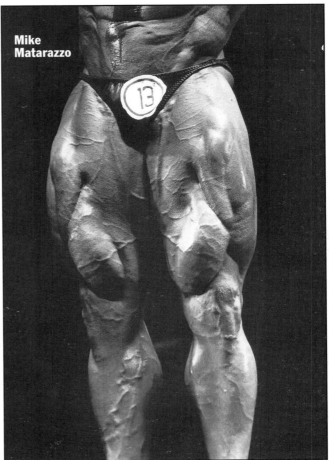

Mike Matarazzo

Johnnie Morant, Jerry Rodgers, Lee Priest and Sonny Schmidt

TUES.-FRI.
Leg presses – *3 x 12-15*
Leg extensions – *3 x 12-15*
Lying leg curls – *3 x 15-20*
Standing calf raises – *3 x 15-20*
Leg-press toe raises – *3 x 15-20*
Seated pulley rows – *3 x 10-12*
Pulldowns – *3 x 10-12*
Seated dumbell curls – *3 x 10-12*
Standing cable curls – *3 x 10-12*

ROUTINE 5:

MON.-THURS.
Squats – *3 x 12-15*
Leg extensions – *3 x 12-15*
Leg curls – *3 x 15-20*
Standing calf raises – *3 x 15-20*
Flat bench presses – *3 x 10-12*
Incline dumbell flyes – *3 x 10-12*
Lying triceps extensions – *3 x 10-12*
Reverse triceps pushdowns – *3 x 10-12*

TUES.-FRI.
Bent-over rows – *3 x 10-12*
Lat pulldowns – *3 x 10-12*
Front shoulder presses – *3 x 12-15*
Bent-over lateral raises – *3 x 12-15*
Barbell shrugs – *3 x 12-15*
Preacher curls – *3 x 10-12*
Concentration curls – *3 x 10-12*
Crunches – *3 x 20-30*
Hanging leg raises – *3 x 15-20*

ROUTINE 6:

MON.-THURS.
Leg presses – *3 x 12-15*
Hack squats – *3 x 12-15*
Leg curls – *3 x 15-20*
Donkey calf raises – *3 x 15-20*
Dips – *3 x 10-12*
Flat dumbell flyes – *3 x 10-12*
Lying triceps extensions – *3 x 10-12*
One-arm dumbell extensions – *3 x 10-12*

TUES.-FRI.
T-bar rows – *3 x 10-12*
One-arm dumbell rows – *3 x 10-12*
Dumbell presses – *3 x 12-15*
Side lateral raises – *3 x 12-15*
Upright rows – *3 x 12-15*
Alternate dumbell curls – *3 x 10-12*
One-arm preacher curls – *3 x 10-12*
Crunches – *3 x 20-30*
Lying leg raises – *3 x 15-20*

ROUTINE 7:
MON.-THURS.
Decline barbell presses – *4 x 8-10*
Flat dumbell flyes – *3 x 10-12*
Barbell rows – *4 x 8-10*
Behind-the-neck pulldowns – *3 x 8-10*
Standing barbell curls – *3 x 8-10*
Concentration curls – *3 x 10-12*
Crunches – *3 x 20-30*
Hanging leg raises – *3 x 15-20*
TUES.-FRI.
Squats – *4 x 8-10*
Sissy squats – *3 x 12-15*
Lying leg curls – *4 x 12-15*
Standing calf raises – *3 x 15-20*
Seated calf raises – *3 x 15-20*
Front military presses – *4 x 10-12*
Lateral raises – *3 x 10-12*
Smith-machine shrugs – *3 x 12-15*
Lying triceps extensions – *4 x 10-12*
Pushdowns – *3 x 10-12*

EVERY-OTHER-DAY SPLIT...

ROUTINE 1:
DAY 1
Incline barbell presses – *3 x 8-10*
Flat flyes – *3 x 10-12*
Chins – *3 x 10-12*
T-bar rows – *3 x 8-10*
Scott curls – *3 x 10-12*
Concentration curls – *3 x 10-12*
Crunches – *4 x 15-20*
DAY 2
Leg presses – *3 x 12-15*
Leg extensions – *3 x 12-15*
Leg curls – *4 x 15-20*
Barbell presses – *3 x 10-12*
Side lateral raises – *3 x 10-12*
Lying dumbell extensions – *3 x 10-12*
Triceps pushdowns – *3 x 10-12*
Standing calf raises – *3 x 15-20*
Seated calf raises – *3 x 15-20*

ROUTINE 2:
DAY 1
Dips – *3 x 8-10*
Incline dumbell presses – *3 x 10-12*

Front pulldowns – *3 x 10-12*
One-arm dumbell rows – *3 x 10-12*
Side lateral raises – *3 x 10-12*
Upright rows – *3 x 10-12*
Crunches – *4 x 15-20*
DAY 2
Squats – *3 x 12-15*
Hack squats – *3 x 12-15*
Lying leg curls – *4 x 15-20*
Leg-press toe raises – *3 x 15-20*
Seated calf raises – *3 x 15-20*
Standing barbell curls – *3 x 10-12*
One-arm Scott curls – *3 x 10-12*
Lying triceps extensions – *3 x 10-12*
Dumbell extensions – *3 x 10-12*

The late, great Andreas Munzer.

EXERCISE DESCRIPTIONS

ABDOMINALS:

Roman-Chair Situps – The Roman chair looks similar to a low incline bench, but it has a pair of foot supports at one end. Anchor your feet under the supports (they are usually round padded rollers) and lean back on the bench. Pause at the bottom and then return to the starting position. Try to use only your abdominals and not your hip flexors.

Comments – Roman-chair situps are very effective for working the lower abdominal region. By bending and locking the legs, it's virtually impossible to cheat. If there's a disadvantage to this exercise it's the stress placed on the lower back. Many bodybuilders find arching the back in this manner very painful. Our advice is to give the Roman-chair situps a try and see how they feel. If there's any back pain, substitute one of the other abdominal exercises.

Muscles Worked – Roman-chair situps primarily work the lower abdominal region, but the upper abs are also stimulated. Depending on the ratio of your leg/upper body length, you may find the hip flexors taking much of the strain. Only you can judge how effective the exercise is for the abdominals. If you feel your abs are doing very little, switch to another exercise.

LEGS:

Hack Squats – You need a special machine to do this exercise. Place your feet about shoulder width apart on the machine's incline foot board. Rest the pads on your shoulders and slowly squat down until your thighs are parallel with the floor. Using thigh power alone, return to the starting position.

Comments – There are two variations of the hack machine. One version uses shoulder pads for supporting the weight. The other relies on two handles placed low on the machine. The user must hold the handles to lift the weight. Most bodybuilders find the shoulder pad version more comfortable.

To get the full benefit of the exercise, make a slight V-shape with your feet (heels together, toes apart). As with any type of squat, don't bounce at the bottom as this places tremendous strain on the knee ligaments.

Muscles Worked – Hack squats will give your outer thighs that nice sweeping look. By bracing your back against the back board of the machine, you greatly reduce the strain often associated with regular squats.

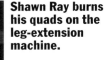

Shawn Ray burns his quads on the leg-extension machine.

Finish

Leg Extensions – If you've ever had a sports related knee injury, this exercise should be familiar. Leg extensions are among the most popular of rehabilitation exercises. Sit down on the bench and place your feet under the padded rollers. Raise the legs to a locked position and squeeze the thighs. Lower back to the starting position and repeat.

Comments – Most gyms have a machine that incorporates the leg curl and leg extension such that you can perform both exercises on the same apparatus. The same weight stack is used, but for leg extensions you sit on the end and use the lower rollers, while for leg curls you lie face down and use the upper rollers. Your gym, however, may have the exercises on separate machines. Many bodybuilders lie on their backs when doing leg extensions. You can't use the same amount of weight, but this disadvantage is made up for by working the thighs through a greater range of movement.

Resist the tendency to drop the weight into the starting position. As with other exercises, 50 percent of the movement is the negative (lowering) phase of the exercise. For variety you can perform extensions one leg at a time.

Muscles Worked – Extensions are great for building the thigh muscles around the knee area. They're also a very effective physiotherapy exercise. Following knee surgery, most athletes are limited in the amount of direct leg exercise they can perform. Leg extensions are great for strengthening not only the lower thigh but also the associated tendons and ligaments.

Sissy Squats – Depending on your strength levels you may need to hold on to a weight during this exercise. Place your feet in a V position and, leaning back, squat down until your thighs are at least parallel with the floor. If you have trouble keeping your balance, grasp a stationary upright for support. When you can do 15 to 20 reps with relative ease, hold a weight with your free hand against the chest.

Comments – You can do this exercise with a dumbell or weight plate held to the chest. Most bodybuilders find the plate most convenient, but it's personal preference. Don't get carried away with the amount of the weight. Save the heavy poundages for your regular squats and leg presses.

Muscles Worked – Sissy squats are similar to hack squats in that they will add a great sweep to your outer thighs. Although more isolated than regular squats, sissy squats involve the glutes to some degree.

Donkey Calf Raises – With your toes resting on a block of wood (at least four inches thick is recommended) bend over at the waist and have a willing training partner sit on your lower back. Flex up and down on your toes, going for the maximum stretch. If you find one rider too light, try to fit a second on your back.

Comments – The bashful might want to avoid this exercise. Also, many upper-class gyms (health spas) advise you not to do them. You see, the general public is intimidated by the sight of people riding on top of each other, especially if they are going up and down!

Aaron Baker performs donkey calf raises on a machine.
Finish

Start

Nevertheless, donkey calf raises are considered by many to be the best calf exercise. Arnold, Larry Scott, Franco Columbu and Frank Zane made extensive use of donkey raises. The exercise is seen less frequently in gyms today. No doubt the presence of fancy new equipment and increased numbers of general fitness trainers have contributed to their decline. Still, if you check out Gold's or World Gyms in California, you will see numerous bodybuilders burning their calves with donkey raises. And one look at their lower legs confirms the effectiveness of the exercise.

Muscles Worked – Donkey calf raises work the whole calf region. If you keep the legs completely locked, most of the work is done by the upper calf. Bend the legs slightly and the lower calves take most of the strain. For variety you might want to include both methods in your training. Remember, when doing the bent-leg variety, you will need to use less weight as the lower calf cannot handle the same load as the upper calf.

Seated Calf Raises – A special machine is required for this exercise. Sit down and place the knee pads on your legs. With your toes on the foot rest, stretch up and down as far as you can.

Comments – Because it works the lower calf, you will need to use less weight. Go for at least 20 reps and try to feel every one of them. No bouncing the weight on your legs. Even though the supports are padded, improper style can injure your knees.

Muscles Worked – Since the legs are bent, most of the stress is placed on the lower calf (soleus), but there is some secondary upper-calf involvement.

Aaron Baker on the seated calf raise machine. Start

Finish

CHEST:

Flat Flyes – Start this exercise in the same position as dumbell presses. Instead of having the dumbells pointing end to end, rotate your hands until the palms are facing and the dumbells are parallel with your body. Keeping your elbows slightly bent, lower the dumbells to either side in a wide arc as far as you can, for a full stretch. Pause at the bottom, and then squeeze the dumbells up and together over the center of the chest.

Comments – Flyes are more of a stretching exercise than a mass-building movement. Still with practice you will eventually be using considerable weight. Always lower the dumbells in a controlled manner, no matter what the poundage. Drop them too fast and you'll rip the pec-delt tie-in. Treatment for such an injury is surgery and many months of rehabilitation.

Muscles Worked – Flyes work the whole chest region. Fully stretching at the bottom works the outer chest region, and squeezing together at the top develops the inner chest. This squeezing gives your chest that clean line up the middle. As there will be some pec-delt tie-in strain, be careful at the bottom of the movement.

Incline Flyes – This is the same exercise as the previous, but you use an incline bench. Once again go for a full, slow stretch at the bottom.

Comments – As with incline dumbell presses, the incline bench dictates lifting the dumbells higher. You may need a partner to hoist them into position. It's probably a good idea to have the dumbells passed to you whether you can lift them or not. Jerking heavy dumbells from the floor puts a great deal of stress on the biceps and lower back. Better to be safe than macho.

Muscles Worked – Incline flyes put most of the stress on the upper pectorals. They also strongly affect your chest/shoulder tie-ins. Once again, by squeezing the dumbells together at the top, you can work the inner chest.

Decline Barbell Presses –

Position a decline bench (the Roman chair is often used) so that the bar can be brought down to the lower chest. The reps are performed in the same manner as flat and incline bench presses.

Comments – Many gyms have decline benches with the bar supports welded to the back of the bench. If the angle of the bench is adjustable, vary it to get the maximum feel in your pectoral muscles. You can substitute dumbells in place of the barbell.

Muscles Worked – Decline presses are similar to dips in that they work the lower, outer chest region. They are a good substitute if you find your front delts taking most of the strain during flat bench presses.

BACK AND SHOULDERS:

Barbell Shrugs – Hold a barbell with a shoulder-width grip. Keeping your arms locked, raise the bar, trying to touch the shoulders to your ears. Squeeze at the top of the movement, and then lower the bar.

Comments – There are a number of variations to this exercise. Instead of raising and lowering the bar in a straight line, you can rotate it in a circular pattern. You're not limited to using a barbell for the exercise. Many bodybuilders find the Smith machine is more comfortable. Instead of taking the bar from the floor, you can have it set at any desired height, making the exercise easier on your lower back. The Universal bench press can also be used for shrugs. In fact more serious bodybuilders use the machine for shrugs than for bench

Start

Midpoint

Finish

Craig Titus puts all of his energy into a set of incline flyes.

Start

Dumbell shrugs as performed by Darin Lannaghan.
Finish

presses! Try to keep the arms, legs and back straight throughout the movement. And watch the lower back!

Muscles Worked – Barbell shrugs are by far the best trapezius-builder. Make them a regular part of your training and you will have traps that give the Incredible Hulk pose! Besides the traps, your forearms, hamstrings, lower back, and rear delts will be indirectly stimulated.

Dumbell Shrugs – This is simply a variation of barbell shrugs. Hold the dumbells about shoulder width apart and perform the movement in a similar manner to the barbell variety.

Comments – You can hold the dumbells parallel or pointed end to end. The choice is yours. If you hold them end to end, watch you don't bang them off your legs. Try keeping them in front of the body and sliding them up the front of the thighs.

Muscles Worked – Dumbell shrugs work the same muscles as shrugs done with a barbell. Since you will be using less weight (you can generally lift more weight with one barbell than two dumbells), the lower back will not have the same strain placed on it. We strongly recommend using dumbells if you have a pre-existing back problem.

Upright Rows – Start the exercise by holding a barbell at arms' length. Using a narrow grip (about three to five inches), lift the bar up the front of the body, keeping the elbows flared to the sides. Squeeze the traps together at the top, and then lower into the starting position.

Comments – Which muscles are worked depends on the grip used. Generally, any hand spacing of five inches or less puts most of the stress on the traps. Widen the grip and the side deltoids come into play. In the routines presented above we are suggesting the exercise as a trap-builder, but you can easily substitute it for one of the delt exercises. Just remember to keep the grip wide when doing so.

If you have weak or injured wrists, you might want to think twice about performing this exercise. Upright rows place tremendous stress on the forearms and wrists. If you experience minor pain when doing the exercise, try wrapping the wrists with support bandages. This should enable you to complete your sets in comfort. Of course you're the only one who can determine if the "pain" is just a nuisance or representative of something more serious. If in doubt skip the exercise.

As with barbell curls, upright rows give you the option of adding a few cheat reps at the end of the set. Limit such cheat reps to one or two. Don't make the mistake of cheating from rep one.

Muscles Worked – With a narrow grip upright rows primarily work the traps with some secondary deltoid stimulation. A wide grip (six inches or more) will shift the strain to the side delts, causing the traps to play a secondary role. The forearms are worked no matter what grip you use.

Lateral Raises – This exercise can be performed seated or standing. With the elbows slightly bent, raise two dumbells to the sides of the body. As you raise them, gradually rotate the wrists so that the little finger is highest. Many bodybuilding authorities, including Robert Kennedy, liken the wrist action to pouring a jug of water.

Comments – You can do the exercise with the arms locked straight, but most bodybuilders find it more effective to bend the arms slightly and use more weight. Lateral raises can be done to the front, side or rear (explained in detail later). Instead of using dumbells, you can substitute a cable. Either version may be performed with one or two arms at a time.

Muscles Worked – You can use lateral raises to work any head of the deltoid muscle. Most intermediate bodybuilders use them for the side delts, as the front delts receive ample stimulation from various pressing movements. Side laterals will give your delts that half-melon look. There's not much you can do to widen the clavicles, but you can increase your shoulder width by adding inches to the side delts.

Bent-Over Laterals – This is the bent-over version of regular side laterals. By bending over, you shift the stress from side to rear delts. You can do the exercise free standing, seated or with your head braced on a high bench. This last position is for those with lower-back problems or people who have a tendency to swing the weight up.

Comments – Concentrate on lifting the dumbells with your rear delts, not your traps and lats. For variation try using a set of cables. You will have to hold the cable handles with your opposite hands, so the cables form an X in front of you. This exercise is popular with bodybuilders in the months leading up to a contest.

Muscles Worked – When performed properly, bent-over laterals work mainly the rear deltoids. There is,

Mike Christian

however, secondary triceps, trap and lat stimulation. If you're not sure what a fully developed rear deltoid looks like, take a look at a recent picture of Paul Dillett. His rear delts contain as much muscle mass as most bodybuilders' whole deltoid region!

Smith-Machine Shrugs – With a shoulder-width grip lift the bar from the supports. Keeping your arms straight, lower the bar as far as the traps will allow. Shrug your shoulders as high as you can, trying to touch your deltoids to your ears. Pause, and then lower to the starting position.

Comments – Smith-machine shrugs are great for those with lower-back problems. Unlike a standard barbell which has to be taken from the floor, the Smith machine allows you to start and finish the exercise at waist level.

Muscles Worked – As with barbell and dumbell shrugs, this exercise targets the trapezius muscles. It also places secondary stress on the delts and forearms.

TRICEPS:

Triceps Kickbacks – Holding a dumbell, and with your body braced on a bench, bend over and set your upper arm parallel with the floor. Extend the lower arm back until it's in the locked position – i.e. your whole arm is now parallel with the floor. Pause and squeeze at full extension, and then lower back to the starting position.

Comments – Resist the urge to swing the dumbell up using body momentum. True, you can use more weight, but the exercise won't give the same triceps development. Keep the upper arm locked against the side of the body. As with bent-over laterals, if you have trouble keeping stationary, or have a weak lower back,

place your free hand on a bench or other such support.

Muscles Worked – Triceps kickbacks are great for giving the triceps that horseshoe look. They are especially useful for developing the long rear head of the triceps. Competitive bodybuilders favor them during the precontest months.

Reverse Pushdowns – This exercise is performed in the same manner as regular pushdowns, the main difference being that you hold the bar with your palms up. Keep your elbows locked against your sides and extend the bar downward. Flex the triceps at the bottom, and then return to the starting position.

Comments – You won't be able to use as much weight in this version of pushdowns, so don't become alarmed if you have to drop it 20 or 30 pounds. Reverse pushdowns are great for finishing the triceps off after a basic movement like lying triceps extensions or dips. Concentrate more on the feel than the weight used.

Muscles Worked – This is another great movement for the long rear head of the triceps. A couple of sets and you will feel your triceps burning from elbow to armpit!

One-Arm Cable Pushdowns – With your body in the standing, upright position, grasp one of the upper cable handles. Push the handle down, lock out the arm at the bottom, and then return to the starting position.

Comments – You can do this exercise either palm up or palm down. You might want to reach across with your free hand and grab your shoulder on the same side that is being exercised. Besides the bracing effect, you have your free hand in a position to spot yourself on the last couple of reps. As with the previously described

Finish

Darin Lannaghan pumps up his triceps with kickbacks.
Start

reverse pushdowns, go more for the burn than for huge poundages.

Muscles Worked – You'll find one-arm cable pushdowns great for finishing the triceps. A palms-up grip will place most of the strain on the rear triceps, whereas a palms-down grip will hit more of the side head.

BICEPS:

Concentration Curls – Sit on the end of a bench and pick up a dumbell. With your elbow resting on your inner thigh, lower the dumbell, and then curl it back up. Perform one set, and switch arms.

Comments – Most bodybuilders perform concentration curls in the seated position. A few (including Arnold Schwarzenegger) like to do the movement in the standing, bent-over position. Instead of bracing the elbow against the thigh, it's held down and away from the body. Keep the shoulder on the exercising side lower than the free side. Resist the urge to swing – use only biceps power. As with all dumbell curls, you may want to supinate the hands when performing the exercise.

Muscles Worked – Concentration curls are generally considered to be more of a shaping and peaking exercise than a mass-builder. Keep in mind that peak and

Edgar Fletcher squeezes his biceps hard on concentration curls.

Finish

Start

shape are primarily due to genetics. Unless you have the genetics, you will never develop biceps peaks like Robby Robinson's. Still, you'll never know unless you try, and this is where concentration curls come in. The exercise cannot change your genetics, but it can maximize whatever potential you might have.

One-Arm Preacher Curls – Instead of using a barbell, try preacher curls with a single dumbell. Remember to lower slowly and not bounce the weight at the bottom.

Comments – By using a dumbell you can adjust your upper body to take some of the stress off the biceps tendon. Many bodybuilders find preachers hard on the forearms and elbows. Using a dumbell allows you more flexibility than is possible with a rigid barbell. A barbell puts the force at 90 degrees to the upper body. A dumbell allows you to vary this angle, thus placing less stress on the forearms and elbows.

Muscles Worked – Dumbell preacher curls place most of the stress on the lower biceps. They treat your forearms and elbows with more kindness than the barbell version!

Finish

warmup exercise. Many body-builders (including Franco Columbu) suggest starting your biceps workout with cables or dumbells. This practice warms up the area and doesn't put the same stress on the elbows and forearms that barbell curls do.

Muscles Worked – Standing cable curls are another so-called peaking and shaping exercise. They work the whole biceps region, and if performed one arm at a time, allow you to really concentrate. For a great pump try finishing your biceps workout with a couple of high-rep (15 to 20) sets of cable curls.

Big Jim Quinn performs one-arm preacher curls.

Start

Standing Cable Curls – For variety try standing biceps curls with a set of cables. Whether you work one arm or both at the same time is up to you. If doing them one arm at a time, hold the machine with your free hand for support. It's extremely difficult to stay stationary when exercising one side of the body.

Comments – As with most cable exercises, go for the feel rather than the amount of weight. Cable curls are an excellent way to finish off the biceps after a basic movement such as standing barbell curls. Of course, you can take the opposite approach and use them as a

Craig Titus

CHAPTER TWELVE

WHAT YOU DON'T KNOW

The dynamic Vince Taylor

Before looking at some common bodybuilding injuries and their prevention or treatment, a word of caution is needed. The purpose of this chapter is not to train the reader to be a physical therapist. Nor would it be possible to outline all the injuries that athletes may receive during their lives. What we'll attempt is to give the reader a general feeling for sports injuries, and suggest some reasons for their causes and possible prevention.

We stress that this is not a self-diagnostic manual. At the slightest sign or indication of a serious injury the athlete should immediately stop training and see a physician.

SORENESS VERSUS INJURY

Ask any bodybuilder how he knows that he's had a good workout. Invariably he'll give you a one-word answer – soreness! Any time you place the muscles under a greater-than-normal load, whether by increasing intensity, resistance or duration, the outcome is muscle soreness. Even though soreness is a form of mild pain, bodybuilders welcome it. In fact they feel they've wasted a workout if some state of soreness doesn't exist the next day!

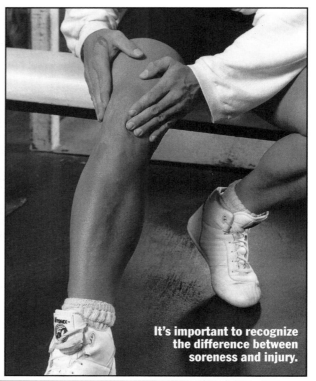

It's important to recognize the difference between soreness and injury.

INJURIES:

"I was pumping up before I went onstage to do my routine and I grabbed a pair of 7-1/2-pound dumbells for some last-minute curls before I went on. But when I did the curl with my left arm, I heard what sounded like a wet rag tearing. The only problem was I felt it too."
– Vince Taylor, top IFBB Pro Bodybuilder

Muscle soreness does concern injury, but the "damage" is at the microscopic level; it's usually not severe enough to warrant therapeutic intervention. Put another way, if athletes visited the therapist every time their muscles got sore, clinics would replace gyms as the main focal point of an athlete's day.

The best bodybuilders, those who are in tune with their bodies, can differentiate between muscle soreness that is symptomatic of a good workout, and soreness that suggests overwork or injury. If postworkout soreness is severe, this pain should warn you that you're subjecting your body to levels of intensity that are too much or too soon after the previous workout. Severe soreness is an indication that you need to take it a little easier in the gym or pace yourself more intelligently in the future.

MUSCLE SORENESS

By now you've probably noticed that when you're performing an intense set, the muscle being exercised begins to burn after the first few reps. The burning sensation is caused by a build-up of metabolic byproducts including lactic acid. If they reach high

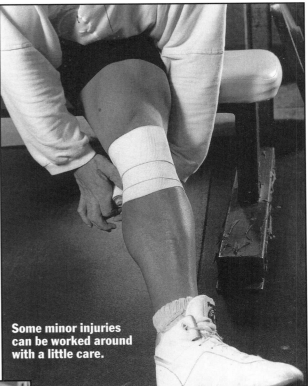

Some minor injuries can be worked around with a little care.

enough levels, muscle functioning may be impeded.

Where did this lactic acid come from? The body's chief energy source is called ATP (adenosine triphosphate). The body can produce ATP through either of two pathways. One uses oxygen and is called the aerobic pathway. The other functions without oxygen and is called the anaerobic pathway.

The aerobic pathway is the source of energy for low-intensity, long-duration exercise such as marathon running. Short-duration, high-intensity exercise such as bodybuilding relies mostly on the anaerobic pathway. One of its byproducts is lactic acid, which may be utilized as an energy source in the future. Unfortunately high concentrations may interfere with many of the body's metabolic functions. Increased acidity can slow down enzymes which are needed for ATP production. In addition, high muscle acidity prevents utilization of glycogen, a primary starting material for ATP production. Finally, the build up of lactic acid produces the muscle soreness that you experience following a workout.

The symptoms of soreness usually appear about 12 hours after the workout, and become more intense the next day. Within a few days the symptoms disappear.

Generally you'll get over simple soreness in a few days. Light, high-rep exercise that gets the blood flowing to the area, stretching, massage or use of a sauna all can speed up the removal of muscle soreness. If soreness persists and the

Meryl Ertunc

COMMON CAUSES OF INJURIES
LACK OF CONCENTRATION

"When I walk through the gym door, I start right in on my workout. I speak to nobody except my trainer and within 45 minutes I'm finished my chest. My sole objective is to focus on the workout and complete it effectively."

– Meryl Ertunc, lightweight national champion

In simple terms, concentration means keeping your mind on your muscles and what they are doing during a set. It also means concentrating on proper exercise form and feeling the muscle work as you do a set instead of just hoisting a weight and then letting it drop.

From novice to competitive bodybuilder the key to injury prevention is mental focus. When you enter the gym try to leave your outside daily life behind. For one or two hours focus on one task – your training. Heavy exercises such as squats, deadlifts and bench presses require total diligence in their execution. Lose this focus and sooner or later an injury will come knocking at your door.

Besides the pressures of daily life, your routine itself may lead to loss of focus. Most bodybuilders tend to follow the same routine day in and day out. On one hand it makes sense to execute programs that work. On the other hand it may lead to boredom. When you find yourself just going through the motions, it may be time for changes. Besides making your training more interesting, you'll also be shocking the muscles into new growth. Finally, performing different exercises leads to a new level of concentration.

OVERTRAINING

"Compared to the secure ball-and-socket joint of the hip, the more shallow shoulder joint is somewhat fragile, relying as it does on ligament and muscle strength for much of its stability. This means that hard-training bodybuilders who blitz their delts regularly tend to incur a lot of shoulder injuries. My solution was always to split my shoulder routine so as not to give too much trauma of exercise stress to the shoulder in any one day." **– Tom Platz, former IFBB Pro Bodybuilder**

As this topic is so important, we shall be discussing it in more detail later in the book. Suffice it to say that a body that is in a continuous state of overtraining is more susceptible to injuries than one in which full recovery has taken place after each workout. In short, overtraining is overtaxing the body to the point that it never fully recovers between workouts. In case you didn't know, muscles don't grow in the gym, but in the hours and days following exercise. Although the time varies, on average a period of 48 to 72 hours is required for a muscle to recover from stressful exercise. Recent evidence suggests that full recovery may take even longer. There is no way you can perform 10 to 15 high-

muscle in question cannot be exercised without intense pain, or things just don't "feel right," the logical conclusion would be that you have injured the affected area.

There is a host of reasons for bodybuilding injuries. The most common are lack of concentration when working out, overtraining, poor exercise technique, too much weight, inadequate warming up, lack of stretching, exercise type, muscle imbalance, reaction to biochemicals and even poor nutrition. Any or all of these circumstances can cause a severe injury. For a better understanding let's take a look at each in more detail.

The legendary Tom Platz

POOR EXERCISE TECHNIQUE

"Training is not just about heavy weights. It's also about really clean form, full mental involvement, and taking the muscle to the point of failure. I don't believe in going beyond failure because that just overstresses the body and makes recovery that much harder. It's like hammering a nail into wood, a comparison you may have heard me use before. If you hit the nail once and get it all the way in, why hit it any more? You'll just tear up the wood."
– Dorian Yates, Five-time Mr. Olympia

What is the most common reason for injuries? Contrary to most people's beliefs, it's neither the amount of weight being used nor the speed at which the exercise is being performed. It's the technique or form that has the greatest impact on potential injuries. Granted a bodybuilder using heavy weights would probably suffer greater damage if an injury were to occur, but as long as good form is followed, that individual is at no greater risk than the person using lighter poundages.

Sudden starts or stops place tremendous strain on the athlete's musculoskeletal system. This is why most chest injuries occur at the bottom of the movement, at the point where the

Paul Dillett, Dorian Yates and Kevin Levrone

intensity sets for your chest on Monday, and expect it to have recovered by Wednesday. Unfortunately many bodybuilders ignore the body's warning signs (chronic fatigue, loss of strength and size, decreased motivation levels) and continue to train this way. Eventually they're in such a state of overtraining that one injury after another occurs.

Often the key to injury prevention is to simply listen to what the body is saying. It makes far more sense to voluntarily take a week off than to be laid up for six months with a torn muscle.

Thierry Pastel

(this is often the only exercise they perform!) dropping the bar to their chest as fast as gravity can carry it, then bouncing it back up. Such technique places tremendous stress on the pec-delt tie-in (the area where the chest muscles and shoulder muscles meet). For the sake of a few extra pounds the trainer is not only defeating the purpose of the exercise, but also greatly increasing the risk of damage. This area is very susceptible to injury in the form of muscle tears. As well, the pectoral tendons may tear away from where they insert in the upper arms. The injury sounds gruesome, feels worse, and worst of all, requires surgery and rehabilitation just to get full arm movement back.

Not to be biased against the bench press, the squat can provide some unique entertainment too. As with bench pressing, most injuries occur at the bottom of the movement, as the direction of movement reverses. It's a wonder that more kneecaps are not removed from gym walls these days. Proper form means squatting in a slow and controlled manner, bending the knees and descending to the floor, not dropping straight down and then bouncing back up. Otherwise you lose about 50 percent of the benefit of the exercise, and more important, place tremendous forces on the supporting structures of the legs and back.

Another area that gets abused by bodybuilders is the biceps and associated tendons. The arms are considered the universal glamour muscle (one other *muscle* has more recognition, but it would be inappropriate to describe it here!) and it's safe to say that every serious bodybuilder wants bigger arms. Unfortunately in their quest for Schwarzenegger-sized biceps, many bodybuilders sacrifice style for weight. The preacher curl gets loaded to capacity, and sooner or later one of two accidents will occur. At the very least, you will tear one of the biceps heads. Besides being painful, full recovery takes several months, necessitating a drastic alteration in your training schedule.

Often the injury sustained is more serious and requires surgery. The biceps is attached to one of the forearm bones by a tendon. If excessive force is placed on this area, the biceps may tear away from the tendon. More often than not the biceps/tendon structure tears away from the forearm bone. In both cases surgery is required for recovery. Injuries of this type don't heal themselves. The two parts don't magically reattach. Some of bodybuilding's greatest stars have suffered biceps/tendon tears. Among them are Lou Ferrigno, Dorian Yates and Tom Platz.

The best cure is prevention. Perform the exercise in a controlled manner, and don't get carried away with the weight you are using. Give it time. Before long you will be using large poundages, and in much better style.

bar is changing direction and exploding off the chest. In fact bouncing or jerking the bar up puts more stress on the chest muscles than if the person were to place more weight on the bar and do the exercise in a controlled manner. Yet go into any gym and observe bench-press technique. You will see bench pressers

TOO MUCH WEIGHT

Closely associated with exercise technique is the amount of weight being used. In fact both are often interrelated. Too much weight leads to improper form, which leads to injuries. If you can't do the desired number of reps in good style, the weight is too heavy. You want to control the weight, not have it control you! Even when performing some of the advanced training exercises (forced reps, rest pause, etc.), you still use good form.

No doubt you have read in *MuscleMag* how So-and-So uses 200 pounds in the preacher curl or 500 pounds in the bench press. Rest assured that these guys didn't start their bodybuilding careers using such poundages. They started like everyone else, using enough weight to stimulate the muscle, but not enough to sacrifice good form. You are strongly advised to do the same.

THE LACK OF A PROPER WARMUP

There are three types of warmups: cardiovascular, general whole-body and a warmup for the muscle you are about to train. At the very least, you must do the third to prevent injuries. If time permits do all three. Not only will the likelihood of injury be reduced, but your whole system will also be prepared to work at its most efficient.

When starting your workout, it's a good idea to get the blood moving, heartbeat elevated slightly, and muscles warmed up. The increased circulation helps get the blood to the muscles more quickly and an elevated heart rate means that the body is better prepared for the upcoming exercises.

Many bodybuilders like to do 5 to 10 minutes on the stationary bike before beginning their workout. Others like to do some general conditioning exercises (jumping jacks, pushups, situps, etc.) before beginning. Whatever your preference, try not to enter the gym cold and go straight to the barbell. If at all possible, ease into your exercise routine.

Besides the heart and cardiovascular system the muscles need to be prepared for your workout. A cold muscle is less flexible than a warm one, and this lack of flexibility may lead to a muscle tear. If it has been properly warmed up, however, the muscle becomes more pliable and flexible. Instead of tearing, it will stretch.

No matter what the exercise, you don't begin with your maximum weight. Start with a light weight and do 15 or 20 reps. Then take a medium weight and do a moderate rep set (12 to 15 reps). Do not attempt your heavy weight until at least the third set. Even this may be too soon. If for example you are working up to 300 pounds in the bench press, you might want to do 4 or 5 intermediate warmup sets. Don't use the full weight from set one. Your bodybuilding career could end in a matter of seconds.

EXERCISE TYPES

No matter how carefully you warm up and perform the exercises, sooner or later you will notice that there are exercises that treat you with hostility. Among these are squats, deadlifts, preacher curls and flyes.

Some bodybuilders find that squats place unwanted stress on the lower back and knees. Even with low weight and good form the exercise still hurts. If this happens to you, avoid the exercise. True, squats are probably the best exercise for thigh development. But they are not worth destroying your lower back over, especially when a combination of other exercises, such as leg presses and extensions, can get the job done.

Laura Creavalle

Preacher curls are another potentially problematic exercise. This movement puts untold stress on the lower biceps/tendon region. Even with proper form and good technique you may find the movement uncomfortable, if not downright painful. Again, give up performing the exercise, as a torn biceps is much more painful. Stick to standing barbell curls, or substitute dumbells.

Everyone's physiology is unique. Just because a certain exercise is considered "the best" for a particular muscle group doesn't necessarily mean it's for you. If any of the exercises that we have outlined in this book is painful to perform, substitute another in its place. Nothing is gospel in the bodybuilding world. If, however, all the exercises for a given muscle are painful, see your physician. This is an indication of an underlying muscle injury which must be treated.

Before we leave this section, we should mention a few exercises that ought never to be performed, period! Avoid the following like the plague:

1. Seated twists
2. Bench squats
3. Weighted side bends
4. Headstands
5. Hyperextensions
   (with the emphasis on the prefix "hyper")

Most of these exercises should be familiar to you. As an example of the potential risks, twists are among the most common warmup exercises performed, yet most people don't realize that the human spine was not designed to move that way. Twists place an incredible amount of strain on the lower spine in the form of torsion. Such a movement can lead to damage of the spinal nerves and also cartilage and ligaments.

Without going into detail on the other four, suffice it to say all place improper stress on the spinal column, particularly the lower spine. Not only are the exercises of little bodybuilding benefit, but they are utterly dangerous. Our advice is to avoid these exercises completely.

POOR EQUIPMENT

While most of the more popular bodybuilding manufacturers produce equipment that's well designed, many gyms rely on homemade jobs. The gym owner may obtain the services of a welder, who constructs the various machines by following a few simple sketches. For the simpler cable machines this approach poses little risk, but the more complex machines are another story. The machines produced by the major manufacturers (Nautilus, Polaris, Universal) have the benefit of being designed by kinesiologists. (Kinesiology is the study of how the body moves.) You can't just slap a few iron bars together and call it a leg press. It must respect the biomechanical movement of the legs. Many homemade machines don't take this factor into account. In fact, besides not working the muscle they were designed to, they may subject it to unwanted stress.

Porter Cottrell,
Vince Taylor,
Sonny Schmidt,
Paul Dillett and
Chris Cormier

A second problem with makeshift machines is their construction. Most welders (unless they happen to work out themselves) have no idea of the amount of weight that their machine will have to support. They construct it for the average person. An average person will use a few hundred pounds on a leg press. An intermediate or advanced bodybuilder will pile on 500 to 1000 pounds. This heavy weight is not taken into account when the apparatus is welded together. The bottom line is, be wary of homemade exercise equipment. If unsure of its safety, *avoid it!*

Homemade equipment does not have a monopoly on poor design. Many of the older machines (1950s and 1960s era) were designed when sports kinesiology was in its infancy. The result was an apparatus that didn't mimic the movements of the human body. The older versions of the Universal leg press are a good example. Many bodybuilders find these machines put severe stress on the knee region. Don't misinterpret us. Many a great set of thighs were built on these machines, but at the same time users frequently developed knee problems.

Another problem with older machines is that they were designed with an average-size person in mind. They don't accommodate larger (6'4"-240+ pounds) or smaller (4'10"-120 pounds) bodybuilders. For example, Lou Ferrigno, Paul Dillett and Ralph Moeller would have trouble using many of the older pec-deks. The newer machines take this variance of body size into account and are adjustable. Still you may find that a particular piece of equipment doesn't suit your body type. If this happens, simply substitute another in its place.

MUSCLE IMBALANCE

The exercise programs in this book have been chosen to train the body evenly – that's to say, to keep the muscles in proportion and balance. This is what nature intended. Unfortunately many bodybuilders focus only on the most visible muscles (i.e. the chest and biceps). In doing so they neglect other such important muscles as the back and triceps. Besides the obvious outcome of distorted proportions, the more serious condition of a muscle imbalance is set up. As we explained earlier, the body's muscles don't work individually, but in groups. Focusing on a select few produces dangerous imbalances. By concentrating too much on the chest, the back muscles (which are used to stabilize the body during various chest movements) become the weak link. The same situation applies to the biceps-triceps complex. Neglecting one or the other will only lead to problems down the road. Trust us. Whether you follow the programs outlined in this book or design your own (as most intermediate and advanced bodybuilders ultimately will), make sure you work the body evenly. Don't go into the gym and perform the "Friday night pump-up" (chest and biceps)! By following a balanced

Lee Priest

training routine, you will produce a more complete physique and the risk of injury will be greatly reduced.

REACTION TO BIOCHEMICALS

Many bodybuilders experience chronic joint pain. Some cartilage injuries heal quickly while others do not. When deterioration reaches the point that full recovery never takes place, osteoarthritis sets in. Arthritis is among the most prevalent yet least understood of medical conditions. A number of theories have been put forward to explain why the condition develops in some, but not in others. Three of the most studied are: reaction to industrial pollutants, food allergies, and high blood acidic levels. Let's look at these in more detail.

One of the unfortunate byproducts of western industrial societies is pollution. A main constituent of pollution is heavy metal toxins. Such contaminants as mercury and lead are pumped into the air and also into water, where they concentrate in seafood. As food works its way up the food chain, the concentration of these metals rises. Eventually they reach the top of the food chain – humans. Because these toxins are not

Vince Taylor graciously accepts fifth place at the 1995 Mr. Olympia.

easily removed by the body, many people develop severe reactions, which often manifest themselves in the form of osteoarthritis. Thus the extreme pain experienced by many bodybuilders may be environmental in nature and not training related.

Much medical and supplement literature states that food allergies may be at the root of arthritis. The theory is that injured cartilage tissue has a reduced resistance to allergens. By definition, an allergen is any substance that causes the body's immune system to respond. In most cases this response is vital to survival, as the allergen is dangerous to the body. In a few cases, however, the allergen is inert – that is, it has no detrimental effect on the body's functioning (e.g. dust, pollen). Often the substance is vital to life. Many people are allergic to milk, shellfish and refined sugar. The body's immune system erroneously thinks these substances are harmful, and initiates defense procedures. Some bodybuilders who have osteoarthritis experience an increase in pain immediately after consuming certain foods. Others have a marked inflammatory response after ingesting supplements.

A third explanation for arthritic pain may lie with blood acid levels. Many bodybuilders who consume mega doses (grams rather than milligrams) of vitamin C experience intense joint pain. When vitamin C dos-

ages are reduced, pain is reduced and frequently eliminated.

Why does vitamin C cause an increase in joint pain? Vitamin C is an acid – ascorbic acid. High acid levels are believed to cause an increase in osteoarthritis. There are other acids besides vitamin C that may be involved. As an example, scientists have suggested that lactic acid, one of the byproducts of muscle respiration, may also lead to joint inflammation. Thus we have yet another good reason not to train through a serious injury.

POOR NUTRITION

"The part nutrition can play in maximizing your chance for complete recovery is not to be overlooked. As a rock-bottom minimum, you should have the recommended daily allowance (RDA) of protein, vitamins and minerals. If you feel your postworkout recovery proceeds at a snail's pace, then I suggest you take a multivitamin tablet as general insurance."

– Robert Kennedy,
founder of MuscleMag International.

Most people are unaware that poor nutrition can lead to injuries. Hundreds of years ago sailors developed a disease called scurvy, which was characterized by a degeneration of the bones. The condition was

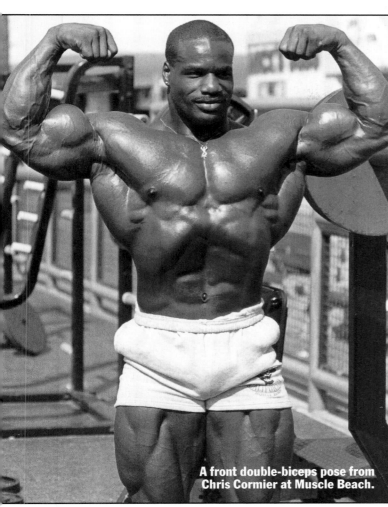

A front double-biceps pose from Chris Cormier at Muscle Beach.

1. Strains – one of the most common forms of injuries. They involve damage to muscle/tendon regions.

2. Sprains – damage to ligaments and joints from over-stress. They're caused by overstretching the ligament or suddenly twisting the area.

3. Tears – partial or complete tearing of tendons, ligaments or muscles. Tears are among the most painful of injuries.

4. Dislocation – condition where the bone comes partially or completely out of its socket.

5. Tendinitis – temporary or chronic inflammation of a tendon. Tendinitis causes collagen-type protein material to adhere to the tendon coverings (called sheaths), acting as a lubricating fluid for the tendon-muscle complex. If this material sticks it causes an irritation of the nerves supplying the muscle.

6. Bursitis – temporary or chronic inflammation of a bursa within a joint. Bursae are saclike bags that contain synovial fluid which protects and lubricates joints. Unlike most injuries, bursitis tends to be amplified by the application of heat. The best course of action is to apply ice and elevate the area to help drain away excess fluid.

7. Spasms – involuntary contractions of muscles. (A milder version is called a twitch.) Most spasms last only a few minutes, but they can linger for hours or even days. They are caused by nerve pressure or electrochemical imbalance.

caused by a lack of vitamin C, and once citrus fruit was included in the diet, the disease was all but eliminated.

While we are confident that today's bodybuilders are in no way comparable to a sailor in Nelson's time, nevertheless if they are following an improper diet, they may be leaving themselves open to injury. For example, with insufficient protein the exercised muscles cannot recover between workouts. Too few minerals and the musculonervous system does not function properly.

Because of the importance of nutrition to body-building, we have devoted an entire chapter to it. If you feel that your diet is inadequate when it comes to any of the required nutrients, take a supplement.

CATEGORIES OF INJURIES

"I've had quite a few injuries over the years, but this year was the worst. I had a torn quadriceps, a torn ligament in my shoulder, a tear in one biceps, and the usual minor tendon pains." 		**– Dorian Yates**
										Five-time Mr. Olympia

While every muscle, tendon or ligament is a potential site, sports injuries can be placed into ten main categories. Keep in mind that humans love classifying things and there is rarely agreement. Another text may list eight or twelve categories.

Jamo Nezzar

The powerful Mike Francois.

8. Cramps – a more intense form of spasms involving unwanted muscle contraction. Cramps are usually of short duration (seconds to minutes).

9. Hernia – a condition where an underlying organ begins to protrude through its protective sheath of connective tissue. Although the problem is rare, a few bodybuilders develop hernias in the lower abdominal region. At the slightest indication of a hernia, see your physician.

10. Fractures – partial or full breaks in the body's bones. These injuries are very rare in bodybuilding, as generally a muscle or tendon will tear before the underlying bone fractures. Still, a few bodybuilders have broken bones by dropping a plate on their foot!

Bouncing the barbell on your chest doesn't do the ribs any good either. Also, it's possible to break a forearm bone when doing preacher curls, but once again the tendon or biceps will probably snap first. As fractures are serious, seek immediate medical attention at the slightest sign.

LISTEN TO YOUR BODY

Of these categories of injuries, numbers 1, 2 and 5 are probably the most common among bodybuilders. The constant stress placed on tendons begins to take its toll. In their quest to develop Olympian arms, impatient and overzealous bodybuilders will load the bar with plate after plate. Unfortunately the arms weren't designed to have such extreme stress placed on them. Eventually the budding superstar will begin experiencing a slight soreness in the area between the lower biceps and forearms. He takes a few aspirin to kill the pain and continues working out in the belief that you can "train through" such a minor annoyance. In some cases the irritation will go away, but often a more serious condition – chronic tendinitis – develops. What could have been cured with a week or two of rest, now takes months, if not years. Now you're in a precarious situation. If you continue to pop pain killers and workout (as most bodybuilders do), you multiply your chances of a serious injury.

The solution to all of these woes is to listen to what your body is trying to say. A couple of days' rest will not only help prevent serious injury, but the bodybuilder often finds that once workouts resume, training intensity and motivation levels are much higher. (The most likely explanation for this phenomenon is that most bodybuilders are in a constant state of overtraining.)

Sprains and strains are other common bodybuilding injuries. Once again improper warming up and technique are usually at the root of the problem. Sometimes a simple overuse of the area is all it takes to cause discomfort. As with most injuries these conditions may be mild, moderate or severe. Often the athlete's response to the first determines the development of the other two. The two characteristic symptoms of muscle sprains and strains are swelling and pain. Because these two symptoms are common to most injuries, you should seek medical attention at the first sign of an injury. There's no need to rush to the physician every time you have a slight muscle cramp or spasm, but if the condition persists, see a doctor. It could be indicative of a more serious problem – e.g. nerve damage.

While no two injuries are alike, there are a few generalizations that should be followed in treatment. These include:

1. Stop training the area and apply ice.
2. See a physician (a sports specialist if possible).
3. Apply heat where necessary.
4. Gradually try to rehabilitate the area with exercise.
5. Be patient and don't rush back into the gym!

Sharon Bruneau and Milos Sarcev

OVERTRAINING

"You build your super athlete from harder training and recovering from it. How do you recover? From super nutrition. Lots of people try to find ways to train harder, but if you can't recover from your workouts, they won't do you any good. The limit is how much you can eat and recover, not how much training you can do."

– John Parrillo, exercise and nutrition expert

"The Dragon Slayer" himself, Rich Gaspari.

Perhaps the biggest impediment to bodybuilding success is overtraining. In their quest for increased size many bodybuilders follow the notion that "if some is good, more is better." This is true, but only up to a certain point. There is a fine line between not doing enough and doing too much. Bodybuilders spend years straddling the line between positive stress (doing enough to cause growth) and negative stress (doing too much and impeding growth).

In simple terms, overtraining means exercising to the point that your body has insufficient time to recover before the next workout. If the body has not recovered, sooner or later you'll experience some type of injury. Many bodybuilding authorities have written extensively on the topic of overtraining. Among these are Dr. Arthur Jones, Mike Mentzer, Robert Kennedy, Willem S. Van der Merwe and Dorian Yates.

From their writings we see that overtraining can be broken down into five categories:

1. Performing too many sets too many days a week, even when the intensity levels are low – in other words expending so much energy that there isn't enough left for muscle recovery.

2. Training with too many sets too many days a week with too high an intensity. The central nervous system is overloaded, the adrenal glands are taxed, and the body as a whole is thrust into a state of total fatigue. If the bodybuilder continues training, injury and muscle loss may result. This condition has been labeled "the overtraining syndrome" by *MuscleMag's* founder, Robert Kennedy.

3. Training with the right number of sets and reps, but for too many days a week. Because the body doesn't receive enough time for full recuperation, the central nervous system overloads. This form of overtraining leads to fatigue, staleness and reduced motivation levels. The result – zero growth.

4. Training with adequate sets but with too much intensity. Once again the nervous system is put into a state of shock. The athlete's system becomes flooded with catabolic hormones such as cortisol, and muscle growth stops, and in many cases, reverses.

5. A final form of overtraining involves exercising the same muscle groups on too frequent a basis. For most bodybuilders hitting the same muscles twice a week is sufficient. For many once a week is adequate.

"The majority of bodybuilders are overtrained in sets and reps and undertrained in intensity. My advice is cut the number of exercises and sets you are doing by 50 percent and double your intensity. Then watch what happens." — **Dorian Yates, Mr. Olympia winner**

Most bodybuilders in a state of overtraining fit into one or more categories. Notice that all have one feature in common – a failure of the recovery system to keep pace with the volume of training. At the very least, muscle growth slows, but in many cases the body starts breaking down muscle tissue.

Not wanting to be accused of misleading readers, we should add that it's possible to add muscle mass while overtraining. In fact most bodybuilders probably fall into this category. Unfortunately these people are expending far more energy than they need to. They work for years to make gains that they could have achieved in a few months. For this reason many bodybuilding writers refer to overtraining as undergaining.

Undergaining means your efforts are disproportionate to your results. If one person is spending twice as much time in the gym as another, he should be gaining muscle mass at nearly twice the rate. Yet how many bodybuilders make such gains for their investment? We can tell you, very few. To compound the problem, once gains slow down, these same people add sets to their routine. In an attempt to halt the downward spiral, they push even harder, trying desperately to keep their lifts and energy levels up. The result is a further deterioration of the body's recovery system and the setting up of a vicious cycle.

The tragic results of overtraining are not always limited to muscle, ligament and tendon damage. Chronic overtraining can lead to a depression of the body's immune system. The latest Russian research indicates that the body's immune system can become so weak that it is unable to fight off harmful germs. The opposite can also occur. The immune system begins to attack harmless substances in the form of an allergic response.

How do we break the overtraining cycle? The first step is to recognize that a state of overtraining exists. Here is a list of the most common symptoms of overtraining:

1. Reduced or nonexistent muscle gains
2. Weight loss
3. Swollen lymph nodes
4. Lack of motivation
5. Irritability
6. Insomnia
7. Frequent injuries
8. Lack of energy
9. Reduced strength level
10. Overall feeling of fatigue
11. Increased blood pressure
12. Abnormal heart rate
13. Headaches
14. Tremors or twitches

Dorian Yates exudes confidence in competition.

If you have a number of these symptoms the odds are that you're overtraining.

Once overtraining has been established, the next step is to take two or three weeks off. That's right – skip the gym completely. After months (or years) of overtraining your body is chronically fatigued. When you take a three-week rest, energy stores are replenished, nagging injuries heal, and motivation levels rise to new heights. Don't worry about losing muscle mass. Two or three weeks will not cause muscle loss. Once you resume training, you will start making the muscle gains that have eluded you for so long.

After your three-week rest no doubt your motivation levels are sky high. Before you take advantage of this newfound euphoria, a word of caution. Picking up where you left off only defeats the purpose. Within a few weeks you will be back to where you started. There must be a total reevaluation of your training program. Be aware that most cases of overtraining happen to the more advanced bodybuilders as they come back from a layoff. Instead of easing back into training, they attack the weights with full intensity. Because of their

Darrem Charles and Lee Priest compare chests.

strength levels they place tremendous loads on their recovery systems. For example, an advanced bodybuilder benching 400 pounds for reps is placing a proportionately greater demand on his system than a beginner bodybuilder benching 150 pounds.

While there are no hard and fast rules for changing your training routine, the following are a few generalizations.

1. Add sets to only one or two bodyparts at a time. Any more than this will overload the body's recovery system. If you decide to specialize on legs, fine, do so, but leave the total number of sets for the rest of the body alone. A good recommendation is to increase the overall workload by no more than 10 percent. This does not sound like much, but over a year it's considerable. Don't make the mistake of adding sets to every bodypart. In fact it might be a good idea to reduce the number of sets.

2. Follow an appropriate routine for your training level. Nimrod King's chest routine or Flex Wheeler's biceps program are far too intense for a novice bodybuilder. You need years of training to build up to this level.

3. Pay close attention to any signals that the body gives you. If you feel tired and sluggish, don't push too hard during that day's workout. A hard day at the office or school may mean adjusting your routine accordingly. Remember, there is a fine line between adequate training and overtraining. When your body gives notice that you've crossed the line – take heed!

4. Do not utilize advanced training techniques (rest-pause, trisets, negatives, etc.) on every set. Don't go to failure on every set. Consider cycling your workouts. Alternate heavy and light days. You can apply this philosophy over the whole year as well. Spend part of the year training with heavy weight and low reps, and part of the year training with light weight for high reps.

5. Pay close attention to your diet. Make sure it provides all the required nutrients. An improper diet can have drastic effects on recovery between workouts. We recommend including B-complex vitamins with your meals, and a protein shake would help as well.

6. Get adequate rest! This is one of the primary ways to fight overtraining. Without proper rest your body is unable to cope with the physical stress placed on it. If for whatever reason you haven't been getting enough sleep, try going to bed a bit earlier, or taking a nap in midafternoon.

Charles Clairmonte

CHAPTER THIRTEEN - OVERTRAINING

Craig Titus

BOOK FIVE

Up the Ladder of Intensity

5

Chapter Fourteen

ADVANCED BODYBUILDING

"Bodybuilding isn't a hit or miss and hope for the best type of endeavor. You must be constantly aware of what is happening to you and mentally note this so as to make the appropriate change in your training, diet, etc., when necessary. Concentration means paying attention to the smallest details – not only to training, but also to diet, recuperation and mental attitude."
– Greg Zulak,
former editor-in-chief of MuscleMag International

Now that you've graduated to the advanced level of bodybuilding, it's time to introduce the various training techniques that will keep your muscles growing. This chapter is divided into two sections: advanced techniques and training routines. We'll discuss the techniques first and then show you how to apply them to your training.

AM I ADVANCED?

As much as we would like to be able to advise you precisely when to proceed to the advanced level of training, realistically we can't. We can, however, narrow it down to a reasonable time frame.

After about a year's training you should have gained around 15 to 20 pounds of muscular bodyweight. Your arms should be in the 17-inch range, and your chest should stretch the tape an additional 3 to 5 inches. Those previously slight thighs will now be filling out your pants, and your waist should have dropped anywhere from 2 to 4 inches. Of course, these are average gains. Some of you will have made such progress after a few months, while others will be only too happy to have reached this level in two years. As everyone is different, these figures can only be used as a rough guide.

Another way to determine if you're ready to proceed is the response to your current training program. The human body has remarkable powers of adaptation. After your first few months of training, you probably experienced a slow-down period. To keep the muscles growing you had to start using intermediate training routines. Instead of one basic exercise per muscle group, you hit the muscles from new angles. And what happened? The muscles began responding! Now after about a year of following such routines, progress has slowed down once more. To address the situation you must apply advanced training techniques to shock the muscles into new growth.

INCREASING MUSCLE MASS

To increase muscle mass you have to increase the amount of work performed in the gym. There are three ways to do this. First you can increase the duration of your workout (more sets, more reps). Second, the amount of time between sets can be reduced (intensity). Or third, you can employ a combination of these strategies.

Increasing workout duration has its place. It's the most widely used of the three, but it has its limits. Doing more sets at the same intensity level will work

Eddie Robinson

Porter Cottrell, Vince Taylor, Charles Clairmonte and Nasser El Sonbaty

only up to a certain point. A beginner going from 3 to 6 sets for chest training will in all probability make excellent gains. Armed with this knowledge, he jumps to 10 or 12 sets, expecting the same results. Unfortunately the gains made don't justify the extra investment of effort. A few bodybuilders (the smart ones) take the hint and drop back to 6 or 8 sets, but most take the opposite approach and add sets. Despite the fact that few if any gains are made, they continue to exercise in this nonproductive manner. A few individuals built phenomenal physiques using this strategy. French bodybuilder Serge Nubret routinely did 30 to 40 sets of 20 reps each on the bench press, and Roy Callender performed anywhere from 60 to 80 sets for his back.

If extending workout duration is not the answer, how about increasing intensity levels? You can do this in two manners: increase the amount of weight used, or decrease the time between sets.

Lifting more weight for the same number of reps is usually not an option because you are limited by strength levels. You don't suddenly decide to lift more weight. You have to be able physically to do so. Besides, if you could lift more weight, wouldn't you be doing it already? The option left is to perform your exercise routines faster. This also can be done in two ways: reduce the time between sets, or speed up individual exercises. Both have limitations.

If you try moving the weight faster, the result is often an attempt to get the weight up at all cost. In effect less emphasis is placed on strict style, and more on cheating. This is not what you want. The other option is to do the same workout but in less time. Instead of 60 seconds between sets, reduce it to 45, or even 30 seconds.

See the problem? You will eventually reach a point where the muscle does not recover between sets. The only way to keep this pace up is by reducing your workout poundages. Now you're back to square one, breaking one of the most fundamental rules of bodybuilding – a muscle adapts by having an increased workload placed on it. The solution is to increase both set duration and intensity at the same time.

You want to do more reps but with a stress level that leads to muscle growth. Doing 20 reps with a light weight will not stimulate muscle growth – the muscle is probably asleep for the first 10 reps. The idea is to make the first 10 reps as productive as the last. The following techniques are among the most effective for increasing workout intensity.

ADVANCED TRAINING TECHNIQUES

CHEAT REPS

Cheating is an ugly word in most sports, but in bodybuilding it takes on a particular significance. Cheating is probably the first advanced training technique bodybuilders discover. Most learn the principle without prior instruction. Remember that last set of barbell curls, how after doing 8 strict reps, you used a little body swing to get an addition 2 or 3. You may not have realized it but you just discovered the cheating principle. Done properly it lets you target deeper muscle fibers. Done incorrectly, it drastically increases your chances for injury.

In bodybuilding terms cheating is the process by which additional muscles help you complete a few extra reps after the target muscles have fatigued. The biceps curl is a good example. After the biceps have tired, a slight assistance from the lower back (in the form of momentum) will allow the completion of 2 or 3 additional reps.

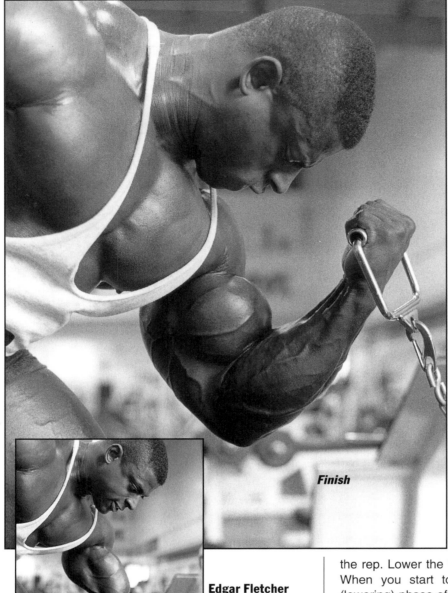

Finish

Edgar Fletcher shows how the one-arm cable curl is done. He should know – look at that gun! Start

the most common bodybuilding injuries result from exercises where bouncing is widespread. Bouncing the bar off the chest to get an additional rep on the bench press is one of the classic mistakes of bodybuilders. Likewise the Scott curl (bouncing the bar at the bottom of the exercise) and the behind-the-head shoulder press (bouncing the bar off the top of the spine) get abused in the same manner. The latter is especially dangerous as it can lead to damage to the spinal cord.

The key to effective cheating is knowing how and when to cheat. For illustrative purposes, let's use the preacher bench (Scott curl) once more. We have already explained how bouncing at the bottom of the rep is dangerous. To cheat correctly on the Scott curl, start by positioning the bench so that you're doing the exercise in a standing posture. Perform your reps to positive failure, and when you can no longer raise the weight, lock your arms and swing the weight up using your upper body. At the same time thrust the hips forward for additional body momentum. This little movement forces the bar past the sticking point (usually at the very bottom) allowing the biceps to complete the rep. Lower the bar slowly and repeat the process. When you start to lose control over the negative (lowering) phase of the movement (on average following an extra 2 or 3 reps), terminate the set. Don't go to the point that you are lifting the bar entirely with momentum, and then dropping it uncontrollably. Such a dangerous practice will only lead to injury. Besides the Scott curl, you can do cheat reps on just about every biceps exercise you can think of, whether barbell, dumbell or cable.

Properly cheating on the shoulder press is a bit more difficult. You need to perform the exercise in the standing position. Once again do your 8 to 10 positive reps, and then on the last rep rest the bar on the shoulders and bend the knees slightly. Start the bar moving with shoulder power and then forcibly straighten the knees. The leg kick will get you past the sticking point. Be careful on this exercise as your vertical posture (unbraced at that) places you in a susceptible position. If you experience any sort of back problem, stop the movement and return to the back-braced version.

Proper cheating should begin only after the primary muscles have failed – in this case the biceps. Improper cheating is using additional muscles to get the weight up at any cost, regardless of the primary muscles. One of the most common forms of bad cheating is bouncing.

Although we looked at this problem in more detail in the chapter on injuries, suffice it to say that bouncing places undue stress on the body's muscles, tendons and other connective tissues. Not surprisingly, two of

Other exercises lend themselves to cheating. After going to positive failure on the lying triceps extension, use the lats to push the bar past the sticking point. Although chins are relatively immune from cheating, most versions of the pulldown are not. When you reach positive failure, use your bodyweight to force out those extra muscle-building reps. For example, when performing front pulldowns, lean back and pull the bar downward with a little bit of body momentum. A few extra reps performed in this manner will do wonders for your lats.

Ironically two of the most basic exercises in bodybuilding are not good candidates for proper cheating. It's possible to arch the back and bounce the bar off the chest on the bench press, but both practices are dangerous. The former can lead to spine damage, the latter to a crushed rib or punctured lung. As for squats, the amount of weight used makes safe cheating all but impossible. Squats are one of the few exercises where any amount of cheating could end your bodybuilding career on the spot.

The leg press is another story. With those knees of yours just begging to be pushed, you can quite easily force out cheat reps. Pile on the plates and bang out 10 to 12 reps to failure. Then using your hands, push your thighs or knees as much as needed to complete the rep. Chances are it won't be the lack of strength but the pain that causes you to end the set! Even though they hurt tremendously, leg presses are one of the most effective means to put slabs of muscle on your thighs.

The most frequently asked question concerning cheating is how many cheat reps to perform. Although the number is a personal decision, there are a few guidelines. Some bodybuilders use a slight cheat from rep one. They make up for the looseness in style by piling on more weight. We suggest leaving this practice until you've got a few years of experience under your belt. For the most part, choose a weight that allows 8 to 10 good reps. After going to failure on rep 10 (or whatever the final rep happens to be), use a slight cheat to overcome the sticking point, and grind out an additional 2 or 3 reps. Any more and you'll overtax the muscle.

A good guide to cheating involves the amount of effort required to keep the bar moving. If you're doing biceps curls and you have to swing, shrug and sway the whole body just to get the bar up, you have probably gone too far.

Cheating is one of the easiest and most effective advanced training techniques. Properly employed it will hit muscle fibers that you didn't even know existed.

BURNS OR PARTIAL REPS

Popularized by California's Vince Gironda, burns are nothing more than a couple of partial reps at the end of a regular set. Say for example you just manage to squeeze out 10 reps on the barbell curl. While performing an 11th full rep may be impossible, lowering the bar

five or six inches and returning it to the top three or four times is probable. These partial reps are called burns, and as the name implies, they *burn!* After a set that includes burns you feel as if the targeted muscle is on fire. Don't let this sensation bother you, as this means you've stimulated muscle fibers that probably were not worked before.

ULTRASLOW REPS

Although the time varies, most bodybuilders take approximately three to five seconds to perform a single rep. For variety, many of today's top stars employ slow-rep training in their workouts.

Using an ultraslow training pace has a number of advantages. For starters it eliminates any cheating or body momentum. Lifting and lowering a barbell slowly takes pure muscle power. Another advantage is safety. Most injuries are the result of sudden stops or starts, either of which can rip tendons, ligaments or muscles. Slow training eliminates virtually all these potentially dangerous actions.

Edgar Fletcher

Michael Francois' shirt says it all.

howling for mercy. Most exercises can be done in an ultraslow manner. The only exceptions are movements where safety is a concern. For example, squats and bench presses done in a slow style may be risky. Make sure a spotter is handy if you give them a try.

Why are slow reps so effective? Well, muscle fibers work on an all-or-none principle. There's no in-between. Muscle power is based on the number of muscle fibers contracting, not a graded response by individual fibers. A light weight will cause a few fibers to contract, while a heavy weight will bring many fibers into play.

During a slow-rep set the muscle fibers tire very quickly, so more fibers have to contract to complete the rep. This is one reason why 3 or 4 ultraslow reps may be better for muscle growth than, say, 8 to 10 standard-speed reps. Another beneficial aspect of slow reps is that they raise the threshold of muscle fibers in much the same manner as giant or descending sets (discussed later).

Finally slow reps raise the threshold of the Golgi tendon organs. These stretch receptors located in the muscle/tendon attachments shut a muscle down if and when the muscle undergoes excessive strain. In many cases muscle failure occurs because of Golgi-tendon firing, not exhaustion. Ultraslow reps help prevent this reaction by resetting the Golgi tendon organs' firing threshold – allowing you to perform more reps before the muscle shuts down.

If you are having trouble achieving a pump in a certain muscle, or have "hit the wall" in your training, give ultraslow reps a try. Not only will the change stimulate new growth, but the strictness of the style will also allow you to feel the muscle being worked.

We also have to take into account the amount of weight used. Lifted slowly, 100 pounds can be made to feel twice as heavy. As greater concentration is needed to lift a weight slowly, your mind is totally focused on the set. A final reason for lifting the weight slowly is that most bodybuilders emphasize a fuller range of motion to make up for the lighter weight used.

If not convinced yet, try the following during your next arm workout. Set yourself up with a dumbell on the preacher bench. Instead of the standard 8 to 10 reps, taking about four to five seconds per rep, try lowering and raising the dumbell over 30 seconds. Take 15 seconds to lower and another 15 to raise. If you're lucky you may get 3 or 4 reps, but don't be surprised if you conk out after 1 or 2.

The same style can be applied to other exercises as well. For a unique chest-training experience, try two or three ultraslow dips. You can blast the shoulders with ultraslow sets of lateral raises (all three directions). Legs? No problem. A set of 2 or 3 ultraslow 30-second reps of leg extensions or leg presses will have them

ULTRAFAST REPS

"I believe that training more quickly with explosive concentric movements activates more of the fast-twitch muscle fibers. These happen to be the ones with the greatest growth potential. Training quickly also serves to burn bodyfat, leading to a leaner level of muscle development."
– Michael Francois
1995 Arnold Classic winner

Having explained the merits of ultraslow reps, now we are going to do the opposite – examine training that uses high-speed reps. Originally attributed to Leroy Colbert, the first man to develop muscular 20-inch arms, high-speed reps are done using the heaviest weight and the fastest speed possible. Now this doesn't mean you bounce the weight around in haphazard form. It means using good technique to perform the reps as fast as you can. Some – with good reason – call it "racing the clock." You perform as many reps as possible in the shortest time. The extra momentum generated by the speed allows you to perform more reps before your muscles fatigue than you would by doing standard-speed reps.

Another advantage to high-speed reps is that you can handle more weight. We think we made this clear in the last section. The slower the reps the less weight that can be used. Conversely, moving the weight at a fast pace allows the use of heavier poundages. Try 6 fast reps. See what we mean? You probably could have used much more weight in this fast set. Not only can you use more weight, but the speed of the sets also means more work in less time.

STRIPPING

As your body adapts to traditional training styles, you must employ new techniques to keep the muscles growing. One of the easiest and most effective to perform is the stripping method. Let's say you are using 200 pounds for 8 reps on the bench press. While the 8th rep may be the last you can perform with 200 pounds, no doubt if the weight were suddenly dropped to 175 pounds, you could squeeze out a few more. The stripping technique permits you to do this. As soon as you complete the last rep, have a training partner remove (strip) 20 or 30 pounds from the bar. Immediately force out as many reps as possible. A 20-pound

drop will probably get you 2 or 3 extra reps. If you want, you can remove an additional 20 or 30 pounds.

The stripping technique is not limited to barbells. A dumbell version known as "down the rack" can also be used in your training. After doing a few warmup sets, perform a couple of standard sets with your regular weight. To push your muscles to failure, grab a lighter pair of dumbells and bang out a few extra reps. Although you can theoretically use the whole dumbell rack, most bodybuilders find 2 or 3 down-the-rack sets sufficient. They are especially effective for shocking the muscles after weeks or months of repetitious exercises.

This technique is very intense and therefore should not be abused. For most novice and intermediate bodybuilders 1 or 2 strip sets will be adequate.

Start

Lee Priest pulverizes his pecs with incline dumbell presses. *Finish*

Gary Strydom's killer calves!

21 is an arbitrary number, and you can perform any number of reps. From 3 x 6 to 3 x 10 the choice is yours. We recommend giving 21s a go during your next biceps or hamstring workout. But do only 1 or 2 sets as the biceps are small muscles and would quickly burn out.

STAGGERED SETS

Let's say after a couple of months of training you notice that your calves are lagging behind the rest of your body's growth. Besides working them in a normal routine, some bodybuilders like to blast calves unsuspectingly while working other muscle groups.

For example, between sets for the back, jump under the calf machine and burn out 20 to 25 reps. Most people find that, while the calves burn like crazy when exercised, they don't fatigue you like such exercises as squats or bench presses. This means that you can get extra calf work without interfering with the rest of your training.

When performing staggered sets, keep in mind that there are a few combinations that wouldn't make much sense. Working forearms along with other exercises would hinder your training, as the forearms are needed for gripping most gym apparatus. Likewise, performing a high-energy exercise like squats would only prevent you from doing justice to the other muscle groups being worked.

NEGATIVE REPS

"Two decades ago exercise physiologists discovered that the negative cycle of an exercise offered at least as much potential for strength and muscular development as the positive cycle of movement. Thousands of bodybuilders worldwide make intelligent use of negative-rep training to achieve maximum physical development." **– Joe Weider, founder of Flex *and* Muscle & Fitness**

Research carried out in the late '60s and early '70s indicated that the downward part of the movement (with gravity) was just as productive as the upward part (against gravity). In fact a workout composed of a high

TWENTY-ONES

Although you can apply this technique to many exercises, it's most suited to curling movements. The name comes from the number of reps performed during the set. To do a set of 21s, take a weight that is about half what you would normally use for a set of barbell curls. (You may find that even this is too heavy.) Now divide the movement into three sections: bottom to midpoint, midpoint to top, and full movement. Perform 7 half reps, curling the weight from the bottom to midpoint. Next, without stopping, curl the bar from the midpoint to the top for an additional 7 reps. By now the burn is so intense you are cursing Bob Kennedy's ancestors. Great. You will have larger biceps than any of them! Finish the set (if you can) with 7 full reps. The name "21s" comes from the number of reps performed (3 x 7= 21).

You may want to add a slight cheat curl to complete the final couple of reps. As you will quickly find out, this is one of the most intense methods to work the biceps. You can't use your normal workout poundage, but don't worry. You don't have to. The partial movements force the biceps to work in ways they never did before. Also,

The Master Blaster, Joe Weider.

percentage of negative reps often left you more sore than one consisting solely of positive reps. Negatives received their greatest boost from the works of Arthur Jones, inventor of the Nautilus line of training equipment. Jones based much of his high-intensity theory on negative training. His two-seconds-up/four-seconds-down concept became the norm in Nautilus gyms everywhere. If Jones could be criticized on one point, it is that he placed too much emphasis on negatives. It's not that negatives aren't effective – they are – but like all bodybuilding techniques, negatives should be done for variety and not as an end-all solution to muscle growth. Don't be misled into thinking that the increased soreness means negatives are more productive than positives. This is just not the case.

To perform negatives, you must have a training partner or spotter on most exercises. Load the bar with more weight than you can lift in the normal fashion, and then lower it in a slow and controlled manner, attempting to stop or even reverse the barbell's direction. Once you reach the bottom, have your training partner assist you in returning the bar to the starting position.

A few exercises allow you to perform negatives on your own. After going to positive failure on the barbell biceps curl, for instance use your lower back and legs to swing the weight up. Now try to lower the weight as slowly as possible, going as far as trying to stop the bar. A couple of reps like this are great for shocking stubborn muscles into new growth.

REST-PAUSE REPS

Another superintense training technique is called rest-pause. To perform rest-pause reps, load the bar with enough weight to allow just 1 rep. Perform the rep and then place the bar back on the rack or floor (or wherever it started from). Wait 10 to 15 seconds and then perform another single rep. Repeat this pattern for 8 to 10 repetitions.

Rest-pause is based on the principle that a muscle will recover about 90 percent of its strength in 10 to 20 seconds. You may find that in order to complete the 8 to 10 reps, the weight will have to be reduced slightly after the first couple of reps. Also, given the intensity of the technique, rest-pause reps should be performed only by intermediate and advanced bodybuilders.

PRE-EXHAUST SETS

Invented in 1968 by *MuscleMag's* own Robert Kennedy, pre-exhaust sets help eliminate the problem of "the weakest link in the chain." Most exercises involve more than one muscle group, even if the exercise is considered to be targeting a single muscle. For example, most chest exercises involve the triceps and shoulders. These muscles often tire before the pectorals. The theory behind pre-exhaust sets is to fatigue the primary muscle as much as possible by using an isolation exercise (or as close to an isolation exercise as you can get), and then perform a

compound movement that utilizes fresh muscles to take the fatigued muscle to greater depths of stimulation.

One of the best examples of the pre-exhaust principle is flat-bench flyes followed by barbell bench presses. The bench press is called a chest exercise, but the triceps and shoulders receive tremendous stress as well. Often it's the smaller triceps that give out first. To get around this difficulty, first perform an isolation exercise like dumbell flyes, which places little stress on the triceps. This will "pre-exhaust" the chest muscles, leaving the triceps in a stronger state. Now when you perform bench presses, the triceps are no longer the weak link in the chain. The relatively stronger triceps can be used to push the chest muscles to failure.

Another great pre-exhaust combination is dumbell lateral raises and barbell shoulder presses. If you start with barbell presses, often the triceps give out before the delts. But if you first pre-exhaust the side delts with

Flavio Baccianini

lateral raises, then your fresh triceps can push the delts to the maximum on the barbell press.

There are a host of pre-exhaust combinations. Among the more popular are the following:
Leg extensions – squats or leg presses
Shrugs – barbell rows
Scott curls – narrow-grip chins
One-arm dumbell extensions – narrow-grip bench press
Crunches – leg raises
Lateral raises – shoulder presses
Flyes – barbell bench presses

SUPERSETS

"If you really want to blast a single muscle group to the limit, you can do a superset consisting of two consecutive exercises for that bodypart. For example, when I was attempting to improve my biceps development, I would do a superset consisting of barbell preacher curls and standing barbell curls. As soon as I finished my set of preacher curls, I'd simply stand back from the bench without even changing my grip on the bar and do my standing barbell curls. I've never felt a deeper or more intense growth burn in a muscle group than with this type of superset."   **– Tony Pearson,**
former Mr. America and Mr. Universe

Unlike straight sets, supersets involve performing two exercises in an alternating fashion. There are two main variations of supersets. The first involves performing two exercises for the same muscle. A set of barbell presses might be followed by a set of dumbell presses. Both exercises are considered among the best general chest movements. A variation of supersets involves alternating a lower-chest exercise like dips with an upper-chest exercise such as incline dumbell flyes. Although both are working the same muscle group, they are stimulating different sections.

The most common form of supersetting involves alternating two exercises for different muscle groups, usually two oppositely working muscles. For example the chest serves to push the arms forward, while the back muscles draw the arms backward. Many bodybuilders capitalize on this connection and alternate a chest exercise such as bench presses with a back exercise such as chinups. Another common superset alternates biceps and triceps exercises. Once again we have two oppositely working muscles being exercised. The following are examples of supersets:

SUPERSETS FOR THE SAME MUSCLE GROUPS

Thighs –
Squats, leg extensions – leg presses, hack squats
Hamstrings –
Lying leg curls, standing leg curls – lying leg curls, stiff-leg deadlifts
Chest –
Bench presses, dips – dumbell presses, dumbell flyes

Bodybuilding legend Tony Pearson.

Back –
Chins, barbell rows – seated rows, front pulldowns
Shoulders –
Front shoulder presses, side lateral raises – behind-the-head presses, upright rows
Biceps –
Barbell curls, concentration curls – Scott curls, incline curls
Triceps –
Narrow presses, pushdowns – lying extensions, dips
Abs –
Crunches, reverse crunches – hanging leg raises, Roman-chair situps
Calves –
Standing calf raises, seated calf raises – donkey calf raises, toe presses

Lee Labrada pumps his quads on the leg press. *Finish*

Start

SUPERSETS FOR ALTERNATE MUSCLE GROUPS

Thighs –
Squats, lying leg curls – leg presses, stiff-leg deadlifts

Torso –
Bench presses, chins – incline presses, barbell rows

Arms –
Barbell curls, lying extensions –   Scott curls, pushdowns

TRISETS

As the name implies, trisets involve performing three exercises in a row. For example, three chest exercises can be grouped together in such a manner that they train the entire chest. A common triset for the chest would be flat bench presses, followed by incline presses, followed by cable crossovers. With this triset the lower, upper and inner chest regions are worked. Trisets are great if you're pressed for time, as they allow you to perform an intense workout in a short period. The following are some examples of trisets:

Thighs –
Leg extensions, hack squats, leg presses –
   squats, sissy squats, leg extensions

Chest –
Dumbell presses, dumbell flyes, dips –
   barbell presses, dumbell flyes, cable crossovers

Back –
Chins, pulldowns, barbell rows – front pulldowns, seated rows, narrow pulldowns

Shoulders –
Rear shoulder presses, lateral raises, upright rows – front shoulder presses, front laterals, shrugs

Biceps –
Barbell curls, dumbell curls, cable curls –
   Scott curls, concentration curls, incline curls

Triceps –
Lying extensions, kickbacks, pushdowns – narrow presses, dumbell extensions, reverse pushdowns

Abs –
Crunches, reverse crunches, hanging leg raises –
   Roman-chair situps, crunches, lying leg raises

Calves –
Standing calf raises, seated calf raises, donkeys –
   donkey calf raises, dumbell calf raises, toe presses

GIANT SETS

Giant sets are really nothing more than an extension of trisets. Instead of three exercises, four or more are performed in an alternating fashion. Giant sets are a very intense form of exercising, and beginners need not perform more than one every couple of workouts. Even then this might be too much.

As a final tip, giant and trisets are great for shocking muscles that have become stale after weeks

Back –
Chins, barbell rows, front pulldowns, seated rows –
T-bar rows, dumbell rows, pulldowns, pullovers, chins

Shoulders –
Front presses, side laterals, shrugs, cable laterals – upright rows, rear presses, front laterals, shrugs

Biceps –
Barbell curls, dumbell curls, Scott curls, cable curls – Scott curls, incline curls, cable curls, barbell curls

Triceps –
Narrow presses, dumbell extensions, pushdowns, kickbacks – pushdowns, lying extensions, dips, kickbacks

Abs –
Crunches, lying leg raises, rope crunches,
Roman-chairs – hanging leg raises, crunches,
Roman chairs, rope crunches

Calves –
Donkey raises, seated raises, standing raises,
toe presses

EXTENDED SETS

Although other forms of training have become more popular, extended set combinations are one of the most effective methods for increasing training intensity. To perform extended set combinations, perform the first set of an exercise to positive failure, and then without stopping, switch over to an exercise that puts you in a better biomechanical position. Let's look at a few examples to illustrate our point.

One of the most popular triceps exercises is the lying triceps extension using an EZ-curl bar. Performed with the elbows close to the head and pointing to the ceiling, the movement is virtually all triceps. Instead of terminating the set at the end of the exercise, switch over to narrow-grip bench presses. The shoulder and chest involvement allows you to force out more reps than if you were doing an isolation movement.

Another useful combination is dumbell flyes and dumbell presses. Start by doing a standard set of flyes, and after the last rep rotate the dumbells and blast out as many reps as possible of dumbell presses. You are stronger in the press than the flye because the press utilizes more shoulder and triceps power. In effect you are using these still fresh muscles to push the chest to greater depths of failure.

**Hanging knee raises target the lower abs.
– Craig Titus**

or months of straight sets. One or two giant sets will shock them into new growth (more on this later). The following are examples of giant sets involving four or five exercises:

Thighs –
Squats, leg presses, extensions, hack squats –
leg presses, sissy squats, lunges, extensions, hacks

Chest –
Bench presses, flyes, incline presses, dips – incline presses, dips, cable crossovers, flyes, pullovers

A third set combination can be performed for the lats. Done with a wide grip, front or rear pulldowns primarily work the upper and outer lats with little biceps involvement. (As you will discover later, totally isolating a muscle is virtually impossible.) After going to positive failure on wide pulldowns, switch over to underhand-grip narrow pulldowns. The underhand grip brings the still fresh biceps into play, thus allowing the lats to be pushed to complete failure. The fact that narrow pulldowns mainly stress the lower lats is another plus, and doing both exercises ensures that the whole lat region is worked.

For a great deltoid workout, try doing 6 to 8 reps of side laterals with a heavy dumbell, followed immediately by dumbell presses. You can also do the same combination substituting barbell presses for the dumbells. Although most people can use heavier weight on presses than on side laterals, doing the exercises nonstop means that you'll probably have to use the same weight for both. Try an experiment first. If you get 10 to 12 reps on the dumbell press, even after doing the laterals, use a heavier dumbell on your presses – not so heavy that you're limited to fewer than 6 to 8 reps, however.

If you're looking for something to jazz up your biceps workouts, try the following: Perform 6 to 8 reps of incline dumbell curls. Without stopping, blast out another 6 to 8 reps of standing barbell curls. (Have the bar set up in advance.) If you really like pain, add a few cheat reps at the end of the barbell curls. You won't need many sets like this to put new inches on your biceps.

Drag curls followed by barbell curls are another good combination. Start by doing 6 to 8 reps dragging

Tonya Knight

Start

Finish

Shelley Beattie performs standing barbell curls.

the barbell up close to the body. After the last possible rep, do as many barbell curls as possible, adding a slight cheat if necessary to keep the bar moving.

To force new growth into the thighs, try front squats and regular back squats. Start by doing 10 to 12 strict reps of front squats. Re-rack the weight and, taking the bar on the shoulders, force out another 10 to 12 (or more) reps of standard back squats. As front squats eliminate most lower-back and glute involvement, these muscles will be fresh when you're performing back squats. A couple of sets and your thighs will beg for mercy!

Finally, you can even work the abs using extended set combinations. After doing 20 to 25 reps on the crunch, switch over to situps. The crunch fatigues the abs to a great degree, and then you can use the hip flexors to force out extra reps on the situps.

CHAPTER FOURTEEN – ADVANCED BODYBUILDING

Sharon
Bruneau

The same holds true for leg raises and knee-ups. Lie on the floor, or if you have the strength, an incline board, and do 20 to 25 reps of leg raises (knees slightly bent). Finish the set by pulling the knees towards the chest. The improved biomechanical position of the knee-up allows you to get reps that you probably could not do on the leg raise.

In conclusion we must add that, as with most advanced training techniques, you can easily get carried away and do too much. For most bodybuilders one or two extended set combinations for each muscle group will be sufficient. Any more and you'll risk overtraining. Then instead of making progress, you'll hinder it.

TEN SETS OF TEN

There are many advantages to training a muscle with several different exercises. Perhaps the most important is that you can hit the muscle from a variety of angles. The more angles you attack from, the more muscle fibers stimulated and the greater overall degree of development. For example you have flat benches for the lower chest, inclines for the upper chest, pec-deks for the inner chest, and dips for the outer chest.

Another advantage to using multiple exercises for each muscle group is psychological variety. Let's face it – doing the same exercise day after day can get pretty monotonous. But if you change your routine and perform different exercises, the variety keeps your enthusiasm levels up.

If there's a disadvantage to this plan, it's the risk of overtraining that crops up anytime you perform multiple exercises for one bodypart. For example the shoulder complex consists of four muscles (three heads plus the traps). Now if you were to perform 3 or 4 sets for each, you could end up doing 16 sets for this one bodypart. For Genetic George this is fine, but most bodybuilders would quickly overtrain if they followed such a routine for an extended period of time. One solution is to utilize the one-exercise-per-muscle-group-per-workout approach.

The concept of doing only one exercise per muscle is not new. Reg Park and Vince Gironda were doing it back in the 1940s and '50s, and Vince still maintains that performing a single exercise for 8 to 10 sets of 8 to 10 reps is one of the best ways to tax a muscle to the limit.

There are numerous advantages to performing only one exercise per muscle group. The most obvious is that once you set the exercise up, your focus remains fixed throughout the workout. You perform 8 to 10 sets and proceed to the next muscle group.

Another benefit is that you don't have to worry about losing the pump between exercises. Unless you have the next exercise set up and ready to go (very difficult to do in a commercial gym given the number of members waiting for equipment), it's going to take at least two or three minutes to grab a bar and put the plates on. (Of course, you don't have this problem with cable and machine exercises.) While two or three minutes doesn't sound like much, it may be enough time to lose that great pump you've worked so hard to obtain. By doing only one exercise, you never go more than 45 to 60 seconds between sets.

A third advantage lies in thoroughness. For the most part you don't even feel the muscle working until you've done 2 or 3 sets of an exercise. In fact you may complete your first exercise and not get anything out of it. However, if you are doing 8 to 10 sets of one exercise, you know that sooner or later the muscle you're targeting will start to burn.

If you're concerned about variety, simply change the exercises from workout to workout. For example, one chest workout could consist of 10 sets of flat benches, and the next could be 10 sets of incline dumbell presses. Future workouts could center around dips, flyes, pec-dek, etc. By training in this manner, you are not only hitting the muscle from different angles, but the variety also keeps you from getting bored.

The following table consists of three sample workouts that you can perform for each bodypart. You still split your workouts up as usual (i.e. three, four or six days a week), but do only one exercise per bodypart. This means that a typical workout will consist of only two or three exercises.

Keep your calf and abdominal exercises in the 20-rep range, thighs and hamstrings in the 15-to-20 range, and the rest in the 10-to-12 range. Finally, don't expect to be using the same weight towards the end of your sets. By the time you reach sets 8 to 10, your muscles will be extremely fatigued, so you'll have to drop the poundage considerably.

MUSCLE	WORKOUT 1	WORKOUT 2	WORKOUT 3
Quads	leg presses	squats	hack squats
Hamstrings	standing leg curls	lying leg curls	deadlifts
Back	chins	bent-over rows	pulldowns
Chest	bench presses	flyes	inclines
Shoulders	shoulder presses	lateral raises	front raises
Traps	upright rows	barbell shrugs	cleans
Triceps	pushdowns	extensions	dips
Biceps	dumbell curls	cable curls	Scott curls
Abdominals	crunches	leg raises	crunches

ADVANCED TRAINING ROUTINES

Now that you've seen the techniques, it's time to start incorporating them into your training. Because of the increased intensity of your workouts, you may want to split your routine into six workouts instead of the current four. The six-day-a-week routine means you have only two muscles to work on the same day. The time normally spent on the third muscle group can be invested in the other two muscles.

You don't have to jump from four to six days a week. Your time budget may not allow such frequent workouts. Everything from work to school to family and friends may dictate that you stick with the four-day-a-week routine. This is fine. Many professional bodybuilders follow such a schedule year round, only switching to a six-day plan in the few months prior to a

contest. You should, however, apply advanced techniques, to make better use of your four days' training.

The following routines are examples of four- and six-day-a-week splits. Where possible, we include various advanced training techniques, and with time you will begin designing your own programs. Where our routine may stress the chest, you may want to hit the back with more intensity. If so, reduce the sets and advanced techniques for the pecs, and apply them to your back exercises. Remember that these programs are meant as a guide, not an absolute. In most cases we use a rep range between 8 and 15. On some of the basic exercises (squats, bench presses, shoulder presses, etc.) you can use heavier weight, and fewer reps (4 to 6). As we discussed earlier, rep range is an individual preference. For illustration purposes we have chosen average rep ranges. You will have to experiment to find what works best for you. By now you probably have already done so.

Koen Balcaen

**Franco
Santoriello**

A FEW WORDS OF CAUTION

Before you jump into the routines, a few words of caution are needed. First, don't make the mistake of using these techniques on every set. If the routine recommends 4 sets of a particular exercise, limit the advanced techniques to the last 1 or 2 sets.

Second, it probably makes sense to perform your advanced sets for each muscle group only once a week. Leave the other workout for straight sets. In other words, alternate an intense workout with a lighter one. This alternation gives the body enough time to recover.

Third, try to limit these techniques to a duration of four to six weeks. Few bodybuilders can handle such intensity year round. You'll quickly reach a state of overtraining if you train too intensely for too long.

Finally, resist the urge to do more! Within a few weeks of starting these techniques you will notice rapid improvements in size and strength. Many bodybuilders then take what they feel is the next logical step. If one or two supersets is good, then three or four must be great. They may be right up to a point, but within a couple of weeks their gains slow down – if not reverse. There is a very fine line between training too much and not training enough. You have to apply the maximum

amount of intensity that stimulates muscle growth without overtaxing your recovery system.

There will be days when your energy level is sky high. Great. Take advantage of it. Do that extra super-set or forced rep. Most of the greatest bodybuilders in the world will tell you that training instinctively is perhaps the greatest of all advanced training techniques. Don't make the mistake of increasing your workout duration on a weekly basis. Only after many years of training will you become fine-tuned with your body. For now use the outline as a guide, and make changes only when you want to prioritize one muscle over another.

FOUR-DAY-A-WEEK ROUTINES

Routine 1
Monday-Thursday

EXERCISE	SETS	REPS
Barbell bench presses	4	8-10
Superset:		
Incline dumbell presses		
Incline dumbell flyes	3	8-10
Bent-over rows	4	8-10
Pulldowns	3	8-10
One-arm dumbell rows	3	10-12
Standing barbell curls		
(Do one or two strip sets.)	4	8-10
Seated dumbell curls	3	8-10
Concentration curls	3	10-12
Crunches	3	20-30
Hanging leg raises	3	15-20

Tuesday-Friday

EXERCISE	SETS	REPS
Squats	4	12-15
Hack squats	3	12-15
Leg extensions	3	12-15
Lying leg curls (Drop the		
weight twice on last set.)	4	12-15
Standing calf raises	4	15-20
Seated calf raises	4	15-20
Military presses	4	8-10
Side laterals	4	10-12
Upright rows	4	10-12
Barbell shrugs	4	12-15
Lying triceps extensions	4	10-12
Superset:		
Triceps pushdowns		
Reverse triceps pushdowns	3	10-12

Routine 2
Monday-Thursday

EXERCISE	SETS	REPS
(Pre-exhaust the pecs with one		
set of flyes and then follow with		
one set of incline presses.)		

Flat dumbell flyes	3	10-12
Incline bench presses	3	10-12
Dips	3	10-12
T-bar rows	4	10-12
Seated pulley rows	4	10-12
Front pulldowns	4	10-12
Preacher curls	4	10-12
Dumbell curls	4	10-12

(Perform the last two sets in a down-the-rack manner. Drop the weight two or three times.)

Hanging leg raises	4	15-20
Crunches	4	20-30

Tuesday-Friday

EXERCISE	SETS	REPS
Leg presses	4	12-15
Hack squats	3	12-15
Leg extensions	3	12-15
Lying leg curls	4	12-15

(On the last two sets strip the weight down two or three times.)

Standing calf raises	4	15-20
Donkey calf raises	4	15-20
Front shoulder presses	4	10-12
Side lateral raises	4	12-15

(Perform the last two sets down the rack.)

Bent-over laterals	4	12-15
Dumbell shrugs	5	12-15

(Down the rack on the last two sets.)

Trisets:

Lying triceps extensions		
Triceps pushdowns		
Narrow upright dips	2	10-12

(Perform these three exercises as two trisets.)

Routine 3

The following routine is an excellent way to specialize on the legs. You divide your routine into upper- and lower-body training.

Monday-Thursday

EXERCISE	SETS	REPS
Squats	4	10-12
Leg presses	4	10-12
Hack squats	4	10-12
Leg extensions	4	12-15
Lying leg curls	5	12-15
Standing calf raises	4	15-20
Seated calf raises	4	15-20
Crunches	3	20-30
Lying leg raises	3	15-20

Tuesday-Friday

EXERCISE	SETS	REPS
Incline barbell presses	4	10-12

Flat dumbell flyes	3	10-12
Dips	3	12-15
Bent-over barbell rows	4	10-12
Seated pulley rows	3	10-12
Pulldowns	3	10-12

Giant Sets:

Front military presses		
Behind-the-neck presses		
Side laterals		
Bent-over laterals	2	10-12

(Perform two giant sets on these four exercises.)

Universal-machine shrugs	4	12-15

Supersets:

Lying triceps extensions		
Standing EZ-bar curls	3	10-12

(Because you have to work three large torso muscles, limit your arm work to 6 sets. By using an EZ-curl bar for both triceps and biceps exercises, you can save time. Perform 3 supersets of these exercises.)

SIX-DAY-A-WEEK ROUTINES

There are two main variations of the six-day split. You can train six days in a row and take the seventh day off (usually Sunday for convenience), or train three days on, take a day off, and then repeat the cycle. The six-day-straight routine allows you to follow the standard

Shelley Beattie

CHAPTER FOURTEEN – ADVANCED BODYBUILDING

Achim Albrecht, Flavio Baccianini and J.J. Marsh

seven days that we live our lives by. Unfortunately training six days straight can be taxing on the body's recovery system.

Conversely, the latter version, does not respect the traditional seven-day week. Within two weeks you will have been in the gym on every day. So if there is one day you can't work out, follow the six-day-straight routine and rest on the day you can't make the gym. The big advantage to the three-on/one-off routine is that the body is getting a day's rest every four days.

When training six days a week (either version), pay special attention to your body's signals. If after a few weeks you notice the signs of overtraining, stop and re-evaluate your program. Don't keep pushing yourself six days a week because you read somewhere that Kevin Levrone follows such a routine. Either cut back on your sets, or revert to the four-day-a-week routine.

Routine 1
Days 1 and 4

EXERCISE	SETS	REPS
Flat barbell bench presses	4	10-12
Incline dumbell presses	3	10-12
Dips	3	10-12
Cable crossovers	3	12-15
Chins	4	10-12
T-bar rows	4	10-12
Pulldowns	3	10-12
One-arm rows	3	10-12

Days 2 and 5

EXERCISE	SETS	REPS
Front military presses	4	10,8,6,10
(Pyramid fashion)		
Side lateral raises	4	8-10
One-arm cable raises	3	10-12
Barbell shrugs	3	10-12

Dumbell shrugs	3	12-15
Reverse pushdowns	4	10-12
Lying triceps extensions	4	10-12

(Pre-exhaust the triceps with reverse pushdowns, and then follow with the lying extensions.)

Standing barbell curls	4	10-12

(Perform the last two sets in stripping style.)

Concentration curls	4	10-12

Days 3 and 6

EXERCISE	SETS	REPS
Squats	4	10-12
Hack squats	4	12-15
Leg extensions	3	12-15
Lying leg curls	4	12-15
Standing calf raises	4	15-20
Crunches	3	20-30
Roman-chair situps	3	20-30

Routine 2
Days 1 and 4

EXERCISE	SETS	REPS
Incline bench presses	4	10-12
Flat dumbell flyes	3	10-12
Dips	3	10-12

(Between your legs hold a dumbell that allows you to get 8 to 10 good reps. Drop the dumbell and rep out as many extra dips as possible.)

Behind-the-neck presses	4	10-12
Dumbell presses	3	10-12
Bent-over lateral raises	3	10-12
Upright rows	4	10-12

(Perform the last two sets in stripping style.)

Barbell shrugs	4	12-15

Days 2 and 5

EXERCISE	SETS	REPS
Bent-over rows	4	10-12
Seated pulley rows	4	10-12
Front pulldowns	4	10-12
Seated dumbell curls	4	10-12
Standing EZ-bar curls	3	21-30

(Do three sets of 21s. You can use any rep range – i.e. 3 x 7, 3 x 8, 3 x 9, or 3 x 10.)

Days 3 and 6

EXERCISE	SETS	REPS
Leg presses	4	12-15
Hack squats	4	12-15
Leg extensions	2	12-15
Squats	2	12-15

(Pre-exhaust the thighs with extensions, and then follow with a set of squats. Do this twice. This is an excellent way to really blast the legs.)

Lying leg curls	4	12-15
Crunches	3	20-30
Hanging leg raises	3	20-30

**Michael Francois'
titanic legs are the
result of years of
squatting.**

TRICKS OF THE TRADE

STICKING POINTS

"Variety is extremely important for continued biceps and triceps growth. The arms get stale doing the same exercises each workout. I like changing the exercises just to keep the muscles off guard." **– Anja Schreiner IFBB Pro Bodybuilder, Ms. International**

Anja Schreiner

Over the five million years of its evolution the human body has developed remarkable powers of adaptation. As soon as it encounters stress, a series of biochemical reactions take place to counter that stress. In fact muscle growth is one form of stress adaptation.

You'll soon discover that at first your muscle gains come quickly. After a few months, however, performing the same routines does not provide the same results. You eat more, train harder, and allow more time for recuperation, yet no matter what you do, the muscles refuse to respond. You have encountered what bodybuilders commonly call a "sticking point." If steps are not taken to address the problem, the condition may last months or even years.

COMING UNSTUCK

Once you have identified a sticking point (it may be one muscle, but more commonly the whole body), you must stop and evaluate the situation. Look at every aspect of your program, especially diet, rest and training. Because of the importance of these three we shall look at each in more detail.

DIET

Like all machines the human body needs fuel to run properly. If the diet is deficient in carbohydrate, you'll run out of energy halfway through your workout. The body also requires the protein, vitamins and minerals that allow necessary repairs to take place. If your diet lacks any of these nutrients, your body's recovery powers are limited.

No less an authority than Vince Gironda has suggested that bodybuilding is 85 percent nutrition. Is it any wonder that your muscles are not growing because of haphazard eating patterns? The road to new growth may lie not in the gym but in your kitchen!

CYCLING YOUR TRAINING ROUTINES

We don't think it's an exaggeration to say that 90 percent of all bodybuilders are in a state of overtraining. In their quest for additional size they are following routines designed for a few genetically gifted individuals. Even the top professionals reduce their training in the off-season. Few follow a 20-set-per-bodypart routine year round. That intensity is mainly limited to precontest training. If the top bodybuilders cycle their training, what makes you think you can handle such intense exercise programs on a regular basis? If you're following this kind of routine, you know the answer to your sticking problem. Often all that is needed to break a sticking point is a return to the old-fashioned basics of just a few exercises which work large groups of muscles. For most bodybuilders this will mean cutting the number of sets in half, if not by two-thirds. Doing 6 to 8 sets for the smaller muscle groups and 8 to 10 for the larger ones is sufficient for just about everyone. More is not necessarily better!

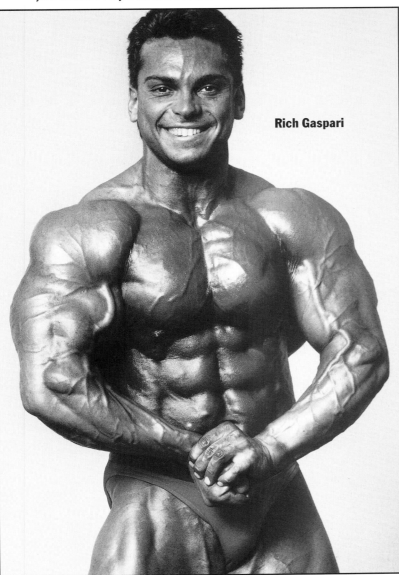

Rich Gaspari

Another way to reduce the chances of overtraining is to follow a heavy-day/light-day schedule. Sure, all the top champions can train heavy, but they don't max out during every workout. They couldn't even if they wanted to. Their joints can't take it. They may train heavy every third or fourth workout, or they may alternate heavy months with light months. But training heavy for long durations is out of the question.

To get around this obstacle, most work the same muscles in a twice-a-week fashion, using one workout for heavy weight/low reps (by heavy we mean 6 to 8 reps), and the other for light weight/high reps (12 to 15). Such a routine provides the best of both worlds. The heavy weight will stimulate muscle size and density, while the high reps will build endurance and promote capillary formation. The biggest advantage to workout-cycling is that the body's recovery system is not taxed beyond its limits.

Most competitive bodybuilders cycle their routines in this manner. Following a contest they take a three- or four-week layoff, allowing injuries to heal and full recuperation to take place. They then resume training three times a week. They work the whole body with just one or two exercises per bodypart. After a few weeks they switch to a four-times-a-week program. This basic mass-building routine lasts for a couple of months. The final phase of the cycle is a six-day-a-week schedule with the emphasis on contest preparation.

You can only increase workout intensity up to a certain point before the law of diminishing returns takes over and you overtrain. By cycling your routine year round, you reduce the risk of burnout and ensure long-term gains.

SHOCK IT TO THEM!

"You should change the order of the exercises from one workout to the next to take advantage of the muscle confusion (shocking) principle. This way your back, chest or thighs never know what to expect in terms of training intensity."
– Rich Gaspari, IFBB Pro Bodybuilder
Three-time Mr. Olympia runner-up

The body's ability to adapt quickly to new situations is beneficial from a bodybuilding perspective. As we increase the load (weight) placed on a muscle, the body adapts by making the muscle bigger and stronger. Eventually even progressively increasing the weight does not stimulate muscle growth. Working out with the same weight, the same time each day, the same days each week, all lead to what we commonly call training staleness. Everything becomes predictable. The body can guess what's coming next. It becomes stubborn and refuses to grow. Your next step should be obvious. You need to wake it up!

CHAPTER FIFTEEN – TRICKS OF THE TRADE

Mike Matarazzo

with several burns or forced reps. Throw in a couple of down-the-rack or stripping sets. A few sets of these and we guarantee your muscles will be shocked into new growth!

Some bodybuilders carry the shocking principle to the extreme by performing a different routine every workout. For most this would defeat the purpose as the body, believe it or not, can adapt to variety. (It sounds like a contradiction in terms but – believe us – it happens!). Further, it's generally accepted that you need a certain amount of regularity in your workouts to gain muscular size and strength. By continuously changing the exercises, you will limit your weight progression. Regularly performing the same exercise leads to a marked increase in strength on that movement.

The shocking principle, like most techniques outlined in this book, is a valuable training tool that should be used but not abused. When the situation warrants, include the shocking principle in your workouts, but don't make it a regular feature. The advantage of shocking lies in its novelty not its uniformity. You'll only be defeating the purpose by relying heavily on it. Still, for that extra spurt of growth, few techniques stimulate the body's muscles like the shocking principle.

By combining the shocking principle with adequate rest, proper nutrition and a simplified training schedule, You can overcome most sticking points. Once growth resumes, the bodybuilder can ease back into a regular training routine.

MUSCLE PRIORITY

"I train my arms on my last training day of the week. It's arms alone, and that consists of the entire arm: biceps, triceps and forearm. This way I can give them all the attention they need while I'm fresh instead of when I'm exhausted from having gone all out during a chest or back workout minutes before."

– Mike Matarazzo
IFBB Pro Bodybuilder, USA National champ

Although we touched on this before (under the topic of exercise order), we think it's necessary to look at it again, this time in more detail.

As the years progress, you will notice that certain muscles respond to training better than others. For example, your thighs have developed into columns of power, but your upper body is only average. Perhaps your triceps are overshadowing your biceps. Or your front delts make your upper chest look shallow. To correct the weakness, you must reevaluate your training. For obvious reasons your best workouts will be those performed when your energy levels are the highest. In most cases these will be the workouts at the beginning of the week. Take advantage of this fact, and modify your schedule so that the weakest muscles are worked on the first or second day. If you are following

One of the best ways to shock the body is to employ variety. Instead of doing 3 sets of 10 reps, surprise it with 5 sets of 20 reps. If you make bench presses the mainstay of your chest workout, substitute declines. You might want to skip all your main exercises for a couple of weeks. By changing exercises you are keeping the body guessing. It "thinks" it's going to be doing shoulder presses at 4 p.m., but instead you hit it with lateral raises at 7 p.m. (or 7 a.m. if you can arrange it!).

If changing the exercises doesn't appeal to you, try changing their order of execution. If you regularly work chest first and back second, try switching it around for a few days. Start your workouts with the back exercises. But don't take this advice to heart and work arms before the major upper-body muscles. That approach may sound good in theory, but in fact you will cut your workout poundages by 30 to 50 percent. The arms are an integral link in upper-body exercises. Tiring them out first will decrease the effectiveness of such movements as bench presses and chinups.

You can also shock the body by utilizing some of the advanced training techniques. Finish your last sets

the four-day split, train your weaker muscles on Monday. If you are following the six-day split, train the weakest muscles on days 1 and 4. You can use muscle priority within one workout as well. Train your weakest muscles at the beginning when you are fresh. If your back is weak, exercise it first, and leave your chest for later.

After a couple of months of such prioritizing, your weak points will be brought back to the level of the rest of your physique. Of course, by then other muscles may be out of proportion. Don't worry. It's a rare bodybuilder indeed who has every muscle growing at the same rate!

SPECIALIZATION

It would be convenient if by hitting each muscle group with equal intensity, the end result was perfect proportions. But unfortunately this is not the case. Sooner or later you'll discover that some muscles grow simply by looking at weights, while others can be tortured almost daily and yet refuse to budge.

Most multijoint exercises such as bench presses, squats, deadlifts and shoulder presses place most of the tension at the midpoint of the exercise. For example, barbell biceps curls mainly hit the central belly of the muscle. The upper and lower sections receive much less stimulation. This means that for total biceps

development you must include isolation movements in your training routine. If you want to target the lower biceps, you need to do various forms of preacher or Scott curls. Likewise, the barbell bench press will develop great lower pecs, but for most bodybuilders creating pecs with that "slabs of armor" look requires isolation exercises for the upper pecs.

These examples illustrate what is known in bodybuilding circles as specialization. As soon as a weakness is recognized, it must be confronted head on. If that means reducing or eliminating a basic "must do" exercise, so be it. As you progress up the bodybuilding ladder, you should be spending more time on single-joint isolation movements than on multijoint basic movements.

Here are a few of the recommended procedures for incorporating specialization into your workouts:
1. Prioritize your weak points by training them first in your workouts. It only makes sense to hit lagging muscles first when muscle glycogen levels are highest.
2. If you have the time, split your daily workout in two. Train your weak muscles first and by themselves. Then come back later in the day for your regular workout.
3. Perform your specialized program on days that are normally nontraining days. For example, if you train on Monday, Tuesday, Thursday, and Friday, try specialized routines on Wednesday and Saturday.

Lee Haney

Aaron Baker and Ken "Flex" Wheeler

movements carried out around the house? How often do you walk across the gym floor carrying a 50-pound weight? When was the last time you balanced a barbell on one shoulder and climbed a ladder? Chances are the answer to both questions is never.

Let's look at it from another point of view. How many times during the day are both your arms or legs performing the exact same movement at the same time? Not very often, we bet. Your day-to-day physical activity most certainly consists of movements that place unequal stresses on the body. There is only one exception to this pattern, and – you guessed it – it occurs when we go for a workout. Just about every exercise in the gym is done in symmetrical fashion. It seems our goal is always to move both arms or legs at the same time.

One of the great misconceptions among bodybuilders is that asymmetric training (training one side at a time) will produce an asymmetric build – i.e. you'll end up looking lopsided. Who wants one 16-inch arm and one 19-inch arm? And this is certainly what will happen if you train one side at a time, right? Wrong, and here's why.

When you lift a bar with both arms, quite often one side dominates and takes a disproportionate amount of the stress. The end result is that certain muscles on one side grow faster. The chest, triceps and front delts, are famous for this problem. But if you could place an equal amount of stress on both sides of the body, then such muscle imbalances would not occur. This is where asymmetric training comes in.

How do you train asymmetrically? Let's say you want to give your lats a good blast. Grab a heavy dumbell, and with one hand braced on a bench, pull the dumbell up with the other arm. As you lower the dumbell, stretch forward slightly to hit the whole lat. One-arm dumbell rows are excellent for bringing out the back's V-flare.

Triceps, no problem. Bend over at the waist and brace your body on a bench. With the upper arm held tight against the body and parallel to the floor, extend the lower arm back until it's in a fully locked position. Called triceps kickbacks, this exercise is great for correcting any imbalances produced by such movements as bench presses and lying extensions.

To avoid burnout, never continue a specialized program for longer than six to eight weeks. If you start experiencing the symptoms of overtraining, stop the specialization and return to your regular routine.

4. Train the weak muscle group on six consecutive days for two to three weeks. While this is one of the more radical methods, it's also one of the most productive. Use light to moderate weight for 4 to 6 sets of 5 to 8 reps.

ASYMMETRIC TRAINING

Have you ever noticed how sore you get after lifting a heavy object in your house or backyard? All those hours hoisting tons of weight, and yet one 50-foot walk with a concrete flowerpot results in two days of torment. Perhaps the criticism thrown at bodybuilders is true – we're all a bunch of useless showpieces!

In all probability the truth lies somewhere short of that extreme. Think of it this way: How much similarity is there between exercises performed in the gym and

If the delts on one side of the body are lagging behind, try incorporating one-arm dumbell raises into your routine. Hold an upright for support, and do 10 to 12 reps per side.

Besides the equality of stress placed on the body's muscles, there's a physiological basis to asymmetric training. Good evidence suggests that the brain has to split nerve impulses to stimulate the muscles on both sides of the body to contract. Training one side at a time allows for the full nervous stimulation of these muscles.

In addition, we have the issue of concentration. It's much easier to concentrate on an exercise when only one muscle group is being worked. Try this little experiment the next time you're in the gym. Do a set of barbell curls and try to concentrate on both biceps. Now do a set of one-arm dumbell curls in the same manner. See the difference? It's much easier to focus on one contracting biceps than having to divide your attention between both.

Perhaps a more basic but equally important point is exercise variation. The body gets stale from doing the same exercises day in and day out. That's why you need to periodically shock it with new movements. A few weeks of asymmetric training serves as a wake-up call, bringing with it new growth.

Although there are too many asymmetric exercises to list here, the following will add variety to your training and help correct muscle imbalances.

BICEPS
Cable curls
One-arm dumbell curls

DELTS
Dumbell raises (front, side, rear)
Cable laterals

TRICEPS
Dumbell kickbacks
One-arm extensions
One-arm cable pushdowns

CALVES
Dumbell calf raises
One-leg calf raises

HAMSTRINGS
One-leg lying leg curls
One-leg standing leg curls

LATS
Dumbell rows
One-arm pulldowns

TRAPS
One-arm shrugs

THIGHS
One-leg extensions
One-leg presses

CHEST
One-arm pec-dek
One-arm crossovers

Just about every exercise you can think of can be done in an asymmetric fashion. However, a couple of precautionary points are necessary. If at any time you feel lower-back pressure, stop the exercise. Try to use just enough weight to work the muscle without twisting the spine. If you have to use spinal torque to lift the weight, it's probably too heavy. Also, a few exercises don't lend themselves to asymmetric training. Under no circumstances should you do one-leg squats (while using a barbell) as too great a risk is placed on the knees and lower back.

Although chest exercises with one dumbell are possible, you might want to give them a pass. It's extremely difficult to brace yourself so that you won't fall off the bench.

Laura Bass

Finally, when trying a new exercise in the asymmetric style, use instinct as a guide. Learn to differentiate between a good muscle workout and a potentially deleterious injury. We're not saying asymmetric training is the cure to all bodybuilding ills, but we think that once you give it a try, you'll be hooked.

Marjo Selin

INSTINCTIVE TRAINING

When you start in bodybuilding you'll be wise to follow an organized, preset program. (Hence this book!) As your knowledge is limited, using routines designed by experts of the sport makes sense. Eventually you'll reach a point however, where you have become fine-tuned with your body. You know its strengths and weaknesses. You know what works and what's a waste of time. In short, you have developed an instinct for training.

The instinctive principle is probably the most advanced of all training philosophies. Its success depends on you and you alone. No one can tell you what works best for your physique. Only after years of experimentation does the full benefit of the instinctive principle surface.

The instinctive principle can be applied both long and short term. Short term applies to modifying your workouts on a daily basis to suit your individual body rhythms. There will be days when your body tells you to take a rest. No doubt you having been training heavy, setting numerous personal goals in the process. Then one day you go to the gym and nothing happens – no motivation, no desire, no longing to attack the weights. You are faced with two options. You can go by the book and continue the workout, risking an injury in the process, or you can listen to your body and vacate the gym. That's right – grab your gym bag and leave. Don't force yourself to go through the motions because the book says not to skip workouts. The most knowledgeable book is your body. Listen to it once in a while.

The instinctive principle can be applied long term as well. As the years progress, you will become aware that some exercises just don't suit your individual body structure. For instance most bodybuilding books (including this one) and authorities consider chins and bench presses to be two of the best exercises, yet some bodybuilders get virtually nothing out of them. If you fall into this category, fine. Avoid them and substitute two exercises that work for you. Remember, you are the best judge in these matters.

REST

"Proper rest is also very important in the recovery cycle. Most anyone who runs around in a hyper state all day, burning up energy like a furnace in the middle of a Finnish winter, will never develop a significant degree of muscle mass."
– Marjo Selin
IFBB Pro Bodybuilder
MuscleMag International *columnist*

We touched on this one before, but we can't stress the issue enough. Your muscles don't grow in the gym. They grow after you leave. You must get six to eight hours of sleep every night. Staying up till 3 a.m. does not facilitate your bodybuilding career. Think about it. In a typical workout you will move tens of thousands of pounds. (Every 10 reps with 100 pounds is 1000 pounds!) There is no way to keep this up for extended periods of time unless you are allowing adequate time for recuperation. Even then it's a good idea to take a few extra days off to compensate. We know, it goes against your training philosophy. But trust us. Your body will benefit greatly from the extra rest. Minor injuries will have time to fully heal. That case of tendonitis may disappear. And your enthusiasm to get back in the gym will reap great dividends. After a period of inactivity your body will be begging for exercise. Instead of failing to grow, you will probably make the best gains of your life!

COMING BACK AFTER A LAYOFF

"Following a major competition, I always like to take one or two weeks off from heavy training – weeks when I go to the gym and train light, more or less in a playful sort of mood. This allows me to completely rest my body from the grind of contest training." **– Ron Love**
IFBB Pro Bodybuilder, Grand Prix winner

We would be negligent if, after advising you to take time off, we omitted to offer guidance on resuming training. You may think returning to the gym is only a matter of picking up where you left off, but it's not that simple. You have to ease back into your training, and because of the poundages used, intermediate and advanced bodybuilders are at the greatest risk. As a general rule, the longer your layoff, the more gradual should be the resumption. For most a few days or weeks is the typical amount of time away from the gym. A few bodybuilders, however, start enjoying their time away from training. It may be an exceptionally hot summer, they may meet a new girl or boyfriend, or nagging injuries fail to heal. Whatever the reason, that planned two- or three-week layoff stretches into a three- or four-month sabbatical. There's nothing wrong with this. In fact, more bodybuilders might want to try it.

Ron Love

All right, you have just picked up the latest copy of *MuscleMag*. One glance at Michael Francois gets the iron-pumping juices flowing. What's the first thing you do? More important, how do you ease back into training? The following advice will virtually guarantee that your return to the gym will be painless and free of injury.

Perhaps no workout is as important as the first following a layoff. Problems arise when the bodybuilder rushes back into the gym and attempts to pick up where he left off. At the very least, the next day his muscles are sore beyond belief. Too often, however, the end result is a serious injury. Let's face it. If it took years to condition your body to rep with hundreds of pounds, what makes you think you can do it again on day one? Even switching exercises in the middle of a training cycle causes severe soreness – and this during an uninterrupted stretch of workouts.

The first step on your return to working out concerns what to wear. If you normally train in a T-shirt and shorts, try switching to a track suit (sweat shirt and full-length pants). This clothing will keep the muscles warm, helping to prevent injury. After a week or so – or when you feel you're back in the training groove – you can change to your normal attire.

The next step is to design a 10-to-14-day introductory training routine. We recommend picking one exercise per bodypart – nothing fancy, just basic exercises. Do 1 or 2 sets, and then move on to the next bodypart. You should be in and out of the gym in about 45 minutes. No doubt you think this seems like a low-intensity workout, and you're right, it is, but after a layoff this is about as much as the body can handle After sitting idle for a few months, you can actually grow on this type of routine!

Keep your reps moderate to high – say, in the 12-to-15 range. Choose a weight that is about half of what you previously used. Even if your strength levels haven't apparently dropped, resist the temptation to put extra weight on the bar. Remember, the goal is to get the muscles accustomed to contracting again. Throwing hundreds of pounds at them will not be taken kindly.

Stick with this introductory routine for about two weeks. You can gradually ease back to regular training poundages, but always make sure you've warmed up adequately. The first month back is a great time for experimentation. As with most bodybuilders, no doubt before your layoff you were set in your ways. Day in, day out it was the same monotonous routine. It could have been boredom that led to the layoff in the first place. Upon resuming training, try new exercises. Instead of flat bench presses, give declines a try. If barbell rows were the mainstay of your back regimen, switch to T-bar rows. Substitute dumbell curls for barbell curls. Besides changing exercises, you might want to alter muscle groupings. Instead of training back

Finish

Start

Michael Francois trains his hamstrings with kneeling leg curls.

and chest together, try exercising back and shoulders on the same day. Eventually you may end up with a totally new routine that is far more productive than what you were following before the layoff.

As a general summary, here are a few pointers to keep in mind when resuming training:

• Always dress warmly to help prevent injuries.
• Don't attempt to pick up where you left off. Ease back into training.
• Select one exercise per bodypart.
• Never do more than two sets per bodypart.
• Keep your rep range moderate to high (12 to 20).
• Keep the poundages light to moderate. Resist the urge to put more weight on the bar.
• After a few weeks try experimenting with new exercises.

The following is an excellent routine for easing back into training. You may switch exercises (e.g. pulldowns instead of chinups), but don't add sets. Perform the workout on three nonconsecutive days. (Monday – Wednesday – Friday or Tuesday – Thursday – Saturday). The goal is to treat your body with kindness and respect. This may sound like a contradiction in bodybuilding terms, but trust us, you'll be better off in the long run.

THE COMEBACK WORKOUT

LEGS
Squats – *2 x 12-15 reps*
Leg curls – *2 x 15-20 reps*
Standing calf raises – *2 x 20-25 reps*

CHEST
Flat-bench presses – *2 x 10-12 reps*

BACK
Chinups – *2 x 10-12 reps*

SHOULDERS
Shoulder presses – *2 x 12-15 reps*

BICEPS
Dumbell curls – *2 x 10-12 reps*

TRICEPS
Triceps pushdowns – *2 x 10-12 reps*

ABDOMINALS
Crunches – *2 x 20-25 reps*

That's it – 18 sets total. Allowing for a minute between sets, you should be able to complete this workout in about 35 to 40 minutes. After two or three weeks you can go back to a split routine if that is the program you were following before your layoff.

Gerard Dente

CHAPTER SIXTEEN

RELAXATION AND RECOVERY

Bodybuilders tend to focus their efforts on what they can lift in the gym. Too often they forget that a good night's sleep is just as important as regularly doing squats. Muscles must be challenged to develop and grow, but to accomplish this they need time to recover from training. In this chapter we examine how to attain a relaxed state, with an emphasis on the art of massage. Much of this section focuses on how massage can speed recovery and actually enhance muscle growth. The Soviet training system that incorporated the use of the sauna is also described.

REST

It was the ancient Greeks who made the second greatest discovery in human medicine (after the invention of fire). They found that if a sick person was allowed to rest, he or she was more likely to recover. At the time this idea was revolutionary! It probably strikes you as being common sense. But did you realize that muscle growth requires rest as well as exercise? Bodybuilders will sometimes take a day off and party all night. This is unfair to your body. You need to give each set of muscles at least 48 to 72 hours to recover, including at least seven or eight hours of solid daily sleep. Infants spend most of their time sleeping. Infancy is also a period of rapid growth. To build muscle tissue you must design your workout schedule (and your social life) to ensure sufficient rest.

MEDITATION IN BODYBUILDING

Many bodybuilders use loud music, coffee or even violent imagery to hype themselves up for a workout. If that's your style, trying to calm down after a heavy gym session can be a challenge in itself. Find a quiet place. Sit or lie on a comfortable chair, sofa or bed. Close your eyes and breathe slowly and deeply. Inhale through the nostrils and exhale through the mouth. Concentrate only on the sound of your own breathing. If you wish, you can create a serene visual image. One bodybuilder found great success visualizing the feather floating in the air from the movie *Forrest Gump*.

Lee Apperson and Debbie Kruck

You will soon find that you feel peaceful and content. This takes only a few minutes, can be performed practically anywhere, and is very easy to do.

To get out of a bad mood, force yourself to smile, and hold it. You'll be surprised to find that your frame of mind improves. These are all very simple biofeedback techniques that are both effective and applicable to bodybuilding.

COMBATING STRESS

The rigors of modern daily life have added a new term to 20th-century vocabulary – *stress!* Although our pioneering ancestors hundreds of years ago no doubt experienced their own form of stress, only in this century has stress become recognized as a life-threatening condition that can be just as deadly as any bacteria or virus. With the cutbacks in staff at most businesses we have a situation where fewer people are doing more of the work. This increased workload at the office, combined with the "after five o'clock" commitments of most married people imposes tremendous pressure.

Increased stress, particularly when prolonged, can lead to difficulties in behavior and emotions. Under stress many people become less tolerant, more perfectionistic and less able to deal with ambiguity. Even under the best of circumstances these tendencies can occur. Many people become detached and abandon relationships.

Preoccupied with possible solutions to their problems, concerned with possible failure, fatigued and possibly depressed, they withdraw from much of the world around them. Many develop a pessimistic outlook, which can lead to thinking that negative outcomes are inevitable for them. Over time they view setbacks as catastrophic, frequently making mountains out of molehills. If they are under pressure too long, they tend to make irrational decisions based upon faulty assumptions.

Aches, pains and other physical ailments become more common, and often people develop irrational fears about their health, believing they have contracted a life-threatening illness. Closely linked with this problem is health neglect. Poor nutrition, lack of exercise and unsatisfactory sleeping patterns often develop. Memory and concentration may be impaired, giving rise to difficulties in making decisions. We now have a snowball effect taking place. Doubts about one's stamina and the ability to continue performing under pressure frequently occur, especially if the subject becomes chronically fatigued and develops health problems. This deterioration in one's self-esteem leads to self-imposed stress, which escalates the problem even further.[1]

RECOGNIZING THE PROBLEM

The first step in addressing the situation is to identify the underlying problem. Much stress is job related.

Jason Arntz

Given the realities of the unemployment situation, simply quitting one's job is not practical or feasible. A more realistic approach would be to learn relaxation techniques. Just as most over-the-counter medications treat only symptoms, not underlying causes, employees should focus their energy on adapting to the problems (symptoms) that stress may produce. This is where massage comes in. Massage is fast becoming recognized as a leading form of relaxation therapy – to the point that many corporations now offer employees health benefits that include massage as a means of dealing with job-related stress.

ATHLETICS

For a bodybuilder in an intense competitive state anxiety is a factor which is known to have a debilitating effect on athletic performance. In many cases an increase in stress leads to a decrease in athletic accomplishment. This decrease in performance in turn often leads to even more anxiety. Once again we have the development of the dreaded snowball effect – factor one leads to factor two, which leads back to more of factor one, which in turn leads to even more of factor two. Throw in the pressure of potential lucrative endorsement contracts (provided that you win!), and the

Sharon Marvel

respiration rate, blood pressure and muscle tension. Further research has demonstrated that an eight-week relaxation program is as effective as an eight-week walk/jog program in reducing anxiety levels in working women.[2]

HISTORY OF MASSAGE

"Do touch. Do talk about it. But do not do it until after the sirens." **– Dr. Ruth Westheimer, sex therapist (during a visit to Israel, commenting on how to have good sex in an air-raid shelter)**[3]

Sex is often confused with massage in the western mind. While both involve touching, and both can provide pleasure, the goals are different. Depending on the source that is consulted, the root of the word *massage* derives from the Arabic *mass* (to touch), the Greek *massein* (to knead) or the Latin *manus* (the hand). Modern definitions usually define massage as "the act of rubbing, kneading, or stroking the superficial parts of the body with the hand or an instrument."

Massage is one of the oldest methods of treating human ills. Writings of physicians, philosophers, poets and historians show that some form of rubbing or anointing was used among both savage and civilized nations from the most ancient of times. In much of written medical history massage and exercise are referred to simultaneously. The very early literature makes little distinction between the two[5].

THE ORIENT

The use of massage was documented by the Chinese 3,000 years ago. The Chinese used massage as a holistic form of medicine and as a way of maintaining the appearance of youth. At one time the top school of massage existed in the Forbidden City of Beijing under the patronage of the Chinese royal family. In modern China massage is still used by many for the same reasons, and now by athletes who wish to improve performance.

THE MIDDLE AGES

Persian doctor Ibn Seena authored an early encyclopedia in 1020 AD. It was a large volume called *The Book of the World*. The medical science section covered these topics:

1. diet
2. medications
3. massage

Ibn Seena recognized that different goals required different forms of massage. He subdivided massage techniques into the following categories:

Strong Massage – for the whole body, to increase strength.

Weak Massage – for the whole body, to relax the muscles and produce a feeling of well-being.

Lengthy Massage Sessions – used to lose weight by exercising muscles through massage. A long-term regimen was claimed to cause weight loss.

end result is often one very stressed-out bodybuilder.

A great deal of research has been carried out in recent years to devise strategies which will not only treat the situations when they arise, but also go a long way in preventing them before they start. There are numerous relaxation strategies that coaches and athletes may employ to reduce stress and prevent burnout.

Most of the procedures and techniques used by athletes, coaches and sports psychologists are variations first proposed by Edmond Jacobson in 1929. Jacobson hypothesized that if the muscles of the body are relaxed, tension and anxiety will be dissipated. From a bodybuilding point of view, it is believed that a relaxation of tension in the muscles will result in smoother and more efficient contractions in voluntary muscular movement. Jacobson's full progressive relaxation procedure involves systematically tensing and relaxing specific muscle groups in a predetermined order. After several months of therapy an athlete should be able to evoke the relaxation response in minutes.

Research has consistently shown that relaxation techniques effectively reduce oxygen consumption,

Intermediate massage (in terms of time and force)
– used to produce beautiful skin.

For athletes, Ibn Seena felt that strong massage should be used before competition to increase strength for better performance. He recommended that after competition weak massage be used to help the muscles recover and to relieve fatigue.

In Finland, Poland, the Baltic Republics and Russia birch saplings were used as instruments of massage. People would sit in searingly hot saunas where they would flagellate (whip) themselves, or a friendly neighbor, with leafy branches. This process was, and still is, believed by practitioners to improve circulation, skin tone and health in general.

In 1812 Peter Henry of Sweden scientifically systematized a massage technique called "Swedish massage." It included first the manipulation of soft tissue, and second the exercising of the joints.[6,7] Henry founded the Royal Institute of Gymnastics and Massage in 1813. To this day the most common forms of massage carry the name Swedish massage. While variation exists, the name has held, giving testament to the precision of Henry's classification. The techniques are comfortable, palliative, and favored by the vast majority of physical therapists and licensed masseurs.

A RUSSIAN TRADITION

Some countries have seen an increase in the practice of massage. In modern Nordic nations massage is such an integral part of the culture that it is considered as normal a feature of daily life as eating and sleeping.

In Russia, before the Revolution, massage was a privilege of the very rich. Since 1922 the Institute of Physical Education has trained specialist masseuses. Programs were developed to meet the many needs of various clients. The old Soviet space program incorporated massage into its cosmonaut training system, and specialized massage was administered to cosmonauts before and after each mission.

The old Soviet system managed to produce world-class massage experts, benefiting cosmonauts to Olympic athletes. Now the wall has come down. The Iron Curtain lies rusting. In this chapter we will present techniques that incorporate many of the Soviet secrets of massage.

SWEDISH AND SOVIET MASSAGE

While both Sweden and the former Soviet Union have their own traditions of massage, no one has attempted to combine them before. The following chapter integrates techniques from the Nordic tradition of relaxation with the intensity of sports-minded Russian ambition.

Swedish massage is a deep muscle-kneading treatment involving stimulation of soft tissues, ligaments and tendons. It helps induce mental and physical relaxation, stimulates circulation and relieves muscle soreness, thus improving the functioning of joints and muscles.

Lee Apperson

There are five methods of applying Swedish massage. The first is stroking (effleurage), which is performed with fingers or thumbs on small areas of the body and with the full hand on large areas. It is applied superficially while stroking muscles toward the heart. This action assists venous blood flow and lymph circulation. Stroking is the technique that accustoms the subject to the physical contact of the massage therapist. It is composed of light gliding movements over the skin with no attempt to manipulate the deeper tissues. Stroking is used to enhance relaxation, prepare the subject for further manipulation and distribute lubricant. It is customarily used at the beginning and end of a session.[4,6]

When the masseuse performs stroking for an extended period of time, the client will reach a state of relaxation. Breathing will slow and a feeling of well-being will be established. The stroking movement is used to relieve tension and as an analgesic for painful sports injuries. Further stroking aids circulation and causes a gentle debriding (removal) of dead skin, increasing regeneration, cleaning the pores, and giving the skin a youthful appearance.

The second method is kneading (petrissage), massaging the muscles in a deep, firm, clockwise, circular motion, or in a straight back-and-forth movement across the muscle. The heels of the hands and

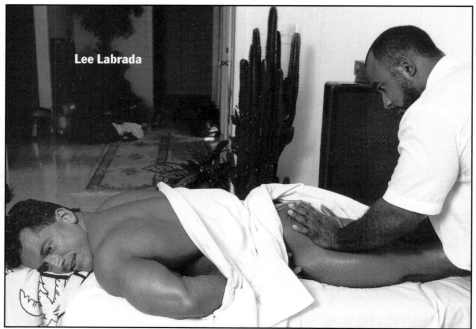

Lee Labrada

which are localized areas of tenderness within the muscle. It is also used to break down adhesions and scar tissue. Pain may result from the application of deep friction massage, so this technique is optional.[4,6] A form of friction is used in Shiatsu, a Japanese technique that is 3,000 years old. Using any part of his or her body, the practitioner applies pressure along acupuncture lines to increase the flow of energy. It is followed by stretching to help relax painful parts of the body. Called cross-friction, Shiatsu involves alternating straight-line movements, followed by the same movements at a 90-degree angle to the first. The practitioner applies both movements at the same point while maintaining continuous contact and pressure with the skin.

The fourth method is chopping (tapotement), which is a percussive movement using both hands alternately in quick blows. Tapotement may also be described as slapping, tapping, hacking or cupping depending on the position of the hands. This technique is used to stimulate the subject and is applied prior to athletic competition or when relaxation is not the desired effect.[4,6] The fulcrum of the movement is at the wrist, not the elbow or shoulder, because striking the patient too hard could be painful and cause injury. Chopping should be both rhythmic and alternating. A slight variation of this movement is the closed-fist technique in which the part of the fingers between the first (closest to the finger tip) and second joint make up the active surface area.

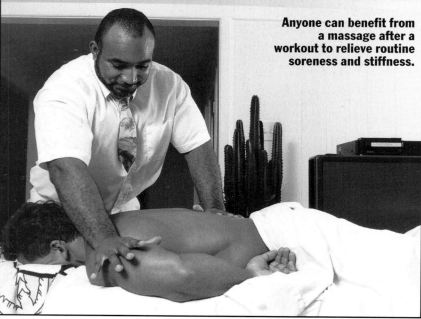

Anyone can benefit from a massage after a workout to relieve routine soreness and stiffness.

the pads of the thumbs or fingers are used. Connective tissue and muscles are gently squeezed and rolled with the fingers in a milking action.[4,6] This technique is more forceful and deeper than stroking. It can be done with objects: flagellation (whipping) and birch branches or toweling the body forcefully with a cloth held between both hands (as if drying off from a shower). A form of kneading involving the use of a cylinder rolled across the muscles (e.g. a rolling pin rolled across the soles of the feet) is referred to as "rolling" in this book.

The third method is friction, the movement of skin over underlying tissue. The edge of the hand, fingers, thumbs or palms can be used in this rapid back-and-forth motion over the top of the skin. This is a deep-penetrating technique to relieve trigger points

Fifth is vibration – making hands or fingers tremble to create a firm, rapid shaking of the deep tissue. The vibration is performed rhythmically in an attempt to enhance relaxation or stimulation.[4,6] A variation of this method is hydro-vibration, which involves resting a part of the body in a water bath that is being vigorously circulated. Whirlpool baths, hot tubs, jacuzzis and small portable foot baths all operate on this principle. Soviet massage incorporates the following techniques:

Edging – All five fingers are held tightly together and kept straight. Using either edge of the hand the masseuse pushes deeply into the flesh in the direction of venous return (towards the heart), squeezing blood along. This technique makes the subject more alert because it speeds removal of waste products from the body tissues. If it is done properly, a brief white patch will be visible behind the hand following each application. While the straight-hand method is fine for most areas, a different approach – called curved edging – must be used with the back. The hand is curved, or spoon-shaped to adapt to the contours of the dorsal region. Beginning at the base of the spine, the masseur proceeds towards the shoulders. For a small surface area the tips of the fingers can be used to form an edge. If more focus is needed, one hand can be placed on the other.

Pinching – This movement exercises the muscle, stimulates energy, increases potential for workload, and improves alertness. It also improves the elasticity of the muscle. Pinching can also be used on such muscles as the buttocks, thighs, trapezius, upper arms, chest (men only!), and very gently on the abdomen. It should never be performed so that it is painful (but ticklish is acceptable).

TIPS TO REMEMBER

If the hands are weak or tired, one can be placed over the other and together pinch the flesh. The hands can follow each other up the limb or along the muscle, following a steady rhythmic pattern. In a version of "Indian sunburn," the hands pinch in opposite directions as they move along. In self-massage it is sometimes easier to use the fingers as anchors and let the thumbs do the pinching. A spiral pattern can also be followed in which the fingers and thumbs dig in deeply and the hands twist along the muscle. This stage of massage is usually concluded with pinching by thumb and pinky alone, resulting in heightened alertness.

There is a gradual increase in the intensity of the technique. The masseur determines which method or methods to use depending on the purpose of the massage. A bodybuilder trying to relax would probably not appreciate blow or vibration movements. Conversely most bodybuilders do not want to be put into a comatose state just before a competition or training session!

SELF-MASSAGE

For obvious reasons it is preferable to have a masseur perform massage. If, however, a friend or fellow bodybuilder is unavailable, self-massage can help the bodybuilder become his/her own therapist. Do some stretching exercises before engaging in self-massage.

One form of massage is auto-rotation. All of the following movements are performed three to five times, and then repeated in the opposite direction three to five times. All movements must be done slowly. They should be performed daily to achieve maximum effectiveness. Some of the following are normal bodybuilding exercises when combined with weights, but in this case they are forms of massage because the movement of the active muscles massages the nonactive ones.

Neck Massage:
1. Rotate the head, using the nose to track a circle.
2. Move the head up and down with the nose tracing a straight line.
3. Move the head from side to side, with the ear leading toward the shoulder.
4. Turn the head from left to right, and right to left, like a vigorous "no" gesture. If you're a parent, practice with your teenager.

Hand Massage:
1. Spread the fingers out and bring them back together.
2. Make a fist and then release.

Arm Massage:
1. Rotate hands at the wrist.
2. Move hands up and down.
3. Bend the elbows, allowing the hands to touch the shoulders.
4. Biceps curl (no weight).
5. Shoulder press (no weight).
(Repeat 1, 2 and 3 with the arms above the head.)

Larry Scott

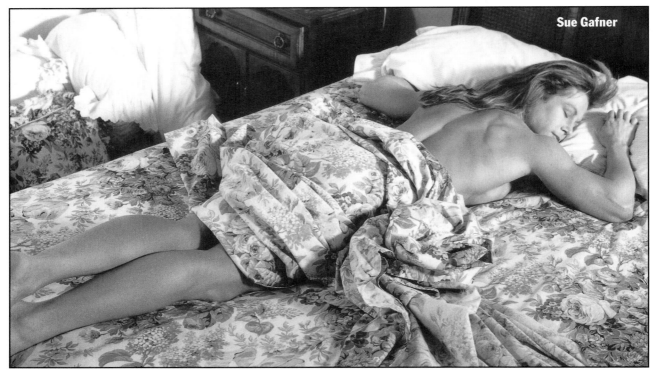

Sue Gafner

Shoulder Massage:

1. Stand or sit with the back straight and the hands on the hips. Rotate the arms with the elbows leading in an alternating fashion.
2. Stand or sit with the back straight, elbows bent with the fists clenched and placed just above the nipples. Then flap the arms up and down.

Leg Massage:

1. Lie down, and with the legs straight and slightly raised, rotate the feet at the ankles.
2. Straight leg raises.

Lower-Back Massage:

1. Stand with hands on hips and rotate the upper body from the pelvis.
2. From the same position bend forward and backward to a vertical position.
3. From the same position bend sideways from left to right and right to left.

Self-massage is one of the means used by bodybuilders to recover from workouts or competition. It offers a number of benefits. First, not every bodybuilder has access to a qualified masseur. Second, self-massage techniques are not difficult to master. Third, self-massage can be performed at the bodybuilder's convenience. Finally, most masseuses tend not to work for free!

As with standard massage, self-massage is used for a number of purposes. It may be athletic, therapeutic or hygienic. In recent years, bodybuilders have discovered that massage before a workout or competition increases work capacity and helps prepare the body for the heavy physical stress that will be placed

on it. Massage before workouts is generally of medium to high intensity as the main objective is to mobilize the body's energy reserves. The main techniques are rubbing, kneading and shaking. The session may last from five to fifteen minutes.

Postworkout massage has as its main objectives the relaxation of the bodybuilder and the facilitation of the removal of waste products. Restorative massage appears as one of the most important methods of restoring and increasing sports work capacity. Its main task is liquidation of nerve, muscular and psychological stress. In brief, it serves to speed up nerve-muscle relaxation.[8] Unlike preworkout massage, postworkout massage tends to be characterized by a slow, soft, gentle touch. Such techniques as light stroking are carried out for durations of ten to fifteen minutes. Experts recommend that postworkout massage sessions begin about two hours after the workout.

Two sessions of postworkout massage are recommended. The reason is that lactic acid, the principal byproduct of exercise, is removed in two steps. The first stage involves the removal of lactic acid from the muscles. The first massage session helps speed up the removal rate. The second stage is removal of lactic acid from the body. (After work it diffuses from the muscles into the bloodstream.) A second massage session helps facilitate this process.[9]

PLEASE DO NOT...

You can do massage by yourself, on yourself, without the need of a specialist. You can do it at home, work, or in school. It can be done to reduce stress before and after work and exams. Like all beneficial treatments, however, massage can be detrimental if used in the wrong situations. Massage is never done in the following circumstances: The bodybuilder is battling a severe flu. (A good massage is like a vigorous workout, and when ill the body needs rest.) The bodybuilder is extremely nervous. (This condition requires a specialist as the massage is more intense than normal, and an inexperienced masseuse may cause harm.) The subject has had blood loss through donation or injury. (The body needs to recover and achieve a normal fluid balance.) Neither should massage be performed on irritated skin because this condition could be aggravated, on varicose veins because the veins have already been weakened, or on a cancer patient unless approved by a physician. Finally, massage is never done on the abdomen during pregnancy (except for stroking) or just after eating. (Blood is needed to supply the organs of the digestive system.)

In addition, certain areas of the body are considered to be forbidden zones for massage. Never massage the backs of the knees and the armpits. Tremendous potential exists for severe nerve damage in these areas if massage is performed. In Soviet massage the buttocks, breasts and groin are taboo areas that are not normally touched. In Western culture touching the buttocks as part of legitimate massage is acceptable.

WATER, WATER, EVERYWHERE

"Momo just froze. Guys who were there said he was like a piece of iron when he died." **– Mike Matarazzo, top IFBB Pro Bodybuilder (commenting on the death of Mohammad Benaziza, who is believed to have died from an electrolytic imbalance brought on by excessive use of diuretics)**

Massage can be physically demanding for both the client and the masseuse. Water should always be consumed in moderate amounts during massage. The amount of water lost daily averages about two liters, although this figure varies with individual activities and the climate. Humans can live for weeks without food, but only a few days without water. For these reasons hard-training bodybuilders should replenish the water lost during physical exercise or massage by drinking enough fluids during and after workouts. Training intensely without replenishing lost fluids can result – and has resulted – in dehydration leading to kidney failure, causing permanent kidney damage and even death.[26] The use of salt tablets has been abandoned as a training aid for athletes, and most coaches ensure adequate supplies of drinking water. In cold weather athletes can become dehydrated because the sensation of thirst is decreased as a result of the lower temperatures. Whatever the weather, indoors or outdoors, physical training causes dehydration, and bodybuilders should make a conscious effort to consume liquids.

Before the massage session the client should consume one glass of water, followed by one glass of water after the massage. If massage is taking place in a sauna, he or she should sip small amounts throughout the session.

A HAPPY "MEDIUM"

"I feel right on the money – energized, but in a relaxed way." **– Brent Mayne, Kansas City Royals catcher (on the effects of his pregame Hindu medicinal regimen, which includes being doused with hot sesame oil and having ginger juice squirted up his nose)[10]**

As early as 3000 BC the writings of Homer suggest that an oily medium was used for massage. In his *Odyssey* he wrote that beautiful women rubbed and anointed the war-worn heroes to rest and refresh them. Herodotus advised that a greasy mixture should be poured over the body before rubbing. Olive oil was used and it was believed that the oil itself had some curative value. From Roman history records we learn that the writer Cicero received great improvement in his health from his anointer.[5]

As a rule, warmup massage is performed with ointments, requiring precise individuality of application. The massage practitioner must know which procedures are best for each athlete. He or she must know

The late Mohammad Benaziza

the duration of the session, which muscles are to be treated and how to massage them, which ointment to use and how much. Incorrect application and alteration of dosage can show negatively on muscle condition. The masseur should standardize oil applications in order to get the maximum benefit.

Frequently a bodybuilder becomes agitated from a burning feeling after liniment application. To avoid these unfavorable situations, the masseur must select the best massage method and the most suitable ointment for each bodybuilder during training. For one athlete a certain amount of one kind of liniment will be satisfactory for warming up the legs, whereas for another it would be entirely insufficient. For a third it might provoke unbearable burning, and for a fourth such undesirable effects as allergy and nausea might be produced. In this last case a change of medium would be necessary.

In recent years many track and field athletes have used heating liniments during warmup massage regardless of weather conditions – even when the temperature is 86 degrees or more. The reason for this practice is that, when heat liniments are used 30 to 90 minutes before the start of an event, the massaged muscles are warmed deeply for this length of time. As a result more blood goes to the muscles, and their work capacity is increased. The muscles and ligaments become more elastic and have greater resistance to injury. Bodybuilders would be wise to imitate this behavior. In warmup massage the most widely used warming liniments are Nicoflex, Dolpic and Algipan (from the Cramer Company). The best approach is to warm the muscles by using liniments which give a sensation of moderate warmth for a long time since not everyone can withstand strong heating for long periods. Sometimes toning-up liniments (Cramer's, Johnson's or others) are used when there is precompetition burnout, apparent muscle sluggishness, and fatigue.

To increase muscle tone during prolonged training, it is better to use liniments which have an oil base (Cramer's) or to add oil (olive is best) to liniments without an oil base. This oil content creates a film which decreases heat loss and maintains warmth longer. The effect of warming liniments generally lasts from two to four hours.[11] Japanese physicians routinely massage patients with shark liver oil to treat muscle pain as well as other ailments.

If the bodybuilder develops an allergic reaction to the liniment being used, a change should be made to another brand. A trainer who must treat an athlete whom he or she has not massaged previously, should inform the athlete how he usually gives massages regarding duration, intensity and which liniments he normally uses.

THE MODERN BODYBUILDER

"Something that has helped me recuperate and feel better is having deep tissue massage. For years I never did anything that would break up the lumps and tightness in my muscles. After a few sessions of deep tissue massage I noticed that my lats actually took on a new shape. The tightness was gone and the muscle now has a flowing look." **– Shelley Beattie**
IFBB Pro Bodybuilder

Modern bodybuilding is characterized by a dramatic increase in achievement levels. Today's bodybuilders are generally thought to be far superior to their historical colleagues. The training intensity undertaken by present-day bodybuilders would frighten the bodybuilder of thirty or forty years ago. Performance levels which were once though to be unattainable are now the norm. No doubt future bodybuilders will look back and view present standards as rather primitive!

The problem is that these new methods of sports training, which are distinguished by increased duration

Lee Apperson

and intensity, can lead to overload, fatigue, and ultimately overtraining. For a long time this risk has led sports coaches and doctors to search for more effective methods which allow in a short period of time the restoration of strength and work capacity of the athlete. Their research has brought about the development of sports massage. Over the years the popularity of training massage has reached the point where it is now an important part of a bodybuilder's program. The benefits include improving physical and psychological qualities, maintaining sports form, and speeding up the elimination of fatigue after physical training.[12]

Sports massage is very important in all stages of training and immediately before competition. It is broken down into training massage, pre-event massage, restorative massage, injury-treatment massage and relaxation. The approach used depends on the goals of the bodybuilder. For ambitious bodybuilders massage is a necessary part of the training cycle. The large volume and intensity of training loads place great physical and psychological demands on the modern bodybuilder. All of this can lead to fatigue, overloading and overtraining. Massage helps combat and prevent these detrimental conditions. One of the reasons that sports massage is so effective is that it excites the nerve endings in the skin, muscle and blood vessels.

DOES MASSAGE WORK?

Although the idea of therapeutic massage has been around for thousands of years, few scientific studies have been conducted to determine why massage works, or if in fact it does work. Generally massage brings relief to sore muscles by increasing the blood supply to the area (thereby helping remove waste products such as lactic acid) and speeding up the healing process. Dr. Norbert Sander, a competitive runner who has won the New York City marathon, is a firm believer in the powers of massage:

"Many athletes believe that if they train hard, the injury will work itself out. The idea of massage is a lot more popular among athletes in Europe than it is in the United States. You see the masseurs at the Tour de France working on the cyclists. I often hear interviews in which athletes thank their masseurs, not their trainers."

Juan Keys, a muscular therapist who worked with members of the Mexican Olympic track team in the 1970s and later worked with boxer Doug DeWitt, goes further and says that regular massage will not only speed recovery, but will also improve performance:

"Muscles that have been relaxed by massage use energy more efficiently. Stretching is not enough. A massage should be part of an athlete's routine to help prevent injuries as well."

Dr. Sander said practically anyone could benefit from a massage after a workout to relieve routine soreness and stiffness. The more endurance a sport

Shelley Beattie

involves, the more a participant's muscles are likely to need attention.

Massage should not be viewed as a mystical cure-all. "It works best for a chronic injury, one that won't go away or one that has you stymied because you can't get back to where you want to be in your training. For an acute injury such as a muscle tear, you need rest and have to let the muscle heal."[13]

BASIC SHIATSU

Shiatsu is the most well-known style of acupressure – a practice equivalent to acupuncture yet involving the manual application of pressure rather than the insertion of needles. Shiatsu practitioners use about 92 of the 360 standard body parts, applying a strong, direct pressure with the fingers. When done properly, the manipulation can be of immediate benefit, especially in the reduction of muscle tension and alleviation of pain. Treatments usually last from one half hour to an hour.

Some theorists believe Shiatsu blocks the transmission of pain impulses by closing gates of the body's pain-signaling system and releasing endorphins – neurochemicals that reduce pain naturally. Therefore, it

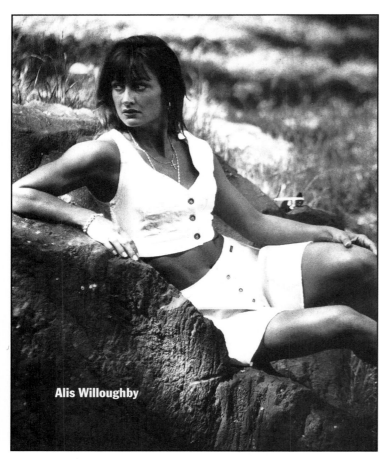
Alis Willoughby

may be of benefit to visit a practitioner if you have a muscle strain.

STRAINED MUSCLES

Perhaps the most common of all bodybuilding injuries is a muscle sprain. This painful spasm can cost the athlete valuable training time and possibly eliminate the athlete from competition. Therefore, Shiatsu may be of benefit – helping to relieve pain and even the associated stresses accompanying bodybuilding competitions. However, if the pain is persistent and/or intense, see a doctor. Never work through such pain![14]

STRETCHING TO PERFECTION

"I stretch out a lot. You've got to stay loose. And I hit the bag two or three times a week." **– Mike Matarazzo, top IFBB Pro Bodybuilder**

Up to this point massage may seem to be the cure for all the bodybuilder's problems. However, not wanting to be accused of being biased, we invite the reader to take a closer look at massage and how it compares to another easily performed movement – stretching.

In Europe soccer is said to be responsible for 50 to 60 percent of all sports injuries. Of all injuries treated in European hospitals, 10 percent are due to soccer. Needless to say, researchers continuously strive to devise strategies to combat this problem. One study has shown that the design of training has an important

effect on the type and number of injuries, and that many injuries can be avoided by a change in training methods. Swedish researchers have been looking at procedures to help reduce the high number of injuries suffered by soccer players.

Muscle tightness seems to predispose athletes to certain injuries. The less flexible the muscle, the greater is the risk of injury. In order to increase their flexibility, Swedish soccer teams have used various techniques. Highlighting the regimens are different stretching programs and muscle massage. In one study eight healthy male volunteers with no history of musculoskeletal or neurological problems were examined. All participated in various exercise programs. The researchers performed four different combinations of experimental procedures: (1) general warming up, (2) general warming up and massage, (3) massage alone, (4) general warming up and stretching.

"...like grab a pole to stretch out your chest. Whatever muscle you're working, find a way to stretch it."
– Mike Matarazzo, top IFBB Pro Bodybuilder

The effects of general warming up and stretching on ranges of motion and leg strength were measured. Thigh muscle strength was not influenced by any of the experimental procedures. Stretching resulted in a significantly increased range of hip flexion, extension, abduction, knee flexion and ankle flexion. Massage and warming up did not produce any significant changes. Only ankle flexion showed any improvement by massage. The researchers concluded that stretching was a superior method for increasing flexibility in the lower extremities.[15]

What's the lesson to be learned from all of this? Stretch! Never stop stretching. You don't have to train like an Olympic athlete, but a little aerobic fitness, supplemented with some stretching movements, will go a long way in preventing injuries and helping you to stay in shape.[16] Bodybuilders should always take the time to warm up and stretch the muscle group before it is challenged.

RECOVERY

In their quest for peak performance bodybuilders tend to focus most of their attention on training, devoting little time to recovery from these intense training sessions. We now realize that recovery plays as big a role in athletic preparation as training and practice do. A bodybuilder who has not fully recovered from one workout is susceptible to injury when diving into the next session. The question that the reader should be asking is, how do you know if you need more recovery time? One of the best indicators of overtraining is the resting pulse as measured just after waking in the morning. If it is elevated, the body is telling you that it's time to slow down and reduce intensity. The only drawback to this method is that the bodybuilder must have an indication of what his or her basal (resting) pulse rate was to begin with. Another indicator of overtraining is decreased enthusiasm and motivation for training. Bodybuilders love to train. If, however, going for a workout becomes a chore and missing a workout becomes a viable alternative, bingo! You know your body is sending you a message that a period of rest is in order. Other signs indicating that more recovery time is needed include excessive pain, fatigue, continued soreness, and nagging injuries that won't go away. If the bodybuilder experiences all – or even some – of these symptoms, he should be devoting more time to recovery. Can you speed up recovery time? Yes! Let's now look at the levels of recovery and the role massage plays in facilitating this important process.

The first level of recovery involves recuperation that occurs during an actual workout or competition. The second level happens right after the workout, the goal being removal of waste products built up through intense exercise. Finally, delayed recovery raises bodybuilders to higher competitive levels. Sports massage works at all three levels. Massage while training helps athletes recover faster from intense workouts and increases training potential. How long the massage lasts depends on the specific muscles involved in the activity. For example, massage before competition can either increase or decrease nerve-cell excitability, again depending on the type, duration and intensity of the massage. Probably the most important benefit of precompetition massage is the prevention of injuries by warming the joints and connective tissue. The last type, restoration massage, speeds muscle

recovery two to three times faster than passive rest. It does this by promoting increased blood and lymph flow and lactic acid removal in muscles.[17]

MASSAGE AND SPORTS PSYCHOLOGY

"Cigarettes, coffee, late nights and booze occasionally."
– Timothy Dalton, former James Bond
(explaining how he keeps fit)[27]

The problem of regulating the psychological emotional stress of bodybuilders is very important. At the same time the effect of such a powerful method of massage has not been fully appreciated. In the arena of million dollar salaries and the glory of competition, it is often forgotten that bodybuilders are human. The rigors of intense training combined with an overabundance of psychological pressure often lead to premature burnout. In recent years sports psychologists have been recommending massage, not just for performance improvement, but also as therapy to help bodybuilders achieve one of the most basic of human states – relaxation!

Warmup massage must take into account the bodybuilder's psychological condition. If you notice that he or she is overanxious, you can decrease the anxiety by gently performing massage at a slow tempo. Begin with stroking and gentle rubbing and shaking movements from the spine. Also massage the lower neck-shoulder, girdle area, the neck and the head. Conclude the session with massage of the leg region, using warming liniments.[11]

Matt Mendenhall relaxes in the sun.

In cases of anxiety or apathy psychological influences can be helpful. The masseur can inspire the bodybuilder by telling her about her readiness to perform well in competition and the good condition of her muscles and joints. He can mention an interesting situation from a previous competition or simply an event which elicits a positive reaction from the bodybuilder.[11] Just as the athlete's body needs physical nourishment, so too does the mind need positive psychological reinforcement.

THE BODYBUILDER'S MASSAGE PROGRAM

Historians have noted that what running was to the 70s, bodybuilding is to the 80s and 90s. Although the public has the perception that bodybuilding is a form of entertainment, it is in fact one of the most physically demanding of all sports. Massage is used to encourage muscle growth, relieve fatigue, and speed up recovery time.

During the workout there are two time periods (called recovery periods) that bodybuilders must consider. The inter-recovery period takes place between groups of sets (for different muscle groups). The intra-recovery period takes place between sets for one muscle group. The beginning bodybuilder is advised to massage only before and after the complete workout. The intermediate bodybuilder, who is now involved in more intense workouts, is advised to massage in the inter-recovery period. The advanced bodybuilder may, in order to overcome a plateau, massage during the intra-recovery period. This treatment is also advisable when preparing for a competition. It relieves fatigue and burnout, and helps relax the athlete.

Massage is not to be performed if the athlete is dehydrated prior to a contest! In order to augment the "ripped" look, some bodybuilders will take diuretics and restrict water intake. This practice is unhealthful, inappropriate, dangerous, and has led to a number of deaths. If the athlete has followed a proper diet and maintained normal fluid intake, massage can be performed right up to the moment he or she steps onstage.

Joe Spinello

Achilles heel:

> Stroking – x 5
> Kneading – x 5
> Stroking – x 5

Calves:

> Stroking – x 5
> Circular kneading – x 10
> Edging – x 10
> Stroking – x 5

Buttocks:

The athlete is lying down for the following...

> Stroking – x 5
> Kneading – x 10
> Edging – x 10
> Stroking – x 5

Back:

> Stroking – x 5
> Kneading – x 10
> Two-hand circular kneading – x 10
> Chopping – x 10
> Edging – x 10
> Stroking – x 5

Chest:

Left of the sternum you massage to the left.
To the right side of the sternum you massage to the right. Simply, massage away from the center of the chest.

> Stroking – x 5
> Kneading – x 10
> Edging – x 10
> Stroking – x 5

Shoulders:

> Stroking – x 5
> Kneading – x 10
> Edging – x 10
> Stroking – x 5

Arms:

> Stroking – x 5
> Circular kneading – x 10
> Edging – x 10
> Stroking – x 5

Hands:

> Stroking – x 5
> Circular kneading with the tip of the thumb – x 10
> Two-hand kneading with the tips
>   of the thumbs – x 10
> Rolling – x 10
> Stroking – x 5

Because of the intensity of the training engaged in, some of the muscle units and fibers deteriorate into the worst possible state. This deterioration can happen when repetitious movements are used, when the muscles are once again challenged before full recovery has taken place, and when injuries are not allowed to fully heal. To prevent serious injury the bodybuilder should learn to recognize the early signs of overtraining. From there, corrective measures can be taken. First, the body-builder should focus on another event during training. Second, he or she should reduce the work load. Finally, massage should be performed to aid in the restoration process. Strained muscles can also be treated with restorative massage.

RESTORATIVE MASSAGE

"It is only the first 100 years of life that are difficult."
– Old Moldovan saying

Sometimes competitive sports are so demanding that a more intensive and involved form of massage is needed to help the bodybuilder recover, particularly if this person is scheduled to compete again within a short time. How can the bodybuilder recognize this situation? First, he will experience slight pain or extreme stiffness. Second, his muscles will lose strength and elasticity. Third, he will find relaxing increasingly difficult. If overloading of the neuromuscular system continues, regeneration and recovery never occur and the bodybuilder is greatly at risk for muscular strains and tears.

Restorative massage is conducted in two stages. The first session lasts eight to ten minutes and is conducted after the first workout. The second session lasts 35 to 40 minutes and is conducted two to three hours after the second workout. The objective of the first session is to remove metabolic products, thus preventing them from spreading to the surrounding tissue. The objective of the second session is to remove metabolic products which have diffused into the blood and other tissues.

Having looked at the reasons for massage, let's now follow that old fitness saying, "Don't just think about it – do it!"

The first massage session starts in the back and progresses downward toward the feet. Light kneading is alternated with percussion of the back muscles. From the back we move to the gluteal area. The glutes are shaken, vibrated and kneaded. Thighs and hips are worked next with alternate percussion and kneading, finished off with light stroking. Finally the lower leg muscles (gastrocnemius) and feet are massaged. Kneading and percussion are again alternated, and the area is finished off with light stroking movements.

The second session of restorative massage, lasting about 40 minutes, takes place about two to three hours after the second workout. The massage time is divided as follows: back, 20 percent, head and neck, 15 percent, and the lower limbs, 65 percent. As with the first session the therapist starts in the upper regions and works toward the lower limbs. Percussion and kneading movements are alternated, and each region is concluded with light stroking movements.

Keep in mind that the effectiveness of the massage depends on the skill and sensitivity of the masseur. The best results are obtained when there is a positive interaction between the bodybuilder and the masseur. Such

Paul DeMayo and Denise Paglia

a relationship can only develop over time. We recommend that bodybuilders limit their sessions to one or two masseurs. In this manner both athlete and therapist can provide feedback to each other and use it in future sessions.[18]

MASSAGE AND CIRCULATION

One must remember how blood and lymph circulation flow to be able to massage in the correct direction. Failure to keep this fact uppermost in mind can cause problems. The direction of movement is always toward the heart (venous return):

> fingers $\rightarrow$ shoulders
> toes $\rightarrow$ groin
> head $\rightarrow$ shoulders

The following are exceptions:

> rib cage $\rightarrow$ groin (to aid digestion)
> sternum $\rightarrow$ right side of chest

MASSAGE IN THE 20TH CENTURY

In a never-ending quest to obtain the winning edge, athletes and researchers alike are continuously searching for innovations that will give the athlete that extra 5 to 10 percent. Manufacturers of sports equipment were quick to come forward and address the demand. The last five years have seen a boom in training-related machinery. This trend has reached the point where a modern gym is now reminiscent of the dungeon of a medieval castle! Every possible combination of weight, pulley, cable, wire, etc., is used in the design of modern training equipment. It was only a matter of time before massage was discovered by technology.

One of the most effective of the new techniques is vacuum massage. Using a device called a Traxator-Minor vacuum massager, therapists have been able to speed up recovery times and increase the functional reserves of intensely training athletes. The device sets up a vacuum (much the same as the standard carpet-cleaning Hoover or Electrolux), which gently tugs on the subject's skin and underlying muscles.

The effectiveness of vacuum massage was evaluated by measuring the speed of blood circulation, tonus of thigh muscles, and skin temperature. Studies have shown that after a procedure of vacuum massage, speed of circulation increases in the blood vessels by 1.4 seconds. The plastic and contact tonus of the quadriceps muscle decreased by one to five myotomes. Skin temperature increased more than one degree celsius.[20]

The evidence indicates that vacuum massage speeds up recovery from intense training sessions. The degree of improvement is very small, but at the level of international sports even the most meager improvement can mean the difference between first and second.

The latest in self-massage resembles a home entertainment system. Manufacturers have designed a capsule shaped much like an Easter egg and about the size of a sofa – large enough to accomodate a man or woman. Equipped with stereo, adjustable programs and even fragrance controls, the capsule permits a user to relax in the privacy of his own home and not have to worry about making appointments, lack of parking space, or therapist fees. The massage capsule can be used by anyone – from top-rank athlete to corporate business executive, from housewife to student – in search of the perfect way to end a stressful day.

"I was working on my computer and he massaged my neck." **– A dream involving President Bill Clinton, (as related by one of his female fans)**[21]

Another option is the Relaxor mat. This portable, pulsating massage mat goes with you anywhere. Much cheaper than massage capsules, and more convenient than going to a massage therapist, the massage mat makes the perfect traveling companion. It operates on low voltage and is complete with AC adaptor. The mat produces a soothing, wave-like massage up and down the user's body.[19]

From vacuum massagers to massage capsules to mats, the art of massage will never look the same again. We can only guess how the ancient Greeks and Romans would view such developments!

SOVIET SECRETS

Since the fall of the Berlin wall and the breakup of the Soviet Union, many of the training secrets of the Eastern Bloc athletes have become known. One of the more popular restoration techniques has been the application of heat, not to one or two bodyparts, but to the whole body. The Soviets (for the purposes of this book we shall refer to all athletes from the former Soviet Union as Soviets) use such heat sources as saunas, steam baths and hydrotherapy. Soviet athletes spend 10 to 15 minutes in a dry-heat sauna after an intense workout. The benefits include increased circulation, neuromuscular toning, the easing of pain, and the speeding up of the removal of waste products.[17]

Bodybuilders and other athletes are now working out much harder than their compatriots of years gone by. Such training is necessary to go beyond the achievements of yesterday's athletes. As effective as heavy training is, it cannot be done without taking steps to ensure that recovery is complete. The athlete must be careful not to overstep his or her physical bounds and go into an overtrained state. You can recover from a mild case of overtraining, but chronic overtraining may need months for full recovery to take place.

In this chapter we have outlined massage programs that will greatly enhance the recovery abilities of bodybuilders. Massage, however, is just one method of speeding up recuperative processes. There are many others. They include sports massage, heat, hydrotherapy (water), electrical stimulation, pressure chambers, and various types of showers. The drawback to most of these procedures is that they require specialized and often expensive equipment. An alternative available to most athletes is the sauna. Although popular in Asian and European countries for centuries, only in recent years have saunas begun to be taken seriously by North American athletes and coaches. Most of the negativism associated with saunas in the US and Canada is due to improper use. This negative coverage downgrades the use of a very effective means of body restoration after workouts. The advantage of a sauna over a steam bath is the low humidity of the former. The dry air of the sauna provides a favorable condition for effective sweating. The sweat can evaporate, thus getting rid of excess heat and maintaining body temperature at a more constant level. Another benefit is that a 20-minute sauna session burns off 300 calories.

Regulated heat is one of the most promising means of recovery in athletics and bodybuilding. It is finding increased use not only in the athletic world but in medicine as well. By using saunas on a regular basis, you will find your body recovering faster, and will be able to to do more work and thus make better gains.[22]

The sauna appears to be one of the most effective means of restoration in the period of intense training of athletes. Increased physical work capacity under the influence of a sauna is explained by the positive changes that take place in the highest nerve centers and in the biochemical processes of muscle contraction. Other benefits include improvement of blood circulation in the peripheral tissues, relaxation of the muscles, activation of the oxygen-restorative processes, and removal (through perspiration) of several end products of the exchange of various substances and toxins. Saunas also improve the rate at which muscle tissues are supplied with oxygen and glycogen.[23]

Research shows that for a one-time exposure, the physiological effect depends on the magnitude of the heat stress undergone for a specific time period. In a sauna an increase in heart rate is indicative and directly related to the body's core temperature. Saunas have been demonstrated to heighten functional blood circulation capabilities without muscular work. From a psychological perspective athletes report an improved sense of well-being, a feeling of confidence, good mood, and increased competitive desire.[24] Greater strength, a feeling of freshness, courage, removal of fatigue and increased energy have also been said to accrue from sauna use.

The sauna is most beneficial when signs of excessive stress and muscle tightness appear. These can be recognized when there is a sudden drop in total physical performance. Before outlining training cycles involving the sauna, we advise adherence to the following guidelines:

1. Use of the sauna for rehabilitation and restoration requires medical supervision.

2. Air temperature in the sauna should not go over 90 degrees Celsius with a relative humidity of 5 to 15 percent.

3. To increase the restorative effect, the athlete should not go into the sauna immediately after intense training. The best time is one or two hours after the workout.

4. Before entering the sauna, wash with soap and wipe the skin dry. This procedure creates the optimal conditions for sweat release and thermal regulation.

5. The stay in the sauna begins on the lowest benches for two to three minutes, gradually moving to the upper benches. On the highest benches the athlete can either lie down or sit, placing the legs horizontally. During the time of perspiration it is important to achieve muscular and psychological relaxation. In the last two or three minutes of being in the hot sauna, it is necessary to sit with lowered legs and only then leave the heat. A sudden attempt to stand could cause dizziness or fainting.

6. The sauna stay ends with a 30- to 40-minute rest, during which time you must replace lost liquids and biologically active substances by using mineral waters and vitamin-rich drinks.[23]

Below is a table of recommended sauna cycles.

Key to Table:
F – Frequency (number of times in the sauna, alternating with rest intervals for one session)
C – Temperature (in degrees Celsius)
H – Humidity (percent)
Ri – Rest interval (minutes, after time in sauna)
Sp – Shower pattern: cool (C) – 20, warm (W) – 40
St – Time in minutes

Types of Cycles:
Prep – Before training
Post – After training
Pre-event – Before competition
Post-event – After competition
Veteran – Hard training (not for everyone!)

For the first four cycles, time in the sauna is limited to ten minutes.[23] The veteran cycle has a sauna period of 30 minutes.[24]

The maximum time spent in the sauna is always 10 minutes.[24] The length of time a bodybuilder devotes to one particular cycle depends on his level of training and competition. The recreational bodybuilder might use the sauna once a week, whereas the competitive bodybuilder may use the sauna after every workout. For an injured bodybuilder (who has already received medical clearance to resume training), the post-event cycle is ideally suited to speed rehabilitation.

A WORD OF CAUTION TO THE READER

The sauna is a valuable training tool, but if used improperly it can be harmful. Before attempting any of the suggested cycles, see a physician for a complete medical and obtain clearance to pursue the program. There could be an underlying medical problem that you might not be aware of. To protect yourself do the following:

1. The bodybuilder should be continuously drinking small amounts of water while in the sauna (on average a small sip every 10 seconds).

2. Not all saunas are created equal! Therefore you must listen to your own body. Monitor your pulse rate. If it becomes rapid and erratic, leave the sauna *immediately*. Speak to an attendant or fellow patron. If you begin to have chest pain call 911. If you are in the sauna and become dizzy or lightheaded, leave the sauna. If assistance is available, ask for it. If you are alone, do not stand up. Crawl out of the sauna and call for help.

3. Saunas do not turn people into bodybuilders. They can help bodybuilders become better bodybuilders. The sauna is merely a training aid that must be used in combination with proper diet and exercise.[24]

DANCE TO THE MUSIC

Music is a great emotional and spiritual booster. From the Monday morning drive to work to the dance floor on Friday night, music has become fixated in twentieth-century life. In recent years sports psychologists have discovered that music accompaniment in training

Sauna Cycles	F	C	H	Ri	Sp	St
Prep	3	90	5	12	C-W-C	30s-5min-30s
Post	3	90	10	10	C-W	30s-5min
Pre-event	2	90	15	5	C-W	30s-5min
Post-event	3	70	15	10	W	5min
Veteran	1	80	30	0	C	1min

sessions significantly increases not only the effectiveness of the training but also the mental attitude of the trainer. A similar approach is now being applied to massage sessions as well. The music can take many forms, and there is going to be much individual preference in choosing what's to be played. Some bodybuilders prefer heavy rock music while others endorse easy listening. Generally most prefer music with a fast tempo during training and light soothing music during massage and relaxation sessions.[25] Because bodybuilding incorporates music into the competition itself, bodybuilders should begin using music early in their training.

All the technical innovations described in this chapter are derived from massage – from warming the muscles to relaxing the athlete. Massage is a vigorous workout that can be tailored to the athlete's needs and sport. While technology will continue to advance, it would be foolish to assume that any of these changes could ever replace the hands-on art that has lasted for over 3,000 years.

IFBB professionals Craig Titus and Ericca Kern.

Dennis Newman

BOOK SIX

6

The Greatest of Sports

Chapter Seventeen

EVERYTHING YOU NEED TO KNOW ABOUT COMPETITIVE BODYBUILDING

Kevin Levrone

"When people see me onstage, they don't realize how little competitive experience I have had. I've always been a confident, outgoing person. I'm very comfortable onstage – something of a showoff – so posing in front of a big audience is easy for me."
– Kevin Levrone, IFBB Pro Bodybuilder
Night of Champions winner

Congratulations! You've arrived! After many months (in most cases, years) of pounding away in the gym, your physique has taken on the shape and size that garners you compliments. It's now time to take that extra step – strutting your stuff on a competitive bodybuilding stage.

This chapter offers many tidbits of information that will prepare you for your first contest. Of course, we realize that not everyone is interested in competing. No problem. In fact, the vast majority of people who work out have no intention of competing. Even so, much of what we discuss in the next few chapters, applies to everyone – whether for the beach or posing platform. So sit back and read about the little things that provide the winning edge.

WHY COMPETE?

Competitive bodybuilders generally fall into one of two categories. At one end of the spectrum you have those who feel they're ready to compete after a couple of months of training. While there are a few genetic naturals who gained 20 to 30 pounds of muscle mass in only a few months, most need to be training for at least a year before they're ready.

Besides the lack of muscle mass, the limited training time means a restricted amount of knowledge. The end result is a crash course in dieting (two to three weeks), a posing routine haphazardly thrown together, and a total lack of contest preparation. Is it any wonder that many such would-be competitors give up the sport for good?

At the other end of the spectrum we have the procrastinators, those guys who train for five to 10 years, gain 50 to 75 pounds of muscle mass, and still feel they're not ready! The problem usually lies with an improper self-image. They constantly compare themselves with Dorian Yates or Vince Taylor, and falling short, decide to wait "just one more year." Unfortunately that one more year becomes five or 10, and before they know it, their best competitive years are behind them. It's a shame really when you see audiences full of bodybuilders who obviously could have placed – or even won – the contest they were watching.

Another benefit of competing is improved progress. The evidence strongly suggests that those bodybuilders who frequently compete make faster progress than those who don't. A number of reasons are put forward to explain this phenomenon. For starters, regular competition necessitates cycling your training. Thus the body is constantly shocked with new training and eating patterns. It never gets a chance to become stale and complacent.

Another reason lies with experience and knowledge. Those who compete regularly make a great effort to learn as much as possible about the sport. With increased knowledge comes increased progress. It's as simple as that.

A third reason is perhaps more basic. There is nothing like competition to bring out the best in someone. A fifth-place finish this year will motivate most to bust their butts in training and place higher next year. This constant effort to be the best can lead only in one direction – to the top!

Whatever the reason for competing, the bottom line is that you should give it some serious thought. Unlike such sports as boxing, judo or wrestling, where getting in over your head can be dangerous, bodybuilding is 100 percent safe, at least from a physical point of view. Granted, your ego may be brought down a notch or two, but our experience is that most competitors use a poor placing to motivate them for future events.

Besides the level of competition, there are other factors to consider. When choosing your first contest, make sure it's far enough down the road that you have enough time to prepare. Deciding to enter an event that's two weeks away is foolhardy. There's no way in such a short time period that you can get into top physical condition and have a posing routine prepared.

For information on contests, check with the gyms in your area, or better still, contact a local representative of the IFBB/NPC. These are the largest professional and amateur bodybuilding federations in the world. Check also the Upcoming Events sections in the large bodybuilding magazines like *MuscleMag International* and *Flex*.

Most larger cities, provinces or states offer several contests each year. Usually events are arranged so that if you win one, you can enter the next contest up the ladder later in the year.

You should use the same approach to contest selection as training – that is, start slowly and gradually work your way up the ladder of intensity. Generally speaking, the order of competition should be city, state or province, regional, and finally national. If you're lucky enough to win the national event, you have the honor of representing your country at the world championships. Win this and it's on to the pro level, and pretty soon Robert Kennedy will be on the phone requesting an interview and photo shoot! Sounds exciting, doesn't it? So think seriously about that upcoming local competition. Afterwards you'll wonder why you didn't do it sooner.

John Sherman

THE TITLES

"Winning the Nationals was a dream come true for me, one I've been cultivating for a long, long time. I've always been pretty athletic and have always liked the look of big, freaky muscles! I loved the way training made me feel and how it changed the way I looked. I still do."
— **John Sherman**
IFBB Pro Bodybuilder
USA National champion

With the reorganization of bodybuilding contests in the early 1980s, the once familiar "Mr." titles are all but extinct. The Mr. and Ms. Olympias are still there, but by and large the Mr. and Ms. titles have been replaced by names that are more in keeping with the legitimate sport bodybuilding has become. For example, the once-famous Mr. America is now called the US National Championships. Other countries have adopted the same naming format. The winners of the respective countries go on to compete in the World Championships, formally called the Mr. Universe (amateur). Of course, athletes don't simply decide to enter their country's national bodybuilding championships. First they have to qualify at local and regional shows. The usual format is to win an all-city contest, and then go on to the state or provincial event. After winning your state or province the next step is often a regional competition, involving a small number of jurisdictions in a common geographical area. If you win a

Larry Scott

Sergio Oliva

Arnold Schwarzenegger

Franco Columbu

Frank Zane

Chris Dickerson

Samir Bannout

Lee Haney

**1996 Mr. Olympia
Dorian Yates**

All these contests fall under the category of amateur bodybuilding. This means there are no cash prizes for the winners or placers. The dividing line between amateur and professional these days however, is very thin. For example, endorsing clothing and food supplements is extremely lucrative, but technically not "income." Therefore an amateur can make a substantial amount of money in this manner but still retain his amateur status. Extreme examples of this arrangement were sprinters Ben Johnson and Carl Lewis, who made millions in endorsements during their careers but retained their amateur status as none of the money was deemed "payment" for winning.)

Once bodybuilders have won the Nationals, North American Championships, or other qualifying event, they receive their professional card. They are then eligible to compete in the sport's various pro contests.

PROFESSIONAL BODYBUILDING

Like most pro athletes, professional bodybuilders receive some sort of financial reward for winning or placing in a contest. In recent years the first place winners at such prestigious events as the Arnold Schwarzenegger Classic and Mr. Olympia have received as much as $100,000. This may not seem like much when compared to earnings in such sports as golf ($250,000 to $300,000) or tennis ($500,000 to $1,000,000), but on the other hand it's a far cry from the days of a handshake and a case of protein powder!

"I know that I can't fight fire with fire, so my approach is to be the finest, the most complete, the most finished physique up there. The other guys may be like two-carat diamonds, but they have slight flaws. So along comes a flawless one-carat diamond. Which costs more? Which holds its value longer?"
– Lee Labrada
IFBB Pro Bodybuilder

For those who plan to go all the way, the top male bodybuilding title is the Mr. Olympia. First held in 1965, this event is considered the Super Bowl of bodybuilding and takes place each fall. Over its 30 years such greats as Arnold Schwarzenegger, Sergio Oliva, Franco Columbu, Frank Zane, Lee Haney and Dorian Yates have used the Olympia to set the sport's standard. As has become the practice in recent years, many top-rank bodybuilders train solely for this event, preferring to give a pass to the other pro contests.

Although relatively new compared to its male equivalent, the Ms. Olympia has also been the scene of many tough physique battles. First held in 1980, the event has been won by female superstars Rachel McLish, Kike Elomaa, Carla Dunlap, Cory Everson, Lenda Murray and Kim Chizevsky.

state or provincial championship, or place in the top three at a regional event, you are eligible to compete at the Nationals.

Most local events are called "closed" championships, meaning you must live in a designated area to compete. Other competitions are called "open" and, as the name implies, are accessible to any entrant, regardless of residence.

The following is a list of all Mr. and Ms. Olympia winners since 1965.

MR. OLYMPIA	MS. OLYMPIA
1965 – Larry Scott	----------------
1966 – Larry Scott	----------------
1967 – Sergio Oliva	----------------
1968 – Sergio Oliva	----------------
1969 – Sergio Oliva	----------------
1970 – Arnold Schwarzenegger	----------------
1971 – Arnold Schwarzenegger	----------------
1972 – Arnold Schwarzenegger	----------------
1973 – Arnold Schwarzenegger	----------------
1974 – Arnold Schwarzenegger	----------------
1975 – Arnold Schwarzenegger	----------------
1976 – Franco Columbu	----------------
1977 – Frank Zane	----------------
1978 – Frank Zane	----------------
1979 – Frank Zane	----------------
1980 – Arnold Schwarzenegger	Rachel McLish
1981 – Franco Columbu	Kike Elomaa
1982 – Chris Dickerson	Rachel McLish
1983 – Samir Bannout	Carla Dunlap
1984 – Lee Haney	Cory Everson
1985 – Lee Haney	Cory Everson
1986 – Lee Haney	Cory Everson
1987 – Lee Haney	Cory Everson
1988 – Lee Haney	Cory Everson
1989 – Lee Haney	Cory Everson
1990 – Lee Haney	Lenda Murray
1991 – Lee Haney	Lenda Murray
1992 – Dorian Yates	Lenda Murray
1993 – Dorian Yates	Lenda Murray
1994 – Dorian Yates	Lenda Murray
1995 – Dorian Yates	Lenda Murray
1996 – Dorian Yates	Kim Chizevsky

Carla Dunlap

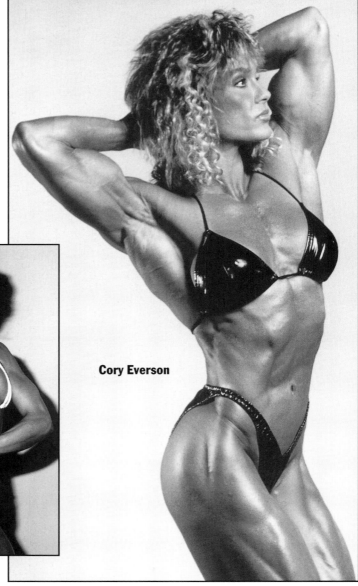

Cory Everson

Rachel McLish   **Kike Elomaa**

Lenda Murray

YOUR FIRST CONTEST

Now that you know what you're aiming for, it's time to think about entering your first bodybuilding contest. The best competitive position for your first contest is the audience. Yes, we're quite serious. It makes little sense to go straight from the squat rack to the posing dais without learning the finer points in between. If you think a bodybuilding contest is only a matter of jumping onstage and hitting a few double-biceps poses, you're sadly mistaken. Most competitors will readily admit that preparing for a contest is nearly as time consuming as training itself. So your first step on the road to the Mr. Olympia is to attend a local contest.

At that first contest don't limit your observations to the competitors and their routines. Sit back and take in what yuppies call the "big picture." Watch the judges. Which competitors do they call out? What seems to impress them the most? How about the audience members? Which music selections get them into the swing of things? Which posing routines put them to sleep? Do the judges and audience members react the same way or differently?

Kim Chizevsky
1996 Ms. Olympia

Besides the Mr. Olympia other pro contests are held each year. Immediately after the Olympia most male competitors fly to Europe for a series of Grand Prix events in various countries – e.g. Germany, Great Britain, Russia, Belgium and Spain. European tours allow pro body-builders to perform for audiences "on the other side of the pond." Besides the entertainment aspect, the contests offer athletes a substantial amount of prize money.

After a few months' break, the pros get ready for North American competitions, including the prestigious Arnold Schwarzenegger Classic, the Ironman Invitational, and the New York Night of Champions. Over the years each has been the scene of some terrific onstage battles, and to be considered one of the sport's greats, a body-builder has to have won one or more of the three.

Lee Labrada, Lee Haney and Gary Strydom

Then there are the various booths set up outside the auditorium. (At the bigger events the gang from *MuscleMag International* often appear, so by all means go over and say hello.) Notice what they're selling. Do you need posing trunks for an upcoming competition? Could you use some new workout gear? A quick walk through the lobby will introduce you to the wide world of bodybuilding paraphernalia.

Bodybuilding contests are divided into two phases, prejudging and the finals. While the evening show is as much entertainment as competition, the prejudging is all business. Usually held in the morning and afternoon, the prejudging gives the judges an opportunity to carefully evaluate the competitors and make as many comparisons as they feel are necessary for accurate placings.

As a future competitor you definitely need to attend the prejudging. In the vast majority of cases the judges have the winner selected before the evening show. By attending the prejudging, you'll become familiar with what's expected of you.

PREJUDGING

The prejudging is divided into various rounds – compulsory poses, comparisons and individual posing routines. Men are required to do seven compulsory poses, women five. For comparisons the judges call out different groups of competitors to have them repeat the compulsory poses one or more times. This process allows the judges to compare physiques in terms of size, symmetry, and definition or muscularity. As you watch the compulsory segment, you'll see that some competitors are repeatedly called out and others virtually ignored. Usually the top five or six competitors will be called out the most often. (If one individual is head and shoulders above the rest, the judges may ignore him completely, having decided with one glance that he or she is the winner.)

After the compulsories and comparisons the prejudging usually proceeds to the individual posing routines. (Sometimes this round is omitted at the prejudging and performed only at the evening show.) Perform a good routine and you'll almost certainly place towards the top. Stumble about and you can kiss the winner's trophy good-bye. It's that simple. Your posing routine can make or break your chances of winning (more on this later as well).

Depending on the number of contestants, the prejudging usually finishes by early afternoon. The competitors by this time feel as if they've gone through ten sets of squats. Posing, especially holding poses, is very tiring. Combine this strain with the hot lights and you end up with a group of beat-out, dehydrated bodybuilders.

THE EVENING SHOW

The evening show usually starts around 7 or 8 p.m. It resembles the prejudging with the exception of the larger audience. If you've never seen, or more importantly, heard a bodybuilding audience, you're in for a treat! The terms *loud*, *noisy*, *obnoxious* and *boisterous*, don't do bodybuilding audiences justice. Nowhere is this characteristic more apparent than at a city or state contest.

A typical audience is made up of camps or cliques, each loyal to one or more contestants. At times inter-gym rivalry borders on war.

Lee Labrada

You should be warned that this is not a night at the opera. Polite applause is not where it's at. As soon as a favorite bodybuilder mounts the posing platform, there erupts a chorus of verbal support: "Come on, Charlie, show 'em what you've got" or "Hey, Susan, let's see those abs." From one corner of the audience you may hear "Squeeze it, squeeze it!" From another it's throaty bellows of "Hold it, hold it!" It seems that no matter how hard the competitor tries, the audience wants more, and when two favorites get together onstage, look out!

Between the shouts of ecstasy and encouragement there is an actual event. The first three rounds are identical to the prejudging, consisting of two compulsory and one individual posing round. After the judges have made their decision, the show ends with what's known as the posedown. Depending on the number of contestants, the judges call forward the top three to six competitors and have them go through a type of posing free-for-all. Each competitor flexes to the roar of the audience, matching shots with his nearest competitor. If one competitor is considered to be the one to beat, the others jockey into position to have a go at him or her by jumping in front and showing the judges their best bodyparts. They are saying to the judges, "Hey, look, my back and abs are better than this guy's, and as for legs well forget it."

After the posedown, which normally lasts 60 seconds, the head judge asks the competitors to relax. (Usually several requests are necessary to settle down the now-pumped-up athletes.) From then on it's a matter of announcing the placings from fifth to first, or third to first, depending on the number of trophies being awarded. You may hear scattered boos when some clique's favorite doesn't place as well as expected, but for the most part the audience goes away feeling contented, and in some cases, more tired than the contestants.

Well, what did you think of your first contest? Exciting wasn't it? Next time you'll be the one onstage being yelled at. Naturally there are a few intermediate steps along the way, but that's where we come in. Read on.

SELECTING YOUR FIRST CONTEST

The first step in your competitive career is to choose the correct contest – that is, the contest most applicable to your physique level. If you're in your teens, the choice is a bit easier as most shows feature a teenage division. To compete in such events you must be 19 years old or younger. Many events feature another category called "junior." To be eligible, you must be 20 years of age or younger, and not have won a previous open-level or junior contest.

If you're above 20 years of age, you may have the option of competing in the "novice" division. These contests are for bodybuilders who have never placed in any previous competition. Not all shows feature this class so you may want to check beforehand.

Front double biceps

Back double biceps

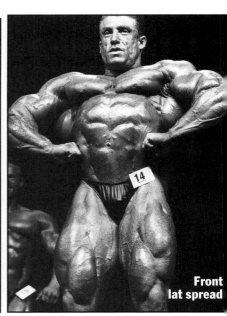

Front lat spread

Dorian Yates demonstrates the seven compulsory poses.

Although there are exceptions, most contests are broken down into weight divisions. Such an arrangement makes competition more equitable for shorter and smaller bodybuilders. In IFBB competition the weight classes are as follows:

Lightweight – under 154 pounds (70 kilograms)
Middleweight – under 176 pounds (80 kilograms)
Light Heavyweight – under 198 pounds (90 kilograms)
Heavyweight – over 198 pounds (90 kilograms)
(Bantamweight and welterweight divisions are sometimes included also.)

The strategy employed by most competitors is to compete at the top of their weight class. It may sound more glamorous to compete in the heavyweight division, but you'll make a far greater impact on the judges competing as a ripped light heavyweight than as a smooth heavyweight. So lose those few extra pounds and be the largest and most complete competitor in your weight class.

SCORING

"The contests are decided by nine judges, whose tastes vary on any given day. I've learned not to get bent out of shape over placings. What concerns me is looking better than ever before." **– Lee Labrada, top IFBB Pro Bodybuilder**

To the untrained eye selecting the winner at a bodybuilding contest may seem rather easy. Ask Joe Average off the street who should win, and chances are he'll say the guy with the biggest muscles. But ranking the contestants in a bodybuilding competition is no simple chore, and behind the scenes the judges work feverishly to accurately determine the fairest placings.

In IFBB competition the judging panel is made up of approximately seven judges (both male and female),

each of whom has been evaluated and certified. Although there have been exceptions, by and large judges work their way up the competitive ladder in the same manner as the bodybuilders themselves. By the time they reach the professional level, judges will have evaluated dozens, and in some cases, hundreds of contests.

Bodybuilding contests are presently scored using the ranking system. After each round (described in the next section), the judges rank the individuals from first to last. At the end of the competition the individual who accumulates the lowest score wins. This system means that a competitor doesn't have to win every round to be declared the victor. Conversely – but rarely – there have been winners who have never placed first in any of the rounds, but won because of their accumulated low scores. Finally, to guard against the possibility that a judge may be biased for or against one competitor, the highest and lowest scores are eliminated at the end of each round.

Now that you have some idea of how you'll be scored, our next task is to explain each of the rounds in more detail. Remember, to win or even place in today's highly competitive bodybuilding, you must make a good impression during each round. Don't devote all your preparation to the free-posing round and ignore the compulsories. Likewise don't step onstage with a haphazard free-posing routine.

THE COMPULSORY ROUNDS

Round 1 – Although the most basic of the four, round one is where you make the first impression on the judges. You'll be first asked to stand facing the judges, hands at your sides. This sounds straightforward, but there are definite do's and don'ts. For starters, don't let your stomach hang out! Keep your abs tensed at all times. While you want your muscles to appear larger, your waist is definitely not one of them. Another thing,

Back
lat spread

Side
triceps

Side
chest

Front abdominals

try to keep every muscle in your body tensed. Years ago standing relaxed meant just that. Nowadays it means standing "tensed." Depending on the number of competitors, you may have to stand there for 20 to 30 minutes. At any time one of the judges may be looking at you, so always maintain a ready appearance. You don't realize how tiring posing is until you try it. And we don't mean for a few seconds. Try standing in a semi-flexed position for five or ten minutes. See what we mean. Your heart rate goes up, you start to sweat, and your muscles may begin to cramp. Now you know why we suggest preparing for a contest months in advance. Arnold Schwarzenegger said afterwards that one of the hardest things he experienced during his comeback in 1980 was holding poses. While his body was close to his 1970s shape (about 90 percent), he was not used to flexing and holding the various poses.

After a close scrutiny the judges will ask you to turn 90 degrees so that you are facing sideways. As before, keep the abs tight and muscles flexed. Oh and one other thing, *smile*!

Another 90-degree turn brings you back-on to the judges. Here such things as V-taper and calf development are analyzed. To bring the calves out, try curling the toes and pressing on the floor with the balls of your feet. This flexes the calf muscle, especially the inner and outer sections.

Your next turn puts you sideways again, this time facing the opposite direction. This may seem redundant, but there's a purpose. Few bodybuilders are perfectly symmetrical. The odds are that one bodypart is less developed on one side. Now in the vast majority of cases the difference is negligible, but in a few cases it stands out. The underlying culprit is often genetics, but injury and improper training technique can also account for it. So this is why the judges want to look at you from both sides. Your final turn brings you back to the front, where the judges may take a final look.

Although muscle size is taken into account during round one, the judges are primarily looking at symmetry, proportion, and to a lesser extent, definition.

Round 2 – All right, this is where you really get to show the judges how you stack up against your opponents. Some have called this the coldest and most clinical of the four rounds. It consists of seven compulsory poses, each designed to show the judges different aspects of your body. These seven have set the standard over the years, and you must have them down pat before you step onstage. As some can be performed from either side, you should practice both. In most cases you can pick your favorite side, but we have seen contests where the contestants were told which side to pose from, so make sure you're comfortable with both.

The seven compulsory poses are as follows:
1. Front double biceps
2. Back double biceps
3. Front lat spread
4. Back lat spread
5. Side triceps
6. Side chest
7. Front abdominals usually called "abdominals and legs," (hands behind the head).

Although you can hide weaknesses in the free-posing round, it's impossible to do so here. The compulsories are designed to let the judges see everything, so if you think arms and pecs are all that's needed, think again.

One other thing we forgot to mention, and that's your opponents! You see, the compulsories do more than highlight your individual strengths and weaknesses. They also show how you compare with the competition. In most cases the judges call two or three competitors forward, and have them hit the same pose. After a few minutes of careful scrutiny, they are asked

Flex Wheeler

No matter which variation you use, don't forget the legs. Many competitors, in their attempt to get the maximum size and hardness out of their upper body, forget to tense their legs. In any front pose start by making a V with the feet and pushing the floor with the balls of the feet. This gets the calves set. Next flex the quads slightly, gradually pushing the floor with your heels. This little movement brings out the inner thighs. It may sound like a contradiction, but it's possible to push the floor with both your heels and the balls of your feet, at the same time. It just takes practice. Once the legs are set, you can bring the arms up and flex the biceps.

When doing the pose from the rear, many competitors like to emphasize the calves by putting one foot back and rising up on the toes. (In many contests you will be asked to do the pose in this manner.) This gives the judges an opportunity to compare calf size with the rest of the body.

Many competitors who have great control over their legs actually point to the calves and quads as they set them. As things start happening (i.e. the thighs separate into both longitudinal and cross striations), judges and audience members often gasp in amazement.

Aaron Baker

to hit another shot, and so on. These contestants are then asked to step back, and another two or three are told to come forward. This procedure is repeated over and over until the judges have the competitors ranked.

Most of the compulsory poses are self-explanatory. The front and back double biceps are probably the best known of all bodybuilding poses. In fact most Joe Averages off the street can hit the pose. (Granted they won't have the muscle to accompany it, but at least their limbs will be in the correct position.)

There are two variations you can use on this pose. The larger competitors hit it straight on – that is, upper arms parallel and lower arms vertical with the floor, weight distributed evenly on both legs, and torso straight up and down. Sergio, Arnold and Haney literally dwarfed other competitors with this shot.

The other variation is usually done by competitors whose physiques are more famous for symmetry than pure mass. Such bodybuilders as Frank Zane, Mohamed Makkawy and Lee Labrada would never hit these poses straight on, but instead twist the body so that the emphasis is placed on graceful proportions rather than absolute mass. By twisting the torso, bending one knee, and holding one arm slightly higher than the other, such bodybuilders could effectively compete against larger opponents.

The side chest and side triceps poses may be done from either side. If given the choice, you should obviously pick your better side. For example, most bodybuilders have one triceps that is slightly larger than the other, so this is the side they show the judges. As for the chest, even though your pectorals may be symmetrical, keep in mind that the side chest shot is more than just pectorals. It's also legs, arms, shoulders, etc., so display the side that emphasizes the strong points. Once again don't forget the legs, especially the calves and hamstrings. When turned to one side, both these muscles must be flexed. You do this by bending the knee that is closest to the judges and rising up on the toes as if you were doing calf raises. Also, instead of keeping the foot pointing straight forward, turn it so that the heel is facing slightly forward. These little movements serve two purposes – the calf is now fully flexed, and the hamstrings are fully visible. Take a look at Dorian Yates or Robby Robinson doing a side chest shot. Yes, friends, those are hamstrings!

Speaking of Robby Robinson, one of his trademarks has always been his intercostals – very visible on those great chest shots of his. If you've got good intercostals, don't be shy. Flex them for all to see.

The front and back lat spreads are identical with the exception of direction. Some competitors tilt back slightly on the front lat spread. This lets the judges see more of the lats as the arms sometimes get in the way. Most competitors like to start the back lat spread by squeezing the shoulder blades and arms together, and then, with the fingers held against the sides of the waist, flare the lats out by moving the arms forward. If you get a chance to see *Pumping Iron,* pay close attention to Franco Columbu. To this day Franco is considered by many to have the greatest lat spread of all time. (In recent years Dorian Yates gets the nod.) His lats looked like a set of bat wings! Not only did they have incredible thickness, but they attached very low on his back – down around the waist area. The result was one of the most fantastic V-tapers in bodybuilding. The front and back lat spreads are not compulsory poses for women.

The final pose in round two is the abdominal pose. Although there are variations that can be done during your free-posing routine, the accepted version for round two is to place both hands behind the head, extend one leg forward and flex. When doing this pose try to twist your upper body off-line with your lower. This practice not only brings out the abs, but also puts the maximum tension on such other midsection muscles as the intercostals and obliques.

Before we move to round three, there is another important point to remember. All the judges are at slightly different angles to you. If you hit your poses straight on, only those judges seated directly in front

will get the full effect. The way around this problem is to twist slightly as you hold the poses. A good practice is to look each judge in the eye as you twist from side to side. Doing so ensures that every judge sees your full physique. It would be sad to lose points simply because of a bad view! If you find yourself involved in a number of these comparisons, chances are you're going to end up near the top, providing you don't blow round three, the free-posing round.

Ed Corney

Round 3 – Free Posing

"Now dat's posing!" — **Arnold Schwarzenegger (commenting on Ed Corney's posing routine at the 1975 Mr. Olympia in South Africa. The event was part of the now famous bodybuilding documentary** Pumping Iron**)**

"If you copy someone else's posing style, that's exactly what it will look like. The judges will see you as a follower, not a leader." — *Cory Everson* **IFBB Pro Bodybuilder, Six-time Ms. Olympia**

Laura Creavalle, Kim Chizevsky and Debbie Muggli

In a close contest the free-posing round is just as important as the compulsory rounds – if not more important. It can make the difference between winning and not even making the top three. It's also the last chance before the posedown to make an impression on the judges. You may have been a "bump on a log" in the earlier rounds, but a great free-posing routine will make them sit up and take notice. Most of the audience didn't attend the prejudging, so they have nothing to judge you on. Win the audience over with your posing routine, and they'll start screaming your name or number, and in a close contest the judges often cast the deciding vote on the basis of audience response. (They're human, remember.)

Posing routines come in all formats. No doubt you remember the different routines from your last contest. There may have been several, boring routines that received polite applause, and then one competitor who literally lit the place up with his stage presence. He may not have had the greatest physique, but what he had was shown to absolute perfection. Remember how he held the audience (and more important the judges) in the palm of his hand. Every move was fluid and dynamic with no stops or starts. It was like watching Baryshnikov with muscles. From the moment he walked onstage until he hit his last shot, time seemed to stand still. This is the impression you want to make, and here's how to do it.

PICKING THE MUSIC

"Many people choose posing music that they themselves react to and get a feeling from. That's fine, but I go a step beyond that and choose what I think a crowd would get a feeling from. Then you have an advantage." **– Francois Muse, top amateur bodybuilder and expert poser**

The first step in preparing any posing routine is music selection. This may not be as easy as it sounds (no pun intended). You may think it's only a matter of throwing on Led Zeppelin and away you go, but it's not that simple. For starters, you must choose a music selection that suits your particular physique. Classical music is fine, but remember, most of the audience has been raised on rock 'n' roll. Lee Haney and Arnold could get away with classical music because they had overpowering physiques, but someone standing 5'8" and weighing 170 pounds would only put the audience asleep with such a combination. There have been exceptions. Two of the greatest posers of all time, Chris Dickerson and Mohamed Makkawy, regularly defeated competitors outweighing them by 50 pounds by using outstanding posing routines designed around classical music. Then there's Ed Corney. While Ed never had the largest physique onstage, he made up for it with his graceful posing. Flexing to the easy tempo of Frank Sinatra's "My Way," Ed regularly brought houses down in the 1970s and early 1980s. Where most bodybuilders looked as if they were combining separate poses, Ed flowed from one shot to the next. If you don't believe us, check out George Butler's *Pumping Iron*.

All things being equal, the best music choice is some sort of upbeat dance music, preferably something that's current and on the charts. Not only is it ideally suited for hitting poses, but it has the added benefit of getting the audience involved. It won't take long for someone to start clapping in time, and before you know it, half the audience (or more) is clapping along. Such audience participation usually has a positive effect on the judges.

Another type of music often used is hard rock or heavy metal, but once again you need the physique to go with it. As the music is very powerful, you run the risk of being overwhelmed if your body is lacking in mass. If you've heard your physique described as "proportioned, symmetrical or graceful," you may want to give heavy metal a pass.

Still a few bodybuilders more famous for their symmetry than for their mass used heavy metal to propel them to victory. Perhaps the most successful was three-time Mr. Olympia Frank Zane. While Frank didn't have the mass of a Mike Mentzer or Robby Robinson, nevertheless he successfully combined rock music (often Pink Floyd) with a beautifully balanced physique.

An important point to keep in mind is that your music selection should complement your posing routine, not obscure it. Back in the late 1970s and early 1980s the success of the *Star Wars* movies meant that a lot of bodybuilders used the movies' music scores in competition. While parts of the songs were fine, other selections were distracting. For example, laser blasts and computer-generated voices tend to distract from the posing routine. Movie themes can be great (*2001 – A Space Odyssey* being one of the most popular), but don't get carried away.

If you have trouble deciding what type of music suits your particular physique, you might want to try the following: As you're driving around, picture yourself posing to the various songs on the radio. As the music goes up in tempo, visualize hitting a double-biceps pose. If the music "crashes down," crunch that most-muscular together. Try to design a whole posing routine around one song. Or you may notice that certain songs have sections that would make great posing segments. Make a mental note of which ones and then use the splicing principle.

In recent years many bodybuilders have spliced together sections from different songs. For example, you can start with a slow piece of classical music, and then gradually up the tempo until you're flexing away to one of Madonna's hit dance songs like "Vogue."

Now a word of caution on splicing is necessary. Nothing sounds as ridiculous as two or three songs spliced together in an amateurish fashion. If you decide to go this route, make sure the pieces flow together without the cuts being obvious. If you have the money, get a professional sound engineer to do the job for you. (Even a friend with a decent tape deck is better than a haphazard job done on a $20 Walkman.) Once you have the tape completed, make one or two extra copies. This may seem trivial but there's a good reason. As you go through life, you continuously fight Murphy's Law – "anything that can go wrong will go wrong!" Numerous competitors have stepped onstage ready to pose, only to have some tape-eating machine destroy their one and only copy! It has also been known that fellow competitors may "misplace" your music selection backstage.

Whatever the reason, make sure you have at least one extra copy with you on the day of the event. Even better, have a friend in the audience hold on to a third copy. This way, no matter what else goes wrong, you'll still have your music ready to go.

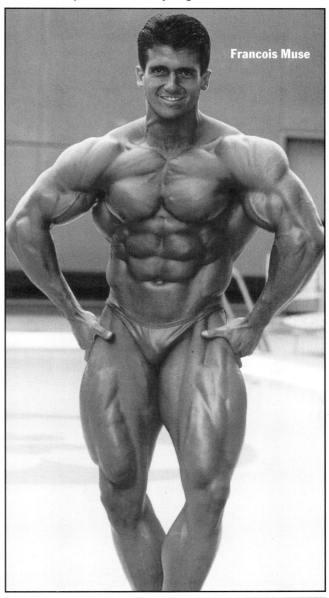

Francois Muse

Make sure the tape is rewound and set at the beginning of the song. Allow 10 to 20 seconds of blank tape so that you can set yourself onstage. It wouldn't look the best to have the music kick in while you're still climbing the posing steps! You can take this lead time to the opposite extreme as well. Standing fixed in one position for 30 seconds onstage while waiting for the music to start is a great way to attract catcalls. Wait long enough and the audience becomes restless. Now you have two obstacles to overcome. Besides having to win the audience back, you are making a poor impression on the judges.

At the amateur level posing music is usually 90 seconds in length. The judges will probably give you a few seconds leeway, but why take the chance? Set your routine to run within the time limit.

If you're talented enough to make it to the pro level, time does not become a factor, at least from the rule point of view. But unless you've got an outstanding routine, try to limit it to two or three minutes. Any more and you risk overstaying your welcome. Any less and the judges won't get a good look at you. A good rule of thumb is to stay long enough to show your body's strong points, but short enough to leave the audience wanting a bit more.

As a final suggestion, start a collection of posing routines on video tape. You can use various sources for this – everything from contests on ESPN and *American Muscle Magazine* to purchasing specific routines through ads seen in bodybuilding magazines.

Aaron Baker, Flex Wheeler and Lee Labrada

Who are the best posers today? Although there is much personal interpretation, most agree that the following rank at the top: Vince Taylor, Lee Labrada, John Brown, Bob Paris, Tom Terwilliger, Shawn Ray, Tonya Knight, Lenda Murray and Laura Creavalle. In the past Ed Corney, Mohamed Makkawy, Chris Dickerson, Arnold and Frank Zane thrilled audiences with their onstage exploits.

WHICH POSES?

"Contest posing is exhausting, and for most of us, emotionally and often physically harder than the workouts that lead to the posing dais." – **Dave Draper, actor, writer and former Mr. Universe**

All right, you've got your music selected. Now it's time to build a posing routine around it. There are two aspects to the free-posing round – the poses themselves and the music selection. Which poses to pick is best determined by answering the question "What's the purpose of a good posing routine?" The answer of course is that you want to show your body to its best advantage, and this means highlighting its strong points and camouflaging its weak points. You may say, "Well, I have no weak points!" Our response to that is: "Poppycock! Every bodybuilder has weak points." From a 15-year-old in a novice contest to the lineup at last year's Mr. Olympia, there isn't a bodybuilder alive (or dead for that matter!) who doesn't have weak points. Dorian Yates and Lee Haney could be criticized for their less than huge arms (at least compared to the rest of their bodies). Paul Dillett could use more lower lat development. Even the great Arnold

did not have the awesomeness in his thighs to match his upper body.

You may say we're nitpicking — and maybe you're right — but the fact remains that every bodybuilder has weaknesses (no matter how small) if you look close enough. The top bodybuilders have designed posing routines that minimize these flaws, and your goal should be to do the same.

The first step is to make a total evaluation of your physique. Unlike picking music, where you're the best judge, objectively analyzing your physique is best left to others. Most bodybuilders see only their good points and choose to ignore (or in all honesty may not see) their less-than-perfect bodyparts. This is where a second or third opinion is valuable. Have someone who is not afraid to hurt your feelings make a detailed evaluation of your physique. Have this person make notes as you go through the compulsory poses. Write down which poses highlight your strong points and which shots are less than flattering.

Using this information, set the poses up in a manner that allows easy transition from one pose to another. Hitting a front lat spread and then trying to follow with a rear double biceps is just not practical. The idea is to hit a few poses from the front, side and rear, all within easy reach of one another.

There are two schools of thought when it comes to the actual poses to use. Many believe that since you already performed the mandatory poses in the compulsory round, you should limit them in your free-posing routine. On the other side of the coin, the compulsory poses generally are the ones that display your physique to its fullest. What it really comes down to is development. If your best poses happen to be the compulsories, by all means use them. Let's face it. The idea is to put your best foot (and any other bodypart) forward. If the mandatory poses detract from your physique, you might want to limit them in your free-posing routine. If your compulsories are weak, you're going to lose points during the early rounds. Also, weak compulsories usually mean a lack of overall development. Still, with a bit of creativity, it's possible to make a good impression even if your physique suffers in the comparison rounds.

When selecting poses, remember you have only 90 seconds to do them. If you allow a couple of seconds for holding each pose, and another couple of seconds to move between them, you'll end up with between 10 and 15 poses per routine.

Once you've got the poses ranked (i.e. great, decent and fair), the next step is to arrange them in a logical order. Start your posing routine with one of your best. For Arnold and Robby Robinson it was often a double biceps because in all probability they had the best arms in the contest. Similarly, Dorian Yates and Mike Francois can't go wrong by hitting a front lat spread.

If you have great arms, use them. Hit a double-biceps pose and get the audience oohing and ahhing. Or do a combination biceps-lat spread. Hold for a few seconds and then drop the arms to the front in a graceful manner, hands open. Now bring both up into a double-biceps pose. With both arms held high you can move to just about any frontal or side shot with relative ease. If your abs are great, put your hands behind the head and twist into an ab shot. By this point the audience and judges realize that you're for real — great

Dave Draper

arms and abs usually mean a high placing — but don't stop now. Twist to a couple of back shots, straight on or three-quarter, the choice is yours. Just remember to highlight your best features. After a few intermediate poses get ready for your finale. Most bodybuilders save the most-muscular or crab shot for last. This pose highlights just about every muscle on the body — everything — veins, striations and muscle fibers will pop out during this one. Remember Lou Ferrigno in *The Incredible Hulk*? All it took was one of Lou's hulking green most-musculars, and the bad guys sought cover! Treat the audience and judges in the same manner. To

Aaron Baker, Flex Wheeler and Dave Fisher

make the effect more dramatic, have your second last pose such that your arms are above your head. This way most of your torso muscles are stretched out and appear thinner. Now as the music crashes down, do the same with your arms. Bring them down and forward. Squeeze them together with all your strength. Pop those traps up around your ears. Flex the chest so that striations look as if they're about to explode right into the first two rows. If they do, so much the better. Now you've got their attention!

What separates average posers from great posers is the way in which one pose flows into another. Many bodybuilders try to remain in a state of flex for the entire duration of the routine, but this approach is counterproductive because you want things to happen as you pose. The best posers relax slightly between poses, so that when they hit the next shot, the muscles, striations, and veins, seem to explode from nowhere. This effect makes much more of an impact on the judges and audience than if you remained tense throughout the routine.

TRANSITION

As the sport became more competitive, many bodybuilders realized that it was going to take more than a collection of individual poses to claim the winner's trophy. If you saw *Pumping Iron,* you probably remember one scene where Arnold and Franco are posing while under the scrutiny of a dance instructor. One of the things that separated Arnold from the rest of the competition was his attention to stage appearance. Guys like Lou Ferrigno and Sergio Oliva carried as much muscle as Arnold, but onstage their posing looked like a collection of pictures, while Arnold

gracefully moved from one pose to the next. (Of course, with time big Lou transformed his own posing routine.)

The art of tying individual poses together is called transition, and it takes as much practice as the individual still poses. Many bodybuilders hire professional choreographers to help with their posing routines, and while in the past men have been reluctant to avail themselves of this specialized assistance, nowadays most realize they need a complete package to win a top event. Cory Everson made frequent use of dance instructors during her record run of Ms. Olympias. Likewise, Rich Gaspari hired a professional ballet dancer to prepare him for the Arnold Classic.

No doubt many readers – most of you probably males – feel that dance and ballet are for sissies. Nothing could be further from the truth. We assure you that after a couple of minutes of posing, whether holding shots or moving from one pose to the next, you will be huffing and puffing like your last set of squats – and squats are not for sissies, right? So if you can afford a few hours with a professional choreographer (or better yet, check around as somebody's girlfriend, boyfriend, sister, brother, etc., may be involved in dance or ballet), go for it. The results will be worthwhile, and before you know it, you'll be famous for your posing.

Before we leave posing we should add another option to improving posing, especially transition moves. For a small fee you can rent a VHS video recorder. (As with choreographers, check around because many people own their own video recorders, especially parents of small children). Have a friend record your posing routine, and then sit back and make a critical analysis. Try different routines using different musical selections, and then pick the one that shows your physique to its best advantage. Don't be shy either. Have as many different people as possible give their opinion. It makes more sense to hear criticism before the contest than after.

If you have a talent for posing (don't be surprised if you do as many individuals had no idea about posing until they have actually tried it) it might be a good idea to put together two or three different routines. The most popular musical selections chosen for posing tend to be current. This means that a popular upbeat song may be selected by more than one competitor. Nothing is as frustrating as having to follow a competitor who selected the same song as you did. Unless you have some outstanding moves in your routine, much of the dramatic effect will be lost. Audiences and judges are only human, and people easily get bored from listening to the same song. But if you have a backup routine ready, you can avoid this complication.

Having said that, it may be to your advantage to use the same song! Let's say the competitor before you did a poor job of posing to a given song (let's forget the diplomacy, they crucified the song!). Now's your chance to go out and show the judges how it's really supposed to look! Of course you have to be absolutely sure that your routine is in fact much more entertaining.

There is another reason for changing songs. Many bodybuilders use one posing routine for the prejudging and another for the evening event. This use of two routines is not necessary, but it does add to the dramatic effect. A word of caution is needed, however. If this is your first bodybuilding event, no doubt you will be a bit nervous. This anxiety is normal and it's rare for a bodybuilder to be emotionless at his or her first event. Ed Corney said that he couldn't wait to get off the stage the first time he competed. (Later on he savored each and every moment onstage). If you decide to use two different routines, make absolutely sure that you are confident with both. Have the sequence of poses and timing down pat. Your first posing display in front of hundreds of people is stressful enough without having to worry about pose order. You should be able to flip through the poses in your sleep. If there's any doubt (and you're the only one who can make this decision), stick with one routine. With time comes experience, and then you can start experimenting with multiple posing routines.

Last but not least are the final touches. Always appear confident onstage. Smile as much as possible (Arnold may not smile much in his movies but take a look at those confident grins from his competitive days!), and make eye contact with both the judges and audience members. Leave nothing to chance, and this includes walking to and from the stage. This detail may seem trivial, but numerous competitors have tripped while walking up or down stairs to the posing platform. If possible practice these seemingly unimportant

movements beforehand – preferably at the actual venue but we realize for most this is not feasible. A good posing routine can take months to prepare, but those who take the time usually end up at or near the top.

Round 4 – Unlike the first three rounds where for all intents and purposes your poses are arranged in sequence, the posedown, as round four is called, is made up on the spot. Although it usually depends on the number of contestants, a typical posedown involves the three to five top competitors. You'll be asked to line up towards the front of the stage, and after a signal from the head judge, begin to hit your favorite poses. Your opponents are doing the same, so the posedown becomes a sort of chess match. The strategy is to draw the judges' attention towards your best features and away from the other competitors.

Although it's difficult to prepare for the posedown, there are strategies to give you the edge. If at all possible, try to have some idea of who you'll be posing against (another reason for seeing your first contest rather than entering it). In most cases they'll hit the same poses in much the same sequence. If this is the case, you can be ready. Let's say your opponents' abs and shoulders are sharper than yours, but you have

Milos Sarcev

the edge in chest and arm size. When they hit an ab shot, you immediately throw up the arms. If they turn around to display their shoulders, you counter with a side chest shot. The idea is to offset their strong points with your own. If they hit a pose that happens to be one of your best, accept the challenge and duplicate it. Of course, your opponent will be doing the same, so think in terms of offense and defense.

Another point to remember is that the posedown is the last component of the contest. This means you will be tired. The combination of posing, nervousness, and dehydration under the hot lights will leave you exhausted by the end of the day. Yet, you still have the posedown to complete (at least if you're somewhere in the medal hunt), so it's a good idea to practice the posedown in the weeks and months leading up to the contest. If you have a couple of willing "competitors," so much the better. The three or four of you can line up and pretend it's the finale at the Olympia. Five thousand fans are screaming, and after dispensing

Lee Priest

with Yates, Wheeler, Francois and others, it's down to you three!

As a typical posedown lasts one to two minutes, try practicing for three or four minutes. This preparation gives you a couple of minutes to play with in the event of an extension, which is quite possible given the competitive nature of modern bodybuilding. Often the difference between first, second, and third is a more aggressive posedown display by one competitor.

POSING AS A FORM OF PRECONTEST EXERCISE

"In preparation for a contest I practice my posing for up to one hour at a time four or five days per week. This is increased to one hour per day over the last two weeks before a show. There's no other way for me to get it right." **– Marjo Selin, IFBB Pro Bodybuilder and MuscleMag columnist**

Besides the actual contest, posing has other uses. After your first posing session you'll realize just how tiring it can be. You probably said to yourself many times, 'This is just like working out.' Well, guess what? You're absolutely right – posing is exercise! Unfortunately many don't realize this until they're up onstage, and by then it's usually too late.

Aside from preparing for the contest, practicing posing has another great benefit. No matter how much you exercise and diet, it's impossible to completely refine your physique. Workouts may develop the larger muscles, but it's the little things that get you the brownie points. Take the intercostals, serratus and teres. Regular exercise helps bring them out, but for that honed, chiseled look nothing beats posing. You may have noticed this after your first or second posing session. The next day you were probably sore in places you didn't even know existed.

Many bodybuilders look their best two or three days after the contest. This is in all likelihood because of all the posing on contest day (something they may have neglected to do leading up to the event). The result – all the sharpness and detail that might have given them the title arrives two days later!

Look at it this way: An amateur can sculpt a decent statue out of clay, but compared to the work of a master it appears rough. Just as the master brings out the detail in stone, so too can the bodybuilder bring out the sharpness in his physique.

If you're not convinced yet, most of the sport's top bodybuilders spend one to two hours each day on posing. They practice everything from the compulsories and holding shots to the free posing and posedown. Every aspect of competitive posing is rehearsed, practiced and then repeated.

POSING FOR THE CAMERA

Another topic related to posing is physique photography. In fact, the two are interrelated. Each month

MuscleMag International brings you some of the greatest physique photography in the world, with every issue packed full of outstanding photos of your favorite stars. While contest coverage accounts for a portion of the magazine, it's the studio shots that comprise the majority.

In many respects, photo sessions are similar to rounds one, two and three of a bodybuilding contest in that the pictures are divided into both compulsories and the individual bodybuilder's favorite poses. Photo sessions can take place in a studio, in a gym or outdoors, with both photographer and bodybuilder working together to obtain the desired effect.

In the following sections we look at both indoor and outdoor photography. It's by no means an all-inclusive course on physique photography, but merely a brief discussion of some tips you can use to obtain good quality pictures.

STUDIO PHOTOS

Over the years many photographers have become nearly as famous as the bodybuilders they shoot. Such camera artists as Art Zeller, Chris Lund, Jimmy Caruso, Russ Warner, Mike Neveux, John Balik, Albert Busek, Garry Bartlett, and *MuscleMag's* own Robert Kennedy have developed reputations as the best in the business. It's safe to say that every top bodybuilder during his or her career has been "shot" by at least one of these men.

As the aforementioned photographers only have time to shoot the top bodybuilding stars, you'll have to be a bit more creative. In most cases a friend with a good Canon or Nikon can suffice, but even then there are things to remember. For starters just about everything is left to you, and this includes oil, tanning and shaving down (all of which will be discussed in more detail in the next chapter).

If the photographer you have chosen is familiar with bodybuilding, you have a head start. He or she will know what to look for in terms of posing positions. If not, bring along a third person who can help line you up properly with the camera. Often how you think you look and how you actually appear are two different things. You can confirm this yourself with the aid of a mirror. Stand in front of the mirror and close your eyes. Now hit a pose, hold it, and visualize what it looks like to a person standing in front of you. Now open your eyes. See what we mean? You thought your arms were straight, but in fact they were too low or too high. Maybe you forgot to tense your legs or abs. Whatever the problem, the only solution is to practice, and this is where the second set of eyes comes in handy.

If your friend has access to a photo studio, so much the better. Studio photos demand a great deal of lighting and other photo technology, so you have an added expense, but the results are worth it. The lighting equipment means that you can have the pic-

Marjo Selin

tures taken anytime during the day, and the seamless backgrounds show your physique off to its fullest.

If the photo studio is not an option, you can still obtain some great pictures. They just take a bit of ingenuity. The most important piece of equipment is obviously the camera. If at all possible, avoid using a cheap instamatic. You know the one where all you have to do is line up the subject and press the switch. Not only do these cameras produce poor-quality originals, but blowing up to an 8 x 10 is virtually out of the question. The lenses in these instant cameras are so poorly manufactured that obtaining a sharp focus is impossible. Even the "expensive" instant cameras are limited by their lack of sharpness.

Nowadays most people have access to a good 35 mm camera. It doesn't have to be a $2000 Nikon or Canon, but it should have such features as a focusable lens, variable shutter speeds, and some sort of light-monitoring system. Another advantage of a 35 mm camera is its ability to accept different lenses. Simple studio shots can be taken with a standard 35 mm lens, but for outdoor and competition shots you'll need such exotics as wide-angle and telephoto lenses.

Perhaps the greatest advantage to a 35mm camera is the sharpness it gives to the photos. There's just no comparison between the craftsmanship that goes into a 35mm camera and its instamatic opponent – with most of the difference found in the lens. With a good 35mm, not only will the originals be sharp, but you also have the option of blowing up to an 8 x 10 or more, without losing much quality.

You have the option of color or black and white film. In this age of brilliance and color it's refreshing to see black and white hold its own and in many cases surpass color photography. Many of the greatest bodybuilding pictures ever taken have been reproduced in black and white. Jimmy Caruso's black and whites of Arnold have become legendary. Robert Kennedy's line of best-selling books are famous for their black and white photography. Likewise Dr. Ellington Darden's "High Intensity" series relies heavily on black and white. Although color has its places (contests and outdoor shots), when it comes to studio shooting, nothing beats the good old Charlie Chaplin black and white.

Getting back to the studio, once you have the assistants and equipment ready, the next thing to address is the background. Unless you and your photographer really know what you're doing, keep it simple. If there's a large, blank wall available, make use of it. You may have to remove a few pictures, but these can be replaced later.

If you don't have access to an appropriate wall, you may want to invest a few dollars in a backdrop. This is nothing more than a large, one-piece sheet that is placed behind the subject. Professionals have backdrops that start at the ceiling and curve out towards the subject. In some cases the subject stands on the leading edge of the backdrop, making it appear as if the subject is within the background. You don't need to spend hundreds or thousands of dollars for the real thing either. For the sake of $15 or $20 you can go into a fabric store and purchase enough material to make your own. All you need is three or four square meters of material and you're in business.

There are two schools of thought when it comes to backdrop colors. Some photographers have a preference for darker colors, particularly black. Jimmy Caruso falls into this category. Others, like Russ Warner, prefer light colors. One advantage to using black and white is that these colors (the physicists among you are no doubt hollering that "black is the absence of color and white is all colors combined!") tend to be the cheapest to buy.

Generally speaking, light colors will show off size, and dark colors emphasize definition and hardness. There's a lot of overlap between the two, and even more important, if your physique lacks size or hardness, no backdrop in the world will make a difference!

Jay Cutler

OUTDOOR PHOTOS

If you thought the backdrop and lighting were important indoors, wait till you try shooting outside. Unlike the studio setting where you have control over the conditions, outside you must be more selective.

Let's start with the background. Initially it may seem a good idea to have such momentous structures as buildings and bridges behind you, but when you get the pictures back you'll see that your physique is overshadowed by these backgrounds. Over the years bodybuilders have discovered that the best outdoor backgrounds are neutral settings like the sky or sea. Another popular background is mountain ranges far off in the distance. Some of Arnold's best pictures (check out the cover of his book *Arnold: The Education of a Bodybuilder*) were taken in rugged settings.

Once the background is decided on, you must position the camera so that the angle is right. If the camera is held too high, your physique will appear smaller. Most photographers position the camera at waist level or slightly lower. This makes the body appear taller and more massive.

You'll probably get the best quality by using shutter speeds of from 1/60th to 1/125th of a second. Using a shutter speed this slow, you'll need a tripod (a three-legged stand used for supporting a camera). It's virtually impossible to hold the camera steady enough without blurring the photo. If you don't have a tripod, rest the camera on the back of a chair or some other waist-high object. Another option is to increase the shutter speed to 1/250 or 1/500 of a second. There is a trade-off, however, as this allows less light into the camera and you'll need high-speed film.

The time of day is also very important for shooting outdoors. You would think that the best time would be noon with the sun directly overhead, but this is not the case. Sunlight streaming straight down causes the shadows that detract from your physique. The best

Clarence Bass

times to shoot outdoors are around ten in the morning and four in the afternoon. At these times the sun is low on the horizon, and while still providing enough light, doesn't give you those unwanted shadows.

One of the biggest misconceptions of outdoor photography is the more sun the better. In fact a clear, sunny, blue sky is often the worst condition for shooting outdoors. Too much sun plays havoc with light readings and you run the risk of overexposure. Overcast days are by far the best when it comes to outdoor photography. You don't have to worry about harsh shadows, too much light or sunburn.

The choice is yours regarding what poses to hit. If the goal of the photo shoot is to provide a visual record of your progress, stick with the compulsory poses. Every two or three months repeat the process and make comparisons. If you've already attained a great deal of size (as most bodybuilders feel they need to be bigger, it's surprising that any photos get taken!), start experimenting with different poses. For example, if you're getting ready for a competition, take photos of all your free-posing positions. If you have the film and time, take two or three pictures of the same pose from different angles. This way you know how each judge will view a particular shot.

THE PRECONTEST DIET

"Exercise physiologists say it's practically impossible to shed a large amount of fat without losing some muscle. If diet alone is used, 75 percent of the loss will probably be lean tissue. If diet and exercise are used, a greater portion of the loss will be fat. Exercise protects lean tissue. The use-it-or-lose-it principle comes into play. If muscle tissue is being used, it's much less likely to be lost." — **Clarence Bass, author of Ripped**

Eating before a contest is not all that different from eating during the off-season. In most cases all it takes is a few minor adjustments and you're in business. If your year-round eating habits are less than satisfactory, then yes, you'll need to make drastic changes.

Male bodybuilders usually need to lower their bodyfat percentage from an off-season of 10 to 12 percent to a shredded contest percentage of 2 to 4 percent. (Yes, this level is unhealthful if maintained for an extended period of time, and we'll see why later.) For women bodybuilders the numbers are 15 to 18 percent and 5 to 7 percent respectively.

The following section is not meant to be a repeat of our nutrition chapter. Instead we will highlight a few points that are especially important to bodybuilders when it comes to precompetition nutrition.

Although there are a few bodybuilders who actually try to add weight before a contest, the usual goal is to gain as much muscular bodyweight as possible during the off-season, and then shed the excess fat in the weeks prior to the contest. The trend twenty or thirty years ago was to gain 30 or 40 pounds during the off-

**Arnold
Schwarzenegger**

expect was a handshake, trophy, and in one or two cases a small cash reward (the exception rather than the norm). Nowadays the top pros have eight to ten yearly events, each offering hundreds of thousands of dollars in total prize money. Besides the contests, top pros (and their amateur counterparts) can earn just as much – if not more – money in posing exhibitions and endorsements. Being in shape has become a year-round, lucrative necessity.

Most bodybuilders today try to keep within 10 to 20 pounds of their contest weight. A lightweight bodybuilder should not have to lose more than 10 or 12 pounds to make his weight class. Similarly, a heavyweight would be best advised not to add more than 20 or 25 pounds during the off-season. (With the increased number of exhibitions that pros participate in these days, the terms *off-season* and *precontest* often overlap.)

HOW THE PROS DO IT

"In general, bodybuilders make the same dietary mistakes as the rest of the population. Time and time again I see competitors come into shows looking drawn and depleted. The reason is obvious: An improper approach to diet has caused them to burn up valuable muscle tissue in their attempt to lower bodyfat levels."
– Arnold Schwarzenegger

"For me contest preparation is very basic. I just change what I eat to lose or gain. I start out the first two weeks eating hamburger meat, the next two weeks it's chicken, and the last two weeks before the show I eat fish. I also include carbs the whole time. To maintain size I eat hamburger meat. I can get hard without putting on fat eating hamburger meat." **– Vince Taylor
IFBB Pro Bodybuilder**

Assuming that you fall within the above parameters, your best approach is to start your precontest diet two to three months before the show. This allows enough time to lose one or two pounds a week in what could be called "comfortable" fashion. Start by cutting high-fat foods from your diet. (By rights you should avoid high fats year round.) At the same time increase your calorie-burning exercises. This two-pronged approach makes far more sense than putting yourself through the misery of an ultrastrict crash diet. Perhaps the best way to illustrate precontest dieting is to give you the philosophy of some of the IFBB's top pros.

USA national champion Tom Terwilliger starts his precontest phase about eleven weeks before a contest. He gradually tightens his diet until he's taking in 3000 calories a day. He maintains this level for two weeks and then begins dropping 100 calories a week until he reaches the 2100 mark. This is maintained until he starts his carbohydrate depletion/loading phase, about a week before the event.

One of the most commonly asked questions at bodybuilding seminars is how low should a person go

season. Called "bulking up," this process made some sense for those people who had trouble gaining muscular bodyweight, but for the most part the disadvantages outweighed the advantages. For example putting on 30 pounds in a few months tends to stretch the overlying skin. The result – ghastly stretch marks! Granted most bodybuilders develop stretch marks, but the practice of bulking up only compounds the problem.

Another reason to avoid bulking up involves the ordeal that you must go through to remove the excess fat. The human body was not designed to undertake rapid weight loss, fat or otherwise. Trying to shed 25 to 30 pounds in a two-month period is both physically and mentally draining.

Perhaps the main reason why bulking up has become a thing of the past involves the current state of bodybuilding affairs. Years ago all the winner could

in terms of calorie intake? The most appropriate answer is, it all depends.

Like most things in life there is a lower limit. Once you reduce to a certain calorie level, the body starts drawing on its fat reserves. Reduce your calories even further and it begins to burn muscle tissue as fuel. In effect you begin to lose muscle size. As no bodybuilder in his right mind wants this, the art of dieting is to straddle the border between what's enough to lose fat, and too much so that the body begins to burn muscle tissue. Few bodybuilders get it right the first time, but once they do, contest preparation becomes a whole lot simpler.

There are certain minimums that must be followed in terms of caloric intake. It's generally accepted that you should not consume less than 1 gram of protein for every 2 pounds of bodyweight. This is an absolute necessity if you want to hold on to your valued muscle mass. Also, try to keep your carbohydrate intake at least 80 to 100 grams a day. Besides fueling the muscles, a certain amount of carbohydrate is needed for proper brain functioning. Deplete your carbs too much, and your cognitive (thinking) abilities begin to suffer. We know this is an extreme example, but the risk is there, so be warned.

North American Championships winner, and IFBB pro Dave Fisher (a regular contributor to *MuscleMag),* begins his precontest dieting 17 weeks before the show. He uses the first two weeks as a sort of "conditioning" phase. Any junk food is eliminated from the diet (not that Dave makes it a regular habit, but he's not immune to the occasional PopTart or peanut butter sandwich!), with a special emphasis on foods high in sugar and fat. These two weeks of training serve as a sort of warmup for the fifteen weeks that follow.

Fifteen weeks out Dave is consuming about 4420 calories on a typical day. This includes 254 grams of protein, which makes up 22 percent of his daily food consumption. He refuses to count the number of grams of fats, as their total is low to begin with. As for carbs, Dave counts only the calories. If he wishes to reduce his bodyfat level even further, he switches from starchy carbs like oatmeal and pasta to fibrous carbs like lettuce and broccoli. In case you're wondering, starchy carbs are utilized by the body differently than fibrous carbs. The result is a greater energy supply even if both are supplying the same number of calories. At this point in his preparation

Dave is doing three 20-minute sessions of cardio a week.

Checking with Dave a month later, we see that his caloric intake has dropped to about 3400 a day. He has also changed the composition of his calories, increasing his protein intake from 22 percent to 34 percent of the total. Besides increasing his protein intake, Dave has reduced his carbs, but is quick to add that everyone is different. One person may have to drop his carbs even further, while another can keep them moderate to high. It takes years of experience to determine your exact nutrient proportions. As Dave is fond of saying, "dieting is an art, and like most art forms, there is a lot of personal interpretation."

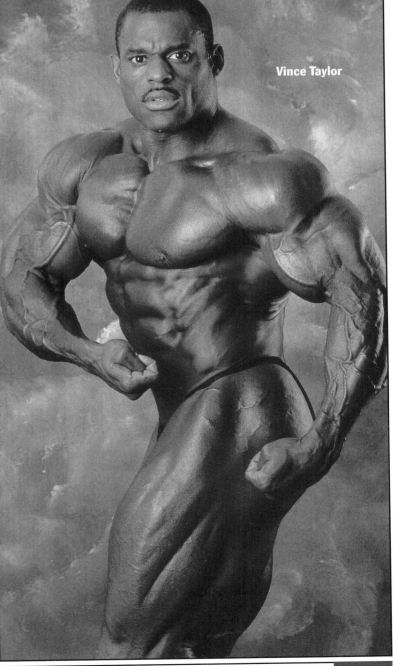

Vince Taylor

As the competition day draws near, supplements play a big role in Dave's dieting plan. To use his own words: "I feel that supplements play a very important role in achieving the condition necessary to win bodybuilding contests."

When he begins his supplement program, Dave is careful not to go too heavy. He likes to build up as the weeks go by and the contest draws closer. As the dieting gets tighter, he gets more liberal with the supplements. His primary reason for using supplements is to give him the necessary nutrients to maintain muscle mass and at the same time continue fat loss. The following is a typical supplement day during Dave's precontest dieting phase. Keep in mind that there are days when he doesn't feel like popping all those pills. He adds, "A few missed vitamins once in a while won't wreck your whole contest."

Dave Fisher's Precontest Supplements:
6:00 a.m. – 5 carnitine
6:30 a.m. – cardio
7:00 a.m. – 5 carnitine, 5 branched-chain amino acids
8:30 a.m. – meal 1, 3 vitamin, 4 vanadyl
1:00 p.m. – meal 2, 3 vitamin, 4 vanadyl
3:00 p.m. – meal 3, 3 vitamin, 4 vanadyl
4:00 p.m. – 5 branched-chain aminos, 5 carnitine
4:30 p.m. – workout, cardio
7:00 p.m. – 10 branched-chain aminos, 5 carnitine
8:30 p.m. – meal 4, 3 vitamin, 4 vanadyl

Dave admits that this is a lot of pills to swallow, but the results are worth it, as he weighed an awesome 210 shredded pounds for the North American Championships. Although swallowing pills is no problem for him, he realizes that many people gag on tablets as small as aspirin. To get around this difficulty, he recommends chewing up the tablets with a spoonful of applesauce or other sugar-free medium. This method may be less convenient than swallowing the tablets whole, but it gets the job done.

Three weeks out from the contest, Dave is to all intents and purposes contest-ready. With striations running up, down and across his entire body, he just has to hold on to this shape. At times this is easier said than done. Dave says that prior to the North Americans he frequently found himself looking into the refrigerator and day-dreaming!

Dave's food intake is now down to 2810 calories a day, which includes 384 grams of protein. This works out to 54 percent which is more than double his intake 12 weeks earlier.

Dave keeps meticulous records during his off-season and precontest phases. Every aspect of dieting, training and precontest preparation is written down for future reference.

CARBOHYDRATE LOADING

We would be remiss if we left precontest dieting without some mention of carbohydrate depletion/ loading. Have you ever noticed

Dave Fisher

Paul Dillett

small and flat. If our aspiring Yates then consumes high-carbohydrate food, the glycogen-famished muscles begin storing the craved sugar tenaciously. In addition the liver and blood also fill with glycogen. The end results are muscles filled with water and greatly enhanced surface vascularity. This whole process can take as little as 10 to 12 hours – hence the improvement that can be seen from one day to the next. Many bodybuilders who appear flat at the prejudging arrive back for the evening show sporting a wholly different physique. Not only have his or her muscles increased in size, but the veins and striations are much more conspicuous.

Perhaps the biggest change occurs overnight. It's common practice for bodybuilders to pig out after the evening show, and such postcontest banquets are famous for their overindulgence. If a bodybuilder's body had not topped up its glycogen levels before the contest, the food binge after the show will complete the process. The next morning the athlete wakes up displaying the physique that should have "arrived" the day before. Of course by then it's too late, and the lesson will have to be saved for next year. Still, this is what bodybuilding is all about – trial and error.

Many bodybuilders make a determined effort to deplete the body's glycogen to abnormally (sometimes dangerously) low levels. A week or so before the show they attempt to cut all glycogen from their diet. Three or four days of this practice leaves the body begging for glycogen. Muscles once full now lose water and flatten out. And as for vascularity, forget it. Dracula would have trouble finding a vein!

Next comes the tricky part. Replenishing glycogen levels can take as little as eight hours or as much as 72 (or more), depending on the individual's biochemistry. If the contest is on Saturday, most bodybuilders start their carb-loading on Tuesday or Wednesday. If the timing is right, by contest day the muscles are full and hard, and vascularity has returned to its once prominent freakiness. In fact, because of a little-understood process called overrebounding, the bodybuilder's physique may be larger than normal.

Without going into too much detail, suffice it to say that after a period of glycogen deprivation the body may store sugar in higher than normal levels. Muscles end up literally bursting with water.

There is another side to overloading. Consume too much carbohydrate and the excess sugar may be stored in the body's tissues. Besides the muscles and veins, water will accumulate under the skin, causing a bloated, fat appearance. All that hard-won muscularity will be blurred. This is the main reason why bodybuilders who look smooth at the prejudging appear ripped at the evening show. All that posing and sweating under the lights drains the excess water, thus allowing the bodybuilder's true muscularity to show through. The problem is that most of the placings are

how some bodybuilders look small and flat one day, and full and vascular the next? In the space of 24 hours their bodies have taken on an entirely different appearance. Many pros will tell you how they "missed their peak," and during the photo shoot the next day displayed the physique which could have won them the contest. The biological mechanism behind this phenomenon involves glycogen levels and the amount of water that the muscles are holding. Time things perfectly and you step onstage big as a house, and hard as a rock. Miss your peak and your physique lacks both size and vascularity. It's that simple, and here's how it works.

The pure form of sugar used by muscle cells is called glycogen. Among its many properties is its ability to hold four times its weight in water. The ultrastrict diets of many bodybuilders deplete their glycogen stores to the point that the muscles don't hold the normal volume of water. This makes the muscles look

Sandra Blackie, Samir Bannout and Dinah Anderson

detail in the nutrition chapter. Keeping fat levels low takes a year-round approach. Holding water, however, usually concerns the bodybuilder only during the weeks and days leading up to the show.

The human body is composed of over 90 percent water. Life seems to have evolved on Earth (at least the only planet we know of in our solar system) because of the abundance of this life-giving compound. Therefore it's only reasonable to assume that any life which evolved on our planet would make use of good old H_2O.

Water can be considered a bodybuilder's best friend or worst nightmare, depending on where it's being stored. We have dealt with the importance of glycogen to water levels in the muscles. We've also described how muscles inflate or shrink, depending on glycogen levels. Trying to eliminate water by reducing glycogen levels is not a good practice. A flat, nonvascular physique is not the look you're after. There are better ways to get rid of excess water without ruining your championship form.

One of the most useful methods to keep tissue water levels down is by eliminating salt intake. Survival kits routinely carry salt tablets, the reason being that salt causes the body to retain water. In a survival situation retaining water is an absolute necessity, but for a competitive bodybuilder too much water in the body (especially under the skin) is counterproductive. One of the biggest culprits in terms of sodium content is tinned food. With its great preservative abilities salt is a frequent medium in which to store food. As soon as you start your precontest diet, avoid any tinned products that contain salt. (Given the other preservatives in such food, you might want to avoid tinned products all year long.)

Another way to limit excess water is to restrict fluid intake in the weeks and days leading up to a contest. Obviously you don't cut out fluid entirely, but don't make a practice of consuming great quantities. If possible drink distilled water as it has all the sodium removed.

determined at the prejudging, and unless the marks were close to begin with, the competitor will place out of the money. The audience is often frustrated, as they can't understand how such a huge, ripped physique placed so low. No doubt their opinion would be different if they had seen the competitor's condition at the prejudging.

As in most aspects of bodybuilding, the solution to this dilemma is experimentation. Only you can determine how your body will respond under a given set of circumstances. You may need as few as 12 hours to carb-load, or it may take a full week. The odds are you won't get it right the first time. But then again, who knows? Maybe you'll peak perfectly for your first contest.

WATER RETENTION

Since we made reference to tissue water in the previous section, we should discuss the subject in more detail here. All things being equal, the bodybuilder who has the most defined physique will place higher. There are two primary reasons why your physique may lack definition. You may be either carrying too much fat or holding too much water. The issue of fat is discussed in

As exercise is a great way to shed water (in the form of sweat), adding such exercises as running and bike riding will keep your water levels down. Posing is great too, and it has the added benefits of hardening your physique and improving mental preparation.

Before you take any drug, check with a physician or other knowledgable medical professional to see how it affects water control. Some drugs like cortisone and anabolic steroids (discussed in more detail elsewhere) cause the body to retain large amounts of water. In the weeks leading up to a contest, many bodybuilders use copious amounts of painkillers to train through injuries caused by increased training, decreased caloric intake and stress. Unfortunately many painkillers, including the over-the-counter variety, cause the body to hold water. So beware, and if in doubt, check with someone knowledgable.

"The general public will surely not miss the irony in one of the world's best bodybuilders, supposedly epitomizing the ideals of health, strength and physique, dying within minutes of being proclaimed a world-beater."
– Robert Kennedy, MuscleMag International founder (commenting shortly after the death of bodybuilding star Mohammad Benaziza)

Speaking of drugs, another recommendation is to avoid such dangerous chemicals as diuretics. These chemicals work by interfering with aldersterone, a hormone responsible for the body's water and electrolytic balance. Many bodybuilders take diuretics a few days before a contest in the hope of shedding a few extra pounds of water. The problem is not so much the water loss but the electrolytes that go with it. Electrolytes are dissolved substances such as calcium, sodium and potassium that are needed for the proper functioning of the body's electrochemical systems. Such biological processes as nerve-cell firing, muscle contraction and heartbeat are controlled by electrolytes.

If the only side effect of diuretics were muscle cramping, maybe the benefits would outweigh the risks, but unfortunately that's not the case. Such potentially fatal conditions as arrhythmia (irregular heartbeat), seizures and heart attacks have been known to occur after heavy diuretic use.

"I'm really sorry. I really am. I feel Mohammad screwed up with his electrolytes. When you take clenbuterol in excessive amounts – you know clenbuterol does block cortisol – you lower your cortisol and you tend to throw up when your cortisol is low. And then not drinking enough fluids, and taking aldosterone antagonists, estrogen antagonists, taking potassium, and taking this and taking that – that's a lot of different things and somehow they're going to interact, you know?"
– Samir Bannout
IFBB Pro Bodybuilder, 1983 Mr. Olympia
(commenting on the death of Mohammad Benaziza)

Two of the sport's more promising members have died as a result of excessive diuretic use. In 1982 Heinz Sallmayer, winner of the lightweight class at the 1980 Mr. Universe, died of a heart attack brought on by an electrolytic imbalance. And just hours after winning the 1992 Belgian Grand Prix, Mohammad Benaziza dropped dead of similar circumstances.

Both competitors had promising careers ahead of them, especially the massive Benaziza, but their misguided attempt at shedding that extra few pounds of water only led to their downfall. Yet for all the publicity generated by their deaths (incorrectly attributed to steroids by the mass media), horror stories still circulate about bodybuilders taking high doses of diuretics, insulin, and other drugs used to shed water. The win-at-any-cost attitude apparently still prevails. No doubt it will take the deaths of a few more bodybuilders before the message sinks in – and then again, maybe it never will.

Paul DeMayo and Denise Paglia

HOW TO LOOK YOUR BEST ONSTAGE

APPEARANCE

Contest preparation involves other aspects besides diet and posing. The following section looks at the various skills that must be mastered if you want to be totally prepared for a bodybuilding contest.

WEARING GLASSES

As many readers probably wear glasses, a few general comments about eyewear may be appropriate. No doubt you've discovered that during training your glasses keep sliding down your nose. This usually presents no problem in the gym, but onstage it has its drawbacks. The combination of posing and hot lights leads to excessive sweating, which in turn means a constant adjusting of your glasses. Extraneous hand motion is annoying while you're standing in the lineup, and it's also very distracting during your free-posing routine.

Many bodybuilders get around this problem by wearing contact lenses. Yes, they'll set you back around $100, but they're well worth the investment. Not only will you have full peripheral vision, but the distractions associated with glasses will be a thing of the past. Wearing contact lenses is not an absolute necessity, and you won't be penalized for wearing glasses, but you might want to think about the matter if you intend to make competition a regular part of your life.

SHAVING DOWN

Although losing his hair may have been detrimental to Samson's lifestyle (as the biblical tale goes, Samson lost all his great physical strength after his hair was cut), a hairless body is an absolute must if you plan to compete. Besides, removing body hair will allow you to acquire a better tan.

Samir Bannout, Flex Wheeler and Paul Dillett

North American culture is, in some respects, counterproductive to the competitive bodybuilder, and nowhere is this contradiction more obvious than on the issue of male body hair. Men are supposed to have copious amounts of hair all over their bodies. Not having a hairy chest is considered unmasculine. So a sport that emphasizes a lack of body hair must be for sissies, right? Try telling that to Dorian Yates as he's doing bent-over rows with 400 pounds, or Paul DeMayo as he flexes one of those massive, hairless quads of his.

There is nothing sissy about removing body hair. You've spent months, if not years building, a great physique, so why keep it hidden by body hair? In fact, after you shave your body the first time, you'll see your physique from a totally different perspective and the odds are you'll want to keep it that way.

You have a number of options for the removal of body hair. The method most frequently used is a razor. Pick up a pack of Bic disposables and go for it. If this is your first time shaving down, the hair is probably fairly long (half an inch or more), so you may need more than one package (razors usually come in packages of five or 10.) As the skin is not used to having a sharp metal blade hauled over it, go easy. Replacing body hair with nicks and cuts is not helping the situation. The phrase "blood, sweat and tears" was not meant to be taken literally in connection with pumping iron!

We strongly suggest that you shave a few weeks before the contest. This body hair approach gives any little cuts and nicks time to heal, and also clears up the skin rash which often appears on a newly shaved area.

If using a straight edge, you might want to do so while in the shower or bath. This way the water can soften the skin and reduce the chances of nicks and cuts. Although most men use some type of shaving cream when shaving their faces, it's probably not a good idea when shaving off body hair. The length of the hair combined with the cream makes for an almost uncontrollable combination. Also, the lather obscures the various ridges and curves of your muscles. You may be entirely familiar with the topography of your face, but how about your calves or quads? Our advice is to skip the shaving cream so you can see where you're going.

If a straight edge is not to your liking, try an electric razor. Most electric shavers have a side attachment for trimming mustaches, and this will do a wonderful job of removing body hair. You can use the regular shaving section (usually two or three circular blades), but keep in mind that these small blades were not designed for cutting long body hair, only short facial growth. If you try to remove long body hair, you'll probably end up yanking more hair than you cut. You also run the risk of burning out the razor's small motor, so stick with the trimmer.

Using an electric razor has a couple of advantages. For starters it's much faster. A good razor will allow you to shave your body in less than half an hour. A straight

Henderson Thorne

edge takes an hour or more. Another advantage is safety. It's virtually impossible to cut yourself with an electric shaver, but a straight edge is another story. Because it doesn't cut as close to the skin as a straight edge, the electric shaver won't produce an associated rash. Straight edges on the other hand are so efficient that they often (especially the double-bladed varieties) cut below the skin surface – the result, an itchy rash. Spectators may accept baseball players scratching themselves on the field, but a bodybuilder doesn't receive any extra points for scratching onstage.

Finally we remind you not to use an electric shaver in the bath or shower – common sense to some but perhaps not to others. Electricity and water don't make a great combination!

The third option for removing body hair is to use some sort of hair removal cream. Although primarily designed for women, these creams will work for men as well. The creams have an active ingredient that breaks down the hair's protein structure. Just smear it on and wait the specified length of time. Some brands work in five to 10 minutes, but others take overnight. In either case you only need to wash the cream and hair off with water. It's a bit frightening at first to see your body hair crumble into fragments, as if you had some disease, but this is how the cream works, so don't be alarmed.

As a word of caution, run a little experiment before you smear your whole body with hair removal lotion. Some people may have an allergic response to the cream. Test a small area of your body with the cream first. If no rash or redness appears you can cover the rest of the body. If you have a reaction, try other lotions. The allergic response may be limited to one brand. If after trying two or three different brands, your skin still exhibits a rash, in all likelihood your body is allergic to the active ingredient, and a razor is your only option.

A fourth - unusual method of hair removal exists. Former Mr. Olympia Franco Columbu apparently wasn't a fan of lotions or shaving. As the story goes, in the weeks leading up to a contest he would pull the hair out with his hands! By the day of the contest his body would be free of hair. A few masochists may want to give this method a try, but we believe the vast majority will prefer to stick with a razor or lotion!

SKIN CARE

Skin care is related to the topic of hair removal. The skin is your body's first line of defense against disease, and its condition can add years to (or subtract years from) your life. All those hours baking in the sun, sweating in the gym, and shaving with cold metal can turn a youthful-appearing body into an aged-looking sack. As bodybuilding success is heavily dependent on appearance, you have to treat your skin with the same care as you give your muscles.

Wrinkle-causing effects are accumulative. While the damage you inflict may not be visible now, 10 or 20 years down the road your once-soft skin will begin to harden and lose much of its elasticity. Two of the main culprits (besides the natural aging process) are excessive exposure to sunlight and a build-up of dead cells on the outer skin layer (epidermis). That grey, ashen appearance may be considered normal if your skin neglect starts at an early age, but one good facial from a skin-care specialist, and you'll be convinced otherwise.

Lee Priest

Many athletes experience skin blemishes from excessive sweating, and bodybuilders are no exception. Conditions from acne to heat rashes are regular plagues of modern athletics. One important difference in bodybuilding, however, is that most athletes don't have their bodies scrutinized by judges.

Before the male readers among you skip to the next section, we remind you that the skin is nonpartisan when it comes to aging. The following skin-care program, performed in the morning and before bed, takes only three to five minutes, yet the results will keep your skin looking healthy and youthful.

CLEANSING

The first step in skin care involves cleaning the skin with a mild non-detergent lotion. If you have to use soap, use unscented brands.

The deodorant types leave a clogging residue behind. Avoid harsh scrubbing with an abrasive cloth as this only irritates the skin and spreads infection, especially if you have a skin problem like acne. Also, use lukewarm water rather than hot.

It's a good practice to clean in the morning and before you go to bed. If you have dry skin you might want to skip the evening session and wash only in the morning.

TONING

The next step to good skin care is toning. If you have oily skin you will need an astringent toner. Otherwise, you can use a nonalcoholic brand. Toners remove the residue left behind by washing. No matter what brand of soap or cleaning lotion you use, there'll still be some slight residue left behind. The best applicator for toning is a cotton ball, but a light cloth will do the job adequately. Use circular motions when applying the toner, and avoid the area around the eyes as they are very sensitive to such chemicals.

Applying a small amount of toner after a workout helps to help clean away some of the dirt left by sweating. Now, guys, if you're afraid of what your gym buddies will say when they see you with cotton balls, try splashing a little toner on as if it were aftershave. No one will know the difference, and in 20 years, while your skin appears youthful, theirs will begin to look like dried prunes!

MOISTURIZING

One of the main reasons why skin begins to wrinkle as it gets older is dehydration. Imagine two pieces of leather left out in the sun, one untreated, the other regularly covered with oil. Which one will dry and crack first? The untreated one, of course, and your skin behaves in much the same way. (If you didn't know already, that's what leather is – the dried hides of such animals as cows, pigs and alligators.)

While your skin is continuously hydrated with water, most of it evaporates to the surrounding air. If,

Taking good care of your skin now will help keep it healthy and youthful looking for the future.

however, you seal the water in with a moisturizer, the trapped water will keep your skin soft and pliable. The type of moisturizer you select is best determined by the individual skin type. If your skin is very dry, you can use a heavy moisturizing cream. Those with slightly oily to normal skin should use a moisturizing lotion. If you have very oily skin, you probably should skip moisturizers altogether.

EXFOLIATION

Besides the three previous steps, which should be performed daily, every two or three weeks (perhaps more frequently depending on your skin type) you should apply some type of exfoliant. Without miring you down with too much biology, exfoliation is the process by which old, dead cells are removed from the epidermis.

Lee Apperson

eyes and lips. After you've finished, rinse with water. Some experts suggest sliding an ice cube briskly over the face.

Regular exercise promotes excessive perspiration. Besides water, such bodily products as salts, minerals and acids are excreted through the skin pores. Thus the sweating process is a natural skin cleanser, but only if you shower and wash afterwards. Failure to do so will leave behind fantastic breeding grounds for bacteria. The result – body odor and in some cases infection. Finally, to promote healthy skin, change clothes regularly, especially socks and underwear.

TANNING – OBTAINING THE GOLDEN LOOK

Bodybuilder or not, everyone these days seems to enjoy spending time "catching a few rays." Lily-white skin, once the symbol of upper-class standing, has now given way to the California bronze look. For those less fortunate living in northern latitudes, pilgrimages to the sunny south have become almost ritualistic. Yet, just when life seems so wonderful, along comes science to spoil our frolicking good time on the beach. Evidently all those chemicals we pumped into the air were not accepted kindly by the atmosphere. Mother Nature responded in her unique style, and now every year she opens her ozone layer to give all below a good dose of ultraviolet radiation. This periodic hole is just a warning, and with proper precautions put in place, the damage can be reversed.

Besides the periodic opening over the Antarctic, the ozone layer has thinned out around the entire planet. Instead of the "don't spend too much time in the sun" warnings of 20 years ago, such orders as "get out of the sun," now regularly blast our collective consciousness.

For those not versed in the finer aspects of meteorology, let's give you a brief description of how the atmosphere works. Surrounding the earth is a thin layer of gas called the ozone layer. Among its many useful properties is its ability to filter out much of the sun's harmful solar radiation, including ultraviolet. This is not to say that the ozone layer stops all solar radiation, but it blocks enough so that life as we know it can continue to exist. Unfortunately mankind's destructive ways over the years have eroded much of the ozone layer's effectiveness. Recent studies suggest a 5 percent reduction in the ozone layer results in a 10 percent increase in ultraviolet rays, which in turn produces a 20 percent increase in skin cancers. Before you cover yourself from head to foot and go underground, understand that it's all a matter of percentages. You won't develop skin cancer by walking to the car, but exposing yourself to the same amount of sun as, say, 25 years ago is statistically more dangerous.

Although your skin sheds these cells naturally, you can speed up the process. Men do this regularly when they shave. A sharp razor blade helps remove dead cells from the face, thus allowing the underlying tissues to grow. This is perhaps one reason why men's skin does not wrinkle as fast or as much as women's.

Many liquid exfoliants are on the market, but be warned. Some are very harsh and can actually redden or damage the underlying skin. Think of it this way: If you're scraping old paint before you put on a new coat, the object is to slough off the old, loose layer without tearing into the underlying wood. The same holds true for your skin. You want to remove old, loose cells without damaging the underlying, regenerative skin layers. Some commercial products will do just that, so be careful. If in doubt, check with a cosmetician or dermatologist.

No matter what type of exfoliant you use, don't scrub too hard, and never rub in the same place for longer than a couple of seconds. Keep moving your hand over the entire face, and once again, avoid the

One of the ironic (and dangerous) trends in modern society has been that, as the ozone layer depleted, so too did the amount of clothing worn on the beach. The late 1960s and early 1970s saw the appearance of string bikinis and briefs that covered only enough to keep the wearer from getting arrested. While such beachwear raises the blood pressure of admirers, there may be a heavy price to pay in the future.

Besides the risk of skin diseases, excessive sun also destroys the skin's youthful elasticity, leaving it dry, wrinkled and looking old. The exposed skin of people who worked outside all their lives tends to be dark, leathery, and covered with various skin moles. Conversely, the skin on the unexposed parts of their bodies is soft, supple and youthful looking.

In light of these warnings you may be surprised to learn that we're going to recommend tanning before your first competition!

NATURAL TANNING

One reason for spending time in the sun before your contest is that regular tanning helps tighten and thin out the skin. This tightening makes the muscles appear more striated and ripped. Even the top black bodybuilders make regular tanning a part of their precontest preparations.

A second and more obvious reason for tanning is the darker color. All things being equal, the bodybuilder who sports a nice, dark tan on contest day will place higher. The bright stage lights that flood down on bodybuilding contestants tend to wash out and blur muscle separation and definition. So while the lights make the competitors more easily visible, they also make them look smooth. The way around this problem is to darken the skin, either naturally with sunlight or artificially with dyes and lotions.

One of the protective mechanisms developed by the body, when it first evolved three to five million years ago, was skin pigmentation. The equatorial sunlight of the African continent (where humans are believed to have originated) necessitated a dark skin color to protect against ultraviolet radiation. As they migrated northward, the reduced sunlight allowed their skin to become lighter. The ability to darken the skin, however, upon excessive sun exposure, remained. This darkening is what's commonly called tanning, which from a biological basis is protection, but from a sociological viewpoint is attractiveness.

True tanning (the process by which skin pigment is darkened) takes place over repeated exposure to sunlight, usually a week to ten days (which just happens to be the average amount of time people spend cruising down south on holidays!). Therefore, spending three or four hours in the sun for one or two days just before a contest makes little sense. Besides the health risk, your body will burn, not tan! Instead of a nice chocolate-brown color, you'll look like an overripe tomato! And if your burn is severe enough, you'll have the puffy look to go with it as one of the body's responses to severe burns is to flood the area with blood plasma.

Be sure to wear sunscreen when tanning outdoors.

The best procedure for obtaining a good tan would be to start weeks in advance of your contest. How early depends on your skin type. For some, two weeks is sufficient, but most people need three to four weeks.

You must tan the whole body. Don't spend all the time lying on your back and front. You'll look cute standing there onstage with a nice dark tan, only to raise your arms for a double-biceps pose and display two white arm pits! As every inch of your body will be displayed during competition, make sure you tan completely. Don't be afraid to lie at awkward angles to the sun, so long as you're well covered with sunscreen. In fact, you should put an extra helping on the less seen areas as they'll probably be more sensitive to the sun's rays.

A few of you may be extremely sensitive to sun exposure. This sensitivity may be social (living year round in northern latitudes) or biological. (Many people of Nordic descent have low skin pigment.) In either case you must be extremely careful when suntanning, and a sunscreen is an absolute necessity. (Given the state of the ozone layer, it's a good idea for everyone to swear some sort of sunscreen, no matter his race or color.)

In the late 1970s the Food and Drug Administration (FDA) developed a system of sun protection factors (SPF) which rates the effectiveness of sun lotions on a scale of 2 to 22. The numbers on the scale do not correspond to hours or minutes. A lotion with an SPF of 5 does not mean you can stay in the sun for five hours! This detail may seem trivial, but many people have this misconception. An SPF of 5 means you can stay out in the sun five times longer than if you were wearing nothing (lotion that is, not clothes!). For example, if you normally turn red after 20 minutes, an SPF of 5 would allow you to stay in the sun for approximately 100 minutes.

Before you get carried away and slap on a 20, thinking you can spend a full day at the beach, consider a few important points. If you plan to play around in the sand and water, swimming, exercising, etc., one application is not enough. The water (ocean, fresh or sweat) will remove most of the lotion's effectiveness, bringing you back to square one. Even if you're doing no more than lying around for a few hours, you're advised to apply lotion periodically.

The numbers on the SPF scale are averages, and while most people can safely go by the label, a few will have to watch their exposure to the sun carefully. In most cases trial and error will determine the level of protection you need. Keep in mind that by the time you notice your skin turning red, it's usually too late to reach for the sunscreen.

The following guidelines can be used for safe suntanning. Just remember that everyone responds differently, so know your limits.

1. Apply the first layer of sunscreen two hours before going out into the sun. This gives the cream time to penetrate the skin.

2. Although requirements vary, you should use a sunscreen of no less than 5 or 6. Most doctors recommend a 15. Some people will have to go higher.

3. Never stay in direct sunlight for longer than 60 minutes, no matter how dark you get.

4. Apply the sunscreen frequently (and liberally) throughout your stay in the sun.

5. As acquiring a good tan takes at least two weeks, start out slowly, increasing the duration slightly each day.

6. If you're going to be exercising, use a water-based sunscreen and apply frequently, as oil-based products interfere with sweating.

7. Some tanners may have to cover sensitive parts of the skin (nose, ears, lips, bald spots) with a sun blocker like zinc oxide.

8. Pay attention to ozone warnings. If the reading is high, stay out of the sun or use a high-SPF sunscreen and limit your stay.

Roland Cziurlok

9. As 50 percent of your tanning will involve lying on your back, wear a good pair of sunglasses. They won't permit you to look directly at the sun, but they help prevent eye damage from accidental exposure.
10. If you are fair skinned and burn easily, avoid direct suntanning altogether. Instead try one of the following methods for acquiring your contest tan.

ARTIFICIAL TANNING

All is not lost if you can't (or for health reasons don't want to) tan outdoors. You can acquire contest-winning color by other means. Many fitness centers have artificial tanning beds that are specifically designed for this purpose. Even though tanning beds treat you like a breakfast waffle (most require you to get in, lie down, and lower the top cover down on top of you!), used properly they will darken your skin sufficiently for competition. No doubt years ago you heard frightening reports of skin cancer resulting from the use of such beds. Rest easy as the newer models produce only tanning rays and not the hazardous cancer-causing ultraviolet rays. Too much artificial light though, will burn you like the real thing, so limit your exposure.

The second option can be considered a lesson in optical illusion or painting, depending on your point of view. In recent years numerous companies have developed coloring agents that will darken your skin. Most of these products work by interacting with enzymes in the skin. Just spread them on, wait a few hours (or overnight depending on the brand) and before you know it, you look like the typical surfer!

Other products give you instant color. In effect they're dyes that you paint on. One minute you're white, and the next you're a golden brown. How dark you turn usually depends on your skin color to begin with. If your skin is very light, you may turn orange or yellow instead of brown. Many inexperienced bodybuilders (and a few pros as well) turn up on contest day looking as if they're in the final stages of liver disease! This is another reason why you should start contest preparations well in advance.

Perhaps the best approach is to combine tanning lotions with brief periods in the sun. Test the product on a small area of skin first as tanning lotions, like hair-removal creams, can produce an allergic response. Most of the popular brands, such as Quick Tan (QT), are accelerated by sunlight. A couple of days of alter-

Roland Kickinger and Milos Sarcev

nating tanning lotion with sunlight will give you as dark a color as you need.

When you apply tanning lotion, make sure you cover the whole body. This point may seem unimportant, but we have good reason for stressing it. In their haste for tanning the body's showy parts (i.e. the muscles), many bodybuilders forget the most conspicuous part of their anatomy – their face!

How often do we see bodybuilders step onstage sporting beautiful tans, only to smile at the audience with lily-white faces! Make sure you apply the same amount of lotion to your face as to the rest of your body. Try to avoid the eyebrows and hairline, however, as most lotions will stain the skin in these areas a darker color than the surrounding skin.

Don't make the mistake of applying the lotion with your bare hands. Your hands are covered by skin, remember, and tanning lotions will darken any skin they come in contact with. Nothing is quite as humorous as a bodybuilder with black palms hitting a hands-open, overhead arm shot. Either use a pair of thin rubber gloves, or have someone else apply the lotion for you.

Tanning lotions are not sunscreens, so don't be misled into thinking you can spend extra time in the sun. You still need to use a good sunscreen if you plan to stay in the sun for extended periods.

From hair to posing trunks, appearance is everything.

Most drugstores devote entire sections to tanning products, so you shouldn't have any problem obtaining such popular brands as Quick Tan, Tan-in-a-Minute or Dy-O-Derm. Another approach would be to check out the various ads in *MuscleMag International*. Numerous companies offer their tanning products for sale through magazine advertisements.

Finally, beware of the products of tanning pharmacology. As with most aspects of society, if you look hard enough you will find a pill that supposedly gives you what you want. Many products on the market are claimed to speed up the tanning process. These pills work (we use the word guardedly) by making the skin extra sensitive to sunlight. Unfortunately most of these products are not FDA approved. This means that at the very least they don't work, but more important, they may be downright dangerous. If you choose to go this route, be extra careful.

HAIR STYLE

Although there are exceptions, most bodybuilders take great pride in how their hair looks on contest day (or for that matter, any other day). And it's not just the women either. Many a male pro bodybuilder has fretted backstage because his hair looked out of place.

Besides the personality of a good hair style, there are also practical considerations. Having a large mass of unkempt hair can make your neck and traps look much smaller than they really are. If you don't believe us, look at photos of Robby Robinson in his younger days. While Robby's hair couldn't be called untidy, nevertheless his large Afro detracted from his traps and shoulders. In recent years he has opted to wear a

shorter hair style, making his upper body appear even larger than it is.

Another reason to avoid long hair concerns the contest itself. Standing and flexing under hot lights will leave you sweating profusely. Much of this perspiration comes from your scalp. Your previously tidy long hair now looks strung out and scraggly. If you prefer wearing long hair, fine. Just keep it tied up and out of the way. The other extreme, which is fast becoming a trend with modern bodybuilders, is to shave most or all of the hair off.

For most, a good hair style lies somewhere between these two choices. Sadly, many bodybuilders these days forget that the sport is based on the complete package, and this includes the hair.

The first step to an attractive hair style is the cut. If you have any doubt, get someone else's opinion – male or female – it doesn't matter as long as it's someone you can trust. A former girlfriend or boyfriend might not be the best person to check with! If you have the time and money, go to a hair salon and try a number of different styles. Have pictures taken so that you can analyze them afterwards. You may even decide to change the color.

Coloring your hair has many advantages. For starters it helps to reflect light onstage. Also, the dye in many coloring agents penetrates the hair fibers, swelling up the hair shaft and making it thicker and fuller. A change of hair color can symbolize a whole new you. You've changed your body over the past few months, so why not a new hair color to go with it?

Different coloring techniques can be applied to your hair. You can lighten or darken it, highlight it, or change its color completely. Perhaps it's time to go for that California beach-blond look!

Conditioning is important for good hair care. As your hair is primarily composed of protein, it needs to be fed. Regularly adding conditioner to your hair gives it that full, healthy look.

Your low-fat diet and regular sweating play havoc with scalp dryness. A good protein-based conditioner helps put moisture back in both the hair and the scalp. Get a brand that contains moisturizing agents and protein. In addition, use a mild shampoo to prevent excessive drying of the scalp and hair. Good two-in-ones (combination shampoo and conditioner) are available, but the best results will be obtained by shampooing and conditioning separately.

"No, if I was going bald I'd just go bald gracefully. I have an ugly head for being bald. It's not round like a Michael Jordan head, but if I was going bald I'd just go bald. I would never get a hairpiece. No thanks."
– Henderson Thorne, IFBB Pro Bodybuilder

For those readers who see baldness fast approaching in their rear-view mirror, there are alternatives. Such products as hair-thickening sprays, root volumizers, and polymer-based shampoos and conditioners will give thinning hair a pumped-up, swelled appearance. Of course, if there is nothing there to swell, you're left with few choices. The most effective is a hair transplant, but many take a simpler, more economical approach and opt for a hairpiece or toupee.

STRETCH MARKS
Closely related to the issue of skin care is the topic of stretch marks. You have probably noticed that many of the larger bodybuilders have unsightly skin tears on their bodies, particularly the pec-delt tie-in region where the upper chest and front shoulder muscles connect. Two main conditions lead to stretch marks: rapid weight gain (usually muscle, but fat tissue can also contribute) and poor nutrition.

If the underlying muscles expand too rapidly – most bodybuilders doubt this could ever happen! – they stretch the covering skin until it eventually tears. The result is purplish streaks or scars along the growth site. The pec-delt tie-in region is very susceptible because of its rapid tissue growth.

A diet that is deficient in essential nutrients, especially vitamin E, can contribute to the formation of stretch marks. Healthy skin is highly elastic and stretchable, but poor nutrition reduces these properties, so the skin tears instead of stretches.

All serious bodybuilders have stretch marks. They're an unavoidable part of the sport. Over time you'll probably develop them yourself. Therefore the emphasis should be on reducing not avoiding. To lessen the likelihood of developing stretch marks, make sure you are following a well-balanced diet that provides all the essential nutrients. If in doubt, fortify your diet with vitamin and mineral supplements. As most bodybuilders tend to get more than enough nutrients, a second suggestion is probably more applicable.

Since stretch marks are the result of rapidly gaining weight, avoid bulking up in the off-season. Bulking up causes the body to lay down excessive amounts of adipose tissue - a polite term for fat. The result – stretch marks. Try to gain only pure muscle tissue. While this will not prevent stretch marks (we have never seen a serious bodybuilder without stretch marks in the chest-shoulder region), it will greatly reduce the extent of their development.

If you have already developed stretch marks, a number of over-the-counter remedies should help. Rub a hand lotion containing vitamin E into the area. This will speed up healing and help prevent future marks. Some bodybuilders report success using many of the popular suntan lotions. Coconut oil is a favorite.

Another method of dealing with stretch marks is cosmetic. A dark tan (natural or artificial) will hide all but the most serious cases of stretch marks. Unless viewed

Dorian Yates

Ronnie Coleman

CHOOSING APPROPRIATE POSING TRUNKS

Perhaps thirty or forty years ago a bodybuilder could slip on any old pair of shorts and hit the stage, but times have changed. Nowadays choosing a suitable pair of posing trunks can be as challenging as designing the posing routine itself.

Many points must be evaluated when you're choosing a pair of posing trunks. Details from color and design to cost and availability must be considered. Since all of this takes time, don't wait until the last minute to start searching. You may find that the only way to purchase what you need is through mail order, and this process usually takes four to six weeks. (*MuscleMag International* contains many ads for high-quality posing trunks.)

Probably the most important characteristic of posing trunks is their style, and you want to choose a style that will complement your individual physique. Leg and torso length generally determines the cut of the trunks. If you have a long torso and long legs, you can get away with trunks that are cut low on the thigh (i.e. with 3 to 5 inches of material between the waist and the hip). On the other hand, a short statured bodybuilder wants to create the illusion of leg length, so he should wear what are called high-cut briefs (2 to 3 inches of material between waist and hip). The higher cut shows more of the leg, thus creating the illusion of height. (Of course this theory works only when the bodybuilder is standing alone onstage. All the illusion in the world will not make 4'1" Flavio Baccianini appear taller than 6'5" Lou Ferrigno!)

Although the trend is towards skimpier posing trunks, a lower limit exists. Go much below 2 inches and your posing briefs might be considered striptease material! Briefs must cover a certain percentage of the glutes. If in doubt, check the contest pictures in the various muscle magazines.

Besides leg and torso length, body type plays an important role in selection of trunks. Competitors with slender builds can get away with small trunks, while those with stocky builds need a fuller variety.

Your condition may influence your choice of posing attire. Let's say the cuts in your thighs extend right up to your waist. Now that's something you really want to show the judges, and a pair of high-cut trunks is just the thing. Conversely, a great set of washboard abs can look good even if you wear a thicker style of posing trunks.

Besides cut, color plays an important role in trunk selection. First and foremost, current IFBB rules state that posing trunks must be a solid color. This means no dots, lines or wavy bands through the base color. Also (and this is a bit harder to define), your posing briefs must not be too shiny. They should absorb most of the light and not reflect it back to the audience.

Personal preference plays a part, but we can

at close range, the marks will be virtually invisible. Remember however, that this solution merely treats the symptoms and not the cause. The skin is the body's first line of defense against infection. If it has tears, outside pathogens (germs) have a route inside. While infection because of stretch marks is rare, you should always pay attention to personal hygiene. Wearing dirty gym clothes increases the likelihood of contracting an infection – besides repelling your gym mates.

suggest a few guidelines for picking the right color. Try to stay with basic colors that are dark in nature. Black, blue, red and purple are the most frequently seen at bodybuilding contests. Naturally there are exceptions. Black bodybuilders do not normally wear black posing trunks. Red or shades of blue and purple are best for them. Such superstars as Shawn Ray, Lee Haney and Flex Wheeler have regularly worn red posing trunks in competition.

Try to avoid light-colored posing trunks. One flip through a bodybuilding magazine should convince you that light colors tend to draw attention to the waist and make it appear larger. Stick to the darker colors.

Where you buy your posing trunks depends on where you live. In larger centers you can probably track down a store that sells men's beach wear. Most swimming shorts are too large, but some of the smaller briefs may be promising. If someone you know is talented at sewing, perhaps you can have a pair tailor-made. Most gyms and many health-food stores carry bodybuilding equipment, so you might want to check there as well. Many pro bodybuilders sell top-quality posing trunks through ads in *MuscleMag* and other bodybuilding magazines.

Although prices vary, men's posing trunks average $20 and women's two-piece posing suits average around $40. These are middle-of-the-road prices, and no doubt posing suits in the hundred-dollar bracket are available if you shop around.

We strongly recommend taking at least two posing suits to the contest. Posing oils and tanning lotions can stain posing attire, and many bodybuilders like to change colors between prejudging and the night show. Competitors have been known to play an assortment of cruel backstage tricks on one another. (Remember Ken Waller swiping Mike Katz's favorite T-shirt in *Pumping Iron?*) Just when you're getting ready to step onstage, lo and behold, some ill-meaning opponent has hidden your only pair of trunks! Have an extra pair on hand to avoid such embarrassments.

There's also the issue of what you wear for tanning. It makes good sense to wear a smaller posing trunk during your tanning sessions. This way, when you wear the larger trunks, you can be sure that all of the goods on display will be tanned. Nothing distracts like tan lines.

Ultimately which style and color you choose will be a personal decision. If you have access to different

Debbie Muggli, Kim Chizevsky and Laura Creavalle

CHAPTER EIGHTEEN – HOW TO LOOK YOUR BEST ON STAGE

Nowadays bodybuilders use oil to highlight the body's shape and musculature. By now you realize that there's more than one way to do most things, and applying body oil is no exception. First, you have two types of oil to choose from – petroleum-based and vegetable oil. Your initial inclination may be to rush out and buy a bottle of baby oil because it's the most familiar. However, we recommend avoiding mineral oils as they lie on top of the skin instead of sinking into it. Rather than highlighting your muscles, mineral oil will make you look as if you're wrapped in cellophane!

Vegetable oils on the other hand sink into the skin and slowly surface as you begin to sweat. In place of the luster produced by mineral oil, such popular oils as almond and olive give the skin a muscle-highlighting shine.

Like a great naval fleet at sea, you should bring an "oiler" with you. Granted there are other competitors backstage to help, but be wary. Do you really think it's a good idea to ask a rival to oil your back? You may find yourself onstage with half your back oiled! No, unless you can trust one of the other competitors, ask a friend to oil your back.

Have your training partner or a close friend practice the oiling technique several weeks before the contest. After a couple of rehearsals you'll know it will be done right.

Choose the right oil to highlight your body's shape and musculature.

Don't get too carried away and follow the "more is better" philosophy either. Large amounts of oil only flatten the muscles, not highlight them. Incidentally, stepping onstage like an advertisement for OPEC will not get you any extra points! In fact, excessive oil could cost you a higher placing.

Finally, common courtesy demands that you wipe yourself down after the contest. Nothing is as disgusting as a competitor walking around backstage dripping oil all over the place. Not only is such behavior uncouth (oil stains are very difficult to remove from carpet and stage curtains), but it's downright dangerous. Oil splattered on a hardwood floor is an accident waiting to happen, so bring an extra towel and wipe yourself off.

kinds (i.e. borrowed from friends or a store close by that sells them), see which pair looks best on you. As with hair style, have a few pictures taken and get different opinions. The bottom line is that posing trunks should highlight your physique to its fullest.

STRIKING OIL

For all their advantages, the bright lights used at bodybuilding contests have some drawbacks. One of these is their tendency to "wash" the body out and make it appear flat. The old-time strongmen found that by applying a light coat of oil, they could largely eliminate the detrimental effect of the lights.

Dorian Yates

THE BODYBUILDING COMPETITION

IT'S SHOWTIME!

Congratulations! You've made it! In a few hours you'll compete in your first bodybuilding contest. All those months of precontest training and dieting will be put to the test. If you've stuck to your diet, chances are you've attained what bodybuilders commonly call "ripped" condition. Your chest has striations from sternum to armpit. All three heads of the delts are fully visible. The biceps and triceps (all three heads) are neatly separated. Grandma continually badgers you about using your abs as a washboard. Even those quads of yours, which

at one time appeared as one solid hunk, now separate into four distinct muscles. Yes, it's time to let it all hang out (figuratively speaking of course!) and show what you've got.

Before leaving home you should pack the following items in a large gym bag. Mentioning some of them may seem redundant, but in the precontest excitement things often get overlooked.

The first item to pack is really two items in one. How many bodybuilders have rushed to the contest only to discover they've left their posing trunks behind! Granted some members of the audience may be thrilled to see you pose in your birthday suit, but sorry, folks, that's against the rules. Remember to take at least two pairs. For convenience you might want to wear one pair to the theater and put the other in your gym bag.

The next item is your body oil. If you're the generous type, pack an extra bottle for the competitor who forgets his or hers.

The odds of towels being supplied free are slim, even at the pro level, so pack two or three of your own. Not only will you need them to remove oil, but they're also handy for drying off sweat. They'll be useful too if shower facilities are available.

Include some sort of tanning lotion, preferably the quick type. With all the sweating you'll do, the combination of body oil and sweat may streak your physique. Having quick tan available allows you to touch up between prejudging and the evening show.

Although optional, it's a good idea to take along some sort of warmup suit. A track suit is best but some competitors have a robe or dressing gown. At the very least warm up in a pair of shorts and T-shirt. Besides speeding up the warmup process, the suit has the added benefit of hiding your physique until the last moment from the other competitors (more on psychological warfare later).

The final item you should take is a small toiletry kit. Put the following items into the kit as throughout the day they'll come in handy:

Rich Gaspari

1. soap
2. shampoo
3. deodorant
4. brush or comb
5. hairspray
6. small mirror
7. small hair dryer
8. toothbrush and toothpaste

You may think of other items, but these are the most frequently used.

You might want to include some sort of portable exercise apparatus. Most venues don't have weights backstage (they tend to damage the hardwood floors), so pumping up will take creativity on your part. A set of chest-expander springs is small, light and easy to fit into a gym bag. You can use them to work virtually all the body's muscles.

The previous items (not counting the towels and chest-expander springs) will set you back 10 to 15 dollars at a drugstore. In all probability you already have most of them at home, so your expenses will be minimal. Other optional items to take include rubbing alcohol (to remove oil), bottled water, slippers to keep your tootsies warm backstage, and a lock to secure your property if lockers are provided.

ARRIVAL

Before you leave the house (apartment, hotel room, etc.), go through your checklist to make sure you have everything. If in doubt, have a second person double-check for you. In all the excitement it's very easy to overlook something.

Although contests vary, it's wise to arrive at the site at least an hour early. If prior instructions told you to be there sooner, follow them. Being late for your first contest is no way to earn points. At the least you'll be rushed getting ready (oiling up, putting on trunks, etc.); at worst you may be disqualified. So have all times and dates memorized beforehand.

If you're in an unfamiliar town or city, memorize the shortest route to the theater. Don't rely on a road map come Saturday morning. Make a trial run on Friday to see how long you need to travel from the hotel to the contest site. The trip will probably take longer on Friday because of traffic, but use this time as a guide. If the drive goes faster on Saturday morning, so much the better. It's virtually impossible to be too early.

If you happen to be in one of the heavier weight classes, you can watch the proceedings from the audience, at least during the prejudging. Evening shows tend to be sold out, so there are usually no extra seats available for competitors. Some promoters allow contestants to sit on the floor after their weight class, but that depends on theater rules, fire regulations, etc. If you're unsure, check in advance. (Incidentally, for a great perspective of what goes on at a prejudging, check out *Pumping Iron*.)

The prejudging is conducted by weight class, starting with the lightweights and working up to the heavies. If there's a teenage division, this will probably be judged first. As most contests feature a women's division, they may follow the teenagers, or be judged after the men's lightweight. Procedures vary from contest to contest so don't be surprised if the order of judging is different.

Also popular these days are guest posers, and since guest posers tend to be the largest bodybuilders present, most promoters put them on at or near the end of the show. It makes no sense to have Paul Dillett come on first, and then follow with the lightweights! Let's face it. After Paul no one would look good. No, in all probability, guys like Paul, Dorian Yates or whoever, would be scheduled before the heavyweights or as the grand finale.

THE GREAT PUMP-UP

Once the head judge or MC calls out your weight class, immediately proceed backstage and get ready. Change into your posing trunks and start pumping up. For those new to the sport, or those who somehow

Berry DeMey

CHAPTER NINETEEN – THE BODYBUILDING COMPETITION

Pumping up before hitting the stage.

reached this far without hearing the term, "pumping up" is the process of performing high repetitions (20+) to force huge volumes of blood into the muscles. There are two distinct viewpoints on pumping up. Former Mr. Universe Bill Pearl generally skipped the practice, preferring to run through his posing routine and leave it at that. Sergio Oliva by all accounts nearly did an entire workout backstage. These are more or less the extremes of the sport, and most bodybuilders nowadays perform a moderate amount of pumping up before hitting the stage.

Why pump up? Well, as you probably have noticed from your training, a pumped-up muscle is larger than an unexercised one. The forcing of blood into the area swells the muscle considerably. Those 17-1/2-inch arms of yours can be pushed to the 18-inch bracket with a few quick pump sets. A good pump in your lats and you feel ready to compare lat spreads with Michael Francois!

Of course (and you probably saw this coming), there are disadvantages to excessive pumping up. A full, tight muscle is generally harder to control than an unpumped muscle. Also, a muscle bloated with blood may lose some of its sharpness and definition. Finally, pump up too much, and you run the risk of shrinking onstage. You may appear huge at the beginning of the judging, but as the blood drains from your muscles, they begin to lose size.

Which muscles to pump? In years gone by, the big, showy muscles received the lion's share of pumping exercises. Bodybuilders backstage would do set after set for their biceps and chest. Nowadays these muscles tend to be the largest to begin with, so most bodybuilders put their energy in other areas. If your chest or biceps are weak, it would make sense to get a maximum pump there before going onstage. But for the most part limit your chest and biceps pumping to one or two quick sets.

Two other muscles to avoid are the forearms and calves. Neither muscle pumps up to a noticeable degree, and perhaps more important, both are notorious for cramping, especially the calves. As most bodybuilders tend to border on dehydration, the low electrolyte levels can cause severe cramping while onstage (a good reason to sip water at every opportunity). Our advice is to forget about these two muscles. At the most do one quick-rep set just to warm them up.

Now that we've told you which muscles to avoid, here's our list of muscles (and the associated exercises) to pump up before hitting the stage.

1. The Deltoids – As the shoulders are seen from every angle, and you can never be too wide, you must do a few pump sets for them. If light dumbells are available perform a couple of sets each of shoulder presses, side laterals and bent-over laterals. If dumbells are not available (or someone else has them), break out your chest expander springs. Using one or two springs (most of these sets allow up to five springs to be attached), grasp the handles and extend your hands to arms' length. (It's ironic that something called a chest

Casey Viator forces some blood into his monstrous arms.

expander does nothing for the pecs.) Do a couple of sets to the side, and then bend over and do a few for the rear delts. Great rear delts are seldom seen at contests – at least at the lower and intermediate levels – so if you've got them, put a good pump in there and show the judges. They're guaranteed to earn you extra points!

2. The Lats – Perhaps the most distinguishing trademark of a bodybuilder is his or her V-shape. Even in clothes this classic shape is visible. Some people walk around with a permanent lat flex even when they don't have the lats to go with it, but the majority of bodybuilders carry themselves with pride.

To pump up the lats, do a few sets of dumbell rows (you'll be lucky to have the dumbells, and a barbell is usually out of the question), chinups if an appropriate overhead bar is available, and towel pulls. As the name implies, towel pulls require a towel and a willing partner. With your partner holding one end of the towel, grab the other end with a narrow grip and pull towards you. The idea is for your partner to apply just enough resistance to work your lats. On one hand you don't want to tear the towel, but on the other hand you want to pump up the lats. Like oiling up, towel pulls with your partner should be practiced before the day of the contest.

3. Chest and Triceps – Nothing beats the good old pushup to pump these two muscle groups. You can do them straight from the floor with your feet on a bench (primarily hits the upper chest) or between two benches

You may have to be creative if no weights are provided backstage.

CHAPTER NINETEEN – THE BODYBUILDING COMPETITION

Tom Platz

(primarily for the lower chest). All you need is a couple of sets to get the blood into your pecs and triceps. Don't go overboard, however, as unless they're lacking in size. Your chest and triceps can get by without much of a pump.

4. Thighs – As the thighs need a fair amount of weight to pump up, there's not much you can do backstage. Sissy squats are one option. Holding an upright with one hand, and leaning slightly backwards, squat down to the floor, trying to tense your thighs with every rep. If dumbells are available, you can do dumbell squats as well. Don't try to perform a full leg workout. Save most of your energy for the posing. You'll need it!

5. Biceps – As your lat-pumping exercises also hit the biceps, you probably won't have to do any direct biceps movements. A few dumbell curls or spring curls (using your trusty chest expander, pin one handle to the floor with your foot and curl upwards with the other handle) will get an adequate amount of blood into the biceps. You don't want to overpump them and lose control or overshadow your triceps development.

You want good control over your midsection (abs, intercostals, obliques), so avoid pumping up that region. A blood-bloated waist is not desirable. The idea is to have a small but sharp set of abdominals, and the best way to achieve this effect is by refraining from pumping your midsection.

While doing these pumping exercises it's a good idea to hit various poses between sets. Not only does posing facilitate the procedure by aiding distribution of blood evenly to all parts of the muscle, but it also helps loosen you up for the show.

Once you've finished pumping up, have a trusted friend or competitor(!) apply a thin layer of oil over your entire body. (Check beforehand as some contests don't allow body oil.) Remember to apply the oil sparingly because a heavy coating of oil only reflects light back to the audience, making you appear smooth.

You'll probably be given a five-minute warning before proceeding onstage, so when it comes, make a few final checks in the mirror. Is the oil applied evenly on your body? Is your hair neat and tidy? Have you pinned your competition number to your trunks (you will be given a number so that the judges can keep track of you), and have you memorized it? The judges will only refer to you as "contestant number so and so." You'll look kind of stupid standing there without reacting to their instructions after two or three references to your number. Soon the announcer will call your weight division onstage, and the road to the Olympia begins!

The first thing you notice when you walk out onstage is the brightness and intensity of the lights. In fact your eyes will take a couple of minutes to become adjusted to the brilliance. Try to avoid staring at the lights. The direct brightness is dangerous, and when you look away you may become dizzy and lose your balance. If there is one advantage to the lights it's their

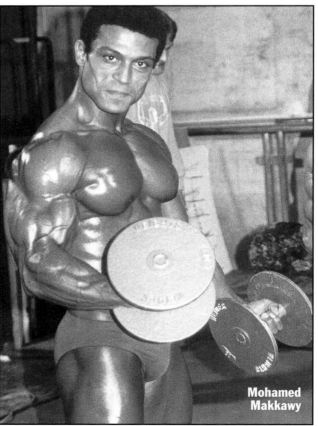

Mohamed Makkawy

Kevin Levrone, Dorian Yates and
Nasser El Sonbaty

ability to block out the audience – a welcome feature if this is your first contest.

After you've been positioned onstage, all you have to do is follow directions. Either the head judge or MC will ask you to perform various compulsory poses. When comparisons are to be made, the competitors will be called out by number, not name. (This is why you should have your number memorized.) As soon as your number is called, step forward and wait for further instructions. (For a complete description of each round, see the posing section earlier in this section.)

POST PREJUDGING

When the prejudging has ended, you want to spend the day in an appropriate fashion. Your first concern should be to replace lost fluids. That bottled water we told you to take along is now worth its weight in gold. After three rounds of posing you probably will have lost three to five pounds (or more) of water. As soon as you get backstage take a few sips, sit back and relax. Don't gulp the whole bottle down at once, for it will only give you gas. Try consuming the water over the next hour or so. If you are severely dehydrated, obviously you want to get the liquids into you much faster.

Before putting on your clothes, remove the oil from your body. If shower facilities are available, use them. If not, you can remove the oil with the rubbing alcohol we suggested you include in your bag. Wipe down with a towel before putting on your clothes. Oil stains are very difficult to remove.

Before leaving the contest venue, check with

someone to find out what time contestants should return. In most cases it will be about an hour before curtain time. Remember that there will be a bigger crowd at the evening show, so parking may be a concern. Leave your arrival too late and you may have to walk a distance to the theater. Also, make sure you have some sort of identification to confirm you're a competitor. (Hopefully your appearance will be all that's required!) You don't want to be accused of trying to sneak in.

Most competitors go for a quick meal in the afternoon – nothing major, just a light snack containing a few carbs, maybe a baked potato or some steamed rice. A little food will keep your energy level up, and in the event that your muscles were not fully "carb-loaded," the extra glycogen will give you a fuller appearance at the evening show. Don't make the mistake of consuming a large meal that will take hours to digest. Not only will it give you a bloated, fat-looking stomach, but it also lessens the control you have over your abdominal muscles.

No doubt you were up early in the morning (and anxiety prevented you from getting sufficient sleep the night before) so a short nap after eating is advisable. Don't forget to set the alarm clock, and limit your sleep to one or two hours. If you "crash" for three hours or more, your body will sink into its deep-sleep mode. Then when you get up the body will think it's morning and you'll need a couple of hours just to "wake up." The idea is to sleep long enough to recharge your batteries, but not long enough to shut you down for the day.

Lee Labrada

The evening show may or may not resemble the prejudging. The free-posing and posedown rounds will be the same, but the odds are there will be fewer comparisons. Contests vary from city to city and state to state, so don't be surprised if you have to go through four complete rounds again. This repetition is especially likely if the judges have still not determined the placings.

"You know, the reason I don't feel so badly about this is that I made so much improvement this year both size-wise and muscularity-wise, with definition. I presented myself in my all-time best shape, and that is the best you can do. The rest of it boils down to the opinion of eleven people, and there's not much you can do to influence that. If they decide that you're not the man, so be it. With a different panel the results might be different." **– Lee Labrada, IFBB Pro Bodybuilder (commenting on his third-place finish at the 1992 Mr. Olympia)**

After the winners are announced, accept the results wholeheartedly. This will be no problem if you place first. The winner always agrees with the judges! If you end up fourth, when first or second seemed assured, don't make a scene. In the vast majority of contests the judges place the contestants appropriately. We know this is not what you wanted to hear, but it's a fact of life. You may have felt like the winner onstage, but you probably looked different from the judges' table.

What if you (and a majority of the audience) feel you were robbed? Simply smile, strike a few of your best poses for the audience, and congratulate those who placed above you. Don't throw your trophy (if you get one), give the judges the finger (it happens), or otherwise make a fuss. One of the greatest lessons to learn from competing is good sportsmanship. When Tom Platz placed lower than expected at the 1981 Mr. Olympia, he didn't react negatively. He didn't storm off the stage cursing. No, like the gentleman he was (and still is), he thanked the audience for their support and then congratulated the winner, Franco Columbu. No doubt this display of professionalism was a big factor in Tom's future business successes. Likewise at the 1994 Ms. Olympia, when Laura Creavalle was announced second, she didn't let the disappointment show through onstage. No doubt Laura was infuriated inside, but she kept her feelings to herself and, smiling, congratulated the winner, Lenda Murray.

If there's a lesson to be learned here, it's that judges are only human and sometimes they make mistakes. We'll be the first to admit that in a few cases politics have determined the placings. We hope you're never the victim of such injustice. It's not fair to put yourself through the hell of precontest dieting and training, only to lose because someone else was friends with the head judge. The odds of this occuring

Before getting dressed you may want to spend a few minutes visualizing the evening's events. Mentally run through your posing routine a couple of times. It's also a good practice to plan a few strategies to deal with your opponents. The prejudging showed what you're up against. By now you have a good idea of who's placing where. If you can narrow your competition down to two or three, visualize their weak points and your strong points. Decide what poses you'll hit when they strike their best. What are their weak bodyparts? Which bodyparts can you go head to head with, and which ones should you avoid? Try to anticipate how the posedown will develop. Granted, there's no way to plan it out pose for pose, but at least you'll have a strategy.

Give yourself a minimum of two hours' preparation time before the evening show – an hour to wake up and get dressed, and an hour to get there. The checklist you followed in the morning also applies in the evening. Check yourself and then have someone else confirm for you.

are very slim, but if it happens, it happens. Yelling, screaming, and making obscene gestures at the judges will not help your cause. You're better off to take a page from Tom's book and appear to accept the decision very graciously. If afterwards you want to go somewhere private and jump up and down, cursing and swearing, so be it. Get it out of your system. Chances are one good postcontest meal will calm you down. Channel the excess frustration and anger towards your training. Ensure that next year the judges will have no choice but to place you first. History loves good sportsmanship, but hates a sore loser.

PSYCHOLOGICAL WARFARE

One of the highlights of the 1960s and 1970s was listening to the great Muhammad Ali before an upcoming fight. With a mastery of the English language that Shakespeare would envy, Ali routinely psyched out opponents with his rantings and ravings. Such proclamations as "I am the greatest" and "I'll knock him out in the eighth round" were frequently heard in the weeks leading up to the fight. Whether such statements bothered Joe Frazier or Ken Norton is unclear, but no doubt many lesser opponents had their confidence shaken by Ali's rhetoric. While psychological warfare has probably existed as long as competition itself, it's safe to say that Muhammad Ali was the first modern athlete to refine it to an art.

The sport of bodybuilding had its own Muhammad Ali in the late 1960s and early 1970s – the one and only Arnold Schwarzenegger! To this day Arnold is the first to admit that a couple of his contests were won with the help of psychology. The most frequent victim of such tactics was the Cuban Myth, Sergio Oliva.

Even by today's standards Oliva was an awesome sight. From that tiny waist to those cannonball-sized delts of his, pound for pound Oliva took a back seat to no one in terms of muscle mass. Arnold, the intelligent competitor that he was, realized he would need more than a great physique to beat him. So at the 1970 Mr. World contest Arnold told Sergio that he should put on a few more pounds if he intended to defeat him. Oliva, being a tad insecure at the time, took Arnold's advice to heart and added another ten pounds. This gain was not to his benefit, however, as much of the weight was fat. Two weeks later, at that year's Olympia, a smooth Sergio placed second to a rather confident Arnold.

Arnold used a different strategy two years later in Essen, Germany. Most agree that the Myth was at his best at the 1972 Olympia. In fact, from a physique standpoint Oliva may have had the edge over Arnold. As the story goes, Arnold persuaded the judges to move the prejudging to another room. What Arnold failed to point out was that the room had dark brown walls, and while Arnold's physique stood out, the Cuban-born Oliva blended right in. A different background might have brought Oliva the title that year,

but Arnold's "advice" saved the day for the Oak.

Then there were Arnold's table-side manners at the 1975 Mr. Olympia. With the film *Pumping Iron* being shot that year, Arnold invited the Ferrigno family to breakfast on the morning of the contest. Nineteen-year-old Lou hung on every word as the great Schwarzenegger expressed the opinion that Lou needed two more weeks to take the title. Then he added that if Lou had another two weeks, he also would have another two weeks, and the outcome would be the same – Arnold would win! The inexperienced Lou took Arnold's comments seriously, and he was never sure of himself afterwards.

In defense of Arnold, he probably would have won those contests regardless of his comments. After all, from 1970 to 1975 he was the sport's number one bodybuilder, and he had the physique to back up his shrewd remarks.

Other bodybuilders used different forms of psychological warfare to better their cause. Franco Columbu

"The Myth" Sergio Oliva

Tonya Knight

supposedly ate pizza in front of other competitors. Frank Zane would keep himself hidden until the last minute before the show. This strategy had the other competitors guessing as to Frank's physical condition.

In recent years the practice of playing mind tricks on opponents has taken a different turn. With the seriousness of modern competitions (due to increased prize money), today's pros limit their psyching to trading barbs in the muscle magazines. The backstage antics of years gone by are rare. With so much money on the line, who's going to risk the wrath of a 250-pound competitor? Stealing someone's T-shirt, as Ken Waller did to Mike Katz in 1975, could be fatal these days!

No doubt at the lower levels some degree of psychological warfare takes place, but it's usually limited to such comments as "I thought your calves were bigger than that" or "Maybe you should have started your diet two weeks earlier." There's no need for you to join in such backstage shenanigans (unless it's good-natured fun with a friend). If you've dieted properly, and your posing routine flows from pose to pose, you have nothing to worry about. Bodybuilders who rely on insulting remarks are usually only attempting to cover up their own weaknesses and insecurities. Our advice is to let distracting remarks go in one ear and out the other.

COMMUNICATION SKILLS

"My television exposure is way more than I ever got from all the bodybuilding magazines. Bodybuilding publicity is great, but the television audience is so much larger."
– Tonya Knight,
IFBB Pro Bodybuilder, former
MuscleMag International *columnist,* **and**
former star of **American Gladiators**

This is one of those topics that on the surface may not appear to have any relationship whatsoever to bodybuilding. However, every form of sporting entertainment seems to be covered on cable TV these days, and bodybuilding is no exception. It's not just the local TV stations either. Chances are state (provincial) and regional shows are going to receive some TV coverage too.

If you win or place high in one of these contests, sooner or later you'll be asked for an interview. Your response to such a request should be an absolute, wholehearted – YES! You can't beat interviews (both TV and print) when it comes to furthering your bodybuilding career. Your next competition may be hundreds of miles away but if the judges have seen your face on some TV show or in a local newspaper, you have a decided advantage over a competitor who has never received prior news coverage.

TALKING FOR SUCCESS

Since most people are slightly nervous when confronted with a microphone, the following section can be used to guide you through your first interview. Perhaps the most important aspect of good public speaking is learning to relax. Remaining calm often takes care of the other facets of communication. If you let yourself get uptight at the first sight of a microphone, your nerves are probably going to have a major effect on what you say and how you say it.

No matter how excited you are, try to speak slowly and carefully. Don't race along trying to put as many words as possible into one sentence. Reporters usually ask enough questions to allow almost anyone to say what's on his or her mind.

**Legends Lou Ferrigno and
Arnold Schwarzenegger battle it out!**

If you have a habit of tossing in foul language during your day-to-day speech, for obvious reasons a certain amount of modification is needed. Vulgarity may be accepted among your peers, but it's a definite no-no on TV.

It might be a good idea to tape record yourself at some point, just to see how you sound. Get a willing friend to play the part of the interviewer. Have him ask you a series of questions like "How long did you diet for the contest?" and "Did you expect to place this high?" If this is your first time on tape, the results may surprise you. Most people don't realize how their voice sounds to others. In many cases they can't even recognize their own voice on tape!

Play back your practice recording several times and analyze it. Pay particular attention to how fast you're speaking and how you pronounce each letter. If you have a distinct dialect or accent, you may want to change it – not that either is wrong, but what you're saying should be clear and understandable. Both Arnold Schwarzenegger and Lou Ferrigno spent years working on their speech – Arnold because of his native German, and Lou because of a hearing loss suffered in childhood. Now both are among the sport's best public speakers.

Chris Cormier and Kevin Levrone at the 1994 Mr. Olympia.

Another problem to avoid is the use of "uhs" and "ahs" in your speech. Don't string sentences together with such idiosyncratic grunts. Finish one sentence and then start the next. If you have nothing to add, say nothing. The interviewer will take the hint and ask the next question (unless this happens to be his or her first interview, in which case the two of you will have some fun!).

Don't use unfamiliar words. Nothing sounds as ridiculous as a person trying to imitate a thesaurus. Be yourself.

If asked to comment on your low placing, don't blame it on the judges. Not only is that a sign of poor sportsmanship, but the odds are some of the same judges will be judging you again in the future. One or two careless or ill-considered criticisms and your bodybuilding career could be over!

Instead of being negative, respond by saying how you underestimated the competition (this will win you many friends), or how it was all a great learning experience and next year – look out!

As a final suggestion, go through your video library and check out how the top pros respond. Most contest coverage includes backstage interviews with the competitors. Such former bodybuilding stars as Chris Dickerson, Frank Zane, Cory Everson and Carla Dunlap have hosted this portion of the events in the past. Frank Zane did much of the commentary and interviewing at the 1994 Mr. Olympia.

After watching the tapes you'll see that most competitors are clear, concise and professional. In essence they are a credit to the sport. Granted, a few could use speaking lessons themselves, but these incidences are few and far between.

If you feel you have a future in bodybuilding (your contest placings should give you an idea), you might consider taking a couple of public speaking courses. Not only will such instruction improve your image at bodybuilding contests, but good speaking habits are an advantage in all facets of life.

Lou "Incredible Hulk" Ferrigno

Tom Platz is intensity!

CHAPTER TWENTY – THE MANY FACETS OF THE SPORT

THE MANY FACETS OF THE SPORT

THE BUSINESS OF BODYBUILDING

"First of all you must get out of the gym and see yourself as a product that must be sold and marketed and packaged. Bodybuilders must see themselves as a product and not individuals outside of the gym."
– Tom Platz, IFBB Pro Bodybuilder, superstar turned businessman

Unlike his counterpart of 30 years ago, the modern bodybuilder can look forward to receiving more than a handshake and trophy after winning a major title. And while not in the same league as, say, tennis or golf, bodybuilding nevertheless can provide a lucrative income for the sport's elite.

"I think you have to be aggressive these days in order to be a success, especially in bodybuilding. You can't just sit around and hope that things will come to you and happen the way you want." **– Tonya Knight, top IFBB Pro Bodybuilder, former MuscleMag International columnist**

For all the opportunities available to the modern bodybuilder, surprisingly very few athletes have capitalized in a big way. For every Arnold, Lou Ferrigno or Tom Platz, there are hundreds if not thousands of bodybuilders out there just waiting for something to happen. But it does not work that way. Bodybuilders must actively pursue their careers by promoting and marketing themselves. Many feel they only have to win one major title and in a few days Robert Kennedy or Joe Weider will be banging on the door begging for a photo shoot. Time after time the sport has seen promising careers go crashing down in flames because all the individuals had going for them were great physiques.

The key to complete bodybuilding success (as opposed to simply winning a few titles) lies in carrying the energy expended in the gym, out into the business world. Just as bodybuilders set long- and short-term goals in their training, so too should they map out a strategy for business success.

As soon as Arnold left competitive bodybuilding, he plunged head first into the entertainment business. First there were acting lessons, then the establishment of social contacts within the industry, and later when financial success came his way, Arnold began to learn the ins and outs of real estate. In short Arnold didn't sit on his ass and wait for people to approach him. He took the bull by the horns and went after them. Former Mr. Universe and pro bodybuilder Tom Platz, summed it up best when he said: "If you sit and wait, nothing is going to come to you. No one is going to come to you unless you make yourself available and function as one

Porter Cottrell

of them." Now we're not suggesting that you'll be the next Arnold – after all there is only one Arnold – but you can achieve great success if you equip yourself with the tools to do so.

The following topics relate to the bodybuilding business world. They range from direct sources of income to approaches that can be used for publicity. If you plan to make a living from the sport someday, this section is a must read.

PRIZE MONEY

"I would like to see the prize money increased for the women. It just does not seem fair that the women, who have to train and diet just as hard as the men, do not receive the same amount or even close to the amount the men get."
— **Kathy Unger,**
world amateur champion

Prize money is one of the least lucrative means of financial reward. The winner of a major bodybuilding contest may win $100,000 but the money remaining for the lower placings falls off rapidly. There are only six to eight major contests each year, so a bodybuilder would have to win a couple, or place in numerous, to make what could be called "real money." And given the highly competitive nature of the sport, only a select few could survive strictly on prize money.

No doubt the future will see the purses for major bodybuilding contests expand, but there's still a long way to go before they reach the $500,000 to $1,000,000 earned by top tennis and golf stars. Still, through the efforts of such people as Ben and Joe Weider, Arnold Schwarzenegger, and *MuscleMag's* own Robert Kennedy, bodybuilding continues to grow by leaps and bounds. With increased popularity will come increased sponsorship and ultimately increased prize money.

GUEST POSING

"One quality I've been complimented on over the past few years is my consistency. It amazes some people, but I diet for a contest for only about four weeks. I pride myself on showing up in top shape for guest appearances and I can be ready for photographs with only a few days' notice."
— **Porter Cottrell**
IFBB Pro Bodybuilder
Night of Champions winner

One of the main reasons why today's bodybuilders remain ripped and massive year round is that they're continually in demand for guest appearances. A local contest featuring Paul Dillett, Shawn Ray, Kevin Levrone or Dorian Yates is virtually guaranteed to sell out. In return, a top pro can earn thousands (in some cases hundreds of thousands) of dollars in extra income. In fact, most pros earn more money in this manner – and from seminars, which is the next topic discussed – than from actual competition.

Guest posing has long been associated with bodybuilding (often to keep the audiences entertained during weightlifting events!), but it was Arnold and Franco who turned posing into a lucrative endeavor, and ultimately brought it the credit it deserved. The great demand for guest posers has resulted in a drastic change in the modern bodybuilder's year-round condition. Years ago the practice was to bulk up to 30 or 40 pounds above contest weight, and then diet down in the weeks prior to the event. In effect the defined appearance featured in the various muscle magazines was seen for only a short time before and after the competition. With the demand for guest posing, today's bodybuilders try to stay within 10 to 20 pounds of their best competitive weight. Of course there are exceptions, and stories circulate of pros who normally compete at 240 showing up for guest appearances weighing in excess of 300 pounds. Instead of a rock-hard statue, audiences are treated to the Pillsbury Doughboy! While a few spectators actually enjoy the excessiveness, most leave disappointed, having expected to see something resembling the magazine image.

For those future (or present for that matter) guest posers out there, here are a few pointers to remember. You should attempt to schedule appearances shortly before or after a major contest, but carrying 40 or 50 extra pounds is just not called for. Keep in mind that word quickly spreads about a guest poser's appearance. Show up two or three times fat and out of shape, and this aspect of your bodybuilding career goes down the tubes!

Be on time. Arriving five minutes before curtain time will give the promoter ulcers. If you're late, the audience turns against you. If you fail to appear at all, your name will be mud throughout the bodybuilding kingdom!

Try to arrive at the contest venue before the competition begins. Not only does this punctuality give you time to mingle and sign autographs, but it also goes a long way in promoting your reputation. News travels fast.

What does a promoter look for in a guest poser? Louis Muia, a Toronto promoter and veteran of over 35 shows, feels that the ideal guest poser should be a total package of conditioning, professionalism, conduct, and attitude. He or she must be socially mature and able to speak professionally. In short the athlete must be promotable. Another promoter, Spence Curry, adds that guest posers should be willing to pitch in and help sell the contest – i.e. reciprocate service for the fee they are receiving.

SEMINARS

Besides guest posing most top bodybuilders earn additional income by giving seminars. The two activities are often combined over the course of a weekend. Top pros commonly give a bodybuilding seminar on Friday night, after the prejudging on Saturday or on Sunday afternoon.

If you get the chance to attend one of these seminars, take it. Nothing beats first-hand knowledge. Nearly every professional (and a large number of amateurs) is a walking storehouse of information. That's one of the main reasons they reached such a lofty status. You can read all the books and magazines you want, but there's nothing quite like the atmosphere of a bodybuilding seminar. Instead of taking weeks or months to solve a particular

Tom Platz

problem, you may need only one answer from a pro bodybuilder.

Most bodybuilders divide their seminars into three broad categories – training, diet and competition. Depending on the bodybuilder, you may ask questions during his/her discussion or afterword in a special question-and-answer period. Feel free to take notes, as a topic that seems irrelevant now may be of the utmost importance two years down the road. If you are at the beginning stage, precontest dieting is of no present concern. But two or three years from now you may decide to enter your first bodybuilding competition, and that's when the pros' advice will come in handy.

PHOTOS

Flip through the pages of *MuscleMag* and other bodybuilding magazines and you can't help but notice ads for 8 x 10 photos of your favorite stars. Some photos – for example those of Sergio Oliva – have become classics.

The photos may be color or black and white, and on average range in price from $5 to $10. In many cases you get a special price by ordering them in sets. Besides showing the compulsory poses, they serve as a great source of inspiration.

When your physique starts winning amateur events, it would be a good idea to have a series of such 8 x 10 photos taken – both color and black and white. Get them done when you're in top condition, and take them with you to seminars and posing exhibitions. Not only will the fans be grateful to receive them, but the photos also serve to further your image. Remember, overexposure in bodybuilding is virtually impossible.

VIDEOS

For years film strips have been available of the top bodybuilders going through their posing routines. With the advent of video there has been an explosion in such products. Advertised through the pages of the various muscle magazines, the subjects of these videos range from the bodybuilders of yesteryear to today's superstars.

There are generally three categories of bodybuilding videos. First are what could be called the classics – those that feature top bodybuilders posing in a myriad of locations from beaches and pools to studios and stages.

The second version are videos covering the major bodybuilding competitions. Every year the Olympias, Arnold Classic and others (both male and female) are recorded by professional videographers, and made available to the bodybuilding public. All it takes is one

Laura Binetti

viewing and the competitive juices start flowing! Although prices may vary, on average they sell for $39.95.

The third video format is a relatively new phenomenon, but if the early response is any indication, promises to be the most exciting of the three. It's one thing to read a magazine article and look at the accompanying pictures, but it's something else when you can watch a bodybuilding superstar on video. Every rep, bead of sweat, and contracting muscle fiber is captured on tape to inspire you to new heights of bodybuilding success. The tapes may be either full-body workouts or individual bodyparts. Your chest workout will never be the same after watching Lou Ferrigno train his. Or how about Dorian Yates blasting his back? If you're still not satisfied, try Kevin Levrone's leg workout. Watching a bodybuilding superstar train on video ranks second only to being there in person. In some respects the tape is superior, because you can review it at your convenience.

If you start winning major titles, you might seriously consider making your own training video. (If you really

Dorian Yates

lished very profitable businesses. Such former super-stars as Gary Strydom and Mike Christian offer a whole range of top-quality, moderately priced gym wear. You can check out their clothes at better sports stores or through ads in various bodybuilding magazines.

TRAINING CONSULTANTS

"When I'm signing autographs, if the line isn't too long I try to write something personal to each person. At a seminar, no matter what the fans ask, I try to answer. When fans write, they deserve a reply, so I always send a form letter with a little note on it. Ideally I'd like to reply personally to each, but realistically I can't as that would take up all my time."
— *Tonya Knight,*
top IFBB Pro Bodybuilder,
former American Gladiator,
former MMI columnist

For most bodybuilders training at a big city gym, expert advice is often only an incline bench away. Go into any large gym and you'll find a full spectrum of bodybuilders, from rank beginners to regional and national competitors. It's quite common for experienced trainers to offer advice to those just starting out in the sport.

But what happens if you train in a small gym or basement where the most experienced person around is you? Well, you have a number of options, ranging from books and magazines to videos and the occasional TV show. If by chance none of these methods answers your questions, don't despair. You have another option – write a pro bodybuilder!

As most pros do their best to answer all their mail, for the cost of a stamp you can jot down a few questions and send them off. A few weeks later back comes your personalized reply. If you want a complete workout designed, check with the pro as no doubt there will be some kind of charge. Most will answer a few questions for free, but a lengthy evaluation and restructuring of your training requires a great deal of time, so charging a fee is only natural.

Although the method varies, many pros will use audio tape to answer questions. Check first, however, before you buy a cassette tape to send.

MAIL-ORDER COURSES

First popularized by Charles Atlas, mail-order training courses are nothing more than an elaborate extension of consulting. For years Arnold, Lou Ferrigno, Dorian Yates, Mike Mentzer, Larry Scott, Tom Platz, Vince Gironda, Franco Columbu, and Lee Haney have offered training courses through the various bodybuilding magazines. The courses are usually divided into two general types – full-body instruction tips and individual bodypart routines. Prices vary, but generally average around $8 per course. Although such courses have given way in recent years to videos, many are still available and contain an abundance of useful information.

make it big, you won't have to worry as video producers will seek you out!) Start with a full-body training video, and see how it goes. If it's successful, you can produce an expanded video for each bodypart. Don't skimp on the production cost either. The video industry is like the photo industry; you get what you pay for. Invest the extra dollars and have a professional videographer do it right. Not only will your fans appreciate it, but word will get around. Develop a reputation for mediocrity and your business dreams end up the same.

CLOTHING – THE FASHION SET

It was only a matter of time before bodybuilders joined the fashion set. Wearing a T-shirt and pair of shorts no longer cuts it in the gym these days. Nothing less than a designer workout suit is acceptable in the fashion-conscious '90s.

Many pro bodybuilders have turned their talents to marketing gym wear, and a few of them have estab-

BODYBUILDING CAMPS

Reading books and magazines is not enough for many aspiring bodybuilders. They want a more personalized touch to instruction. To meet this demand a number of pros have established training centers offering one-on-one instruction. For a fee (which ranges from a few hundred to a few thousand dollars, depending on the length of stay, type of instruction, etc.) you can train, sleep and breathe bodybuilding.

Perhaps the greatest benefit of training camps is the degree of individual attention. As no two physiques respond the same, a knowledgeable instructor can observe your training and make adjustments where needed. That kind of evaluation is virtually impossible through the mail. In the past bodybuilding camps such as Bodybuilding Expo and Zane Haven (run by three-time Mr. Olympia Frank Zane and his wife, Christine) have helped thousands in their competitive body-building careers.

Bodybuilding camps may not be for everyone. Besides the cost of the camp you have to consider transportation costs and time away from work or school. Still, if money and time are no problem, two weeks in California or Florida may be just what the bodybuilding doctor ordered.

BOOKS AND MAGAZINE ARTICLES

While bodybuilding magazines always featured training tips from the stars, these articles were mostly written by staff writers. Even articles attributed to a certain pro were probably ghost written. Only in the past 15 to 20 years have bodybuilders taken pen in hand to write their own articles. A few – e.g. Rick Wayne and Mike Mentzer – have become as famous for writing as for competing. Mike has influenced millions with his theories on training and recuperation, and Rick's articles are considered classics by the bodybuilding community.

Besides magazine articles, many pros including Arnold Schwarzenegger, Lee Haney, Franco Columbu, Tom Platz, Mike Mentzer, Lou Ferrigno, Bill Pearl, Rachel McLish, Cory Everson, Bob Paris, and most recently, Dorian Yates, have released their own body-building instruction books. In most cases the books are part biography and part instruction. Among the more famous are Arnold's *Encyclopedia of Modern Bodybuilding* and *Arnold: The Education of a Bodybuilder,* Bill Pearl's *Keys to the Inner Universe,* and Franco Columbu's *Coming on Strong.*

In addition to the many pro bodybuilders, other highly knowledgeable people have thrown their hat into the journalistic ring. The late Bill Reynolds produced dozens of outstanding books during his productive career. Other notables include Joe Weider, Dr. Ellington Darden, George Snyder and Bill Dobbins.

Finally we have *MuscleMag's* own Robert Kennedy, perhaps the most successful and prolific bodybuilding writer ever. At last count Bob had authored or co-authored over 40 books on the subject. This is in addition to his running of *MuscleMag International* on a day-to-day basis.

Milos Sarcev and Sonny Schmidt

CHAPTER TWENTY - THE MANY FACETS OF THE SPORT

Rod Ketchens

Although Bob never won the Olympia ("didn't have the genetics," as he's fond of saying!), there's no doubt that when it comes to bodybuilding do's and don'ts, he takes a back seat to no one!

SUPPLEMENTS

By far the biggest industry in the bodybuilding world is the food-supplement business. Each year manufacturers of such supplements as Twinlab, MET-Rx, Strength Systems and Hot Stuff, gross millions of dollars. The supplement industry as a whole is collectively worth billions of dollars, with the Weider corporation accounting for between three and four hundred million.

The marketing of supplements has meant big bucks in other areas as well. Most of the revenue generated by the various bodybuilding magazines comes from advertising, and a big chunk of this is supplement-related promotion. Flip through any copy of *MuscleMag, Flex, Muscle & Fitness or Ironman,* and you'll see page after page of eyecatching advertise-

ments. While perhaps annoying at times (the ads tend to split articles up over numerous pages and readers often have to search for the final few paragraphs), nevertheless they are necessary to keep the magazines in circulation.

Another supplement-related topic is the endorsement contracts paid to bodybuilding stars. With the primary goal of any manufacturer being to encourage people to buy their product, many supplement manufacturers hire top bodybuilders to represent their products. Nothing sells a can of protein powder like a picture of Lou Ferrigno or Dorian Yates on the label. If the aspiring bodybuilder believes that the champion actually uses the product, chances are he'll buy it himself.

So competitive has this area become that a few of the bigger corporations like Weider and Twinlab have offered superstar bodybuilders hundreds of thousands of dollars. Clearly the simple days of liver tablets and brewer's yeast are long gone!

CONTEST PROMOTING

Just as many actors decide to become directors, so too do many bodybuilders try their hand at contest promotion. Instead of worrying about diet, tanning and holding water, new considerations like lighting, venue, and lining up sponsors become major concerns. Rich Gaspari, Nimrod King and Kevin Levrone, have all promoted their own competitions.

As in many aspects of the sport, the most successful bodybuilder turned contest promoter is Arnold Schwarzenegger. In conjunction with his partner Jim Lorimer, Arnold annually promotes the Arnold Classic, held each spring at the Veterans Memorial Auditorium in Columbus, Ohio. Over the years Kevin Levrone, Michael Francois and Flex Wheeler have added the coveted ASC to their list of titles.

SO YOU WANT TO BE A CONTEST PROMOTER

Like any business venture, contest promotion has its risks, and for a promoter to be successful, he or she must cover all the bases. The following is not meant to be an all-encompassing guide for contest promotion. Instead we'll touch on the main points that need to be addressed if your contest is to be a success in terms of both revenue and public acceptance.

Contest promoters don't just decide on the spur of the moment to hold contests. They first become affiliated with a major bodybuilding federation, and then follow the specific guidelines of that federation. Let's say the regular contest promoter in your city had decided to call it quits after this year's event. Being the entrepreneur you are, you jump at the opportunity and decide to promote it. You may not be the only interested party. Two or three other would-be promoters may have the same idea. This means the four of you will have to bid to receive the rights to run the show.

And just as with a business tender, the lowest bidder usually gets the contract. (Make sure your estimates are well researched!)

Let's assume you are successful in your bid to hold the contest. You now have a year or two of frenzied preparations. The job can be done in less time, but if you want to make your first contest a success, give yourself plenty of time to iron out all the bugs. Although it's not necessary, your first step might be to have a chat with the previous promoter. If he (or she) is the friendly type, and contest promotion has not left a sour taste in his mouth, chances are he'll be only too happy to help you. If you discover that he lost money five years in a row, you might want to rethink the whole venture!

Most of the contacts the former promoter had are probably still around, and much of your trouble can be eliminated with a few phone calls. Also, people with prior experience can give you a rundown on all the little problems that will pop up, and we assure you that they will. Armed with a decent plan of attack, you now can start the actual preparations.

Your first concern is acquiring a contest site. For a small, local competition, you can probably get by using a high school gym, but as you rise up the contest levels, both contestants and spectators expect better facilities. Most cities and small towns have arts centers with raised stages and sloped audience seating. Of course the ritzier the venue, the higher the renting cost, so you'll need to factor this expense into the price of the tickets. Don't expect to book the auditorium two weeks in advance. As most better theaters are booked solid for Friday and Saturday nights, you'll need to phone months, if not years, in advance.

Another concern is the lighting. While most facilities have their own lights, they may not be appropriate for a bodybuilding contest. You don't need fancy colors either. Most shows get by with plain white light. If the place you're using has limited lighting spend the extra dollars (ranging from a few hundred to a few thousand depending on the quality and quantity of the contractor's time and equipment) and do it right. And once again, start checking around months or years in advance, as lighting personnel may be booked as tightly as theaters.

Once the venue is taken care of, the next step is to promote the contest. If you leave the advertising too late, most of the eligible competitors will pass on the event because a bodybuilder needs a minimum of two or three months to get ready for a competition. You don't just stop training and hop onstage. Bodybuilders have to develop a posing routine, start a precontest diet, and revamp their training, all of which takes months. If at all possible let the gyms in your contest area know at least four to six months in advance. At the very least

give three months' notice. This lead time allows potential entrants to make up their mind and start preparing.

Besides notifying local gyms, send a brief description of your event to the major bodybuilding magazines. Most will list the contest in the upcoming events section. For example, *MuscleMag International* has its What's On page, and *Flex* has a similar section called Coming Events.

Another method of advertising is through the various media outlets. If you have a contact at the local newspaper, try to get a brief article in the sports pages. Not only does a bodybuilding contest give them something "different" to write about, but you also get free advertising.

If you have the cash, a brief mention on the radio wouldn't hurt either. Radio ads reach a wide audience and, compared to TV, are relatively inexpensive. Most cable TV companies have a local news channel for upcoming events. Prices are very reasonable, and given that '90s disease called remotecontrolitis, the odds are good to excellent that a large number of TV viewers will see the ad.

Have a local printer run off the required number of tickets. Don't make the mistake of overselling. If your theater seats 1000 people, this is the number of tickets

Dave Fisher

CHAPTER TWENTY - THE MANY FACETS OF THE SPORT

Lee Haney and Dorian Yates pose off at the 1991 Mr. Olympia.

to print. There have been cases where contest promoters had 200 angry (and in most cases, LARGE!) fans turned away at the door because of overselling. Unlike airline travelers, the vast majority of the bodybuilding public actually go to the contest.

If your auditorium has numbered seats, the numbers should appear on the tickets. Keeping this in mind, you may want to line up a few ushers to direct spectators to their seats.

Depending on the level of your contest, you may or may not have to arrange accommodations for contestants and judges. Normally this responsibility applies only to pro events, but it's something to be aware of.

One person you must arrange lodging and transportation for is the guest poser. Moderate interest in a contest can be greatly boosted by the presence of a well-known bodybuilding champ. If fans know that someone of the caliber of Dorian Yates, Paul Dillett, Shawn Ray, or Kevin Levrone will be guest-posing, you probably won't have to worry about unsold seats. Instead your biggest concern may be scalpers!

Another individual whose importance is second to none is the MC (master of ceremonies). This can be anyone from a local celebrity to a highly respected international bodybuilding figure. One piece of advice should be noted, however. If you are relying on the services of someone who's not familiar with bodybuilding, make sure he doesn't belittle the sport. Nothing is as demeaning to bodybuilders as some wisecracking comedian using the contest as an occasion for his string of antibodybuilding jokes. If there's any doubt, get someone else.

Contest day will be both the most hectic and the most satisfying of your life – provided all goes as planned! Everything from looking after the contestants, judges and guest poser to audience management must be addressed. To reduce your stress level, it's a good idea to delegate responsibilities to a few trustworthy helpers. Getting volunteers shouldn't be a problem as most bodybuilding fans love the opportunity to get closer to the competitors. Let one person look after the guest poser, another can coordinate audience seating, and a third can work backstage. Such an arrangement gives you the freedom to oversee the whole operation.

While contest promotion may not be for everyone, for those looking for a challenge, it can't be beat. Unless you flop completely, you'll probably decide to promote next year's contest as well. And with each year comes experience. If you develop a highly respected reputation, someday you may be asked to promote a professional Grand Prix event. Don't laugh – most of today's promoters got their start at the local level and worked up. There's no reason why you can't do the same. Good luck!

MAGAZINE PUBLISHING

"I have worked out every day of my life since I was a teenager. Bodybuilding in fact has been my life. I didn't wake up one day in middle age and ask myself if my goals and self-image were worth preserving. I never fooled myself. Even at 17 with seven dollars to my name, I decided to publish a bodybuilding magazine. I saw the possibilities in bodybuilding at an early age."
**– Joe Weider, publisher of Flex, Shape
and Muscle & Fitness**

The unofficial journals of the bodybuilding world are the numerous muscle magazines, most of which are published on a monthly basis. Every conceivable bodybuilding topic is covered from training and diet to contest results and star profiles.

Over the years bodybuilding virtuosos Joe Weider and Robert Kennedy have become as famous as the bodybuilding stars they profile. Virtually every star owes much of his or her success to Weider's and Kennedy's monthly promotion. One training article in *Flex* or *MuscleMag* can boost a bodybuilder's career to dizzying heights.

In addition to the training and profile articles, bodybuilding magazines also contain advertisements for a wide variety of products and services. Although the former appeal most to readers, it's the latter that provide most magazines' operating revenue. Everything from food supplements and clothing to training aids and videos is featured. If an item is bodybuilding related, it probably will be sold through bodybuilding magazines.

Among the more popular bodybuilding magazines are *MuscleMag International, Flex, Muscle & Fitness, Shape, Ironman, Muscular Development* and *Muscle Media 2000.*

Berry DeMey

ACTING

"My dreams go so far that I will see myself riding on a horse, with long blond hair, in a movie called 'Conan the Barbarian, Part Six'."
    – Berry DeMey
    IFBB Pro Bodybuilder

Probably no one else has done as much to further the popularity of bodybuilding as has Arnold Schwarzenegger. It started with *Pumping Iron,* continued with *Conan the Barbarian* and *The Terminator,* and most recently *Eraser, Jingle All the Way* and *Batman and Robin.* In terms of box office sales Arnold's movies have grossed more than those of any other actor in history. Not bad for a guy who stepped off a plane in California 27 years ago with nothing else going for him but a great physique.

After establishing himself as the world's number one bodybuilder, Arnold set his sights on Hollywood, and the rest, as they say, is history. Not being one to forget his roots, Arnold continues to be the greatest ambassador of the sport, regularly giving speeches on fitness, and promoting his annual Arnold Schwarzenegger Classic in Columbus, Ohio.

Although Arnold is the most famous bodybuilder-turned-actor, others have striven for Oscar gold. One of the first was Steve Reeves, who starred in a number of Hercules movies back in the 1950s. With his boyish good looks and outstandingly symmetrical physique Steve became an international movie star.

"It helps tremendously. Now is the time Hollywood has accepted bodybuilding, so the two go together perfectly. If I had made a comeback ten years ago, it would have been just for bodybuilders, but today you'd have the public, Hollywood, and the bodybuilding audience come together. It would generate a lot of excitement because, I feel, my comeback would bring back the old days. The old pictures. The blood, sweat, and tears of the sport!"
    – Lou Ferrigno
    IFBB Pro Bodybuilder, former Mr. Universe and star of The Incredible Hulk

If Arnold is the most famous bodybuilding movie star, the title of most successful TV star goes to Lou Ferrigno. In the late 1970s and early '80s Lou became famous as TV's *Incredible Hulk.* The show was so successful that Lou recreated the role in the early 1990s as a TV movie. Between appearances as the Hulk were several moderately successful movies like *Hercules* and *Cage.*

Other bodybuilders who have turned up on TV or in the movies include Dave Draper, Mickey Hargitay, Reg Park, Cory Everson, Frank Zane, Franco Columbu, Rolf Moeller, Vince Gironda, Sergio Oliva and Serge Nubret.

"I've been in hundreds of movies. I know that I appeared in my first movie in my mother's arms when I was six months old in New York. I don't remember the name. Later on I did whatever they needed a guy with a build to do. I never had any big roles though."
— Vince Gironda, "The Iron Guru"
(who not only appeared in hundreds of movies, but has trained hundreds of actors and actresses for their own movie roles)

Besides competitive bodybuilders, many actors rely on bodybuilding as a means to get into outstanding physical shape for movie appearances. The most famous of these was Sylvester Stallone, who rocketed to stardom in the mid 1970s with his outstanding performance in *Rocky*.

Rambo and *Rocky* sequels found Stallone sporting a physique that many competitive bodybuilders would envy. In fact Stallone relied on none other than two-time Mr. Olympia Franco Columbu to help prepare him for many of these movies.

Other actors who rely on bodybuilding to further their acting careers include Clint Eastwood, Charlie Sheen, Dolph Lundgren, Jean-Claude Van Damme, Stephen Seagal, Mr. T and Danny DeVito (just kidding!).

We would be neglectful if we failed to mention two of the sport's most colorful characters. Depending on your viewpoint, the Barbarian brothers, David and Peter Paul, are both actors and bodybuilders, or neither! The Barbarians first came to prominence in the early '80s. With their construction-worker garb and feats of strength, they gave bodybuilding an idiosyncratic shot in the arm. Their appearance in the movie *D.C. Cab* only helped to further the duo's popularity.

SO YOU WANT TO BE AN ACTOR

"Well, ya got a guy in a rubber muscle suit claiming to be a superhero and ya got a guy that's like 6'4", 250 standing beside him. What are ya gonna do? You're not lookin' like DC Comic."
— Andrew Bryniarski
bodybuilder turned actor
(commenting on his scenes from
Batman II being cut)

As many movies require a "heavy" or two, there are lots of minor acting roles open to bodybuilders. Unfortunately, to get your foot in the door, you almost certainly need to be based in Los Angeles. Now before you pack your bags and head to the airport, there are a few facts to consider.

Acting is one of the most difficult occupations to break into. Every year thousands head to Tinseltown looking for that first big break, and while a few actually realize their dream, the vast majority get lost in the crowd. We don't mean to sound negative but you have to be realistic. In your hometown you may be the big fish, but in LA you're just another minnow in a sea of sharks. For every small movie role there are hundreds if not thousands of actors seeking the same part.

Nearly every bodybuilder who became an actor achieved a high level of competitive success first. Every bodybuilder in our previous list holds at least one major title, including the Mr.'s America, Universe and Olympia. In fact their bodybuilding success brought them to the attention of TV and movie producers. It's virtually impossible for an unknown to hop off a plane in Hollywood and walk right into a picture.

If you're still determined to be an actor, our advice is to try to break into the business in your own region. Move to a larger city in your state or province. Not only will there be less competition, but you'll also get a feel for big-city life. If you can't handle living in a small city, how do you think you will survive in LA, given that everything is magnified many times over?

Andrew Bryniarski

BODYBUILDING GYMS

"I think you'll never have another era like that again. I was blessed to have experienced that because I felt I was training with the best of all time. That's not to say the guys today aren't great too, because they are – there are a lot of excellent physiques out there – but as far as characters and personality are concerned, there was much more to write about back then. It was incredible to have so many great physiques training together in one small gym at one time."
– Danny Padilla
IFBB Pro Bodybuilder, former Mr. Universe
(commenting on the atmosphere at the original Gold's Gym in the early 1970s)

Sooner or later the idea of owning a bodybuilding gym or store may enter your mind. Years of plugging away in an overcrowded gym get you thinking about the business side of the sport. Or perhaps you see the need for a clothing/food supplement store. Whatever the interest, the concept of going into business on your own is very appealing. In the following section we will briefly discuss the different aspects of opening your own bodybuilding establishment.

PRIVATE GYMS

Bodybuilding gyms fall into two broad categories – privately owned and franchises. Most gyms are owned by one or two enterprising operators who started the business from scratch. They saw the need for extra training space. Perhaps the local YMCA was becoming overcrowded or maybe there was no gym to begin with. In either case the money was raised and the establishment started.

What privately owned gyms offer is atmosphere, including personalized instruction. As most are owned by persons dedicated to bodybuilding, the level of attention tends to be better in such gyms. In addition, the owners keep the equipment in top condition whereas maintenance often gets overlooked in bigger franchise gyms.

FRANCHISE GYMS

The large chains or franchises – such famous establishments as Gold's, World Gym and Powerhouse – have become fixtures in the minds of bodybuilders the world over. (There are many others, too numerous to mention here.) Joe Gold opened his famous gym in Venice Beach, California. In the late '60s and early '70s Gold's hosted the biggest names in bodybuilding. On any day you could see such stars as Arnold, Franco, Frank Zane, Bill Grant, Ed Corney, Robby Robinson and Ken Waller, going through their paces. With the limited exposure and popularity of bodybuilding, the sport's stars saw themselves as a sort of tight knit fraternity.

In the early 1970s Joe Gold sold the gym and its famous name. He later wanted to get back into the gym business, but since his last name was now a trademark, he called his new facility World Gym. With the rapid growth of bodybuilding the respective owners of Gold's and World decided to license out their names. The result was a plethora of such gyms across Canada, the United States and around the world.

If there is one advantage to training at a major franchise gym, it's equipment variety. Most feature nearly every conceivable piece of bodybuilding equipment available. Granted, you don't need half of it to build a great physique, but if you want it, it's there.

GETTING STARTED

Starting a gym may be the greatest challenge of your life. If you do it properly you can make a comfortable living. Managed improperly, the venture may put you in debtor's prison!

Your first step in opening a gym is to decide which route to take – franchise or private. The advantage of going franchise is the immediate recognition of the name. Virtually everyone in bodybuilding has heard of Gold's and World. As soon as you open one of those gyms, you attract a large clientele based solely on the name. In addition, most franchise owners receive a great deal of advice on starting up. Of course this

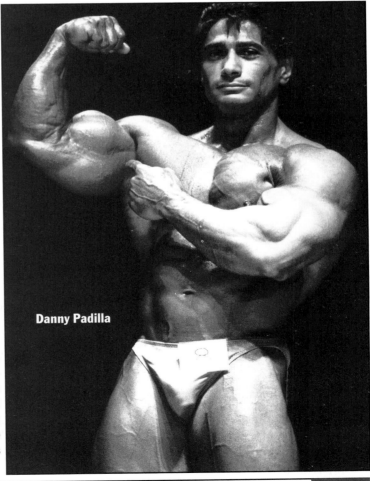

Danny Padilla

CHAPTER TWENTY - THE MANY FACETS OF THE SPORT

Sonny Schmidt and Vince Taylor

works both ways. Before you approach Gold's or World for a license, you need a business proposal. Let's face it. Nobody wants to lend his name to a venture that will be bankrupt in six months. In your proposal you need to consider such topics as location, demand, start-up cost, and maintenance cost. Only after considering the feasibility of your proposal will a major gym chain grant you a license.

The other option is to go it alone. (If you can find a willing partner, so much the better.) All of the previous considerations still apply (location, cost, demand, etc.), but instead of approaching Gold's or World, you go to a bank or other financial institution. (We are assuming that most aspiring gym-owners will need a loan to start their gym.)

If the bank grants your loan, the next step is to make the various contacts for opening the gym. You have to arrange for equipment, shower facilities, food supplements and other purchases. It wouldn't hurt to advertise in advance either. If you can swing it, have a grand opening featuring a well-known guest poser.

Nothing draws potential members like a top body-builder. Even if your star attraction appears for only an hour or two, the name will bring out the curious.

The first few months will be hectic as you get the bugs ironed out, but with time your membership will increase and you may even begin to see a profit. Keep the operation simple at the beginning and hire only one or two employees to look after maintenance and instructing. You can save on instructor fees by offering free memberships to experienced bodybuilders willing to volunteer their time. Just make sure, however, that they're qualified. You don't want a lawsuit because some idiot instructor showed a member the wrong way to do squats!

Likewise if you're not handy in the maintenance department, see if any of your members have a background in such work. Once again payment may be as simple as a free membership.

We have touched on only the basics – a whole book could be devoted to the topic – but if you follow our advice, you may find that in a few years you'll have paid off the loan and have established your gym as "the place to be." Who knows? Maybe someday someone in another city or town will approach you wanting to use your name as a franchise!

THE MUSCLEMAG INTERNATIONAL STORE FRANCHISE

If you think that this is self-advertising, you're absolutely right. It is! But it's also a chance to introduce to you one of the fastest-growing phenomena in bodybuilding.

Bodybuilding's greatest spin-off is merchandise sales. The health-food industry alone is annually worth billions of dollars. Clothes, equipment and cosmetic products (tanning lotions, etc.) are also big sellers. It seems no city or town is complete nowadays without a store that supplies these products.

The problem for many potential store owners is legitimacy. "Ron's Supplement Store" or "Judy's Bodybuilding Shop" just doesn't carry much weight (with all due respect to the Judys and Rons out there!). This is where we come in. For over 20 years *MuscleMag International* has been supplying the bodybuilding public with a host of top-quality products, and it's now possible for your business to have our reputation from the beginning.

As a franchise holder, you get to carry the MuscleMag International logo on your store. In addition, everything from letterheads and flyers to business cards and advertising will carry the name recognized around the world. In short, your store will carry legitimacy from day one.

Besides the paper work you have the satisfaction of knowing that you're part of a much bigger operation. As Robert Kennedy adds: "We become a family, providing you the support and guidance necessary to own and operate your own business, along with many other benefits."

If your goal in life is to own your own business, a *MuscleMag International* franchise may be just what you're looking for. If interested contact:

•**USA** –
Jerry Cooper
MuscleMag International Corporation (USA)
1625 Barclay Blvd.
Buffalo Grove, Illinois 60089
Phone 847-229-8461 or Fax 847-229-8469

•**Canada and International** –
Marianne Butler
MuscleMag International Corporation
6465 Airport Road
Mississauga, Ontario L4V 1E4
Phone 905-678-3496 or Fax 905-678-9236

Britain's Dorian Yates

Sonny Schmidt

BOOK SEVEN

Training with the Champs

7

Prelude to
Book Seven

TRAINING WITH THE CHAMPS

"You should strive to improve your body a little at a time. Don't push the mind too much either. Let the mind stay hungry for more. Tease the mind a little bit."
– Arnold Schwarzenegger
Seven-time Mr. Olympia

Arnold Schwarzenegger

acquired is then presented to our faithful readers every month. Everything from diet and nutrition to contest preparation and recovery is found in each issue of *MuscleMag International*. Of all the articles featured, by far, the most popular are the training routines of the superstars. We gave you Arnold's chest routine, Lou's arm-training program, Shawn's leg-training secrets and Dorian's tips on building bigger delts. It's safe to say that *MuscleMag*, at one time or another, has featured at least one training routine from every champion. One of our guiding principles is to give readers what they want, our established practice of featuring the best the sport has to offer.

"Lee Haney is the greatest bodybuilder ever, Arnold is the smartest, and Victor Richards is the freakiest."
– The Barbarian Brothers

Peter and David Paul

The following section can be considered a "best of *MuscleMag*" in terms of training programs. We have selected some of our more popular articles featuring the top bodybuilders in action. Where possible we have tried to include routines from champions famous for the relevant bodypart. For example we have Arnold's chest routine, Tom Platz's leg workout, Nimrod King's back and Paul DeMayo's calf program.

Throughout *MuscleMag's* twenty-four-year history our writers have interviewed thousands of amateur and professional bodybuilders. The advice and wisdom

Don Ross

builder is following an entirely different routine. This apparent discrepancy is normal, as one of the best ways to keep a muscle growing is with variety. The odds of a bodybuilder following the same program year after year are pretty remote. With time and experience you will discover that you need to do the same to keep your muscles on their toes.

Perhaps the greatest value of the following routines lies in their educational benefit. No doubt you will find that a particular champ had the same problem developing a muscle group as you are having. In most cases the article will outline how the champ overcame the dilemma. Often you can take the same approach to bringing up your own lagging muscle group.

"You need to find out first whether you want to lose weight or gain, and then go from there. I would explain that we get out of bodybuilding what we put into it, and that results are not dependent just on training but also on rest, nutrition and of course, mindset." **– Robert Kennedy, founder and publisher of MuscleMag International**

Finally, although the odds are against it, a few lucky readers will eventually reach the national and professional levels of bodybuilding. In this case the programs featured here will suit you perfectly. In fact, sooner or later *MuscleMag* will be calling you for advice on training arms or legs or calves or…

"In our years as bodybuilders, trainers and writers, we have met most of the champions. Each one has his or her own routine and training theory. Each has a different diet as well, yet all achieve similar results. We have found one common denominator. Every one was absolutely sure of success from the start. Each had the ability to visualize his or her goal."
– The late Don Ross, bodybuilding writer

Before you jump right in, a few cautionary points must be brought to your attention. The programs presented are not intended for beginning-level bodybuilders. Even intermediates would quickly overtrain if they followed these routines for extended periods of time. As a matter of fact, the champs themselves only follow these programs for a couple of months at a time. If you are an intermediate or beginning bodybuilder, think twice about doing 20-plus sets for a given muscle group. The trend these days is to do fewer sets but with more intensity.

Most champion bodybuilders change their routines frequently, so what you see here is really a moment in time. You may read elsewhere that the same body-

Robert Kennedy

SUPER
Hardcore Women

Chapter Twenty-one

BACK

AS WIDE AS ALL OUTDOORS

"Chins, chins and more chins. Any width grip and if you work at it long and hard enough you can't help but come out with a good back. Personally I do 5 x 8 every back session."
– Bill Pearl
Four-time Mr. Universe winner

The trademark characteristic of the bodybuilding physique is the V-shape. A well-developed back always draws favorable comments. It creates the illusion of a small waist and enhances a massive upper body. Bodybuilders famous for their great back development include Franco Columbu, Arnold Schwarzenegger, Dorian Yates, Flex Wheeler, Michael Francois, Sergio Oliva, Nimrod King, Robby Robinson, Roy Callender and Lee Haney.

ANATOMY

The bodybuilder's classic V-shape is primarily due to the large latissimus dorsi muscles. Properly developed, these muscles will give the owner that "wingy" look. The lats start under the armpits and stretch right down to the waist. (A few bodybuilders have what are called "high lats," in which case the lower lat insertions connect fairly high on the back.) The main function of the lats is to draw the arms back and downward.

Other back muscles include the teres (major and minor) and the rhomboids. Both muscles attach to the lats around the shoulder blade region. Their primary function is to stabilize and move the shoulder blades. They also assist the lats in moving the arms.

Although often trained with the shoulders, the trapezius are really part of the back-muscle complex. The traps are the large triangular-shaped muscles located at the base of the neck, extending down the

Flex Wheeler, Mike Francois and Andreas Munzer compare rear-biceps shots at the 1995 Arnold Classic.

Dorian Yates

Width exercises develop the outer edges of the lats so that the V-shape becomes more pronounced. They also stretch the scapulae (shoulder blades) to widen the muscle-bone structure. You will use various chinning movements and pulldowns to increase back width.

Thickness exercises increase the density of the central back muscles. Many bodybuilders have wide backs but very little muscle covering the central back region. Their backs appear shallow. To increase back thickness, you have to perform numerous rowing movements.

"When you look at young, up-and-coming bodybuilders from the front they appear to have very good development until they turn around. That's when you notice they're all too deficient in their back development."

– Albert Beckles, IFBB Pro Bodybuilder, "The Ageless Wonder"

The following are some of the more popular widening and thickening exercises. We have included exercises for the spinal erectors with the thickening exercises. The various pullover exercises will be found in the chest-training section as most bodybuilders do pullovers on chest day, even though the exercise is as much a lat movement as a pectoral exercise. Likewise, trap exercises are found in the shoulder-training section as most bodybuilders train traps with shoulders. You can include them with your back training if you wish.

center of the back. Their main function is to lift and rotate the shoulder-girdle complex.

Finally, the lower back is made up of two snake-like muscles called spinal erectors. Although the lats and traps are more glamorous, it's the spinal erectors that will be the limiting factor in many of your mass-building exercises like squats, bent-over rows and shrugs. So even though they're small, you must not neglect them in your training. The spinal erectors work in conjunction with the abs and obliques to keep the upper body erect.

TRAINING

"You must keep the back arched during your back workout. Far too many people round their shoulders and this takes the stress off the lats. Many bodybuilders don't even know what it feels like to have a full back contraction!" **– Dorian Yates**
IFBB Pro Bodybuilder, Five-time Mr. Olympia

All back exercises (with the possible exception of exercises for spinal erector) can be divided into two types – those for width and those for thickness.

Widening Exercises:
1. Wide-grip chins
2. Narrow-grip chins
3. Chins using V-shaped handles
4. Reverse chins
5. Front pulldowns
6. Behind-the-neck pulldowns
7. Narrow-grip pulldowns
8. Pulldowns using V-shaped handles
9. Reverse pulldowns
10. One-arm pulldowns

Thickening Exercises:
1. Barbell rows
2. T-bar rows
3. One-arm dumbell rows
4. Seated pulley rows
5. One-arm cable rows
6. Stiff-leg deadlifts
7. Hyperextensions

Flex Wheeler

Flex and company start their back workout with wide-grip pulldowns. They begin with light weights and move up to extremely heavy weight, shooting for a minimum of 10 reps on every set. Even though they train heavy, good form is never sacrificed. Flex emphasizes, "We pull the bar to the top of

Flex Wheeler performs seated pulley rows.

Start

Finish

THE CHAMPS' ROUTINES

FLEX WHEELER – *outlining how he and his training partners love to slap on plates… "The only thing about our workouts that you can even consider different or unusual is our use of heavy weight – extremely heavy weight."*

One of the sport's newest superstars, Flex Wheeler has become known for his superwide back. His training strategy is simple – use as much weight as possible as long as the style is not sacrificed. But he cautions beginners about using excessive poundages: "If someone next to you is outbenching you, screw him! Who cares? As long as you're using a weight that's heavy for you, you can forget the other guy."

the chest and release fully to get a good stretch. The same goes for pulldowns behind the neck – we bring the bar down to the base of the neck."

The next exercise on the agenda is the seated pulley row. Again they train as heavy as possible: the full stack plus an additional 45-pound plate and two 50-pound dumbells!

The third exercise is the one-arm dumbell row. They start with a 110-pounder and graduate to a 200-pounder for the last couple of sets. They insist on good style. "A lot of people use this kind of weight but end up bouncing the dumbell up and down – we don't do any of that whatsoever. The key to these dumbell rows is getting a full stretch. Rest your supporting hand on something high enough to allow you to get that stretch."

The last movement Flex and crew perform is the close-grip pulldown. Once again they strive for a minimum of 10 reps. Of course, if one of them does 11 or 12 reps, the other two see this as a challenge and reciprocate. Such intrapartner competition is what makes their training so effective.

Flex Wheeler's Back Routine:

1. Wide-grip pulldowns to the front – *5-6 sets of 10 reps*
2. Seated pulley rows – *5-6 sets of 10 reps*
3. One-arm dumbell rows – *5-6 sets of 10 reps*
4. Close-grip pulldowns – *5-6 sets of 10 reps*

SONNY SCHMIDT – *explaining how much time he devotes to his back training… "My average back workout takes about two and a half to three hours, mate."*

Besides kangaroos and Crocodile Dundee, Australia has another feature it's famous for – Sonny Schmidt's back! He believes that many of today's bodybuilders have weak back development because they don't invest the time required to build the area. "They just don't seem to train their backs as hard as they do other bodyparts," he states. "If you ask most body-builders whether or not their backs hurt the next day after a back workout, very few can truthfully tell you that they do."

Sonny has come under criti-cism for his lengthy back workouts. He is quick to respond: "Some people say I overtrain, and I do train a long time, but if my mind's not satisfied, the workout's not done. Besides, I've

Australia's Sonny Schmidt

Wide-grip chins

Start

Finish

got a few training partners who follow my workout and they're really starting to grow. They train with me, they enter contests, and they win contests. If that's overtraining, well, I'll just keep overtraining, thank you."

He says to work the back effectively, you have to lift the weight with your upper-back muscles, not the traps or lower-back muscles. He continues, "Make style the focus, not how much weight you can lift." Early in his career, he liked doing low reps for the back, but over the years he's discovered his back, like the legs, needed higher rep ranges to grow.

His first two exercises are chins and behind-the-neck pulldowns. He experiments with different grips to hit the outer lats from all angles. "The angle you use and the width of your grip will determine how the exercise affects your lats. I always vary both the width of the grip and the angle of the exercise to keep surprising the muscles."

Next, he moves on to his thickening exercises. For this he relies on barbell rows, T-bar rows and seated cable rows. He adds: "It's one thing to have very wide lats, but true champions have thickness too, and that's why the middle-back exercises are so important."

For variety, Sonny substitutes dumbell rows for one of the previous exercises. To work the lower lats, he makes sure to include a few sets of close-grip pulldowns. Sometimes he throws in one-arm cable rows also.

To finish his back workout, he does hyperextensions, but he is quick to add that he gets a lot of lower-back stimulation from his barbell and T-bar rows. Here is a recap of Sonny's back workout. Although it may be too taxing for most, we are confident that if you can handle it, it will give you the back you always dreamed about.

Sonny Schmidt's Back Routine:

1. Chins – *4 sets to failure*
2. Pulldowns behind the neck – *5 sets of 10-15 reps*
3. Close-grip pulldowns – *4 sets of 10-15 reps*
4. Seated cable rows – *4 sets of 10-15 reps*
5. Barbell rows – *4 sets of 10-15 reps*
6. T-bar rows – *4 sets of 10-15 reps*
7. Hyperextensions – *4 sets of 15-20 reps*

SHAWN RAY – *1994 second-place Mr. Olympia, describing the importance of a well-developed back... "The back is your largest body area, so don't neglect training it just because you can't see it well in the mirror."*

When it comes to overall body proportions, few bodybuilders can compare with IFBB bodybuilding superstar Shawn Ray. One of his best bodyparts is his outstanding back. Shawn believes in a total approach to back-training. He says, "Many bodybuilders have great upper backs, but have greatly deficient lower backs." For a complete back, he follows a routine that works all areas of the back – inner, outer, upper, lower and overall thickness.

He is quick to point out the dangers of going too heavy and not using strict form on back exercises. "Don't get caught up with just loading the weights on. Pay good attention to form."

Shawn begins his back-training with front pulldowns, using a wide grip. He finds this an excellent exercise to start with as it does a great job of warming up the back. "I get a full stretch at the top, and then when I pull the bar down to my chest I squeeze as hard as possible and exhale completely, getting out all the air. Make sure you pull with the lat muscles and not the biceps." He pyramids the weight in 30-pound increments, doing 4 or 5 sets of 10 to 15 reps.

His second exercise is seated cable rows. He learned this one from 1982 Mr. Olympia and multi-

Shawn Ray

T-bar rows
Start

Finish

Grand Prix winner Chris Dickerson. Chris taught him the importance of fully stretching and contracting the lats. Proper style for Shawn starts with knees slightly bent. He leans forward to get a full stretch and then pulls the handles to his abs. He brings his elbows toward the rear and squeezes his back muscles hard. Again he does 4 or 5 sets of 12 to 15 reps.

Next it's on to the T-bar row. He finds this both a good mass-builder and a source of motivation. "I picture Arnold when I'm doing T-bar rows," he says. "I've seen inspirational pictures of him doing this exercise very intensely."

Shawn bends his knees but keeps his back straight. He holds the T-bar with his hands about thumbs distance apart. He pulls the bar to his midsection, using only his arms, and not the lower back. He pauses at the top, and then lowers the bar slowly, concentrating on getting a full stretch at the bottom. Although he may work up to seven 45-pound plates, he still does 4 to 5 sets of 12 to 15 reps.

He finishes his back-training with chinups. (For variety he sometimes starts his back routine with chins.) He doesn't use any weight, but concentrates on squeezing and contracting the upper back. "Chinups can widen your back by working the large outside portion of your lats, and – as Robert Kennedy points out – they widen the shoulder girdle by stretching the scapulae. This stretching helps create a V-taper to the upper body."

Because he has a weak grip, Shawn uses straps when doing chins. He varies his grip from time to time, using close, medium and wide grips. He stresses the importance of pulling your chest to the bar, not yanking or swinging your body up. He routinely does 4 sets of 12 to 15 reps.

Shawn considers these four basic exercises the best for building back width and density. For beginners and intermediate bodybuilders he suggests limiting the machine exercises and concentrating on basic free-weight movements. "A lot of bodybuilders like to do trendy machine exercises," he says, "but it's essential to start using free weights early in your career so that you can develop your whole back."

Shawn Ray's Back Routine:
1. Front pulldowns – *4-5 sets of 12-15 reps*
2. Seated cable rows – *4-5 sets of 12-15 reps*
3. T-bar rows – *4-5 sets of 12-15 reps*
4. Chins – *4-5 sets of 12-15 reps*

Lee Haney,
eight-time
Mr. Olympia.

(hands about 5 or 6 inches wider than shoulder width) and get as many reps as possible. His favorite width exercise was narrow pulldowns to the chest. He arched the back on the exercise and concentrated on pulling the elbows down and back, squeezing his shoulder blades together at the bottom.

For thickness he did a variety of rowing movements. He started with barbell rows, standing on a block to get a full stretch in his lats. He emphasizes the need to keep the knees slightly bent, so as not to place undue stress on the lower back.

On seated cable rows Lee recommends using a set of handles that allow a narrow grip. Pull the handles to your lower abdomen, arch your back, and squeeze your shoulder blades together. Stretch forward as far as possible, once again keeping your knees slightly bent.

His third thickness exercise was often T-bar rows. He advises keeping the back parallel with the floor and raising it only slightly as you pull the bar up. He found this exercise great for both spinal erector and midback mass.

Although he's not as rigid about reps and sets any more, in a typical back workout he did four exercises for 3 or 4 sets of 8 to 12 reps. The following is a standard Lee Haney off-season back workout:

Lee Haney's Back Routine:
1. Barbell rows – *4-5 sets of 6-12 reps*
2. Front pulldowns – *3-4 sets of 8-10 reps*
3. Seated pulley rows – *3-4 sets of 8-10 reps*
4. Dumbell shrugs* – *3-4 sets of 10-15 reps*
*Lee alternates traps with his back
and shoulder routines.

LEE HANEY – *Not since Arnold Schwarzenegger had a bodybuilder dominated the Olympia stage like Atlanta's 250-pound Lee Haney...*

With eight Olympia titles to his credit, Lee set the standard for years to come. From head to toe the Georgian behemoth displayed one of the most impressive physiques of all time. The centerpiece of his massive torso was a back that was both the widest and thickest on the Olympia stage.

When he trained back, Lee emphasized all four aspects of the muscle; consequently, he did exercises for width, thickness, upper back (traps) and lower back (spinal erectors). As the years progressed, he modified this approach to add balance to his back. Early on he did a lot of direct lower-back work, but soon his spinal erectors were getting adequate stimulation from rowing exercises. Adding width to his back was relatively easy, so instead he concentrated on adding thickness.

If you're having trouble adding width to your lats, Lee recommends a program heavy on chins, both to the front and behind the head. Take a medium grip

ALBERT BECKLES – *Although famous for his peaked biceps, Albert Beckles, "The Ageless Wonder," had one of the widest backs on the pro bodybuilding circuit during the 1970s and 1980s. When asked how he developed such a flaring back, Albert replied, "Chins gave me the width – 4 sets of wide-grip chins, 12 reps each set."*

For his first exercise Albert attached a weight around his waist. He didn't stop chinning until he had completed the desired 12 reps. He used a very wide grip and pulled himself up until his chin was above the bar. After a few minutes' rest he moved on to the second back exercise, barbell rows.

When he did this exercise, Albert stood on a bench and grabbed an Olympic bar with a wide grip. He found this movement great for adding thickness and density to the center part of his back.

The third and fourth exercises were a superset of pulldowns and bent-over laterals. "I found the wide-grip pulldowns great for developing the outside of the lats," says Albert, "and the bent-over laterals hit the center and upper part of the back. On the pulldowns I used a lot of heavy poundage but on the laterals I used only light stuff. I liked the idea of heavy and light and I really got pumped up after 4 supersets of these two exercises."

Albert Beckles's Back Program:

1. Chins – *4 sets of 12 reps*
2. Barbell rows off bench – *4-5 sets of 12 reps*
3. Pulldowns/bent-over laterals –
   4 supersets of 12 reps

Bob Paris

Albert Beckles

BOB PARIS – *Mr. Symmetry, Bob Paris, carefully designed his back-training program. Not satisfied with mediocrity, Bob devised a way of mentally picturing his back as he worked out. He explained: "The visual connection that's so easy to get with other bodyparts was missing when I trained my back, so I memorized how my back worked by studying it in the mirror when I wasn't exercising it. I then burned the image of it into my mind so that I could easily call up a mental picture of what was happening during a back workout. It was almost like watching my back in a mental mirror."*

Using this strategy, Bob developed a back routine that hits his back from an assortment of angles. He includes exercises for lat width and thickness, and exercises that build the traps, lower back and rear delts. Although a typical workout may not work every area, he ensures that his whole back is covered in two workouts. Nothing is left to chance.

A typical back workout starts with front pulldowns to the chest. "I like to do these using different grips," he explains. "I find that the back gets affected in different ways with each variation."

Bob flexes his back throughout the exercise, as if he were doing a double-biceps pose. He says this technique gives him the desired feeling in the movement.

His next back exercise is often behind-the-neck pulldowns. Keeping his upper body in line with the action of the machine, he pulls the bar down to his neck, squeezing the muscles on every rep.

Start

Bob Paris demonstrates the lat pulldown.

Finish

For back thickness Bob alternates barbell rows and dumbell rows. He stresses that you must always be conscious of the lower back when doing any rowing exercise. He suggests using the legs as shock absorbers with the knees bent to take much of the strain off the lower back.

On average, he trains his back twice in a 7- to 10-day period. Anything more, he adds, is overtraining. He has good advice against overtraining: "Forced reps are probably the most abused training method. When you do something that goes beyond your own capacity to move a weight, you're tapping that much further into your recuperative ability. I would use forced reps very judiciously – no more often than a couple of forced reps on an exercise, and no more than every couple of workouts."

Bob Paris's Back Routine:
1. Front pulldowns – *4-5 sets*
2. Behind-the-neck pulldowns – *4-5 sets*
3. Barbell rows – *4-5 sets*
4. Dumbell rows – *4-5 sets*
5. Seated cable rows – *4-5 sets*
Bob varies the reps between 6 and 30 depending on the exercise, grip, and amount of weight used.

LEE LABRADA – *"First of all I treat my back a little differently than my other muscle groups. As you know, I never do more than 10 sets for any muscle group, and for smaller muscle groups, like biceps, I usually do only 6 to 8 sets. But the back consists of so many different* muscles that I feel I have to do more sets than usual to train it properly. I divide my back into three regions – lats, upper back and traps, and lower back. I do exercises for all three areas."

Two-time Mr. Olympia runner-up Lee Labrada readily agrees that he will never have the mass of a Lee Haney or Dorian Yates, but don't try telling him his muscularity and detail are inferior. Some people feel that in the back department he can hold his own with anyone. At one time Lee's back suffered greatly in comparisons with other top pros, but since he redesigned his back-training, he readily trades back shots with all comers. "In the past my back was fairly thick and well developed," he says "but compared to guys like Lee Haney, Dorian Yates and Vince Taylor, it lacked thickness and density. I felt the back was the only bodypart where Haney had a definite edge on me, so I had to bring mine up."

Lee starts his back work-out with various lat exercises. These are followed in sequence by upper back, traps and lower back. His first back exercise is some sort of seated pulley rowing. For variety he alternates between a narrow V-shaped bar and a straight bar. If he uses a straight bar he pulls it to his belly button. He pulls the narrow bar to the top of his abs. With either bar he pauses and arches his chest to get a better back contraction. He does 3 sets of about 10 reps.

The next exercise is medium-grip pulldowns, although every now and then he substitutes chins. He explains: "I used to chin a lot, but now I do chins maybe 20 percent of the time. The lat pulldown allows me a greater range of motion and I can get a better contraction with it, so I stick with the pulldown probably 80 percent of the time. If I do chin, I use a parallel shoulder-width grip."

Lee's third back exercise is the one-arm dumbell row. He does these with one knee resting on a flat bench for support. He pulls the dumbell to his waist, not his rib cage. This style, he feels, isolates his lats better. Once again, it's 3 sets of around 10 reps.

The fourth and final lat exercise is either the barbell or T-bar row. To protect his lower back, he keeps his knees slightly bent and pulls the bar in a smooth, controlled motion. No bouncing, no heaving. Again it's 3 sets of 10 reps. He tries to keep the reps around 10 per set, but for variety he goes up to 15 during every fourth or fifth workout.

Unlike many bodybuilders, Lee trains traps with back, not shoulders. His main trap exercise is the dumbell shrug, and during a typical back workout he does 5 or 6 sets of 10 to 12 reps. He keeps his palms facing forward on this exercise, rather than facing the sides or rear. "The reason," he says, "is to throw more stress on the rear traps where I need it."

Lee ends his back workout with 3 sets of 15 reps of either hyperextensions or deadlifts. He alternates these lower-back exercises every other workout.

He does the same back workout year round. During the precontest phase of his training he drops the poundages slightly (more out of necessity than choice), but the exercises, sets and reps remain the same.

Lee Labrada's Back Routine:

1. Seated pulley rows – *3 sets of 10 reps*
2. Medium-grip pulldowns – *3 sets of 10 reps*
3. One-arm dumbell rows – *3 sets of 10 reps*
4. Barbell (T-bar) rows – *3 sets of 10 reps*
5. Dumbell shrugs – *5-6 sets of 10-12 reps*
6. Hyperextensions or deadlifts – *3 sets of 15 reps*

SELWYN COTTERILL – British bodybuilding champ Selwyn Cotterill has a problem that most bodybuilders would die for. He has to limit training for his back so that it doesn't grow too fast. He explains, *"My back grows easily for me. I don't have to concentrate on it as much as other bodyparts. In fact I often have to limit my back-training to one workout per week, so that it doesn't get too big."*

Lee Labrada

Start

Seated pulley rows
Finish

Mike Francois and Flex Wheeler

A typical back workout consists of 4 sets of 8 to 12 reps of four different exercises. Selwyn varies the exercises and order to keep the muscles guessing. Among his favorite back exercises are lat pulldowns, T-bar rows, seated pulley rows, straight-arm pulldowns and chins.

When doing pulldowns, he is careful to force his elbows back as far as possible. This technique, he says, stretches his lats to the maximum.

Selwyn prefers T-bars over barbell rows. He finds he can concentrate more on his lats. He keeps his torso parallel to the floor and bends his knees slightly. He does not bounce the weight or jerk it up with his lower back. Nothing moves but his arms and the weight.

He does seated pulley rows with his knees slightly bent and chest arched to get the full lat stretch. In the fully contracted position his upper body is perpendicular to the floor, handles touching his lower rib cage.

If there's one movement that Selwyn tries to do first, it's the straight-arm pulldown. He uses the lat machine and bends forward, starting the bar just above face level. Keeping his arms straight, he pulls the bar down to waist level.

He uses a V-grip handle for chins. He finds this grip takes most of the biceps out of the movement and works his lats more. When he's in the top position, he arches his back and squeezes his lats together for two or three seconds. Because of this unique approach, Selwyn doesn't need to use any extra weight for this exercise.

Selwyn Cotterell's Back Routine:
1. Lat pulldowns – *4 sets of 8-12 reps*
2. T-bar rows – *4 sets of 8-12 reps*
3. Seated pulley rows – *4 sets of 8-12 reps*
4. Straight-arm pulldowns – *4 sets of 8-12 reps*
5. Chins – *4 sets of 8-12 reps*
* *In a typical back workout Selwyn will pick four of these exercises.*

STEVE BRISBOIS – *"I can chin more than any other bodybuilder in the world. But I don't think anyone will take me up on it. They wouldn't want to lose."*

He may stand only 5'4" and weigh 160 pounds, but Canadian Steve Brisbois can compare backs with anyone. In fact he takes great pleasure in going head to head with the IFBB's "big guys." Steve follows a three-on/one-off routine with back-training occurring on day two of the cycle. Realizing that he can never match most of the top pros in mass, he is careful to ensue his physique is balanced from head to foot. "I do a thorough back routine" he states, "because I want my physique to be equally strong and solid both front and back – no differential, no disappearing act when I turn around."

Steve begins his back-training with seated pulley rows. His feet are together and he is facing forward. He starts the movement in the fully stretched position, and pulls the handle to his lower rib cage. In the fully contracted position his upper body is leaning slightly back from the vertical.

His next exercise is the front pulldown using a wide grip. He pulls the bar down to chest level and slowly returns to the arms-locked-out position. Many bodybuilders stop short of locking out, but Steve goes for the full stretch. For his third exercise he does close-grip pulldowns through the entire range of movement.

Steve's favorite back exercise is the standard, wide-grip chinup. He hangs down completely at the bottom, and then pulls himself up until his head clears the bar. No partial or half-reps here. Every rep is done throughout the fullest possible range.

His final back exercise is the one-arm dumbell row. He places one knee on a bench and pulls the dumbell up close to his side. He cautions, "If the dumbell is a distance away from the body you're not working your back as you should."

Roy Callender

Steve Brisbois's Back Routine:
1. Seated pulley rows – *3-4 sets of 10-12 reps*
2. Front pulldowns – *3-4 sets of 10-12 reps*
3. Close-grip pulldowns – *3-4 sets of 10-12 reps*
4. Chins – *3-4 sets of 10-12 reps*
5. One-arm dumbell rows – *3-4 sets of 10-12 reps*

ROY CALLENDER – During the late 1970s and early 1980s one of the greatest backs to grace bodybuilding stages belonged to Canadian Roy Callender. From his snake-sized spinal erectors to his wide sweeping lats, Roy's back was the envy of everyone. He made it a point to "turn his back" on the audience whenever possible!

Roy attributed his great development to his love of training, especially his back workouts. On a typical back day, he would do 10 to 15 different exercises for back alone. His favorite exercise? Chins of course. During the early '80s the rumor went around that Roy was routinely doing 50 to 60 sets of chins in a typical back workout. When asked about this, he confirmed the rumors – he was doing 60 to 90 minutes of chins with little rest between sets! He figured he was doing about 60 sets of chins during his back workouts. As if the chins were not enough, he also did pulldowns in his back workout. On average he would do 8 to 10 sets of about 10 reps per set.

For thickness he did about 10 sets each of T-bar rows, seated pulley rows and one-arm dumbell rows. He kept the reps around 8 to 10, but on the last couple of sets dropped to 5 or 6. The drop was not due to an increase in weight but to a decrease in energy.

Because of a lower-back injury suffered in 1979, Roy tailored his back program to include some lower-back exercises. He reasoned that in all the years of training his upper back, he had neglected to keep his lower back up to par. The result was a muscle imbalance and ultimately an injury. For his lower back he did a lot of stiff-leg deadlifts and hyperextensions.

Roy observes that most bodybuilders would over-train if they followed his back routine. He recommends modifying it to suit your own specific needs and abilities.

Roy Callender's Back Routine:
1. Chins – *30+ sets of 8-10 reps*
2. Pulldowns – *8-10 sets of 10 reps*
3. T-bar rows – *8-10 sets of 10 reps*
4. Seated pulley rows – *8-10 sets of 10 reps*
5. Dumbell rows – *8-10 sets of 10 reps*
6. Hyperextensions – *8-10 sets of 12-15 reps*
7. Stiff-leg deadlifts – *8-10 sets of 12-15 reps*

BRIAN BUCHANAN – In September of 1989 *Ironman* magazine profiled one of the most exciting bodybuilding stars to emerge in years. The cover showed the upper body of a bodybuilder doing a double-biceps pose. What made the effect so eyecatching was that the man appeared to be sculpted out of clay. The model for the cover was British bodybuilder Brian Buchanan, and, as we shall see, the editors of *Ironman* had good reason to choose Brian for this particular pose.

Not since Sergio Oliva had a bodybuilder displayed such a waist-chest differential. His waist stretched the tape to a paltry 28 inches, while his chest was 53-plus. The result: the most impressive V-flare in bodybuilding! Although Brian concedes that genetics played a big role in determining his taper, he stresses that without years of heavy rows and chins he would never have recognized his potential.

Brian started his back training with chins. He did the first 3 sets with no additional weight attached. They served as a warmup. He then strapped 100 pounds around his waist and forced out 4 additional sets of 8 to 10 reps.

His next exercise was barbell rows, and to get a full stretch, he stood on a 6- to 8-inch block of wood. He used a medium-width grip, and kept his knees slightly bent to take much of the stress off the lower back. He found using a reverse (palms-up) grip placed most of the stress on the lower lats. He pulled the bar to his lower rib cage, and paused for a split second to get that extra contraction in his lats. For added variety he sometimes supersetted chins with barbell rows.

Brian did his next two exercises in superset fashion. He combined wide-grip pulldowns with seated pulley rows, keeping his elbows back on both exercises and squeezing his shoulder blades together.

He finished his back-training with another superset combination, this time T-bar rows and lever rows. He did 3 supersets of these two exercises, making sure to flex and contract the back muscles on every rep.

To further bring out his back detail, Brian concluded his back-training with a few minutes of posing. Recognizing that vigorous posing is a form of isometric exercise, he hit various back shots (double-biceps, lat spread, etc.) and held them for 10 to 20 seconds each. Not only did posing stimulate his muscles for further growth, but it was also great practice for competition. He recommends setting up two mirrors so that you can see your back muscles as you pose.

Brian Buchanan's Back Routine:
1. Chins – *6 sets of 8-10 reps*
2. Bent-over rows – *5 sets of 8-10 reps*
3. Seated cable rows/pulldowns* – *3 sets of 8-10 reps*
4. T-bar rows/lever rows* – *3 sets of 8-10 reps*
3 supersets

NIMROD KING – It is no exaggeration to say that Nimrod King is easily one of the most massively developed bodybuilders ever to emerge from Canada. From his 29-inch-plus thighs to his gargantuan upper body, Nimrod's physique is packed with the slabs of muscle needed for competing on the pro circuit. His 1989 US Pro Championship win gives testament to his awesome potential.

Nimrod's back is complete in every sense of the word. His lats sweep out like two great fans, and as for density, they must be at least two inches thick! Completing the package are his neck-covering traps and python-like spinal erectors.

In developing his massive physique, Nimrod had an advantage over most in that he started training at a very young age. While most bodybuilders don't take up the sport until 16 or 17, he was lifting away at the tender age of 12. And to show that he was doing things right from day one, he follows much the same back routine now as he did all those years ago. He started with the basics, and continues to make them the focal point of his workouts.

Nimrod's back routine starts with chins (which he calls pullups). He alternates

Brian Buchanan

Robby
Robinson

Nimrod's final exercise is the one-arm dumbell row. He does 3 sets of 12 reps, and once again every rep is done for the full stretch.

We'd assume from looking at Nimrod's traps and spinal erectors that he'd spend hours blasting them with shrugs and hyperextensions. Not so. He does (are you ready for this?) *no* trap or lower-back exercises! His traps get all the stimulation they need from shoulder exercises, and squats keep his spinal erectors in top shape. Most bodybuilders are not so lucky and have to do specific exercises for these muscle groups.

Nimrod King's Back Routine:

1. Chins – *4 sets of 12-15 reps*
2. Narrow front pulldowns – *4 sets of 12-15 reps*
3. Behind-the-neck pulldowns – *4 sets of 12-15 reps*
4. Seated cable rows – *4 sets of 12-15 reps*
5. T-bar rows – *4 sets of 10-12 reps*
6. One-arm dumbell rows – *4 sets of 10-12 reps*

ROBBY ROBINSON – Just when you thought he'd hung up the posing briefs for good, lo and behold, up he steps and takes the first Masters Mr. Olympia title! Robby "The Black Prince" Robinson has been competing since the mid-'70s and apparently has no intention of calling it quits. And why should he? With those grapefruit-sized biceps, complemented by that incredible waist/chest differential, Robby can hold his own with anyone, regardless of age!

When one lists the greatest backs in bodybuilding history, the name Robinson is sure to be near or at the top. Robby's back is – in one word – complete. Every sector is loaded with dense, striated muscle, from those wide, flaring lats to his column-like spinal erectors.

Robby starts his back workout with that old standby, chins. To hit the various regions of his lats, he varies his grip. One workout he does wide chins behind the head; the next he may do narrow chins to the front. Unlike many bodybuilders who strap enormous poundages around their waists, Robby adds at most an extra 20 to 25 pounds. He prefers to make the exercises as hard as possible by doing each rep in a slow, controlled manner.

To hit the middle and lower back, he does 4 or 5 sets of T-bar rows. He finds that a narrow grip on this exercise stresses the lats where they attach to the center back. To reduce back strain, he keeps his knees bent and lifts the bar using only his lats and arms.

Robby's final upper-back exercise is the seated cable row. In pulling the handles to his waist, he keeps his elbows close to his sides. He finds executing the exercise in this manner works the teres, rhomboids and lower lats.

For his lower back Robby alternates good mornings with hyperextensions. He usually does 4 or 5 sets of 15 to 20 reps.

between pulling behind the head and pulling to the front. On a typical back day he does 4 sets of 12 to 15 reps.

Next are pulldowns, both with a wide grip behind the head and narrow grip to the front. He goes for the feel in each exercise, and doesn't get carried away with weight. He firmly believes that it's better to use lighter weights in strict form than heavy weight in loose form. Besides getting a better pump, he greatly reduces the risk of injury.

After the chins and pulldowns it's on to T-bar rows and seated rows. Nimrod used to do rowing first in his routine, but he discovered that it took too much out of him and he was unable to do justice to his chins and pulldowns. By doing the chins and pulldowns first, he still has energy left to complete the heavy rows.

When he says "heavy" rows, he means it. How's a set of 10 reps with 445 on the T-bar for starters? Yet for all the weight used, he does every rep with immaculate style. There's no bouncing or swinging of the back – just smooth, controlled reps. He does both forms of rows for 4 sets of 10 to 12 reps.

Robby Robinson's Back Routine:
1. Chins (varied grip) – *4-5 sets of 8-10 reps*
2. T-bar rows – *4-5 sets of 8-10 reps*
3. Seated cable rows – *5-6 sets of 8-10 reps*
4. Hyperextensions/good mornings –
   4-5 sets of 15-20 reps
5. Barbell rows* – *4-5 sets of 8-10 reps*
6. One-arm rows* – *4-5 sets of 8-10 reps*
* Precontest only

SERGIO OLIVA – Nicknamed "The Myth," Cuban-born Sergio Oliva ranks among the all-time greats in bodybuilding history. The nickname is justified, for after one look you begin to wonder, 'Is he real or is he a myth?' Pound for pound Sergio Oliva carried as much muscle mass as any bodybuilder in history. When he hit his famous double-biceps shot from the rear, all eyes in the audience focused on perhaps the greatest combination of delts, arms and back in the sport.

Compared to most accepted ways to train back, Sergio's approach was unique. Realizing that most of the body's muscles evolved to work in pairs, he would train back and chest together, often in superset fashion.

His first exercises were supersets of chins and bench presses. In doing his chins, he did not follow the age-old adage of doing a full range of movement. He didn't bring his body completely above the chin bar, nor did he extend his arms to a fully locked position. Instead he stressed the middle third of the exercise. He found this part of the exercise formed the bulk of the movement, and the top and lower portions merely increased the speed at which he tired.

Sergio's next back exercises were front and rear pulldowns. He liked to alternate both, doing a set of behind-the-head pulldowns first, waiting a few seconds to catch his breath, and then doing a set of front pulldowns.

Then came seated cable rows, performed in alternating fashion. During a typical back workout Sergio alternated wide grip and narrow grip. Unlike most bodybuilders who treat this exercise as a power movement, he preferred to use less weight and go for a full stretch.

After seated rows it was back to two additional versions of pulldowns. Sergio alternated narrow pull-downs with bent-bar pulldowns. He had a special bar that resembles a bicycle handlebar and when he pulled down, the bar brought his hands close to both sides of his head.

For his lower back he alternated deadlifts with good mornings. As with seated rows, he was more concerned with style than amount of weight lifted on his deadlifts. He preferred to use a regular grip on this exercise (most do deadlifts with a reverse, palms-

Sergio Oliva

facing-up grip), and kept his hands as wide as possible. He does good mornings in the traditional manner with bar behind neck and bending at the waist.

His final back exercises were T-bar rows and pullovers. As you probably have guessed, he alternates the two exercises – one for thickness and one for width.

Sergio Oliva's Back Routine:
1. Wide-grip chins/bench presses –
   4-5 supersets of 8-10 reps
2. Close-grip chins/bench presses –
   3-4 supersets of 6-8 reps
3. Wide/close-grip cable rows –
   3-4 sets each of 6-8 reps
4. Narrow-grip/bent-bar pulldowns –
   3-4 sets each of 6-8 reps
5. Deadlifts/good mornings –
   3-4 sets each of 6-8 reps
6. T-bar rows/machine pullovers –
   3-4 sets each of 8-10 reps

VICTOR RICHARDS – *"To a lot of people I'm just a 275-pound monster. I realize that there is nobody with a physique like mine, but I don't judge people only by what type of body they have. I'm more interested in the type of person someone is and what I can learn from him rather than how much he can bench press."*

In terms of posing exhibitions and seminars he's one of the most popular bodybuilders in the world. His fans consider his advice on gaining mass, gospel. He weighs around 275 pounds in hard condition, yet stands only 5'8". To top off the mystique, he's never competed in a pro contest! This marvel of muscle is Victor Richards, and he may well be the most massively developed man in history.

Although many of his professional colleagues argue that big Vic has yet to prove himself, others are happy that he has chosen to remain on the sidelines. He is absolutely loaded with potential. From calf to neck he has brought new meaning to the word *development.*

Given that his heroes are Arnold, Sergio and Haney, it's not surprising that Vic is a great believer in bodybuilding basics. With few exceptions he tries to use the maximum weight on all his exercises. He also relies heavily on instinct. if he gets into a groove on a particular exercise, he might spend one or two hours doing nothing but that exercise.

His first back exercise is the behind-the-head pulldown. He progressively adds weight with each set, and then reduces it for additional sets. In a typical back workout, he does anywhere from 10 to 15 sets of 6 to 15 reps.

From rear pulldowns it's on to front pulldowns. Vic varies the grip on this exercise, alternating between wide and narrow. For the narrow variety he uses a V-shaped bar and pulls it to his navel. Although he goes by how his muscles feel, on average he does 10 to 12 sets of 6 to 15 reps.

For back thickness he does seated cable rows – 10

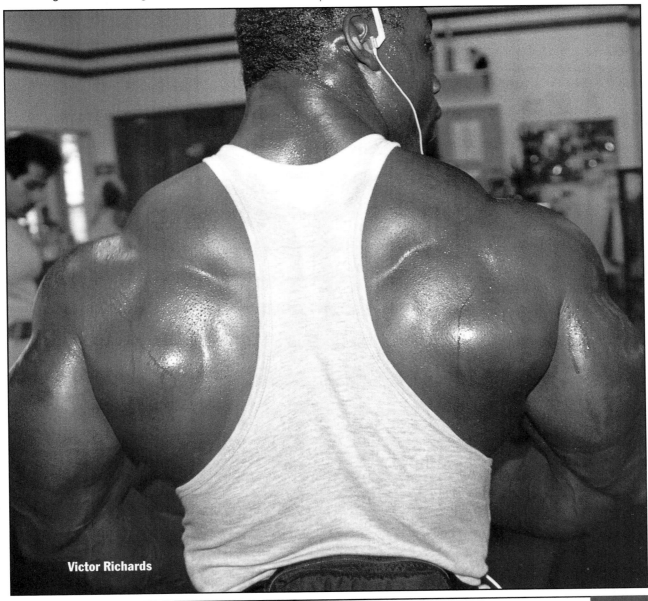

Victor Richards

CHAPTER TWENTY-ONE - BACK

Laura Binetti

constantly being punished by judges for being too muscular, Laura stuck to her belief that sooner or later the powers-that-be would see women's bodybuilding for what it truly is – copious amounts of shredded muscle!

After turning pro in 1990 Laura suffered disappointment after disappointment. Unlike others who would have hung up their posing suits and called it quits, she persevered and was rewarded in 1994 with a Canada Pro Cup victory.

Laura's road to her first pro victory started back in elementary school. "I was always athletic," she recalls "I can remember being involved in all the track events at school. I really got serious about running in junior high. I did some track events also, but in grade seven I mainly focused on cross-country running. It wasn't until I started university that I found every person to be specialized in some sport."

Laura soon met up with Olympic high jumper Greg Joy, and he put her on a regular weight-training program. Before long she was lifting every day, and the results showed. She gained mass so fast that Greg suggested she try bodybuilding, and the rest, as they say, is bodybuilding history.

In short order Laura won the Hamilton Steel City Classic and was invited to compete at the 1990 Ms. International. After placing fourth among the amateurs, she was granted her pro card. "It was one of the most exciting shows I've ever done because we were really treated like athletes. I couldn't believe it when I got my pro card because I never really expected to go that far."

After placing out of the top ten at the '93 Ms. Olympia, and eighth at the 1994 Ms. International, Laura set her sights on the 1994 Pro Cup. Although winning was certainly on her mind, Laura's main goal was to requalify for the Ms. Olympia. Her victories at the 1994 Canada Pro Cup and 1996 European Pro Classic guarantee that great things can be expected from this Canadian superstar in the future.

One of Laura's best bodyparts is her outstanding back. As with many bodybuilders early in their careers, this was not always the case. While developing thickness was never really a problem, Laura felt her width needed improvement.

She has restructured her training schedule. Instead of training on a three-on/one-off schedule, Laura now

to 15 sets of 6 to 15 reps. He trains as heavy as possible while carefully maintaining good style. He neither bounces the weight nor uses body momentum to hoist it. Every rep is done in a controlled manner.

Vic's last back exercise is the one-arm dumbell row. He finds this exercise excellent for the lower lats as well as the traps and rear delts. Sometimes he substitutes T-bar rows, but he prefers dumbells as they place less stress on the lower back.

Victor Richards's Back Routine:
1. Pulldowns behind the neck – *10-15 sets of 6-15 reps*
2. Front pulldowns – *10-12 sets of 6-15 reps*
3. Seated cable rows – *10-15 sets of 6-15 reps*
4. Dumbell rows (T-bar rows) – *6 sets of 6-15 reps*

LAURA BINETTI – If placing first were based solely on sheer determination, Toronto's Laura Binetti would win hands down. The bodybuilding highway is littered with the remains of bodybuilders who gave up after one or two bad placings. But not Laura. Even though she was

trains one bodypart a day for five or six days. Having adopted this new system, she wonders how she ever trained more than one bodypart in the same workout. The one-bodypart-a-day routine allows her to hit each muscle with more intensity without draining her recovery system.

Like most bodybuilders, Laura changes her exercises around to keep the muscles guessing. She has four different routines which she rotates from day to day. If she happens to do the same exercises, she modifies the sets and reps.

On all her exercises Laura is careful to get a full range of motion. She goes for a complete stretch and contraction on each rep, keeping a moderate training tempo. She believes it's extremely important to move the weight with muscle power, not momentum or inertia.

Laura doesn't do any direct work for her lower back. She feels it's thick enough from all the heavy squats, deadlifts and bent-over rows.

Laura believes in stretching after each set. She holds a beam or upright support with both hands and stretches her lats. This technique has helped tremendously in correcting her previous width problem. Also, all that stretching has given her much better control over her back muscles – an important point, considering today's highly competitive contests.

Laura Binetti performs bent-over rows with picture-perfect form.

Laura Binetti's Back Routines:
Routine 1
1. Seated cable rows – *8 sets of 8-12 reps*
2. Reverse pulldowns – *5 sets of 6-10 reps*
3. Bent-over rows – *4 sets of 8-12 reps*
4. Reverse barbell shrugs – *4 sets of 10-12 reps*
5. Lat pulldowns – *3 sets of 10-12 reps*

Routine 2
1. Bent-over rows – *6 sets of 6-12 reps*
2. Reverse pulldowns – *4 sets of 8-10 reps*
3. One-arm rows – *5 sets of 10-12 reps*
4. Reverse barbell shrugs – *4 sets of 10-12 reps*
5. Lat pulldowns – *4 sets of 10-12 reps*

Routine 3
1. Lat pulldowns – *8 sets of 8-15 reps*
2. Seated rows – *6 sets of 8-20 reps*
3. Bent-over rows – *4 sets of 8-10 reps*
4. Reverse barbell shrugs – *3 sets of 10-12 reps*
5. Straight-arm pulldowns – *3 sets of 12-15 reps*

Routine 4
1. Wide-grip chins – *6 sets to failure*
2. Reverse pulldowns – *5 sets of 6-10 reps*
3. Seated cable rows – *4 sets of 12-15 reps*
4. Straight-arm pulldowns – *4 sets of 12-15*
5. Lat pulldowns – *4 sets of 12-15*

Start

Finish

Chapter Twenty-two

CHEST

POWERFUL PECTORALS

"Chest power is vital in sports. This mighty muscle group is responsible for all forward pushing movements of the upper body. All sports involving throwing, pushing or punching are improved by a program of chest work." **— Jim Quinn, IFBB Pro Bodybuilder (commenting on the importance of a strong chest to many sports)**

Jim Quinn

Next to the biceps, the pectorals are probably the most trained muscle group. How many aspiring bodybuilders have gazed admiringly at the chests of Arnold, Serge Nubret, Lee Haney or Lou Ferrigno? Go into any gym and chances are a high percentage of members are doing some sort of chest exercise.

Several reasons exist for such a preoccupation with chest-training. For starters the chest is the center of upper-body strength. Most upper-body exercises depend heavily on pectoral power. A second reason is its location. The chest is usually the first area your eyes focus on when you look at a bodybuilder's physique. During many exercises for the chest you can watch it flex with every rep. Unless you use a mirror, you can't get the same effect with back-training. Another reason for the popularity of chest-training is the response of the pectoral muscles to exercise. Most bodybuilders find their chests grow fairly easily with regular training. Even if regular exercises like bench presses and dips don't work, it's usually only a matter of switching to another exercise to make the chest respond.

A final reason is how the chest feels during a workout. Unlike calves, forearms and thighs, which can be termed "high-pain" muscles (i.e. they quickly take on a burning sensation with each successive rep), the pectorals are very pleasant to train. They readily pump up, and soon the bodybuilder feels he's added inches to his chest measurement.

ANATOMY AND TRAINING

"A long time ago it occurred to me that the champions who were most admired for their pectoral development all had one thing in common: they practiced the dip between parallel bars religiously. There is no better pectoral developer than the dip."
— Samir Bannout, 1982 Mr. Olympia

Chest-training can be divided into various facets. For purposes of training, most bodybuilders divide the chest into upper and lower. With time you will need to specialize, and the terms *outer*, *inner*, and pec-delt tie-in will become relevant.

When we talk about the chest we are really referring to the large pectoral muscles. The pectorals can be subdivided into the pectorals major and pectorals minor. The pectorals major are the large fan-shaped muscles that cover the front of the whole upper torso region. The pectorals minor are located underneath the

Samir Bannout

THE CHAMPS' ROUTINES

"The bodybuilder who wins out over the bench press and goes on to test the true limits of his strength simply learns to trust his power rather than fear the pain. And that's a far more significant test of concentration than brute strength."
— **Dr. Franco Columbu**
Two-time Mr. Olympia

ARNOLD SCHWARZENEGGER – Few would argue that Arnold Schwarzenegger's chest ranks among the greatest sets of pectorals in bodybuilding history. From rib cage to sternum to pec-delt tie-in, his chest development was the envy of every aspiring bodybuilder.

Arnold attributed his phenomenal chest development to basic exercises. His routine might even be described as mundane. He was never partial to machines or fancy cable exercises, but stuck with basic mass-building exercises, and you can't deny the results. There's a good lesson here for beginning bodybuilders. Don't get caught up in every new fad that comes along. We often hear engineers and architects

Arnold Schwarzenegger

majors, and although they add to the bulk of the chest, bodybuilders usually don't think about them during a chest workout. For the purposes of this section, when we refer to pecs, we mean the pectorals major.

The primary function of the pectoral muscles is to bring the arms and shoulders forward. An exercise physiologist can give you a more precise definition, but for bodybuilding purposes the chest muscles are responsible for drawing the arms towards the center of the body. The angle of the arm movement with respect to the upper body determines which part of the pectorals is involved.

At the intermediate level of bodybuilding you want to do at least one exercise for the lower chest and one for the upper chest. By the time you reach the advanced level, you may need to specialize on particular areas of your chest muscles. The programs that follow were designed to hit the chest from every angle.

COMMON CHEST EXERCISES

1. Flat barbell bench presses
2. Incline barbell bench presses
3. Decline barbell bench presses
4. Dumbell presses
5. Dumbell flyes
6. Dips
7. Cable crossovers
8. Pullovers
9. Pec-dek flyes

Lou Ferrigno

talking about going back to the drawing board. The same principle holds true for bodybuilders. Stick with the basics, and resist the urge to do elaborate shaping exercises. Lay down a good foundation before you start adding exercises.

Arnold's chest routine consisted of what are generally regarded as the best mass-building exercises. The routine we present is the same one that he followed in the early to mid-'70s. Keep in mind that in a competitive career that spanned over 15 years, he used many different chest routines. This is but one of them.

Arnold usually started his chest routine with flat or incline bench presses. He alternated the two, depending on how he felt on a particular day. Although he included forced reps from time to time, he generally did his sets in a standard positive-failure format. In fact he often terminated his set just short of failure. He did 5 sets of each exercise, about 8 to 10 reps per set.

After the two basic mass-building exercises he (and often his training partner, Franco Columbu) moved on to an isolation exercise like flat dumbell flyes. Those wishing to see intensity should rent *Pumping Iron* and watch Arnold doing flyes. If this doesn't inspire you, change sports!

To finish his chest training, he did 5 sets of cable crossovers with each rep performed in a slow and controlled manner – no bouncing, jerking or yanking the weight up. Arnold made a special point of pausing and squeezing his pecs together when his arms were in the extended position.

Arnold's Chest Routine:
1. Incline presses – *5 sets of 8-10 reps*
2. Flat bench presses – *5 sets of 8-10 reps*
3. Flyes – *5 sets of 8-10 reps*
4. Cable crossovers – *5 sets of 10-15 reps*

LOU FERRIGNO – *"People don't believe me when I tell them my chest isn't naturally large and that I've had to work damn hard to bring it up. My chest was actually small and underdeveloped during my first few years of training because my arms were so long."*

Next to Arnold Schwarzenegger, Lou Ferrigno is perhaps bodybuilding's best-known star. In the late 1970s and early 1980s big Lou entered the hearts of millions as TV's Incredible Hulk. His most-muscular pose (albeit with a slight greenish tinge!) became the most recognized pose in bodybuilding history. When Lou (playing the Hulk) hit this pose, an assortment of bumps, bulges and protrusions would explode from his body, and at the center of this eruption was his 60-inch chest.

Although he uses machines and cables in his training, Lou makes free weights the focal point of his chest workouts. In this respect he is from the same school as Arnold and Sergio – two of his early heroes.

In a typical chest workout he uses both dumbells and barbells. This variety, he says, ensures that the pecs are hit from all angles. His first chest exercise is some sort of pressing movement, usually with a barbell, but occasionally he will substitute dumbells. He normally does 4 or 5 sets of 8 to 10 reps. Next he does flyes, either flat or incline, 4 or 5 sets of 8 to 10 reps, dropping the weight on the last set.

Lou's third exercise is another pressing movement, often flats or inclines. For variety he sometimes adds a few sets of declines or dips. Once again it's 4 or 5 sets of 8 to 10 reps, with reduced weight on the last set.

To finish his chest workout, big Lou throws in a few sets of cable crossovers and dumbell pullovers. The pullovers help tie the pecs and lats together, and bring out the serratus. He uses the crossovers, not as mass-builders, but to flush the pectorals with blood. They give his pecs the maximum pump before he moves on to another bodypart.

Lou Ferrigno's Chest Routine:
1. Barbell/dumbell presses – *4 sets of 8-10 reps*
2. Flat/incline flyes – *4 sets of 8-10 reps*
3. Flat/incline presses – *4 sets of 8-10 reps*
4. Decline presses, flyes or dips* – *4 sets of 8-10 reps*
5. Pullovers* – *3-4 sets of 10-12 reps*
6. Cable crossovers – *3-4 sets of 10-12 reps*
*Done only occasionally

DORIAN YATES – *"Although my arms and calves responded fairly quickly when I started training, my chest was pitifully weak with no peak muscle to speak of at all. I used to dream of having massive bulbous pecs like those of Arnold."*

If Arnold dominated the 1970s, and the 1980s belonged to Lee Haney, then massive British bodybuilder Dorian Yates is making the '90s his domain. With five Mr. Olympias to his credit (and no sign of slowing down) Dorian is setting the standard that will take bodybuilding into the next century. Although his chest was formerly one of his weakest muscles, specialized training has made it one of the thickest on the pro circuit. Here's how he did it:

"The most common mistake made by eager body-builders is overtraining. I regularly see beginners doing 15 to 20 sets of chest work and wondering why their pecs aren't growing. It may surprise those beginners to learn that I perform only 6 or 7 heavy sets in a chest workout. It's only by avoid-ing the pitfalls of constant overtraining that I have been able to make good gains in the chest area."

No doubt these comments will come as a shock to many. Mr. Olympias are supposed to do 25 to 30 sets per bodypart, right? Wrong! At least not in Dorian's case. He is one of a growing number of bodybuilders who have found doing fewer sets gives better results. Instead of five or six recovery-draining exercises, he puts every-thing into three exercises done for 2 sets each. He doesn't do anything fancy either, just the good old basics – flat bench presses, incline presses and flyes.

Dorian's first chest exercise is either flat or decline bench presses, which he alternates from time to time. Before starting his barbell work, he warms up with a few light sets of dumbell presses or flyes. After these, it's on to barbell presses. Even though he does only 2 heavy sets, what sets they are! He does each rep in a slow, controlled manner, and when he has reached positive failure he has a training partner assist with a couple of negatives. Both sets consist of 5 to 8 reps.

The next exercise on Dorian's agenda is the incline barbell press. He explains:

"I use an angled bench of 30 degrees as I find a steeper angle puts too much stress on the frontal delts. After I have done my first exercise, my chest is suffi-ciently warmed up for me to go straight into the heaviest weight I can handle on the incline bench for 5 to 8 reps. Again the reps are performed without any build-up of momentum, which I feel robs the muscles of deep stimulation."

Dorian Yates

He does 2 sets of inclines to failure. Although many bodybuilders periodically substitute dumbells on this exercise, Dorian finds them too awkward. He says he spends too much effort concentrating on control rather than working his chest.

His final chest exercise is flat flyes. With his arms slightly bent, palms facing upward, he presses the dumbells up to just short of touching:

"I don't bring the dumbells all the way up to touch at the top position as I prefer to keep tension on the pecs throughout the movement."

Once again, he does only 2 sets of 8 to 10 reps to failure. For variety he goes down the rack on this exercise, doing an additional 5 or 6 reps.

Dorian Yates's Chest Routine For Beginners:
1. Bench presses – *3 sets of 8-10 reps*

Dorian Yates's Chest Routine For Intermediates:
1. Bench presses – *3 sets of 6-8 reps*
2. Incline flyes – *2 sets of 8-10 reps*

Lee Haney

Dorian Yates's Personal Chest Routine:
1. Flat barbell (or incline) bench presses – *2 sets of 5-8 reps*
2. Incline barbell presses – *2 sets of 5-8 reps*
3. Flat flyes – *2 sets of 5-8 reps*

LEE HANEY – *"I have always believed in using basic exercises and avoiding overtraining my chest. There are a lot of guys who aren't even winning local titles yet who regularly blast their chests with 25 to 30 total sets three days a week. It's their training approach that holds them back."*

With his record eight Mr. Olympia victories Lee Haney is unquestionably one of the greatest bodybuilders to have ever graced a competitive stage. In fact many argue he is the greatest, bar none. (Of course, others counter, "What about Arnold or Sergio or Dorian or…?") In any case, few would dispute that Lee developed one of the most massive physiques of all time. At the center of this gargantuan frame are two enormous slabs of meat that he calls his pectorals. The list of adjectives that mere mortals use to describe Haney's chest is too long to include here!

When in serious training, he started his chest routine with 2 high-rep (15 to 20) sets of flat bench presses. These sets served to warm up the pecs for his heavier sets, which consisted of 6 to 8 reps using anywhere from 315 to 415 pounds.

After flat barbell presses he switched to flat dumbell presses. In a typical workout he did 3 sets of 6 to 8 reps. He pyramided the weight, usually starting with 120-pound dumbells.

To hit the upper chest, Lee did 3 sets each of incline barbell and dumbell presses. He used a 30-degree bench for both exercises, as over the years he discovered the 45-degree bench was placing too much stress on his front delts.

His off-season chest workout concluded with 4 or 5 sets of flat dumbell flyes. As he was doing this exercise more for shape than size, he used less weight than on the dumbell press.

In his pre-Olympia training phase Lee supersetted 4 sets of cable crossovers and dips. Instead of the usual 6 to 8 reps, he kept the reps higher – in the 15 to 20 range.

Lee stresses that his routine is too advanced for most bodybuilders. He recommends reducing both the number of exercises and number of sets. With time you can gradually add new exercises.

Lee Haney's Chest Routine:
1. Barbell bench presses – *3 sets of 6-8 reps*
2. Dumbell bench presses – *3 sets of 6-8 reps*
3. Incline barbell presses – *3 sets of 6-8 reps*
4. Incline dumbell presses – *3 sets of 6-8 reps*
5. Flat bench dumbell flyes – *3 sets of 6-8 reps*
6. Cable crossovers* – *4 sets of 15-20 reps*
7. Dips* – *4 sets of 15-20 reps*
Precontest training only

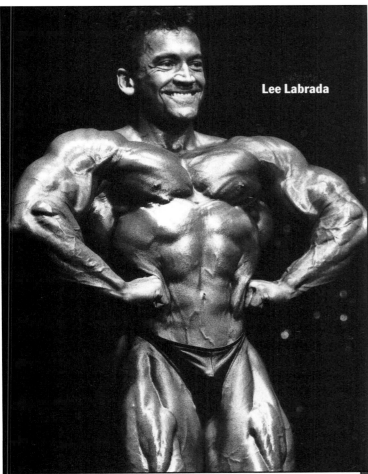

Lee Labrada

proceeded immediately to his heaviest weight. He squeezed out 10 pure reps with this weight, and then reduced it by approximately 10 percent for his next set. After doing 3 sets in this fashion, he moved on to his next chest exercise. He alternated two routines in his chest workouts.

Lee Labrada's Chest Routines:

Routine A
1. Incline barbell presses – *3 sets of 10 reps*
2. Incline dumbell flyes – *3 sets of 10 reps*
3. Flat dumbell flyes – *3 sets of 10 reps*

Routine B
1. Incline barbell presses – *3 sets of 10 reps*
2. Incline dumbell flyes – *3 sets of 10 reps*
3. Flat dumbell flyes – *2 sets of 10 reps*
4. Flat bench presses – *2 sets of 10 reps*

SERGIO OLIVA – If a list were drawn up of the most massive bodybuilders of all time, the name Sergio Oliva would rank near or at the top. Even in today's age of giants like Yates, Dillett and Francois, most fans would concede that the Cuban-born "Myth" carried as much muscle mass as anyone. We can only imagine what he might have looked like had he had access to today's state-of-the-art supplements, training apparatus and knowledge.

To say Oliva's chest was among his best bodyparts would be doing a disservice to his other muscles. All of Oliva's muscles were his best bodyparts! From calf to

Samir Bannout and Sergio Oliva

LEE LABRADA – *"For chest training I keep it very simple. I start with my upper-pec work, doing 3 sets of heavy incline presses. I follow this with heavy incline dumbell flyes for another 3 sets. Then I go to the flat bench and do 3 sets of flat dumbell flyes. That's 9 sets. This is actually more sets than I'd normally do, but I specialized on my pecs this year."*

Known as "Mr. Symmetry" and "Mass with Class," Lee Labrada was frequently criticized early in his professional bodybuilding career for his weak upper pectoral development, but not any more:

"I felt that I had an upper pec weakness and I've brought it up through a lot of heavy inclines, flyes and presses. I took the approach that one workout I'd concentrate mostly on my upper pecs and then next chest workout I'd do mostly flat bench presses and flyes with a little upper-pec work. That system worked well for me."

Lee decided to focus on the basics to bring his upper chest up to par. Instead of using a lot of cables and machines, he went heavy on barbell and dumbell exercises. Whereas other pros were doing 25 to 30 sets for their chest, he limited his workout to 8 or 10 sets total.

Lee did not pyramid the weight as most bodybuilders do. Instead he did 1 or 2 warmup sets and

neck everything was in proportion. That is as proportioned as huge can be! With his 29-inch waist and 54-inch chest, Sergio's upper body had to be seen to be believed. His chest and back were thick beyond belief, and as for his deltoids, well, we look at those in more detail later.

In terms of chest-training, he was from the old school – that is, nothing fancy just time-proven exercises like bench presses, inclines, declines and flyes. His reps ranged from 8 to 15 and he usually did 5 sets of an exercise.

Like most bodybuilders, he started his chest training with flat bench presses. Early in his career he focused mostly on the amount of weight lifted, but later he emphasized quality.

After bench presses Sergio moved to flyes and decline presses, both for his normal 5 sets of 8 to 15 reps. To finish his chest, Sergio added 5 sets of cable crossovers – being careful to flex and forcibly contract the pecs at the top (hands-together position) of the movement. For variety he often substituted dips and inclines for one or two of his regular exercises. Sometimes he supersetted chest and back together. Few bodybuilders are as impressive as the Myth with a full upper-body pump. Awesome!

Sergio Oliva's Chest Routine:
1. Bench presses – *5 sets of 8-15 reps*
2. Decline presses – *5 sets of 8-15 reps*
3. Flat dumbell flyes – *5 sets of 8-15 reps*
4. Cable crossovers – *5 sets of 10-15 reps*

SELWYN COTTERILL – Standing 6'2" and weighing between 260 and 270, British bodybuilder Selwyn Cotterell is one of the sport's stronger competitors. Incline presses of 405 pounds are the norm, and he routinely works up to 500 pounds.

"You know how people always say that bodybuilders are weak? Well, I wanted to show 'em they're wrong, so I entered a couple of powerlifting meets – and won!"

Even though he has yet to win a pro IFBB show, Selwyn is kept very busy guest posing around the world. This is not surprising as bodybuilding fans love huge size, and he has it in abundance.

He follows a four-on/one-off routine, and hits chest on day one. He does four exercises, keeping the reps at 6 to 10. Although he uses extremely heavy poundages, he is careful to maintain good style on all his exercises.

Selwyn begins his chest-training with incline barbell presses. He does 5 sets, starting with 250 pounds, working up to an incredible 500 pounds. He lowers the bar just short of touching his chest.

Selwyn Cotterill

"It doesn't touch the chest because that would break the tension. I want to keep tension on the chest muscles at all times."

His next exercise is the incline dumbell press, which he calls "arch-back flyes." He calls them this because he likes to arch his back when doing the exercise. He keeps his feet wide apart and holds his elbows straight out to his sides. As with barbell presses, he doesn't lock out at the top, preferring to keep tension on the muscles throughout the whole range of movement. Where most bodybuilders are completing their inclines with 90 pounders, Cotterill is starting with this weight! He goes from 90- to 150-pound dumbells on this exercise, doing 6 to 10 reps.

The third exercise is a variation of the decline barbell press. Instead of lowering the bar to the lower chest (around the nipple area), he brings it to the middle chest.

"A lot of people bring the weight down to the lower pecs, but I bring it to the midchest. People say this exercise is just for the lower chest, but I find it hits the upper chest as well."

Selwyn starts with around 300 pounds and works up to 450. He does 4 sets of 6 to 10 reps.

The fourth and final exercise is the cable crossover. He does 3 sets of 10 reps, going from 130 to 200 pounds (respectable bench poundages for many bodybuilders!). To start the exercise, he stands directly between the uprights with his feet about four inches apart and upper body bent slightly forward. He squeezes his arms together but stops short of touching his hands. For variation he steps forward to perform the exercise. This change of position puts a slightly different stress on the pectorals.

There you have it – the chest routine of one of the biggest bodybuilders on the pro circuit. While you may not be able to handle the same poundages (few can!), we are confident that following such a routine will add inches to your chest.

Selwyn Cotterill's Chest Routine:
1. Incline presses – *5-6 sets of 6-10 reps*
2. Incline dumbell flyes – *4 sets of 6-10 reps*
3. Decline presses – *4 sets of 6-10 reps*
4. Cable crossovers – *3 sets of 10 reps*

NIMROD KING – With the possible exception of Lee Haney, Dorian Yates and Paul Dillett, few bodybuilders have the muscle mass of Canadian sensation Nimrod King. From sternum to front delt Nimrod's pecs hang like two enormous sacks. He attributes his great pec development to two training modifications – switching from low to high reps, and separating chest from delts and triceps.

"Making these changes has brought about a 50 percent improvement in my chest in the last two years. When I trained chest, delts and triceps in the same workout I'd be benching as heavy as I could just trying to skip through my chest workout so I could get to my shoulders, and hoping I had enough energy left over to train my triceps. Now I train chest and calves in the morning and shoulders, triceps and abs at night. Therefore I can put 100 percent concentration into my chest workout and train my chest much harder and more thoroughly."

Nimrod takes the view that training chest, shoulders and triceps together is fine for beginning and intermediate bodybuilders, but for advanced bodybuilders like himself it's better to train the muscles separately.

Besides changing his routine, he modified his rep range. Now instead of low and medium reps (5 to 10), he does 15 to 25 on all his chest exercises.

"You can even tell how someone trains just by looking at his physique. The people who do only low reps are thick, puffy and bloated. They're big, of course, but someone who trains with high reps will look even bigger and have more density, cuts and muscularity. The person who does high reps will look better than the person who does just low reps."

Like all top bodybuilders, Nimrod attacks the chest from different angles. From the upper and lower pecs to the inner and outer pecs, no part of his chest goes untouched. His present workout consists of seven or eight exercises, 4 or 5 sets of each for 15 to 25 reps. That's a lot of work to be sure, but the results speak for themselves.

His first chest exercise is the flat barbell bench press. Instead of locking out, he keeps the bar moving in a piston-like motion.

"I do not extend my arms to lockout, except on the last rep, because extending all the way up burns me out too fast and takes the tension off the pecs."

Barbell inclines follow flat presses, and once again Nimrod limits the reps to short touch-and-gos – no locking out. Despite the high reps he rests less than a minute between sets, and in a typical workout he'll do 5 sets of 15 to 25 reps.

The third exercise is flat dumbell flyes for 3 sets of 12 to 15 reps. He reduced the number of sets so that he has energy remaining to do other chest exercises. Unlike his barbell exercises, Nimrod prefers a full range of motion on flyes. He brings the dumbells as low as possible and then presses up to an arms-locked position.

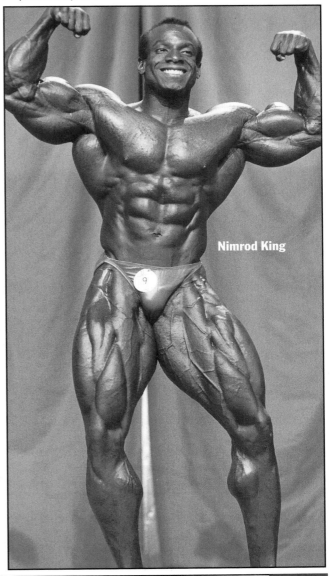

Nimrod King

He finishes his inner pecs with 2 sets of pec-dek flyes, contracting his pecs fully on every rep. As with barbell flats and inclines, he does the reps in a continuous motion.

Decline dumbell flyes are next, and Nimrod does 4 sets of about 15 reps. He uses a decline angle of about 30 degrees, and follows the style of his regular flat flyes – i.e. full range of motion.

To complete his chest workout, he blasts out 2 sets of machine presses. He feels this is a great way to give his pecs a pump.

Many will argue that Nimrod's chest routine is not for the average bodybuilder, and he readily agrees, but it has brought him the type of chest development he wanted. In the sport of bodybuilding one of the underlying principles is to do whatever works, so if your chest is lagging behind, give this program a try, and see if it's for you.

Nimrod King's Chest Routine:
1. Barbell bench presses – *5 sets of 15-25 reps*
2. Incline barbell presses – *5 sets of 15-25 reps*
3. Flat dumbell flyes – *3 sets of 12-15 reps*
4. Dumbell pullovers – *3 sets of 12-15 reps*
5. Cable crossovers – *1-2 trisets of 12 reps*
6. Pec-dek flyes – *2 sets of 15 reps*
7. Decline dumbell flyes – *4 sets of 15 reps*
8. Machine presses – *2 sets of 15-17 reps*

MICHAEL FRANCOIS – With his wins at the 1994 Chicago Pro Invitational and Night of Champions and the 1995 Arnold Classic and San Jose Invitational, Michael Francois has established himself as one of the top bodybuilders in the world. This in itself is pretty amazing, but what's even more astounding is that he achieved these accomplishments after only five years of serious training!

Michael is one of a new breed of bodybuilders who believe strongly in the relationship between size and strength. Consequently, you won't find him doing light pumping sets. Much of his density comes from basic exercises like squats, deadlifts, benches and shoulder presses.

"From the very beginning I've always known powerlifting; however, I didn't really incorporate it into my program until about a year ago. Now it's a staple part of my training."

He is not alone in his belief in heavy training. Superstars Dorian Yates, Chris Cormier and Kevin Levrone all practice the hard and heavy training philosophy.

Unlike many bodybuilders, big Mike doesn't rely much on fancy training methods like drop sets, supersets and staggered sets. He prefers old-fashioned straight sets.

"I try to work myself up to a certain weight and then just use that. Usually after I've done one chest exercise – unless the next one's going to be a totally different angle or something – I don't even warm up when I go on to the next one. I just jump right into the heavier weights."

Michael Francois

To stretch the rib cage, pectorals and serratus, he does 3 sets of cross-bench pullovers. He uses a dumbell and aims for 12 to 15 good-quality reps.

To hit the inner pecs, he utilizes a rest-pause triset on the cable crossover. He does 12 reps with the selected weight, stops for 5 to 10 seconds, and then bangs out as many more reps as possible. Most bodybuilders would stop here, but not Nimrod. He pauses a second time and tries a few additional reps. Instinct determines whether or not he will do a second triset.

Berry DeMey, Lee Haney and Mike Quinn

Heavier weights for Michael means using 405 pounds for sets of 8 on flat bench presses and sets of 12 with 315 on incline presses. He doesn't start with this weight, but works up to it in 90-pound jumps. Once he reaches his top weight, he does on average 3 good sets.

Given his preference for heavy training, Mike's first chest exercise – the flat barbell bench press – is not surprising. Even though the reps are fast and piston-like, he keeps the weight under control at all times. With such a promising career ahead of him, why take a chance on an injury because of poor exercise technique? He starts at 135 pounds and proceeds to 405 (i.e. 135, 225, 315, 405), with which he does three sets.

Incline presses are next, and once again he works up to his top weight (around 315) for 3 sets. He doesn't have a preference for barbell or dumbells, but lets instinct determine which to use. If his shoulders are sore, he'll probably use the dumbells, but on days when everything feels "just right" heavy barbell inclines are his choice. If he uses a barbell he brings it down high on the neck, similar to Gironda presses. He finds this version great for putting slabs of meat around the collarbone area.

Mike uses two rep styles in his training. During the off-season he usually stays in the 6 to 8 range, but occasionally drops as low as 4. In his precontest phase he does sets of 10 to 15. Still, even while on a strict diet, he tries to keep his weights heavy. This, he says, helps him retain muscle mass.

After the heavy barbell work, it's on to variations of the dumbell flye. Depending on the day, he may use an incline, decline or flat bench. As contest time approaches, he adds variety to his flyes by including cable versions.

For his last exercise Mike throws in an often neglected exercise – the dumbell pullover. He has such a liking for this movement that he does it for both his chest and back. On chest days he keeps his arms bent all the way though the range of motion and pulls the weight over the middle of his chest. At the top he squeezes his pecs together as hard as possible. During the precontest season he substitutes cable crossovers in place of pullovers.

Taking a cue from Dorian Yates and Lee Labrada, Mike rarely exceeds 10 or 12 sets total during his off-season training. He feels that if you are training heavy and hard, doing more than 10 or 12 sets is not only unnecessary but also almost impossible. With the perils of overtraining constantly in his mind, he trains each bodypart only once a week. This schedule gives the muscles a chance to recover fully before being attacked once again.

With his convincing win at the 1995 Arnold Classic, this 240-pound sensation is a sure bet to give such stars as Dorian Yates, Paul Dillett and Kevin Levrone a run for their money at the Mr. Olympia. If five years of training can bring him four pro titles, what will another five accomplish?

Michael Francois's Chest Routine (Off-Season):
1. Flat bench presses – *3 sets of 6-8 reps*
2. Incline presses – *3 sets of 6-8 reps*
3. Dumbell flyes – *3 sets of 6-8 reps*
4. Pullovers – *3 sets of 6-8 reps*
5. Cable crossovers* – *3 sets of 10-12 reps*
Precontest only

Chapter Twenty-three

SHOULDERS

TOUCHING BOTH SIDES OF THE DOORWAY

"I have always emphasized deltoid training because since my earliest days in bodybuilding I was told that the key to developing a great body was to build the abdominals, calves and deltoids to the absolute maximum." **– Lee Labrada, IFBB Pro Bodybuilder Mr. Olympia runner-up**

Lee Labrada

It's said that of all the body's muscles, the shoulders are the hardest to hide. With a bit of creative posing you can disguise a weak back, and putting a clean line under the pecs will create the illusion of great chest development. But no matter what strategy you employ, it's virtually impossible to camouflage poor shoulder development. The explanation for this problem lies with anatomy. Regardless of the body's position (front, back or side), at least two of the shoulder's three muscles will be visible.

ANATOMY

When we speak of the shoulders we are referring to a whole complex of muscles. The shoulders (called deltoids or delts) are composed of three submuscles called heads – the front (anterior), side (lateral) and rear (posterior). Each head raises the arm in a slightly different direction. The anterior delt raises the out-stretched arm to the front, the lateral delt raises the arm to the side, and the posterior delt raises the arm to the rear.

For maximum shoulder impressiveness bodybuilders must have all three heads equally developed. Unfortunately this balance is rarely seen. Most bodybuilders have large front delts from years of heavy benching and other chest exercises, yet their side and rear delts are woefully weak. While most back exercises hit the rear delts, many bodybuilders find they need to train the area on a regular basis to bring it up to the quality of their front delts. Although in recent years various rear-delt machines have come on the scene, many gyms don't have them yet because of cost. If your gym falls into this category, don't despair. A number of dumbell and barbell exercises can do wonders with the rear delts.

"The lateral raise is one of the most popular shoulder exercises but also one of the most frequently performed incorrectly. All too often bodybuilders become trapped into swinging up weights that are far too heavy to provide benefit." **– Lee Labrada IFBB Pro Bodybuilder**

You can never be too wide. If you are blessed with a wide bone structure to begin with, regular training of the side delts will give you that "yard wide" look. For those with average or less than average shoulder width, regular side-delt training is a must. No exceptions. You may fear that having a narrow shoulder structure will keep you from the winners' circle, but take a look at bodybuilding's first Mr. Olympia, Larry Scott. Larry realized from the beginning that unfavorable genetics had limited his shoulder width, but instead of sulking about it, he immediately went to work and built deltoids among the largest ever seen. You can't change shoulder structure, but you can add inches to shoulder width by enlarging the side delts.

Besides the delts, the shoulders also include the trapezius (called traps) muscles. These large, fan-like muscles start at the base of the neck and extend downward to the middle of the back. Because of their location, the traps may be worked with either shoulders or back. As most bodybuilders train traps with shoulders, we will include the exercise descriptions here.

The first step in shoulder-training is the warmup as the shoulders are especially vulnerable to injury. Next to the lower back and knees, the shoulder area is the most common site of bodybuilding injuries. Plunging headfirst into a heavy set of military presses or bench presses is only asking for trouble. A few stretching and arm-rotation exercises can save you months – if not years – of aggravation. One of the most depressing aspects of shoulder injuries is that they are cumulative – that is, a series of small, perhaps unnoticeable injuries will eventually add up and produce one major injury. Often the damage is done before you have time to take preventative steps (reducing the weight, changing the exercises, etc.). The bottom line is that you should take a couple of minutes and loosen up the shoulders with a few warmup exercises.

John Terilli

TRAINING

"If you can't spur growth in your delts, you should first check to see that you aren't overtraining in the muscle group. Since your delts do much of the work in many chest and back exercises, it is rather easy to overwork them. I seldom do more than 12 sets of delt-training. When I did 20 to 25 sets I got no results. With half that amount of work I now receive many times the gains."

– John Terilli
IFBB Pro Bodybuilder

Shoulder exercises can be divided into two types – basic compound movements that simultaneously work more than one region of the shoulders, and isolation exercises that primarily hit one muscle at a time. Intermediate and advanced bodybuilders should perform at least one of each in their workouts.

One of the more popular routines for training shoulders is Robert Kennedy's pre-exhaust system. Start with a set of dumbell laterals to isolate and fatigue the delts, and then follow with a compound movement like military presses. Even though the delts are tired, the muscles of the arms and upper chest can push the delts past the failure point.

The primary exercises for working the traps are variations of shrugs and upright rows. Shrugs can be done using a barbell, dumbells or a machine. Upright rows are one of the those exercises where the grip determines which muscles will be worked. When performed with a wide grip, upright rows primarily work the side deltoids. (Vince Gironda swears by this movement.) When performed with a narrow grip, the trapezius muscles are strongly affected. In fact many bodybuilders do upright rows solely as a trap exercise.

Although virtually every top pro bodybuilder has outstanding shoulder development, any number have become famous for sporting huge, ripped delts. Among the greats who have developed outstanding shoulders are Arnold Schwarzenegger, Larry Scott, Scott Wilson, Mike Christian, Ron Love, Kevin Levrone, Paul Dillett and Mike Matarazzo. The last two have been the subject of debate in recent years as to who is wider. Certainly Dillett and Matarazzo possess two of the largest pairs of shoulders in bodybuilding history. Both have their fans and advocates, and no doubt the debate will rage for years. In the comparison frenzy, however, we must not forget the biggest shoulders of all – those of the Cuban Myth, Sergio Oliva.

DELTOIDS:

Compound Exercises
1. Behind-the-neck barbell presses
2. Front barbell presses
3. Machine presses
4. Dumbell presses

Isolation Exercises
1. Front dumbell raises
2. Lateral raises
3. Bent-over lateral raises
4. Upright rows
5. Cable raises

Traps
1. Barbell shrugs
2. Dumbell shrugs
3. Machine shrugs
4. Deadlifts
5. Upright rows

THE CHAMPS' ROUTINES

LAURA CREAVALLE – *"There was a time when I never really enjoyed working shoulders because they used to be a problem area. It has only been in the last two years that I have learned to work them more intelligently, and, as the photos will show, my deltoids are now round, capped and full. This development accentuates my V-taper and gives me the symmetry I need to win."*

Since the fall of 1994 Laura Creavalle has firmly established herself as one of the top female bodybuilders in the world. At the 1994 Ms. Olympia she pushed the ultimate winner, Lenda Murray, to the limit. In fact, if the audience response is any indication, Laura was the winner. She followed this sensational performance by winning the 1995 Ms. International competition, and many feel that she is destined to take the coveted Ms. Olympia title one day.

Few female bodybuilders possess Laura's combination of ripped muscle and femininity. Although once a weakness, her shoulders are now among her best bodyparts. Through trial and error she found that her delts responded best to sets of 10 to 12 reps. She is also a great believer in variety when it comes to training shoulders, and to keep her muscles "off guard," she routinely varies the exercises, sets, and repetitions.

Most of her shoulder-training depends on basic exercises.

"I do not do lots of cable work or isolation movements. I much prefer to stay with basic movements. The greatest deltoids, on legends like Arnold and Sergio, were built using basic exercises."

Laura begins her shoulder workout with that old standby – barbell presses. She alternates behind-the-neck presses with front presses. She does not lock out, preferring instead to keep tension on the delts throughout the exercise's middle range of motion. This

Laura Creavalle

is a good practice as the bottom third of the movement is primarily traps, and the top third is mainly triceps. (Of course, this diversity is what makes the shoulder press such a great all-around mass-builder, and beginners should do the exercise through the full range of movement. As an experienced bodybuilder, Laura has modified the exercise to suit her specific needs.)

Her next exercise is the side lateral raise. A typical workout will include 3 or 4 sets of 10 to 12 reps. Again she limits her range of movement, and never raises the dumbells above parallel as doing so switches the stress from the delts to the traps. Unlike many bodybuilders who cheat slightly on the exercise, she does side laterals in the strictest of style, and this means no swinging or jerking the weights up.

Not being one to neglect her rear delts, Laura finishes her shoulder routine with bent-over lateral raises. Even though there are numerous machines that work the rear delts, she prefers to use dumbells for 3 or 4 sets of 10 to 12 reps.

Laura usually concludes her shoulder workout at this point, but for variety she sometimes includes upright rows to finish off her delts. To vary the angle, she alternates stance and bar position during the exercise. She does a few sets fully erect, and leans slightly forward on others.

In the age of 20- to 30-set shoulder workouts Laura is an exception in that she never does more than 12 sets total for her shoulders.

Laura Creavalle's Shoulder Routine:
1. Front (rear) shoulder presses – *3-4 sets of 8-10 reps*
2. Side lateral raises – *3-4 sets of 8-10 reps*
3. Bent-over lateral raises – *3-4 sets of 8-10 reps*
4. Upright rows* – *3-4 sets of 8-10 reps*
Occasionally

STEVE BRISBOIS – When you're "five foot something" and outweighed by a hundred pounds, you need characteristics that will make you stand out for the judges. Canadian Steve Brisbois has taken this philosophy to heart. Not having the height or mass of such giants as Haney, Christian and Yates, Steve had to rely on quality and proportion.

At the center of his outstandingly balanced physique are fully developed shoulders. All three delt heads are proportionally developed, giving his physique that wide and powerful look.

In 1991 Steve suffered a shoulder injury that necessitated a revamping of his shoulder training. He had to give up most barbell exercises and rely solely on dumbells and cables. Besides switching exercises, he had to change his attitude towards workout poundages and reps. Lower reps and heavy poundages were placing too much pressure on his injured shoulder, so

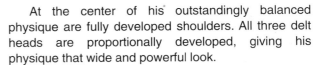
Dumbell shoulder presses

Start   *Finish*

he cut back the weight and compensated by doing more reps. He found that his delts responded best to rep ranges between 10 and 20.

Don't make the mistake of believing that his shoulder workouts were less intense. Using lighter weight forced him to do his reps with increased concentration. He raises and lowers the dumbells (or cables) in slow and immaculate style with no bouncing or swinging.

"Many bodybuilders try to go too heavy when they train delts. The delts are actually a small muscle and don't require tons of weight to grow, but they do require high-intensity work and strict form to keep the leverage on the shoulders. I use a weight heavy enough to tax the muscle but light enough to control and to allow for higher reps. If you use medium-heavy weights, strict form and deep concentration, really forcing the delts to do all the work as you lift the weight, your delts will grow."

Steve divides his shoulder training into sections. He works front and side delts after chest, and hits his rear delts after his back-training.

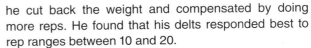
Steve Brisbois

Jackie Paisley

too wide, he does 6 or 7 sets of 12 to 20 reps of this important exercise.

Although Steve likes to split his shoulder training, from time to time he follows a one-bodypart-a-day schedule. When he's on such a program, he does all his shoulder exercises during one workout.

Steve Brisbois's Shoulder Routine:

1. Dumbell presses – *3-4 sets of 10-15 reps*
2. Side lateral raises – *6-7 sets of 12-20 reps*
3. Front dumbell raises – *4-5 sets of 10-15 reps*
4. Cable upright rows – *4-5 sets of 10-15 reps*
5. Bent-over lateral raises – *6-7 sets of 12-15 reps*

JACKIE PAISLEY – One of the most popular lecturers on the pro bodybuilding scene is 1989 Ms. International winner Jackie Paisley. In fact she frequently groups her seminars together to form a personal trainer's certificate course offered through Gold's Gym.

One of Jackie's best bodyparts is her shoulders. She uses three different routines to keep them that way.

"Once I work them by themselves, another time I group them with back, and the next time I group them with arms. I try to isolate my deltoids as much as possible. I don't use my back at all, and I don't even wear a belt any more, except for squats."

With her constant traveling, she had to discover new ways to stimulate the muscles with different equipment. She pays more attention to form than weight, and adds:

"Heavy or light don't have much meaning to me. I just slap on some weight and go to work."

Another point to make is that Jackie emphasizes different exercises in each of her three shoulder workouts. One day she may start with heavy barbell pressing movements, and the next she may be doing dumbell exercises. Then there are days when machines and supersets play a big role in her training. It all depends on how she feels.

Another area of variation is the number of sets and reps she does.

"The total number of sets I do depends on how I feel. I cut way back any time I feel the need to. I don't really change the structure of my workouts during pre- or postseason. I just adjust the total volume of work I do. I don't have a set pattern of reps that I follow for specific exercises either. I vary that all the time."

Jackie trains her whole body over a three- or four-day period, depending on how she groups her bodyparts and what her travel schedule is. She usually takes a day off between training cycles, but that may vary too. The following is a sample routine that she uses to develop her contest-winning delts. She varies her program from workout to workout.

For his front delts he does 3 or 4 sets of front dumbell raises. To really hit the area, he does his front raises while sitting on an incline chair. He lifts the dumbells to eye level, pauses, and then slowly lowers them.

For rear delts, he likes to follow his back-training with 6 or 7 sets of bent-over laterals. Although he keeps the reps high, he does every rep in a smooth, controlled manner.

For his side delts he does 4 or 5 sets of 10 to 15 reps of machine or dumbell presses. As he found locking out aggravates his shoulder injury, he reverses the exercise about two inches short of a lock.

Steve's second side-delt exercise is the cable upright row. He prefers the cable for three reasons: it keeps the tension on the muscle, the angle of pull is not limited to one plane as with a barbell, and most important, it places less strain on his injured shoulder. He does 4 or 5 sets (10 to 15 reps) of upright rows.

The mainstay of Steve's side-delt training is the dumbell lateral raise. Since he feels you can never be

Jackie Paisley's Shoulder Routine:

1. Rear-delt machine – *4 sets of 10-12 reps*
2. Lateral raises – *4 sets of 10-12 reps*
3. Rear cable laterals/Arnold presses –
   4 supersets of 10-12 reps
4. Side laterals/upright rows –
   4 supersets of 10-12 reps
5. Dumbell presses – *2 sets of 10-12 reps*

DORIAN YATES – He may not have the aesthetic lines of a Lee Haney or Shawn Ray, but England's Dorian Yates takes a backseat to no one when it comes to rock-hard, freaky muscle. Dorian is probably the thickest competitor on the scene today. Certainly he has few equals in pure muscle density.

Perhaps his greatest asset is his ability to improve from year to year. Most top pros reach a certain level and then plateau, but not Dorian. A comparison of pictures taken in 1992 and 1997 shows the five-time Mr. Olympia gained a considerable amount of rock-solid muscle each year. The guy keeps on getting bigger and bigger – and it's good-quality beef too, none of this soft adipose tissue that some competitors display. The mind boggles to think what the guy will look like in three to five years!

Unlike most pros, Dorian works out just once a day, but what a workout it is! Heavily influenced by the writings of Mike Mentzer, he follows a high-intensity format in his workouts, basically using as much weight as possible for 8 to 10 reps per set. Although Mentzer advocated 1 or 2 sets per bodypart, Dorian finds that he needs 6 sets to fully fatigue his muscles. This total usually breaks down to 2 sets each of three different exercises.

Over the years, he has found that he actually needs to spend less time in the gym to achieve the same results.

"My training has changed slightly from last year. I'm now training my whole body once every seven days compared to once every five days. I feel that, as I'm getting bigger and stronger, I need more rest and recuperation."

Picking a best Yates bodypart is no easy task. While his back probably receives the most votes, his delts are not far behind. All three heads are massive, clearly separated and shredded.

He usually begins shoulder-training with seated dumbell presses. He finds this exercise great for his side and front deltoid heads. He does 1 or 2 warmup sets, followed by 2 high-intensity sets to failure, using the maximum weight he can handle for the desired number of reps. He lets instinct determine the amount of weight used. If the first set feels light, he moves up in poundage on the second set, but if it feels heavy, he uses the same weight or drops it slightly.

To isolate the medial (side) delt, he does side lateral raises. Because his delts are sufficiently warmed up by this point, he jumps right into his 2 workout sets. He does 2 sets to failure, again using as much weight as he can handle for 8 or 10 reps. He then drops the weight and does a second set of 10 to failure. Another weight drop brings about a third set of 10 reps. Dorian does 2 of these triple-drop sets, going to failure on each set.

For his third and final delt exercise, he does 2 triple-drop sets of bent-over flyes. He keeps his reps in the 8 to 10 range.

To finish his shoulders, Dorian throws in 2 sets of shrugs on the Universal bench-press machine. After a warmup of 10 reps he does 2 of his patented high-intensity sets to failure.

Although he does "only" 6 sets total for his delts, keep in mind that 4 of the sets are drop sets. So in fact he is really doing 14 sets (3 x 2 x 2 + 2).

Dorian Yates

Kevin Levrone

Those bodybuilders who are experiencing difficulty in developing their shoulders may be able to benefit from Dorian's philosophy. Instead of increasing the volume of your training (i.e. adding sets), try upping the intensity. Remember, what counts is not how long you're in the gym, but what you're doing when you're in there!

Dorian Yates's Shoulder Routine:
1. Seated dumbell presses – *2 sets of 8-10 reps*
2. Side laterals – *2 triple-drop sets of 8-10 reps per set*
3. Bent-over laterals –
   2 triple-drop sets of *8-10 reps per set*
4. Machine shrugs – *2 sets of 8-10 reps*

Dorian does a warmup set of 10 reps before starting each exercise.

KEVIN LEVRONE – Mention great genetics, and the names Arnold, Sergio, Haney and Yates come to mind. In recent years, however, a new force has appeared on the bodybuilding scene, and already he is being compared with the greats of the past. His name is Kevin Levrone, and most bodybuilders would love to be blessed with his genetic potential.

Kevin took the pro bodybuilding scene by storm in 1992 by winning the highly touted Night of Champions contest in New York City. Superstardom seemed assured when tragedy struck. He severely tore one of his pectoral muscles while doing heavy bench presses. His promising career seemed to be over before it even started. Not wanting to disappoint his legions of fans (or himself), he sought immediate medical attention (there's a lesson to be learned here) and much to the chagrin of his bodybuilding rivals, regained his outstanding competitive form. He hit the 1994 pro circuit with a vengeance, and won both the Arnold Classic and San Jose Invitational. The year ended with a third-place finish at the Mr. Olympia and a second at the German Grand Prix. Kevin Levrone was back!

What makes the Levrone physique so outstanding is that it's the complete package. Every muscle is full, striated, and in balance with the rest of the body. Anchoring his superb frame are two cannon-ball sized delts that seem to stretch his shoulders to a yard wide.

Kevin follows a three-on/one-off routine, hitting chest, shoulders and triceps on day one. Although he likes to spice up his workouts with variety, he utilizes four exercises as the mainstay of his shoulder program.

He relies on dumbell presses for shoulder mass, doing 4 or 5 good-quality sets of 10 to 12 reps. The dumbells typically range from 100 to 150 pounds. Using such poundages means that he has to rely on a spotter to get the dumbells into starting position. Whenever possible, he braces his back against a vertical support, which keeps excessive pressure off his lower spine.

Next he does front raises. On a typical day he does 4 sets of 12 reps, using 50-pound dumbells. Like Steve Brisbois, Kevin likes to pause when the dumbell is level with his eyes.

He hits his side delts with 4 sets of bent-over lateral raises. He uses a cable rather than a dumbell for this exercise, and prefers doing the movement one arm at a time. He grasps the cable on one side of his body and pulls it across and up to the other side.

To finish his delts, Kevin does 4 sets of side lateral raises, with cables once again taking precedence over dumbells. He does the exercise one arm at a time while standing erect.

The simplicity of this program is surprising. It contains no exotic exercises, just time-tried and proven basics. While some may dismiss Kevin's success as being all genetics, thousands of hours of training were required to bring him to this level. He also pays meticulous attention to his diet. Genetics are an asset only if you train hard, and Kevin does this with single-minded intensity.

Kevin Levrone's Shoulder Routine:
1. Dumbell presses – *4 sets of 12 reps*
2. Front raises – *4 sets of 12 reps*
3. Bent-over laterals (cable) – *4 sets of 12 reps*
4. Side laterals (cable) – *4 sets of 12 reps*

NIMROD KING

One of the most massively developed men to emerge from the 1980s bodybuilding scene was 1989 US pro champion Nimrod King. With his huge chest and back, Nimrod realized that to keep his delts in proportion, he would need to spend many hours training them.

After reading his chest and back routines, you would have noticed that he prefers moderate to high reps. He is always careful to avoid injuries and for this reason he starts his shoulder-training with 3 sets of high-rep machine presses.

"I use the machine to warm up because I find the barbell front press hard on my joints. I try to stay away from exercises that strain my joints so I avoid injuries that might set me back for weeks or even months."

Nimrod's first "heavy" exercise is the barbell press behind the neck. He does 3 sets of 15 to 20 reps with each rep lowered all the way down. His objective on this exercise is to get as much blood into the area as possible, and the only way to do this is by utilizing high reps.

For his front and side delts he does 3 sets of upright rows.

"I prefer to burn out on the upright rowing. I do 15 reps, and after 10 reps it's really hurting! Those 5 extra reps bring out the muscularity."

Nimrod's fourth exercise is the seated dumbell lateral raise. He varies the weight throughout the year. During the off-season he averages about double the weight of his precontest training. Once again, proper form is the rule of the game on this exercise. He keeps his back straight, and lifts the dumbells using only his side delts. At the top of the movement he tries to stop

CHAPTER TWENTY-THREE - SHOULDERS

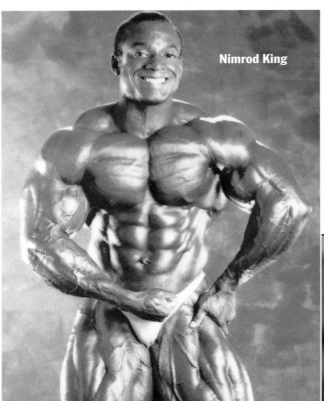

Nimrod King

LEE PRIEST – Standing only 5'4", Australia's Lee Priest packs an incredibly striated 190 pounds on his frame. Showing some of the gusto that made compatriot Paul "Crocodile Dundee" Hogan a hit back in the mid-'80s, he routinely brings ulcers to guys outweighing him by 50 pounds or more. Pound for pound he is one of the largest bodybuilders currently on the pro tour.

To say Lee was blessed with favorable bodybuilding genetics would be an understatement. Besides winning three bodybuilding contests at 13 years of age, he was competing at the Mr. Universe when he was just 17! Lee adds that he probably has his mother to thank for such great genetics.

Lee Priest

the dumbells for a split second before lowering them slowly to take advantage of negative resistance.

To hit the famous King traps, Nimrod does 4 sets of dumbell shrugs. As his traps get substantial stimulation from back training, he feels the shrugs are sufficient and no additional direct trap exercises are required.

He knows that only large, fully developed rear delts will take him to the winners' circle, so he concludes his shoulder-training with 4 sets of rear laterals on a 45-degree incline bench. To get the most from the exercise, he raises the dumbells to ear level.

Nimrod does no direct front-delt exercises. He feels he receives all the front-delt stimulation he needs from chest training.

Nimrod King's Shoulder Routine:
1. Front machine presses –
   3 sets of 15-20 reps
2. Presses behind the neck –
   3 sets of 15-20 reps
3. Upright rows – *3 sets of 15 reps*
4. Seated dumbell lateral raises –
   4 sets of 10-15 reps
5. Dumbell shrugs – *4 sets of 10-15 reps*
6. Rear laterals (45-degree bench) –
   4 sets of 15 reps

Lee Priest performs presses behind the neck.

Start

Finish

"I think I got my genetics from my mother. She took up bodybuilding at age 38 and won the state title after only eight months of training. She still trains and competes and does really well."

His training can be summed up in simple terms – heavy and basic. Not one for fanciness, he prefers straight basic sets over trisets and drop sets. He follows the popular four-days-on/one-day-off training schedule and hits delts on day three. Generally he picks four exercises and does 5 sets of each for a total of 20 sets.

Most delt workouts begin with a heavy barbell exercise like front or behind-the-neck presses. Lee does 2 light warmup sets and then bangs out 5 good-quality sets, keeping the reps in the 6 to 8 range. He does each rep in a slow deliberate manner, making sure to move the weight through the full range of motion.

His second exercise is usually dumbell side laterals. Pyramiding the weight up on the first 2 sets, he once again does 5 sets of 6 to 8 reps. Although he emphasizes strictness, he uses a slight cheat to complete the final few reps when necessary.

Lee's third exercise is dumbell bent-over laterals. He blasts his rear delts with five sets. As with the side laterals, he uses about 85 to 90 percent strict style on this exercise.

To finish his shoulders, he does 5 sets of shrugs or upright rows, depending on how he feels. Given the size of his traps, he must be feeling pretty good!

To catch his muscles "off guard," Lee occasionally does 5 trisets for his shoulders. Alternatively he may change the order of his exercises while still doing straight sets.

Lee Priest's Shoulder Routine:
1. Barbell shoulder presses – *5 sets of 6-8 reps*
2. Dumbell side laterals – *5 sets of 6-8 reps*
3. Bent-over laterals – *5 sets of 6-8 reps*
4. Barbell shrugs or upright rows – *5 sets of 6-8 reps*

SHAWN RAY – *"Normally I try to avoid machines at all costs unless I'm doing leg extensions or some back exercise where I have to use a machine. But I'm a barbell, dumbell kinda guy. Machines don't really do anything for me. The range of motion is too restricted and they're just not as heavy as free weights. So I don't advocate machines at all, particularly when working shoulders."*

Although routinely outweighed by his fellow competitors, sometimes by as much as 50 pounds or more, Shawn Ray has developed what many consider to be the most perfectly balanced physique currently on the pro scene. His second-place finish at the 1994 Olympia only seemed to confirm these opinions.

Shawn Ray

Shawn's next exercise is behind-the-neck barbell presses. In a typical workout he does 4 sets, using a grip slightly wider than his shoulders. As his triceps fatigue before his delts, he has a spotter help him with the last few reps. The next day he trains shoulders, he will substitute dumbell presses in place of the barbell.

"I like to keep variety in my workouts so that I'm always hitting the muscles from a different angle."

To hit his rear delts, Shawn does 4 or 5 sets of bent-over laterals. On this exercise he sits on the edge of a bench and bends over as far as he can, trying to touch his head and chest to his knees. He lifts the dumbells out to the sides as far as possible. If he feels he's cheating he drops the weight to regain proper form.

Dumbell shrugs
Start

Finish

Unlike many bodybuilders, he doesn't have a fixed routine for training shoulders. On any given day he may change everything from sets and reps to exercises and order. The only constant is his selection of four exercises to work his delts. He typically does 4 or 5 sets of 12 to 15 reps, with the first set serving as a warmup.

As he has developed most of the overall shoulder mass he needs, Shawn focuses his attention on bringing out the fine detail necessary for bodybuilding competition. His first shoulder exercise is often the dumbell lateral raise.

"While I'm doing side laterals I visualize the striations on the side of my deltoids when I'm onstage hitting a side chest shot, or my profile as I'm standing sideways onstage in the symmetry round. I try to see in my mind the caps on the side of the deltoids going into the triceps."

His style on side laterals is very strict. With a slight bend in his elbows, he raises the dumbells using only the power of his side delts. He stops the dumbells at shoulder level, keeping his elbows higher than the dumbells, and then lowers.

"You have to remember, it's not the poundage that dictates growth – it's the form and consequent burn."

He finishes his shoulder workout with 4 or 5 sets of either upright rows or dumbell shrugs. During each rep Shawn visualizes hitting a most-muscular pose with his traps bulging right off his delts! Whether he's doing shrugs or uprights, he keeps his body erect and squeezes his traps at the top of the exercise.

Shawn doesn't change his shoulder training much close to a contest. Any adjustments he makes are intended to burn more calories. His rep range remains the same, but he adds a couple of drop sets to really blast his delts.

Shawn Ray's Shoulder Routine:
1. Side lateral raises – *4 sets of 12-15 reps*
2. Behind-the-neck presses – *4 sets of 12-15 reps*
3. Bent-over laterals – *4 sets of 12-15 reps*
4. Shrugs (uprights) – *4 sets of 12-15 reps*
Shawn frequently changes exercises, sets, and reps.

AARON BAKER – The phrase "pound for pound" gets tossed around pretty loosely these days. It was first used to describe 1950s boxing sensation Sugar Ray Robinson. Most in the boxing game considered Robinson the best boxer, pound for pound, who ever lived. What this means is that only his bodyweight prevented Robinson from winning the heavyweight title. (He fought as a middleweight.) Many boxing aficionados believe that if Robinson's weight had been scaled up proportionately, he could have easily beaten the best heavyweights of the day. (Of course Marciano fans would probably disagree!)

Throughout bodybuilding history, numerous bodybuilders have embodied the phrase "pound for pound," and Aaron Baker is one such competitor. Weighing around 240 in contest shape, Aaron is one of the thickest bodybuilders on the pro circuit. From calves to traps he has it all. No weaknesses. Yet for all the accolades, he has yet to walk away with any of the IFBB's major titles. Many experts (including former *MuscleMag* editor Greg Zulak) consider Baker to be the world's most underrated bodybuilder. In fact, his name (along with Flex Wheeler's) has been put forward as one of the few bodybuilders capable of displacing Dorian Yates in the sport's number one spot.

Aaron Baker

Aaron's delt-training is reminiscent of Nimrod King's with its emphasis on moderate to high reps. He keeps his reps in the 12 to 15 range, but frequently goes up to 25 when the desire is there.

He starts his shoulder training with a couple of light sets of dumbell presses or lateral raises. Then, depending on his mood, he does straight sets of presses and laterals, or supersets the two together.

Side lateral raises

Start

Midpoint

Finish

If he's doing the superset routine, he starts with laterals, using 60- to 70-pound dumbells. He aims for 15 to 20 reps on the laterals, and then does a set of dumbell presses, using 110- to 125-pound dumbells. He does only 2 such supersets, but feels that the important factor is not the number of sets, but what you get out of each one.

"I do fewer sets than most guys do, but I rely on my ability to get more out of what I'm doing at this level – to get the most out of every rep and set. I have to compensate for a lack of volume with extra intensity."

CHAPTER TWENTY-THREE - SHOULDERS

For variety Aaron sometimes substitutes machine side laterals in place of the dumbells. To hit his rear delts, he uses bent-over lateral raises. Because his shoulders are already warmed up from the previous presses and side laterals, he doesn't do light warmup sets of rear laterals. Instead he jumps right to the 70-pound dumbells and blasts out 2 sets.

Usually, that's all he does for shoulders. Every now and then he will throw in a set or two of upright rows. He feels his traps are thick enough, so he does high reps (15 to 20) on the uprights, using moderate weight of 135 to 140 pounds.

Aaron's entire shoulder routine consists of 8 sets, and he is puzzled when he sees intermediates routinely doing 15 to 20 sets for their shoulders. He suggests that if your delts are not responding to 20 sets, you should try cutting your workout in half. In most cases the problem is not one of doing too little, but of doing too much!

Aaron Baker's Shoulder Routine:

1. Light side laterals or presses –
   2 sets of 15 to 20 reps
2. Side laterals – *2 sets of 15 to 20 reps*
3. Dumbell presses – *2 sets of 15 to 20 reps*
4. Bent-over lateral raises – *2 sets of 15 to 20 reps*
5. Upright rows* – *2 sets of 15 to 20 reps*

Done occasionally

TONYA KNIGHT – Former *MuscleMag* columnist Tonya Knight attributes much of her success to receiving some great advice early in her career.

"During one of my first photo shoots I was told that I would someday be a champion if I brought my shoulders up. So from then on, every time I went into the gym to train shoulders, I did behind-the-neck presses to build mass. I'd try to see exactly how strong I could get on them. I kept myself motivated by trying to lift heavier weights each time. I knew that if I was getting stronger, my shoulders had to be growing."

Realizing that bodybuilding judges go for the complete look, Tonya took the advice to heart and made outstanding gains. She feels the exercise that made the most improvement to her shoulders was the behind-the-neck press.

Unlike many bodybuilders who do the exercise in a touch-and-go manner, she is careful to move the bar through the full range of movement. She lowers the bar until it touches the base of her neck, and then pushes it back up to an arms-locked-out position. She is very firm on the last point.

"I lock it out, but just for a slight second. I hate it when people hardly straighten their arms – they're just not getting much out of the exercise."

Tonya Knight demonstrates bent-over laterals.

Tonya lets instinct determine the number of reps. On some days it's 15 to 20, but on others she struggles to complete 6 to 8 with a heavy weight.

Her second exercise is the side lateral raise. Depending on how she feels, Tonya uses either dumbells or cables. Correct form for her is arms slightly bent, elbows held higher than the wrists, and a slight rotation of the hands at the top of the movement (to use the common analogy – as if you were pouring a pitcher of water). She alternates between doing the exercise standing or seated. She also alternates between heavy and loose, and light and strict. By loose she means doing 8 strict reps, and then using a slight cheat to grind out 4 or 5 additional reps. She never uses a weight that prevents her doing the first 6 to 8 reps in strict form.

For her rear delts Tonya does 4 sets of 12 reps of bent-over dumbell laterals. She does the exercise in the standing position, pausing at the top to squeeze and fully contract her rear delts.

She doesn't do any direct front-delt work, as she feels her front delts get adequate stimulation from her various chest exercises. Her traps, however, are another story.

"I think there's a point where women can have traps that are too big, but I don't have that problem at all. Of course, not having big traps has probably helped me on the modeling side of bodybuilding. If you ever look at good models, you'll notice that they have long, thin necks. Build your traps up too much, and you'll have no neck at all."

Tonya's trap work consists of either upright rows or shrugs. When doing shrugs she wears a pair of wrist straps. This way she can use the maximum amount of weight, and not worry about her forearms giving out. She keeps her arms straight and pauses at the top, thus ensuring that her traps, and not her biceps or shoulders, are doing most of the work. As with presses, she likes to alternate light with heavy days.

On upright rows she takes a narrow grip (slightly less than shoulder width), and pulls the bar to below her chin. At the top she squeezes her traps, and then rolls her shoulders forward as she lowers the bar. As with her other shoulder exercises, she does 4 sets of 12 to 15 reps.

Tonya Knight's Shoulder Routine:
1. Behind-the-neck presses – *4 sets of 6-20 reps*
2. Lateral raises – *4 sets of 12-15 reps*
3. Bent-over laterals – *4 sets of 12-15 reps*
4. Upright rows/shrugs – *4 sets of 12-15 reps*

VINCE TAYLOR – When he won the 1989 Night of Champions (NOC) contest, and placed third in that year's Mr. Olympia, newcomer Vince Taylor was suddenly thrust into the bodybuilding limelight. This attention caught Vince off guard, as the NOC contest was his pro debut! He shouldn't have been surprised,

Tonya Knight

for he displayed one of the most complete physiques ever to hit the posing platform.

In looking at his shoulder routine, we see he doesn't pay any attention to the accepted rules of overtraining. Most bodybuilders feel that anything over 20 sets is too much, but not Vince. He tried the 12-to 15-set route and ended up losing shoulder size. He found that to adequately train his delts he needs upwards of 35 to 40 sets! For most bodybuilders this volume of work would be grossly overtraining, but it brought Vince his greatest shoulder gains to date. Fellow competitors even came up to him after the 1989 NOC contest and complimented him on his marked shoulder improvement. Over the course of time he has also found that his delts respond best when he alternates one month of high reps with one of low reps.

Vinces high-rep routine starts with 10 minutes of light (maximum of 60 to 70 pounds) presses behind the neck. After this warmup he puts 130 to 140 pounds on the bar and bangs out 5 sets of 15 reps.

Vince Taylor

Next up are dumbell raises. He does 6 sets of side raises, 5 sets of rear raises, and 5 sets of front raises. He then repeats the three exercises using cables. Altogether he does an average of 30 sets of various types of raises.

Now for the real mind-blower: Vince is actually doing double sets on each set. He does a set for 12 to 15 reps, puts the weight down, pauses a few seconds, picks the weight up and does another 10 to 12 reps. Even though most people would call this 2 sets, Vince considers it 1 set. Therefore, when we say he does about 30 to 35 sets for his shoulders, in reality he is doing upwards of 70 sets!

During his heavy workouts he warms up with one-arm dumbell presses. Holding onto a machine for support, he does 5 sets each of front, side and rear raises. He uses only dumbells during his heavy phase, giving the cables a pass. He cheats slightly to get the dumbells moving, but not enough to sacrifice good form.

Vince Taylor's Shoulder Routine:
1. Behind-the-neck presses – *warm up for 10 minutes*
2. Behind-the-neck presses – *5 sets of 15 reps*
3. Front raises – *5 sets of 12-15 reps*
4. Side raises – *6 sets of 12-15 reps*
5. Rear raises – *5 sets of 12-15 reps*
Vince uses cables and dumbells during his high-rep month, but uses only dumbells during his heavy phase.

ARNOLD SCHWARZENEGGER – One of the principal reasons why Arnold dominated bodybuilding in the early to mid-'70s was the completeness of his physique. Even though a few bodybuilders had individual bodyparts as good as Arnold's, none had his overall degree of development. From that 57-inch plus chest and those 22-inch plus arms to his outstanding back and calves, the Schwarzenegger physique had few weaknesses.

Not wanting his upper body to be dominated by his massive chest, Arnold made a point of training his shoulders with great intensity. Typically he started his deltoid-training with some form of shoulder press. Although the number of sets and reps varied, he normally did 4 or 5 sets of 8 to 10 reps. He alternated front barbell presses with presses behind the neck. For variety he sometimes substituted dumbell presses, using both the standard (palms facing forward) form and a modification which down through the years has become known as the "Arnold press." In doing this movement, he would start with his palms facing upward, as if he had just finished a dumbell curl, and then press the dumbells up while rotating his thumbs inward. The result is a movement that's half lateral raise and half dumbell press. This exercise is great for hitting the front and side delts.

His next shoulder exercise was some version of the lateral raise. In a typical workout he included standing, lying and bent-over laterals. He also did a form of laterals that involved lying on an incline bench. The exercise was seldom seen until Arnold was observed including them in his workouts. After that everyone seemed to be doing lying lateral raises. The exercise is relatively simple to do. Lie on your side on an incline bench (the abdominal board is used most frequently) and raise a dumbell with the opposite hand. You'll find this style of lateral raise effective for putting a cap on the side delts.

To finish his delts, Arnold used different versions of cable laterals. For his traps he would choose from four basic exercises – shrugs, upright rows, cleans and power pulls.

Unlike the current philosophy of limiting sets to 15 to 20 per bodypart, Arnold frequently did 35 to 40 sets for his shoulders. In fact his shoulder training often involved 50 sets or more.

Arnold Schwarzenegger's Shoulder Routine:
1. Seated presses behind the neck – *4-5 sets of 8-10 reps*
2. Dumbell presses (Arnold's version) – *4-5 sets of 8-10 reps*
3. Side laterals – *4-5 sets of 8-10 reps*
4. Bent-over laterals – *4-5 sets of 8-10 reps*
5. Cable side laterals – *4-5 sets of 8-10 reps*
6. Upright rows – *4-5 sets of 8-10 reps*
7. Shoulder shrugs – *4-5 sets of 8-10 reps*

LEE HANEY – When he won his eighth consecutive Mr. Olympia title in 1991, Atlanta's Lee Haney accomplished what few thought possible – beating Arnold Schwarzenegger's record of seven wins. It wasn't that Lee didn't have the equipment. He was tall, had long muscle bellies, and possessed one of the greatest waist/chest differentials in bodybuilding history. But most observers believed that with the competitiveness of modern bodybuilding, no single athlete would dominate as Arnold did back in the '70s. Lee proved them all wrong, and now the saying is "No one will beat Haney's record of eight!"

His early inspiration was the Cuban Myth, Sergio Oliva. Since both has similar bone structures, copying Oliva's style made sense. As the years progressed, however, Lee began to realize that no two physiques are alike. True, copying Oliva's training made sense early on, but as he worked his way up the competitive ladder, he found his body telling him to make modifications.

It was around the time that he won the '82 Nationals that Lee first started seriously thinking about

Arnold Schwarzenegger

Lee Haney

from the old school. His main delt exercise was the shoulder press, and he alternated between barbell and machine versions.

Lee usually kept his reps between 8 and 10, but numbers depended on the day and mood he was in. He used a nonlock style on his pressing exercises, preferring to power through the set with a piston-like motion.

For his rear delts he favored the bent-over lateral raise. He used dumbells most of the year, but during his precontest phase, switched to cables. He found cables great for peak contraction and etching in that extra detail needed for the Olympia stage.

Rounding out his shoulder training were various forms of standing lateral raises. Although he favored presses, for variety he periodically blasted his front and side delts with lateral raises. He would do the first 6 to 10 reps in strict style, and then cheat slightly to grind out 2 or 3 additional reps.

The following is a sample shoulder routine used by Lee. Keep in mind that he frequently changed his program.

Lee Haney's Shoulder Routine:
1. Presses behind the neck –
   3-4 sets of 8-10 reps
2. Front machine presses –
   3-4 sets of 8-10 reps
3. Side lateral raises –
   3-4 sets of 8-10 reps
4. Bent-over lateral raises –
   3-4 sets of 8-10 reps

pursuing bodybuilding as a career. Until then his training had had one main theme – heavy! He did all exercises with the heaviest weight possible, paying little attention to form, technique or shape. Soon after he restructured his training, he began to totally dominate the sport.

One of the most important lessons Lee learned was that to keep the muscles growing you have to add variety to your training. The body soon accustoms itself to the same routine. You must consistently shock it with new exercises, poundages and training styles. Failure to do so usually leads to stagnation.

During his record run of eight Olympias Lee's lat spread was widely accepted as the greatest in existence. With his tiny waist leading up to those incredible lats, he literally hid the two competitors unfortunate enough to be standing next to him. Adding tremendously to his lat spread were two cannonball-sized delts.

Although he is one of the sport's most recent champs, his philosophy on shoulder-training is right

MIKE CHRISTIAN – Although Haney won a record eight Mr. Olympias, it wasn't all fun and games for Lee. One of his strongest opponents was Mike Christian, and in terms of shoulder development, many feel that big Mike had the advantage.

He admits that his delts always responded quickly to training. In fact prior to the 1988 Olympia, he rarely worked them in the off-season! His delts received all the stimulation they needed from chest- and back-training. He changed all this following the 1987 Mr. Olympia. He realized that if he was going to beat Lee Haney, he would have to hit every muscle group equally hard – no exceptions – and that included shoulders.

Besides adding regular delt-training in the off-season, Mike made another major change. He began to cycle his workouts. One workout would be reserved for heavy weight and low reps (around 8), and the next would be a lighter session using reps in the 10 to 12 range.

He usually began his shoulder-training with a good all-round delt-builder like barbell or machine presses. Although he occasionally did front presses, he preferred the behind-the-neck variety. Whereas the front presses are nearly all front and side delts, the behind-the-neck press brings the rear delts into play. Mike did each rep in a nonlock style. He paused at the top, but his arms never locked out completely.

His next exercise was often side lateral raises. Unlike most who do the exercise with two arms, Mike preferred to work one arm at a time. Holding an upright pole for support, he raised the dumbell slightly higher than his shoulders, and then slowly lowered it back to the starting position.

To stress his front delts, he used 4 sets of front dumbell raises. Again he did them one arm at a time. Occasionally he alternated arms.

For rear delts he did either bent-over dumbell laterals or the machine version. As a personal preference, he was partial to the machine. Beginning bodybuilders would do well to follow Mike's advice on this point. Towards the end of a workout, with fatigue setting in, there is a tendency to forget about proper form and do the last exercises haphazardly. Because most bodybuilders conclude their shoulder-training with rear delts, it's bent-over laterals that usually get abused. The problem is that the exercise puts you in a dangerous position, as any excessive jerking or swinging places great stress on the lower back. Therefore, Mike recommends using a rear-delt machine if one's available. The machine forces you to do the exercise in a strict and safe manner. The upright pad prevents any swinging or bouncing which can lead to lower-back problems.

Mike Christian's Shoulder Routine:

1. Behind-the-neck presses (barbell or Smith) – *4 sets of 8-12 reps*
2. Side lateral raises – *4 sets of 8-12 reps*
3. Front lateral raises – *4 sets of 8-12 reps*
4. Rear delts (machine or dumbell) – *4 sets of 8-12 reps*

Mike Christian

QUADS AND HAMSTRINGS

BUILDING PILLARS OF POWER

"When I train my legs, or any other muscle group, I move the weights with a specific purpose in mind. I want to feel the involvement of the muscle fibers in the muscles I'm working. Loading the leg-press machine with 1000 pounds and using total effort to move the weight, just to say I did it, isn't my approach at all." **– Lenda Murray, IFBB Pro Bodybuilder Six-time Ms. Olympia**

Lenda Murray

Just as a building is only as good as its foundation, so too is bodybuilding success largely dependent on leg development. Most sports require an abundance of leg power. Where would a boxer be without his legs? How long would a hockey player last if his legs were lacking in power? Bodybuilding is no different in that the legs must be in balance with the upper body; 50-inch chests teetering about on 23-inch legs just won't cut it with bodybuilding judges. And while it's true that bodybuilding contests are judged strictly on appearance, it's safe to say that you'll never develop size without increasing leg strength. The two go hand in hand.

Perhaps the best example to illustrate the importance of great leg development is the cover of Robert Kennedy's *Hardcore Bodybuilding*. Millions of bodybuilders have been inspired by that picture of Tom Platz's mind-blowing legs. From thigh to calf to hamstring Tom's legs are considered by most to be the best in bodybuilding history. Other bodybuilders with outstanding leg development include Dorian Yates, Nimrod King, Samir Bannout, Roy Callender, Paul DeMayo, Paul Dillett, Lee Priest, Tim Belknap and Mike Francois.

ANATOMY

Bodybuilders generally divide the legs into three main muscle groups: thighs (quadriceps), hamstrings (leg biceps) and calves (soleus and gastrocnemius). The main function of the thigh is to extend the lower leg at the knee joint. It is analogous to the triceps of the upper arm in that the thighs are the extensors of the legs. The hamstrings are the direct equivalent of the arm biceps, for they flex or curl the leg toward the body. Walking or running involves the contracting and relaxing of both muscles.

The primary muscles of the lower legs are the calves, those diamond-shaped (if they're not shaped that way now, they soon will be!) muscles located on the back of the legs below the knees. They allow you to stand up on your toes. Most gymnasts and ballerinas have great calves from years of such tiptoeing. Since most bodybuilders treat their calves as an entity all their own, and not just another leg muscle, we shall discuss calf-training later in the book.

TRAINING

"I attribute the outer sweep of my thighs to front squats. I find the exercise is one of the hardest and most effective in my training schedule. One of the reasons the movement is so difficult is that you can't fully expand your lungs to catch your breath. I usually do 4 x 8, in the off-season going as heavy as 315 pounds."
– John Hnatyschak, IFBB Pro Bodybuilder

Most bodybuilders start their leg workouts with the thighs, and for good reason. The thighs are the largest muscles in the legs and require the most energy to train. Granted, if your hamstrings are sadly lacking in size, it may be a good idea to train them first, but for the most part, start your leg-training with the quadriceps.

The best all-round leg exercise, and the one that will give you massive, powerful thighs, is the squat. Although the leg press is a good substitute, it's the squat that separates champions from the average bodybuilder. Doubtless every top bodybuilder has squatted sometime during his or her career. And while some no longer use the exercise (e.g. Lee Haney, Renel Janvier), all will readily admit that the fastest way to herculean thighs is by spending many hours at the squat rack.

Despite all that, there are a few good reasons why you might want to avoid squatting. For starters the exercise places tremendous stress on the lower back and knees. For most, these areas will keep pace if you gradually increase the weight over the years. A few, however, will begin to notice slight problems creeping in. Others will make the mistake of neglecting a proper warmup and jump right to their top poundages – the result a potentially career-ending injury. Finally, people new to the sport of bodybuilding often have nagging knee and back injuries from playing other sports. If you fall into any of these categories, we strongly suggest you either skip squats or drastically reduce the weight you use on them.

A second reason for de-emphasizing squats lies with proportions. In some cases, squats place most of the stress on the glutes, and not the thighs. (Vince Gironda uses this argument for avoiding squats altogether.) The result is an overly developed gluteus region. Of course you need some glute development to keep the area in proportion with your thighs. Also, narrowing the stance may be all that's necessary to shift most of the stress from the glutes back to your thighs.

If you don't have pre-existing injuries, and your goal is developing your thighs to the maximum, we strongly suggest making squats a regular part of your leg-training. At the very least, finish your leg routine with a few sets of light squats. We can't overstress the importance of regular squatting, especially at the beginning and intermediate levels.

The other primary thigh-building exercise is the leg

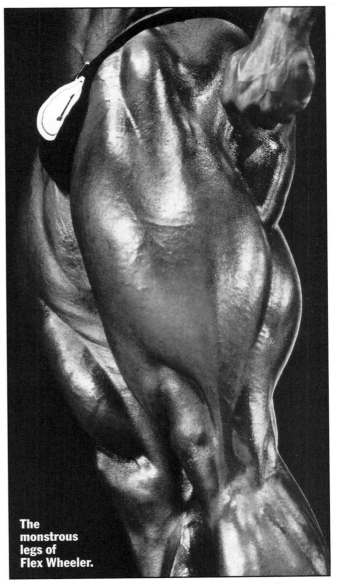

The monstrous legs of Flex Wheeler.

press, which, if done properly, gives much the same degree of development as squats. The main advantage of leg presses over squats is that they eliminate lower-back strain. They also limit the amount of glute involvement. For these reasons leg presses are a great substitute for those with lower-back injuries or those wishing to eliminate gluteal development.

Leg presses have one other benefit and that's the reduction in knee stress. As many people find squatting hurts their knees, the leg press allows the user to employ a wide range of foot positions, thus eliminating most knee strain.

Without repeating our description of the exercise from the training chapters, we must stress an important piece of advice. Within a few months you'll be capable of pressing hundreds of pounds on this exercise. Although most books (including this one) emphasize using a full range of motion on all your exercises, the leg press is one where you might want to stop short of locking the legs out.

Given the amount of weight used, and the fact that most trainers "slam" the legs into the locked position, there is a risk of hyperextending the legs at the knee joint. In fact most physical therapists recommend doing leg presses in three-quarter style – in other words, stopping the exercise before the legs lock out.

If you decide to do leg presses in the locking-out style, please do so with care. You can still do forced reps by pressing the knees. Just don't forcibly snap the legs out straight.

If squats and leg presses are the best mass-builders, leg extensions and hack squats are by far the best isolation exercises. While they contribute to thigh mass, their primary benefit is to give the thighs the shape, cuts and striations needed to win contests. (Of course, if you have a layer of fat over your muscles, those prize-winning striations and cuts won't be visible.) Virtually all bodybuilders include at least one mass and one isolation exercise in their leg-training.

The two main exercises for working the hamstrings are the lying leg curl and the stiff-leg deadlift. The hamstrings are the one muscle group where you are limited by the number of available exercises. There are dozens (and in some cases hundreds) of exercises for the other major muscles, but you have three good hamstring exercises, and that's it.

A WORD OF ADVICE BEFORE YOU GET STARTED
Because of the nature of leg-training (heavy weight, lower back and knee stress), we stress the importance of a proper warmup. Walking in cold off the street and then jumping to your maximum weight is asking for trouble. One set of 135 pounds on the squat is not a warmup. It's an injury waiting to happen. If you're working up to 300 on the squat, start with 3 or 4 good warmup sets. The knees and lower back were not designed to have 300 pounds suddenly dropped on them. Both areas must be thoroughly prepared. It's not only the squat and leg press that require a few warm up sets either. You should warmup on all your leg exercises – leg extensions, leg curls, hacks, etc. A few extra minutes is not much time to invest if it provides a lifetime of injury-free leg-training.

"Some bodybuilders complain of knee problems when doing heavy leg presses. For me it has been just the opposite. Leg presses have actually eliminated what chronic joint problems I had, and I can now execute the exercise without concern for injury." – *Vince Taylor*
IFBB Pro Bodybuilder
1995 Masters Olympia Champion

Thigh Exercises:
1. Squats
2. Leg presses
3. Hack-machine squats
4. Leg extensions
5. Front squats
6. Sissy squats

Vince Taylor

Hamstring Exercises:
1. Lying leg curls
2. Standing leg curls
3. Stiff-leg deadlifts

THE CHAMPS' ROUTINES

"Legs are the basis of your upper-body strength. They have to support you during all standing exercises. They are the source of your drive and speed in all sports. They are a large muscle group that requires a lot of oxygen to train." – *Paul "Quadzilla" DeMayo*
IFBB Pro Bodybuilder
USA National champion

JOE SPINELLO – Although he has competed in fewer than a dozen major contests, Joe Spinello is regarded by many to be one of the best bodybuilders ever to come out of Canada. Most feel it's only a matter of time until his name is placed right up there with such other notable Canadians as Paul Dillett, Nimrod King and Steve Brisbois.

One of Joe's best bodyparts is his tree trunk-sized legs. No matter what pose he hits, you can't help fixing your eyes on those beautiful sweeping thighs. Here's how he built them.

Joe starts his leg-training with extensions. A couple of warmup sets are followed with 4 heavy sets of 10 to 15 reps. To stress different sections of his thighs, he alternates his foot positions. With his toes pointing inward, the outer thighs receive most of the benefit. Point them out and the reverse happens – the inner thighs are hit. He prefers a slow exercise tempo.

"I do my reps medium slow. I'm not a person who likes fast reps. I work to feel both negative and positive parts of the movement."

After leg extensions Joe moves on to leg presses. Like most bodybuilders, he once made squats the focal point of his thigh-training, but he soon realized that his upper body was lagging behind. To address this problem, he cut back on squats and did more extensions and curls until his upper body caught up. Since then he has used leg presses as his main thigh-builder.

Joe Spinello performs lying leg curls.

"Squats were at one time my baby, but when you attain a certain amount of mass, you want to be able to work that mass at different angles. I can do this better with leg presses. I usually do 4 or 5 sets of 10 to 15 reps."

Joe does leg presses through a full range of motion because he feels partials are not productive for building mass. As with leg extensions he varies the angle of attack. On some sets he lowers the weight to his chest, using a narrow stance, whereas at other times he lowers it to the sides using a wide, duck-like stance. He finishes his thigh workout with hack squats – using the same set and rep range as in previous exercises.

To work his hamstrings, Joe usually starts with lying leg curls. Because leg curls are one of the few exercises that directly work the hamstrings, he likes to vary his foot position. In a typical workout he does 6 sets – 2 with the feet pointing in, 2 pointing out, and 2 pointing to the center.

Joe Spinello

Start

Finish FLEX

CHAPTER TWENTY-FOUR – QUADS AND HAMSTRINGS

After lying leg curls he moves on to standing leg curls. Customarily he does 4 sets of 10 to 15 reps. On some days he substitutes stiff-leg deadlifts in place of the standing leg curls. During the off-season he does only two exercises for his hamstrings, but close to a contest he trisets the three movements together.

Joe Spinello's Leg Routine:

1. Leg extensions – *4 sets of 10-15 reps*
2. Leg presses – *4 sets of 10-15 reps*
3. Hack squats – *4 sets of 10-15 reps*
4. Lying leg curls – *6 sets of 10-15 reps*
5. Standing leg curls – *4 sets of 10-15 reps*
6. Stiff-leg deadlifts* – *4 sets of 10-15 reps*

Substitute for standing leg curls

MIKE MENTZER – Few men have had the impact on bodybuilding as "Mr. Heavy Duty," Mike Mentzer. Besides winning the Mr. America and Mr. Universe titles, he went on to become one of the sport's most respected writers. In fact Mike's writing is probably his greatest contribution to bodybuilding, even more than the titles he won.

In the late '70s and early '80s he gained fame as the promoter of the heavy-duty style of training. Whereas most bodybuilders traditionally added sets with time, he took the opposite track and reduced sets.

Mike based much of his training style on the works of Dr. Arthur Jones, inventor of the Nautilus line of machines. As discussed earlier in the book this type of training is based on the belief that the stronger you get, the more taxing training is to the body's recovery system and the fewer sets you need to do to achieve the same results. Too many sets can quickly lead to overtraining. The debate still rages as to whether heavy-duty training is more effective than the classical high-sets variety. Not one champion bodybuilder has yet built his or her physique exclusively with this form of training; nevertheless, Mike's ideas have led to a revamping of many people's training.

Today most bodybuilders follow exercise programs that are shorter than their counterparts of 20 or 30 years ago. Although they may not subscribe to Mike's theories in full (i.e. 1 or 2 high-intensity sets to failure), they certainly have been influenced by them.

Watching Mike train legs was a lesson in brutality! On a typical leg day he would start by pre-exhausting his thighs with a set of leg extensions. He held each rep in the legs-locked-out position for two seconds and then slowly lowered. After 6 to 8 such reps he would have a partner help him grind out another 2 or 3. Then to completely fatigue his thighs, the partner would lift the weight into the top position so that he could do 2 or 3 negatives.

After one set of such ruthlessness Mike rushed to the leg press, and without pausing, did another set to failure. As his legs tired, he pushed his knees with his arms, providing just enough resistance to keep the weight moving.

Mike Mentzer

Sometimes he substituted squats in place of the leg presses. Because of safety factors he did the squats only to positive failure.

To hit the hamstrings, Mike did 1 or 2 sets of lying leg curls. As with the leg extensions, the set consisted of 6 to 8 reps to positive failure, 1 or 2 forced reps, and 1 or 2 negatives (usually on every second leg workout). And that, dear readers, was Mike Mentzer's entire leg routine – 3 or 4 sets!

Obviously this program is not for everyone, but if you've been slugging away with multiple sets and getting no results, perhaps Mike's leg routine is just what you need to shock your legs into new growth. At the very least, his method is great for those with limited time available for leg-training.

Mike Mentzer's Leg Routine:
1. Leg extensions* – *1 set of 6-10 reps*
2. Leg presses* (or squats) – *1 set of 6-10 reps*
3. Lying leg curls* – *1-2 sets of 6-10 reps*
Includes forced and negative reps

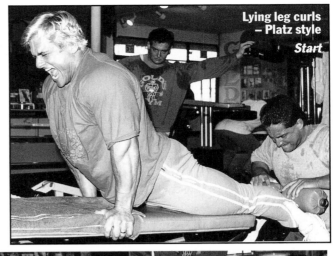

Lying leg curls – Platz style
Start

Finish

Tom Platz

TOM PLATZ – Given the thousands of bodybuilders who have become champions at the national or international level (besides the many thousands more who placed just slightly out of reach), it's a bold statement to say that one bodybuilder has the best particular bodypart in history. If you say Arnold had the best chest, others will counter with Lou Ferrigno or Serge Nubret. Yates currently has the best back, but what about Haney or Francois? For delts you have Oliva, but don't forget Dillett and Christian. And so it goes. For every "best" there is a "counterbest".

When it comes to legs, however, it's generally accepted that Tom Platz had the greatest pair in bodybuilding history. This opinion is shared by fans and competitors alike. When Tom put his hands behind his back, stuck one leg forward and flexed, the audience erupted into musclemania frenzy. A few additional flexes and his thighs became a mass of cross-striations. If contests could be won by legs alone, he would have been a champion for life. Many have suggested that his legs actually held him back. There may be some merit to this view, as throughout his competitive career, he never quite managed to raise his upper body to the level of his gargantuan thighs. Still, in the eyes of his legions of fans, the highlight of any contest occurred when he hit his famous thigh shots. Awesome!

Watching Tom train legs was like witnessing a locomotive careering out of control. How do 600-pound squats for 15 to 20 reps grab you? And he would consider that his light day!

True low-fat definition extends to the glutes as well as the hams.

NIMROD KING – Many said that when Nimrod King burst onto the bodybuilding scene, it was like the second coming of Tom Platz. His legs were not only huge in size, but also had striations and cuts that made them appear even larger than they were (which was somewhere in the 30-inch category).

Although Nimrod's thighs rivaled Tom's in size, their training styles had little in common. Whereas Tom would frequently alternate heavy and light days, Nimrod keeps workouts relatively light and uses high reps. He seldom, if ever, uses fewer than 20 to 25 reps on his leg exercises, and prefers the burn and feel of the exercise to the amount of weight used.

"I believe in going for the burn. Those extra 5 to 10 reps mean a lot. They bring out the cuts, the density and the striations. Just going from 15 to 20 reps or from 20 to 25 reps can mean the difference between building good legs and great legs."

Because his leg workouts take so much out of him, Nimrod has to psych himself up beforehand. He often starts preparing for his leg workout the night before.

"My leg workout is my most intense for any of my bodyparts. It takes a lot of hard work, and totally drains me. I find I am so intense training legs that the morning of my workout I am totally preoccupied with it. I can't think of anything else. In fact when I go to bed the night before, I find my mind is already concentrating on the next day's workout. By the time I get to the gym I'm so psyched up I'm in another world."

Nimrod's first leg exercise is the king of all thigh movements – squats. A typical workout will see him do 4 sets of 20 to 25 reps. The first set is a warmup, followed by a moderate set using additional weight. Finally, he puts on about 315 pounds for 3 sets of 20 to 25 reps. Upon completion of squats his legs look like two overfilled balloons.

Next Nimrod moves on to his favorite leg exercise, one-leg leg presses. Nimrod explains why:

"I love one-leg presses. I have been doing them for the last three years. They have really worked for me. They have also balanced out my legs. For a while my left lower thigh was smaller than my right lower thigh, but by doing the one-leg press, I got my thighs balanced out."

In a typical workout he does 3 or 4 sets of 20 to 25 reps for each leg.

His last thigh exercise is the leg extension. Not being one to shy away from hard work (and remember, this is what it takes to build tree trunk-sized thighs), he does his first 4 to 6 sets in triset fashion. He selects a weight that allows about 15 reps to positive failure. He

In one of his more popular cycles he divided his thigh-training into three routines. On day one he would do barbell squats and hack squats. Day two consisted entirely of hack squats. On day three he would do high-rep squats. Close to a contest he added leg extensions to his day two routine.

For hamstrings Tom did lying leg curls, usually for 6 to 10 sets of 10 to 15 reps. Besides straight sets he often utilized such advanced training techniques as forced reps and negatives in his leg-training.

In determining reps and sets, he preferred to let instinct take over. On heavy squat days he might do 8 or 10 sets of 5 to 15 reps. On others he might be content with sets of 30 to 35 reps. The choice depended on how he felt. Aware of the pitfalls of overtraining, he rarely exceeded 10 or 12 sets total for his thighs. Beginners take note: If Tom Platz needed only 10 sets for his thighs, why on Earth would you want to do 20 or 25? As Tom is quick to add, it's not the quantity but the quality that counts.

A Typical Tom Platz Leg Workout:
1. Squats – *8-10 sets of 5-35 reps*
2. Hack squats – *5-8 sets of 10-15 reps*
3. Leg curls – *6-8 sets of 10-15 reps*

then gets up, shakes his thighs for 5 to 10 seconds, and then hops back on the machine and grinds out another 10 to 12 reps. Is he finished yet? Not likely. Another 5 to 10 seconds of shaking is followed by another 10 reps. This he calls one set. He does not reduce the weight on any phase of the movement.

At this stage most bodybuilders would either move on to another exercise or give up completely, but Nimrod does 3 or 4 additional sets of leg extensions – one leg at a time. Once again the reps are in the 20 to 25 range, and each is done in a slow, controlled manner.

Dave Fisher

To work his hamstrings, Nimrod does 8 to 10 sets of lying leg curls. After all the thigh work, training hamstrings is a chore for him, but he realizes that only complete legs are winning contests these days so he forces out the sets and takes pride in the fact that his hamstrings are in balance with his massive quads.

From looking at Nimrod's leg routine, one can easily see that he's partial to one-leg movements. He is in the minority on this point. Still, one-leg training has worked wonders for him, and –who knows?– if you're in a rut and your legs are not growing, maybe it will do the same for you.

Nimrod King's Leg Routine:
1. Squats – *4-5 sets of 20-25 reps*
2. One-leg presses – *4-5 sets of 20-25 reps*
3. Leg extensions* – *5-6 sets of 25-30 reps*
4. One-leg extensions – *3-4 sets of 20-25 reps*
5. Lying leg curls – *8-10 sets of 20-25 reps*
Each set consists of 3 rest-pause sets of 10-12 reps.

DAVE FISHER – 1991 North American champion Dave Fisher is a firm believer in intense leg-training. He's also not one to listen to so-called "experts" voicing concerns about the pitfalls of squats.

"I believe in heavy, full squats with my ass right to the floor – none of this half- and quarter-squats or bench squat stuff people do. Those are just lazy ways of ruining a great thigh exercise. I hate these guys who come into the gym with their girlfriends along to watch, put four plates on the bar, and then do quarter-squats. They yell and scream and think they're so awesome. Give me a break. Let's see you put your ass through the floor with four plates, buddy, and see how strong you are."

If you've read Dave's articles and columns in *MuscleMag,* you know he's a great believer in the relationship between size and strength. Following the old adage, "the stronger you get the bigger you get," he devotes much of his leg-training to powerlifting.

"On squats I have done lots of triples, even working down to singles and maximum single attempts. Anyone with really skinny thighs should devote a lot of time and most of the first few years of training to heavy power-style training on basic exercises too. Get a big squat and you'll get big thighs."

Like most top bodybuilders, Dave likes to divide his training so that legs are trained by themselves on one day. A typical Fisher leg workout starts with squats – lots and lots of squats. A total of 8 to 10 sets is not out of the ordinary, and he increases the weight with each set until he is forcing out singles, doubles and triples.

After squats he moves on to hack squats and leg presses. During a typical workout, Dave does 5 sets of each, keeping the reps in the 12 to 20 range. On some days he employs a shock routine. He and his

Start

Finish

Dave Fisher performs leg presses.

"I try to do 2 or 3 sets on every leg-curl machine in the gym. That's fun. You do a couple of sets on one machine, then find another one and do a couple more sets, and go to another one, and so on. By the time you're finished, you've done 20 sets of leg curls, and you don't even realize it. You can't believe how sore your hamstrings are the next day, but I like doing that."

Dave Fisher's Leg Routine:
1. Squats* – *8-10 sets of 1-15 reps*
2. Leg extensions –
   5 sets of 12-20 reps
3. Leg presses –
   5 sets of 12-20 reps
4. Lying leg curls –
   6 sets of 12-20 reps
5. Stiff-leg deadlifts –
   3-4 sets of 12-20 reps
Pyramid style

SHAWN RAY – Another bodybuilder who prefers to go by feel rather than worry about the amount of weight is 1994 Mr. Olympia runner-up Shawn Ray. Of the current crop of bodybuilding superstars, Shawn is considered by many to have the greatest symmetry and proportions.

He trains legs twice a week, and although he doesn't religiously stick to the same routine, his workout always revolves around the same core of exercises. A normal leg day will see him starting with squats. Unlike some, he never lets his ego get in the way of proper form on this king of all thigh-builders.

training partner occasionally cut their leg-press weight in half and go for 75 to 80 reps, pushing each other all the way! To make the workout more fun (if you can call high-rep leg presses fun), they treat the workout as a mini competition.

"Well, he did 70 reps with three plates and I ended up doing 75 with four plates. Believe me, that was a brutal set, but that's what it takes to shock the muscle and get it growing."

To work hamstrings, Dave does 6 sets of lying leg curls and 3 or 4 sets of stiff-leg deadlifts. Even though he doesn't like deadlifts, he forces himself to do them because he realizes one exercise alone is probably not enough to adequately work the hamstrings. For variety he goes to Gold's Gym and takes advantage of the assortment of training apparatus there.

"The goal with squats is not the maximum poundage but deep, full squats. Personally, I've never had any of the knee or back problems associated with squats, and that's because of the attention I pay to my technique. When squatting, I keep my head perpendicular to the ground and let the weight take me down as far as I can go. I don't do any partial reps or forced squats."

Shawn tries to flex his quads on every rep and usually does 4 sets of 12 to 15 reps. He prefers the feeling high reps give his thighs, and believes rep ranges of 4 to 6 are better for powerlifters than bodybuilders.

Another favorite Ray mass-builder is the leg press. Again the emphasis is on form and feel, rather than weight. While some bodybuilders may slap 12 to 15 plates on each side, he uses eight, but makes those eight feel like 12. He uses a narrow foot spacing on the exercise, and makes sure to bring his knees down until they touch his shoulders. Occasionally he likes to do leg presses in a descending-sets fashion to give his thighs a wake-up call. He does 10 reps, and then has a partner strip off two 45s. He forces out another 10 reps, has two more 45s removed, and – yes, you guessed it – completes 10 further reps.

Shawn often does squats and presses on the same day. On the next he substitutes lunges and hack squats. Although most consider hacks more of a shaping exercise for the outer thigh, he doesn't get that specific.

"People always say that hack squats are for the outer thigh or the inner thigh, but I don't care what part of the thigh is involved – I just know the quad muscles are working. I do 4 or 5 sets of 12 to 15 reps."

When doing hacks, Shawn keeps his feet close together and toes pointed outwards. He places his hands on his belt for balance, and explodes upward from the bottom. To get the full range of movement, he squats as far down as his legs allow.

Lunges are perhaps Shawn's favorite leg exercise.

"I like lunges because they're not only good for shaping and bringing out the separation in the upper thigh, but they're also good for separating the hamstrings from the quadriceps."

As he lunges forward, he touches his back knee to the ground, a mandatory part of the exercise that many forget to do. He keeps his body as upright as possible and looks straight ahead in the mirror. This last point is important for both form and safety. If you drop your head and lean forward, the odds are you'll lose your balance. You'll be eliminating much of the effectiveness of the exercise, and also placing your knees and lower back in a compromising situation. Shawn prefers high reps to heavy weight, and has been known to do sets of 50 in his workouts.

If there is one exercise that Shawn faithfully does every leg workout, it's the leg extension. Even before doing any other leg exercise, he does a few sets of medium-heavy leg extensions. Usually it's 3 sets of 25, and this serves to warm up the thighs. Later, after he's finished his other quad exercises, he returns to the leg extension and blasts out 3 or 4 additional sets, this time with more intensity. As with leg presses, he does descending sets on the leg extension. He drops the weight twice, doing about 30 reps in 10-rep sets. A typical leg-extension routine looks like this:

1 x 10 with 200 pounds
1 x 10 with 150 pounds
1 x 10 with 100 pounds

Keep in mind that Shawn does these 3 sets back to back with no rest. He includes 3 or 4 such drop sets in a normal leg workout. He completes his leg workout with 5 or 6

Shawn Ray

B

CHAPTER TWENTY-FOUR – QUADS AND HAMSTRINGS

sets each of leg curls and stiff-leg deadlifts. He does the stiff-legs standing on a block or bench. He grips the bar with a shoulder-width grip and keeps his feet close together and knees slightly bent. Like all successful bodybuilders, he puts total concentration into each rep.

"As I come to the bottom of the movement, I relax completely. There's this famous picture of Tom Platz bending over, touching his palms to the ground and with his hamstrings looking just like an anatomy chart. That's what I try to imagine my hamstrings looking like in that stretch position."

A typical workout poundage would be 150 pounds for 15 to 20 reps.

Shawn does his leg curls on an angled bench with a pad under his thighs. Doing them this way keeps the lower back out of the exercise and also allows for a full stretch at the bottom. He usually does 6 sets, the last 2 being drop sets.

Shawn Ray's Leg Routine:

1. Leg extensions – *3 sets of 15-20 reps*
2. Squats – *4 sets of 12-15 reps*
3. Leg presses* – *4 sets of 25-30 reps*
4. Hack squats – *4 sets of 12-15 reps*
5. Lunges – *4 sets of 50-100 reps*
6. Leg extensions* – *3 sets of 25-30 reps*
7. Stiff-leg deadlifts – *4-5 sets of 15-20 reps*
8. Leg curls – *6 sets of 15-20 reps*
Drop sets of 10 reps

SANDY RIDDELL – Anyone who thinks serious training is only for the guys should check out Sandy Riddell's leg routine. Not content to let stubborn legs hold her back, Sandy created a training program that brought her within an inch of the Ms. Olympia title.

Shawn Ray performs the king of all thigh-builders – squats.

Despite a brief foray into powerlifting, her legs never developed as fast as her upper body. She finally managed to force growth into her legs by varying her exercises.

Sandy trains her legs twice a week, and although her routine may vary, she generally does 3 or 4 sets of four different exercises. For a change of pace she sometimes picks one exercise (the leg press being her favorite for this) and does 10 to 12 sets for her leg workout.

Her first exercise is often barbell lunges. To get a full stretch, she places one foot on a standard flat bench. She does 3 or 4 sets of 10 to 15 reps, one leg at a time. Correct posture for her is torso erect and the head tilted slightly back.

For her second exercise Sandy does 3 or 4 sets of dumbell lunges. Instead of placing one foot on a bench, she keeps both feet on the floor. This position shifts much of the strain from the glutes and hamstrings to the front thighs. Keeping the reps in the 10 to 15 range. She finds this exercise great for warming up the thighs for her next exercise, the 45-degree leg press.

Unlike most bodybuilders who do 4 or 5 sets of leg presses and then move on, Sandy varies her foot position on this exercise. She uses four different placements on the leg press, each one designed to target a different part of her legs. With feet close and high on the pressing board she works her glutes and hamstrings. Feet wide and high stresses the inner thighs. Placing feet low on the pressing board targets the quads again – wide for inner and narrow for outer.

Start

Finish

With the exception of leg presses, Sandy's leg workout can be done with a barbell and two dumbells. There's nothing fancy – just good, old-fashioned free-weight exercises. Instead of using elaborate machines, she relies on foot position to attack her legs from different angles. Her program shows you what can be accomplished with a bit of creativity.

Sandy Riddell's Leg Routine:
1. Barbell lunges – *3-4 sets of 10-15 reps*
2. Dumbell lunges – *3-4 sets of 10-15 reps*
3. Leg presses* – *3-4 sets of 6-12 reps*
4. Squats* – *4-8 sets of 6-25 reps*
Sandy varies her foot position on these exercises.

CHRIS CORMIER – One of the best-rounded bodybuilders to hit the stage in recent years is 1988 Ironman champion Chris Cormier. With a ripped 214 pounds on a 5'10" frame, Chris is one of the more deceptive bodybuilders currently on the scene. His great proportions and shredded muscle make him look much larger than his actual weight. In fact he can stand next to competitors who outweigh him by 20 to 30 pounds and not appear out of place.

Sandy Riddell

Lunges

Start

Finish

Sandy's last exercise is the king of leg movements, the barbell squat. As with leg presses, she varies her foot position on this exercise. If her goal is more inner thigh and glute development, she takes a wide stance and, with the toes pointing outward, descends into a full squat. To hit the lower and outer thighs, she does the squats with a narrow, toes-pointing-forward stance, and squats only to parallel. In a typical leg workout, she does 4 to 8 sets of 6 to 25 reps. She divides her squat routine into four distinct workouts. The first workout involves moderate weight, her second is her heavy day, the third is a light-weight/high-rep day, and for her fourth workout, she emphasizes stretching and isolating the quads.

Chris attributes much of his superb leg development to great genetics.

"First of all, my legs are short. I notice guys with longer legs having a harder time developing a good sweep and shape. I am also blessed with good muscle insertions on my hamstrings."

He also gives credit to his athletic background of wrestling, track and field, and football. The football was especially beneficial as it always emphasized some sort of leg exercise and that "push harder and harder" mentality.

CHAPTER TWENTY-FOUR - QUADS AND HAMSTRINGS

Chris Cormier

15 to 25 reps. For variety he sometimes likes to substitute hack squats in place of the machine squats. As with leg presses, the reps are misleading. He routinely does 6 sets of 15 to 25 reps on this exercise, in the process using twenty 45-pound plates. (Are you counting? That's 900 pounds plus the weight of the machine – 1000 pounds!) He likes to finish his thighs with some light stretching exercises – that is, if he has the energy left to get into a stretching position!

The second half of Chris's leg-training takes place on day two. He starts with 5 sets of standing leg curls, averaging around 25 reps per set. Next it's 6 sets of 15 to 20 reps on the lying leg curl. On this exercise he keeps his feet together and emphasizes both the raising and lowering phases.

To finish his hamstrings, he blasts them with 3 sets of stiff-leg deadlifts. Because of the risk of injury to the lower back, he is careful to use only moderate weight and do each rep in a slow, controlled manner with no bouncing at the top or bottom. Unlike his leg presses, for which he loads on huge poundages, Chris uses only moderate weight on the deadlifts.

Chris Cormier's Leg Routine:
Day 1
1. Leg presses – *8 sets of 15-20 reps*
2. Leg extensions – *6 sets of 30-60 reps*
3. Machine squats – *4 sets of 15-20 reps*
or…
4. Hack squats – *6 sets of 15-20 reps*
Day 2
1. Standing leg curls – *5 sets of 25 reps*
2. Lying leg curls – *5-6 sets of 15-20 reps*
3. Stiff-leg deadlifts – *3 sets of 15 reps*

Chris divides his leg-training into two workouts – quads and hamstrings. He trains thighs on day one with the first exercise being the leg press. He typically does 8 sets of 15 to 20 reps. Don't get the impression that the high reps mean light weight though. On most days he starts with 315 pounds and works up to over 1000 pounds. He keeps his feet high on the pressing platform and moves his legs through a full range of motion.

Next it's leg extensions. A standard workout includes 6 sets of 30 to 60 reps on each set. You don't know what pain is until you've done 60 reps on this exercise.

Most bodybuilders would be finished at this stage, but Chris immediately moves on to the squat machine, where he bangs out 4 sets of

Start

Finish

Horizontal leg-press machine

SUE PRICE – *"In the past couple of years I've become known for my legs, especially at the Nationals in 1991, when my bodyfat got so low that my legs even freaked me out!"*

Unlike many bodybuilders who put leg-training in the same category as visiting the dentist, pro bodybuilder Sue Price has always loved training legs.

"It's the one bodypart that you can just let loose on and unleash every bit of energy you have. A leg workout is where you get to dig deep, use all your emotions and all your drive and put yourself to the test."

Sue and her training partner divide their leg workouts into four different routines, doing just about every conceivable exercise during one of the four. Reps vary from as low as 10 to as high as 100. The masochists among you may want to try the latter!

Sue often supersets two exercises to save time and add variety to her leg workouts. Stiff-leg deadlifts and seated leg curls are a favorite superset, as are Smith-machine squats and sissy squats.

Following are Sue's four leg routines:

Sue Price's Leg Routines:
Routine 1
1. Squats – *4-5 sets of 12-20 reps*
2. Leg presses – *4-5 sets of 10-15 reps*
3. Leg extensions – *4 sets of 8-12 reps*
4. Seated leg curls – *5 sets of 12-15 reps*
5. Stiff-leg deadlifts – *4 sets of 12-15 reps*

Machine squats

Finish

Start

Sue Price

Routine 2
1. Squats – *1 set of 100 reps*
2. Leg presses – *1 set of 100 reps*
3. Hack squats – *1 set of 100 reps*
4. Lying leg curls – *1 set of 100 reps*

Routine 3
1. Seated leg curls – *4 sets of 10-12 reps*
2. Leg extensions – *4 sets of 12-20 reps*
3. Lying leg curls – *4 sets of 15-20 reps*
4. Leg presses – *3 sets of 10-12 reps*
5. Glute/ham machine – *3 sets of 20-25 reps*
6. Smith-machine squats – *4 sets of 20 reps*

Routine 4
1. Seated leg curls/deadlifts – *3 sets of 12-15 reps*
2. Hack squats – *4 sets of 10-15 reps*
3. Leg extensions – *4 sets of 10-12 reps*
4. Smith squats/sissy squats – *3 sets of 15-20 reps*

CHAPTER TWENTY-FOUR – QUADS AND HAMSTRINGS

LEE HANEY – Although famous for his upper body, Lee Haney developed a set of legs that combined both mass and separation. But perhaps the greatest tribute to his training and determination is the fact that he has them at all.

For those new to the sport or unfamiliar with Lee's history, it was leg-training that got him hooked on bodybuilding in the first place. As a football player in high school, he had great ambitions to make the NFL. Unfortunately two serious leg injuries came between him and his dream, and football's loss became bodybuilding's gain.

While undergoing rehabilitation for his legs, Lee first noticed the rapid changes that exercise created in his physique. He had worked with weights as part of his football routine, but only when he began training legs following the injuries did the iron bug really bite. Soon he started thinking of going all the way in bodybuilding. (With eight Mr. Olympia titles to his credit, it's safe to say that he succeeded!)

If one word could describe Lee's leg-training, it was *controlled.* He did every rep of every set in the strictest fashion in a conscious effort to prevent re-injuring his legs and a desire to get the utmost benefit from each exercise.

Lee Haney

He divided his leg workout into two sessions, training quads in the morning and hamstrings later in the day. He usually started his thigh-training with leg extensions. At one time he began with heavy squats, but he felt his knees and lower back were being stressed without a proper warmup, so he made a few adjustments, and did 4 or 5 sets of leg extensions to adequately prepare his legs for the heavier exercises to follow. As with all his leg movements, he kept his reps in the 10 to 15 range.

After leg extensions he moved on to the vertical leg press. For years he used the incline version, but later in his career switched over to the vertical type where you lie under the weight and push straight up. Because of the greater safety built into leg presses, he could go really deep on this exercise. Not only did he hit the whole thigh region, but also at the bottom of the movement (legs fully bent) his hamstrings were brought into play.

To finish his thighs, Lee did 4 sets of squats, using moderately heavy weight. Conscious of his old leg injuries, he kept his squat poundage around 315 to 405. Beyond that, he says, you spend too much time trying to get the weight up at any cost. He preferred to make up the additional 200 pounds or so that other men might have used by putting 100 percent intensity into each rep.

He would return to the gym later for hamstrings. In a typical workout he did 4 sets of lying leg curls and 3 or 4 sets of stiff-leg deadlifts, keeping the reps at 8 to 12.

Lee's legs may not have matched the standard of his upper body, but they were good enough to win him the sport's top prize eight years in a row!

Lee Haney's Leg Routine:
1. Leg extensions – *4-5 sets of 12-15 reps*
2. Leg presses – *4-5 sets of 12-15 reps*
3. Squats – *4-5 sets of 10-12 reps*
4. Lying leg curls – *4-5 sets of 10-12 reps*
5. Stiff-leg deadlifts – *3-4 sets of 8-10 reps*

MOHAMED MAKKAWY – With his string of Grand Prix wins in the early '80s, Egyptian (and Canadian citizen since 1986) Mohamed Makkawy became famous for his outstanding symmetry and vascularity. This was not always the case, however. While his calves and upper body showed the results of years of training, his thighs once lagged woefully behind.

"I didn't get into my leg workouts as much as I now know I should have. I was pretty good at squats and, although I didn't get the kind of leg development I wanted, I still used to do an awful lot of regular squatting in my training."

A trip to the "Iron Guru," Vince Gironda, changed all that. After first modifying Mohamed's eating patterns, Vince set out to bring his thighs up to par. His first exercise was leg curls on the leg-curl/leg-extension machine. He did a set of 20 reps, and then without rest flipped over and did an equally intense set of leg extensions. Each rep was slow and controlled with no lifting of the legs or glutes off the bench. At the top of the leg extensions Vince had Mohamed flex and forcibly contract his thighs for one or two seconds. For the third exercise of his triset he hit the hack-slide (squat) machine. With his heels only a few inches apart and his toes flared out wide, he dropped slowly into the full squat position, letting his knees spread out very wide as he approached the bottom.

During his stay at Vince's Gym, Mohamed would run through his triset three times with very little rest after each one. Within a few months his legs were in balance with the rest of his physique. During the next few years he was one of the most dominant bodybuilders on the Grand Prix circuit.

Mohamed Makkawy's Leg Routine:
1. Leg curls – *3 sets of 15-20 reps*
2. Leg extensions – *3 sets of 15-20 reps*
3. Hack squats – *3 sets of 15-20 reps*
Note – Perform as 3 trisets.

KEVIN LEVRONE – With his 1992 Night of Champions victory and third place in the 1994 Mr. Olympia, Kevin Levrone has established himself as one of the premier bodybuilders in the world, and one of the few given a realistic chance of dethroning current Mr. Olympia Dorian Yates. He is another bodybuilder who feels the only way to develop tremendous thighs is to bust your ass at the squat rack. He usually begins by banging out 20 quick reps with 225 on the bar. This set serves as a wake-up call and gets the blood into his thighs. His next set is 315 for another 20 reps. By now his thighs are starting to wish they were located on someone else, but no such luck! His third set consists of 20 reps with 405 pounds. He keeps going in this fashion (90 pounds a set in a pyramid manner) until he reaches 700. Of course by this time the rep range has dropped back to 5 or 6. Still this number of reps for that amount of weight is impressive by anyone's standards.

Hack squats are Kevin's second thigh exercise. He starts with 315 pounds and works up to 600. On all his sets he tries to squeeze out 12 good-quality reps. He normally does 4 or 5 sets of hacks.

To finish his thighs, he does 4 or 5 sets of leg extensions with the weight ranging from 100 to 160 pounds. He keeps the reps around 12 until the last set where he drops the weight and does a "rep set" of 20. For those about to jump to the conclusion that he skips leg presses, read on.

Every second leg workout Kevin adds (notice we said "adds" not "substitutes") 6 sets of presses with the weight ranging from 800 to an incredible 1500 pounds. Although other bodybuilders prefer high reps on this exercise, Kevin finds sets of 12 the most rewarding.

To hit his hamstrings, he does 6 sets of standing and lying leg curls, and 6 sets of stiff-leg deadlifts. To give an idea of his leg power, he routinely does 12 reps

Mohamed Makkawy

with up to 140 pounds on the standing leg curl. (That's one leg at a time, remember.) You don't appreciate how impressive that is until you realize that the average bodybuilder uses that weight for lying leg curls – with two legs!

Lying leg curls are next. He does 6 sets of 12 reps, using anywhere from 80 to 140 pounds.

Kevin finishes his hamstrings with 6 sets of stiff-leg deadlifts – 3 with 225 and another 3 with 315. He does 8 to 10 reps in both sets.

Kevin Levrone's Leg Routine:
1. Squats – *6 sets of 12-20 reps*
2. Hack squats – *5 sets of 12 reps*
3. Leg extensions – *5 sets of 12 reps*
4. Leg presses* – *6 sets of 12-15 reps*
5. Standing leg curls – *6 sets of 12 reps*
6. Lying leg curls – *6 sets of 12 reps*
7. Stiff-leg deadlifts – *6 sets of 8 reps*
Every second workout

Kevin Levrone

This doesn't seem like much, but remember proportion is uppermost in Aaron's mind. He feels this is all he needs to keep his thighs in tiptop shape.

We would be misleading you if we left the impression that this is the only routine Aaron followed. Early in his career, when gaining leg mass was a priority, he made good use of squats and hacks (in addition to extensions and lunges). Taking a page right from Arnold's leg-training, he would do 4 or 5 sets of each of these exercises. With time he noticed his quads overtaking his upper body. In the manner of a future champion he modified his training, giving special attention to his upper body. If he notices his legs beginning to lag behind, you can be sure that Aaron will once again be back at the squat rack.

Aaron Baker's Present Leg Routine:
1. Leg extensions* – *12-20 reps*
2. Sissy squats* – *12-20 reps*
3. Lunges* – *12-20 reps*
4. Leg curls – *4-5 sets of 12-15 reps*
5. Stiff-leg deadlifts – *4-5 sets of 12-15 reps*
All three exercises are done as 1 triset.

Aaron Baker

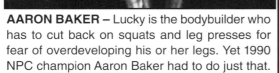

AARON BAKER – Lucky is the bodybuilder who has to cut back on squats and leg presses for fear of overdeveloping his or her legs. Yet 1990 NPC champion Aaron Baker had to do just that.

With symmetry foremost in his mind, Aaron has put squats and presses in the background, preferring instead to make extensions, sissy squats and lunges the focal point of his thigh workouts. In a typical thigh workout he combines these three exercises into a triset, going to failure on each set. To work his hamstrings, he does leg curls (standing and lying) and stiff-leg deadlifts.

Finish

After a couple of light "pumping sets" to get blood into the area, he blasts out four good-quality work sets. Aiming more for muscle quality than mass, he uses "only" eight plates on his hacks.

"Since I'm gifted genetically I don't need that much weight. I have the muscle there. I just wanna stimulate my quads and develop the muscle maturity. Believe me, I could go heavier if I wanted to, but I don't."

Using a piston-like style on the hack machine, he stops just short of a lock at the top and then goes back down, keeping constant tension on his thighs. He doesn't rest long between sets either. During the off-season he averages about 90 seconds, but once into his precontest mode he reduces rest intervals to 45 to 60 seconds.

PAUL DEMAYO – "Legs on me are primarily genetic. They just grew no matter what I did. Asking them how I developed them is like asking Flex Wheeler, 'Why are your muscles so round? How do you train for that?' I mean, what the heck can he say? It just happened."

Nicknamed "Quadzilla" because of his freaky leg mass, 1994 USA Nationals winner Paul DeMayo has the potential to be one of the most exciting bodybuilders on the pro circuit. After sweeping to victory at the Nationals, Paul was swamped with offers for posing exhibitions and seminars. Not being one to miss a business opportunity, he decided to put competitive bodybuilding on hold but you can be sure that eventually he will start wreaking havoc in the pro ranks.

Not since Tom Platz has bodybuilding seen such an awesome set of thighs. Reliable estimates put Paul's quads over 30 inches.

Like most bodybuilders famous for their thighs, he made squats the mainstay of his early leg workouts. "Back when I was 20 or 21 I used to work up to sets of 505 pounds for 8 to 12 reps. I learned to squat with my heels up on a two-by-four block of wood, and I can't squat flat-footed. I definitely feel the squat played a major role in developing my quads, but now I don't want them to get freakier than they already are."

In recent years he has redesigned his thigh training, placing less emphasis on squats and more on leg extensions and hack squats. He usually starts his leg workout with hack squats on the Flex machine.

Aaron lunges with perfect technique.

Start

Paul DeMayo

sions to just 3 sets. On days when the energy is there, he adds an extra set or two.

As with hacks, Paul concentrates on quality rather than quantity when doing extensions. On a typical day he uses about 100 pounds, and after completing as many reps as possible to failure, he finishes the set with partials.

Hack squats and extensions form the basis of Paul's present thigh workout, but occasionally he starts his leg-training with a few sets of squats. As for leg presses, he found the exercise difficult to do.

"I always had a problem with leg presses because I felt as if all the weight was coming down and crushing my stomach. I could never do much weight on leg presses, and I never really used them."

To work his hamstrings, he relies on lying leg curls, standing leg curls and stiff-leg deadlifts. He usually starts with lying leg curls on the Cybex machine, and does 4 sets of 8 to 12 reps. He does the first 2 sets using 140 pounds, and then drops to 120 for his third set. To finish off his lying leg curls, he does one drop set with 100 pounds down to 80 pounds.

After lying leg curls it's on to the one-leg standing variety on the Flex machine. Paul treats this exercise like dumbell concentration curls, and uses it for isolating his hamstrings. He normally does 3 sets with 60 to 70 pounds.

He completes his hamstring-training with 4 or 5 sets of stiff-leg deadlifts. Although the weight varies, he uses between 135 and 225 for sets of 8 to 12 reps.

For those having trouble building great legs, Paul has this piece of advice:

"If you want to make progress in your leg-training, or for any other bodyparts, your mind has to be into it. Most people with under-developed legs dread leg-training because they know if it's done right it'll take the life out of ya. So a lot of people avoid the hard work. You have to be positive, but more importantly you have to be willing to put forth the maximal effort."

Paul DeMayo's Leg Routine:
1. Hack squats – *4 sets of 8-12 reps*
2. Leg extensions – *3-4 sets of 8-12 reps*
3. Lying leg curls – *4 sets of 8-12 reps*
4. Standing leg curls – *3 sets of 8-12 reps*
5. Stiff-leg deadlifts – *5 sets of 8-12 reps*
Note – Paul makes frequent use of drop sets and partial reps.

After hack squats Paul moves on to leg extensions, using either the Cybex or Icarian machines. He lets instinct determine how many sets to do. If his legs are particularly fatigued from hacks, he limits the exten-

The incredible thighs of
Flex Wheeler.

Chapter Twenty-five

CALVES

BODYBUILDING'S DIAMONDS

Although some bodybuilders have been blessed with favorable calf-building genetics, for the most part only years of training will put meat on what bodybuilders often call "the lowers." If one word can describe calves in terms of training, it's *stubborn*. How often have you heard the complaint "I really blast them, but they refuse to grow." There may be some truth in this statement but often the individual's idea of "blasting" consists of a few sets of calf raises at the end of a workout. After several

Sammy Ioannidis

months of such mediocrity our Mr. Olympia wannabe gives up, citing "unfavorable genetics" as the reason for his lack of calf progress. What our misguided friend fails to realize is that the calf is composed of very dense muscle fiber. Throwing in a few haphazard sets at the end of a workout does not build 20-inch diamonds.

Sure, there are exceptions. Some men spend years bombing their calves from all angles, using a multitude of sets and reps, yet years later are still hobbling about on 15-inch calves. Then we have the opposite extreme – those genetically blessed (cursed by many!) wonders who walk into the gym displaying 18-inch cows and promptly boast that they never did a calf raise in their life! If they survive the fury of their less-endowed gym mates, our gifted brethren go on to say how their mother, father and great-aunt Matilda all went through life atop 18-inch pillars. Such bodybuilding superstars as Mike Mentzer, Chris Dickerson and Johnny Fuller fall into this category. Mike frequently credited his father as having two of the greatest calves he'd ever seen. Chris Dickerson, one of a set of triplets, said that his brothers had nearly the same-sized calves as he did, yet they never worked out with weights. And then there's the irrepressible Johnny Fuller, who said his calves were 18 inches before he started training. Such is the benefit of choosing your parents wisely!

No doubt most readers of this book fall somewhere in between. This means you have good potential to build great calves, but you'll need to bust your ass to do so.

Why are the calves so difficult to develop? Well, for starters training the little buggers hurts! Next to forearm- and thigh-training, calf workouts are among the most uncomfortable you can do. Many bodybuilders are unwilling to put up with such pain, especially when the results are slow in coming.

Another reason for calf neglect is their location. When someone says, "Show me your muscle," you don't roll up your pants and flex your calf. You pop up a biceps or two. Unless you are lucky enough to live in a warm climate, your calves will spend much of the year covered up. Many bodybuilders ask themselves, "Why bother to spend all that valuable time training a muscle that will rarely be seen?"

A final reason has to do with the calves' response to training. They are generally among the most stubborn muscles when it comes to growth. You spend hours doing standing calf raises, donkey calf raises, seated raises, etc., and what do you get in return? An extremely sore muscle but little observable growth. It seems that, unlike other muscles which begin showing results in a matter of months, the calves take years to respond.

All of these reasons can be used to explain the less-than-distinguished calf development on many bodybuilders. Yet if you plan to compete, you absolutely have to make calf-training a regular part of your workouts. Even if competitive bodybuilding is not in your future, nothing looks as stupid as a bodybuilder walking about on 28-inch thighs and 15-inch calves. So let's get to the gym and start turning those calves into cows!

ANATOMY

The calves are not one muscle but a whole complex of muscles. You have the gastrocnemius, tibialis anterior, soleus, extensor digitorum longus, plantaris, tibialis posticus, flexor digitorum longus, and a few others that we need not mention here. For bodybuilding purposes we need only focus on the gastrocnemius and soleus. Granted you will be training all the smaller muscles, but bodybuilders tend to focus on these two.

The bulk of the calf is made up of the gastrocnemius, the large U-shaped muscle at the rear of the lower leg. The primary function of the gastrocnemius is to lift the body onto the toes. Take a look at the outstanding calf development of gymnasts and ballerinas. If you don't believe us, stand on your tiptoes and look down. Most of what you are looking at is the gastrocnemius. Beautiful, isn't it? And with a little help from us, it's going to look even more impressive!

The other main calf muscle is the soleus, a broad, flat muscle located below the gastrocnemius. It too helps raise the body onto the toes, but is more strongly stressed when the knees are in a bent position.

TRAINING

Few pursuits in life are easy and calf-training is no exception. But don't despair – you're in good company. The one and only Arnold Schwarzenegger started his bodybuilding career in such a manner. Only after spending years developing that gargantuan upper body of his did he realize that his calves even existed! The point was further driven home as he watched former great Reg Park using upwards of 1000 pounds on the calf machine. Arnold's days of calf neglect were over.

Chris Cormier

Some people argue that calf genetics is unevenly arranged among races. Supposedly African-Americans have a disposition towards poor calf development. Some blacks do have inferior calves, but then some of the greatest black bodybuilders in history are famous for their lowers. Just look at Sergio Oliva, Chris Dickerson, Vince Taylor and Flex Wheeler, all of whom exhibit 20-inch monsters.

Calf-training is generally divided into two types of exercises – standing and seated. The primary standing exercise is the standing machine calf raise. This apparatus allows you to pile on hundreds of pounds of weight, thus stimulating the gastrocnemius muscles to the maximum. Another effective exercise is the toe press on the leg-press machine. Instead of lowering with the thighs, you keep your legs straight and press the weight using only your feet. The most popular seated calf exercise is the seated calf raise, once again done on a special machine. As the legs remain bent throughout the full range of the exercise, the primary stress is placed on the soleus muscles.

Of course calf-training is not limited to machines. Flip through back issues of *MuscleMag International* and other bodybuilding magazines, and you'll see pictures of Arnold working calves with one or two people on his back. The exercise is called donkey calf raises, and while you might not want to do it in a health spa, the results are outstanding. The exercise is done in a bent-over position with the body braced on a waist-high bench. What's unique about the exercise is the weight source. Instead of plates or weight stacks you use another person (a cooperative one naturally!) who sits on your lower back as you do the exercise. Another popular calf exercise is the dumbell calf raise. All you need for this one is two dumbells and a block of wood.

Besides the exercises themselves there are variations of foot position that you can use. Pointing the toes inward, outward or straight ahead all stress different parts of the calf. You can also do calf raises with bare feet. Many trainers swear by this technique, claiming the absence of shoes allows for a better stretch. But be careful. Removing your sneakers takes away much of the ankle support that is needed. Let's face it. Doing 500-pound calf raises places tremendous stress on the feet and surrounding connective tissues. Also, many gyms have strict rules against removing footwear. You can go halfway and leave your socks on, but then you have the problem of traction. Trying to keep your feet firmly anchored on a block of wood while wearing socks is difficult if not downright dangerous.

Our suggestion is to wear foot support on your heavy basic exercises like standing calf raises. You can try doing lighter stretching exercises barefoot. The bottom line is to use your best judgment, and if in doubt, wear footwear.

Before we look at the champs' routines, we must emphasize a few important points. Research has determined that the calf is one of the body's most endurance-capable muscles (in the same category as the forearms). Think about it. You use your calves in just about every day-to-day activity – everything from running and walking to standing and sitting up. This means your calves have tremendous powers of recovery. To adequately fatigue them, experts recommend that, instead of resting between sets, you use the time to do low-intensity exercises such as no-weight calf stretches. In this way you keep continuous tension on the calves, thus increasing the training intensity.

Generally speaking, you should work the larger gastrocnemius muscles first, leaving the soleus till later. The reason has to do with fiber types. The gastrocnemius muscles are mainly composed of fast-twitch or white muscle fibers that tire quickly. Conversely, the soleus muscles are chiefly composed of slow-twitch or red muscle – i.e. high-endurance fibers. If you do seated calf raises first, you may not have the energy left to adequately train the gastrocnemius muscles. If, however, you start with the larger, low-endurance gastrocnemius muscles, you should still have sufficient energy left to hit the soleus.

Bodybuilders usually train calves after the rest of the leg muscles. This practice is fine as long as your calves don't lag behind. If your thighs begin to overshadow your calves, don't hesitate to revise your schedule. For example you may want to hit calves on a day of their own, or train them on a less intense day, such as arm day. Finally many bodybuilders use what's called staggered sets in their calf-training. Between sets for another muscle group they throw in a set or two of calves. Over the duration of a workout the number of such sets could add up to 15 or 20. A few months of such training can do wonders for lagging calf development.

Roger Stewart

Whatever calf routine you follow, treat calves as another muscle group. This means hitting them at least twice a week with a variety of exercises. Now let's look at how the champs built some of the greatest calves in history!

Calf Exercises:
1. Standing calf raises
2. Seated calf raises
3. Toe presses on leg-press machine
4. Donkey calf raises
5. One-leg calf raises holding dumbell
6. Reverse calf raises on hack machine
7. Barbell calf raises

THE CHAMPS' ROUTINES

ARNOLD SCHWARZENEGGER – What else can be said about the one individual who has done more for bodybuilding than perhaps any other? When the "Austrian Oak" first landed in the United States, few realized the impact he would have on the sport. Within ten years he was bodybuilding's undisputed king, and within twenty he had conquered Hollywood. Not bad for an Austrian kid who had nothing going for him but a 240-pound physique!

Arnold's road to the top of the bodybuilding hierarchy was not without its obstacles. True he had the raw material (about 250 pounds of it), but years of training were required for his physique to take on the polish that would bring him his seven Mr. Olympia wins. Early in his career he focused his training on basic exercises intended for increasing overall body mass. He soon realized, however, that there was more to bodybuilding success than muscle size. After much encouragement from such notables as the "Master Blaster," Joe Weider, and the "Iron Guru," Vince Gironda, Arnold began to take notice of his lagging bodyparts, chief among these being his calves. Until he came to America, he had relied heavily on his upper body to dwarf his opponents. This he did easily. But America was a whole new ball game. No longer would a set of 22-inch arms and 57-inch chest suffice. Refinement was the key, and with refinement came completeness.

It's hard to believe that a man famous for his calves (among other bodyparts) had at one time neglected them almost entirely. After repeated goading from others, including Joe Weider and Reg Park, Arnold took to calf-training with a frenzy. To motivate himself further, he cut the lower legs off his sweat pants. With his weak calves on display for all to see and ridicule, he went to work in bringing them up to the level of his massive upper body.

For his first calf exercise Arnold did 6 sets of donkey calf raises. He would stand on a three-inch block of wood and have one or two training partners hop on his back. After lowering his heels as far as possible, making sure to get a full stretch in his calves, he then flexed up on his toes as far as he could. In a typical workout he would do 6 sets of 15 to 20 reps.

Next he did 5 or 6 sets of standing calf raises. Before he met Reg Park, Arnold did the exercise using 300 to 400 pounds. After watching Reg blast his calves with upwards of 1000 pounds, Arnold took the hint and made increasing the weight a major priority. Before long he too was bombing his calves with 1000 pounds.

Arnold Schwarzenegger

Reg Park

REG PARK – Since we started this section with Arnold, it seemed appropriate to follow his routine with the man who inspired Arnold the most – Reg Park. A native of South Africa, Reg started bodybuilding in September of 1948. Although the rest of his physique quickly took on herculean proportions, his calves lagged way behind. After noticing the improvement Clancy Ross had made to his calves in three short years (1945 – 1948), Reg vowed to attack his own with the same intensity.

In December of 1949 he met up with Joe Weider at Weider headquarters, then located in Jersey City. Joe made arrangements for him to go out to California and train with his idol, Clancy Ross. Before long the two were seen working out together.

"The workouts I had with Clancy at the time consisted of three complete body workouts a week on a Monday-Wednesday-Friday basis, when he did 3 sets of 20 reps on the standing calf machine. On the completion of this work he did 3 sets of free-standing heel raises which he used for pump purposes and also to emphasize the full range of heel raising and lowering."

He went on to say that Clancy may have done other exercises, but while he trained with him, that was all he did. Although Reg gave Clancy's calf routine a try, the results were slow in coming. Joe Weider suggested he shock his calves by training them three times a day. Reg took the advice to heart, and visitors to the Weider building frequently saw him doing donkey raises with 250-pound Charlie Smith (a writer for the Weider organization in those days) on his back. By mid-1951 his calves had caught up to the rest of his body, and soon others were seeking him out for advice on bringing up their own stubborn "lowers."

After he learned the secrets of calf growth, there was no holding Reg back. Self-conscious about his weak calves, he continued to blast them, even when he was stuck for time. This supreme effort paid off, as he soon developed the greatest calves of his era. All he needed was 2 or 3 sets and his calves were fully pumped.

Reg relied on the basic exercises – standing calf raises, seated calf raises, donkey calf raises, and toe presses on the leg-press machine. He would do 3 or 4 sets of each, aiming for 15 to 20 reps. On donkey raises he often went to failure, then had his training partner hop off his back, and ground out another 10 to 15 reps or went to failure, whichever came first.

Unlike many bodybuilders who did high (20+) reps on this exercise, he treated it no differently than any other. He routinely did sets of 10 to 12, using as much weight as possible.

His third exercise was the seated calf raise. He would load a weight on the machine that allowed him 15 good reps. On each rep he would lift his heels as high as possible and then lower for a full stretch.

Finally Arnold would do 5 or 6 sets of toe presses on the leg-press machine. After 12 to 15 good reps he pumped his calves for a few additional reps. Pumping involves a rapid flexing of the calves, trying to go a little higher on each successive rep.

Within five years of specialized training Arnold's calves evolved from being one of his worst bodyparts to one of his best. In fact they rank among the best of all time. We won't guarantee that by following his calf routine you'll get the same results, but we are sure that anyone can make great improvement to his calves by training with his dedication.

Arnold Schwarzenegger's Calf Routine:
1. Donkey calf raises – *5-6 sets of 15-20 reps*
2. Standing calf raises – *5-6 sets of 12-15 reps*
3. Seated calf raises – *5-6 sets of 12-15 reps*
4. Toe presses on leg press – *5-6 sets of 12-15 reps*

Reg Park's Calf Routine:
1. Seated calf raises – *3-4 sets of 15-20 reps*
2. Standing calf raises – *3-4 sets of 15-20 reps*
3. Toe presses on leg-press machine – *3-4 sets of 15-20 reps*
4. Donkey calf raises – *3-4 sets of 15-20 reps*

NIMROD KING – Anyone who maintains that black bodybuilders can't build huge calves has never met Canadian sensation Nimrod King. When you have quads the size of Nimrod's (30+ inches by some accounts), outstanding calf development is a must.

Nimrod doesn't train his calves on leg day. He prefers to train them separately, usually on trap-delt day. No matter what the exercise, he uses a full range of motion when he trains calves.

"I try to go all the way up, hold at the top, and flex for a second before I lower slowly."

His first exercise is usually toe presses on the Nautilus leg-press machine. As with most of his exercises, he keeps the reps high, usually in the 20 to 25 range. As he feels this is his main mass-builder, he doesn't hesitate to do 7 intense sets.

Next up it's 8 sets of seated calf raises, once again using a rep range of 20 to 25. His third exercise is toe presses on the 45-degree leg-press machine.

His fourth and final calf exercise is the standing calf raise. As his calves are pretty fatigued at this point, he does only 3 sets.

You may think that 24 sets is too much for one muscle group, but Nimrod disagrees. A few years ago his calves were among his weakest muscle groups. Especially noticeable was their dreaded "high-calf" appearance. To attack the problem head on, Nimrod had a friend design a special seated calf machine angled at 45 degrees. The angle allowed him to stretch his calves a few additional degrees. He trained with the machine in his house every second day for two years – doing thousands of sets and tens of thousands of reps in the process. The hard work paid off, as his calves grew two inches.

Although he is the first to admit that he will never have the fullness or calf length of guys like Vince Taylor or Chris Dickerson, Nimrod is proud that he has brought his own "lowers" to their present size. He refuses to believe that blacks cannot build huge calves, and he is living proof that with determination and hard work anyone can turn mediocrity into bodybuilding success.

Nimrod King's Calf Routine:
1. Toe presses on the Nautilus leg press – *7 sets of 20-25 reps*
2. Seated calf raises – *8 sets of 20-25 reps*
3. Toe presses on 45-degree leg press – *6 sets of 20-25 reps*
4. Standing calf raises – *3 sets of 20-25 reps*

PAUL DEMAYO – Throughout the 1970s and 1980s the one bodybuilder who came to represent the epitome in leg development was "The Golden Eagle" – Tom Platz. Tom's legs were so outstanding that they overshadowed his upper body. Even when he added inches to his upper torso, his legs stole the limelight. He went on to become a very successful body-builder/businessman. The bodybuilding public seemed unconcerned that Tom's competitive wins were limited. What mattered was that anyone who had ever hoisted a barbell knew perfection when he saw it, and Tom's killer quads were the ultimate.

In recent years a new phenomenon has emerged on the scene. They call him "Quadzilla," and for good

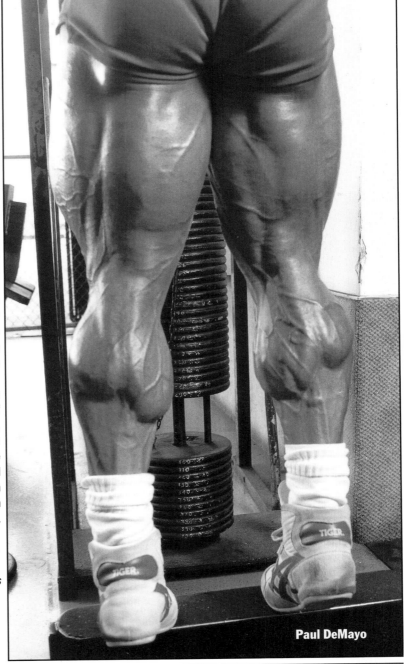

Paul DeMayo

Paul DeMayo

motion on each rep, and stretching his calves after each set. He also increased the frequency of calf-training, hitting them twice in a four-day period. Finally he made use of the muscle priority principle. With his thighs as large as he needed them, he could afford to leave them until the end of his leg workout. This way he could devote most of his energy to training calves and hamstrings.

Paul's first calf exercise is the standing calf raise. In contrast to most bodybuilders who stretch all the way down, he limits his

Reverse calf raises on a hack machine demonstrated by Paul DeMayo.

reason. One look at Paul DeMayo's legs and memories of the mythical Japanese creature are brought back. Estimates on his thighs range from 30 to 34 inches. The exact figure is not important. When you are confronted with such slabs of beef, about the only response is "Those things can't be real." Ah, but that's where you're wrong. They are real. Just ask the competitors at the 1994 USA, NPC Nationals, where Paul flexed his way to victory.

Although early in his career he suffered the same criticism as Tom Platz (upper body not up to the standard of his lower), Paul took the less-than-flattering remarks in a positive manner. He went to work blasting his torso muscles with hellish intensity. The result – one of the most massive and complete competitors to ever take the US Nationals.

Although his thighs grew rapidly, the road to massive calves was bumpy for DeMayo. As luck would have it, he trained at the same gym as the one man who was quickly becoming famous for his calves, Mike Matarazzo. As Mike strutted around the gym, sporting those 20-inch lower monsters, Paul vowed to start training his own calves seriously. Looking back, he admits that his calves were by no means emaciated, but his thighs were growing by leaps and bounds, so even a moderate set of calves was going to look small.

At first he approached calf-training like any other muscle group, and that meant using as much weight as possible, regardless of style. While his ego received a tremendous workout, his calves refused to respond. He finally admitted that his lower back and Achilles tendons were taking the brunt of the weight. Putting his pride on hold, he lowered the poundage and began doing the exercises in strict style. He put total concentration into his calf workouts, doing a full range of

reps to the upper half. He made the switch after noticing his Achilles tendon taking most of the strain on the lower part of the exercise. He still goes all the way up on his toes, but stops about halfway down. Although he doesn't count reps, he figures he does about 20 to 25 per set. During a typical workout he completes 5 sets of standing calf raises, starting with 400 pounds and working up to over 500.

Paul's second exercise is seated calf raises. As his calves are already warmed up he jumps straight to his workout weight. He does sets of 20 to 25 reps, using about 200 pounds on each set.

For his final exercise he uses a sled-type machine. He throws on about 200 pounds and burns out 4 sets of toe presses.

Paul always stretches his calves between sets regardless of which exercise he is doing. He feels this is the only way to bring the calves to a state of complete exhaustion.

With his win at the 1994 Nationals Paul "Quadzilla" DeMayo earned his pro card. No doubt many a pro has been dreading the day when he steps up onstage and flexes those mighty legs. It's a safe bet that Paul will have "a leg up" on most competitors!

Paul DeMayo's Calf Routine:

1. Standing calf raises – *4-5 sets of 20-25 reps*
2. Seated calf raises – *3-4 sets of 20-25 reps*
3. Toe presses on sled machine – *3-4 sets of 20-25*

LEE LABRADA – When it comes to winning contests, second-place Mr. Olympia Lee Labrada knows the importance of great calves. As he is often outweighed by 50 pounds or more, he has had to make sure every inch of his physique stands out.

"Good calves are a mark of a champion. A champion doesn't just have big arms and a big chest. He's developed proportionately all over, and that means calves too."

Lee adds that because calves are such a stubborn muscle group, many beginners skip them, preferring instead to concentrate on the more glamorous muscles like arms and chest. But he warns, you've got to treat all muscles the same.

His calf workout usually consists of three or four exercises for 4 or 5 sets each. He stresses that your mind should be totally focused on the exercise. In other words feel each and every rep, and know which muscles you're working. The more you know about your calves, the more effectively you can train them.

Lee's first exercise is usually toe presses on the leg-press machine. He keeps his hips and lower back pressed firmly against the soft pad, but holds his neck and head vertical, not leaning back. With his toes about four inches apart, he pushes with the balls of his feet, extending the weight as far as he can. Sometimes he varies his foot position so that he can hit the calf from different angles. Since he wants to hit the upper gastrocnemius, he keeps his legs straight. Bending the knees will shift the stress to the soleus if that's what's desired.

After toe presses Lee moves on to the seated calf raise. Once again posture is important, and he keeps his upper body perpendicular to the floor. With the balls of his feet resting on the footbar, he lowers his heels as far as he can, and then presses up on his toes as far as

possible. He emphasizes keeping constant tension on the calves throughout the full range of movement. Stretch all the way down and all the way up.

"Most people don't go down far enough. You have to use as complete a range of motion as possible on each rep."

Unlike standing calf raises, where foot position determines the angle of attack, there is not much you can do with your knee position limiting your variety of foot position. Lee keeps his feet pointed straight ahead and uses mind control to vary the stress.

"Put your mind into the muscle. If you apply pressure from the ball of your foot, then you stress the inner head of the calf. On the other hand if you apply pressure from the outside part of the foot, you throw more stress on the outside part of the calf."

Lee Labrada

Lee concludes by offering this advice to aspiring bodybuilders:

"If you want calves you have to work for them. Put in the time and effort. Prioritize your calves and don't baby yourself! Go full bore. Be tough. Then you can develop killer calves to blow away the rest of the lineup."

Lee Labrada's Calf Routine:

1. Toe presses on leg-press machine –
   4 sets of 15-20 reps
2. Seated calf raises – *4 sets of 15-20 reps*
3. Standing calf raises – *4 sets of 15-20 reps*

THIERRY PASTEL – Even though he stands only 5'2", France's Thierry Pastel is not afraid to mix it up with the sport's big boys. Besides his ripped-to-shreds physique, Thierry sports two of the biggest arms currently on the pro tour. In fact when you take Thierry's height into account, pound for pound his arms may be the largest.

Lee Labrada demonstrates the seated calf raise and the standing calf raise.

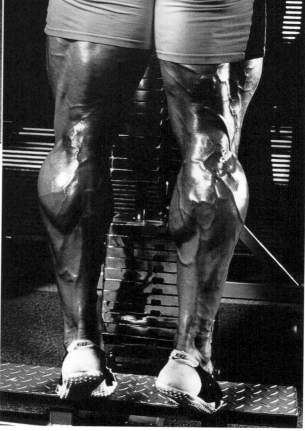

His third calf exercise is standing calf raises. Before jumping to this exercise, he ensures that his calves are properly warmed up because he will be using extremely heavy weights.

"I use a medium pace and sometimes slow motion. You have to be very careful if you're using heavy weights in this exercise. Never come down too fast or use jerky movements – you can rip your Achilles tendon."

He positions himself in the machine with his shoulders placed squarely under the supports. He then rises on his toes as high as possible, contracting fully at the top. Again he emphasizes the importance of feeling the muscle as it's being worked.

Lee often substitutes donkey calf raises, one-leg calf raises and hack-machine calf raises (facing the machine, legs kept straight). He finishes each calf workout with various calf-stretching exercises. For example he sometimes uses the runner's stretch, an exercise where one foot is placed in front of the other and both heels kept firmly on the floor.

"Many people don't realize the value of stretching to strengthen and elongate the muscle and help it grow."

Among his early heroes while growing up on the West Indies island of Martinique was superstar French bodybuilder Serge Nubret. Thierry became so infatuated with Serge that he moved to Paris to train under him. When he stated his intention of building a huge chest and arms, Serge pointed to his less-than-adequate calves and told him those are the muscles that win contests. Thierry took Serge's advice and, after winning a host of non-IFBB events, captured the 1990 German Grand Prix.

He trains calves on day one of his three-day split, hitting them after his chest, shoulder and hamstring training. He constantly rearranges his program. One day he may do 5 or 6 sets of 3 or 4 different exercises, and the next 6 to 8 supersets. He loves supersetting seated and standing calf raises. He averages 15 to 20 reps on each, resting about 10 seconds between exercises and 90 seconds between supersets. He prefers machines for calf-training (as opposed to donkey raises) because they allow him to concentrate more intensely.

Thierry Pastel's Calf Routine:
1. Standing calf raises* – *6-8 sets of 15-20 reps*
2. Seated calf raises* – *6-8 sets of 15-20 reps*
He does both in a superset manner.

VINCE COMERFORD – Another bodybuilder who can hold his own mass-wise, despite his relatively small stature, is Vince Comerford. Sporting a physique packed with as much mass as humanly possible, Vince steps onstage ready to do battle with everyone, big or small.

He has this to say about leg-training:

"You don't casually walk into the gym and decide to do some leg-training. No way! If you have that attitude you should get the hell out of there. Each time I go to the gym to train my legs, it's war."

Vince trains calves separately from his other leg muscles. He picks two exercises and does 5 sets of each, averaging about 15 to 20 reps. His favorite exercises are toe presses on the leg press, donkey calf raises, and both standing and seated calf raises.

If he starts with seated calf raises he does the first set or two as a warmup. He then does 5 intense sets with a medium-heavy weight. Other days he employs the drop-set principle in his training. Upon failing at about rep 12, he has a training partner remove some weight, and he bangs out another 12. Not content to stop there, he does a third drop set of 12 in this manner. In a typical calf workout he completes 3 such drop sets.

Following seated calf raises Vince often moves to the 45-degree leg-press machine. He uses the machine to do 5 sets of toe presses, doing 15 to 20 reps. Instead of drop sets he does rest-pause sets. After 12 or 13 reps he gets up, shakes his legs, and then sits down and bangs out another 5 reps. Again he pauses, shakes his legs, and does a final 5 reps.

"These reps are slow and when I say slow, I mean s-l-o-w! At the very end of each set I pop the weight up, hold it in the contracted position for a few seconds and then slowly lower it. Between sets of toe presses I also stretch my calves out."

Thierry Pastel

Vince emphasizes doing all exercises in good style, utilizing a full range of motion. He also recommends hitting the calves with as much intensity as possible.

"Declare war on your legs. Get into the gym and bomb the hell out of them!"

Vince Comerford's Calf Routine:
1. Seated calf raises* – *5 sets of 12-15 reps*
2. Toe presses on leg-press machine** –
   5 sets of 20-25 reps
*Occasionally doing drop sets of 12
**Rest-pause sets of 13, 5 and 5.

DAVE FISHER – The 1991 North American champion and *MuscleMag International* columnist, Dave Fisher, prefers to train calves separately from other leg muscles.

"I don't train calves on the same day as I do my quads and hamstrings. I fit them in other workouts during the week. Normally they get hit once or twice a week."

A typical Fisher calf routine takes about 45 minutes. Dave alternates between medium reps with heavy weight and high reps with light weight during the same workout. His favorite exercises are standing calf raises, toe presses and seated calf raises.

Rather than count sets, he goes by the feel in his calves. He doesn't stop until his calves are so pumped and burn so much that he can hardly walk. This usually means about three exercises of 5 sets each. Dave is a firm believer in basic training, and his calf-training mirrors this philosophy.

Train calves with as much intensity as possible
– Vince Comerford.

"It's nothing real fancy, just basic hard training, but for me hard and basic is best."

Dave Fisher's Calf Routine:
1. Standing calf raises – *5 sets of 15-50 reps*
2. Toe presses on leg-press machine –
   5 sets of 15-50 reps
3. Seated calf raises – *5 sets of 15-50 reps*
Dave alternates between high- and low-rep workouts.

LISA LORIO – When she was in junior high school, top pro bodybuilder Lisa Lorio was very self-conscious about her calves. Unlike most untrained individuals, she had "lowers" that stood out among her classmates.

"I used to hide my calves by pulling my socks up to my knees because they were bigger than everybody else's."

But don't be misled into thinking Lisa neglected her calf-training when she took up bodybuilding. Many torturous hours in the gym were required to capitalize on her genetic gift. She may have had the blueprint, but turning a set of plans into reality takes hard work.

She feels the key to her phenomenal calf development has been cross-training. She points out that most track stars have great calves and they certainly didn't develop them

Vince Comerford and Kathy Unger

Dave Fisher

sets of seated calf raises, once again doing 20 to 25 reps per set.

Giant-set day consists of 3 giant sets of the following exercises:

1. Standing calf raises
2. Seated calf raises
3. Donkey calf raises
4. Leg-press toe raises

She uses about 75 percent of her normal weight and aims for 10 to 25 reps on each set. To allow for nearly full recovery, she rests about one minute after each giant set. Lisa sums up her calf-training in the following manner:

"Pound your calves every which way you can to shock them into growth."

Lisa Lorio's Calf Routine:
Heavy Day

1. Donkey calf raises – *3 sets of 8-10 reps*
2. Standing calf raises – *3 sets of 8-10 reps*
3. Seated calf raises – *2 sets of 8-10 reps*

Lisa Lorio

in the gym. Lisa took the hint and frequently spends time at the track running 50-yard sprints.

She divides her calf-training into three workouts – heavy, light and giant-set day. Her rep range is in proportion to the amount of weight. Besides these regular routines she throws in extra sets on her noncalf days. For example, on chest day she does 3 or 4 sets of calves just to pump them up and get the blood into the area.

Her heavy day consists of 3 sets of donkey calf raises and standing calf raises followed by 2 sets of seated calf raises. She averages 8 to 10 reps on each set, using as much weight as she can handle – up to 400 pounds on both the donkey and standing calf machines.

A light day starts with 3 or 4 sets of toe presses on the leg-press machine. As she is using light weight, Lisa often goes as high as 50 reps on this exercise. Next it's 4 sets of standing calf raises. She uses about half her heavy-day weight, and does 20 to 25 reps per set. To finish her light-day calf routine, she does 3 or 4

Seated calf raises
– Lisa Lorio

Start

Finish

Light Day

1. Toe presses on leg-press machine – *4 sets of 50 reps*
2. Standing calf raises – *4 sets of 20-25 reps*
3. Seated calf raises – *3 sets of 20-25 reps*

Giant-Set Day

1. Standing calf raises
2. Seated calf raises
3. Donkey calf raises
4. Toe presses on leg-press machine

For each exercise – 1-3 giant sets of 10-25 reps

RICH GASPARI – When he strutted his stuff in the mid-1980s and early 1990s, pro bodybuilder Rich Gaspari was famous for the rock-hard condition he brought to each contest. Even fellow competitors would stop and compliment him on his outstanding vascularity. Like many other hopefuls, he was held back in his quest for the Olympia by one man – Atlanta's Lee Haney!

Besides praise for his freaky muscular condition, Rich garnered many words of encouragement for his exceptional calves. But if you compare his recent photos with those taken when he won the 1984 World Championship, you'll see that he was not born with great calves. He sweated out hundreds of hours of calf raises to develop his average-potential calves into those worthy of a Mr. Olympia contender.

Rich says his goal in calf-training is to keep the muscles so confused that they can't adapt to any one program. There are many ways to increase training intensity, and his favorite is descending sets. As an example he does donkey calf raises with extra weight tied around his waist and a training partner on his back. He does 12 to 15 reps in this manner and then has the training partner hop off before grinding out another 10 to 12 reps. Not being one to shy away from pain, he usually does 5 such drop sets. At this stage his calves feel as though they've been torched, but he's not finished yet!

After donkeys Rich goes on to either the standing calf raise, or supersets of seated calf raises and toe presses on the leg-press machine. He may also do one-leg calf raises holding a dumbell in his hand. He rarely does the same workout two days in a row. If there is one exercise that he uses consistently, however, it's the seated calf raise. As he points out, this is about the only exercise specifically designed for hitting the soleus muscle. Other machines can be used to hit the soleus if you keep your legs bent while doing the exercise, but those machines were primarily designed to hit the larger gastrocnemius muscle.

Although Rich frequently varies the exercises, he nearly always keeps his reps in the 12-to-15 range, only occasionally going down to 6 or 8 or as high as 20 to 30. He tries to keep sets around 12 to 15 reps. Any more, he says, and he overtrains. Finally, he employs numerous advanced training techniques (e.g. descending sets, forced reps) to increase the intensity of his calf workouts.

Rich Gaspari's Calf Routine:

1. Donkey calf raises – *5 descending sets of 12-15 reps*
2. Standing calf raises – *4 sets of 12-15 reps*
3. Seated calf raises – *4 sets of 12-15 reps*
Rich occasionally increases the reps to 20 to 30, or decreases to 6 to 8.

The freaky muscles of Rich Gaspari.

FRANK ZANE – When it comes to making do with what you've got, you need look no further than three-time Mr. Olympia winner Frank Zane. Unlike many of his 1970s contemporaries (Arnold Schwarzenegger, Lou Ferrigno, Mike Mentzer), Frank was not blessed with great bodybuilding genetics. Although he had the height (5'10"), his bone structure was on the light side. To make matters worse, his metabolism didn't seem to gain muscle mass easily. Together the two problems left him with an uphill battle. Lesser men would have quit before they got started, but not Frank. Grabbing the bull by the horns so to speak, he set out to make the most of his limited genetics. He was probably the first bodybuilder to spend as much time learning about gaining weight as actually training.

Realizing that he could never match the mass of some of his larger opponents, he decided to concentrate on completeness. If Arnold and Sergio Oliva can be considered the first bodybuilders in terms of extreme mass, Frank was the pioneer of contest preparation (with all due respect to Vince Gironda). In fact he used his outstanding refinement to hand Arnold one of his few losses at the 1968 Mr. Universe. (Of course Arnold learned his lesson well and the rest, as they say, is history.) Throughout the 1970s Frank used his more refined physique to beat competitors who outweighed him by 20 pounds or more. His career peaked in the late '70s when he won the Mr. Olympia three years in a row (1977-1979).

The key to Frank's success can be summed up in one word – *perseverance*. Not content to let poor genetics stand in his way, he undertook to prove that with an intelligent plan under his belt, a person can achieve almost anything. How many bodybuilders with far greater genetics than Frank's, but little of his drive, gave up after encountering the first obstacle?

Early in his career, he recognized that with his limited mass potential he would need to concentrate on refinement and proportions, and this meant developing every muscle to its maximum. After seeing the progress Arnold made to his calves, he was determined to do the same to his own.

Two of his early influences were Reg Park and Chris Dickerson. He was lucky enough to train with the great South African, Park, for two weeks in 1978. As Reg was famous for his calves (Arnold later said that Reg influenced his calf-training more than anyone else), Frank paid particular attention to how Reg

Rich Gaspari

trained his calves. Everything from foot position and exercise speed to the time between sets was mentally filed away by the inquisitive Zane.

The other man who influenced him was Chris Dickerson. The future Mr. Olympia winner (1982) was an example of what can be accomplished *with* great calf genetics. Most bodybuilders spend years bringing their calves up to the rest of their body, but Chris had to do the opposite – let his body catch up to his calves!

Great genetics or not, Dickerson was careful to include regular calf-training in his workouts, and one of the details Frank noticed was his full range of motion. He estimated that Chris moved his heels a full 5 or 6 inches during his seated calf raises. He did every rep from a full stretch at the bottom to a high contraction at the top.

After years of trial, error and observation Frank came up with several calf routines that added inches to his calves. The basis of his calf-training was variety – at least two exercises per workout. His favorite exercise was the seated calf raise. To hit both major muscles on the calf, he alternated between pulling his heels straight up (mostly targeting the soleus) and rolling outward on the balls of his feet (both soleus and gastrocnemius). Although he always did seated raises in his routine, he never started with that exercise as it placed too much strain on his Achilles tendon. He always did another exercise first to serve as a warmup.

Frank also credited donkey calf raises on the Nautilus machine for developing his calves. Before he discovered the machine, he did the exercise with a training partner on his back (who was often holding a 50-pound plate). Prior to the 1978 Mr. Olympia he was doing 10 sets of 20 to 25 reps. He usually needed only the first 2 or 3 sets to bring an intense burning sensation to his calves. The last 7 sets were bloody murder, but the results were worth the effort as he won his second Mr. Olympia title.

In the early 1980s Mike Mentzer introduced Frank to the Nautilus donkey-raise machine. He used the machine to do both one- and two-leg donkey raises. Soon he was using the entire stack plus additional weight. To provide more resistance, he would have his wife, Christine, sit on his back as well. The total weight then approached 500 pounds. After 15 reps Christine would hop off his back, and Frank would grind out another 10 reps. Without stopping, he would remove the extra weight (usually four 45-pound plates) and blast out a final 10 reps.

Although retired from competition, Frank still finds time to train and write about the sport that has given him so much. With 40 years of training under his belt, he is regularly sought for his advice by younger bodybuilders.

The following is an example of his calf training. He varies the routine from time to time, alternating between straight sets, supersets and trisets.

Frank Zane's Calf Routine:
1. Standing calf raises – *3 sets of 25-30 reps*
2. Seated calf raises – *4 sets of 15-20 reps*
3. Donkey calf raises (machine) – *3 sets of 15-20 reps*

Frank Zane

Dorian Yates

Chapter Twenty-six

BICEPS & TRICEPS

MOUNTAIN PEAKS AND GIANT HORSESHOES

"The best size exercise I can possibly imagine for triceps is the lying French press. It was Sergio Oliva's favorite. We're talking a generation ago, but who has ever been better in that department?"
– Mike Matarazzo, IFBB Pro Bodybuilder USA champion (outlining one of the secrets to better triceps development)

Mike Matarazzo

There are countless reasons why individuals take up bodybuilding. For some it's to supplement another sport. For others it's to attract members of the opposite sex. But for most, however, the number one reason for first grabbing a barbell is to develop bigger biceps. When Arnold Schwarzenegger dominated the Mr. Olympia title back in the 1970s, often the first pose he hit was the front double biceps. Why? Because he knew that while a few others had arms as large (Lou Ferrigno, Sergio Oliva), none had his peak and separation. How many aspiring bodybuilders have stared for hours at the cover of *Arnold: The Education of a Bodybuilder?* It's safe to say that no other bodybuilder ever duplicated that picture of Arnold hitting a single biceps pose.

"The largest muscular arm that I ever measured or saw, was Sergio Oliva's, which accurately measured cold was 20-1/8 inches. Arnold Schwarzenegger's arm was 19-7/8, slightly pumped, probably 19-1/2 cold." **– Dr. Arthur Jones, Nautilus Inventor**

To limit our discussion of arms to Arnold would be doing an injustice to countless others who have maximized bodybuilding's most coveted muscles. The first Mr. Olympia, Larry Scott, was renowned for his large, full biceps development. When Sergio Oliva emerged on the scene, he literally dwarfed the two competitors standing next to him with his trademark double-biceps poses. Other behemoths with great arm development include Casey Viator, Flex Wheeler, Vince Taylor, Paul Dillett, Kevin Levrone, Boyer Coe, Robby Robinson, Chuck Williams, Bill Grant, Mike Matarazzo, Paul DeMayo, Larry Scott, Albert Beckles, Aaron Baker, Manfred Hoeberl and Vic Richards.

The last two are examples of just how awe-inspiring huge arms are to bodybuilding fans. Neither Manfred nor Victor has won a significant bodybuilding competition. Manfred is renowned as a strongman competitor, and Vic refuses to compete head to head with the current crop of top pros. Yet both are among the most sought-after bodybuilders for seminars and posing exhibitions. The reason behind their popularity is simple. Both sport two of the largest pairs of muscular arms in the world. Vic's stretch the tape to between 22 and 23 inches, and as for Manfred, estimates put those guns in the 24-to 25-inch range!

ANATOMY

What is often lost in discussions of arm development is the fact that it's not the more familiar biceps that make up most of the upper arm's bulk, but the less glamorous triceps. Think of the arm as just a smaller version of your legs. In fact the two are the same, but since humans walk upright, we tend to think of the arms and legs as being two separate entities. With the exception of the great apes, every other mammal has four legs. And even the great apes spend most of their time hobbling about on all fours.

What's the largest muscle in your leg? Why, the thigh or quadriceps of course. And what's the smaller muscle that counteracts the thigh? It's the hamstring or leg biceps. The same holds true for the upper arm. The triceps is analogous to the quadriceps – not only is it the largest muscle on the limb, but it's also responsible for extending the lower arm into the locked position. The biceps (both leg and arm) is the smaller muscle which curls or bends the two sections of the limb towards each other. Therefore, does it make sense to devote most of your leg training to the thighs and yet ignore the triceps of the upper arm? Yet go into any gym and you'll observe – bodybuilders doing 10, 15 or 20 sets for the biceps and significantly less for the triceps. If you want huge arms (and what bodybuilder doesn't) you must train the triceps as hard as – if not harder than – the biceps. Granted they may not impress the average person as much as a peaked biceps, but remember, not only does the triceps make up about two-thirds of the arm's mass, but it also contributes heavily to such movements as bench presses and shoulder presses. Often a weak shoulder or bench press is the result of an underdeveloped triceps muscle. Have we convinced you yet?

TRAINING

"Knowing my arms were genetically big, I was eager to capitalize on a natural gift and simply followed a basic human impulse. The more my biceps stood out, the bigger I wanted them to be! The bigger they became, the more I worked them. Big arms, after all, are the most famous symbol of bodybuilding, more so than any other bodypart." — **Ronnie Coleman, world amateur champion**

If you were to ask Joe Average on the street to demonstrate a weightlifting exercise, chances are he would pretend to curl a bar with his biceps. Of the thousands of bodybuilding exercises, the standing barbell curl is probably the best known and most frequently performed. There are a number of reasons for this popularity.

Ronnie Coleman

For starters it's the exercise that develops the biceps, right? You can be sure that any exercise that works the biceps is going to get a lot of attention. Another reason is its simplicity. All you need is a bar and a few plates. That's it. No fancy cables, pulleys or machines are required. Finally, you can do curls just about anywhere – gym, basement, hotel room, etc. Few exercises offer such a promising list of characteristics.

Besides barbell curls, bodybuilders make use of dumbells, cables and machines. Dumbells are popular as they place less stress on the elbows and forearms. Cables are great for precontest training as they keep tension on the muscle throughout the full range of motion. The effectiveness of machine curls can be debated. You might want to include them for variety, but try to center your biceps-training around barbells and dumbells.

The key to large arms is triceps development. Unlike biceps-training where there is one favorite exercise (the barbell curl), bodybuilders have a wide range of preferred triceps exercises. Among the most popular are lying barbell extensions, lat-machine pushdowns and dumbell extensions.

"I burn out if I push my biceps past failure too often. On other muscle groups I can bust past the failure point much more frequently."
– Lee Haney
IFBB Pro Bodybuilder
Eight-time Mr. Olympia

Biceps and triceps receive an enormous amount of stimulation from training the large torso muscles (chest, back, and shoulders). Any time you do pressing movements (bench press, shoulder press) your triceps are heavily involved. Likewise, the biceps get a blast when you work the lats. This means it's very easy to overtrain your arm muscles. Let's face it. After doing 15 to 20 sets of chest or back work, your biceps or triceps are close to fatigue. It makes no sense to bomb them with an additional 15 to 20 sets. Even the superstars with years of experience would quickly overtrain if they followed such a practice for extended periods of time. While many do additional sets for precontest training, they usually do no more than 10 or 12 sets during the off-season.

Common Biceps Exercises:
1. Standing barbell curls
2. Standing dumbell curls
3. Preacher (Scott) curls
4. Concentration curls
5. Alternate curls
6. EZ-bar curls
7. Cable curls
8. Machine curls

Common Triceps Exercises:
1. Lying extensions
2. Pushdowns
3. Dumbell extensions
4. Kickbacks
5. Reverse pushdowns
6. French presses
7. Narrow-grip bench presses
8. Dips

THE CHAMPS' ROUTINES

ARNOLD SCHWARZENEGGER – We begin this section with perhaps the most famous set of arms in bodybuilding history. Much of Arnold's competitive success could be attributed to those 22-inch hams of his. (Of course the rest of his physique didn't hurt either!). Often all it took was the opening double-biceps shot and it was all over.

Arnold's arm-training was as simple as it was productive. Although he varied the exercises from time to time, he made sure to include a couple of barbell and dumbell movements during each arm workout. He divided his arm-training into two phases: nine months for mass-building (off-season) and three months for shaping (precontest). During the off-season, he mainly

Lee Haney

did straight sets. His precontest training consisted of biceps and triceps exercises supersetted together.

OFF-SEASON

On most days he started with standing barbell curls, doing 5 or 6 sets of 8 to 10 reps. To increase the intensity of the set, Arnold frequently made use of the cheating technique. He chose a weight that allowed 4 to 6 reps in good style, and then forced out an additional 3 or 4 reps using a slight body swing.

Another favorite biceps-builder was Scott or preacher curls. Unlike most bodybuilders who do the exercise on the inclined part of the foam pad, Arnold frequently turned the pad around and let his arms extend straight down.

His favorite dumbell exercises were standing alternate curls, concentration curls and seated incline curls. The concentration curls deserve special mention. Most people brace the exercising arm against the inner thigh. Arnold, however, preferred to do the exercise with the arm held free or away from the thigh. Whereas most do the exercise while sitting, he would stand in a bent-over position.

PRECONTEST

About three months before a contest he changed his arm-training. After spending nine months focusing on mass-building, it was time to hone and refine the new muscle. The first major change was to increase his arm workouts from two to three a week. Also, instead of straight sets, Arnold supersetted biceps and triceps together. For example he would do a set of incline dumbell curls and then follow it with triceps pushdowns. Other supersets he did included standing dumbell curls with dumbell extensions and Scott curls with lying EZ-curl bar extensions. A typical workout consisted of 4 supersets of each exercise combination, doing 8 to 10 reps per set.

Arnold Schwarzenegger's Mass-Building Routine (Sample):
1. Standing barbell curls –
   4-5 sets of 8-10 reps
2. Standing dumbell curls –
   4-5 sets of 8-10 reps
3. Concentration curls –
   4-5 sets of 8-10 reps

Arnold's Precontest Routine (Sample):
1. Standing dumbell curls/dumbell extensions –
   4 supersets of 8-10 reps
2. Incline dumbell curls/triceps pushdowns –
   4 supersets of 8-10 reps
3. Scott curls/lying triceps extensions –
   4 supersets of 8-10 reps

DENNIS NEWMAN – Although he didn't win the two contests he was favored to take in 1993 (the USA and NPC National Championships), California's Dennis Newman is considered by many to be one of the best amateurs on the bodybuilding scene. Unfortunately, his diagnosis with leukemia has prevented him from wreaking havoc on the pro scene.

What makes the Newman physique so impressive is its completeness. It's not an overstatement to say he has it all – size, symmetry, stage presence, and screen-idol looks. Among his better bodyparts are his huge, well-shaped arms. He is proud of his arms, and rightly so. He has spent the last couple of years

Arnold Schwarzenegger performs preacher curls.

bringing them up to par with his huge delts. Early in his career, Dennis recognized that his fast growing delts were overshadowing his arms. He was faced with two choices – decrease his delt size or increase the size of his arms. When it comes to muscle mass, the word "decrease" is rarely used in a bodybuilder's vocabulary. Subsequently, he chose to increase the size of his arms.

Like many experienced bodybuilders, he let instinct play a major role in his training. He rarely follows a set routine, and often enters the gym unsure of exactly which exercises he will perform:

"No two workouts are ever the same. I vary things all the time. Sometimes I start with cables and machines and end with heavy barbell/dumbell stuff. Other times I start heavy and finish with cables. The only consistency is that I always incorporate barbells and dumbells into each workout because basic movements build muscle."

Dennis Newman demonstrates one-arm preacher curls.

Dennis trains arms on day four of his four-day cycle. He has no favorite exercises – one day he'll start with triceps, the next day it's biceps. He likes to shock his muscles and keep them guessing, and one of the best ways to do this is by constantly changing the order of the exercises.

If he starts his arm training with biceps, the first exercise is usually Scott curls. He completes 2 light warmup sets, and then begins adding plates. He does 2 wide and 2 medium-grip sets, using 135 to 140 pounds. On most days he does reps of 10, but occasionally he adds a few extra plates, and reduces the reps to 6.

Dennis's next exercise is alternate dumbell curls. Since his arms are warmed up, he jumps right to his workout poundage. A typical day sees him perform 4 or 5 sets, starting with 75-pound dumbells and working down to 60 pounders. Proper style for Dennis is like reading a page from bodybuilding history. With an image of Arnold Schwarzenegger fixed in his mind, he starts each rep with his palms facing towards his body. Then, as the dumbell is lifted, he rotates his palms until they are fully supinated (facing upwards). He finds this little movement gives his biceps that extra bit of contraction.

Dennis considers these first two exercises his mass-builders, which means that his third and fourth exercises are primarily for peaking the biceps. He has a repertoire of three or four exercises from which he chooses. On some days it's one-arm cable curls, on others he performs 90-degree preacher curls. Then there's his favorite – cable preacher curls. No matter what the exercise, Dennis performs 4 sets of 10 reps.

To finish his biceps, he completes 4 sets of 8 to 10 reps of dumbell concentration curls. Rather than perform them with his arm held away from the body like Arnold, Dennis prefers to remain seated with his elbow braced against his inner thigh:

"This position feels better because it steadies me for increased biceps isolation. I can curl the dumbell smoothly up to my shoulder without rocking my body."

After a few minutes' rest, he moves on to his triceps. In most cases he begins his triceps training with lying extensions using an EZ-curl bar. Since this is his first triceps exercise, Dennis does two light warmup sets. He follows with 3 sets of 10 to 12 reps, adding weight with each set. With regards to technique, Dennis lowers the bar to the middle of his skull. (Keep in mind that there is much personal preference on this issue. Some bodybuilders lower the bar to the bridge of their nose, while others lower the bar behind their head. Our best advice is to try different positions and pick the one that's most comfortable).

His next exercise is triceps pushdowns on the lat machine. Although many bodybuilders like to use a V-shaped bar, Dennis prefers the straight bar. Most bodybuilders consider pushdowns a shaping exercise, but Dennis disagrees. Perhaps it has something to do with the 300 to 400 pounds of weight he uses! Using such a large amount of weight requires the assistance of a training partner to hold him down to the floor. Even though he uses horrendous poundages, he is careful to maintain good form. As he pushes the bar down, he turns his head to the side, and only brings the bar up to his midsection before reversing its direction. For variety, he occasionally substitutes a rope in place of the bar. Of course this means using less weight, but he still forces out his usual 10 to 12 reps.

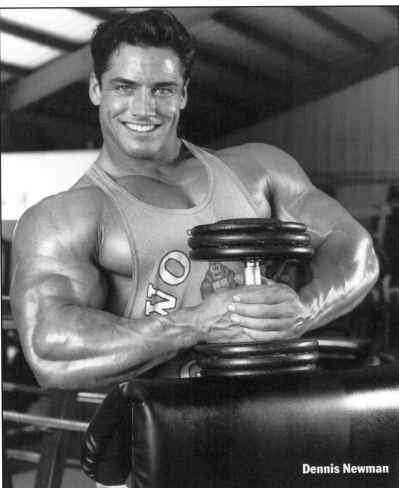

Dennis Newman

For his third exercise, he performs either reverse triceps pushdowns or lying triceps extensions using a dumbell. On the pushdowns, he raises the bar to his forehead and pushes it down to an arms-locked-out position. Dennis finds that this particular exercise is excellent for his lower triceps.

For lying dumbell extensions, he starts with a 45-pound dumbell and works up to a 60 pounder. For those not familiar with the exercise, it's done in the following manner. Lie on your back on a flat bench, and grasp the dumbell with your palms facing your body. Keeping the elbows locked and pointed upwards, lower the dumbell so that it just grazes the ear. You can perform the exercise using two dumbells, but most bodybuilders prefer doing them one arm at a time. For variety, Dennis will occasionally throw in a few sets of dumbell kickbacks. As with his other exercises, it's 4 sets of 10 to 12 reps.

To finish his triceps, and leave them with an awesome burn, he reps out on what he calls "reverse pushups". Most know them as dips between two benches. Dennis does 3 high-rep sets to failure.

Although he changes his routine from week to week (often from day to day!), the following is a sample arm routine that he frequently uses to send shivers up the spines of his fellow competitors.

Dennis Newman's Arm Routine:

Biceps

1. Preacher curls –
   4 sets of 10-12 reps
2. Standing dumbell curls –
   4 sets of 10-12 reps
3. Cable preacher curls –
   4 sets of 10-12 reps
4. Concentration curls –
   4 sets of 8-10 reps

Triceps

5. Lying triceps extensions –
   3 sets of 10-12 reps
6. Triceps pushdowns –
   4 sets of 10-12 reps
7. Lying dumbell extensions –
   4 sets of 10-12 reps
8. Dips between benches –
   3 sets to failure

SAMIR BANNOUT – When one talks of complete arm development, the name Samir Bannout frequently gets mentioned. In fact, few bodybuilders have had Samir's completeness when it comes to arm development. His biceps run the complete length of his upper arm and the three heads of his triceps are fully developed and clearly defined. Samir used these qualities to take the sport's most coveted title, the Mr. Olympia, in 1993.

He believes in training heavy most of the time, but occasionally shocks his muscles with high reps. Samir emphasizes the fact that he always listens to his body, and if it feels right, he does it. He is also a firm believer in the perils of overtraining. For this reason he limits his training to no more than twice a week for each muscle group:

"I allow 72 hours for the muscle to recuperate. I believe that the biceps are just like the abdominals, calves and every other bodypart. Some people think it's necessary to train certain muscle groups three times a week, but I don't agree with that."

Laura Creavalle

For ultimate development, Samir tries to hit the biceps from all angles. He accepts Arnold's belief that the body becomes complacent if it receives the same stimulation over and over again, without change.

Samir's first biceps exercise is often the barbell preacher curl. He uses a wide grip and a weight that limits him to 7 to 12 reps. Although it may vary, he usually does 3 or 4 sets.

His next exercise is alternating dumbell curls, either seated or standing. Once again it's 3 or 4 sets of 7 to 12 reps.

For maximum peak, Samir performs an exercise that is sort of his own creation – squatting cable curls. He starts the exercise with his hands facing the inside of his opposite leg. He then rotates his palm up as the weight is lifted. By the time his biceps are fully contracted, his palms are nearly facing outward. Unlike most bodybuilders who go light on this exercise, he uses as much weight as he can handle, and sticks to his patented 7 to 10 reps.

Before concluding we should mention that Samir frequently changes the order of his exercises. For example, he often substitutes standing barbell curls in place of preacher curls. Other exercises, such as concentration curls and cable barbell curls, are also utilized routinely. He says that the bottom line is to listen to your body:

Samir Bannout

"Use heavy weights for ultimate muscle density with a lot of feeling. Don't use heavy weights if you can't feel the muscles working. Listen to your body, be in control, and focus. Try to hit the muscle from all angles for maximal development."

Samir Bannout's Biceps Routine:
1. Barbell preacher curls – *3-4 sets of 7-12 reps*
2. Alternating dumbell curls – *3-4 sets of 7-12 reps*
3. Cable concentration curls – *3-4 sets of 7-12 reps*

LAURA CREAVALLE – Few female bodybuilders can match Laura Creavalle when it comes to arm development. In fact, many consider her front and back double-biceps pose the best in the business. No doubt those impressive arms of hers were one of the reasons she came so close to winning the 1994 Ms. Olympia.

Start

Finish

What makes Laura's biceps and triceps so outstanding is not just their size, which she has to spare, but their quality. When Laura hits a triceps shot, all three heads separate into shredded muscle, with the rear head extending from her shoulder to her elbow.

Now Laura is the first to admit that the length of her triceps is genetic, but all of the genetic potential in the world is useless if it's wasted by unproductive training. And training is one area where she shines. Every rep is done in immaculate style with little or no cheating. Laura usually begins her triceps training with close-grip bench presses. She does one warmup set, and then 4 sets of 6 to 10 reps. She finds this exercise great for triceps thickness and density.

Laura's second exercise is triceps pushdowns, and once again she performs 4 sets of 10 reps. For variety, she alternates between the one and two-arm versions. If she's performing the one-arm version, Laura turns her wrist out at the bottom to put more stress on the outer head.

For her third exercise she performs bent-over rope extensions. Laura keeps the reps slightly higher on this exercise and leans away from the machine to get a full stretch. With her elbows wide and shoulders locked, she pushes her arms to a locked-out position. Once again she does 4 sets of 10 to 12 reps.

The three previous exercises usually make up Laura's complete triceps routine, but every now and then she adds an extra set or two. Also, close to a contest she will include a few sets of one or two-arm dumbell extensions.

Laura Creavalle's Triceps Routine:
1. Close-grip bench presses – *4 sets of 6-10 reps*
2. Triceps pushdowns – *4 sets of 8-10 reps*
3. Bent-over rope extensions – *4 sets of 10-12 reps*
4. One or two-arm dumbell extensions*– *2-3 sets of 10-12 reps*
*Precontest only

RENEL JANVIER – During the early 1980s, one of the sport's greatest stars was Louisiana native, Boyer Coe. With his third place finish at the 1980 Mr. Olympia (still hotly debated to this day) and numerous Grand Prix wins, Boyer's physique was often the standard by which other competitors

Samir Bannout works his biceps with preacher curls.

**For truly massive arms the triceps must be fully developed.
– Renel Janvier**

they're composed of steel cords – look no further than Renel Janvier. He used his great guns to place third in three consecutive shows (Ironman Invitational, Arnold Classic, and the Pittsburgh Invitational) in 1991.

Renel has a unique training system in that he only trains one bodypart per day. This means he doesn't need to take any days off. And training only one muscle per session means he can go all out and totally annihilate it.

Even though Renel's schedule calls for biceps training only once a week, there are occasions when he will skip them completely:

"Yeah, it's true, sometimes I skip a whole week between biceps workouts. If I work them once a week, they don't respond. I need to blast them once every other week. I train my back so hard that my biceps get tons of work from pulling. I really don't do biceps work that frequently. But when I do, I stick with the basic movements, and I work hard."

Another Janvier idiosyncrasy is to use only one exercise when training a muscle. Instead of performing 4 or 5 sets of 3 or 4 movements, he will pick a single exercise and stick with it for the entire workout.

His favorite biceps exercise is standing barbell curls. He usually does 6 to 12 reps, pyramiding the weight from 100 to 160 pounds. With regards to sets, he doesn't have a fixed number:

"I'll just do as many sets as I feel are necessary. I know when my biceps have gotten enough work. On my last set I may do a descending set where I do the first few reps with my maximum weight, and then keep stripping the weight and bombing the biceps all the way."

A second favorite exercise is the seated incline curl. Once again he may use the exercise for his entire biceps workout, or perform them in conjunction with other movements. As with barbell curls, Renel keeps the reps in the 6 to 12 range. He performs the exercise in an alternating fashion, supinating his hands on every rep.

Another preferred exercise is preacher curls. He does several different variations of this exercise. One day it will be done standing, the next day it could be seated. Or if he's in the mood, he may skip the barbell and use dumbells.

Even though he may add some isolation movements like dumbell and cable concentration curls as a competition draws nearer, the bulk of his workout remains the same. The only real change is in his diet and the amount of cardio work, which includes 90 minutes on a StairMaster.

Renel Janvier's Biceps Routine:
1. Standing barbell curls
2. Incline curls
3. Preacher curls

For each exercise Renel pyramids the weight performing 4-5 sets of 6-12 reps.

were measured. Among Boyer's greatest bodyparts were his two "baseball-sized" biceps, which Boyer had the ability to split – almost at will. With their great size, and near-perfect balance and symmetry, Boyer's arms were the envy of millions.

In recent years a new force has emerged on the bodybuilding scene, and when Haitian born Renel Janvier hits a double-biceps pose many observers feel they are witnessing the re-emergence of the great Cajun. Renel's arms are that good.

If you're looking for an arm that has everything – grapefruit-sized biceps, triceps with all three heads fully developed and separated, and forearms that look like

Note – He prefers to let instinct determine his exact biceps routine. He occasionally sticks to one exercise for an entire workout.

MIKE ASHLEY – After he won the 1990 Arnold Classic and placed second in the Ironman Invitational, Mike Ashley realized that he could compete and beat the best in the sport. What's more important is the fact that Mike trains and competes without the aid of performance-enhancing drugs. He is living proof that, given the right genetics, dedication to training, and frame of mind, an individual can reach the top of the bodybuilding hierarchy without chemical assistance.

When it comes to arm training, he likes to alternate between three distinct routines. He trains for a month using light weights and high reps, follows with a month of medium weight and intermediate reps, and finally devotes a third month to low reps and heavier weights. About a month before a competition, Mike combines all three routines in his precontest preparation. The end result is one of the most dangerous pair of arms on the pro circuit!

Mike Ashley's Biceps Routines:

Heavy Day
1. Seated alternate dumbell curls – *5 sets of 6 reps*
2. Preacher curls – *5 sets of 6 reps*
3. Seated dumbell curls – *5 sets of 6 reps*

Medium Day
1. Preacher curls – *5 sets of 12 reps*
2. Seated dumbell curls – *5 sets of 12 reps*
3. Barbell curls – *5 sets of 12 reps*

Light Day
1. Standing barbell curls – *5 sets of 15 reps*
2. Preacher curls – *5 sets of 21s*
3. Seated dumbell curls – *5 sets of 15 reps*

JOHN TERILLI – The sport of bodybuilding had its own version of "Crocodile Dundee" appear on the scene in the mid-'80s. After winning his class at the 1982 Mr. Universe, Australia's John Terilli packed up his posing briefs and vitamin supplements, and headed for Brooklyn, New York. When he burst on the pro scene in 1983, John was a virtual unknown. Yet, in short order, he placed 5th at the Night of Champions, 2nd at the Caesar's Cup, and 9th at the 1986 Mr. Olympia. Then, when it seemed he was a permanent fixture on the pro circuit, he "disappeared" as fast as he arrived! In reality there was nothing mysterious about his leaving competitive bodybuilding. After three or four grueling years on tour, he decided to settle down and move back "down under".

Although you'd never guess by looking at him, John's arms were always one of his more stubborn bodyparts. Not being one to easily give in, he decided to shock the muscles into new growth:

"The best shocking method I had ever applied to my arms involved taking a barbell into my house and doing a set for biceps and a set for triceps every half-hour, for the whole waking day. Sometimes I did it two days in a row. It worked like magic. I won't even bother to tell you how much I gained. You wouldn't believe it, and neither would anybody else."

Over the years John discovered two things: He was lifting far too much weight and his protein intake was inadequate. To solve the problem, he cut back on his workout poundages and concentrated on "feeling" the weight. As for protein intake, this was easily remedied by loading up on amino acids. The result of these two changes was dramatic:

"Once I found the right workout and the proper food intake, my arm development took off!"

What's surprising is that as his arm workouts evolved they became simpler, not more complicated. In a typical workout he performs a few sets of alternate dumbell curls and then a few sets of barbell curls, using either the EZ-curl or straight bar. He sometimes reverses the order but consistently uses lighter weights with dumbells, and heavier weight on the barbell. Close to a contest, John adds a few sets of cable or concentration curls.

Mike Ashley

For triceps it's usually 3 or 4 sets of lying triceps extensions (using a straight or EZ-curl bar), followed by 3 or 4 sets of triceps pushdowns on the lat machine (using a straight bar or rope). To finish his triceps, he adds a few sets of one-arm cable extensions. With regards to exact sets and reps, we should let John explain:

"All of my exercises vary, but I generally do from 2 to 4 sets, and my reps range from 6 to 15. I don't worry about doing anything too strictly, and I don't go too heavy, but I always concentrate on getting the right feel."

Occasionally, John will incorporate advanced training principles into his workouts. For example, he has a training partner give him a few forced reps, or instead of doing straight sets he will throw in some supersets and trisets. Perhaps his favorite routine for arms includes giant sets. For instance, when working on his triceps he'll pick four different exercises and do them one after another. A popular triceps giant set includes lying extensions, narrow-grip triceps presses, triceps pushdowns, and triceps kickbacks.

Despite his love of giant sets, he is careful not to abuse a good thing. He knows that the human body can only endure such intensity for a limited time. For this reason, he performs giant sets every third or fourth workout.

John Terilli's Arm Routine:

Biceps
1. Alternate dumbell curls – *3-4 sets of 6-15 reps*
2. Barbell curls – *3-4 sets of 6-15 reps*
3. Cable/dumbell concentration curls* –
   3-4 sets of 6-15 reps

Precontest only

Triceps
1. Lying triceps extensions – *3-4 sets of 6-15 reps*
2. Triceps pushdowns – *3-4 sets of 6-15 reps*
3. One-arm cable extensions – *3-4 sets of 6-15 reps*

NIMROD KING – When he first burst onto the Canadian bodybuilding scene, most agreed that it was only a matter of time before the Trinidadian-born competitor would be strutting his stuff with the IFBB's top pros. In fact, Nimrod's appearance at the Canadian championships led many audience members to believe that he was the guest poser and not a contestant – he was that huge!

Among the most awesome appendages on the pro bodybuilding circuit, Nimrod's arms resemble two over-sized Christmas hams. He prefers to train biceps and triceps on separate days, biceps being trained on day one, following his back workout, and triceps after shoulders on day two.

Regarding repetitions, he has taken a page from the works of Serge Nubret. Instead of the traditional 8- to 12-rep range, he prefers the 15 to 25 range. He finds that, not only does this give him the size he wants, but

it also keeps his arms vascular and highly defined – giving him the best of both worlds.

Also unique is Nimrod's fondness for keeping the weight constant on all his sets. He selects a weight that allows 20 to 25 reps on the first set, and then attempts to get the same number of reps on each additional set.

Nimrod's first biceps exercise is the hammer curl. He finds this great for both biceps and brachialis mass. Unlike most bodybuilders who perform the exercise while sitting on a flat bench, he prefers to do the movement on a 45-degree angle bench. He does 4 sets of 20 to 25 reps during a typical workout.

His second exercise consists of 4 sets of barbell preacher curls. He believes that the bench's angle strongly affects lower-biceps development.

To finish off his biceps, Nimrod completes 4 sets of concentration curls, bracing the elbow against his inner thigh. By the time he finishes, his biceps have seemingly swelled to twice their original size. What started out as arms which looked like baseballs now resemble softballs. But these are only his biceps, and the following evening it's back to the gym to hit the triceps.

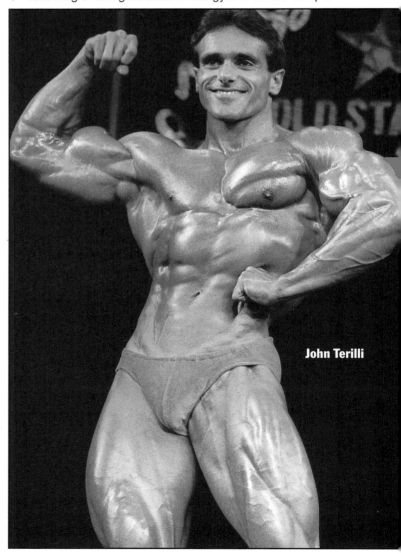

John Terilli

Triceps work begins with standing pushdowns on the lat machine. Nimrod favors a narrow grip on this exercise, and grabs the bar with an overhand grip.

His next exercise is lying dumbell extensions. He lies down on a flat bench and holds a dumbell in each arm. With his palms facing together, elbows pointed upwards, the dumbells are lowered to the side of the head. He is careful to keep the elbows stationary throughout the full range of the exercise.

His third triceps exercise is the one-arm cable pushdown. Of all his triceps exercises, he finds this one the best for bringing out the muscle's horseshoe shape. He does 3 sets of 20 to 25 reps on each arm.

To finish triceps, Nimrod performs 4 or 5 sets of rope extensions. Using a lat machine or a wall pulley, he grabs the rope and faces away from the weight stack. With his elbows held close to his head, he extends his arms to a fully locked out position.

On both days (biceps and triceps) Nimrod concludes his arm training with a forearm exercise. On a biceps day it's reverse wrist curls using a dumbell. After triceps training, it's 4 sets of normal (palms facing up) wrist curls.

Nimrod King's Arm Routine:

Biceps
1. Hammer curls – *4 sets of 15-25 reps*
2. Preacher curls – *4 sets of 15-25 reps*
3. Concentration curls – *4 sets of 15-25 reps*
4. Reverse dumbell wrist curls – *4 sets of 15-25 reps*

Triceps
1. Pushdowns – *4 sets of 15-25 reps*
2. Lying dumbell extensions – *4 sets of 15-25 reps*
3. One-arm cable pushdowns – *4 sets of 15-25 reps*
4. Behind-the-head rope extensions – *4 sets of 15-25 reps*
5. Dumbell wrist curls – *4 sets of 15-25 reps*

GARY STRYDOM – One of the largest bodybuilders to appear in the mid-'80s was South Africa's Gary Strydom. After taking up residence in the US, Gary hit the Grand Prix tour with a vengeance. Success came quick, and his best year was 1989, when he won four contests. Just when it seemed that Gary was to be an immortal fixture in IFBB contests, he skipped town and joined the short-lived rival WBF organization. After serving a mandatory suspension, Gary was reinstated and bodybuilding fans began looking forward to a "second coming" of the South African behemoth.

Although criticized for his less than perfect back (it didn't help matters that his main rivals, Mike Christian and Lee Haney, had two of the greatest backs in history!), the same cannot be said of Strydom's arms. In fact, because his chest and shoulders are so thick, his arms appear smaller than they really are.

When Gary was competing in the late '80s and early '90s, he trained arms using a split routine. In the mornings he hit biceps, and later in the day, usually around supper time, trained triceps.

Gary Strydom

Gary is a firm believer in the perils of overtraining, so he limits his arm training to 12 total sets:

"Every arm session I do two or three exercises per bodypart, and rarely exceed 12 sets in total. I mix up my choice and sequence of exercises regularly, and even when doing the same exercise, I vary the angle of stress from workout to workout."

With regards to reps, he prefers to let instinct play a major role. On heavy days he does as few as 4 or 6 reps, but on most occasions he stays in the 10- to 15-rep range. Prior to the 1989 Olympia, Gary was doing

Flex Wheeler always amazes crowds with his freakish guns.

sets of 35 to 40 reps. The following is a typical Strydom arm routine, but be aware that he rarely performs the same workout two days in a row.

Gary Strydom's Arm Routine (Favorite Exercises):
Triceps
1. Close-grip bench presses – *4 sets*
2. Lying triceps extensions – *4 sets*
3. Triceps pushdowns – *4 sets*
4. One-arm cable pushdowns – *4 sets*

Biceps
5. Alternate dumbell curls – *4 sets*
6. EZ-curl bar curls – *4 sets*
7. Preacher curls (dumbells) – *4 sets*
8. Concentration curls – *4 sets*

FLEX WHEELER – Even though the TV comedy *Twin Peaks* may have been cancelled, there is no doubt that the twin peaks of bodybuilding sensation, Flex Wheeler, are here to stay.

Few bodybuilders garnered the attention that fell on Flex as he worked his way up the amateur ranks. But these things happen when you're blessed with as complete a bodybuilding package as Flex. From calves to chest to biceps, the Wheeler physique was built with one purpose in mind – blowing away the competition! After his win at the 1993 Arnold Classic, many felt that the Olympia was his for the taking, however, the massive Britisher, Dorian Yates, had other ideas, and once again took the coveted crown.

A near fatal car crash derailed his 1994 aspirations but Flex returned to competition in 1995, winning the Ironman and South Beach Pro Invitationals. A second-place finish at the Arnold Classic confirmed that Flex was one of the favorites at the 1995 Mr. Olympia.

To favor one of Flex's bodyparts over another would be doing the man injustice. Of the current crop of pros, Flex probably has the most balanced physique of anyone, save Shawn Ray. Included in this package are two of the greatest arms on tour. If other bodybuilders have baseball-sized biceps, than Flex's are analogous to grapefruits! When David Lynch coined the title "Twin Peaks" for his TV series, he must have had Flex Wheeler in mind.

Flex's biceps workout consists of three main exercises, the first being seated concentration curls. Besides serving as a great warmup, the exercise brings out a full biceps peak. Flex does 4 sets of 7 to 12 reps, being careful to use perfect style:

"While sitting on a bench with my legs wide apart, I place the elbow of one arm on the inside of my thigh. Then I lean almost backwards from the weight so I'm putting immediate tension on the lower part of the biceps. I bring the weight all the way up, and squeeze it."

Flex's next exercise is one-arm alternate dumbell curls. Although considered a mass-builder, he finds that supinating his hands at the top of the movement really brings out biceps peak. He performs each rep

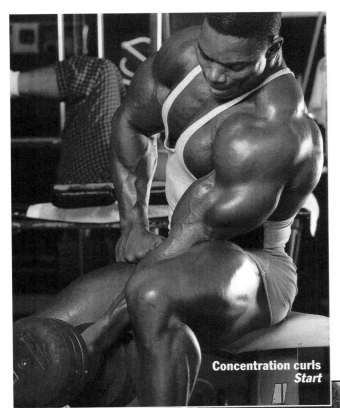

Concentration curls
Start

Finish

"This is an exercise I do when I really want to get some blood into the area. I like it because of the way the low pulley works; it creates tension from top to bottom, and I get an extreme pump in the area even if I already have a pump from some previous biceps exercise. With one arm holding onto the machine for support, I curl the weight with my other arm all the way up and squeeze hard."

While most bodybuilders alternate heavy and light days, he tries to go heavy on every workout. Of course there are days when his body requires light days, so Flex listens. But for the most part, if he can go heavy, you can be assured he will. As for cheating, he tries to maintain strict style throughout the exercise, but he's not immune to adding a few cheat reps at the end of a set:

"It's all about stimulating the muscle, so I guess it's better to cheat than quit prematurely. I don't remember ever cheating, but I'm quite sure I've done it."

Flex Wheeler's Biceps Routine:

1. Concentration curls –
   4 sets of 7-12 reps
2. Seated alternate dumbell curls –
   4 sets of 7-12 reps
3. Standing one-arm cable curls –
   4 sets of 7-12 reps

ROBBY ROBINSON – Look up the word "enduring" in a dictionary, and chances are you'll see a picture of Robby "the Black Prince" Robinson. Except for a few breaks here and there, Robby has been competing (and very successfully we might add) since the early 1970s. From his win at the 1975 American championships, to his first-place finish at Joe Weider's inaugural 1994 Masters Mr. Olympia, Robby has come to symbolize those characteristics that make a true champion. In between these two great contests lie a host of Grand Prix titles.

At 5' 9" and aproximately 210 pounds in contest shape, Robby is not quite as massive as some of today's superstars. But one area where he dominates (past and present) is the front double-biceps pose. Has there ever been a bodybuilder that displayed such perfection in arm development? From his ham-sized triceps and fantastic forearms to those breathtaking biceps – all we can say is that they're perfect.

using a medium-slow tempo, squeezing the biceps throughout the full range of the motion. Again, he does 4 sets of 7 to 12 reps.

For his third exercise, he completes 4 sets of standing cable curls:

Recognizing an advantage when he saw one, Robby was quick to cash in on his above-average arm development. Like Arnold, he often began his posing routine with a front double-biceps pose. Let's face it, when you've got such superiority, you might as well play it to the hilt. A couple of front and back biceps shots and Robby usually found himself somewhere in the money.

If one word could summarize Robby's arm-training philosophy, it was "variety." Using instinct as a guide, he continuously changed his sets, reps, exercises, and poundages. Incidentally, he is proud of the fact that no two workouts are ever the same!

Robby Robinson

A typical Robinson arm workout consists of about 20 to 22 total sets – 8 to 10 for biceps and 10 to 12 for triceps. As for reps, one day it could be 10 to 12, while other days it might be 6 to 8. Robby lets instinct guide him when determining a rep range, preferring to go by feel rather than counting repetitions.

Although his arm workouts vary from day to day, the following is a sample routine he used to build what were perhaps the greatest arms in bodybuilding history.

Robby Robinson's Arm Routine:
Biceps
1. Incline dumbell curls – *3 sets of 8-10 reps*
2. Standing barbell curls – *4 sets of 8-10 reps*
3. Concentration curls – *3 sets of 10-12 reps*

Triceps
4. Pushdowns – *4 sets of 10-12 reps*
5. French presses – *4 sets of 8-10 reps*
6. Lying dumbell extensions – *3 sets of 8-10 reps*

AARON BAKER – Often called the most underrated bodybuilder on the pro tour, Aaron started the 1995 season with a bang – placing second to Flex Wheeler at the South Beach Pro Invitational and Ironman Invitational.

It's no secret that Aaron has a pair of the deadliest arms in bodybuilding. And while his biceps may resemble two over-sized grapefruit, it's his triceps that garner most of the attention. Not only are they huge, but they are deceptive in their quality. From a distance it appears that he has four or five triceps heads present. Only when viewed up close does one realize that it's his muscle density and hardness which provide the illusion.

Aaron Baker

When Aaron trains triceps he usually includes them with his delts and biceps, letting instinct determine which muscle to hit first:

"I prioritize my bodyparts according to the muscles I feel need the most improvement or work. Delts seem to require more energy than arms so I train them first, while I'm my most physically and mentally alert. Then I'll move on to arms. Even though the triceps are a bigger muscle group and demand more work, I train biceps next because they need more emphasis than my tris."

Unlike most bodybuilders, Aaron limits his triceps training to just 6 to 8 heavy sets. His favorite triceps exercise is the lying triceps extension using an EZ-curl bar. He has been performing this exercise since day one and feels it has done the most for developing his triceps mass. With his elbows close to his ears, he lowers the bar behind his head and then pushes it to a locked-out position. He does one warmup set with aproximately 95 pounds for 15 to 20 reps, and then proceeds to do 2 or 3 sets using 140 pounds. He usually lets instinct determine rep range, but in most cases it's in the 8 to 12 range.

For his second exercise, he does 3 or 4 sets of pushdowns, using the Icarian machine. With the first set serving as a warmup, Aaron pyramids up in weight from 100 to 130 pounds.

To finish his triceps training Aaron adds a couple of sets of dips or one-arm dumbell extensions. When doing dips, he straps an additional 100 to 120 pounds around his waist. If he's doing triceps extensions, he pyramids the weight from a 40-pound dumbell to a 70 pounder.

Even though he only performs 6 to 8 sets, Aaron is quick to add that each set is done to failure:

"I don't quit on a set, it's just that when I'm training, the contraction is so severe and the muscle gets so fatigued that it shuts down. It's not that I want to stop. I simply can't go on any more. That's probably the main reason why I don't need to do as many sets as most bodybuilders do."

Aaron Baker's Triceps Routine:

1. Lying triceps extensions –
   2-3 sets of 8-12 reps
2. Icarian machine pushdowns –
   2-3 sets of 10-12 reps
3. Dumbell extensions or dips –
   2-3 sets of 10-12 reps

SHAWN RAY – With his second-place finish at the 1994 Mr. Olympia, Shawn Ray established himself as one of bodybuilding's dominant figures. Shawn's high placing was not a surprise, as he had been slowly rising up the competitive bodybuilding ladder. In fact many of Shawn's fans insist that their man won the contest and that it was only Dorian's reputation which saved the day. In any case, most authorities associated with the sport agree that, pound for pound, Shawn Ray has the most perfectly balanced physique currently on the pro circuit.

Shawn divides his arm training into two distinct routines, heavy and light. Heavy days consist of basic movements, heavy weight, and low reps. On light days, he employs more isolation exercises in his training and prefers to go by feel rather than amount of weight. The following is a detailed breakdown of his arm training.

Shawn starts his heavy biceps routine with standing barbell curls. Unlike most bodybuilders, he performs

Shawn Ray

the exercise in ultrastrict fashion. This means no yanking, arching, or swinging the weight. At the top of the movement, he pauses and forcefully squeezes his biceps. He then lowers the bar in a very slow manner, making sure to bring it all the way down to an arms-locked-out position. Once again, he pauses, and then curls the bar back up to his chin.

Shawn's second biceps exercise is the concentration curl. Although he alternates between standing and sitting variations, he prefers sitting. By bracing his elbow against the inner thigh he is forced to do the movement more strictly. As with barbell curls he pauses at the top and bottom of each rep to get a full stretch and contraction.

For his third and final biceps exercise, Shawn moves to the preacher bench. Even though the exercise works the entire biceps region, it primarily stresses the lower biceps. For this reason he makes sure to lower the bar all the way down. Failure to do so would eliminate the most effective part of the movement.

He performs the previous exercises for 5 sets of 6 to 8 reps. He rests for about 90 seconds between each set, and uses as much weight as he can handle in good style.

For his light biceps days Shawn switches exercises and uses a 10- to 15-rep range. His first exercise is one-arm preacher curls, and he aims for 15 reps using a medium weight. Even though he is using less weight and moving at a quicker pace he makes sure to pause at the top and bottom of the exercise to get a full contraction.

Shawn's second, light biceps exercise is standing cable curls. He uses a straight bar so he can work both arms at the same time. This is one exercise where he may go beyond the usual 12 to 15 reps, sometimes as high as 20 to 25. After 4 sets of these, his biceps are really burning and aching. At this point lesser mortals would call it a day, but Shawn immediately grabs a pair of dumbells and bangs out 4 sets of standing alternate dumbell curls.

Over the years Shawn has discovered that the key to this exercise is not how much weight you can swing up, but the concentration you apply to each rep. Like most bodybuilders, he starts the exercise with his palms facing inward, supinating them as he raises the dumbells.

Shawn hits triceps on day two of his three-day (three on, one off) cycle. As with biceps, he divides his

Edgar Fletcher demonstrates the barbell curl. *Start*

triceps training into light and heavy days. On heavy days he starts with lying triceps extensions using an EZ-curl bar. He usually lowers the bar to this forehead but if the mood grabs him, he might lower it down behind his head. As with biceps, Shawn squeezes his triceps at the top of the movement when his arms are fully locked.

His next exercise is triceps pushdowns, which he finds great for bringing out the triceps' horseshoe-shape. He uses a short, straight bar and takes a 2- or 3-inch wide grip. As he raises and lowers the weight, he keeps his elbows tucked tight against his sides. He slowly brings the bar up to his chin, pauses, and then lowers to an arms-locked-out position. At the bottom he employs his now familiar squeeze.

Shawn's third and final heavy triceps exercise is the one-arm behind-the-head dumbell extension. He alternates between standing and sitting, and works up to a 50- to 55-pound dumbell. To maintain most of the stress on the triceps, Shawn keeps his upper arm

Finish

his arm is in a fully-locked position. For variety, he performs the two-handed variety using a straight bar.

As a final note, Shawn advises beginners to limit their cable exercises and focus instead on basic dumbell and barbell movements. Only after laying down an adequate foundation should you start employing shaping exercises.

Shawn Ray's Arm Routines:
Heavy Day – Biceps
1. Standing barbell curls –
   5 sets of 6-8 reps
2. Concentration curls – *5 sets of 6-8 reps*
3. Preacher curls – *5 sets of 6-8 reps*

Heavy Day – Triceps
1. Lying triceps extensions –
   5 sets of 6-8 reps
2. Triceps pushdowns – *5 sets of 6-8 reps*
3. One-arm dumbell extensions*–
   5 sets of 6-8 reps

*Shawn squeezes out as many reps as possible which is often above the standard 6-8.

Light Day – Biceps
1. One-arm preacher curls –
   4 sets of 15 reps
2. Standing cable curls – *4 sets of 15 reps*
3. One-arm alternate dumbell curls –
   4 sets of 12-15 reps

Light Day – Triceps
1. One-arm cable kickbacks –
   4 sets of 12-15 reps
2. Dips between benches –
   4 sets of 12-15 reps
3. Reverse pushdowns –
   4 sets of 12-15 reps

vertical with the floor (i.e. pointing his elbow at the ceiling). He then lowers the weight down to his opposite ear, being careful not to drop the dumbell in an uncontrolled fashion.

On light days, Shawn starts with one-arm cable kickbacks. He keeps his elbow close to his body and bends his torso at the waist. For support, he braces his free hand on his knee. During the exercise he does not allow the weight to pull his elbow down, and makes sure the exercise's effectiveness is directed to his triceps.

Shawn's second exercise is weighted bench dips. He either places a 100-pound plate across his thighs or has a training partner push down on his shoulders. In either case, the hands are kept close together and Shawn lowers himself as far as possible in order to get a full stretch.

To conclude his triceps training, he does 4 sets of one-arm cable pushdowns. Using a reverse (palms facing up) grip, he pushes the cable handle down until

EDGAR FLETCHER – One of the top bodybuilders on today's amateur scene is Edgar Fletcher. The fact that he has yet to win the NPC Nationals is testament to the competitiveness of modern bodybuilding. With two second-place finishes, a third at the Nationals, and a fourth at the 1994 North Americans, many feel it's only a matter of time before this Pittsburgh native (presently living in Germany) earns his pro card.

Although he is only 5'6", Edgar weighs 220 pounds in competitive shape, and sports arms in the 21-inch range. In fact it's his arms that immediately draw your attention, and many feel that they resemble those of Robby Robinson or Arnold Schwarzenegger.

While hard to believe by looking at them now, Edgar says his biceps were flat and unimpressive just a few years ago. Gaining size was never a problem, but Edgar realized that if he was going to win the Nationals his biceps needed quality – and this meant peak, definition, and separation.

CHAPTER TWENTY-SIX – BICEPS & TRICEPS

To address the problem he totally revamped his biceps training. His first major change was in reducing the amount of weight on his biceps exercises – particularly barbell curls. Instead of using the lower back to get the weight up at any cost, he started using strict form on his biceps exercises.

Another significant modification involved using the "continuous tension" technique. Instead of hoisting the weight up and letting it drop, he now lowers the weight in a slow and controlled manner – emphasizing both the positive and negative aspect of the curl.

Edgar's third major change was to add variety to his biceps training, particularly isolation exercises such as alternate dumbell curls, concentration curls, and hammer curls.

Although it varies he usually selects three exercises for his biceps, performing 3 sets of each in the 6 to 10 range. As his biceps grow easily, Edgar limits his intensity to keep them in balance with the rest of his physique.

The following are Edgar's favorite biceps exercises. On a typical day he'll pick 3 exercises and perform 3 sets of each.

Edgar Fletcher's Biceps Routine:
1. Barbell curls (warmup) – *3 sets of 10-15 reps*
2. Hammer curls – *3 sets of 6-8 reps*
3. Seated alternate dumbell curls – *3 sets of 6-8 reps*
4. One-arm concentration curls – *3 sets of 6-8 reps*
5. Barbell preacher curls – *3 sets of 6-8 reps*

VICTOR RICHARDS – Over the past years, readers of *MuscleMag International* have been treated to the exploits of Vic Richards. It would be an understatement to say Vic is one of the most popular bodybuilders around. His schedule for seminars and posing exhibitions is constantly full, and audiences hang on his every word. All this would be routine except for one important fact – big Vic has yet to compete in a major bodybuilding competition! And if recent comments are any indication, he has no plans to do so in the near future.

Why then is this California superman so popular? Could it be his rock hard, 275-pound physique packed on a 5'9" frame? Or possibly those 33-inch thighs? Or how about his arms that hover somewhere between 22 and 24 inches? Whatever the reason, Vic Richards will probably go down in history as one of the greatest bodybuilders ever, titles or no titles!

Speaking of those arms, we thought that since we started this section with Arnold, then concluding with Vic Richards would only be appropriate. (Think of it as two pairs of 22-inch bookends!)

It will not surprise you to learn that Vic's arms were not built by doing light concentration curls. Having worshiped at the altar of Olivia, Schwarzenegger, and Robinson, big Vic spent most of his early days blasting out set after set of cheat curls. In no time, he was hoisting over 200 pounds for reps. In fact standing curls (barbell and dumbell) were his only biceps exercises. A typical workout saw him do 8 to 10 sets of 6 to 12 reps, of both exercises. He did no direct triceps work as he felt they received enough stimulation from chest and shoulder exercises.

After a few years, Vic added EZ-bar curls to his biceps training, and also began to train his triceps. Although he's not sure how many sets of EZ curls he did, he estimates that it was somewhere in the 10 to 15 range.

Having built his arms to 21 to 22 inches, Vic decided to concentrate on shape rather than size (let's face it, when you've built arms the size of Vic's, what's another inch!). Nowadays he divides his arm training between just three exercises: standing alternate curls, concentration curls, and standing dumbell extensions. He does 8 to 10 sets on the two biceps exercises, and 6 to 8 sets on the triceps movement. Unlike the past where weight was everything, nowadays Vic is careful to maintain good style throughout the exercises' complete range of motion – although he still throws in the occasional cheat rep or two at the end. He keeps his reps in the 10 to 12 range, but on alternate curls may do a few sets with as few as 3 reps. His triceps exercise is done for sets of 10 to 12.

Vic feels the key to his success lies with the fact that he ignores the traditionally accepted rules of bodybuilding. Supposedly you have to do more than 6 to 8 reps to gain size, but Vic has built one of the most dense physiques of all time using 3 to 5 reps. Obviously, few individuals are going to develop Vic's mass using such a system, but who knows, maybe the key to your success lies somewhere in the bodybuilding philosophy of "Mr. Big" – Vic Richards!

Victor Richards's Arm Routine:
1. Standing alternate dumbell curls –
   8-10 sets of 3-12 reps
2. Concentration curls – *6-8 sets of 8-12 reps*
3. Behind-the-head dumbell extensions –
   6-8 sets of 10-12 sets

Arnold claims his last bodybuilding title – the 1980 Mr. Olympia.

Chapter Twenty-seven

FOREARMS

DEVELOPING FOREARMS OF STEEL

Throughout the ages the general public have maintained a fascination with the exploits of circus strongmen. These carnivalistic showmen thrilled millions with their great feats of physical power. Yet these individuals sported physiques that were tame by today's standards. If there was one trait that they all had in common, it was a grip that would make an oyster wince.

Most of the old timers' strength lay in their forearms – the result of countless years of grabbing, clutching, and hoisting. In many cases these individuals possessed limited upper body strength, but this was more than made up for by a vice-like grip.

With the advent of the industrial revolution, professions which depended on physical strength were suddenly made redundant. For example, a modern sailor would probably go into a state of shock if called on deck at 3 a.m. to reef the mainsail! Granted a sailor from Nelson's time would gladly trade places with his modern counterpart, the point is, the continuous splicing and reefing produced great physical strength and conditioning. For all the abuse and malnutrition suffered by the old-time sailor, the British "limy" was probably in far superior physical condition than today's couch potato!

The fascination with the gripping power of the windjammer sailor was immortalized by the exploits of one "Popeye the sailor man." From the cartoon version to Robin Williams's movie portrayal, all it took was a can

Tim Belknap flexes his outrageous forearm.

of spinach and our big-armed hero would discombobulate anyone who came between him and his beloved Olive Oil!

ANATOMY

Contrary to popular belief, it's the muscles of the forearm and not the hand that produce a strong grip. True, there are small muscles that curl and straighten the fingers but their effect is minuscule when compared to the power of the larger muscles located on the radius and ulna (forearm bones).

The forearm is made up of a system of flexor and extensor muscles. Muscles such as the flexor digitorum, flexor carpi ulnaris, and extensor carpi radialis longus all interact to bend the wrist and squeeze the fingers. Granted a kinesiologist can give you a more detailed description, but for our purposes the forearm muscles allow you to do things such as hold a barbell and bend the wrists up and down. In fact when it comes to training the large torso muscles, the forearms are often the weak link in the chain. For example, many bodybuilders find that their forearms give out before the lats when performing pulldowns or chinups. For this reason training straps they use to improve their grip on the bar.

Mohammed Makkawy blasts his forearms with barbell wrist curls.

TRAINING

The forearms can be considered analogous to the calves in that they are composed of extremely dense muscle fiber. In fact, it's a toss up as to which muscle "burns" the most when being exercised. It's this unique physiological characteristic that allows both of these muscles to sustain intense exercise for long periods of time. This means that standard rep and set ranges often don't work. During a typical day the forearms and calves are continuously in motion. Just about every movement has some degree of calf or forearm involvement. Evolution compensated for this by placing an overabundance of dense muscle fibers in both areas. From a biological point of view this makes sense. From a bodybuilding stance, however, training can be pure hell!

Properly fatiguing the forearm muscles requires extreme effort on the part of the bodybuilder. Before getting into the actual exercises, we have to say a word about the different philosophies of forearm training.

There are two general viewpoints when it comes to forearm training. For a few genetically gifted individuals,

forearm growth comes in the form of indirect stimulation. This means certain people develop exceptional forearms by simply working other muscle groups (i.e. grabbing a bar, holding a cable handle, etc.). Casey Viator and Mike Mentzer were famous for their forearms, yet they did little or no direct forearm training during their competitive careers. In their case, a combination of genetics and gripping huge poundages during their workouts led to their outstanding forearm development.

On the flip side of the coin, we have those less fortunate bodybuilders who must train the forearms as if they were any other muscle. Even within this group there is debate as to which rep range is most efficient. Some prefer heavier weights for a standard rep range (8 to 12), while others use moderate poundages for high reps (15+). Our advice is to experiment with both types and choose which works best for you. As most bodybuilders are inclined toward the higher rep range, don't be surprised if you have to do 20 reps or more to get your forearms to respond.

Forearm exercises come in all forms, but most fall into two categories: wrist curls and reverse curls. Standard wrist curls involve holding a barbell with the palms facing up. With your forearms braced on your knees or on a bench, the bar is moved up and down

Forearm development is essential in building great arms.
– Kevin Levrone

through the full range of motion of your hands. This exercise primarily works the muscles of the inner forearms. You can also perform reverse wrist curls using a palms-down grip, thus shifting most of the stress to the outer forearm muscles.

Another popular forearm exercise is the standing reverse curl. The movement is identical to the biceps curl, except that you use a palms-facing-down grip. Doing so shifts much of the stress to the brachialis muscles – located halfway between the forearm and upper arm. When properly developed they help fill in the gap between the upper and lower arms.

Many bodybuilders like to finish their biceps training with an exercise called Zottman curls. In this exercise two dumbells are substituted for a barbell and curled upwards with the palms facing the body. Once again, the brachialis is strongly affected.

A final comment should be made about the various machines that can be used to work forearms. Most of these are based on either a rolling or squeezing type of movement. While a few bodybuilders swear by them, the majority prefer using barbells and dumbells. Our advice is to give them a try and decide for yourself.

WHEN TO TRAIN

Unlike most muscle groups which can be trained in different sequences without much of a problem, there are some definite no-no's when it comes to forearm training. Every upper-body exercise requires some degree of forearm involvement and, as stated earlier, the forearms are often the weak link in the chain. If you train forearms first chances are that you won't have sufficient gripping power left to do justice to the other exercises. Next time you perform a set of chins notice how fatigued the forearms are after the set. Now picture what it would be like trying to do that set if the forearms were tired to begin with. There's no need to check for yourself. Take it from us, it's virtually impossible. What all of this means is that you should leave forearm training for the end of your workout.

Most bodybuilders train forearms after training the upper-arm muscles. It naturally follows as the forearms will already be warmed up by the various biceps curls and triceps extensions. If your forearms are particularly weak you might want to train them on a separate day altogether. Or better still, purchase a small barbell set and train them at home. Do a couple of sets before breakfast in the morning, after school, or even before bed. A couple of months of such specialization will bring great results, and it won't affect your workouts. In fact it will only help, as a stronger grip means you can use more weight on such exercises as pulldowns, shrugs, and barbell curls.

POPULAR FOREARM EXERCISES
1. Barbell wrist curls
2. Barbell reverse curls
3. Zottman curls
4. Machine wrist rollers
5. Reverse barbell wrist curls
6. Machine squeezes

THE CHAMPS' ROUTINES

ARNOLD SCHWARZENEGGER
When you've built the kind of upper-arm mass Arnold has, it only makes sense to try and keep the forearms in proportion. Not content to rely on indirect stimulation, Arnold made sure to include regular forearm exercises in his workouts.

Although he varied the exercises from time to time, his forearm movements were usually variations of wrist and reverse curls performed with a barbell.

A typical workout saw Arnold begin with standing reverse curls. Using a medium weight he kept his elbows close to his sides and curled the bar up using a reverse (palms-facing-down) grip. He typically performed 5 sets of 8 to 10 reps on this exercise.

For his next exercise, he did 5 sets of reverse preacher curls. The exercise is performed in the same manner as standard preacher curls, except a reverse grip is used. As with the standing version, reverse preacher curls primarily work the brachialis muscle located between the lower and upper arm. Once again, Arnold aimed for sets of 8 to 10 reps.

For his third and final forearm exercise, he did 5 to 7 sets of 8 to 10 reps of heavy wrist curls. With his elbows resting on his thighs or a bench, he curled his wrists up as far as possible. He would forcibly squeeze his forearm muscles at the top and then slowly lower. This exercise primarily works the flexors of the forearm.

Looking at Arnold's forearm routine it is interesting to note that his reps fall in the lower end of the spectrum. Most bodybuilders (those who perform direct forearm exercises) use a higher (15+) rep range. By trial and error, Arnold discovered his forearms responded best to a lower rep range. There's an important lesson to be learned here. Just because "most" individuals use a certain rep range, doesn't mean you have to. Don't be afraid to experiment. If there's a key to bodybuilding

Start

Finish

Rich Gaspari uses barbell wrist curls to build and sculpt his Olympian forearms.

Greg Deferro

straining to burst free of their attachments! When it seemed another rep was impossible, he somehow found the determination that champs are famous for, and blasted out one more. As with wrist curls, he aimed for 12 to 15 reps on this exercise. A typical workout saw "Rocky" do 4 such alternate sets.

To finish his forearms, he did 4 sets of dumbell wrist curls. With his forearms braced on his thighs, he pounded out rep after rep until his forearms were virtually on fire. The unique position of this exercise keeps the tension on the meaty inner section of the forearms.

Greg's choice of exercises was not coincidental, as each of the three movements hit the forearms from a slightly different angle. The result, a set of forearms that complimented his massive upper arms.

Although he disappeared for much of the late '80s and early '90s, Greg returned to the competitive fray at the first Masters Olympia in 1994. He had to withdraw because of illness, but the bodybuilding world is still looking forward to future appearances of "Rocky."

Greg Deferro's Forearm Routine:
1. Barbell wrist curls – *4 sets of 12-15 reps*
2. Standing barbell reverse curls –
   4 sets of 12-15 reps
3. Dumbell wrist curls – *4 sets of 12-15 reps*

success, it's finding out what works best for you.

Arnold Schwarzenegger's Forearm Routine:
1. Standing reverse barbell curls – *5 sets of 8-10 reps*
2. Reverse preacher curls – *5 sets of 8-10 reps*
3. Wrist curls – *5 sets of 8-10 reps*

GREG "ROCKY" DEFERRO

One of the most densely muscled bodybuilders on the pro circuit in the early 1980s was Greg Deferro. With his striking facial resemblance to actor, Sylvester Stallone, it was only a matter of time before Deferro picked up the nickname "Rocky".

Greg was noted for the superintense manner in which he trained his various muscle groups – forearms being no exception. One of his favorite exercise combinations was barbell wrist curls and standing reverse curls. He started by bracing his elbows on a flat bench (tilted on a slight decline) and grabbed a bar with a narrow (4 or 5 inch) grip. With his wrists extending over the lower part of the bench, he curled the bar up as far as his wrists would allow. He then lowered until his hands were nearly pointing straight down. At the bottom of the movement "Rocky" let the bar roll to the tips of his fingers, only stopping when it seemed the bar would fall from his hands. After an average of 15 reps, he put the bar down and stood up to do his second exercise, standing reverse curls.

Using a shoulder-width grip, he curled the bar up to a point just below his chin. After a couple of reps his outer forearms and brachialis muscles were literally

Charlie Thomas demonstrates the reverse curl.

JUSUP WILCOSZ

When he competed back in the early to mid-'80s, massive German bodybuilder, Jusup Wilcosz, impressed fans with his rugged, masculine physique. Standing six feet tall and competing at a weight in excess of 245 pounds, Jusup was usually one of the larger body-builders onstage. A particularly unique feature was his full, but neatly trimmed beard. With body-building being a sport that emphasizes an absence of hair, many spectators found Jusup's facial growth a welcome challenge.

Besides his Mr. Europe and two Mr. Universe wins (pro and amateur), Jusup competed in five Mr. Olympias, placing a respect-able third in 1984. Jusup's com-petitive career was put on hold in 1986 when he and his wife opened a gym together. Just when it seemed Jusup might return to the stage, tragedy struck. His wife, Ruth, fell ill with cancer, and passed away in 1990.

Since the gym was a joint project between him and his wife, Jusup decided to sell the estab-lishment. After obtaining a position at one of Germany's larger training centers (AKUF Gym, near Frankfurt) Jusup was once again bitten by the competitive bug. A special invitation to compete in the 1995 Mr. Olympia insured that the bodybuilding world would once again be treated to the physique of the "Stuttgart Strongman".

One of Jusup's trademarks are his outstanding forearms, the result of many years of Olympic lifting. Those forearms led Jusup to three German national champion titles. Jusup has definite views when it comes to forearm training. For starters, he says the size of the forearms is dependent on the amount of weight used. If you're constantly throwing around huge poundages in the gym, then you need an appreciable amount of forearm strength just to hold onto the bar. With strength comes size, and vice versa. Another point Jusup emphasizes is that arm size is very much related to overall body size. In other words, if you want to increase the size of the forearms you must gain overall body size. As the forearms comprise only about 1/15 of the body's weight, it would be impossible to put

Jusup Wilcosz

size on them without adding size all over the body.

With regards to actual exercises, Jusup does little forearm work now. But when he was in serious training, he had four or five forearm exercises that formed the basis of his routines. A typical workout consisted of two or three exercises, performed for 3 sets of 12 to 15 reps. Among his favorites were Zottman curls, reverse curls, wrist curls (both barbell and dumbell versions) and behind-the-back reverse barbell wrist curls.

Jusup Wilcosz's Forearm Routine:
1. Zottman curls – *3 sets of 12-15 reps*
2. Reverse barbell curls – *3 sets of 12-15 reps*
3. Wrist curls off bench – *3 sets of 12-15 reps*

Chapter Twenty-eight

ABDOMINALS

DEVELOPING WASHBOARD ABS

Lee Labrada

"I'm amazed at how many people still believe that all you have to do to get good abs are abdominal exercises. You still hear people say things like 'Yeah, I'm going to work off my beer belly. A hundred situps a day for a month ought to do it.' But that's the fallacy about spot reducing. The persistence of this myth is what sells needless gimmicks to the public. Little do they realize that all they have to do is their ab workouts and avoid the refrigerator."
– Lee Labrada
IFBB Pro Bodybuilder (voicing his opinion on the fallacies of spot reduction)

From competitive bodybuilder, to high school student, to middle-aged parent, it seems just about everyone wants a smaller, tighter waist. In fact, this is the primary reason why manufacturers of those fancy home-training apparatus reap such huge financial rewards.

Just about everyone who takes up bodybuilding has done so with one main purpose – reducing the size of their midsection. For the average person, holding the fort so to speak is satisfactory. For the competitive bodybuilder, however, an average waist just won't suffice. You must display a fat-free midsection which immediately draws the attention of the judges. Anything less will result in a poor placement on the competitive ladder.

In addition to the bodybuilding scene, a small waist is highly favored in everyday society. Surveys show that, next to a small butt, women like a tight, slender waist on a man's body. The "beer belly" look is definitely out!

It's at this point that we're going to burst a few bubbles and dispel a few myths. You cannot, we repeat, cannot significantly reduce the size of your waist by doing endless sets of situps. Sure, situps will tone the waist to a certain degree, but they won't melt the fat away as some fad programs claim. (Besides, there are other exercises that are far safer and more effective than the situp, which we will discuss later.) If you have a layer of fat over the abdominals, (referred to as abs in gym lingo), the only way to remove it is by burning it off. Abdominal exercises will burn calories, however, exercises such as cycling, swimming or running are far more effective. Also, the body does not selectively burn fat from a given area. In other words, you will not remove fat from the waist alone. Fat will be removed in small amounts from the entire body.

John Hnatyschak

Perhaps *MuscleMag International* founder, Robert Kennedy, summed it up best when he said 'super abdominals are built with exercise and honed with diet.' What this means is that a two-pronged approach needs to be taken. Devote a small portion of your training to abdominal exercises, and keep your diet under control. Doing hundreds of situps is not the answer.

A final point to be made concerns stomach distension. Your stomach can be compared to a spring. If you stretch it, it will flex back to its original size and shape. But if you overstretch it, it may never go back to its original size. Overloading the stomach with food or liquid, especially alcohol, (this is where "beer bellies" come from) can lead to a stretching of the stomach – another reason why you should eat four or five small meals a day instead of two or three large ones.

ANATOMY

"Have you ever noticed that you can gain an accurate appreciation of a person's general health by the condition of his or her midsection?"

– Juliette Bergman, top female bodybuilder

When we speak of the abdominals we are primarily talking about the rectus abdominus. These muscles start below the rib cage and extend down just below the navel. A properly developed midsection exhibits layers of muscle, resembling an old-time "washboard," hence the term "washboard abs."

A person may possess between three and four abdominal layers due to human evolution. From a kinesiological perspective, there's no advantage to having either type of arrangement. Individuals with three layers are just as capable as those with four. From a bodybuilding point of view, all things being equal (i.e. bodyfat percentage, development), a bodybuilder displaying four layers will appear more impressive than one with three. Of course, judges will not hold innate differences against you. As long as your abs are highly defined, you'll probably place at or near the top.

The primary function of the abdominals is to flex the spine. Therefore, when the abdominals contract, they bend the body forward at the waist. The range of motion varies between individuals, but on average, the abdominals bend the waist forward six inches. Now think about it, if you move your upper body two or three feet during a situp, another muscle group must be performing 80 percent of the exercise. The other muscle doing most of the work is the hip flexors. For this reason most bodybuilders omit standard situps from their abdominal training.

Besides the rectus abdominus, there are other muscles that make up the waist area. Located at the sides of the lower waist region are the obliques, responsible for twisting and bending the upper body sideways. Two other muscle groups located in the midsection are the intercostals and serratus. Take a look at Robby Robinson performing a side-chest shot. Granted his chest and arms receive most of the attention, but look at the finger-like muscles along his side. Robby is famous for his intercostals and serratus, and he has put them to good use over his 20-year competitive career – including his 1994, Masters Mr. Olympia win.

TRAINING

"There's something extra to having great abdominals. Well-toned abs go hand in hand with total health and lower back integrity. There is also great psychological value to having tightly muscular abdominals."

– John Hnatyschak, IFBB Pro Bodybuilder

Although dozens of abdominal exercises exist, they can be grouped into one of two types – leg raises or crunches. In general, leg raises work the lower abdominal region and crunches work the upper section. Of course, some argue that both types of exercises work the entire abdominal region. There is even strong evidence to suggest that many versions of the leg raise do nothing for the abdominals as it's the hip flexors that take all the strain.

Another practice that's all but been eliminated is doing hundreds (in some cases, thousands) of reps. In years gone by it was believed the only way to a small, tight waist was by doing endless sets and reps. Nowadays, top bodybuilders treat their abdominals like any other muscle group. They pick two or three exercises and do 15 to 25 reps. The only difference is with respect

Kevin Levrone, Dorian Yates and Nasser El Sonbaty

to the amount of weight used. On most exercises the goal is to gradually increase the amount of weight. But no one wants to increase the size of their abdominals, so bodybuilders perform their abdominal exercises with no additional weight. Occasionally they use a 10-pound dumbell on a crunch or situp exercise, but for the most part all of the exercises are done using only bodyweight.

Is it possible to overtrain the waist? The answer to this question depends on your individual training philosophy. One of bodybuilding's most outspoken characters is California's Vince Gironda. Vince maintains that too much abdominal work will cause an overtonus in the midsection, producing the opposite effect of what's desired – a tight, hard waist! In addition, he believes that overtraining the midsection causes a hormonal imbalance which may lead to a loss of muscle tissue in other parts of the body. Now whether you subscribe to Vince's theory (he calls it fact!) or not, is entirely up to you. What's important to remember is that any muscle can be overtrained, and this includes the abdominals. Keep this in mind as you train your way to ripped, eye-catching, prize-winning abdominals!

COMMON WAIST EXERCISES
1. Situps
2. Lying leg raises
3. Crunches
4. Roman-chair situps
5. Reverse crunches
6. Hanging leg raises
7. Rope crunches (pulldowns)
8. Side bends

THE CHAMPS' ROUTINES

"I don't do a lot of abdominal work – probably once a week off-season (crunches, reverse crunches and running stairs) and twice a week precontest. I find that once my abs are in shape, I don't have to do too much to maintain them. Too much ab work causes thickening of the waistline."
– Dorian Yates
IFBB Pro Bodybuilder, Five-time Mr. Olympia

Even though there is debate about the effectiveness of some abdominal exercises, you'll notice that most champs use variations of crunches and leg raises. When someone like France's Thierry Pastel tells you that he attributes his outstanding midsection (one of

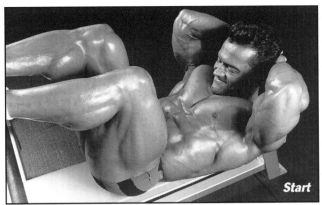

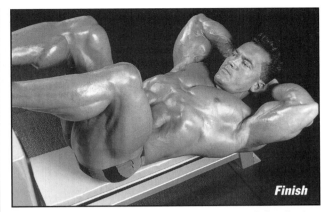

Start

Finish

Lee Labrada crunches his way to awesome abdominals.

the best currently on the pro tour) to numerous sets and reps of leg raises, you believe him. So although the latest kinesiology research may suggest that leg raises are not as effective as once thought, most top bodybuilders still perform them.

Perhaps the best advice we can give you, when training abdominals, (and this refers to other muscle groups as well) is to pick six to eight exercises that effectively work for you. Perform two or three for each ab workout, making sure your whole abdominal region has been hit. The next ab day you can select a new comination of two or three exercises, and so on. Over a two or three-week period you will have effectively hit the midsection from every possible angle. Now let's see how the champs have chiseled those abs of granite!

THIERRY PASTEL – As we have made reference to Thierry earlier, it's only appropriate that we begin this section with his routine.

How do you describe Thierry's rise to bodybuilding stardom? – meteoric. Within two years of taking up the sport, he won the titles of Mr. Martinique, Mr. Europe, and Mr. World.

Perhaps the most eye-catching aspect of Thierry's physique is his mind-boggling midsection. There's not an ounce of fat covering it, and each abdominal layer (Thierry is blessed with that much coveted fourth layer!) looks as if it's carved out of stone. Before we look at his abdominal-training routine we should briefly mention Thierry's philosophy on diet. After all, diet is an important part of maintaining a fat-free waistline.

Unlike many bodybuilders who have two distinct seasons – off and on – Thierry remains in contest condition year round. No bulking up for Mr. Martinique! He doesn't believe in the process of losing 20 or 30 pounds for an upcoming contest. Thierry's dieting consists of tightening his food intake, and are you ready for this – one week before the show! With such die-hard constitution towards appearance, is it any wonder Thierry displays such a phenomenal midsection.

Aside from his all-important diet, Thierry trains his abdominals hard, very hard:

Thierry Pastel displays flawless abdominal development.

"I do abdominals every day. I train them like any other muscle, not like Americans who do five minutes of crunches and think they've worked abs. I usually train them for at least 45 minutes, but the mirror is what tells me how long I should train. I look in the mirror and say, 'Does this bodypart need any more training?' Like today I said, 'Okay, my abs tell me they need 60 sets.' Two weeks from now they may tell me they need only 10 sets. My muscles talk to my mind and ultimately guide what I do."

Thierry usually does four ab exercises in a typical workout. Although he performs them in no set order, for the sake of argument, let's say he starts with leg lifts.

Thierry starts this exercise by lying flat on a bench and grabbing the sides. He then raises his legs until they are nearly vertical, and then slowly lowers, stopping about six inches from the bench. When it comes to reps, Thierry is from the old school of thought. He typically does 5 sets of 50 to 100 reps per set. That's 500 reps! Even more, it's only his first abdominal exercise!

Thierry performs 5 sets of crunches for his second exercise, once again for reps of 50 to 100. He does the exercise with his back on the floor and his legs on top of a bench. On some sets he performs the exercise straight on, while on others he may twist on the way up (hands behind the head, left elbow touching right knee and vice versa), thus bringing his obliques into play.

Another favorite Pastel exercise is hanging leg raises. Grabbing a chinup bar, he raises his legs until they are slightly above parallel. Once again he varies the movement, raising the legs straight up or to the side. Unlike crunches and bench leg raises, he doesn't count reps on this exercise:

"The only thing that matters is concentration. Thinking about the exercise, concentrating, is of true importance. You think about the way to do the exercise, and you think about the muscle so you can shape the body the way you want. We don't work with weight – we work with the mind. The mind is more important than the actual amount of weight."

Thierry's fourth exercise is usually cable crunches. Kneeling down, he reaches up and grabs an overhead cable or rope. He contracts his torso until his forehead almost touches the ground. He pauses, squeezes his abs, and then returns to the starting position. Because of the nature of the movement, this is one exercise where he uses extra weight.

Looking at Thierry's abdominal routine, we see that he is no stranger to hard work (upwards of 1500 to 2000 reps per abdominal workout). Undoubtedly, his ab routine is too strenuous for most, but for him it means developing some of the most coveted abdominals on the competitive stage.

Vince Taylor, Flavio Baccianini and J.J. Marsh

Thierry Pastel's Abdominal Routine:

1. Bench leg raises – *5 sets of 50-100 reps*
2. Crunches – *5 sets of 50-100 reps*
3. Hanging leg raises* – *5 sets of 50-100 reps*
4. Cable crunches* – *5 sets of 50-100 reps*

Thierry lets instinct determine the number of reps and sets on each of the exercises.

LEE LABRADA – With three second-place finishes to Lee Haney at the Mr. Olympia, 180-pound Lee Labrada has established himself as one of the top bodybuilders in the world. His critics say he is too small, but he routinely kicks butt against guys outweighing him by 50 pounds or more, and his Night of Champions victory, as well as numerous Grand Prix titles, help dispel such arguments.

What makes Lee such a formidable competitor is his impeccable shape and symmetry. Coming into each show ripped to shreds hasn't hurt either. Perhaps this fact, more than any other, makes Lee one of the most "in demand" guest posers in the world. Some competitors carry more size and thickness, and others occasionally beat him out in cuts and symmetry, but few bodybuilders surpass Lee on all fronts. In short, Lee is complete.

Lee is well aware that the center of a great physique is a set of rock-hard abdominals. It's usually the first thing that catches a judge's eye (providing they're visible to begin with). If a judge sees washboard abs and granite-solid intercostals, he'll be impressed enough to start looking for more.

Nothing beats a great set of abs!

Start

Francesca Petitjean shapes her lower abs with hanging leg raises.

Finish

Besides their striking appearance, sharp abs improve the image of other muscles. For example, a moderately wide set of shoulders will look a yard wide if they are complemented by a small waist. Lee recognized this fact early in his career, and no doubt this is why he has never placed less than fifth in any pro contest he's entered!

Lee is one of the many legions of young bodybuilders who has been heavily influenced by the writings of Mike Mentzer. Lee took much of Mike's high-intensity philosophy and modified it to suit his own needs. Where Mike recommends performing 1 or 2 high intense sets of low reps, Lee prefers to use moderate weight for an intermediate number of sets, averaging about 9 or 10 sets for larger muscles and 6 to 8 for smaller.

Lee trains abs three times a week, usually on Monday, Wednesday, and Friday. If you could sum up his ab training in

Alternate broomstick side bends and side bends with dumbells are both excellent oblique exercises. – Lee Garoutte

explosive in nature. If he's relying on bodyweight, then he slows things down and tries to keep continuous tension on the muscle.

After regular crunches he does a variation of the exercise which he calls side crunches. Instead of having his feet pointing towards the ceiling, he turns his knees to one side. Now in addition to hitting the abs alone, Lee's intercostals and serratus are brought into play. In a typical workout, he does 3 sets per side, not bothering to count reps:

"Well, this time I don't really count reps. I just go for the fatigue factor, doing as many reps as possible each set. If I'm not using extra resistance, the total reps will probably be close to 100 per side. If I'm using resistance, the reps will come down quite a bit, maybe half that many."

Laura Creavalle

two words, it would be "short" but "intense." Lee likes to keep things simple, devoting most of his energy to one basic ab exercise:

"My ab training is basically centered around the crunch, which I feel is the best ab exercise. The crunch, as you know, is a relatively short movement. It's done by rolling the sternum towards the pelvis – like rolling up a carpet – and squeezing or crunching the abs together. I do them with my legs over a bench to increase the intensity."

Lee performs his crunches in two ways. One workout he uses weight and does low reps, in the 15 to 20 range, and the next he just uses bodyweight and goes to positive failure, not bothering to count reps. If he uses weight it's usually in the form of a 25-pound plate held across his forehead. As he gets tired, Lee lowers the plate closer to his midsection. Even though the weight remains the same, the reduced fulcrum makes it seem lighter.

With regards to speed, Lee likes to alternate. If he's using weight, he'll try to up the pace and make the movement more

The grandfather of all abdominal exercises – the situp.

Start

Finish

For his third ab exercise, Lee alternates between hanging leg raises and lying reverse crunches. Hanging leg raises are pretty self-explanatory, but reverse crunches may be unfamiliar to some. Lee performs them lying on a decline bench with his head resting at the high end. While he's grabbing a part of the bench behind his head for support, he pulls his legs up, trying to touch his knees to his chin. He does 3 sets of about 30 to 40 reps per set. Lee finds this exercise very effective, but only if done properly:

"The emphasis for this exercise is all in the tuck at the top. I feel you could almost do this exercise without bringing your legs down past the halfway point. Straightening the legs or lowering further only works the hip flexors, not the abs. It's that reverse crunching tuck at the top that works the abs."

Lee follows the same ab workout during the off- and precontest season. He goes to failure on each set, only resting long enough to catch his breath, which works out to about one minute between sets. Finally, although many bodybuilders swear by them, Lee avoids any type of twisting movement, maintaining that the exercise is pretty much useless.

Lee Labrada's Abdominal Routine:
1. Crunches – *3 sets of 20-30 reps*
2. Side crunches* – *3 sets of 20-30 reps*
3. Reverse crunches – *3 sets of 20-30 reps*
Lee doesn't count reps on his sets but tries to do about 100 total for the 3 sets.

LAURA CREAVALLE – Even though bodybuilding audiences are famous for voicing their displeasure at contest placings, few could have envisioned the vocal eruption that followed the 1994 Ms. Olympia. After placing second in the 1992 Ms. Olympia, and third in 1993, many in the bodybuilding community felt that 1994 was to be her year. And if the audience reaction is any indication, it was! Without taking anything away from the winner, Lenda Murray, it was simply a case of the reigning champ being slightly off, and Laura being in the best shape of her life. When she was announced second, Laura's fans in the audience (which appeared to be most of those present) erupted in unanimous displeasure.

Laura came to the attention of the bodybuilding public when she won the 1982 Novice Ontario Championship. To this day she claims that it was her ab development that won her the show:

"I recall thinking, 'Okay, I have a contest in six months. Which is the muscle group I can develop the fastest and that can look the most impressive in that amount of time?' Abs of course. There was no way I could have developed big arms or pecs or lats in just six months, so I trained abs very hard."

After reading that Candy Csencsits trained her abs with 2000 reps every day, Laura figured that if Candy could do it, so could she. Laura would train abs for half an hour in the morning and then another half hour before bed. The result – she won her first show and received scores of compliments on her outstanding abs.

To this day, Laura makes ab training an integral part of her workouts. And unlike many others, she has no on- or off-season – she trains them intensely year round:

Mohammed
Makkawy

"I train my abs every day for 15 to 30 minutes. I prefer to warm up my body by training my abs rather than riding the bike or stretching as so many other people seem to do. Training my abs first really gets my blood flowing and sweat pouring. I train my abs as if I were doing an aerobic routine – that means no rest periods at all. I train for a deep ache and burn in my abs and intercostals."

Laura is a firm believer in treating the abs like any other muscle group. Spending an hour on back- or chest-training, and then performing 1 or 2 half-hearted sets for abs just doesn't seem logical to Laura. Even in the off-season she spends a minimum of 10 minutes training abs. That doesn't sound like much, but she doesn't rest between sets, so she easily does 8 to 10 sets.

To increase the intensity of her exercises, Laura uses enough weight to limit her sets to 10 to 50 reps. The exception is hanging leg raises, where she finds her legs are heavy enough as it is.

A typical Creavalle ab workout consists of four exercises. She usually starts with leg raises on a hip-flexor machine. For variety, she alternates lifting to the side (for the intercostals) and to the front (for the lower abs). She aims for 50 reps on the first set, 30 to 35 on the second, 20 to 25 on the third, and 10 to 15 on

the fourth. Often she will superset leg raises with knee-ups while sitting on the end of a bench. She pulls her knees into her chest, tenses, and then straightens her legs out. Once again, she performs 4 sets of 20 to 50 reps (or however many she can accomplish).

Since the first two exercises primarily work the lower abs, Laura chooses two upper-ab movements for her third and fourth exercises. Her favorite is crunches, done for 4 sets of 10 to 20 reps. As she feels her upper abs need more thickness, Laura uses a heavy weight while doing the exercise.

To finish her ab routine, Laura does 4 sets of Roman-chair situps, again using weight to help thicken her upper abs.

Laura Creavalle's Abdominal Routine:
1. Leg raises using hip-flexor machine – *4 sets of 15-50 reps*
2. Knee-ups on flat bench – *4 sets of 20-50 reps*
3. Weighted crunches – *4 sets of 10-20 reps*
4. Weighted Roman-chair situps – *4 sets of 20 reps*

MOHAMED MAKKAWY – Another bodybuilder who recognized the need to develop every muscle to its fullest is Egypt's world champion, Mohamed Makkawy. When you weigh 170 to 175 pounds in contest shape, and you're rubbing elbows with 245-pound behemoths like Mike Christian and Lee Haney, your only chance for success lies in presenting the judges with a complete package. Mohamed did this on numerous occasions, winning a string of Grand Prix victories in the early 1980s. Included in this incredible three-year run were no less than five victories over future eight-time Mr. Olympia, Lee Haney!

Mohamed followed the same bodybuilding philosophy as other under-200-pound bodybuilders. He ignored trying to match mass with the big guys, instead focusing on refining his physique. He realized that nothing less than perfect proportions would be needed

Flex Wheeler, Charles Clairmonte and Michael Francois

to compete successfully against Haney and company, and the key to this was a trim, well-developed midsection.

Much of Mohamed's abdominal development can be attributed to treating the muscle group like any other. This means training them year round, using standard reps and sets. He never subscribed to the "diet alone will bring out the abs" theory. He believes that only regular training can develop a rock-hard midsection.

In terms of actual exercises, his favorite is the hanging leg raise from a chinup bar. He varies the exercise to hit different parts of his midsection. Bringing the knees up to the front develop his abdominals, while lifting to the sides brings the intercostals into play. To increase the intensity, he occasionally performs the movement using extra weight.

After 4 or 5 sets of hanging knee raises, he switches to the bench version. With his buttocks resting on the edge of the bench, he raises his legs (knees kept bent) to slightly above shoulder height.

Mohamed's third exercise is often crunches or incline situps. He is also partial to stick twists, but under no circumstances does he perform side bends. He isn't interested in large obliques and a thicker waist.

Two weeks out from a contest, Mohamed gives up all ab exercises, with the possible exception of hanging leg raises. This he says, allowed for better ab control on the day of a competition.

Mohamed Makkay's Abdominal Routine:
1. Hanging knee-ups – *4-5 sets of 15-20 reps*
2. Bench leg raises – *4-5 sets of 15-20 reps*
3. Crunches – *4-5 sets of 15-20 reps*
4. Stick twists – *4-5 sets of 40-50 reps*

BEV FRANCIS – For many, the sport of female bodybuilding didn't start until Bev Francis emerged on the scene. Up until then, female bodybuilders had more in common with their beauty contestant rivals than male counterparts. All that was to change when Bev first stepped onstage. With years of powerlifting under her belt (including the world record in the bench press), Bev had developed the kind of muscle density that was believed impossible for female athletes. Switching to bodybuilding, she began to shape all of that muscle into a work of art. Throughout the 1980s she routinely gave Cory Everson and other bodybuilders a tough battle at the Ms. Olympia. Many fans voiced the opinion that she was penalized because she carried too much muscle. True or not, to this day she remains one of the sport's most dominant figures. With today's trend toward bigger, more muscular women, many feel Bev's time has yet to come.

Bev's abdominal training consists of 5 to 10 giant sets. She usually starts with decline situps, which gives her the upper-ab development she wants. After 20 to 25 reps she moves on to leg raises, performed off a flat bench. To keep the strain on her lower abs and off her back, she keeps her knees slightly bent throughout the exercise.

Bev's third exercise is situps done on the hyperextension bench. She lowers her body almost to the floor, forcing her abdominals to stretch to the limit. She then curls up into a full crunch position. Once again she keeps her knees bent throughout the exercise.

She then performs side leg raises to hit the intercostals. These are followed by crunches on the Nautilus

Bev Francis

ab machine. For her final exercise, Bev performs rope crunches. Instead of pulling to the front, she alternates pulling to each side. This guarantees that her whole midsection is worked.

She does all of the previous exercises as 1 giant set. She averages 20 to 25 reps per set, performing anywhere from 5 to 10 giant sets per ab workout.

Bev Francis's Abdominal Routine:
1. Decline situps – *20-25 reps*
2. Leg raises off flat bench – *20-25 reps*
3. Situps on hyperextension machine – *20-25 reps*
4. Side leg raises – *20-25 reps*
5. Crunches on Nautilus machine – *20-25 reps*
6. Rope crunches – *20-25 reps*

MIKE ASHLEY – After his wins at the 1988 Detroit Grand Prix and 1990 Arnold Classic, Mike Ashley finally established himself as one of the premier bodybuilders on the pro scene. Only his being a trifle shy in the mass department has kept him from the sport's most coveted title – the Mr. Olympia. Competing with some of the thickest bodybuilders to have ever graced a stage (Dorian Yates, Flex Wheeler, Lee Haney), has not helped Mike either. Yet, mass aside, Mike sports a pair of the greatest arms in the sport, and his abdominals are second to none. Combine this with his always-in-shape physique, and you have a package that can do battle with anyone.

Speaking of abs, Mike trains them on day four of his four-day split. Although he had to put many hours in to develop them, Mike quickly admits that genetics played a major role in producing his outstanding midsection:

"Now I'm not going to say genetics didn't play a part, because not everyone can develop abs like mine. There are a lot of pros out there who train their abs hard and they don't have ab development like me, so I must give some credit to genetics."

Another reason for his great midsection is the type of training Mike engaged in while participating in track and field events. At his peak, he routinely did 70 situps while holding a 45-pound plate behind his head. If that doesn't impress you, how about 10 reps using two 45-pound plates! During gym class Mike could easily do 65 situps in 60 seconds.

Mike's current ab-training philosophy centers around variations of the crunch:

"All of the situps and crunches I have done over the years have really stimulated my abs, and are largely responsible for my ab development. Now I do quite a lot of crunches, reverse crunches and even crunches on my side for the intercostals and sides of my waist. I also do cable crunches."

Because he continuously varies the exercises, Mike doesn't have one specific ab routine. A typical workout will see him pick three or four exercises for 4 or 5 sets of 25 to 50 reps. One thing that he keeps constant is his selection of exercises that work the entire abdominal region – both upper and lower abdominals, and intercostals. He may do supersets of leg raises and crunches, or reverse crunches and Nautilus crunches.

With regards to frequency, he prefers to train his abs once every four days, but close to a contest he may add a second ab workout to his four-day cycle. He doesn't subscribe to the theory that you need to train abs every day of the week:

"Some people try to train their abs every day, but you ask them how intense their ab workout is, and you watch them, and it's like "forget it." It's like they're just going through the motions. I prefer to train my abdominals less frequently, but with superintensity."

For Mike, superintensity means supersets of crunches and leg raises for 50 reps per set, with no rest between sets. Then he moves on to side crunches.

Mike Ashley

Mike Ashley's Abdominal Routine:
1. Nautilus crunches – *5 sets of 50 reps*
2. Reverse crunches – – *5 sets of 50 reps*
3. Side crunches – *5 sets of 50 reps*
4. Leg lifts (raises) – *5 sets of 20 reps*

TONYA KNIGHT – IFBB contestant, former *MuscleMag International* columnist, and one of TV's *American Gladiators,* Tonya Knight was perhaps bodybuilding's most recognizable star in the late '80s and early '90s. Although currently in a state of semi-retirement, Tonya still finds time to pursue her true love – hoisting iron. Her legions of fans wait anxiously for the day that she ventures back into the shark-infested waters of IFBB competition.

Speaking of competition, Tonya admits that much of her success was dependent on her tight, well-muscled midsection. Over the years, she made two major changes to her abdominal training. For starters, like thousands before her, Tonya relied almost entirely on thousands of endless reps of situps. It wasn't until she moved to California that she learned variety was the key to developing an outstanding midsection.

Another mistake involved neglecting abdominal training until a few months before a contest. She wasn't long on the California scene before realizing that to be competitive she had to train her abs year round. The result – an IFBB pro win – and a placing in the top five at her first Ms. Olympia.

Tonya Knight

The basis to Tonya's abdominal-training is year-round variety. She's a strong believer in shocking the muscles, changing her ab workouts from day to day. For example she may select different exercises, change the exercise order, employ different rep ranges, or vary her training tempo (slow and controlled or fast and piston-like). Not only does such variety work her mid-section to the maximum, but it also keeps Tonya's enthusiasm high.

Tonya's ab-training also varied from season to season. During the off-season, Tonya trained abs three times per week. When she switched to her contest phase, she hit them every other day. This resulted in an extra two ab workouts per week.

In all, Tonya had about 10 distinct ab programs to choose from, and even within each, she employed variety. She let instinct determine which routine to follow on a particular day. Her only rule – that each workout was different from the last. Close to a contest she would spend hours practicing her posing, especially ab shots. She would do up to 100 separate contractions for her abdominals, with special emphasis on the mandatory abdominal pose. Tonya attributed much of her abdominal cuts and separation to such isotension.

In terms of specific exercises, she relied heavily on variations of the crunch. Some days she performed the exercise using a rope, while on other days she used a machine. To increase the intensity on her rope crunches, she alternated between crunching to the front, and side to side. She found the side crunches particularly helpful in bringing out her intercostals.

Another favorite exercise was leg raises. Once again, she varied the angle of attack – either by doing the exercise hanging from a chinup bar, or seated on a bench.

Besides straight sets, Tonya liked to lump four exercises together and do 3 giant sets, averaging 50 reps per set, although slightly less on the hanging leg raises.

Finally, Tonya would occasionally perform what she called a high-intensity ab workout. She would choose one exercise, often incline situps, and do 3 sets using weight. For example, she would do 20 reps using a 10-pound plate, and then drop the 10 pounder and pick up a 25-pound plate, and bang out another 20 reps. Not content to stop there, Tonya would drop the 25 pounder and squeeze out an additional 20 reps. 3 sets of such madness was all it took to make her abs extremely sore!

The following is a sample routine that Tonya Knight frequently followed. Keep in mind that no two ab workouts were ever the same, and she constantly varied her routines from workout to workout.

Tonya Knight's Abdominal Routine (Sample):
1. Machine crunches – *3 sets of 30 reps*
2. Hanging leg raises – *3 sets of 30 reps*
3. Rope crunches – *3 sets of 60 reps*

Chapter Twenty-nine

SERRATUS, LOWER BACK AND NECK

CONTEST-WINNING FINGERS

Although not technically part of the abdominal region the location of the serratus allow them to be exercised with other muscles of the midsection.

Top Olympian competitor Shawn Ray.

ANATOMY OF THE SERRATUS

For those not familiar with the serratus, they're the finger-like projections located between the obliques and lats. They tie the lats, obliques, and abdominals together. When properly developed, they frame the muscles of the midsection, and give your physique that polished look. All things being equal, a bodybuilder with great serratus development will in all likelihood beat a much larger, but less complete individual. Frank Zane used this strategy to win three Mr. Olympia titles.

TRAINING THE SERRATUS

Like the abdominals, you have to approach serratus development on two fronts – diet and exercise. The diet aspect is discussed earlier in this book, so we will not go into any detail. Suffice to say, the greatest midsection in the world will not impress the judges if it's covered by a layer of fat. If you want rock-hard abdominals and serratus, you have to remove the excess adipose tissue – there is no question here.

Training the serratus is very straightforward. Frank Zane always favored the cross-bench pullover.

"Make sure to lie across the bench and keep the hips down. As the dumbell is lowered behind the head, it's very important to get as much stretch as possible on every rep. At the same time, make sure to tense the serratus hard at the top of the movement."
– Frank Zane, Three-time Mr. Olympia

Another bodybuilder who favored the dumbell pullover was Steve Davis. Steve is an example of a bodybuilder who never let his lack of muscle mass hold him back (in fact Steve totally transformed his physique, losing over 100 pounds of fat in the process!). Steve adds that besides working the serratus, pullovers lengthen the look of the torso by stretching the pectorals, lats, intercostals, and rib cage. Instead of a bunch of individual muscles, pullovers tie them all together. Try to do at least 3 to 5 sets of dumbell pullovers, twice a week. Keep the reps in the 12 to 15 range, and emphasize the stretch at the bottom.

The straight-arm barbell pullover is also a great serratus-builder. Instead of lying across the bench, lie lengthwise. Also keep your arms locked, as bending them brings the triceps into play. Don't worry about the amount of weight used. Most people don't use more than 40 to 50 pounds for 3 or 4 sets of 12 to 20 reps.

This exercise is a favorite of former Mr. Universe, Serge Nubret.

In addition to the two exercises described previously, movements performed for other muscle groups also work the serratus. Close-grip chins and pulldowns, while primarily lower-lat exercises, simultaneously bring the serratus into play. Vince Gironda considers the wide-grip dip an excellent serratus-builder. The lower part of the exercise spreads the ribs and stretches the serratus, while the top section contracts and knots them together. If you plan on using this exercise for serratus development, there are a few points to keep in mind: Keep the upper back rounded and the elbows straight out to the sides while using a grip that is at least 32 inches wide, and keep your feet forward.

A simpler, but equally effective exercise, is the straight-arm cable pulldown to the thigh. To perform the exercise, grab an overhead pulley handle and with the arms locked, bring the hands down to the thigh. As with pullovers, don't use too much weight as this forces you to bend the arms and bring the triceps into play. Try using light weight for 3 or 4 sets of 15 to 20 reps.

A great way to work the serratus and finish the lats is by performing straight-arm pulldowns on the lat machine. Grab the bar with a slightly less than shoulder-width grip, and bring it down to the thighs. Keep the arms locked solid and aim for at least 20 to 30 reps.

Another great serratus exercise is kneeling rope pulldowns. Most gyms have a short piece of rope with two knobs on the end. It's primarily used for working the triceps, but it's invaluable for doing crunches and pulldowns.

Kneel on the floor, about three feet from the machine, and reach up and grab the rope with both hands. Lean forward and pull the rope to the floor. At the end of the movement you will be in what resembles a fetal position, with your hands on the floor. Slowly return to the starting position, trying to keep tension on the serratus throughout the full range of motion. Not only does this exercise work the serratus but your abs will get quite a blast as well!

"The Equalizer" Gary Strydom

The splendid back of Francis Benfatto.

Another exercise you can perform, provided you have access, is the Nautilus pullover. While considered a lat and chest exercise, the machine's circular motion strongly stresses the serratus and intercostals. To avoid having the chest and lats do most of the work, you might want to perform pullovers at the end of your chest or back routine. Nautilus pullovers are an excellent way to finish the larger torso muscles, and begin midsection training.

A final method of training the serratus is posing, especially behind-the-head ab shots. One of Frank Zane's most impressive poses was the vacuum pose. Place both arms behind the head, and with the hands resting on the upper neck/lower-head region, point the elbows straight up into the air. Now gently push forward with the hands, and at the same time take in a huge volume of air. Hold for 15 to 20 seconds, and try to flex the serratus as hard as possible. Relax, and then repeat the whole process. Do 4 or 5 sets of these after each serratus/abdominal workout. Not only will it bring the muscles out, but it's great practice for competition.

THE NEGLECTED LOWER BACK

"Lower-back development is important not only for appearance, but also to protect oneself against injury. My favorite exercise for this area is straight-leg deadlifts, with a fairly light barbell, while standing on a block of wood. The trick here is to come only about a quarter of the way up so that constant pressure is kept on the lumbar region. I suggest 4 sets to failure."
– John Hnatyschak, world middleweight champion

It's unfortunate that many bodybuilders spend countless hours working the big, showy muscles like chest and arms, and yet totally neglect the one muscle that could potentially save their bodybuilding careers.

When was the last time you watched a bodybuilder come into the gym and say that he was going to work his lower back? Chances are, probably never. It's true that many bodybuilders throw in a few sets of good mornings or hyperextensions at the end of a workout, but for the most part, the lower back is a highly neglected muscle group. What's ironic is that the lower back is one of the most frequently injured areas. Besides the knees and front delts, the lower back has ended more athletic careers than any other muscle group. The solution is to make lower-back training a priority. Not only will you strengthen it and help prevent injuries, but you'll develop a set of spinal erectors that will turn the heads of bodybuilding judges.

ANATOMY OF THE LOWER BACK

The lower back consists primarily of the long spinal erector muscles that start at the base of the spine and extend up to the base of the neck. For bodybuilding purposes, it's the lower region that concerns us – the upper region is covered primarily by the traps and lats.

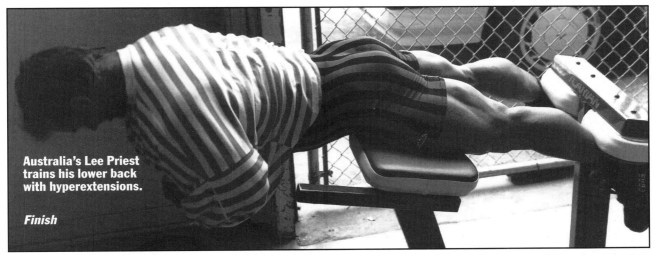

Australia's Lee Priest trains his lower back with hyperextensions.

Finish

Start

CHAPTER TWENTY-NINE - SERRATUS, LOWER BACK AND NECK

Check out the "Christmas tree" in Ali Mala's lower back!

When properly developed, the spinal erectors look like two snakes emerging from the spinal base. A few bodybuilders (Victor Richards, Flex Wheeler, Kevin Levrone, etc.) virtually have pythons running up their backs!

The main function of the spinal erectors is to extend the torso. Contrary to popular belief, the erectors are relatively relaxed in the standing position, and only come into play when the torso bends backward. The erectors work in conjunction with the abdominals to flex and extend the spine, and can be compared to other opposing muscle groups such as the biceps/triceps and quadriceps/hamstrings.

TRAINING THE LOWER BACK

The first rule of thumb in training the lower back is to avoid exercises that cause pain in this area. Now we're not talking muscle soreness, but any pain that is felt deep within the spinal column. The idea is to strengthen the lower back, not put you in traction for six months!

Another point concerns the amount of weight used while performing lower-back exercises. Contrary to popular belief, you don't need excessive poundages to train the lower back. Yes, powerlifters can hoist some impressive weights in the deadlift, but we assure you they didn't start out that way. And besides, proper deadlifting technique utilizes more hip and leg power than simply the lower-back musculature.

Keep the weight light to moderate and the reps in the 15 to 20 range. Above all, perform the repetitions in a smooth and controlled manner. Lower-back exercises are definitely not movements to cheat on.

You should start your lower-back training with an easy warmup exercise. Hyperextensions are fine, but you may find the exercise difficult to perform, so start with good mornings. Stand with your feet about shoulder width apart, and hold a light bar across your back (start by using a broomstick and progress to a small barbell and then a larger version). With your knees locked, bend forward so that your upper body is parallel to the floor. Don't bounce, as this can put unwanted stress on the lower back. Aim for 15 to 20 reps, and when this gets easy, add a few pounds to the bar. Resist the urge to put excessive weight on the bar. It may look impressive but it will eventually catch up with you.

After the lower back is warmed up, you can proceed to hyperextensions. With your legs anchored under the special training apparatus and your hips resting on the pad, lower your upper body as far as comfortably possible. Raise yourself until you are parallel with the floor. Don't hyperextend (this is where the name of the exercise is misleading) your back and arch upwards. The human spine was not designed to move in a hyperextended position and such extreme ranges of motion may only add to existing problems. Once again, aim for 15 to 20 reps. If this seems easy, try putting your hands behind your head. This increases the resistance on the upper body and makes the movement more difficult.

For your final exercise do 2 or 3 sets of lightweight deadlifts. Keep the bar close to the body as you lift and try to maintain constant tension on the spinal erectors. If you have an existing back problem, wear a training belt. Always perform the exercise nice and slow, with no sudden jerks or bounces.

There you have it. Three great exercises to prevent lower-back injuries and help you develop a "python-like" set of spinal erectors. For variety, you might want to triset the three exercises together.

A NECK ABOVE THE REST

How often have you heard a football player being described as having no neck? For all the accolades heaped on the chest, arms, and shoulders, nothing stirs the sports' reporters imagination in the same manner as a bull-like neck. Yet with all this praise waiting in the wings, few bodybuilders make neck training a priority. In fact most avoid it all together, adopting the attitude that only wrestlers and football players have big necks. This may have been fine 10 or 20 years ago, but given the highly competitive nature of today's bodybuilding contests, a strong muscular neck is a necessity. With almost every top bodybuilder sporting great pecs, biceps, and quads, it's the little "extras" that garner the brownie points. Such stars as Shawn Ray, Bertil Fox, Paul DeMayo, and Jeff King, are famous for their outstanding neck development.

ANATOMY OF THE NECK

The neck region contains perhaps the body's most complex musculature. The various capitis and hyoid muscles interact to move the head in virtually any desired direction. In addition, these muscles provide support and protection for the skull and assist in such processes as chewing food and swallowing.

PREVENTATIVE MAINTENANCE

Like most bodyparts, the neck is relatively easy to develop – provided it's trained correctly. Before we look at specific exercises, we need to talk a little about preventative maintenance.

Most individuals (bodybuilders included) are not even aware of their neck until they strain it, or wake up some morning with what's commonly called a "stiff neck". Just as the lower back can cause grief when injured, so too can the neck if treated unkindly. Several of the most common exercises place a great deal of stress on the neck. Many bodybuilders perform the bench press in shoddy style, by arching the back excessively. The result – the person's bodyweight becomes balanced on their glutes and head (neck). The next morning they wake up with a stiff neck and wonder where it came from. The ailment usually gets blamed on a virus, when in fact the real culprit was the errors made during the previous day's training session.

Other exercises may aggravate the neck as well. For example, there is a tendency to force the head back against the bar when performing squats. The result is a tremendous strain being placed on the neck muscles. Likewise, exercises such as shoulder presses, incline presses, and shrugs, can injure the neck if not done carefully.

Our advice is to try and keep the neck neutral when performing most exercises. Obviously this is almost impossible on exercises such as squats, deadlifts, and shrugs, however, excessive arching on chest movements should be avoided.

TRAINING THE NECK

Besides indirect stimulation, the neck can be trained directly using the following exercises. In many cases the exercises require a bit of creativity, as neck-training equipment is limited in most gyms. This is not due to an unwillingness to buy the appropriate equipment but because, for the most part, it doesn't exist! With the exception of the Nautilus neck machine, and a few head straps attached to cables, equipment manufacturers have neglected to design the necessary apparatus.

One of the simplest but most effective exercises for the neck involves lying on a flat bench and supporting a plate wrapped in a towel across your forehead. With your head off the end of the bench, lower it as far as possible, holding the plate in place with your hand. Now tilt the head forward until your chin touches your chest. Try doing 3 sets of 10 to 12 reps.

A well developed neck is a necessity in the competitive world of bodybuilding.

Start

Finish

Another great exercise is the wrestler's bridge. Lie on your back and arch up using the neck and legs, so that only your head and feet touch the floor. Now slowly and gently rock back and forward on your head. You can count a rep as being one full forward and backward motion. This exercise may be difficult for beginners, as it requires the use of your total bodyweight. If you can only perform one or two reps you might be advised to stick with other exercises until your neck has sufficient strength to support your bodyweight.

The other extreme is being able to bang out 20 or 30 reps with ease. In this case you'll need to add additional resistance. Wrestlers have a partner sit on their chest. If you have the strength (and technique) to do this, fine. But be careful. Supporting an additional person's bodyweight places tremendous strain on the neck musculature. It might be a good idea to initially have your partner hold a weight on your chest. When this becomes easy, increase the weight until you can support your partner's weight.

There are a few exercises that can be performed on neck training machines, the most popular being the Nautilus version. In most cases the machines allow you to change sitting position. This lets you train the neck from the front, back, and both sides. The muscles on the side of the neck (sternocleidomastoids), give you that wide, bull-necked appearance. The rear neck muscles tie into the traps, giving a completeness to the

Danny Hester trains his neck on the Nautilus neck machine.

back. There are two approaches to using the neck machine. You can do straight sets in each direction, or perform 1 or 2 giant sets.

If your gym doesn't have a neck machine, use a neck harness. They can be purchased specially made for the job, or you can easily make your own. Slip the harness over your head and support a weight from the end. From here it's just a matter of rotating your head back and forth in a slow and controlled manner. By leaning forward, you are primarily working the rear neck muscles. If you lie facing upward on a bench, you can target the front neck muscles.

Besides these direct neck exercises, a number of trap movements also hit the neck. Most forms of shrugs (whether dumbell, barbell, or machine) will add mass to your neck/trap tie-in. One of the best exercises in this regard is the standing calf machine shrug. Stand under the machine and rest the pads on your shoulders. Instead of standing up on your toes, as you would for calf raises, keep your legs straight and shrug your shoulders. You won't have the same range of motion as a regular barbell or dumbell shrug, but the effect is very pronounced for the rear neck and traps.

If you have competitive bodybuilding aspirations, then a well-developed neck is a necessity. How big

Tim Belknap performs the wrestler's bridge to build his neck.

Kevin Levrone

should it be? This depends on the rest of your physique. You don't want your shoulders to appear sloped or bunched. But on the other hand, your neck should be in proportion with the rest of your physique. The old norm was to have the calves, neck, and arms, stretching the tape to the same measurement. It's doubtful, however, if many of today's champs have 22-inch necks to go along with their 22-inch arms (how many can say the same about their calves?). Still, your neck measurement should be within an inch or two of your arms. A 16-inch neck in no way complements a 20-inch arm!

The other advantage to a strong neck is it's usefulness in many sports. For those involved in activities such as judo, wrestling, rugby, and football, a strong and powerful neck will not only improve your performance but may also save your life.

Unless you were blessed with great genetics, you will probably have to train the neck on a regular basis. Select two or three of the exercises described previously and perform 2 or 3 sets of each. For the sake of two neck workouts a week, lasting 10 to 15 minutes each, you too can be referred to as having "no neck"!

Franco Santoriello

The wide World of Bodybuilding

8

BODYBUILDING ON THE ROAD

The fact that people are always on the move is a reality of modern-day life. Whether for business, vacation, school, or simply for pleasure, contemporary means of travel allow people to cover great distances in short periods of time. For "Joe or Jill Average," this moving about may not cause much of an inconvenience, but for the aspiring bodybuilder, it can create havoc. In fact getting to a gym can become almost impossible. Granted most cities have gyms, but the majority of small towns don't. If your job consists of many one-night stands (musician, salesperson, lecturer, etc.), you have to be creative if you intend to keep that great physique of yours.

Besides the traveling aspect, there are other reasons for not making that gym appointment. For many beginners, undecided on their long-term inten-tions, spending hundreds of dollars on a gym membership may not be a wise investment. What happens if, after plunking down $500, you decide to call it quits within a few weeks? Get your money back – fat chance! Unless you make prior arrangements (and have it in writing!), chances are you're out $500. For these individuals, obtaining a few inexpensive pieces of equipment and working out at home makes far more sense.

Although the following section is primarily designed for those on the road, who lack the appropriate training apparatus, it can be followed by just about anyone. You can exercise your body to a substantial degree by using a few inexpensive pieces of equipment commonly found around the house (or hotel room). Not only will you maintain your present condition, but you might improve on it.

For simplicity we have divided the body into specific muscle groups. The exercises are arranged to hit the largest muscles first, followed by the smaller

There are many ways to maintain your physique while away from home.

Jason Arntz

are numerous nonweight exercises and here are just a few of them.

1. Sissy Squats

One of the best thigh exercises (weighted or not) is the sissy squat. If you're not sold on the merits of this exercise, check with Vince Gironda and Mohamed Makkawy. For years Mohamed was held back by a lack of upper thigh impressiveness. A couple of months of sissy squats, while under Vince's ever watchful eye, and Mohamed's thighs were totally transformed.

To perform this exercise, grab a doorway with one outstretched arm. Bend your knees and lower down until your thighs are parallel with the floor. Keeping the upper body straight, raise back to the upright position. Throughout the exercise, keep your thighs tight and try to keep your butt forward. If your upper body bends forward most of the stress will be taken by the glutes, and you don't want this.

The first 8 to 10 reps may feel light and easy, but will you say the same after 20? Perform 3 sets of sissy squats and you'll know what the word "burn" really means!

If you have some sort of weight present (small suitcase, heavy book, etc.), hold it to the chest with your free hand. You'd be surprised how much difference five or 10 pounds makes.

2. Chair Lunges

Most hotel rooms have at least one chair available, but the baseboard at the lower end of your bed will suffice. Place one foot on the chair, and with the other leg kept straight, lunge forward until your hamstring touches your calf. Pause at the bottom, and then with the torso

For extra muscle isolation try limbo squats in your hotel room. – Marla Duncan

muscles. In most cases we describe three or four exercises for each muscle group. Pick one or two for each muscle and away you go. You can perform straight sets, or group them together into super, tri, or giant sets.

EQUIPMENT NEEDED
- Two chairs
- Two books
- Set of spring chest expanders
- Hand grips
- Bed (to use, not lie on!)

LEGS
Granted your typical hotel room is not equipped with a squat rack and stacks of 45-pound plates, but that's not a good enough reason to give your leg muscles a rest. There

Start

Finish

held erect, return to the starting position. Perform 15 to 20 reps and then switch legs, doing 3 sets of each.

3. Limbo Squats or Between-the-Door Squats

Open the bathroom door (you can use the main door to the hotel room but it may garner you a few questionable stares!) and grasp both sides with your hands. With your body leaning as far back as possible, squat down until your thighs are at least parallel with the floor. This exercise is similar to the sissy squat except you lean back further, thus isolating the thighs more.

4. One-leg Squats

If you have knee problems (or very weak legs) you might want to skip this one. This exercise is similar to regular squats except that you hold on to an upright for support. Squat down to parallel on one leg and then return to the starting position. Don't be surprised if you can only perform 5 or 6 reps. Many people only get 2 or 3 reps. The bottom line is to do as many as possible, until you reach 10 to 15 reps per set.

For added effectiveness, the four previous exercises can be grouped together as 1 or 2 giant sets. Perform 15 to 20 reps per set of each, without stopping, and we guarantee your thighs will be begging for mercy!

5. One-leg Calf Raises

All you need for this one is a two or three-inch object to stand on. A thick book will do, but you may want to bring along a short piece of wood. Perform the exercise in a doorway, as balance may be a problem. Also, the lack of weight will require doing high reps. That's fine, as your calves are probably used to doing 15 to 20 reps with heavy weight. The change will do them good (to be honest, it will shock the hell out of them!).

With one leg bent, lower your heel as far as possible with the other leg. Remember you'll have to make up for the lack of weight by doing a slow, full stretch. Do at least 25 to 30 reps (or more if you can take it) per leg, for 3 sets.

6. Squat-down Calf Raises

As the previous exercise is performed in the straight-leg fashion, most of the stress is placed on the upper gastrocnemius muscle. If you bend the legs, to the point of being in a squat position, the strain is shifted to the lower soleus muscle. As this is an extremely difficult exercise, you may want to use both legs at the same time; this way you can hit both the inner and outer

Start

Finish

Use a book or other similar object to do one-leg calf raises. – Marla Duncan

soleus. If possible, do 20 reps per set. If you find yourself doing 30 or more, try the exercise one leg at a time.

CHEST

What's that you say, "I need a barbell to hit the pectorals." Nonsense! One of the most effective chest exercises is dips. And what's more, by varying the angle you can work both the upper and lower chest.

7. Pushups

Along with situps, pushups are among the most basic of nonweight exercises. Besides the pectorals, pushups also work the shoulders and triceps. You can think of this exercise as a reverse bench press. Instead of lying on your back and pushing the bar up, you lie on your stomach and push the body away from the floor. We recommend doing pushups as a warmup, before any of the following exercises.

For those who are not familiar with the exercise, here's a brief description. Kneel down on the floor with

Basic exercises, like pushups, give your body a good workout.

Start

Finish

doing the exercise this way, try it with the knees resting on the floor. This eliminates much of your leg weight. Do 3 sets of 15 to 20 reps (or as close as you can get to this rep range).

8. Dips Between Chairs

Place two chairs about shoulder width apart. With your feet on the floor and your hands placed firmly on the seat of the chairs, slowly lower your body between them. As this exercise places a great deal of strain on the pec-delt tie-in, don't drop in an uncontrolled manner. What would your gym buddies say if they found out you tore your pecs while dipping between chairs! Unfortunately, this can happen if you're not careful. Although the whole chest region is stressed, this exercise primarily works the lower-chest region.

9. Dips Between Chairs with Feet Elevated

You'll need a third chair or the end of your bed to perform this exercise. With the feet elevated, lower yourself between the other two chairs. If

your hands placed about shoulder width apart. Straighten the legs so that your body is resting on your hands and toes. Lower down to within an inch or so of the floor, and then push back up to arms' length while keeping your back straight. For those who have trouble

Finish

Start

Even though you're not using weights, you still need to be careful to avoid injury when doing dips.

CHAPTER THIRTY - BODYBUILDING ON THE ROAD

Chins between chairs will round out your routine while on the road.

Start

Finish

the chairs and lie down between them. Grab the bar as close to the chairs as possible (not only is this the most appropriate width, but there is less chance the bar will break) and pull your upper body to the bar. Pause at the top, and then lower. Try to keep your body as rigid as possible throughout the exercise. If the bar is of sufficient strength (a round metal pipe would be best), you can perform this exercise with a narrow grip. Try to do a minimum of 10 to 12 reps per set, but of course it's going to depend on your strength level.

12. Spring Pullups
We included this one because many individuals have access to a portable chest expander set. In fact if you do a lot of traveling, you might want to pick up a set. The apparatus consists of two handles joined by adding a spring. The more springs, the more tension – it's that simple. Although they are called chest expanders, it's virtually impossible to work your chest with them! They're great, however, for hitting the delts, arms, and lats, and here's one for the latter.

You'll first need to anchor one of the chest expander handles to the floor. Try lifting up the end of the bed and placing one of the legs through the handle. Stand at arms' length and grab the free handle with both hands. Bend slightly at the waist and pull the handle to the lower rib cage. Pause, and then stretch out to arms' length. Try to position yourself so that the tension remains on your lats throughout the full range of the exercise.

The exercise can also be done while standing on a chair. With the handle secured through one of the chair legs, pull the other handle up as if doing a T-bar row.

Whether doing the bed or chair version, it's a good idea to stretch your lats after each set. Grab a doorknob, and with the arms locked out, try twisting the waist to the left and right to give the lats a good stretch.

DELTOIDS
Although the deltoids will have received some work from the various chest exercises, you may want to perform one or two direct exercises for them. You will need one or two heavy books, and a chest expander set.

13. Front, Side or Rear Lateral Raises
Since the exercises are similar, we will describe all three here. Holding a book in each hand, raise the arms to the front, side, or rear. If doing rear laterals,

you place the chairs slightly wider, you stretch the pecs more, but once again, watch the lower part of the exercise. With the angle changed, most of the stress is raised to the center- and upper-chest region.

10. Pushups with Legs Elevated
This exercise is probably the most difficult of the four. Position your body so the feet are on a chair (the end of the bed will suffice). With the hands resting on the floor, shoulder width apart, perform the exercise like a standard pushup. The exercise's angle places most of the stress on the upper-chest.

As with leg exercises, the previous can be performed for straight sets, or as 1 or 2 giant sets.

LATS
It's difficult to effectively work the lats at home or in a hotel room without some piece of specialized equipment – but it can be accomplished. All you need are two chairs, a short piece (3 or 4 feet) of wood or pipe, and a chest-expander set.

11. Chins Between Chairs
Place the chairs three to four feet apart (or slightly less than the length of your stick). Position the stick across

Melissa Coates

place your head on a chair or other such support. Unless the books used are extremely heavy (hardcover edition of Grey's Anatomy, etc.), keep your arms as straight as possible. This will isolate the delts and limit cheating. If by chance you have a heavy book, then you can do the exercise like a standard dumbell raise (arms and legs slightly bent, a small cheat to get the weight moving, etc.).

If you prefer, the exercise can be performed one arm at a time, just grab a door (or other such upright) for support.

14. Spring Laterals

Instead of using a book, try your trusty chest expander. Secure one handle with a foot, and raise the other with your free hand. Unless you have delts like Paul Dillett, use only one or two springs for this exercise.

For variety, try the exercise with two hands. With both handles gripped in front of you, push the arms to a locked-out position (the instructions for this gizmo, back in the '50s and '60s, said that doing the exercise in this manner would greatly expand your chest). This is an excellent

Albeit a dumbell would be more convenient, books can double as weights for raises.

Finish

Start

Roland Cziurlok

movement for both the rear and side delts, but it's possible to isolate the rear delts even more by bending over at the waist.

15. Upright Rows

Once again, you'll need the chest expander to do this exercise. With one handle anchored to the floor, grab the other handle with both hands and flare the elbows out to the sides. Now raise the handle up as if you were holding a barbell. This exercise not only hits the delts, but also brings the traps into play. Do 3 sets of 15 to 20 reps.

On any of the previous exercises involving the chest expander, make sure the anchored handle is secure. If it slips, or the bed or chair leg breaks, the odds are good to excellent that it will rebound and strike you in the head. You can imagine the force generated by four or five fully outstretched springs. If there's any doubt, skip the exercise.

ARMS

There are a wide range of nonweight exercises that can be performed for the biceps and triceps. Granted a small dumbell would give you a better workout (a small bar and 20 to 30 pounds of plastic-coated plates is a good investment for frequent travelers), but with a bit of creativity you can give the arms a good workout, and here's how to do it.

16. Triceps Dips

This exercise is done exactly the same as the gym version, using two flat benches. Place two chairs wide enough apart so that you have enough room to dip between them. With your heels resting on one, and your palms on the other, lower yourself. Be careful that the chair your hands are on does not tip. Keep your hands as far away from the edge of the chair as possible. This keeps the center of gravity down through the chair and not on its edge. Do 3 sets of 15 to 20 reps.

17. Close-grip Pushups

Done with a wide grip, this exercise places most of the stress on the chest and front delts. Using a narrow (6 to 8 inch) hand placing gives the triceps a good workout. If you're strong enough, try the exercise with the feet elevated. Once again, go for 15 to 20 reps.

18. Spring Curls

Anchor one handle of the chest expander to the floor, and curl the other up using biceps power. For variety you can lift straight up (with the anchored handle and lifting arm on the same side), or lift to the side (with the anchored handle on the opposite side of the lifting arm). Do 3 sets of 15 to 20 reps for each arm.

19. Book Curls

This one will take a bit of practice, as curling a book is nowhere near as convenient as curling a dumbell. Using one or two books (grab a meaty book like the Encyclopedia Britannica), curl the arm up as if using a dumbell. The shape of the books makes supinating (twisting) the hands virtually impossible, so leave that till you get back to the gym. Instead, concentrate on making the book feel heavier than it actually is. Do each rep in an ultraslow fashion, making the biceps burn. 3 sets of 15 to 20 reps should do it.

ABDOMINALS
20. Lying Leg Raises

Sit on the edge of a bed or chair, and with your legs slightly bent, raise them to about 45 degrees (any more than this will increase the stress on the hip flexors). Lower to parallel and repeat. If you've got the abdominal strength, pause for a second at the top and bottom.

21. Crunches

Nothing fancy here. Instead of using a flat bench, place your lower legs on a chair. Perform the exercise in the same manner as you would in the gym. Do 3 sets of 20 to 25 reps.

Like any of the previous muscle groups, you can superset the abdominal exercises together, or perform straight sets.

There you have it – 21 exercises that will keep you fit and trim while on the road. Don't be mislead into thinking that nonweight exercises are nonproductive. Many bodybuilders have the attitude that it's necessary to throw around hundreds of pounds of weight to get results, but this is not always the case. Muscles grow in response to new stimuli, and this can take many forms. The most common is an increase in weight, but changing the exercises can also force the muscles to adapt. Ever notice how sore the muscles get when you try something new? Chances are you were sore in places you didn't even know existed.

The exercises described in the previous section were chosen for a number of reasons. Besides their simplicity and convenience, they're also novel. That is, in all probability, you never did them before. And what does a muscle do when faced with a new exercise – it adapts, it responds, it grows!

Before we leave this topic, we have one further suggestion. If your job requires an extensive period of travel, then you may want to invest a few dollars in a "traveling workout kit." There is no need to lug around hundreds of pounds of plates, but a few accessories wouldn't hurt. The following list contains various items that can be included with your toothbrush, shaver, socks, etc.

THE TRAVELER'S WORKOUT KIT

1. One pair of hand grips
2. One five-spring chest expander set
3. 40 to 50 pounds of weight (more if it's convenient)
4. Two short dumbell bars and collars
5. EZ-curl bar

Most of these items will fit into a large suitcase, and although not appropriate for a commercial gym, plastic weights (remember your first York set consisting of 110 pounds of plates and a 25-pound bar?) are ideal for traveling. Not only are they kind to suitcases, but they treat hotel floors with consideration.

If you travel by car or truck, then there's no limit to what you can carry. 150 to 200 pounds of plates won't make much difference in gas mileage (it's the equivalent to another person in the car), and it takes up little room. Stack the plates in the trunk and put your bar along the floor in the back seat. Throw in a chest expander and a set of hand grips, and you will have a "traveling Gold's Gym"!

Paul DeMayo and Denise Paglia

Chapter Thirty-one

PUMPING IRON AT HOME

It's widely assumed that building a great physique requires a membership at a large, commercial gym. Yet survey after survey has found that a large percentage of individuals skip World or Gold's, and rely on the comfort of their own basements. In fact when you look at the advantages of training at home, it's not surprising that many would-be Mr. Olympias prefer to hoist some basement iron.

The biggest advantage to working out at home is convenience. There's no waiting for equipment, looking for a parking spot, or having to wipe a bench down after some inconsiderate gym member dripped sweat all over it!

Another plus is the expense. After the equipment is bought, it doesn't cost you a cent to work out. Compare this to a $500 to $1000 annual gym membership.

Other benefits include: choosing your own music and how loud it's played, working out whenever you wish, and periodically hitting the refrigerator!

Training at home doesn't require a lot of fancy equipment. In most cases a barbell and a few adjustable dumbells are all that's needed. Remember those old pictures from the glory days of Muscle Beach. Bodybuilders such as Vince Gironda, John Grimek, and Steve Reeves, all built outstanding physiques using only barbells and dumbells. Even the top pros competing today would agree that the bulk of their training centers around free-weight exercises.

If after a couple of months (or years for that matter) you realize you're hooked, then by all means join a gym. But in the meantime, there's no reason why you can't develop a great physique at home.

The exercises in this chapter are described with the assumption that you have access to the following pieces of equipment:

Paul Dillett, Flex Wheeler and Lee Labrada

1. Straight barbell
2. EZ-curl bar
3. Dumbells
4. Flat bench
5. Adjustable bench with
   leg extension/curl attachment*

There is a wide spectrum when it comes to home-training apparatus. They range from a simple, flat bench, to a multi-station training apparatus. Some of the more sophisticated ones have attachments for shoulder presses, leg extensions, lat pulldowns, and pec-deks. If you've got the room (at least the size of a small bedroom) and cash ($500 to $1000), then go for it. Supplemented with free weights, you could build a championship physique in your basement.

We have divided the following into two sections – routines and exercises. The routines are presented first, succeeded by the exercise descriptions.

The routines are to be performed on alternate days. We have chosen a slightly higher rep range, as for most of you, this will be your first experience working out with weights. After a few weeks you may want to increase the weight and lower the rep ranges. Be careful on any exercise where you could get trapped under the bar (bench presses and squats in particular). If you are doing bench presses alone leave the collars off. If you get stuck you can force the bar up on one side, then the other side becomes heavier and drops, allowing the remaining plates to fall off.

The previous suggestion is only to be used as a last resort, as it's not a good practice to train to failure on bench presses if you are alone. If in doubt, skip parallel bench presses and do dumbell presses or flyes instead.

THE ROUTINES
Routine 1:
Sissy squats – 3 sets of 15-20 reps
Lunges – 3 sets of 15-20 reps
Leg curls – 3 sets of 15-20 reps
Dumbell calf raises – 3 sets of 15-20 reps
Dumbell rows – 3 sets of 12-15 reps
Dumbell presses – 3 sets of 12-15 reps
Shoulder presses – 3 sets of 12-15 reps
Upright rows – 3 sets of 12-15 reps
Barbell curls – 3 sets of 10-12 reps
Dumbell extensions – 3 sets of 10-12 reps
Crunches – 3 sets of 20-25 reps

Routine 2:
Leg extensions – 3 sets of 15-20 reps
Front squats – 3 sets of 15-20 reps
Leg curls – 3 sets of 15-20 reps
Dumbell calf raises – 3 sets of 15-20 reps
Lat pulldowns – 3 sets of 12-15 reps
Bench presses – 3 sets of 12-15 reps
Dumbell lateral raises – 3 sets of 12-15 reps

Tonya Knight

Dumbell shrugs – 3 sets of 12-15 reps
Alternate dumbell curls – 3 sets of 10-12 reps
Lying dumbell extensions – 3 sets of 10-12 reps
Leg raises – 3 sets of 15-20 reps

Routine 3:
Leg extensions – 3 sets of 15-20 reps
Front squats – 3 sets of 15-20 reps
Lying leg curls – 3 sets of 15-20 reps
Dumbell calf raises – 3 sets of 15-20 reps
Barbell rows – 3 sets of 12-15 reps
Dumbell flyes – 3 sets of 12-15 reps
Dumbell shoulder presses – 3 sets of 12-15 reps
Upright rows – 3 sets of 12-15 reps
Barbell curls over a chair – 3 sets of 10-12 reps
Triceps pushdowns – 3 sets of 10-12 reps
Crunches – 3 sets of 20-25 reps

Routine 4:
Sissy squats – 3 sets of 15-20 reps
Leg extensions – 3 sets of 15-20 reps
Stiff-leg deadlifts – 3 sets of 15-20 reps
Barbell calf raises – 3 sets of 15-20 reps
Narrow pulldowns – 3 sets of 12-15 reps
Incline dumbell presses – 3 sets of 12-15 reps
Barbell shoulder presses – 3 sets of 12-15 reps
Dumbell shrugs – 3 sets of 12-15 reps
Incline curls – 3 sets of 10-12 reps
Lying barbell extensions – 3 sets of 10-12 reps
Lying leg raises – 3 sets of 20-25 reps

David Dearth

EXERCISE DESCRIPTIONS

Although many of the exercises were described before, we have added some relevant information for home training.

LEGS

1. Sissy Squats

Hold onto an upright structure for support (door, weight rack, etc.). Lean slightly back, and with your feet about shoulder width apart, descend to the floor. Go down to at least parallel, pause, and then return to the starting position. You can perform this exercise holding on with one or two hands. When you can do 25 to 30 reps with relative ease, hold a weight plate against the chest with your free hand. If you find the glutes taking most of the strain, check your stance in the mirror. Chances are that you're not leaning back far enough.

2. Front Squats

Position the bar on the squat rack and step under it. Instead of resting the bar behind the head on your shoulders, place it on the upper chest, just below the chin. Now keeping your back as straight as possible, bend the knees and squat down. Don't bounce at the bottom as this may injure your knees.

If you don't have access to a squat rack, try cleaning the bar from the floor. This involves grabbing the barbell with a reverse grip (palms facing down), and hoisting the bar to chest level (check out the Olympic lifters on TV) primarily using the thighs and hips. Since the legs are capable of squatting far more weight than

most people can clean, you're going to be limited in your leg training. For this reason, and if at all possible, invest in a squat rack. At the very least, have a friend weld something together from scrap metal. Not only will you get a much better leg workout, but your lower back will last a whole lot longer!

3. Leg Extensions

Sit on the end of the bench and place your feet under the leg pads (rollers). Extend your legs until they're in a locked position. Pause for one or two seconds, squeezing the muscles in your thighs. Slowly lower to the starting position.

To obtain cuts, high in the thigh area (what Robert Kennedy calls 'thigh roids'), try performing leg extensions in a lying position. As before, place the feet under the rollers, but instead of sitting up, lie back on the bench. Now try extending your legs. Don't be surprised if you have to drop the weight. Vince Gironda did wonders with Mohamed Makkawy's thighs using this version.

4. Lunges

Many bodybuilders, particularly males, consider this exercise a shaping movement. Performed properly however, this exercise will build a decent set of quads. They also strongly effect the hamstrings, so in this respect they're superior to other leg exercises such as leg extensions and hack squats.

Place a barbell behind the head, and with one leg in front of the other, lunge forward, keeping the weight on the front leg. Try to keep the rear leg as straight as possible, and don't get carried away with the amount of weight used.

Another version of the lunge involves placing the front leg on a chair or bench. This allows an additional stretch at the bottom of the movement.

If you're not convinced of the benefits of lunges yet, superstar bodybuilder, Shawn Ray, makes lunges one of the mainstays of his leg training, and during a typical workout will perform sets of 50 reps.

5. Leg Curl

Lie face down on the bench and place your heels under the leg rollers. Keeping the butt down, curl the lower legs up as far as possible. Don't swing or throw your hips up in the air, as this defeats the purpose of the exercise.

For variety, try doing the exercise one leg at a time. Even better, after doing a set with each leg, rep out using both legs. Given the limited number of hamstring exercises available, you constantly have to look for new ways to shock the muscles.

6. Stiff-leg Deadlift

Stand on a bench or chair and grab a barbell. With the legs slightly bent (straight-leg exercises are murder on the lower back), slowly bend forward, trying to stretch the hamstrings as much as possible. Once again, don't sacrifice technique for the sake of a few extra pounds on the bar.

7. Dumbell Calf Raise

Stand on a piece of wood (at least three inches thick) and with a dumbell in each hand, stand up on your toes. Pause for a second and then lower, trying to touch your heels to the floor. If doing the exercise two legs at a time causes a loss of balance, switch to the one-legged version and grab something for support.

8. Barbell Calf Raise

Instead of holding two dumbells, try the exercise with a barbell. Not only can you use more weight, but the long bar helps you maintain balance. As before, go for a maximum stretch at both the top and bottom of the exercise.

BACK

9. Dumbell Rows

With one hand resting on a bench (or chair) grasp a dumbell and lower it slightly forward. Sawing wood is a perfect analogy. Just as the saw moves up and down on a forward angle, so too should the dumbell. Squeeze the lats at the top, and then stretch out at the bottom.

10. Lat Pulldowns

Sit on the bench and grab the overhead lat bar with a slightly wider than shoulder-width grip. Pull the bar down in front or behind the head. Purists will argue that the two variations are distinct exercises, but in reality there's not much difference. Generally speaking, the behind-the-head version hits more of the upper lats and the smaller teres muscles. Pulling to the front shifts some of the stress downward so that the lower lat insertions are hit. Unless you've reached a specialization phase of training, don't worry too much about which version you use. For variety you might want to alternate the two (one day to the front, the next behind the head, or alternate one with the other during the same back workout).

11. Barbell Rows

Stand on a bench or chair and grab a barbell. With the legs slightly bent, pull the bar up to the lower rib cage. Squeeze the shoulder blades together, and then lower the bar back down to arms' length. Don't loosely drop the weight, as you can easily damage the lower back. Remember, perform smooth reps while maintaining a flat lower back.

12. Narrow Pulldowns

If you have a V-shaped (triangle) bar attachment, so much the better. If not, take a narrow (2 to 4 inch) underhand grip on the regular bar. Lean back slightly and pull your hands to just below the rib cage. Not only is this a great lower-lat exercise, but it also hits the biceps (in fact the biceps are often the weak link in the chain).

CHEST

13. Bench Press

With the barbell positioned above you on the weight support rack, lie back and grab the bar with a slightly

Aaron Baker

wider than shoulder-width grip. Lower it down to the mid-chest region and then push it back to arms' length. Don't bounce the bar off the chest. Not only are you losing most of the exercise's effectiveness, but you can easily break a rib that way. Considered king of the chest exercises, bench presses will also strengthen your delts and triceps.

14. Dumbell Press
Although there are different ways to start the exercise, this is probably the easiest. Sit on the end of the bench, with the dumbells at your feet. Clean them up to your knees and then lie back. Rotate the dumbells so that the ends face one another (i.e. the two dumbells are in a straight line across the body), and slowly lower to your sides. Aim for a full stretch at the bottom. Be careful however, as dropping the dumbells too fast is a great way to tear the pec-delt tie-ins.

15. Dumbell Flyes
This exercise is similar to the previous but with a few modifications. Instead of keeping the dumbells in a straight line, have them facing one another. Also, start by positioning the dumbells at arms length above the chest, with your elbows slightly bent, and then lower in an arc. Most bodybuilders use less weight too. This exercise is as much a stretching movement as a power exercise.

Lenda Murray

16. Incline Dumbell Press
Identical to the flat version, except you use an incline bench. If you have an adjustable bench, set the angle so most of the strain is placed on the upper chest and not the front delts. It's probably going to take a couple of sets to determine the correct angle. If you only have a flat bench, try propping one end up on a box, chair, or another bench. It makes no difference as long as the bench is secure and at the right angle.

Although we didn't include them in the four previous routines, exercises such as incline flyes and barbell presses can also be done on an incline bench. Feel free to substitute them into your workout.

SHOULDERS
17. Barbell Shoulder Press
Sit on the end of a bench and clean the barbell to shoulder height. Press the bar to arms' length and then lower, either to the front or behind the head. If possible, try to use a bench with a vertical support. A regular kitchen chair is ideal for this exercise. You can also do the movement while standing, provided you have the ceiling room. If you have a belt (most serious lifters do), definitely use it on this exercise. A belt won't make you lift more, but it will provide support to your lower spine.

18. Dumbell Press
Done in the same manner as the barbell version, except you use two dumbells. Once again, brace the back and wear a belt.

19. Lateral Raises
Sit or stand, the choice is yours. Hold two dumbells by your sides with the palms facing inward. With the elbows slightly bent, raise both arms to shoulder height (any more and the traps take over). As you lift, rotate the dumbells so that the heel of the hand is facing upward at the top of the movement (the analogy of pouring a pitcher of water is frequently used). You can do this exercise to the front, side, or rear. Rear laterals are performed with the head braced on a high bench or chair. This keeps you from swinging and reduces the stress on your lower back.

20. Upright Rows
Stand with your feet approximately shoulder-width apart. Grab a barbell with a medium grip (about 8 to 10 inches apart) and lift it in front of your body along a straight line. Not only will this put a great cap on the side delts, but it also stresses the traps (you can make it more of a trap exercise by narrowing the grip). This is an excellent movement for finishing the shoulders.

21. Shrugs
With a barbell, or pair of dumbells held at arms' length, shrug the shoulders up as far as possible, trying to touch the traps off your ears! Some bodybuilders prefer doing the exercise straight up and down, while others like to rotate the shoulders in a circular-type motion. Our advice is to try both and pick the one that hits the traps most effectively. If there's no difference in the feel of the exercise, you can alternate versions.

BICEPS

22. Standing Barbell Curl

You can use either a straight or EZ-curl bar. Standing barbell curls are probably the most familiar of all bodybuilding exercises. They're also one of the most effective, provided they're done properly. Do at least 10 good reps before even thinking about cheating, and even then, limit it to 2 or 3 cheat reps. If you have to cheat from the beginning, then chances are you're using too much weight (or you have no concept of good form whatsoever!).

23. Alternate Dumbell Curls

This is another exercise that can be performed standing or seated. Grab two dumbells and curl them to shoulder height. For that extra bit of effectiveness, rotate (supinate) the dumbells from a palms inward to upward position.

24. Incline Curl

With the incline bench set at 45 degrees, curl the dumbells up to shoulder height. You can alternate the arms, or curl both at the same time. Incline curls are great for the long head of the biceps.

25. Barbell Curls Over a Chair

In a way we're substituting this exercise in place of Scott curls, as most don't have a preacher bench in their basement (of course if you do, then by all means use it). Stand behind a chair and brace your upper body by resting your armpits over the chair's back. Now perform the exercise like a regular preacher curl. Granted the angle is 90 degrees (versus the preacher's 45 degrees), but trust us, your biceps will pump up like crazy after a few sets.

TRICEPS

26. Seated Dumbell Extensions

While seated on a bench, lower a dumbell behind your head and then extend it to arms' length, keeping the upper arm vertical and pointed towards the ceiling. For support, try placing your free hand just below the elbow of the working arm.

27. Lying Barbell Extensions

Although you can use a straight bar, the EZ-curl bar is much more convenient. Lie down on a flat bench and position the bar at 90 degrees above you (at arms' length). With the upper arms held stationary, lower the bar to the forehead, or slightly behind, and then extend back to the arms-locked-out position.

28. Lying Dumbell Extensions

This exercise is identical to the previous with the exception of using two dumbells in place of the barbell.

29. Pushdowns

Take a narrow grip (4 to 6 inches) on the lat-pulldown bar and, with your elbows held close to your sides, extend the forearms downward. The standard version is to use a reverse (palms facing down) grip, but for isolating the rear head of the triceps, try a palms-up grip. You can't use the same weight, but the isolation of the movement makes up for it.

The legendary Lee Labrada

ABS

30. Crunches

With the realization that most forms of situps primarily work the hip flexors, the crunch has become the number one waist exercise. With the lower legs resting on a bench or low chair, crunch your upper body as far forward as you can. When the hands-by-the-side version becomes too easy, place them behind your head.

31. Leg Raises

Sit on the end of a bench with your legs extended outwards. With your hands under your buttocks for support, raise your legs to about 45 degrees. A great way to burn out the abs is to alternate leg raises with leg crunches. Instead of raising your legs pull them towards your upper body, trying to touch your knees to your chest. 2 or 3 sets of these and your midsection will take on a new appearance.

Well, there you have it, 31 exercises that will create a whole "new" you (provided you're not satisfied with the "old" you). You can stick with the previous format indefinitely, or after a few months switch to a split routine. Feel free to substitute exercises, provided you have the equipment to do so.

Most home trainers start with a barbell and a few dumbells, and then add equipment as time goes on. Many of the multi-stations are designed with that in mind. One Christmas you can add a pulldown, and the next it's a pec-dek. After three or four years it's possible to have a mini gym set up in your own basement. Get a few friends together and who knows where it may lead, maybe a Gold's or World Gym franchise!

CHAPTER THIRTY-ONE – PUMPING IRON AT HOME

Chapter Thirty-two

AEROBICS

AEROBICS FOR BODYBUILDERS

"During the off-season I ride the stationary bike in the morning on my day away from training. Before a show, starting 16 weeks out, I will begin to increase the frequency of cycling to three times a week, again in the morning. I will usually not ride more than three times a week and I ride only once a day, always before breakfast."
– Kathy Unger,
world amateur champion

Although once frowned upon, it's now generally accepted that aerobics can be beneficial when added to a bodybuilders training schedule. Most competitive bodybuilders include aerobic training during their precontest phase. Not only does it remove unwanted fat, but it improves the cardiovascular system – a major plus as you get older.

When oxygen enters your lungs, it is latched onto by red blood cells and transported to the body's tissues. The oxygen is exchanged for carbon dioxide, which is then carried back to the lungs and exhaled. One of the greatest benefits of aerobic training is that after time, blood volume actually increases. An average-sized male may increase his blood volume by nearly a quart in response to aerobic training. More blood means more red blood cells. More red blood cells means more oxygen and waste-carrying capacity. You can see how both are important to a hard-training bodybuilder. Not only will the muscles receive more oxygen, but waste products will be removed faster.

To compensate for the increased blood volume, the body increases the size and number of blood vessels. Besides the biological effect, the increased number of blood vessels gives the bodybuilder a more vascular look (an important point in bodybuilding competition).

Another favorable aspect to aerobic training is the relaxing effect it has on the body. Studies have shown that such relaxation promotes better digestive abilities, increased mental alertness, and a more positive outlook on life.

Kathy Unger

STARTING AN AEROBICS PROGRAM

"I changed my aerobic activity around. I think it's enabled me to be even better and crisper than I normally have been in my prior shows. I normally would do nothing but the stationary bike, but this time I implemented the StairMaster, treadmill and stationary bike! I think more than anything, the StairMaster has made an incredible difference." **– Porter Cottrell**
IFBB Pro Bodybuilder

Like most forms of physical activity, there is a right and wrong way to start aerobic training. Many enthusiastic trainees make the mistake of plunging right into an advanced aerobic routine. If you've never run before, start off by running two or three times a week. Another thing, just because your squat-produced legs are powerful, doesn't mean the rest of you will stand the rigors of your first jog. In many cases the knees, lower back, or shins give out during a bodybuilder's first run. This is especially true if you are on the large side. Jogging in high school weighing 150 pounds is not the same as going for a run weighing 240 pounds.

"You need it. If you do aerobics all the time, your body's more efficient at burning fat. I do my main aerobic exercise on the days I don't train. I'll do low intensity on the bike to get my heart rate up to 60 percent of max. Precontest, I do aerobics every day: 30 minutes first thing in the morning before I eat, in order to help burn fat, and then 30 minutes in the evening. I'll alternate the stationary bike and fast walking." **– Dorian Yates**
IFBB Pro Bodybuilder, Five-time Mr. Olympia

Years ago, bodybuilders were limited in their aerobic options, but today the choices are endless. Besides regular running, there are stationary bikes, rowing machines, treadmills, step machines, regular bikes, and aerobic bikes. You also have the old standbys of walking, swimming, and skipping rope.

The beauty is, one is as good as the other when you're consistent. By consistent we mean performing the exercise at least three or four days a week. How long you spend at each session depends on your goals. If it's for general cardiovascular conditioning, then 15 to 20 minutes is probably sufficient. But if you want to burn stored fat, most authorities recommend sessions of thirty to forty minutes.

For many, a thirty-minute run or swim is just not possible, at least initially. But if you slowly work up to it over a few weeks thirty minutes of aerobic activity won't be too strenuous. Don't compare your times with others, or try to keep up with well conditioned individuals. Set small goals, obtain them, and then set new goals.

When it comes to starting an aerobics program, many bodybuilders are often their own worst enemies. Instead of easing into things, they attack the program like it was a set of 500-pound squats. After years of

Porter Cottrell

ignoring pain, many bodybuilders fail to take heed of the body's warning signals. You must condition the body over time, and not subject it to brutality from day one!

We will illustrate how to ease into an aerobics program using the stationary bike.

It may not garner much respect among hardcore aerobics trainers, but the stationary bike is a great way to condition the body for more intense aerobics. Not only is it easy on the lower back, but it doesn't create havoc with the knees in the same manner as jogging. Another advantage is its indifference to the weather outdoors. Come rain, sleet, or snow, the lowly stationary bike will keep you dry during a 20-minute workout.

Start out by doing two or three, 12- to 15-minute weekly sessions. After a few weeks, 15 minutes will seem easy, so add on five or ten minutes. Eventually, you'll be doing sessions of 40 minutes with ease. Not only will your heart and lung conditioning improve, but you may even begin to see your abs (no doubt on the missing list since high school)!

Besides duration, another good indicator of aerobic effectiveness is heart rate. Although it varies with age,

Bike riding is one of the best forms of aerobic exercise.
– Frank and Christine Zane

most aerobic charts recommend keeping your heart rate between 120 and 150 beats per minute for the duration of the aerobic workout. One way to really push the heart rate up is to spend the first three or four minutes riding comfortably along, and then tighten the tension gages on the bike. This increases the resistance on the pedals and forces you to expend more energy. It simulates riding up a hill, and you know how difficult that is. After 25 to 30 minutes, reduce the tension and conclude your session with four or five minutes of comfortable pedaling.

When checking the pulse, take it on the side of your neck, just to the side of the windpipe. Measure with your finger, as the thumb has its own pulse. If you have the grit, you can hold your finger at the neck for a full minute, but a simpler method is to measure for 10 seconds and multiply by six. For example, 20 beats in 10 seconds gives a pulse rate of 20 x 6 = 120 beats per minute.

Your next concern is deciding on what days to perform your aerobic routine. It doesn't make much sense to run or bike on leg day. Hitting the squat rack after a five-mile ride is a sure way to end up on the floor (not to mention what it does to your reputation when you fall to the floor with 150 pounds on your back!). The opposite is also true. It's very difficult to do justice to an aerobic routine after a grueling leg workout. Finally, intense leg training (especially high-rep squats or leg presses) is itself partially aerobic. So why waste energy doing two aerobic activities on the same day.

There are numerous aerobic/weight-training combinations. If you're following a four-day split, try running on your three days off. Another popular split is to run on two of your off-days and your lightest weight-training day (i.e. arms, shoulders, etc.). Our advice is to try different combinations and select the one that gives you the best results.

Before you head off to the Boston Marathon, we should bring one final point to your attention. Like all forms of physical activity, it's possible to take aerobic training to the extreme. As a bodybuilder, your aerobics training is meant to complement your bodybuilding progress, not hinder it. Don't fall into the "if some is good, more is better" routine (sound familiar!). Spend too much time running or swimming and that precious muscle mass of yours will go the way of the dinosaurs. Whenever the body's fat level goes below four or five percent muscle tissue is broken down and used as a fuel source; a major concern for a competitive bodybuilder on a precontest diet. The low caloric intake, combined with the low fat level, puts the bodybuilder in a dangerous situation.

Many top bodybuilders, including Boyer Coe, Mike Matarazzo, and Gary Strydom have fallen into this trap. The combination of dieting and aerobics eroded much of their hard-earned muscle, and all three have entered contests way below their best competitive weights.

If you're on the ectomorphic side to begin with, you may want to skip aerobics altogether. After you put on a substantial amount of muscle mass, you can incorporate aerobics into your training. For those who tend to carry too much bodyfat we suggest including a few aerobics sessions into your routine, on a year-round basis. As competition approaches you can increase the frequency of aerobic training.

Aliś Willoughby and Bill Davey

Chapter Thirty-three

FEMALE BODYBUILDING

WOMEN'S BODYBUILDING

"As soon as you're in the public eye, you're a role model. That's not to say that each individual wants to be one... I don't mind it because I enjoy being a role model in health and fitness." **– Cory Everson**
IFBB Pro Bodybuilder, Six-time Ms. Olympia

Cory Everson

Every topic included in this book applies as much to women as men. Not withstanding, we decided to include a separate chapter that addresses some of the more specific concerns of female bodybuilders.

HISTORY

"Today literally millions of women lift weights and each one of them stands out as a symbol that a women can be strong, aggressive and in control, both physically and mentally, and still be very much a woman."
– Joe Weider

It was only a matter of time before women realized that bodybuilding gyms were not just the domain of men. Women had always been associated with the sport, but for the most part these women were included to add a sense of sex appeal to bodybuilding magazines. It wasn't until the late '70s/early '80s that the sport of female bodybuilding was accepted for what it was – female bodybuilding!

Although numerous women can lay claim to having been the first female bodybuilder, it was Lisa Lyon who was the sport's true pioneer. Before her, female contestants used weight training to shape and tone the body. Lisa, however, added a new dimension to her training. She trained in the same manner as the guys, and the results showed. Instead of a slim fashion model, Lisa treated the audience to what was then, unequaled female muscularity. Of course, like any pioneer, Lisa was initially considered a curiosity. But with time came acceptance, and before long other women had tailored their training styles after Lisa's.

With the emergence of the 1980s, a whole new generation of female weight trainers had surfaced. To address this recent phenomenon, the major bodybuilding federations restructured their competitions to regularly include female bodybuilding. Now Ms. Americas and Ms. Olympias would rule alongside their male counterparts (with the exception of the Ms. Olympia, all the "Ms." titles were soon changed in the same manner as male titles; that being from Ms. America to national women's champion).

In the early '80s female bodybuilders such as Rachel McLish, Lynn Conkwright, Stacey Bentley, Laura Combes, Shelly Gruwell, Carla Dunlap, and Georgia Miller Fudge became household names in the bodybuilding community.

"I view bodybuilding as an athletic pursuit. I train as hard now as I ever have. However, many males feel it is not lady-like for women to lift heavy weights as in competitive powerlifting or to develop muscle shape as in bodybuilding." — **Cory Everson**
IFBB Pro Bodybuilder, Six-time Ms. Olympia

The mid- to late '80s were dominated by Cory Everson (whom many consider the greatest female bodybuilder ever). From 1984 to 1989, Cory reigned as female bodybuilding's queen. The key to Cory's success was her combination of muscularity, symmetry, presentation, and most of all – femininity.

The nineties are an exciting time for women's bodybuilding, as outstanding competitors such as Kim Chizevsky, Lenda Murray, Laura Creavalle, Diana Dennis, Sandy Riddell, Debbie Muggli, and Sue Price grace the stage.

DISPELLING THE MYTHS

I don't want to look like that!
The first thing women need to realize is that two months of bodybuilding will not turn them into Arnold Schwarzenegger! Bodybuilding does mean, however, re-shaping the body and lowering bodyfat levels. It's a biological fact that women's bodies do not have high enough concentrations of natural (we'll discuss synthetic forms – anabolic steroids – later) testosterone to build large amounts of muscle mass. Yet this is the main fear of numerous women when they join a bodybuilding gym. How many instructors have heard the expression "I don't want to build muscles, just tone up"?

Some women who take up weight training have fears about developing masculine-looking muscles. If only it were that easy. Millions of men spend four to six days a week in the gym, eat thousands of calories a day, and even take anabolic steroids, and yet still have trouble gaining weight. So rest assured, developing Arnold-sized muscles is virtually impossible.

Most women who are afraid of training hard and heavy are usually uninformed about the physiology of body shaping. They assume that by lifting heavy weights they'll build large muscles; so by lifting light weights they'll tone, right? Wrong!

Muscular toning is in itself a form of growth, and requires progressive resistance. Using light weights will not stimulate muscular adaptation. Training hard and heavy will. In males, the end result is greatly enlarged muscle size. Females, however, develop a small amount of muscle mass and a great deal of tone. As we said before, these differences are primarily the result of unequal concentrations of testosterone between the sexes.

Perhaps women would be more at ease if we replaced the word bodybuilding with bodyshaping. After all, the sport is about changing the appearance of the body so that it has better proportions. This can mean reducing as well as increasing. Most male body-

Cory Everson and Marjo Selin

builders follow this strategy as well. If one area becomes too large, they cut back on the exercises for this bodypart, and invest the energy somewhere else. As an example, Robby Robinson actually had to reduce the size of his hamstrings to bring them in balance with his calves and quads. For many women, the opposite may hold true, their calves might be on the large side and need to be reduced to complement the hamstrings.

The beauty of bodybuilding is that you can modify the routine to suit your specific needs. This is one of the main advantages of bodybuilding over other sports. Most sports emphasize one side of the body more than the other. The results are muscle imbalances and unequal symmetry. In fact this is one of the primary reasons why sports' teams make use of strength coaches – to correct and prevent such muscle imbalances.

What's all the silly equipment for?
Besides the fear of developing a masculine appearance, women hold other concerns about bodybuilding, one of which is the gym itself.

For most women (and men for that matter), the first day at a bodybuilding gym can be a combination of bewilderment and anxiety. This is a normal response, and falls under the category of "fear of the unknown".

The beautiful
Marjo Selin

physique takes time and knowledge. That 240-pound guy over in the corner doing 200-pound curls didn't get that way overnight. The odds are good to excellent that he's a walking storehouse of bodybuilding information. If you have a question, feel free to walk over and introduce yourself (just wait until he finishes his set!). Not only will you be assured of getting good advice, but in all likelihood you'll flatter the guy's ego (for more information on this topic see the chapter on bodybuilding sociology)!

But they'll all laugh!

Another fear women may have is how they'll appear to other members. They think that because they're new and inexperienced, other members will ridicule and laugh at them. Nothing could be further from the truth. Everyone was a beginner at one point, and just like you, had to start from scratch (hopefully this book will give you a head start). Without bringing back memories of kindergarten, everyone makes mistakes, and one of the most basic methods of learning is to make such mistakes. Nearly every exercise is easy to learn, and with the help of instructors and other members, your workouts will progress smoothly and safely. After four to six months of regular training (and learning), you'll find yourself being approached by novice members looking for advice. Congratulations, you're not a beginner any more. You've joined the ranks of knowledgeable bodybuilders.

A new look at reality…

"I like the muscle-to-fat ratio you get from bodybuilding. I hate fat, and the amount of muscle you get from training overcomes the fat. The correct dieting, along with correct training habits, can make your body very hard. I love a hard, trim body. It's like a nice cut of lean meat with no marble through it." **– Kathy Unger, women's world amateur champion**

Joining a gym is like starting a new job – you don't know what to expect. New people, new equipment, perhaps even a new schedule. But your first workout has one important advantage, making a fool of yourself will not cost you your job!

With regards to the equipment, yes some of it looks complicated and downright nasty, but don't worry, there are friendly instructors around to show you the ropes. (This is one of the things to look for when joining a gym. If the staff don't appear knowledgeable and friendly, look elsewhere.) If an instructor is unavailable, don't be shy. Gyms are among the friendliest places to visit (except during the precontest season when many are on a strict diet!), and should you have a question, feel free to ask another member. And don't be intimidated by the larger folk either. Let's face it, to develop a great

Although Albert Einstein is not famous for his bodybuilding exploits, his concept of relativity certainly applies. Many women feel that everyone in the gym has a perfect body, and that theirs will stand out like a sore thumb. But remember that everything is relative. A

160-pound woman may seem on the large side until she's compared to someone weighing 250. Likewise, 120 pounds seems slim until a 95 pounder walks by. If you focus on nothing else, keep in mind that there'll always be individuals in better shape than you, and conversely there'll always be those in much worse shape. The object is to improve your appearance so that the number of people in lesser shape than yourself proportionally increases.

Many women (we keep saying women because this is the focus of this chapter, but most of what we are saying applies equally to men) avoid gyms because they feel everyone there has a perfect body. But this is just not the case. Think of it this way, if they were perfect, why would they spend so many hours in the gym trying to improve?

If there are women in the gym who are in better shape than you are, don't be intimidated, be inspired. Use their image to motivate and challenge you to improve your appearance. The odds are that they went through the same thing when they first started working out.

I wanted to lose weight, not gain it!

"Weight is a mystery to some women. We've become slaves to the scale, but that instrument can only weigh body mass – with no distinction between muscle and fat. The inadequacy of the scale becomes clear when we realize muscle weighs at least six times as much as fat. For example, a piece of fat will weigh much less than a piece of meat the same size. When a woman's body consists of lots of fat, say 35 percent, she can be the same height and weight as another female whose body contains only 15 percent fat. The woman with the higher fat content will be larger because fat displaces more volume."
– Gladys Portugues,
former IFBB Pro Bodybuilder

For those women who are without a bathroom scale, don't bother to buy one. For those who have one, open the trash can and chuck it out. Few household items have caused as much grief as that detested little measuring device. There you are, just out of the shower, soaking wet, but proud of the fact that you've stuck to your diet for the last three weeks. With the moment of truth having arrived, you step onto the scale, and horror of all horrors, you've actually gained 5 pounds! Dejected, you throw up your hands in despair and raid the refrigerator.

The unfortunate part of the previous example is that this scenario repeats itself thousands of times on a monthly basis across North America. What's even sadder is that most of the "victims" had probably made progress.

The problem lies with our preoccupation with weight, which is itself a relative term. A 120-pound woman may look fat, whereas a 140-pound woman may appear slim and trim. What's important is not your bodyweight, but your muscle to fat ratio. A lot of women become scared when after three months of bodybuilding they discover that they weigh more than when they first started. Years of equating weight with fat lead many to believe that all their training has gone to waste. You need to realize that muscle weighs more than fat. But at the same time, muscle is more compact. So while you may have gained muscle, you are probably smaller in size. A good indication is clothing size. Many women find that even though they're five pounds heavier, they're wearing a dress that is one or two sizes smaller.

Perhaps the most perplexing example of this is when someone trains for six months and gains 10 pounds of muscle, but loses 10 pounds of fat. Now if you go by the scales, the net effect is zero. But to say they've made no progress is ludicrous. Everything from muscle tone and size, to fat percentage and skin appearance, has changed. In effect, there's been a total transformation, yet the scales say you've done nothing! You would be better off trading in the scale for a full-length mirror.

SELECTING A GYM

Although we discussed this earlier, a recap probably wouldn't hurt. To get the most out of your workouts, the gym you select must meet certain criteria. First and foremost, it should be conveniently located. If you have to drive or walk for an hour, then you might want to reconsider. Of course, your town may only have one gym so you'll have to make the best of it.

Gladys Portugues

If you have access to more than one gym, don't be afraid to shop around. Don't be misled into thinking the best gym is the one with the most shiny equipment. Many machines are poorly designed and don't work the body through a full range of motion. If you check out a training facility and all they have are machines, move on to the next gym. Free weights are an absolute must if you want to develop and reshape your body.

Another point, don't be afraid to ask questions. Here's some that you definitely must ask:

1. What are the gym's hours of operation?
2. How much does it cost for a year's (month's, week's, etc.) membership?
3. How many instructors are on staff?
4. What are their qualifications?
5. Does the gym keep regular holidays?
6. When is the gym crowded?

These are just some of the questions you'll need answered when selecting a gym. Besides checking with staff, feedback from members would be an asset. Find out what the parking is like at peak periods (will you have to leave the car two blocks away?). Ask the members if they enjoy training there and would they recommend you join? Finally, sit back and take in the big picture. Can you picture yourself working out in this particular atmosphere? First impressions are often a good guide as to whether a gym is for you.

WHAT TO WEAR

No, we are not being sexist, as this applies to both males and females. If you want to improve your chances of blending in from day one, then go out and buy some decent training attire. If the stores in your area only carry sweat pants and tops (these went out years ago), pick up a copy of *MuscleMag International* and start browsing. There are many superb clothing lines to choose from, and for an investment of $40 to $50, you'll really look the part.

To cap off your workout gear, buy a set of good-quality footwear. Designer clothes look kind of stupid when complemented by $10 running shoes. Other items you might want to purchase include a training belt (this one is really a must), a pair of gloves, a headband, and one set each of knee wraps and lifting straps. If you show up on day one with all of this equipment people will think you've been training for years (yes it's an optical illusion but so what, it can be our little secret).

GETTING STARTED

"Muscular arms on women are becoming downright chic. One of the reasons Terminator II *was so popular (in addition to Arnold of course) was that many people loved Linda Hamilton's arms!"* – **Tonya Knight**
IFBB Pro Bodybuilder,
former MuscleMag *columnist*

Alright, you've picked a gym, obtained the latest in training attire, and have read this book from cover to cover. You might say you're ready for combat. Great, nothing replaces a positive attitude when it comes to working out.

Your next step is to select a program that fits your fitness level. As most of you are beginners, this is the first routine we'll describe. Beginners should concentrate on working the major muscle groups using basic exercises. These are movements that generally work more than one muscle group at a time.

Bodybuilders divide the body into six broad categories, as follows:
• Legs (thighs, hamstrings, and calves)
• Back (lats, teres, spinal erectors)
• Chest (lower, upper, pec-delt tie-in)
• Shoulders (three deltoid heads plus traps)
• Arms (biceps, triceps, and forearms)
• Midsection (abs, intercostals, obliques)

As you gain experience, your workouts will start to incorporate more isolation exercises that primarily (we say primarily because it's virtually impossible to totally isolate a given muscle area) target individual muscle groups and sections.

Tonya Knight

Your emphasis at this stage should be on exercise technique and form, not how much weight you can lift. If you attempt to go all out from week one, you'll end up very sore at the least, but in all likelihood will suffer an injury that will set you back weeks if not months. Your break-in workouts should be effective, light, fun, and above all else – safe!

Most women need to emphasize different muscle groups than men. For example, men generally target the large torso muscles like the chest, back and shoulders. Women on the other hand, should focus on the thighs, hips, and abs. It doesn't mean women should skip the other muscle groups, but merely do less sets for them. For example, a woman might do 3 or 4 sets for her thighs and abs, but only 1 or 2 sets for her chest and shoulders.

We recommend training in the previous manner because of the different ways men and women store bodyfat. Men tend to store fat around the waist and upper thighs, while women tend to put it in the glutes, hips, and inner thighs. Therefore, women would be encouraged to concentrate on toning and reducing the hips and thighs, while increasing the size of the upper body to improve symmetry.

With time, you (or a knowledgeable observer) will notice weaknesses developing in your body. Don't despair, every bodybuilder has weaknesses, and it's a biological fact that no physique is perfect. But this is why bodybuilding is so great. As soon as a weakness is spotted, you immediately restructure your training to address it. Within a short period of time the weakness disappears and some other bodypart needs extra attention, and on it goes. Five or ten years down the road you'll have one of the best bodies in the gym and yet you'll still be trying to improve. Sounds fun doesn't it, so let's get at it!

THE BEGINNER'S ROUTINE

For the first four to six weeks of training, you should hit the whole body three times a week. The most popular routine is a Monday-Wednesday-Friday split, but Tuesday-Thursday-Saturday works as well. It all depends on which days are convenient for you. The only rule is not to train two days in a row. Your muscles need on average, 48 to 72 hours to recover. It would be counterproductive to hit the same muscles on two consecutive days.

During your first week we advise performing 2 sets per exercise, for 10 to 15 reps per set. After the first or second week, add 1 set per exercise to the routine. If you're unfamiliar with the terms, sets and reps, refer to Chapter 3 – Everything You Need to Know. Likewise, the exercise descriptions can be found in the Beginner and Intermediate Training chapters.

The following are two examples of beginning level routines that can be performed on three nonconsecutive days.

Routine 1:

Thighs – Leg presses – 2 sets of 10-15 reps
Hamstrings – Lying leg curls – 2 sets of 10-15 reps
Back – Lat pulldowns – 2 sets of 10-12 reps
Chest – Bench presses – 2 sets of 10-12 reps
Shoulders – Shoulder presses – 2 sets of 10-15 reps
Triceps – Pushdowns – 2 sets of 10-12 reps
Biceps – Dumbell curls – 2 sets of 10-12 reps
Calves – Standing calf raises – 2 sets of 15-20 reps
Abs – Crunches – 2 sets of 15-20 reps

Routine 2:

Thighs – Squats – 2 sets of 10-15 reps
Hamstrings – Lying leg curls – 2 sets of 10-15 reps
Back – Dumbell rows – 2 sets of 10-12 reps
Chest – Incline presses – 2 sets of 10-12 reps
Shoulders – Lateral raises – 2 sets of 10-15 reps
Triceps – Triceps extensions – 2 sets of 10-12 reps
Biceps – Barbell curls – 2 sets of 10-12 reps
Calves – Toe presses – 2 sets of 15-20 reps
Abs – Reverse crunches – 2 sets of 15-20 reps

Sue Price

Although you may be advised otherwise, to make progress, you must gradually use more weight. Muscles adapt very quickly, and whether your goal is to increase muscle mass, or to firm and tone, using the same weight for extended periods of time will only hamper your progress. It's absolutely essential that you increase the workload placed on the muscles. Doing so forces the muscles to become stronger, bigger, and well toned.

Please don't let the word "bigger" frighten you. As we said before (and it deserves repeating), women cannot develop the same amount of muscle mass as men. So the next time someone in the gym advises you "not to use too much weight," politely and diplomatically tell them, thanks for the advice, but you're there to make progress, not waste time.

SPLITS – UPPING THE INTENSITY LEVEL

There comes a point in time when it's very difficult to make progress on a three-day-a-week routine. Your muscles have matured to the point that, in order to stimulate them adequately, you would need to be in the gym for two or three hours. As most people don't have the appropiate recovery systems (or time for that matter) to handle such volumes of exercise, a new strategy is needed.

Now before we launch into the merits of split routines we should make one point. If you've made tremendous progress on a three-day-a-week program, and it suits your particular lifestyle (family, work, school, social life, etc.), then there is no reason to alter your current training routine. After all, if it works, why change it? Some of the best bodybuilders in the world swear by such programs. The following section is for those who desire a training program that is a bit more challenging. And even though it's the next logical progression from a three-day-a-week routine, it's not a mandatory progression.

There are many advantages to splitting your training over different days of the week, the primary one being it allows you to do more sets and exercises for each muscle without overtaxing your recovery system. The most common split is a four-day-a-week routine where you hit each muscle twice a week. Even though you train two days in a row, you hit separate muscle groups.

Although individual preference plays a major part, most bodybuilders follow a Monday-Tuesday-Thursday-Friday split; Wednesdays and weekends are spent resting. Such a routine means you train half the body's muscles on Mondays and Thursdays, and train the other muscles on Tuesdays and Fridays.

The following are sample four-day-a-week split routines which you can begin after four to six weeks of

**Kim Chizevsky, 1996
Ms. Olympia champion**

As we said before, after a few weeks of breaking in, add 1 set to each exercise, so that you are performing 3 sets for each muscle group. It's also a good idea to start some sort of aerobics training early in your training as well.

No need to be elaborate. 15 to 20 minutes of the stationary bike or StairMaster will suffice. You can do it after your weight-training workouts or on your days off. For variety, try a rowing machine, or go for a quick run.

With regards to weight, start increasing your work-out poundages after a couple of weeks' training. But don't sacrifice form in the interest of lifting a few extra pounds. Use your rep range to determine how much extra weight to use. If you can do 100 pounds on the leg press for 20 easy reps, add enough weight to make 12 to 15 reps difficult. Conversely, if you are only getting 6 to 8 reps, when you want 10 to 12, then you are obviously using too much weight.

Start

Christa Bauch works
her biceps with
concentration curls.

Finish

Routine 1:
MONDAYS AND THURSDAYS
QUADS, HAMSTRINGS, CALVES, ABS
Quads:
    Squats – 2-3 sets of 12-15 reps
    Leg extensions – 2-3 sets of 15-20 reps
    Hamstrings:
    Lying leg curls – 3 sets of 12-15 reps
Calves:
    Standing calf raises – 2-3 sets of 15-20 reps
    Seated calf raises – 2-3 sets of 15-20 reps
Abs:
    Crunches – 2-3 sets of 15-20 reps
    Hanging leg raises – 2-3 sets of 15-20 reps

TUESDAYS AND FRIDAYS
CHEST, BACK, SHOULDERS,
BICEPS AND TRICEPS
Chest:
    Flat bench presses – 2-3 sets of 10-12 reps
    Incline dumbell presses – 2-3 sets of 10-12 reps
Back:
    Pulldowns – 2-3 sets of 10-12 reps
    One-arm dumbell rows – 2-3 sets of 10-12 reps
Shoulders:
    Shoulder presses – 2-3 sets of 10-12 reps
    Upright rows – 2-3 sets of 10-12 reps
Biceps:
    Standing barbell curls – 2 sets of 10-12 reps
    Concentration curls – 2 sets of 10-12 reps
Triceps:
    Pushdowns – 2 sets of 10-12 reps
    One-arm extensions – 2 sets of 10-12 reps

Routine 2:
MONDAYS AND THURSDAYS
THIGHS, CHEST, SHOULDERS, TRICEPS
Thighs:
    Leg presses – 2-3 sets of 15-20 reps
    Hack squats – 2-3 sets of 15-20 reps
Chest:
    Incline bench presses – 2-3 sets of 10-12 reps
    Flat dumbell flyes – 2-3 sets of 10-12 reps
Shoulders:
    Shoulder presses – 2-3 sets of 10-12 reps
    Lateral raises – 2-3 sets of 10-12 reps
Triceps:
    Lying triceps extensions – 2-3 sets of 10-12 reps
    Pushdowns – 2-3 sets of 10-12 reps

TUESDAYS AND FRIDAYS
BACK, BICEPS, HAMSTRINGS, CALVES, ABS
Back:
    Bent-over rows – 2-3 sets of 10-12 reps
    Seated pulley rows – 2-3 sets of 10-12 reps
Hamstrings:
    Lying leg curls – 2-3 sets of 15-20 reps
    Stiff-leg deadlifts – 2-3 sets of 15-20 reps

initial training. On average you perform two exercises per muscle group, for 2 or 3 sets of 10 to 12 reps each. The first example requires you to train the upper body one day and the lower the next. The second is what's commonly called a push-pull routine.

Biceps:
- Scott curls – 2-3 sets of 10-12 reps
- Incline curls – 2-3 sets of 10-12 reps

Calves:
- Standing calf raises – 2-3 sets of 15-20 reps
- Seated calf raises – 2-3 sets of 15-20 reps

Abs:
- Crunches – 2-3 sets of 15-20 reps
- Reverse crunches – 2-3 sets of 15-20 reps

PREGNANCY AND THE FEMALE BODYBUILDER

"My doctor said: squat, deadlift… do anything you were doing before you became pregnant. I trained a little but I was tired and sick all the time. I was working full time, then training people after work, and I felt terrible! Little did I know at the time that I was carrying two babies!"

– Clare Furr, IFBB Pro Bodybuilder USA champion and Ms. Olympia runner-up (commenting on the difficulties of exercising while pregnant. Carrying twins no doubt doubled her problems!)

For the serious female bodybuilder, pregnancy can be both a blessing and a misfortune. On one hand, the woman is overjoyed because she is bringing new life into the world. On the other, her slim physique, built over hundreds of hours, will disappear in a few months.

Ten or twenty years ago, the prevailing attitude was that pregnant women should avoid all forms of physical activity and "take it easy". Luckily, this viewpoint has changed and it's becoming more common for "mom's to be" to exercise during much of the nine-month gestation period. Many doctors recommend exercising to maintain good health and facilitate the delivery process.

Besides the pre-delivery benefits, regular exercise can speed up the recovery process after the baby is born. With this in mind, a pregnant bodybuilder should make the following goals a priority when designing and following a pre- and post-delivery exercise program.

1. Provide the healthiest environment for the baby's growth and development.
2. Avoid exercises that may be contraindicative to both the mother's and baby's health.
3. Develop a level of strength and flexibility that facilitates the delivery process.
4. Follow an exercise program that speeds up the recovery process after delivery.

A WORD OF CAUTION

Before we provide a few useful tips for the pregnant bodybuilder, we should stress that everyone is unique. Prior to starting any exercise program, make sure to clear it with your physician first. There may be valid health concerns for limiting or avoiding exercise during your pregnancy. Only your doctor will know for sure.

GENERAL TRAINING TIPS FOR THE PREGNANT BODYBUILDER

"I had planned to train right through to the day I delivered. I thought I would hold on to at least some of the muscle I had gained if I kept training. Finally, I couldn't do it any more. I was too big and didn't fit in some of the machines any more. I felt as though I wasn't really accomplishing anything."

– Debbie Ashby, Canadian bodybuilding competitor (commenting on how pregnancy affected her training)

Exercising while pregnant can be very beneficial.

It's generally accepted that most women can exercise right up to anywhere between the seventh and eighth month of delivery. Beyond this point, the emphasis should be on stretching and flexibility. Now this sounds great in theory, but realistically speaking, most women cease training long before the eighth month. Besides the nausea that many women experience, the growing baby depletes the mother's energy reserves. For most women, a bodybuilding gym is no place to be when feeling nauseous.

Still, for those that have the energy and desire, a good workout may be just what the doctor ordered. Not only will it keep your body in great physical shape, but the post-workout calm that most individuals experience (due to enkephalin and endorphin release), can help alleviate some of the stress associated with pregnancy.

Perhaps the greatest change to your training will be with respect to the midsection. It's recommended that women gradually reduce ab work from the first few months until around the fourth month. After this point, ab exercises should be eliminated altogether. The reason is that the developing baby needs room to grow. And the only way this can happen is if the midsection region is allowed to relax and stretch.

The opposite holds true for the lower back. With the weight gained during pregnancy, the lower spine is forced to support much more weight than normal, and most women report back aches during pregnancy. To help strengthen the lower back, and prepare it for the increased load it will have to support, make lower-back training a priority during the early months.

Regular deadlifts and machine exercises will do wonders for the spinal erectors, making the 25- to 30-pound weight gain less stressful on the spine.

One lower-back exercise to avoid, however, is the hyperextension. This movement puts a great deal of pressure on the stomach, and could cause serious implications during pregnancy.

Another exercise to watch is the Scott curl. As the pregnancy progresses, and the baby grows in size, the bench's incline pad starts putting pressure on the midsection. Initially you may be able to work around the problem (perform the exercise one arm at a time), but sooner or later your increased size will mean avoiding the exercise altogether.

DELIVERY

Although it might be assumed that female bodybuilders would have an easier time delivering than sedentary women, studies seem to indicate that there's little difference. Most female bodybuilders admit that giving birth was the most difficult time of their lives, and that regular squatting never came close!

Sharon Marvel

If there is one advantage to being a bodybuilder, it is the post-delivery frame of mind. As female bodybuilders are overly concerned about their appearance, regaining the desire to work out usually doesn't take long. In fact most female bodybuilders resume training within one month of delivery. In a few cases, the first workout came as early as two weeks following birth.

We should add that before you resume working out, check with your physician. Pregnancy takes a tremendous physical and emotional toll on any woman. You may be mentally ready to start working out, but your body may still be recovering. If there's any doubt, give it a few extra weeks to make sure.

ADVANCED TRAINING AND COMPETITION

"Female bodybuilding should be judged as a sport and not a beauty pageant. Half the show's outcome could be judged in the gym and the other half onstage. People who only see us onstage have no idea what we're capable of in the gym. For our sport to be more Olympic, we need to make the move to more athletic events."
– Sharon Bruneau,
top IFBB Pro Bodybuilder

Sharon Bruneau

to seven percent), that individual muscle fibers, striations, and veins, are clearly visible.

Obtaining the ripped look is accomplished in two ways – diet and aerobic exercise. As both of these topics are discussed in great detail elsewhere in the book, we won't repeat ourselves here. But there is one important issue that female athletes should be aware of, and that's the relationship between bodyfat level and the menstrual cycle.

In their attempt to rid the body of as much fat as possible, many female athletes begin noticing menstrual irregularities. In many cases they stop altogether. This condition is called amenorrhea, and since such an occurrence is often the first sign of pregnancy, it comes as a shock to many females (if they were trying to avoid pregnancy to begin with). The loss of menstrual periods due to low bodyfat percentage is well known in sports such as running and gymnastics. But female bodybuilders began reporting the condition only after the criteria for women's bodybuilding changed.

When fat levels drop below six to eight percent, the body goes into a sort of survival mode. It assumes the low fat levels are the result of starvation, and all activities that are not necessary for life are reduced or shut down. As the menstrual cycle is not necessary for an individual's survival, it's often one of the first biological systems to be affected.

We are by no means saying this condition is normal. If the menstrual cycle is affected, then chances are, other systems are being affected as well. Contrary to popular belief, the human body needs a certain amount of fat to survive. Things such as hormone production, nerve insulation, and energy production, depend on fat. As soon as levels drop below a certain amount, the body has to search elsewhere for fat sources. Carry things to the extreme and your body will start breaking down muscle and organ tissue.

Given the highly competitive nature of women's bodybuilding, it can be assumed that more and more women will experience this phenomenon as time goes on (or until the judging criteria changes).

For 90 percent of you competition is the furthest thing from your minds. Having said that, most of today's top female pros felt the same way when they first started training. If you plan to compete some day, the next section is a must read. For those only concerned with toning and shaping, there is still some valuable information to be learned, so don't skip over it.

DIET AND THE MENSTRUAL CYCLE

One of the biggest changes in women's bodybuilding over the years has been the contest appearance of the competitors. The "ripped" look is no longer the exclusive domain of the guys. Nowadays, the ladies are coming in just as "cut" and "hard". In case these terms are new to you, they all the mean the same thing – a very low percentage of bodyfat. So low in fact (five

As a final note, there is no hard evidence to suggest whether or not amenorrheic women ovulate. Therefore, it would be foolhardy to rely on the condition as a form of birth control.

BIRTH CONTROL PILLS

For those women taking birth control pills, there are a couple of concerns if you decide to compete. Because of the estrogen and progesterone components in these pills, there's often significant water retention, especially just before the menstrual cycle begins. Given that the ripped look is preferred by judges these days, it might be a good idea to discontinue use a few weeks before the contest (of course this brings with it more practical concerns – so beware).

Another issue pertains to progesterone as it has catabolic properties. This means it will increase the rate at which muscle tissue is broken down – the exact opposite of what a bodybuilder desires. When combined with a strict diet this problem is compounded further. If there's any doubt, check with your doctor before starting your precompetition diet.

BODYBUILDING DRUGS

"It's apparent that many people don't understand the way drugs work. Once the steroid is out of the tissues and blood, you lose all the effects gained from the drugs. Any endocrinologist will confirm this. Ever see a person who has used steroids for a long time and then stopped? He shrinks right back to his original size."

– Cory Everson, IFBB Pro Bodybuilder
Six-time Ms. Olympia

Like diet, this topic is discussed in more detail elsewhere in the book. Still, there are a few points concerning female bodybuilders, so we'll touch on them here.

It was only a matter of time before female bodybuilders followed their male counterparts into the arena of chemical warfare. With the emphasis being placed more and more on muscularity, many women decided to employ the use of anabolic steroids.

As a recap, these drugs are synthetic versions of the hormone, testosterone. Testosterone is often called a "male" hormone because it's found in higher concentrations in men. But women's bodies contain the hormone as well, just as men's bodies contain estrogen, often called a "female" hormone. It's the relative concentrations of both that result in men on average, being larger and stronger than women.

Anabolic steroids were initially developed to treat endocrine problems. But when athletes learned of the drug's muscle-building/fat-reducing properties, it didn't take long for their use to become widespread.

The issue of whether steroids work or not is still debated, but informed individuals accept the fact that an athlete using steroids will gain muscle mass and strength quicker, and to a greater degree than a nonuser.

FIRST APPEARANCE

Although the exact date when steroids made their debut in female bodybuilding is unknown, it's generally accepted that within a year or two of female contests gaining popularity (and subsequently the increase in prestige and prize money), the first use began. No doubt, female use began in a similar fashion to use among males. A few competitors tried the drugs and discovered the advantages, and before long, minor dosages became mega dosages, and moderate muscle gains became great muscle gains. With each subsequent year, female bodybuilders became more massive and more muscular (the two chief advantages of using the drugs).

The increase in muscularity has raised some heated debates over the direction in which women's bodybuilding is heading. For the most part, the extremely massive and muscular look is only accepted by a small, hardcore section of the bodybuilding public – and almost none of the general public. Of course the women who fit within this category continue to argue that they're being discriminated against. Bodybuilding, after all, is about muscles, right? If the guys are allowed to take things to the extreme, why not the women?

Others counter that when muscularity is gained at the expense of femininity, the original goals of the sport are compromised. But even this viewpoint is questioned, as is the concept of femininity, which is really just a set of attractiveness characteristics set down primarily by men!

Compounding the problem is the ever changing judging criteria. One year it's the massive muscular look, while the next it's the more feminine physiques that get top votes. All of this leaves the competitors guessing as to what the judges are looking for.

SIDE EFFECTS

"Thank God for steroids. The uglier my competitors get, the more work I get."
– Penny Price
IFBB Pro Bodybuilder

The issue of side effects is a very touchy subject, with all sorts of authorities arguing both sides of the issue. In most cases, the argument taken depends on the individual's background (i.e. athlete, sport's official, doctor, etc.).

Besides the increased muscularity (a combination of increased muscle mass and decreased bodyfat), many women exhibit some of the more unpleasant cosmetic side effects associated with steroid use. A close examination of female contestants will reveal maladies such as increased acne, facial hair that has been shaved off, the wearing of wigs (from the loss of scalp hair), and postcontest interviews featuring extremely masculine voices!

These conditions are, for the most part, transitory (although the deepened voice from the result of vocal chord masculinization may be permanent), and therefore return to normal after drug use is stopped. But such appearances only serve to decrease the popularity of women's bodybuilding events. There is no way the general public (or much of the bodybuilding public for that matter) will ever accept such obvious biochemical transformation.

Having said all this, rest assured, most women bodybuilders are perfect examples of what regular weight training can do for the female physique. Superstars such as Cory Everson (considered the greatest female bodybuilder ever), Lenda Murray, Tonya Knight, Shelley Beattie, and Anja Schreiner, all combine the best of both worlds – moderate muscle size, beautiful proportion and symmetry, and above all, distinct femininity.

as for the guys, a stage full of shapely beauties, dancing around in bikinis, has been known to get the average hot-blooded male's testosterone flowing!

If anyone feels these contests are nothing more than beauty pageants, think again. The contestants are among the fittest female athletes in the world, having attained this condition from regular weight training and aerobics. In fact, much of the final score is based on the athlete's individual fitness routine.

The old chauvinistic cliche of curvy bimbos definitely does not apply to these women, and one of the events (George Snyder's Ms. Galaxy) even includes an obstacle course.

With the popularity of such contests growing by leaps and bounds, many of the competitors are developing followings, comparable to mainstream

THE WAVE OF THE FUTURE

"Most of the serious fitness competitors with whom I am associated have tried bodybuilding and/or powerlifting competitions at least once in their careers. Like me, they were turned off by the strong drug-enhanced looks of some of the female athletes."

– Marla Duncan
Ms. Fitness USA winner, and
regular MuscleMag International
columnist (commenting on the
state of affairs in
women's bodybuilding)

In response to the masculinizing of women's bodybuilding (this is a strong word but it's essentially what is happening) many promoters have resorted to running various Ms. Fitness-type contests. Such competitions have far outpaced female bodybuilding contests in popularity. The reason is obvious. There is less emphasis placed on pure muscle mass, and more on the combination of feminine appearance and conditioning. In short, there is no mistaking the contestants for what they truly are – beautiful women!

As expected, such competitions receive flak from the hardcore element of bodybuilding. But things must be looked at from the promoters' point of view. These contests invariably sell out, and TV networks have no qualms about coverage, as sponsors are more than willing to advertise.

Many women watch such contests, as it shows the type of physique that can be built with regular exercise. And

Penny Price

Marla Duncan

Ursula Alberto

Only time will tell if such Ms. Fitness contests will continue to grow at current rates. Certainly their popularity has sent shock waves through the mainstream bodybuilding establishment, as evident with the splitting of the Ms. Olympia into separate fitness and bodybuilding categories. Yes, we've come along ways from the days of Lisa Lyon, and you can be sure that things will continue to evolve.

CONTROLLING YOUR PHYSICAL DESTINY

Well, there you have it, an assortment of tips and techniques to develop a whole new you. Whether you want to redistribute a few inches over your body, get back in shape following pregnancy, or compete in a bodybuilding or Ms. Fitness contest, we think that you can attain these goals by following the principles laid down in this chapter. The only limiting factor is your determination. Only you are in control of your body, and only you can take it to the limit. Go for it!

bodybuilding stars. And most are earning far more money in endorsements and modeling than any Ms. Olympia competitor.

TYPES OF PROGRAMS

CIRCUIT TRAINING

Remember back in the '50s and '60s when coaches preached about the horrors of weight training, how regular weightlifting would stunt your growth and make you muscle bound. Further arguments focused on the supposedly nil effect weight training had on the cardio-vascular system. Nowadays we know differently, but occasionally the old misconceptions still surface, especially among aerobic trainers.

Nowhere is the fear of weight training more pronounced than in the female population. It's this fear of weightlifting that's made aerobics such a popular activity. Now we're not knocking aerobics, but do you really think those shapely females on TV got that way from endless aerobic classes? We seriously doubt it. Even the queen of the 20-minute workout, Jane Fonda, admitted a few years back that she regularly includes weight training in her physical fitness regimen.

Samir Bannout, Mike Christian and Gary Strydom

Perhaps the best argument for including weight training in your day to day activities lies with biology. Muscle is biologically active. It requires energy to sustain itself, even when just sitting. The more muscle you build, the higher the metabolic rate and the faster you burn fat. This is one reason why a 250-pound male can eat 6000 calories a day and still maintain a six percent bodyfat level. These individuals are burning calories even when they are sitting around the house.

Fat, on the other hand, is just layers of biologically inactive insulation. Two of the sport's most prominent bodybuilding writers, John Parrillo and Dr. Scott Connelly, have been saying for years that if you want to get lean, you must build muscle first. Then by combining weight training and aerobics, you get the best of both worlds: a larger, leaner, well conditioned physique.

Conversely, trying to starve off weight only lowers the metabolic rate, reduces lean muscle tissue, and in many cases actually increases fat levels. Studies have consistently shown that people who combine weight training with aerobics lose much more bodyfat than those who rely solely on aerobics.

By now you are probably wondering where the previous arguments are heading. How is it possible to combine both weight training and aerobics? The answer is circuit training of course.

As the name suggests, circuit training involves selecting 10 to 15 exercises and performing one set of each without stopping. Two or three circuits will benefit both the muscles and cardiovascular system.

As with any form of aerobic activity, the objective is to keep moving so the heart rate is kept in the target zone. You want to raise the heart rate and get an aerobic effect, without training to the point of collapse. This means starting with light weights for the first few circuit workouts, at least until you know how much weight you can handle without exceeding your target zone or collapsing (whichever comes first!).

A good guide for establishing your target zone is to take 75 percent of your maximum heart rate. To calculate maximum heart rate, subtract your age from 220. For example, if you are 40 years old, your maximum heart rate will be 220 − 40 = 180. Now use this value to calculate your target zone, which will be 75% x 180 = 135 beats a minute. If you exceed this value you run the risk of straining the heart (it's a muscle after all) or worse, if you're in poor condition, a heart attack.

It will take a few workouts to select the poundages that give you the previous values, but if there's error to be made, go too light rather than too heavy. Also, don't forget to perform a warmup. After all, this is weight training, even if the poundages are less than normal. And besides, a warmed-up body performs efficiently.

THE PROGRAMS

For those couch potatoes among you, this, in all likelihood is your first attempt at real exercise. If so, before plunging into a 20-exercise circuit routine, it might be a good idea to undergo a stress test. No they won't stick needles in you and remove all your blood. But any heart abnormalities (self-inflicted or otherwise) can be detected before you collapse on the gym floor. Not only will the other gym patrons appreciate this, but the rookie gym instructor may not know CPR!

When selecting the exercises, choose movements that are compound in nature. That is, exercises which work more than one muscle group at a time. For example, squats, deadlifts, pulldowns, and bench presses, will make you breathe much harder than such isolation movements as kickbacks, concentration curls, and lateral raises. It's not that isolation exercises are unimportant (they are), it's just that compound movements do a better job of increasing heart and respiratory rate.

Another piece of advice, rotate the exercises every three or four workouts. Just as you get stale following a regular weight-training program, the body can also adapt to the same circuit routine.

Although you may have your own preference for exercise order, it's generally best to start with a leg exercise like squats, and then perform an upper-body movement like bench presses. From there you can shift to a pulling movement like lat pulldowns, and then another pressing exercise like shoulder presses.

Remember, try to avoid resting between sets. Also, for the maximum aerobic effect, keep the reps in the moderate to high range, say 15 to 25 per set. Let's face it, this is not the time to be maxing out!

NOVICE CIRCUITS
Routine 1:
1. Squats
2. Bench Presses
3. Pulldowns

Routine 2:
1. Leg presses
2. Incline presses
3. Deadlifts

Vince Taylor

CHAPTER THIRTY-FOUR – TYPES OF PROGRAMS

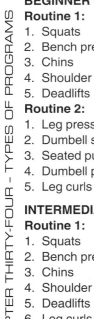
BEGINNER CIRCUITS

Routine 1:
1. Squats
2. Bench presses
3. Chins
4. Shoulder presses
5. Deadlifts

Routine 2:
1. Leg presses
2. Dumbell shoulder presses
3. Seated pulley rows
4. Dumbell presses
5. Leg curls

INTERMEDIATE CIRCUITS

Routine 1:
1. Squats
2. Bench presses
3. Chins
4. Shoulder presses
5. Deadlifts
6. Leg curls
7. Pulldowns
8. Dumbell pullovers

Kevin Levrone, Dorian Yates and Nasser El Sonbaty

Routine 2:
1. Leg presses
2. Chins
3. Dumbell presses
4. Leg curls
5. Dumbell shoulder presses
6. Deadlifts
7. Pulldowns
8. Bench presses

ADVANCED CIRCUITS

Routine 1:
1. Leg presses
2. Bench presses
3. Pulldowns
4. Shoulder presses
5. Pullovers
6. Squats
7. Incline dumbell presses
8. Leg curls
9. Seated pulley rows
10. Barbell curls

Routine 2:

1. Squats
2. Pullovers
3. Shoulder presses
4. Bench presses
5. Chins
6. Leg presses
7. Dumbell presses
8. Pulldowns
9. Barbell curls
10. Leg curls

SUPER-ADVANCED CIRCUIT

1. Squats
2. Bench presses
3. Lat pulldowns
4. Shoulder presses
5. Barbell curls
6. Leg curls
7. Dumbell presses
8. Chins
9. Leg presses
10. Incline dumbell flyes
11. Pullovers
12. Shrugs
13. Standing calf raises
14. Deadlifts

The great thing about circuits is that there is no limit to the exercise combinations. There are dozens, if not hundreds, of exercises for each bodypart. Boredom should never enter into the scheme of things unless you dislike weight training altogether. If this is the case, then try some other form of exercising.

One final note to circuit training. Obviously a lengthy circuit will be difficult to perform in a crowded gym. There's no way you'll be able to perform the exercises in the desired order. As soon as you approach a piece of equipment, somebody is bound to get there first. There are a number of ways to avoid this.

The easiest method is to forget about exercise order and do what's available. Start with a leg exercise and go from there. If the lat machine is in use, perform the bench press. Likewise if that's in use, do your shoulder presses. It's not going to make much difference in the long run.

Another solution is to reschedule your workout sessions to a less crowded time period. Most gyms are filled between 5 and 7 p.m., so forget about doing a decent circuit during these times. If your job or school schedule allows, try training in the morning or later in the evening.

The most radical solution is to change gyms. If your gym is crowded most times of the day, then not only will your circuit routines be affected, but your regular weight training will suffer as well. Of course, if you live in a one-gym town, as many do, then you'll just have to be creative and work around things.

If you're tired of running, or the monotony of the StairMaster, give circuit training a try. Not only will your heart and lungs benefit, but your muscles will harden and take on a much more attractive appearance.

Gary Strydom

Chapter Thirty-five

BODYBUILDING IN THE GOLDEN YEARS

Frank Zane

BODYBUILDING FOR THE YOUNG AT HEART

"I talk to Arnold and Dave Draper every now and then, but our lives have gone in different directions. I like all those guys, but I don't consider myself an old-timer."
– Frank Zane, Three-time Mr. Olympia

"You know Joe Weider is so busy making money and telling readers of his magazine that he created (his favorite word) this system or that principle, that people forget he actually still loves to train. Joe, himself, doesn't volunteer the information. Most see him as a self-promoting businessman. Yet at 74, Joe gets up early every morning, walks over from his house to his home gym in an annex, turns up the music (real loud) and goes to town with the weights… and stays with it for an hour every day. It's been like that for 60 years. Now that's what I call impressive." **– Robert Kennedy, founder and editor of MuscleMag International**

Before Vince Gironda has us stripped and publicly flogged, let's start by saying that when we refer to the "older" bodybuilder, we are not necessarily alluding to chronological age. By old we mean someone who's system has slowed down and has lost some of the attributes and qualities of a younger person. For many, "old" only refers to their birth certificate, and both mental and physical qualities are as sharp as people half their age. Nevertheless, it's a fact of life that as we get older our biological systems begin to slow down. Things such as digestion, elimination, reflexes, and flexibility, all suffer at the hands of father time. In addition, oxygen uptake declines by as much as one percent per year. Finally, muscle tissue declines to two-thirds of what we had earlier in our lives.

Drs. William J. Evans and Irwin H. Rosenberg have broken aging down into the following categories. They can be considered general biological markers to measure biological vitality.

1. Muscle mass
2. Strength
3. Basal (resting) metabolic rate
4. Bodyfat percentage
5. Aerobic capacity
6. Blood-sugar tolerance
7. Cholesterol/HDL ratio
8. Blood pressure
9. Bone density
10. Internal temperature regulation

Besides the biological aspects, we have psychological concerns to think about. As in most sports, enthusiasm and energy levels generally decrease as you get older, and there comes a point in time when the "law of diminishing returns" takes over. No matter how

Ed Corney

taking deterioration. And by now you probably guessed that one of the best ways to decelerate the aging process is exercise!

Arnold Schwarzenegger once said that, "It's not that you're too old to bodybuild, but you're too old not to!" Granted, someone who takes up the sport at 50 or 60 years of age is no threat to Dorian Yates or Paul Dillett, but look at the positive effects that bodybuilding will have on their bodies.

No doubt, many readers have heard of the famous Boston nursing home study involving 86- to 96-year-olds. The volunteers were put on a three-times-a-week program which involved lifting light leg weights. After eight weeks the researchers measured both thigh size and strength. Not only had size increased, but in many cases the subjects had doubled the strength of their quadriceps. Besides the performance on the weight test, all the subjects could walk faster and with greater control. In two cases, the subjects even threw away their walking canes. If there was an unfortunate aspect to the study, it was after the researchers left, no one bothered to keep the exercise going, and the subjects quickly reverted back to their prestudy form.

Perhaps the greatest lesson to be learned here is the importance of leg strength to an elderly person. The great Paul Anderson once said that when leg strength goes, you go. Just about every survival act we perform requires leg strength. For an individual in a nursing home tasks such as going to dinner or using the washroom can be curtailed if the person's legs are weak. Leg power brings independence.

hard you train, you just can't maintain your original form because of the secondary growth factors mentioned previously. There are exceptions of course, but for the most part, the passing of time means that many bodybuilders change their values and attitudes to training. The question is, should they?

Vince Gironda would bury most guys half his age in a typical workout. Likewise, bodybuilders such as Reg Park, Steve Reeves, and John Grimek, still train and look great in their sixties and seventies. The great Bill Pearl, a man in his 60s, still looks fit enough to stand in a pro lineup, and many say Ed Corney was at his best while in his 50s.

Then there's the ageless wonder, Albert Beckles, who won a pro bodybuilding contest in 1984 at the age of 52 (some have suggested that Albert was being conservative with his age)!

No doubt, with the advent of the first Masters Olympia in 1994, many bodybuilders who once thought of retiring will change their minds and keep pumping iron.

"Bodybuilders often speak of the "best years" of their training life, a time when they were most competitive and in their best shape. For me, this was between ages 14 and 41. Good bodybuilders are certainly like old soldiers. Their physiques don't die or fade away if they stay on a regular training program."
– Frank Zane, Three-time Mr. Olympia

If the previous examples haven't convinced you yet, let's look at it another way. If muscle size diminishes with age, and gaining fat becomes easier, then we should be doing something to reverse these changes. In simple terms, we should kick and scream and do whatever is possible to slow down such life-

Boyer Coe

1994 Masters Olympia champion Robby Robinson.

THE SPECIFICS OF MUSCLE-AGING PHYSIOLOGY

To fully understand the aging process, we must look inside the cell to see what's going on. Each of our muscle cells contain about one hundred small energy-producing organelles, called mitochondria. These "cell powerplants" take in fuel derived from the food we eat, and combine it with oxygen to produce ATP (adenosine triphosphate). ATP in turn serves as a fuel source for muscle cells. It's easy to see that if levels of ATP decrease, athletic performance declines as well.

Besides the decrease in athletic performance, there is another significant effect brought on by reduced ATP levels. Without adequate ATP supplies, muscle cells begin to die off, and once dead, these cells are gone forever. Research indicates that no amount of exercise can prevent it. Aerobic exercise can increase the number of cellular mitochondria, but cell death continues just the same.

For those who think such degenerative biochemistry begins in later life, recent evidence suggests that mitochondrial failure begins as early as age 20. Over an average lifetime, cellular energy levels are estimated to fall by over 50 percent.

Although the exact biological mechanism for such failure is not fully understood, recent studies suggest that the mitochondria's own chemical reactions produce genetic damage over time. About the only way to prevent such deterioration is to reduce the number of fuel molecules burned by mitochondria. This can be done with diet, but it's hardly a practical solution for an athlete. The most realistic solution for athletes is to boost mitochondrial ATP levels, despite the accumulated genetic damage. And one method (recommended by Anthony Linnane of Australia) involves diet.

Linnane suggests that one plan of attack might be to increase the amount of transport agents or redox agents in our diets. These agents move electrons between the various electron-transport chains that are responsible for ATP production, and it's these chains which fail because of accumulated genetic damage.

The two most important transport agents are coenzyme Q10 and vitamin C. When used in combination on a long term basis, these agents could help maintain the production of energy needed by our cells over a much longer period of our lives. As both these agents are available in most health food stores, athletes will have no trouble obtaining them. The recommended dose of Q10 is 60 to 120 milligrams per day. Since it's fat-soluble, it need only be taken once a day. Vitamin C on the other hand is water-soluble and must be taken several times a day.

THE KEYS TO BODYBUILDING LONGEVITY

The key to bodybuilding longevity is to make adjustments where necessary. You must realize that you simply don't have the recuperative powers that you had earlier in life. You will get far more benefit from a brief training session lasting between 45 and 90 minutes than from those two and three-hour workouts of the past (on the other hand if you love three-hour workouts, and continue to make progress, then by all means keep going).

Another consideration is what type of workout to perform. Even with the passage of time you can still train for maximum size and strength, but now it's more important than ever to include cardiovascular stimulation in your workouts. Besides the benefit to bodybuilding, a strong heart and lungs are essential for warding off the effects of time. This last point deserves a closer inspection.

A muscle that is completely fatigued in the absence of oxygen will build up lactic acid at rates 25 times the normal level. A fatigued muscle can only generate one-tenth of the energy of a muscle that is rich in oxygen. And since oxygen is brought to the muscles in only one way, the cardiovascular system, it's absolutely essential that yours is working at peak efficiency.

There are a number of ways to accomplish the previous. You can alternate weight training days with aerobic workouts. Or you can combine the two into a circuit routine as described in the previous chapter. A third option is to utilize the Peripheral Heart Action (PHA) system of training, popularized by former 1966 Mr. America, Bob Gajda.

This unique training style combines circulatory fitness with the muscle-developing effects of weight training. Although a short-lived fad at one time, it's fast regaining popularity with bodybuilders who are primarily interested in optimum health and physical conditioning.

The PHA system consists of sequences of groups of four to six exercises, each one for a different muscle group of the body. Instead of exercising the same muscle twice in succession, you move on to another muscle without resting. Later in the chapter we will provide sample PHA routines, but for now we will give you a few pointers when it comes to designing your own routine.

Because there are literally no rest pauses between exercises in a sequence, many bodybuilders will initially have a problem with labored breathing. If this is the case, arrange your exercises so that a heavy compound movement is followed by an isolation movement. For example, perform a set of barbell curls or light dumbell pullovers after a set of squats. This alternation will allow you to maintain decent poundages on most of the exercises.

Another point to remember is not to put two exercises for the same muscle group in a sequence. This interferes with the continuous flow of blood throughout the body. Likewise, don't schedule two heavy pressing exercises in the same sequence. For example, follow bench presses with lateral raises, not shoulder presses. The reverse also holds true. Follow dumbell flyes with shoulder presses.

If you plan to include some sort of forearm training in your PHA routine (and you should), leave the exercises till last or else you may have trouble holding onto the equipment.

Finally, alternate heavy days with light days. For example, Monday and Friday could be light days, and Wednesday a heavy day. The following week you could reverse things, with Monday and Friday being heavy days. Like any form of weight training, you will quickly burn out if you attempt to go all out in every workout.

The following are examples of PHA sequence routines. Select the one that is most appropriate to your conditioning level, and perform it three times a week (on alternate days). With time you may want to design your own sequences. If so, refer to the recommendations earlier in the chapter.

Albert Beckles

Danny Padilla and Olev Annus

Sequence 2:
Donkey calf raises
Lateral raises
Crunches
Dips
Narrow pulldowns
Squats
Sequence 3:
Seated calf raises
Dumbell presses
Twists
Leg curls
Deadlifts

ADVANCED PHA COURSE
3-4 sets of 8-10 repetitions each
Sequence 1:
Seated dumbell presses
Concentration curls
Donkey calf raises
Crunches
Hyperextensions
Reverse curls
Sequence 2:
Squats
Straight arm pullovers
Wide-grip pulldowns
Wrist curls
Standing calf raises
Twists

BEGINNERS PHA COURSE
1-2 sets of 10 repetitions each
Sequence 1:
Shoulder presses
Crunches
Standing calf raises
Barbell curls
Sequence 2:
Bench presses
Lying leg raises
Bent-over rowing
Seated calf raises
Sequence 3:
Squats
Reverse crunches
Straight-arm pullovers
French presses
Sequence 4:
Deadlifts
Upright rowing
Crunches
Wrist curls

INTERMEDIATE PHA COURSE
2-3 sets of 10 repetitions each
Sequence 1:
Standing calf raises
Presses behind the neck
Lying leg raises
Bench presses
Wide-grip pulldowns
Barbell curls

Charles Glass

Sequence 3:
Upright rows
Flat dumbell flyes
Sissy squats
Chinups
Crunches
Neck-strap raises (or machine)

Sequence 4:
Barbell incline presses
Lateral raises
Wrist curls
Leg curls
Dumbell extensions
Seated calf raises

FINAL CONSIDERATIONS

If you follow the advice laid down in this chapter (and for that matter, throughout the whole book), there is no reason why you can't continue to make progress, even in your 50s, 60s, 70s, or beyond. Remember that age can be a relative term, and one of the first steps to conquering it, is to maintain a positive mental attitude. Instead of statements such as "I used to squat this" or "I once benched that," try "I'm going to press this," or "Let's do a few extra reps." Not only does it sound a whole lot better, but you'll garner legions of fans with your enthusiasm.

Besides mental attitude, there are other considerations to take into account. First and foremost, you must be consistent. This means regularly going to the gym, three or four times a week. Start skipping workouts and you'll end up looking like some chain smoking, pot-bellied, 65-year-old. If this is what you want, fine. But don't blame us if you suddenly start to feel old.

Another point to highlight is intensity. Although this one is much more individualistic in nature, nevertheless, there is no reason to hold back just because your birth certificate is over the half-century mark. If you've got the energy, desire, and recuperative powers, then by all means give it your best.

One of the best ways to keep motivation levels high is to train with a much younger person. His or her youthfulness will keep you inspired and your age will keep them on their toes. Let's face it, what 20-year-old wants to be out-worked by a 50 or 60-year-old!

As a final note, don't be afraid to supplement your meals with vitamins, minerals, and extra forms of protein. As your digestive abilities are probably not what they once were, you may be deficient in one or more essential nutrients. Take a good multi-vitamin, and extra vitamin C wouldn't hurt either. Feeling sluggish during workouts? Try an energy bar beforehand. To speed up recovery after workouts, make good use of amino acids and desiccated liver tablets.

Katsumi Ishimura

THE BODYBUILDING SUBCULTURE

BODYBUILDING SOCIOLOGY

"I don't think I have any friends. I don't make 'em easy. I'm friendly with people, but I don't think these guys make friends. You know what the problem is? Bodybuilders are selfish; all they think about are themselves."
– Quote from a bodybuilder talking to sociologist Alan Klein

Perhaps one of the most neglected aspects of bodybuilding has been gym etiquette: the proper behavior and manners that should be followed to produce the most harmonious social exchanges in the weight room. This chapter examines various situations and behaviors, and furnishes a list of guidelines to provide direction. We are not trying to be dogmatic, merely pragmatic. Bodybuilders often have a very poor image among the general public. This is invariably linked to rude and obnoxious behavior observed in the gym. All sports attract a few 'bad apples', but bodybuilding tends to tolerate, and at times even condone, poor behavior. As bodybuilders, we expect a great deal from our bodies; as a community we must learn to expect more from each other. Just as we demand hard work from our tired muscles, we must demand politeness and correct behavior from our fellow bodybuilders.

GROSS BEHAVIOR IN THE GYM

"Never have I seen a people of more perfect physique; they are all tall as date palms and reddish in color... They are the filthiest of God's creatures. They do not wash after discharging their bodily functions, neither do they was their hands after meals. They are as stray donkeys... Ten or twenty of them may live together in one house... A girl brings her master a huge bowl of water in which he washes his face, hands, and hair, combing it out also over the bowl. Then he blows his nose and spits into the water. When he has finished, the girl takes the same bowl to his neighbor, who repeats the performance – until the bowl has gone around the entire household."
– Ibn Faldan
Arab ambassador of the Caliphate of Baghdad (describing the appearance and hygienic practices of his Viking hosts, in 922)

Picture this: You're having one of the best workouts ever. You've pumped more iron than Amtrak sees in a month! You're firm, pumped, and serene. This is the moment when the joy of bodybuilding crystallizes inside you. Body and soul are one. You get in line to use the water fountain. A certain hard-body that ignored you only months before can't get enough of your brilliant conversation. And then the person in front of you spits a huge wad of green mucus into the water basin...

Michelle Ralabate and Rozann Keyser

Bodybuilding is about being the best person that you can be. This does not mean spitting into the gym water fountain! Besides being a good way to spread hepatitis (a liver disease), mononucleosis (the so-called 'kissing disease' that is guaranteed to knock you out of training for a considerable length of time) and numerous other illnesses, it's disgusting behavior that gives bodybuilders a bad rap. In case you didn't know, "bodybuilders are big and dumb," at least that's what the general public says. And such behaviors only reinforce the negative stereotypes. If a regular Joe does something stupid perhaps another person will comment; but bodybuilders who love giving advice on how to lift weights usually turn a blind eye to this behavior. Enough! If your gym doesn't already have them, have the owner post some rules; and see that they're enforced. If people want to act like they're in a barn, we're sure there are some farmers who could use the extra muscle.

TAKING THE OFFENSIVE AGAINST BEING "OFFENSIVE"

"Be home in three days. Don't bathe." — ***A brief love letter to Josephine from her husband, Napoleon Bonaparte.***

A good workout usually results in a good sweat. That's healthy and normal. Unfortunately, the bacteria that live in our pores produce odors that can be offensive. Most people are not like Napoleon: most are taller, have no ambitions for global domination, and most are put off by body odor.

Ever hear the phrase, "This place smells like a gym?" The point is, it shouldn't. Wash your gym clothes regularly. Not once a month, but every day if you're working out heavy. Some bodybuilders use the "stick" test on socks. If they throw the socks and they stick to the wall, then it's time to throw the socks in the wash. If your socks are sticking to the wall, it's time to throw them into the incinerator! Socks and underwear should be washed daily, and change your socks right after your workout. If washing every day doesn't appeal to you, try purchasing extra workout clothes. Three different sets of gym attire will mean having to wash only once or twice a week.

The next piece of advice is to shower after you workout (it sounds redundant, but you'd be surprised how many individuals leave the gym and go straight to a social situation without showering). Some bodybuilders believe that it's unhealthy to wash immediately after a workout. Some people believe in the tooth fairy. Get back to reality and grab a bar of soap.

It wouldn't hurt to brush and floss your teeth before you workout either. You're going to do some heavy breathing, and it's awful hard to find someone to spot you when you've got jungle mouth.

Do not share your razor with anyone in the locker room. Not only is it a good way to spread minor skin

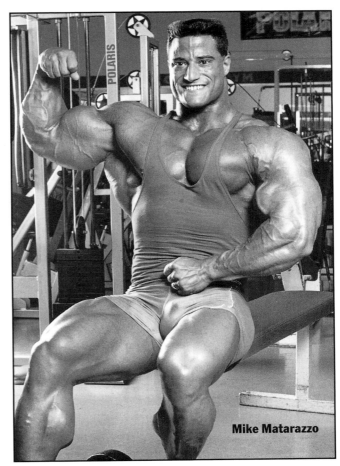

Mike Matarazzo

infections, but sharing blood products is one way to get AIDS.

Do not share your comb with anyone. Head lice are not as uncommon as you think, and regular shampoos won't kill the lice.

Do not share your water bottle with anyone. Flu, colds, mononucleosis, and hepatitis B can all be spread by sharing food and fluids.

No doubt most of you reading this already follow the previous hygiene tips. Great, keep it up. The remainder should rethink their attitudes – bodybuilding is about developing the whole person, not just the muscles.

GETTING ALONG IN THE GYM

"…I'm not a nice person in the gym. When I train, it's like responding to a bell in boxing. Do your work and get out; otherwise, you lose motivation and energy."
— ***Mike Matarazzo, top IFBB Pro Bodybuilder***

"I was always turned off by team sports. Never had any rational reasons, I just didn't like being part of a team and the back-slapping and groping, sweating and all that shit. I would rather spend the day by myself in the basement pumping iron." — ***Quote from a bodybuilder talking to sociologist Alan Klein***

There is a hierarchy in the gym, so you had better get used to it. Socially, new bodybuilders are at the bottom of the totem pole. Next up are the regulars. This includes people who've been working out in one gym for six months or more. The top are the veterans, bodybuilders who've been working out for years, and who have competed or are competing, or are recognized by the other veterans as being successful bodybuilders in their own right. The owner of the gym may be well-liked or despised, depending on how he or she maintains the gym and treats the clients and staff.

As in any hierarchy, there are certain unwritten rules. People who are getting ready for a contest have priority over any piece of equipment in the gym. Doesn't matter if you waited an hour to use the squat rack, move over and wish them luck. Real bodybuilders respect each other. Because of the starvation diets that many people in pre-competition follow, these competitors may be surly and downright aggressive. Just think of a time when one of your family members was on a strict diet or trying to quit smoking. Remember what a barrel of laughs they were? This situation demands tolerance. The Bible gives an excellent piece of advice, "A soft answer turneth away wrath." Be polite, supportive, and you will eventually be accepted. The veterans will never accept you if you violate the gym taboo of not deferring to people getting ready for a contest.

Be careful answering advertisements in the gym. You may see an ad posted by a photographer offering money to take pictures of a bodybuilder. Often these photographers want to take nude photographs; and as the following quote illustrates, they sometimes want more:

*"I knew a gay guy back in New York – one gay guy, and I liked him. I respected him. When I came out here I had guys hitting on me, and I didn't even know it. I had a guy hand me a card that said he was a photographer. He said, "If you wanna make some bucks, give me a call." I said, "Geez thanks. That's great! Here's a guy doin' me a favor, wants to take photos of me." I didn't have any in my portfolio. That's great. Boy did I learn. It was my ass he wanted." – **Quote from a bodybuilder interviewed by sociologist Alan Klein***

Don't stare directly at someone in the gym; use the mirrors, that's why they're there. Humans are primates, and any monkey psychologist will tell you that making direct eye contact with wild monkeys is an aggressive provocation. We don't like being stared at because it makes us feel vulnerable. There are times we want to be noticed, and that's the reason many people go into bodybuilding. But in the gym, we only stare if we have been asked to spot, or observe a movement in order to

Lee Priest

offer advice on how to correct it. Homophobia is rampant in bodybuilding, and staring can be misinterpreted as sexual interest. You do not want to confront a group of angry, homophobic bodybuilders! And guys, contrary to popular belief, most women, like most men, are at the gym just for the exercise. In fact many of them would kick your ass at the squat rack, so don't misinterpret a great figure and sweet smile as a sign of weakness!

A LESS SAVORY SIDE

"If you get too tied up in it, it can sort of drag you down. People pretend to be friends to your face, and when you turn your back they'll be talking about you. They're always going on behind your back, or to your face, about 'oh, you're so fat' or 'he looks like shit' during the off-season. And when you're back in shape, they say, 'You look great… I knew you could do it!'… and all of the other garbage. Then you have your people who strut around and think they're huge… think they're great… but obviously can't see themselves in the mirror too well."
– Lee Priest,
top IFBB Pro Bodybuilder
(commenting on the LA gym scene)

Generally, the gym is a fun place to go. Your fellow bodybuilders are into the sport for the enjoyment of it; most have families and careers to occupy the rest of their time. Bodybuilding is seen as recreation, another way of relaxing after a hard day's work. This sort of gym/health centre/spa maintains an atmosphere that allows camaraderie to grow. Genuine friendships are found here. Bodybuilders help each other out and shout encouragement. And there's a simple reason for this – no one is in competition with anyone else.

"I don't talk to anyone in the gym, I just do my workout. I don't hang around, nothin'... I'm outta there. Then people are amazed that I make progress because they're convinced you have to be in there four, five or six hours a day. More isn't better. It's what you do in that amount of time." **– Paul DeMayo, US National champion, aptly nicknamed "Quadzilla." (A very serious bodybuilder, he doesn't consider the gym to be a social club)**

The LA scene is a very different story. Southern California is the hot spot for professional bodybuilding. It is also competitive in the most Darwinian (survival of the fittest) sense. The smiling faces and back-slapping found in the magazines are sometimes replaced by two-faced comments and back-stabbing in the gym. You have a large number of people all striving for the same goal: the Olympia, followed by endorsement fees, guest-posing contracts, movie stardom, and ultimately fame and fortune. When the stakes are that high, people will justify anything that appears to help them reach their goal. Many head out to California with nothing but a gym bag, and ten years later that's still all they have. In that sort of a 'dog-eat-dog' atmosphere, some gym members look at the latest greenhorn as something to be exploited, manipulated, and if he's talented, sabotaged so that he can't compete successfully. Bottom line, if you're into bodybuilding for recreation and for making friends, stick to gyms outside of the bodybuilding meccas.

Paul DeMayo

"Bodybuilding is great, but your education is just as important. I don't know where bodybuilding will take me, but I do know where a good education will. A person should always have something to fall back on. Neglecting education is a mistake too many athletes make." **– Fred Bigo, businessman**

Some of you might be planning to head for Southern California, train in the hardcore gyms with the pros and become the next Mr. or Ms. Olympia. Our only advice is, go for it – after you have obtained an education or trade. There are millions of amateur bodybuilders, but the number of individuals who make it to the pros might total a few hundred worldwide. And of these, only a few earn the six-figure salaries. A bodybuilder must have something to fall back on, given the likely event they will never make the pros. Those who don't have an education can look forward to bodybuilder jobs: laborer, bouncer or working for a collection agency. These jobs at least provide the time to work out. The problem is they pay very little. Some bodybuilders supplement their incomes by hustling (male prostitution). Their clients are gay males who prefer bodybuilders. As degrading as prostitution is, some young bodybuilders are drawn into it by the prospect of big money:

"A friend of mine who had never done anything before got into the idea of it. I told him, "Don't get into that sick shit," but he got some rich guy, originally from Oklahoma, to dig him. He demanded $500 and a plane ticket. Like if you get a lot of cake, it makes it alright. Well, there are rates for that sort of thing, and the guy told my buddy to screw off. Within two days he was going for $50." **– Quote from a bodybuilder being interviewed by sociologist Alan Klein**

Not surprisingly, heterosexual relationships are disrupted, the bodybuilder undergoes tremendous anxiety and internal conflict, and attempts to stop hustling are sabotaged by the lure of easy money. Not all hustlers can cope: some attempt suicide, while others give up on hustling and bodybuilding altogether.

This sport does not encourage people to build up their bodies so they can degrade them. Bodybuilding is about self-respect. Gay or straight, have the sense to share your body with someone who cares for you, not someone who purchased you. A bodybuilder who sells sex is not a bodybuilder, he's just a prostitute who lifts weights between tricks.

ON GIVING ADVICE

"…I respect a man who can say what's on his mind 'cause so many guys in California just lie and bullshit all the time. One thing about me, I've always been brutally honest. People don't like my honesty sometimes, and so I tell them, 'Well, if you don't like the answer I'm giving, you shouldn't have asked the question!'"

– Lee Priest, Australian IFBB Pro Bodybuilder

Offering advice can be a double-edged sword. By all means, offer assistance if someone looks as if they're going to injure themselves or damage the equipment. But don't read one training article and then strut around as if you're Vince Gironda!

Some new bodybuilders memorize whole sections from the latest bodybuilding magazine, and rush around like a world-famous consultant, spouting gibberish and using terms they don't understand. This is caused by enthusiasm, insecurity, and a desire to be accepted. Acceptance takes time. The smart strategy is to ask one of the veterans for advice on a particular exercise. The veteran will be impressed. The new person has brains, because they asked one of the people who know what they're doing. This kind of recognition is flattering, and everyone wants to be recognized as having expertise in something.

On the other hand, don't be a patronizing nuisance. Ask for advice on diet and training once a week, or every two weeks, but not every five minutes. There is a fine line between flattering someone's ego and getting on their nerves. Please try not to cross it.

USING THE EQUIPMENT

"Are you in here?" **– Question most often heard in the gym during rush hour, it means: Are you using a particular piece of gym equipment?**

There are a set of phrases and customs that are unique to the use of equipment in the gym. "Strip the bar," means take all the weights off the bar and put them back. "Rack the weights," means put all the hand weights back in place on the rack. People join a gym to work out, not to clean up after another bodybuilder. Always put the weights back after you use them.

It is taboo to hog the equipment. If someone asks, "How many more sets?," he or she wants to know when you're going to be finished. Never ask the question during a set, nor should you answer if you are in the middle of a set. It distracts from concentrating on the exercise at hand.

Lee Labrada, Flex Wheeler and Andreas Munzer

Lenda Murray

casual conversations and offering suggestions. Soon the normal gym banter and joking starts, and you're part of the crowd. Before you offer to spot, make sure you know how to do it. Observe before you volunteer, and ask questions to know what is expected of you.

Being seen means being noticed. One way is to wear a variety of T-shirts and sweatshirts with humorous statements on them. People will look your way just to read the joke. Not only do you end up providing someone with a laugh, they begin to see you as a fun-loving person. Other gym members will even start looking around for you when they go in for a workout, thinking, 'What's that comic wearing today?' Remember, bodybuilding is not a means to an end. We won't all end up built like Dorian Yates or Shawn Ray, but we can enjoy the process.

THE DRUG SCENE

"I set up a communication system using a network of satellite pagers that enabled me to do deals without talking to anyone, and it was virtually untraceable. I could contact any one dealer or all of them at once. Information was transmitted in a series of codes. For example: 010750000803010218425769 meant I (01) sent Dave (07) five thousand (5000) Deca (08) by UPS (03), to be delivered the next morning (01) to the second pre-arranged address (02), and the airbill number was (18425769). After that, I would wait for the dealer to confirm the message by paging me back with his number. When the package arrived, he would page me again with his number and the airbill number. We could communicate the exchange of money the same way..." — **Sergio Oliviera, a former steroid dealer (describing how his distribution system worked)**

A significant number of bodybuilders use anabolic steroids. Some gyms have members who are quite open about their use, while other gyms may consider such talk taboo and grounds for expulsion. Steroid use is as controversial as abortion, and there's no safe middle ground to run to. As a new member, never initiate a conversation about steroids. If asked, give your opinion, pro or con. If the other person disagrees with you, then pleasantly agree to disagree. Don't let a different opinion prevent a person from liking you.

Asking strangers a great deal of questions about an illegal practice can be dangerous. You might give people the false impression that you are a user. The anti-steroid crowd may shun you or the owner could kick you out. You might make a drug dealer nervous, with the resulting black-glove treatment in the gym

"Can I work in?" means can he or she alternate sets with you. It is impolite to refuse, unless you're waiting to do your final set. If you're resting between sets, then let someone else do a set, then jump back in. As you alternate you can spot each other and engage in small talk. Such chance encounters often lead to life-long friendships.

SEEKING FRIENDSHIP

I just want to be liked. That's a normal aspiration for anyone. Believe it or not, bodybuilding is one of the best ways for a person in a big city to enlarge their circle of friends. And it's all based on social psychology. The key is becoming familiar. This is not the same as forward. You have to be seen, and seen often. When you first join a gym, you often find that people are cold and distant. There is a simple reason for that. The majority of new members quit. Why invest time making friendships with people you aren't going to see again? Go to the gym often, and try to arrange it so that part of your workout period overlaps with a peak period of use. By being seen at the gym regularly, you become associated with the gym. And we tend to like what we are familiar with. After a while, if you offer to spot someone (and everyone appreciates this), you will find that even some of the veterans will start engaging in

Ben Weider, Michael Francois and
Arnold Schwarzenegger

parking lot. Bottom line: If you don't need to know, then don't ask. Keep the steroid debate where it belongs, out of the gym.

If you are approached by a steroid dealer, just say "no" and continue with your workout. If steroids are legal in your country and you want them then you can get a prescription from a doctor and buy them at a pharmacy. If they are illegal in your country, say no and obey the law. Undercover cops have great fun using sting operations with bodybuilders, and they get great media coverage.

REVERSE ANOREXIA

"No, I feel small. I should be bigger than I am now. I'd feel big if I was 50 lbs. heavier. Right now, I feel small."
   – Steroid-using bodybuilder, responding to the question, "Are you satisfied with your size?" The person being interviewed was, at the time, 265 lbs.

A common problem among male bodybuilders (steroid-users and nonusers alike) is reverse anorexia. No matter how big they get, they don't feel big enough. And just like the emaciated anorexic who can look in the mirror and only see fat the reverse anorexic can look at his own reflection and perceive a small person who should be bigger. Why?

In a theory put forward by sociologist Alan Klein, it may have to do with how many young males become involved with bodybuilding. Unlike sports such as hockey, where a male will join because he has confidence in his abilities, many young men turn to bodybuilding because they want to improve their feelings of low self-esteem. The skinny kid with pimples, who no one notices, creates a new identity based on the muscular images found in bodybuilding magazines. As his muscles respond to dedicated training, his new identity becomes based on his new physical form. This is both normal and healthy.

The problem arises when the new bodybuilder begins to form unrealistic goals, while at the same time ascribing negative values to the former 'self'. Though the muscles may have enlarged, it is still the same person inside. The bodybuilder creates an identity based on an image that exists only in his mind. Thus the sense of 'self' (or ego) becomes directly proportional to physical size.

Despite the above-average musculature in the reflection, the image cannot match the grandiose image which exists inside the viewer's mind. This discrepancy leads to feelings of inadequacy preventing some bodybuilders from developing the self-confidence that so many others have found in the sport.

Reverse anorexia can destroy a bodybuilder's personal relationships. With low self-esteem, how can he cope to have someone like him, when he doesn't like himself? This disorder can have a more subtle effect as some bodybuilders cannot diet down for a contest because they are unable to deal with the loss of mass. It is also the ultimate intimidation tactic. Many competitive bodybuilders exploit this problem and make negative comments about other bodybuilders' muscular development. The goal is to sabotage their training by having them work on a bodypart that is already strong so they ignore the part that is still weak.

How to treat it? Often, it is enough to recognize reverse anorexia for what it is – a distorted self-concept. Once the problem is recognized, the bodybuilder should start setting realistic goals, and sticking to them. Negative comments from other bodybuilders should be ignored. But most important, base your identity on more than physical size. Things such as: talents (music, dance, writing), relationships, education, job and hobbies all help define who and what we are. As bodybuilders, we have a responsibility to ourselves and to each other – to ensure that bodybuilding enhances the self-esteem of those who take part.

BODYBUILDING FACTS OF LIFE

"We met at World Gym. I was in the seminary at the time and she trained at the gym. We got together on New Year's Eve, 1989. I had returned to school early, so classes hadn't started yet. We went out to dinner, and things took off from there." **– Michael Francois**
IFBB Pro Bodybuilder, Arnold Classic winner

What we're about to tell you is a surprising statement to find in a bodybuilding book, but it's the truth. Studies and surveys consistently show that the majority of women prefer men who are lean and toned, and not overly muscular. In short, big biceps place much lower on the popularity pole than a nice tight butt!

Amy Fadhli and Jim Quinn

"I always have sex before a show, but I'll still jump out of bed when it's over and start posing in front of the mirror. I'm veiny, hard as hell. If they could push me onstage right after having sex, I'd be so ripped and vascular you wouldn't believe it." **– J.J. Marsh**
IFBB Pro Bodybuilder
(adding a new technique to contest preparation)

The opposite holds true as well. Most men are turned off by extremely muscular women. Just look at a cover from any bodybuilding magazine, and you'll see a male bodybuilder sharing space with a bikini-clad model or aerobics instructor. It's a publishing fact that the majority of magazine buyers are males between the ages of 15 and 25. A magazine with a 200-pound female on the cover will sell nowhere near the same number of copies as one featuring a Ms. Fitness contestant. Female bodybuilders argue that it's not fair, and maybe they're right. But look at it from the publishers' point of view. Compiling, printing, and marketing magazines costs millions of dollars, and the primary method for recouping the investment is through sales. Sales in turn attract advertisers. So while many muscular female bodybuilders shout prejudice, magazine publishers look at it in terms of dollars and cents.

"At the primal level – and that's a good word to describe it – women can be dependent on a man. And whether we like it or not, the dependency kind of holds us back. A lot of women don't want to admit it, but we give up more in a relationship than men. A woman will give up more choices and sacrifice more to be with a man than a man will to be with a woman." **– Amy Fadhli, Ms. Fitness winner**

Why is it that you can flex your magnificent muscles, and that knock-down beautiful brunette is with that pot-bellied bald guy, and obviously happy to boot? Why is it that a female bodybuilder can train and diet and produce a body that wins loud applause onstage, and at the end of the night she goes home alone?

Our physical appearance is usually all that we have to initially spark an interest. If that doesn't work, we have to have other attributes to ignite the flames of passion. The fat bald guy may be a powerful politician, and power has a very erotic quality. The lonely female bodybuilder might be a highly-trained professional (and most female bodybuilders are), and witty and fun-loving, but her outstanding physical appearance scares most guys off before they can get to know her.

"I guess I've always intimidated men. And I'm not saying it has to do with my body or my voice or anything. I think it's because I'm very painfully honest. I'm very bold. I say what's on my mind." **– Sharon Bruneau**
1991 IFBB North American champion

Another reason why dating opportunities are limited for bodybuilding women is the basic fact that they're go-getters. Their independent lifestyle and aggressive outlook can be intimidating for many men. Sexist attitudes still exist in the gym. A woman may be unfairly labeled an "Ice Queen" simply because she exudes self-confidence. One must also consider that most female bodybuilders have professional occupations; thus a male bodybuilder with poor job prospects would hardly be considered 'husband material'. It is not unusual for a female bodybuilder to be married to, or living with a man, who is not personally involved in bodybuilding!

The bottom line is this: taking up bodybuilding to meet a member of the opposite sex is fine, but remember there's more to a person than their physique. There are a lot of lonely bodybuilders out there. Yes, magazines give the impression that if your biceps begin to bulge then you're going to have a beautiful partner hanging off you arm. However reality is much more sobering, and you have to be into bodybuilding for yourself. If you want to attract a partner, then you need to develop other talents or skills as well. It is a fact of life that the bouncer with big muscles is not nearly as attractive as the skinny lawyer next door.

DATING AND THE GYM

"I refuse to date a woman who has more testosterone in her system than I do." **– A male bodybuilder (stating why he would never consider dating a professional female bodybuilder)**

"I'd pick her up in my Lexus coupe, and we'd listen to some soft music on our way to a nice restaurant in Santa Monica or Hollywood. We'd have a nice down-to-earth conversation at dinner and get to know each other. Then we'd go for a walk on the beach. Back at her place, we'd engage in intimate kissing, and afterwards I'd think how she's the one I want to spend my life with." **– Jim Quinn, IFBB Pro Bodybuilder (describing the ideal romantic date)**

For you singles out there, the gym is as good as any other place to meet someone decent. But there are some things you should consider, because it's not all that different from an office romance.

If he or she says no, that they're not interested, then move on. One complaint to the owner and you're out. Persistently bothering another person is called harassment (and nowadays it applies equally to men and women), and the gym owner has no desire in becoming part of a civil suit. Besides, do we really need a tabloid talk show to air a program on 'Bodybuilding Stalkers'?

Should you go slow or fast? We suggest that the first thing you propose is dinner and a movie. As a bodybuilder, you've probably been blowing your money on gym memberships, supplements, magazines, and bodybuilding books (such as this particular purchase). In other words, you're broke. And now you've got a date. No problem. As long as you have a VCR.

Let him or her know in advance that it's going to be a homemade meal and a video. If it's you they're interested in, that'll be fine. It's also a lot less stressful. Here's how the date goes, from the guy's point of view: Pick her up, compliment her on her hairstyle, or her biceps, or her tattoo. Then drive straight to… the grocery store! Pick out a cart, and go shopping. Some of you are now saying, that's nuts! Is it though? What is more domestic, more relaxing, than a happy couple browsing among the fruits and vegetables? Compare this to the strained small-talk that would accompany an expensive dinner you can't afford. Besides, if the date is a flop, you've still got leftovers!

While you're coasting the aisles, confiding your secret temptation for cheesecake, you can mention how dad used to make baked ham, or how mom used to make the Christmas turkey. Food is central to almost every celebration (and few things interest bodybuilders like food), and there are a lot of good stories to share. Before you both know it, you'll be gabbing away as if you'd been dating for a long time.

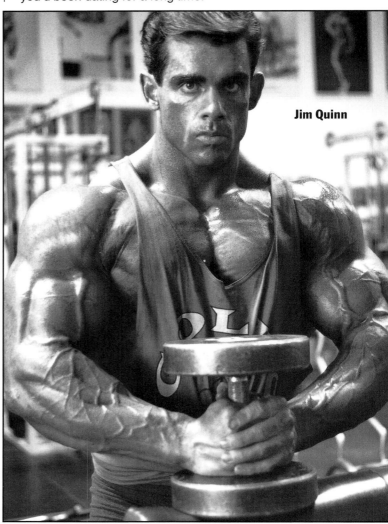

Jim Quinn

Next, it's time to put your relationship to the ultimate test, the Video Store! You want to watch *Die Hard,* and she wants *Fried Green Tomatoes.* Our advice, get a scary movie. They're like jumping out of an airplane, terrifying at first, but afterward they produce the opposite reaction. You'll find yourselves laughing to kill yourselves. Or get a comedy. But avoid anything that's explicit. If you've found someone that's decent, then treat them decent.

Next, your place. And you know the room you're both headed for... the kitchen! Peeling potatoes and scraping carrots is another domestic scene that allows conversation to flow freely. Think about it. Where do you and your friends usually sit? In the kitchen. Where did you have those long chats with mom and dad? In the kitchen. The kitchen, despite all the sharp knives, is (at least symbolically) the place we feel the safest. And if you're safe, you can relax.

Eat the meal. Watch the movie. Then you two can decide the rest.

Sharon Bruneau

Many readers might be saying, but I'm a woman. Can I ask a guy out? Of course! Women do it all the time. The days of 'nice' women never asking a man out are long gone. As we age, the ratio of men to women changes, so that the number of available men decreases. This has made many single women more aggressive in finding a man. And some guys are just plain shy when it comes to asking a woman out. Remember, the big guy at the squat rack may have a bad case of reverse anorexia, so he might think you would never be interested in a 'skinny' guy like him. You'll make his day!

TRAINING PARTNERS

No matter what the personal endeavor, few people achieve success without assistance from others, and bodybuilding is no exception. There will be days when working out is the last thing on your mind. It takes all your energy just to make it to the gym. This is where a training partner can play a major role. On days when you feel lethargic, your training partner can provide the motivation and encouragement to make it through a workout. On other days you can reciprocate. The odds are good to excellent that one of you will arrive at the gym begging for a workout.

Besides the mental push, you and your training partner can enter into little training competitions. If he gets six reps, you go for seven. If she does ten reps you try eleven. Continuously try to push one another to higher levels of success.

Another benefit of training partners is their honesty. You may feel that you have no weaknesses, but a training partner can quickly bring you back to earth. For example, your training partner may inform you that your upper pecs are too shallow. At first you may deny it, but eventually you'll realize that he or she was right.

CHOOSING A TRAINING PARTNER

There are a number of things to consider when choosing a good training partner – first and foremost is positive attitude. It doesn't matter if they can bench as much as you. What's important is his or her mental approach to training.

The reciprocal to the above is avoiding a negative training partner. Nothing can ruin a good workout like such statements as "don't you think that's enough for today?" or "let's skip calves and go for a bite to eat." The problem with such negative statements is that they spread like a virus – in other words their highly contagious!

Dorian Yates, Lee Haney and Vince Taylor

Perhaps the only benefit to being around such negativity is that it can spur you to push harder (if the whole gym has such an atmosphere, then switch gyms). If your training partner says "I think that weight is too heavy today," this can drive you to blast out additional reps. In all honesty, however, try to avoid such individuals as potential training partners.

A less obvious but equally important factor is your training partner's ability to concentrate. Most people go to the gym to escape the stress of daily life. If your partner spends more time talking about the office than exercising – trade him or her in! You don't need the aggravation. Such negativity will only spill over into your training. Of course if you and your partner are good friends, then you may be able to offer advice. But if you are playing counselor more than training partner, you might want to re-evaluate your workout relationship.

Another great characteristic to look for is competitiveness. If after doing ten reps with a given weight, your training partner does eleven or twelve, personal pride will force you to go for thirteen or fourteen (you may not get the reps, but it won't be because of laziness). A training partner who brings out your best is a definite plus.

The trait of consistency is also very important. You may have the greatest partner in the world in terms of drive, attitude, and endurance, but these attributes are useless if he or she is hardly ever in the gym. Anyone can miss the occasional workout. It's a fact of modern-day life that sooner or later something will come up. But if you find yourself frequently waiting half an hour, or working out alone, then it's time to make changes. What your training partner is saying is that working out is not very high on his or her priority scale.

Besides the previous advice, there are a few practical considerations in choosing a training partner. Perhaps the most important is time compatibility. If both of you train at different times then obviously one of you will have to change your schedule. Second, both of you should be following the same training routine. If you favor high reps, high sets, and he or she prefers low reps, low sets, it makes little sense to team up together. Casey Viator and Mike Mentzer initially trained together as both were following the heavy duty style of training. Later, Casey decided to switch to a higher set style of training, necessitating the end to their training partnership.

Perhaps the most famous training partners in the sport's history were Arnold Schwarzenegger and Franco Columbu. They made great training partners, given their love of high set training, similar backgrounds, and most importantly, their incredible drives. Although Franco was stronger on a few of the exercises, overall they complemented one another in the gym.

A third point is strength levels. Both of you should be comparable on the major exercises. It wouldn't make sense to continuously be changing 45-pound plates (although a few bodybuilders prefer to train with stronger individuals as it pushes them to catch up). Granted, adding or taking off five to 10 pounds is no big deal. In fact the odds are you won't be using identical poundages on the exercises. You'll find that you're stronger on some movements, while your partner is stronger on others. For example, you may be stronger on pushing exercises, while he/she has the advantage on pulling movements. This is normal and can in fact be beneficial as both of you will no doubt try to catch up to the other.

We should add an exception to the previous. If a top bodybuilder (pro or amateur) offers to train with you – jump at the opportunity! You've been given the

Lori Ann Lloyd

chance of a bodybuilding lifetime. No doubt the individual has countless years of experience under his or her belt. You can advance your own career by watching and listening to such a bodybuilder. Who cares if there's a wide discrepancy in the workout poundages. If it doesn't both the top pro (he or she would have taken this into account before asking you to work out together) it certainly shouldn't annoy you.

Another practical concern is safety. You need someone who spots properly (they don't just lift the weight off you, or conversely leave it on you!). Granted you can teach someone correct spotting technique, but it must go beyond that. A good training partner can sense when you need assistance, and when to push you for an extra rep. If your partner is consistently sloppy in his or her spotting technique, get rid of them out of safety concerns.

All of the previous may lead to the question – should individuals of the opposite sex train together? Many hold the belief that because of the differences in workout poundages, men must train with men, and women with women. Well, for starters, many of the women these days are no slouches in the strength department. But more important, can you answer "yes" to the following questions – do you both have the same goals? Is he or she consistent in his or her training? Does he or she have a positive outlook when working out? Finally, are you both compatible training together?

If the answer to the previous is "yes", then it makes no difference whether your training partner is male or female, cat or dog, vegetable or mineral! As long as the two of you are complementary in your workouts, nothing else matters.

Overall the benefits of a training partner are numerous, and no doubt after your first couple of workouts together, you'll wonder how you ever managed without one.

BODY MODIFICATION

"I'm into really intense experiences." – **Quote from a body modification aficionado explaining a video he had which depicted him having his lips sewn together in a feature story in Equinox magazine. He also added that this girlfriend had recently left him.**

Many individuals like to adorn their bodies with body decorations, so we thought this topic would appropriately follow dating. Tattoos, body piercing, branding and scarification are all forms of body modification. It's your body, change it as you wish. Just remember, virtually all are taboo in bodybuilding competitions. In fact many bodybuilders later regret the foolishness of their youth. An expensive tattoo laid on by a pro is meant to last for life. Removing such skin blemishes takes time, money, and in many cases, a great deal of pain. So, while it may seem macho at fifteen years of age to get a tattoo, remember, you may regret it four or five years down the road.

WHAT ABOUT MY HAIR?

If you've still got it, flaunt it! Bring a can of hairspray or tube of gel in your gym bag, and do your hair before you work out. Many bodybuilders get perms. There's nothing more annoying than hair in your eyes during rope crunches. For female bodybuilders, a fancy hairstyle is a strong feminine statement. But don't get too fancy! One of the authors once helped rescue another bodybuilder when her ponytail got caught in the hook of a heavily weighted universal pulley. For safety reasons, if your hair is very long, then keep it up and out of the way.

Henderson Thorne

CONDUCT OUTSIDE THE GYM

"I took up weight training because there was really very little going on out there. And I really was very skinny."
– Sean Connery, actor who took up bodybuilding as a hobby at the age of 19. At the time (1949), he had just been discharged from the Royal navy with a stomach full of ulcers. In 1951, he placed runner-up in the Mr. Universe contest in London. This led to a series of acting jobs, culminating in 1962 with his audition for the role of 'James Bond'. The rest is history.

Very few bodybuilders are fortunate enough to have jobs in the bodybuilding industry. And it may surprise you to find out that a muscular body might be a hindrance to a male bodybuilder finding a job! Women bodybuilders will find the opposite, as it is generally obese women who are discriminated against. Many people are intimidated by big muscles. This means you must carry yourself with both pride and dignity. Walking around in the middle of winter wearing a weightlifting belt and strap shirt is not doing our sport any service. This sort of behavior only reinforces the public's misconception of bodybuilders.

"I wear nothing but silk shirts, tailor-made pants and suits. I dress good."
– Mike Quinn
Jr. Mr. America champion

Try to dress in a way that makes people comfortable with your size. Just look at pictures of bodybuilding stars such as Arnold Schwarzenegger, Tom Platz, Lee Haney, Dorian Yates, Shawn Ray, or Lee Priest. Invariably, when these pros are out of the gym, they dress casually, or if the event necessitates, they wear full business suits. The same holds true for the top female stars. Unless they're attending a fitness exhibition, most can be seen wearing track suits, dresses, gowns, or other attractive attire.

Such style sends a message that 'I am approachable.' The well-developed muscles are hidden and fashion has produced a metamorphosis from massive bodybuilder to friendly guy on the street (we have to admit, no amount of clothing will hide Vic Richards or Paul Dillett!).

Another point concerning pro male bodybuilders. What else do we notice about them? Facial hair? Most have none. Earrings? Once again, with few exceptions, most pros do not wear them. Overall hairstyles? Short, conservative, and not a hair out of place. This last point needs to be expanded on.

As hair length changes with the times, we cannot say for certain how long yours should be. The trend nowadays is for males to wear it short. Occasionally, one does come across a picture spread of a bodybuilder with long wild hair that flows over his shoulders, giving him a rock-star image of aggressive sexuality. Now this may be fine for a top pro making a living from the sport, but in the "real world", long hair still gets

Albert Beckles

Seriously though, try to match your appearance to whatever is considered socially acceptable. It's true there's much variation, but every society has definite no-no's.

The previous are some of the common features that most successful bodybuilders display. If you have any ambitions to become a pro, then you must remember that the powers that be are looking for a package that can be marketed beyond the bodybuilding community. Dressing conservatively and avoiding tattoo parlors is a step in the right direction.

John T. Molloy, author of *Dress for Success*, advises large men to avoid dressing too authoritatively. Their size can be intimidating to their smaller bosses. Ambitious executives and assistant managers should wear light colored suits (avoid pinstripes) and sport monochromatic, pastel ties. This is only applicable to white males. While bodybuilding is generally devoid of racism, the business world is not. Mr. Molloy advises minorities to dress very conservatively in order to be taken seriously. He goes on to advise African-Americans to avoid wearing Afros at all costs. From his interviews with African-American and white bosses, almost all said that they would not employ someone with an Afro.

AVOIDING THE BODYBUILDING RUT

"…First I must say that I am 100 percent devoted to the bodybuilding lifestyle. When I'm not in the gym, I'm home either reading the magazines, listening to audios or watching videos on this favorite lifestyle of mine. If I'm not doing that, what else is there but to talk about it for hours on end? My wife of five years started hollering at me the other day, and she was getting darned sick and tired of my stale old talk about bodybuilding. She told me to get a life. I don't see what the big deal is, but I haven't had a square meal in the last week or so because she still has a mad on. What should I do? Divorce her?…" **– Excerpt from a letter sent to the Ask Bob column in MuscleMag. Robert Kennedy agreed with the wife.**

"People are often taken aback that someone so big is also intellectual. Sometimes they're intimidated. They forget that physical development doesn't negate equivalent intellectual development."
– Jim Quinn, IFBB Pro Bodybuilder

As a final suggestion, don't become one of those people who eats, sleeps, and talks bodybuilding morning, noon, and night. Most people don't care how much you lift, or if you lift, or what you lift. So why bore them? If someone is genuinely interested in your workout, then they'll ask. In the meantime, watch CNN, read a newspaper every day, and make it a point to read one book a month that has no connection with bodybuilding. Bodybuilding is meant to enrich your life, not to become your life.

frowned upon. Try applying for a job sporting a pony tail. Employers start thinking such things as: (1) he really hates his parents, (2) how can I give this guy any responsibility when he can't even take care of his own hair, and (3) I thought the Woodstock reunion was last year.

CHAPTER THIRTY-SIX – THE BODYBUILDING SUBCULTURE

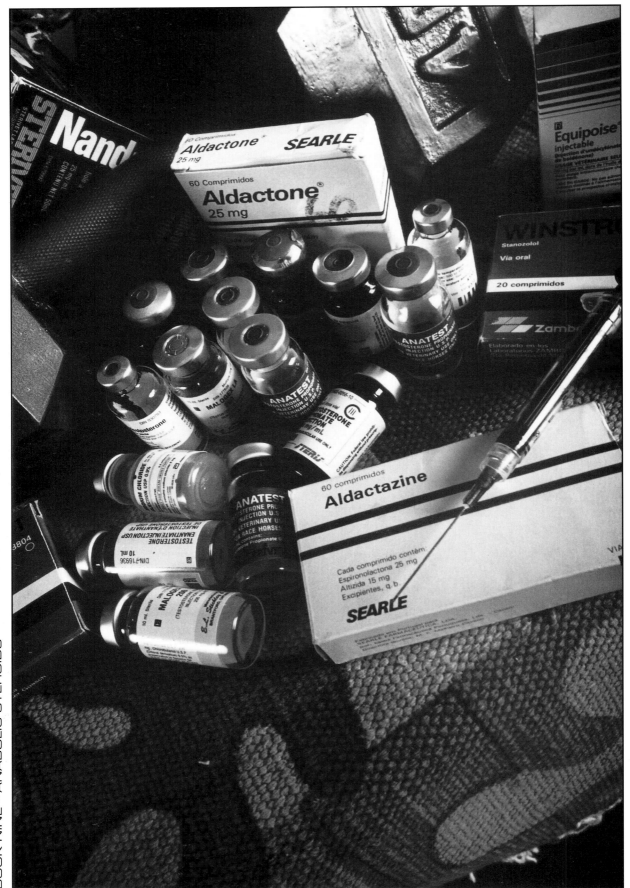

BOOK NINE

9

Anabolic Steroids

ANABOLIC STEROIDS

"…Steroids didn't make me a pro. I never took anything until I was 255 lbs. They should test the audience – 99 percent of guys in the audience are on steroids!"
– Mike Matarazzo, IFBB Pro Bodybuilder

"…they're always full of drugs and they take all this shit. When I tell them what small amounts I've taken, they don't believe me. The person asking is probably taking five times as much as I do. They figure, 'Well, he's five times bigger than me, so he must be using more.' There are so many guys in that gym who use drugs and look like shit! They're skinny, they hold water, and when they stop using them, they lose all their size. They don't believe that size comes from hard training, genetics, and the way you eat." **– Australia's Lee Priest**
IFBB Professional Bodybuilder

If there is one topic that *MuscleMag International* has not shied away from over the years, it's the issue of anabolic steroid use. While other magazines have ignored or distorted the issue, *MuscleMag* has consistently tried to give the readers a balanced perspective, given the public hunger for information about this fascinating class of drugs.

When Canadian sprinter, Ben Johnson, tested positive for anabolic steroids at the 1988 Seoul Olympics, he did more than fail a drug test. He set in motion a chain of events that put anabolic steroids on the front pages of every newspaper, worldwide. While anabolic steroid use has captured the attention of the public, many do not realize that steroids have been used in sports for the past sixty years. With the attention that the media has given steroids since 1988, one of the points they keep stressing is the danger anabolic steroids present to the user. Nine out of ten

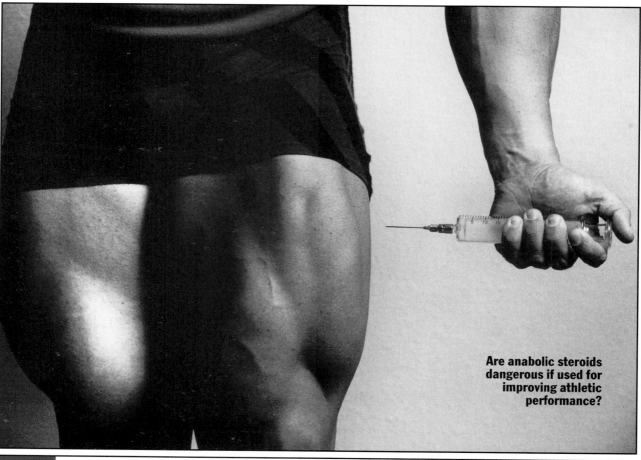

Are anabolic steroids dangerous if used for improving athletic performance?

steroid articles carry a list of horrendous side effects an athlete will experience when using these drugs. Are anabolic steroids dangerous if used for improving athletic performance? Probably not – if used by adults past their mid-twenties, while under medical supervision.

Before we look at the issue in more detail, let us make clear that we in no way condone steroid use. Like any drug, anabolic steroids, when taken without medical supervision, may produce serious side effects. This chapter is not meant to be a "how to" guide to steroid use. Instead, we look at the various facets of drug use in bodybuilding. It is impossible to understand a behavior without describing it. If after reading this chapter you decide not to use anabolic steroids, then one of the chapter's primary goals has been met.

THE DEVELOPMENT OF ANABOLIC STEROIDS

"...animal testicular substance injected into the human body does exert decided effects... relieving pain of obscure origin and promotion of bodily well-being."
– Dr. Leo L. Stanley, resident physician of San Quentin Prison, California, in 1920.
Dr. Stanley carried out testicle transplants using prisoners as both donors and recipients. When the human supply ran short, he substituted goat, deer, ram and boar testes. Surprisingly, his operations appear to have been successful.[1]

Anabolic steroids are the byproduct of over a century's research into hormones. Early researchers were not attempting to find substances which could improve athletic performance. Rather they were searching for the fountain of youth. In 1889, Dr. Brown-Sequard, upon injecting himself with an extract derived from dog testicles, claimed a rejuvenating effect (he was 72 at the time), especially when it came to satisfying his new, young wife. He was not taken seriously by his colleagues, his wife walked out, and he died five years later.[2]

To early researchers the failure of extracts meant that a new approach was needed. Therefore, in the first half of this century actual testicle transplants (supplied by recently executed prisoners and one generous volunteer who parted with one of his gonads) were carried out on sexually dysfunctional or older men. The operations worked and sexual potency was restored.[1] Not all surgeons met with such success, and these operations did not always increase lifespans. Indeed the main side effect of monkey testicle transplants was to give the human recipients monkey syphilis.[2]

Dr. Laqueur, a German pharmacologist, succeeded in isolating crystals from bull testicles in 1935. The chemistry of the crystals was determined by Dutch chemists and given the name testosterone. In the same year Swiss chemists succeeded in synthesizing testosterone from cholesterol.[3] Researchers discovered that some of these newly synthesized drugs, which

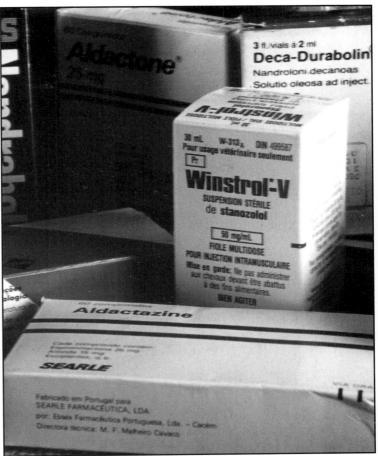

Steroids are the byproduct of science's quest for the fountain of youth.

belonged chemically to a class of compounds called steroids, could cause muscle-building (anabolic) effects. Therefore they were called anabolic steroids.[4] One of the researchers, Charles D. Kochakian, often referred to as the 'father of anabolic steroids', suggested the possibility that androgen therapy might restore protein tissue and stimulate growth in patients suffering from a wide range of disorders.[1] These drugs were clinically successful, and therefore became very profitable to market. German scientists held most of the patents for industrial synthesis, and formed a cartel to control production and drop in prices, in a manner similar to modern-day OPEC. The cartel was broken in 1938 when a British group of scientists developed a cheaper method of synthesis.[4]

THE NAZI CONNECTION

"The first abuse of steroids occurred shortly after the testosterone structure was isolated and manufactured in 1935. Nazi Germany was attempting to take over the world, and German scientists were aware that testosterone increased aggressive impulses in man. The Nazi hierarchy figured it would be a good idea to give German infantry men an added boost of aggressiveness via testosterone injections. While history does not record the results of this particular experiment, Germany did lose the war anyway." **– Jerry Brainum**
Muscle & Fitness *magazine*[5]

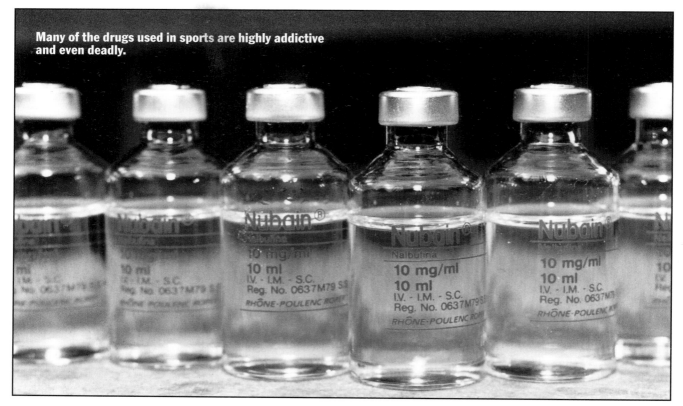

Many of the drugs used in sports are highly addictive and even deadly.

Part of the steroid folklore is that the Nazis gave these drugs to their troops before battle.[6] The idea was that German soldiers would become more aggressive and have no qualms about killing people. There is no evidence that these soldiers were ever given steroids. There are no first-hand accounts in literature, and no wartime and postwar (1945-1946) articles in major medical journals that mention the use of anabolics by German troops.

The rumor that the Germans used steroids could quite likely be a case of mistaken identity. A common stimulant used by both sides during World War II was amphetamine. One writer reports that up to 150 million amphetamine doses were used by the US and Great Britain during WW II. In addition, both the Germans and Japanese used this drug. Since amphetamines not only make the user alert but also more aggressive,[7] and because amphetamines were the drug of choice among athletes after the war (until anabolic steroids became available), it's easy to see how the rumor might have started.

Today this rumor is spread for economic reasons and as a scare tactic. By associating steroids with that ultimate form of evil, the Nazis, steroids become objects of revulsion in the eyes of the public. This serves the purposes of medical doctors opposed to drug use in sports, as well as manufacturers of diet supplements for athletes. While doctors are concerned about health, manufacturers are concerned about profits. Diet supplements are big business, worth hundreds of millions of dollars annually in North America alone. If steroids were legally available the industry would be hurt financially. Therefore supplements are often advertised as steroid replacers. Perpetuation of this myth as fact helps to prevent steroids from becoming socially acceptable and legal in the United States.

Historically, there was widespread use of anabolic steroids in Germany during World War II, but only after the Nazi concentration camps were liberated in 1944-1945. Emaciated survivors of the Holocaust were treated with anabolic steroids to help restore physical health. Ironically, the individuals who benefitted from the effects of anabolic steroids were not the Nazis, but their victims.

ANABOLIC STEROIDS MAKE THEIR DEBUT IN SPORTS

*"In using Rejuven I have been astounded by its vitalizing effect on the body. By using Rejuven it is possible to train much more intensely." – **Paavo Nurmi and Nils Engdahl, Swedish Olympic athletes in the 1920s and 1930s, in a 1931 advertisement for the German drug Rejuven (recently revealed to have contained a natural anabolic steroid).[8]***

The first use of anabolic steroids by athletes is alleged to have been in the 1930s. In 1931, four Swedish Olympic athletes admitted using the drug Rejuven as a training aid. Rejuven was a German manufactured drug that contained the anabolic agent testosterone (derived from a natural source). Athletes were unaware that they were taking an anabolic steroid at the time. There were no rules against anabolic steroid use because anabolic steroids as a class of drugs did not exist.[8] The use of Rejuven in sports appears to have been an isolated incident. Clinical studies associating these drugs with anabolic effects led to the suggestion in 1939 that anabolic steroids had potential for improving athletic performance.[9]

"I lost interest in fooling with IQs of that caliber."
– Dr. John Zeigler
(commenting on steroid users in his study)[6]

In 1954, Dr. John Zeigler, team physician to the American weightlifting team competing in Vienna, was told that Soviet weightlifters were receiving testosterone to boost their performance. It was apparent to Ziegler that the Soviets were using steroids on their female athletes as well. Because steroids have masculinizing effects, it became difficult at times to identify an athlete's gender.[6]

The first steroid use among bodybuilders in North America was in California. In 1958, successful bodybuilder Bill Pearl (Mr. America, Mr. Universe) was told by Arthur Jones (inventor of the Nautilus exercise machines) about a new "chemical" that the Soviets were using. This aroused his curiosity and he began to do some research on his own. At the University of California, a veterinarian informed Pearl about the anabolic steroid, Nilivar. This drug was used to promote strength and growth in cattle. Pearl took this drug for three months and gained 25 pounds of muscle mass. He also experienced a dramatic increase in strength.[10]

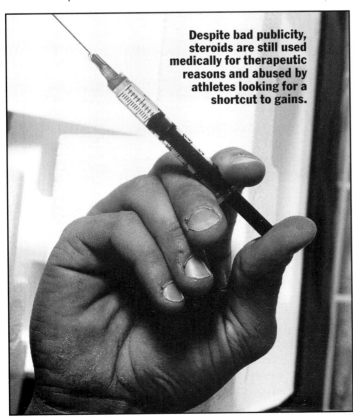

Despite bad publicity, steroids are still used medically for therapeutic reasons and abused by athletes looking for a shortcut to gains.

North America's first medically supervised studies of anabolic steroids and their effects on athletic performance were carried out by Dr. Ziegler in California, in 1959. The drug used was Dianabol, and subjects reported tremendous gains in strength and size while using the steroid. However, Ziegler found that when he substituted a placebo (a medically non-active substance) for the drug, bodybuilders reported the same results. He terminated the study when he learned that some of the bodybuilders were taking up to 20 times the recommended dosage.[6]

WHAT ARE ANABOLIC STEROIDS?

"I wouldn't know what a steroid looked like. If I want to pump up, I'll drink a case of beer."

"...So what you're saying to America's kids is, don't take steroids, drink beer?"

"Well, no." **– Art Donovan, NFL veteran**
(discussing the finer points of professional football with late-night talk show host David Letterman)[11]

"I went from 190 pounds to 200 by eating a lot, and then I went up to about 300 pounds from the steroids."
– Lyle Alzado, NFL veteran[12]

Now that you've been given a brief introduction to anabolic steroids, the next step is to look at the drug's underlying pharmacology. Anabolic steroids are synthetic substances which have actions similar to those of the naturally occurring hormone, testosterone. Testosterone has masculinizing properties (androgenic effects) that are responsible for the development of the male sex organs and secondary sex characteristics (such as facial hair, deepened voice, etc.). These drugs were designed to have the high anabolic activity of testosterone while minimizing its androgenic properties. Since complete dissociation of anabolic and androgenic effects is not possible, many of the actions of anabolic steroids are similar to those of male sex hormones. Furthermore, testosterone receptors in the body are tricked by the similar molecular structure of anabolic steroids, hence steroids are able to mimic testosterone. From a biochemical point of view, steroids cause the body to retain increased amounts of nitrogen, calcium, sodium, potassium, chloride and phosphate ions. This results in an increase in skeletal weight, water retention, and of importance to bodybuilders, an increase in muscle tissue.

THERAPEUTIC USES

Anabolic agents are usually prescribed, in conjunction with an adequate diet, for conditions characterized by protein and bone wasting. They are administered for medical conditions such as: osteoporosis (degeneration of the bone from calcium loss); crush-fractures due to corticosteroid

The late NFL veteran Lyle Alzado and Raye Hollitt.

treatment; the alleviation of low backache after menopause; during post-operative recovery; during convalescence after chronic illness; and for the treatment of pain from inoperable breast cancer. When given in conjunction with a high-calorie/low-protein diet, they may be of value in the treatment of glomerularnephritis (kidney inflammation). They are also used to prevent extensive nitrogen loss after severe burns and may be used to treat cases of retarded growth in children.[13]

ROUTES OF ADMINISTRATION

The two most commonly used methods of taking anabolic steroids are orally and by intramuscular injection (i.m). Less common methods of taking steroids are sublingually (absorption across the mucosa under the tongue), subcutaneous implantation (under the skin) of drug pellets, and transdermally (the drug is dissolved in a medium which can be absorbed through the skin). Since reunification, it was revealed that the East Germans developed an anabolic steroid nasal spray. It was developed for the 1988 Olympics, and traces of its use would disappear after three days.[14]

MECHANISM OF DRUG ACTION

"I played against a lot of guys that I know for a fact were using steroids. I'd play them one year and the next year they'd come back 15 pounds heavier, stronger and they looked different. They played better and hit harder.

That was one piece of the pie in my decision... I will do anything to become the best lineman in the NFL... if they (NFL) don't like it, screw them. This is a business. They're not naive to the situation."
— **David Cadigan, the New York Jets lineman**[15]

Most drugs interact in a specific manner with target sites in biological systems. Such sites are pharmacologically defined as what is called a drug-receptor complex. This complex initiates a series of chemical reactions, the ultimate result of which is a biological response. These responses are graded according to the amount of drug administered.[16] For example, two athletes taking the same dosage of anabolic steroids, all other things (training, nutrition) being equal, may experience differing levels of anabolic effects. The most likely explanation for this is genetics. It has been suggested that some athletes may possess more receptors for a particular drug.

DRUG DOSAGES

Two types of drug dosage will be considered in this section. The therapeutic dosage is what's used as a treatment for a particular medical problem. The other type of dosage is what we will refer to as the "gym dose". This is the amount of steroid reportedly used by athletes to enhance performance. This dose will be expressed either as a dosage (in milligrams or international units), or as a percentage of the therapeutic dose (for purposes of comparison).[17, 18]

Dr. Fred Hatfield, steroid authority and champion powerlifter, states that the maximum dosage of steroids considered beneficial is one milligram per kilogram of bodyweight each day. He claims that dosages beyond this amount increase the risk/benefit ratio. The risks simply start outweighing the benefits.[19] Many of the adverse effects of anabolic steroids are dose-related; therefore the lower the dose, the less likely that side effects will occur.

A lethal dose (the drug dosage that causes mortality in 50 percent of cases) has not been established for anabolic steroids. To put this into perspective, if a person was given a choice between rapidly ingesting a bottle of aspirin, a bottle of anabolic steroids, or a 40 ouncer of alcohol, only the bottle of steroids would not be life-threatening.

ORALS

Physicians and athletes agree that orally administered steroids are more taxing on the liver than their injectable counterparts. Oral steroids have been modified to increase their absorption rate and lifespan. They are more likely to become concentrated in the liver than injectables.

An orally administered drug must first pass through the digestive system, where a high percentage of it will be deactivated before it can enter the bloodstream. Before such a drug can enter general circulation it must first pass through the liver, where more of the drug will be deactivated. With each pass through the circulatory system, more of the circulating drug is metabolized and deactivated. Some athletes experience side effects such as stomach upset, headache, nausea and lack of concentration when they take orals.[18] These side effects can be avoided by using injectables.

INJECTABLES

"I had injected so much that a few years ago a plastic surgeon operated on my butt. I had these lumps under my skin from where the needles went in. He went in and removed one ball-sized mass of tissue and then found a bigger one underneath." **– Lyle Alzado (describing the surgical removal of lumps of scar tissue which were the result of years of steroid injections at the same site)[12]**

The other popular route of administration of steroids is via intramuscular injection (i.m.). There are two types of injectables: water-based and oil-based. This simply means that the steroid is dissolved or suspended in a liquid medium such as water or oil. Injectables diffuse from the muscle into the bloodstream in a slow and steady fashion. As a result, the drug can circulate throughout the body before reaching the liver where it will be deactivated. Since the circulating drug concentration will be small, relative to the amount injected, there will not be an accumulation of

high concentrations of the drug in the liver. Injectables, however, create new problems for the athlete. A hypodermic needle must be used to administer the drug, and the procedure of injecting a drug into one's own body is no simple task. The needle must be the correct length for an intramuscular injection – approximately one and a half inches is the accepted standard. Anything less is not long enough unless the individual is extremely lean. The area of injection is generally determined by personal choice. Since the injection is intramuscular (into a muscle) and not intravenous (into a vein), athletes report that the best areas for self-injection are the thighs (quadriceps) and the buttocks (gluteus maximus). The buttocks, having fewer nerve endings than the thighs, are a less painful site of injection, but much harder to reach. Conversely the thighs are a more painful site of injection, but are easier to reach.

The use of needles is an acquired skill that should only be attempted after instruction from a medical professional, such as a doctor or nurse. Pushing a needle into the skin may seem a simple task, but there are dangers. Without knowledge of the body's anatomy, an artery, vein or nerve may be hit. A damaged nerve can cause partial loss of sensation or movement. Another important factor is the risk of infection. Any time you break the body's protective layer (skin) you are greatly increasing the likelihood of infection. Physicians with the US Olympic Committee Drug

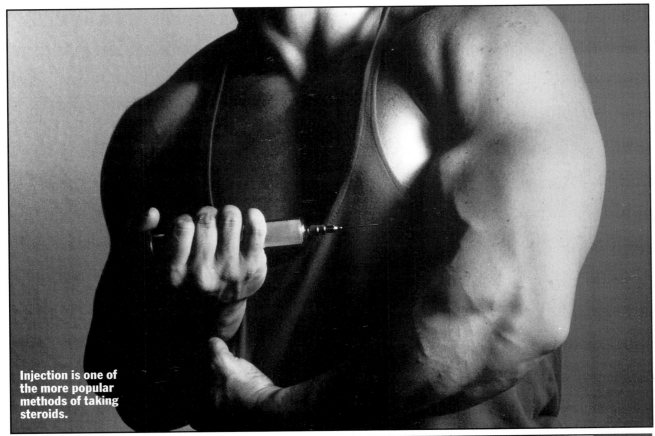

Injection is one of the more popular methods of taking steroids.

Control Program reported the case of a male bodybuilder who became infected with the AIDS virus after sharing a needle for steroid injections with a fellow bodybuilder 60 times over two and a half years. During this period the needle was kept on a locker shelf and never cleaned. Four months prior to seeking medical attention, the patient discovered his friend was homosexual, had developed AIDS related symptoms, and was later diagnosed with AIDS. The patient, who was heterosexual, had been married for five years, and had no extramarital affairs. The examining physicians ruled out every other means by which the individual could have contracted the AIDS virus. The physicians, therefore, concluded that the infection was due to the sharing of an unsterilized needle, which was used to inject anabolic steroids.[20]

OIL-BASED AND WATER-BASED INJECTABLES

Injectable anabolic steroids are found in two types of medium: oil and water. The oil medium is frequently sesame seed or cotton seed. Many anabolic steroids are relatively water insoluble, and most water-based steroids are in fact suspensions. A suspension is basically a steroid powder which has been so finely ground that the crystal size is small enough to pass through a regular gauge needle without clogging. The powder, once ground up is mixed with sterile water. If left to settle the crystals fall to the bottom of the vial. Shaking the vial resuspends the crystals.[21]

DRUG TERMINOLOGY IN THE GYM

When an athlete uses more than one steroid at a time, that particular group of steroids is referred to as a "stack". The practice of taking more than one steroid at a time is referred to as "stacking". The stack may be composed of both orals and injectables, as well as nonsteroid drugs, provided that the purpose of taking the nonsteroid drug is to enhance the positive effect of the steroids, or to help prevent side effects from the steroids. Stacking, however, may increase the likelihood of problems because unknown drug interactions may lead to side effects. Some athletes throw caution to the wind and take as many steroids at one time as they can obtain; this practice is known as "shotgunning".

The practice of alternating periods of steroid use with periods of abstinence is referred to as "cycling". The purpose of alternating a period of time during which the athlete is using steroids with a period of abstinence is to allow the body's depressed natural hormone levels to return to their presteroid state. Another reason for an athlete entering a period of abstinence would be to pass a drug test.

BOGUS DRUGS ON THE BLACK MARKET

"I honestly believe that if I'd told people back then that rat manure would make them stronger, they'd have eaten rat manure." **– Dr. John Zeigler (commenting on the willingness of athletes to try anything to improve performance)**[22]

The majority of athletes obtain their steroids from illegal or black market sources. There are basically two types of bogus (fake) steroids on the black market. The

Because of legal resitrictions many steroids are sold on the black market.

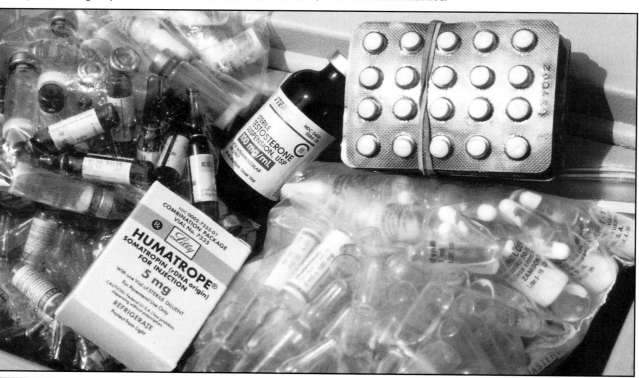

first type is not bogus in the usual sense, but rather semibogus. They are real anabolic steroids, but they have fake labels, and the dosages listed are usually incorrect. These drugs are not manufactured by licensed pharmaceutical companies. Steroid users are well aware of this, but insist that as long as a drug works, and is easily obtainable, they are not concerned.

The second group of bogus drugs are fake in every sense of the word. For example, users have reported athletes buying bottles of clear liquids (such as distilled water) from other athletes. These bottles have no labels and are often not the type of bottle normally associated with the packaging of the drug.

A LIST OF ANABOLIC STEROIDS

(Gym dose usually given as a percentage of therapeutic dose).

ORALS:

Trade Name: **Winstrol**
Generic Name: stanazolol
Tablet Size: 2 mg
Therapeutic Dose: 6 mg per day
Therapeutic Use: Angiodema
Gym Dose: 50 to 700 percent

This drug is considered to be a weak steroid by most athletes. When combined with Maxibolin, however, it has been reported by athletes to be one of the more potent oral stacks.[18,23] Charlie Francis, Ben Johnson's former coach, claimed that this drug was used sparingly because of its tendency to make sprinters stiff.[21] This drug was popular among athletes because up until 1987 there was no effective drug test for the metabolites of Stanazolol (that year, a test for the metabolites of Stanazolol was implemented).

Trade Name: **Maxibolin**
Generic Name: ethylestrenol
Tablet Size: 2 mg, also available in liquid form
Therapeutic Dose: 4-8 mg per day
Therapeutic Use: Antirheumatic
Gym Dose: 150 to 400 percent

Maxibolin is a progesterone-based steroid. Thus, while it acts like a male hormone it is in fact a female hormone.

Trade Name: **Dianabol**
Generic Name: methandrostenolone, methandienone
Tablet Size: 2.5 and 5 mg
Therapeutic Dose: 5 mg per day
Therapeutic Use: Post-menopausal osteoporosis
Gym Dose: 50 to 800 percent

One of the most commonly used steroids, it is known as the steroid for "beginners". It can be considered to be an instant gratification drug because individuals who use it report dramatic and rapid gains in size and strength[23]. The brand produced under the trade name Dianabol is no longer manufactured, but out of habit, bodybuilders continue to refer to the generic as Dianabol.

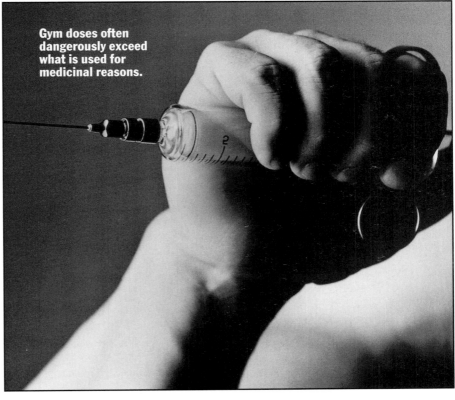

Gym doses often dangerously exceed what is used for medicinal reasons.

Trade Name: **Nilevar**
Generic Name: norethandrolone
Therapeutic Dose: 10 mg per day[24]
Therapeutic Use: A veterinary drug, used for size and strength in cattle.
Gym Dose: 300 percent

The company (Searle) that originally marketed this drug replaced it with Anavar, which reportedly has fewer androgenic properties.

Trade Name: **Anavar**
Generic Name: oxandrolone
Tablet Size: 2.5 mg
Therapeutic Dose: 5-10 mg per day
Therapeutic Use: Antiosteoporotic
Gym Dose: 250 to 350 percent

Anavar is considered by bodybuilders to be one of the milder steroids.[18] It tends to be used primarily for increasing strength and promoting muscle density rather than increasing mass.[23] It is very popular with women because of its low androgenic effects.[25] Users report that they have to take at least 3 tablets (7.5 mg) per 100 lbs. of bodyweight to get the desired effect.[23] In recent years, Anavar has become one of the more commonly faked steroids on the black market.[23]

Trade Name: **Primobolan**
Generic Name: methenolone
Tablet Size: 5, 25 and 50 mg
Therapeutic Dose: 10-20 mg per day
Therapeutic Use: Wound healing
Gym Dose: 50 to 380 percent

Bodybuilders consider Primobolan to be one of the best orals for precompetition training. Users find that it has excellent muscle-sparing properties while they are on strict diets.[23] Because it is low in androgenic effects it is considered to be one of the safest orals for use by females.[25]

Trade Name: **Halotestin**
Generic Name: fluoxymesterone
Tablet Size: 2, 5 and 10 mg
Therapeutic Dose: 2-30 mg per day
Therapeutic Use: Endocrine deficiency
Gym Dose: 100 to 175 percent

This drug should be avoided by female bodybuilders as it has very high androgenic effects.[25]

Trade Names: **Anadrol-50**
Generic Name: oxymetholone
Tablet Size: 5, 10 and 50 mg
Therapeutic Dose: 5 mg per day
Therapeutic Use: Endocrine deficiency
Gym Dose: 500 to 1000 percent

This drug is considered to be a more potent anabolic than Dianabol.[18] Anadrol-50 is also highly androgenic and should be avoided by female bodybuilders.[25] The results are dramatic and quick although it does promote excessive water retention. Users also find that a high dosage is necessary to obtain results.[18]

Trade Name: **Metandren**
Generic Name: methyltesterone
Tablet Size: 5, 10 and 25 mg
Therapeutic Dose: 50 mg per day
Therapeutic Use: Endocrine deficiency
Gym Dose: 140 percent

This drug is taken sublingually and is both highly androgenic and anabolic, and should be avoided by

female bodybuilders.[25] Some users report a motivational "boost" from this drug because it promotes increased levels of aggression.

INJECTABLES:
(In all cases the injection is intramuscular.)

Trade Name: **Deca-Durabolin**
Generic Name: nandrolone decanoate
Therapeutic Dose: 50-100 mg every 3-4 weeks
Therapeutic Use: Antianemic
Gym Dose: 300 to 600 percent

Deca-Durabolin is one of the more commonly used injectables.[17] It is, however, one of the easiest to detect in a drug test. It can be traced as far back as 18 months from last use.

Trade Name: **Android**
Generic Name: testosterone
Therapeutic Dose: 50 mg, 3 x per week
Therapeutic Use: Endocrine deficiency
Gym Dose: 50 to 400 percent

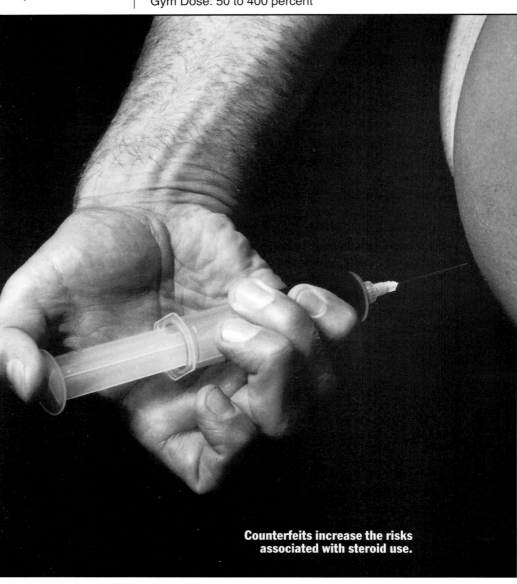

Counterfeits increase the risks associated with steroid use.

Trade Name: **Oreton, Perandren**
Generic Name: testosterone propionate
Therapeutic Dose: 25 mg, 2-4 x per week
(also available in 10 mg tablets; 1-2 tablets per day)
Therapeutic Use: Endocrine deficiency
Gym Dose: 50 to 400 percent

Trade Name: **Depo-Testosterone**
Generic Name: testosterone cypionate
Therapeutic Dose: 100-400 mg every 2-4 weeks
Therapeutic Use: Endocrine deficiency
Gym Dose: 50 to 400 percent

Trade Name: **Delatestrl**
Generic Name: testosterone enanthate
Therapeutic Dose: 100-400 mg every 2-4 weeks
Therapeutic Use: Endocrine deficiency
Gym Dose: 50 to 400 percent

All of these testosterone derivatives (Android, Oreton, Depo-Testosterone and Delatestrl) are highly anabolic, but they also rate among the highest for androgenic effects. For this reason, female body-builders should avoid them.[25] These drugs are among the cheapest to obtain on the black market; hence it is not a financial problem to use high doses.[18]

Trade Name: **Equipoise**
Generic Name: boldenone undecylenate
Therapeutic Dose: 0.125-0.5 mg/.45 kg/2 weeks
Therapeutic Use: Veterinary drug, used to treat debilitated horses.
Gym Dose: 800 percent

Trade Name: **Winstrol-V**
Generic Name: stanozolol
Therapeutic Dose: 25 mg/45 kg/wk or 5 ml/wk for an average size horse.
Therapeutic Use: Veterinary drug, used to treat debilitated animals.
Gym Dose: 400 percent

Winstrol-V is regular Winstrol (oral) suspended in a base of water. Bodybuilders report little water retention when using this drug.[23] It is a favorite for precompetition because it allows bodybuilders to become more muscular and make a lower weight class than they would have made without the drug.

Trade Name: **Teslac**
Generic Name: testolactone
Tablet Size: 50 and 250 mg, also available in aqueous solution.
Therapeutic Dose: Oral - 150 mg/day, i.m. 100 mg/week
Therapeutic Use: Endocrine deficiency
Gym Dose: 23 to 100 percent

Trade Name: **Durabolin**
Generic Name: nandrolone phenlypropionate
Therapeutic Dose: 50 to 100 mg per week
Therapeutic Use: Endocrine deficiency
Gym Dose: 100 to 200 percent

NONSTEROID DRUGS USED IN STACKS

"Incredible. But everybody is different. I knew a guy who spent $15,000 on it and only got pimples. I wake up pumped when I'm on it. Some guys refuse to come off GH."
– Mike Matarazzo
(commenting on growth hormone)

Trade Name: **Pregnyl**
Generic Name: human chorionic gonadotrophin (HCG)
Therapeutic Dose: 1000-4000 units 2-3 x per week
Therapeutic Use: To treat hypogonadism males
Gym Dose: 2 cc every other day

This drug, a hormone preparation, induces the testicles to boost production of testosterone. Recovery time between steroid cycles can be shortened, allowing the user to increase the number of cycles before a competition. There is no information available on how HCG use would affect a drug test such as the testosterone/epitestosterone ratio test.

Trade Name: **Humatrope, Protropin**
Generic Name: human growth hormone
Therapeutic Dose: 0.2 iu/kg/3 x per week
Therapeutic Use: Used to produce growth in children who are deficient in HGH.
Gym Dose: 100 percent

This drug is claimed by some steroid users to have phenomenal properties in terms of muscle growth. Its use is not widespread, principally because of its high cost. Therapeutic doses over one year would cost approximately $14,000 dollars. In 1990, during an attempted comeback (at the age of 41) as a professional football player, the late Lyle Alzado spent $4,000 for a 16-week cycle of HGH.[12] This drug is primarily used by the elite corps of bodybuilders and Olympic athletes.

Potential side effects range from enlargement of the bones in the face and extremities to hypertension (high blood pressure), arthritis and heart failure. There is also a possible cancer connection in people with acromegaly (a condition caused by an excess of HGH), or dwarfism (a condition caused by a lack of HGH) who are treated with HGH. There are at present no medical studies showing whether or not HGH is beneficial to athletic performance, or whether or not there are health risks for healthy athletes who use HGH.[26] At one time the only source of HGH was human cadavers, which carried the risk of Creutzfeldt-Jakob disease through viral contamination. (This disease causes neuronal degeneration of the central nervous system. The disease is caused by a virus that is resistant to the usual methods of sterilization. It can be transmitted through a blood transfusion. There is no effective therapy for this disease, and death will occur 12 to 16 months after the onset of symptoms.) In 1985, this risk was eliminated by advances in bioengineering which

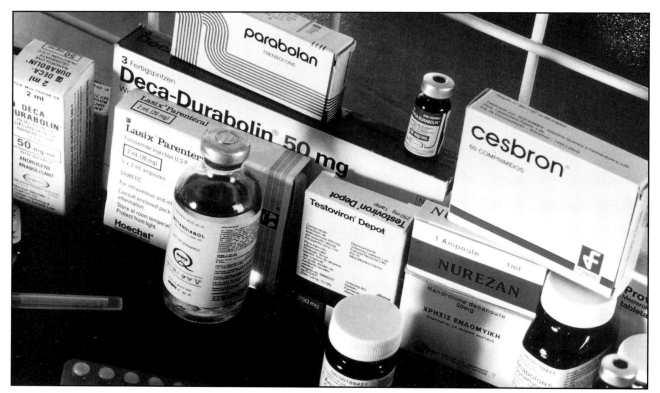

provided new sources of HGH.[12] At present there is no drug test available for HGH.

Trade Name: **Nolvadex, Nolvadex-D**
Generic Name: tamoxifen citrate
Tablet Size: 10 mg (Nolvadex), 20 mg (Nolvadex-D)
Therapeutic Dose: 10-20 mg/2x/day (Nolvadex)
20-40 mg/day (Nolvadex-D)
Therapeutic Use: Breast cancer
Gym Dose: 50 percent

Athletes include tamoxifen citrate in their stacks in the belief that it's antiestrogenic properties will prevent feminizing effects in males, and reduce bodyfat in both sexes. Its mechanism of action is to compete with estrogen for estrogen-receptor sites.

Attempts to minimize estrogen activity in a steroid user may be counterproductive to the objective of increasing muscle mass. Androgen receptors in skeletal muscle are induced by estrogens. This suggests that suppressing estrogen effects may reduce the opportunity for androgens to act at the desired target site, reducing the anabolic benefits of steroids. Some of the undesired effects of androgens may also be reduced by estrogen and are worsened by reduced estrogen action.[27]

STEROID CYCLES

"I go off for long periods of time and stay off as long as I can. I know guys who spent $40,000 to $50,000 getting ready for the Arnold Classic. I stay off as long as possible, and then I'm under the supervision of a very good doctor."
— Mike Matarazzo
(commenting on steroid use)

Alternating drug use with a period of abstinence allows the body's depressed natural hormone levels to return to their presteroid state.

Bodybuilders who use steroids plan their drug programs according to the season. As with training, there is both an off-season steroid cycle and a precompetition cycle. Bodybuilders must tailor their drug cycles in a manner that will enable them to pass drug tests at competitions where steroid use is banned. Five standard patterns of steroid use can be distinguished among bodybuilders. We have named these "straight-arrow," "cliff-hanger," and "ski-slope," "pyramid," and "noncyclic."

Straight-arrow Pattern
The "straight-arrow" pattern consists of a steroid stack in which the doses taken by the bodybuilder remain constant for each drug during the cycle. The addition of drugs after the start of the cycle does not change this designation, provided the drug added is taken at a constant dosage during the cycle. In one study, eight of the ten respondents reported using a straight-arrow pattern.[28]

Cycle A: 5 weeks
Weeks 1-5
Equipoise (i.m.) – 100mg/week
Anavar – 7.5mg/100 lbs/day
Primobolin – 100mg/day[25]

Cliff-hanger Pattern
The "cliff-hanger" pattern involves an overall increase in dosage during the cycle. This pattern would only be used during the off-season, as a bodybuilder would not

pass a drug test with such a high concentration of steroids in his/her system. The big disadvantage of this pattern is that the body's hormonal system is not given a chance to normalize at the end of the cycle. As a result, the bodybuilder often experiences problems with low sex drive, impotence, and a general lack of motivation. These symptoms are transitory and will disappear once the body's own hormonal system kicks back in, or the bodybuilder begins another cycle.

Cycle B: 10 weeks
Weeks 1-10
    Anavar – 12.5mg/day
Weeks 4-8
    Winstrol – 100mg/week
Weeks 8-10
    Winstrol – 200mg/week
Week 11
    All drugs stopped.[27]

Ski-slope Pattern
The "ski-slope" pattern of steroid use can be described as a stack in which steroid dosages decrease over the duration of the cycle. This pattern has an advantage over the other patterns, from a health perspective, because a decreasing dose pattern of steroid use limits the risk of taking the drugs. This pattern is seen in many bodybuilders during the precompetition phase of their training – the rationale being that this pattern will result in very low levels of drugs in the bodybuilders' systems near or at the time of a drug test.

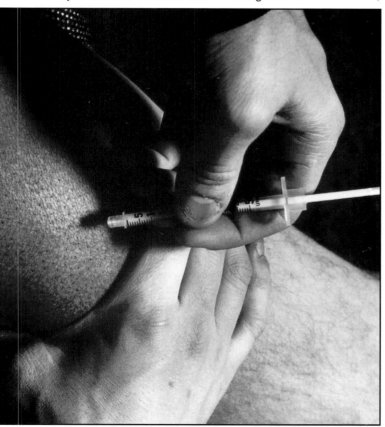

Cycle C: 14 weeks
Weeks 1-7
    Amount taken according to personal preference
Weeks 8-11
    Winstrol-V – 1 cc/3 days
Weeks 8-10
    Proviron – 2 tabs/day
Week 8
    Dianabol – 35 mg/day
Week 9
    Dianabol – 30 mg/day
Week 10
    Dianabol – 25 mg/day
Week 11
    Dianabol – 20 mg/day
Weeks 11-13
    Proviron – 1 tab/day
Week 12
    Dianabol – 10 mg/day
    Winstrol-V stopped
Week 13
    Dianabol – 5 mg/day
Week 14
    All drugs stopped.[23]

Pyramid Pattern
The "pyramid" pattern is characterized by a cycle that can be broken down into three consecutive phases. The first phase is one of increasing dosage, the second phase is the highest dosage reached, and the third phase is marked by a decreasing dosage. Once again, as with the "ski-slope" pattern, this pattern is favored as a precompetition cycle. Because it leaves low levels of drugs in the system, the bodybuilder has a better chance of passing a drug test.

Cycle D: 15 weeks
Weeks 1-8
    Primobolan (oral) – 100 mg/day
Weeks 1-2
    Winstrol (oral) – 4 mg/day
    Maxibolin (oral) – 4 mg/day
Weeks 3-5
    Winstrol – 6 mg/day
    Maxibolin – 6 mg/day
Weeks 6-10
    Winstrol – 4 mg/day
    Maxibolin – 4 mg/day
Weeks 8-14
    Primobolan – 50 mg/day
Weeks 11-12
    Winstrol – 2 mg/day
    Maxibolin – 2 mg/day
Week 15
    All drugs stopped.[23]

Drug cyles are carefully designed to help avoid detection or reduce negative side effects.

Noncyclic Use

"I'm convinced that my biggest mistake was never going off a cycle. According to the guys around the gym, if you go on steroids for six to eight weeks, then you're supposed to stop for the same number of weeks. Me, I'd be on the stuff for 10 or 12 weeks, and then I'd go off for only two, maybe three weeks, and I'd feel that was enough. It was addicting, mentally addicting. I just didn't feel strong unless I was taking something." **– The late NFL veteran Lyle Alzado (describing his steroid use)**[12]

Most steroid users alternate their steroid use with periods of abstinence. There are some bodybuilders who never stop taking drugs, remaining on steroids all year long! It's widely accepted among researchers and athletes that the likelihood of adverse effects increases with the length of time steroids are used.

It's also believed that the risk of adverse side effects can be reduced by taking small amounts of a few different steroids, rather than large doses of one, because each drug follows different metabolic pathways.[25] Conversely, the use of a variety of drugs at one time can produce a "cocktail effect", in which side effects result from drug interactions in the bodybuilder's system. The tendency among bodybuilders is not only to use a greater variety of drugs, but also to use higher dosages. This attitude that "more is better" has led some bodybuilders to abandon the four traditional patterns in favor of noncyclic use. We emphasize that the use of steroids for improving athletic performance or for cosmetic reasons is primarily a question of ethics. Any class of drugs poses risks to the user, but these risks can be minimized, and even eliminated with medical supervision.

PROFESSIONAL BODYBUILDING

"An athlete exists to excel. He breathes to excel. And his rationale is to do everything possible to be able to excel. A pro athlete makes his living from his sport, so it's no exaggeration to say that he believes he was put on earth to be the best athlete possible."
– Tom Platz, former IFBB Pro Bodybuilder[29]

"The pressure on those of us who were bordering on success became enormous. Men whom I had been competing against for years, and even beating on a good day, were suddenly making me look like a novice. Even worse, some of last year's novices were zooming past the nonsteroid campaigners, as though we'd given up the weights for boozing and debauchery."
– John Budd, IFBB Professional Bodybuilder[30]

Of all sports in which anabolic steroids are used, nowhere is it more prevalent than in the sport of bodybuilding. And a number of retired professional

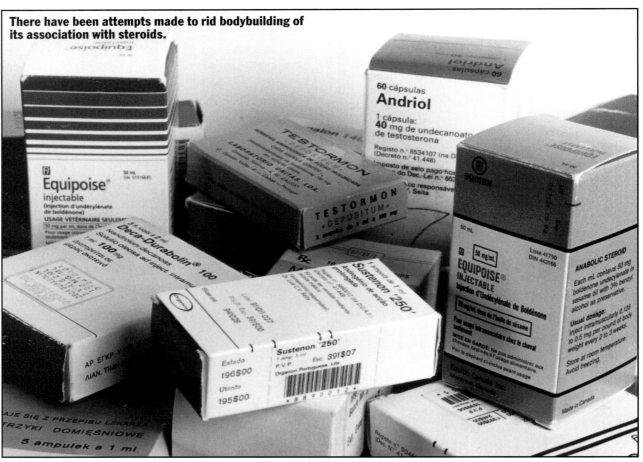

There have been attempts made to rid bodybuilding of its association with steroids.

bodybuilders (including Arnold Schwarzenegger, Tom Platz, and Mike Mentzer) have admitted to using steroids during their athletic careers.

Unlike most sports where steroid use usually starts when the athlete nears, or reaches the top, for the most part, bodybuilders begin much earlier. The majority of bodybuilders who use steroids are noncompetitive amateurs, in most cases falling between the ages of 15 and 25.

WHY BODYBUILDING?

"One of the biggest misconceptions is that you can build a pro-quality physique without steroids... that it just takes longer. People say, 'I won't take steroids. I'm willing to train harder for my muscles and I don't care if it takes five years longer.' The truth is that a hard-training bodybuilder who eats well and trains progressively hits a wall after a few years, and simply cannot get significantly bigger without getting fatter. I know dedicated bodybuilders who have been slogging away with regular high-quality training for 10, 15 and 20 years without gaining even a half-inch on their arms. Five years of all-out training will not give you the gains of a three-month steroid cycle. Sad but true."

– Robert Kennedy
MuscleMag International *founder and editor*

In bodybuilding, the desired physical qualities are large, well-defined muscles with the barest minimum of bodyfat. Anabolic steroids cause the body to increase the amount of tissue and to metabolize bodyfat. As a result, a bodybuilder can use these effects to his/her advantage. And because the public has become used to seeing huge athletes onstage, it's unlikely they would accept anything less. In other words, with each new standard set, there's no turning back. Once the Genie has been let out of the bottle it's difficult to send him back.

"More than positive. It was great, especially initially. The pay was super, we got fine treatment, and there wasn't a lot of work. All we had to do was train and stay in shape so we could show up in good condition for the contests. All of the business aspects – such as arranging schedules, getting airline tickets, and so on – were completely taken care of for us."

– Jim Quinn
IFBB Pro Bodybuilder
(commenting on the now defunct
WBF Bodybuilding Federation)

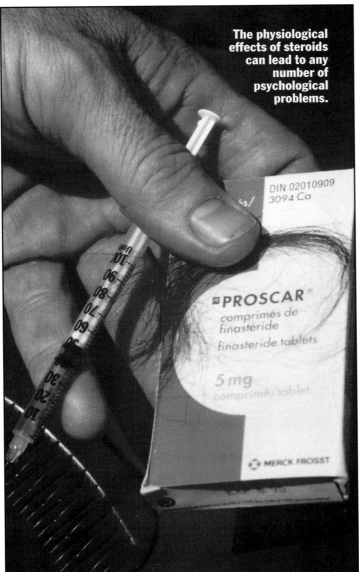

The physiological effects of steroids can lead to any number of psychological problems.

Most amateur bodybuilders will never be tested because they do not enter contests. All they want is to improve their physiques, and it's unlikely in the foreseeable future that anabolic steroid use will decline in the sport. There was a movement by the International Federation of Bodybuilders (IFBB) to rid the sport of drug use. The achieve this end, drug testing was introduced at the Amateur World Championships and some of the pro contests; the first being the Arnold Schwarzenegger Classic held in March, 1990. Four of the athletes, including the winner, Shawn Ray, were disqualified for testing positive for steroid use.

After the introduction of drug testing an interesting development took place. A number of top athletes 'jumped ship' and competed in contests held by the newly formed World Bodybuilding Federation (WBF), which was owned by the World Wrestling Federation (WWF). For a while, none of their contests were drug tested. But as soon as the authorities started leaning on the WWF owners, and drug testing was implemented, the quality of the competitors' physiques dropped drastically. The end result was a collapse of the WBF.

Once they realized that they were losing many of their top stars, the IFBB followed suit and quietly dropped drug testing from their contests.

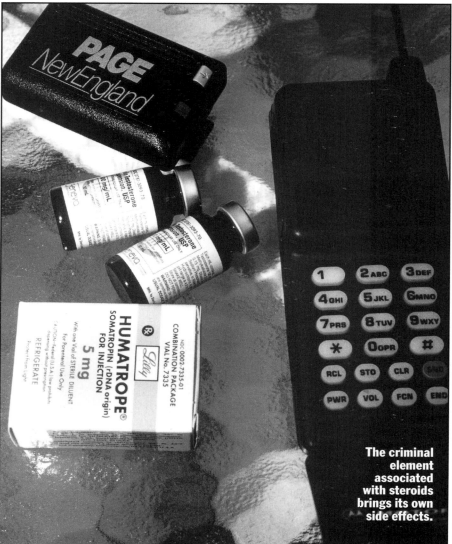

The criminal element associated with steroids brings its own side effects.

One of the prevailing beliefs about steroid users is that they are overly hostile and often the initiators of violent confrontations. While most users admit that their aggression levels rise while on a cycle, the issue of whether this increased aggression manifests itself in the form of physical violence is open to debate.

Anabolic steroids alone usually do not cause violence. Other factors are involved. For example, many steroid users take jobs as bouncers. Thus the opportunity for physical confrontation is much greater. So here we have one factor that is more situational than biochemical.

Another reason may be the individual's background to begin with. It's quite possible that someone who's naturally aggressive will have the condition compounded by steroids.

A third factor may be the individual's athletic pursuits. If the person is involved in aggressive sports, then the opportunity for violence is much greater. For example, some sports require physically aggressive athletes. Sports such as football and rugby are no places for the meek and mild.

A final and more plausible explanation for steroid use and aggression may have to do with the presence or absence of alcohol. In fact virtually every example put forward by antisteroid advocates involves heavy drinking by the user.

Alcohol has the power to release inhibitions, and can be a potentially dangerous drug for steroid users. They experience heightened levels of aggression, but most are able to cope with these feelings. Alcohol prevents the individual from inhibiting his/her hostility.

In one case it was claimed that anabolic steroid use was a contributing factor to a domestic dispute that resulted in homicide. A 32-year old amateur bodybuilder began using steroids three months before the murder. About four weeks prior to the crime he had become quarrelsome and began consuming increasing amounts of alcohol. On the night of the crime both he and his wife had been drinking heavily. He claimed to have snapped after listening to her talk about her infidelities. She was severely beaten and died later. While he had a history of episodes of drunken violence, there was no significant previous psychiatric or criminal history.[32]

BEHAVIORAL EFFECTS: AGGRESSION

"When Smith stepped onto the mat to face Sarkissian, his left ear was bandaged; it had been drained of blood seven times in two weeks. The three middle fingers of each hand were taped together to protect them; all had been broken at least three times. Two nights earlier a Bulgarian opponent had fractured Smith's nose, and a Mongolian had attempted to conquer him with an injury default ("He got on my leg and tried to rip it off and take it home," said Smith). But he wasn't complaining."

– A description of American wrestler and gold medal winner John Smith, and the sportsmanlike atmosphere of Olympic wrestling.[31]

"Yes, I have started a violent physical confrontation. For example, I've thrown knives, chairs, yelled at inanimate objects, and have lost my temper over stupid, silly things. The steroids were a definite contributing factor."
– Steroid user[28]

While steroid use was a possible contributing factor to this tragedy, the fact that the user had a history of abusing his wife indicates that this is simply a case of domestic violence escalating to murder. Unfortunately, this is a tragically common occurrence. The murder may well have happened even without the involvement of steroids. Therefore, given the history of violence in this case, one cannot make any solid conclusion as to whether there was a synergistic (combined) effect from alcohol and steroid use.

There are similar examples which don't need to be repeated here. Suffice to say that in the vast majority of cases it was the steroid user's abuse of alcohol, and previous history of violence, that most likely led to the incidents.[33]

ROID RAGE OR ROID BLAME?

"I miss the violence of the game."
– The late Lyle Alzado at the time a steroid user (answering why he wanted to return to the NFL, during an interview with Maria Schriver on her show Person to Person)

While increased aggression may be beneficial for some athletes, "roid rage" is a controversial side effect that has been used to explain outbursts of violent criminal behavior. Roid rage is defined as an uncontrollable physical outburst of anger and violence, and usually, but not always, of short duration. It's believed that roid rage is transitory, and disappears with cessation of steroid drug use.

The problem with validating roid rage is that the few examples cited in medical journals are all case studies. Further, they all involve individuals who are using roid rage as a legal defense. Invariably alcohol and a history of violence are the two common factors. These two factors are ignored because creative defense lawyers are trying to use any excuse to diminish their defendant's responsibility in the eyes of the law.

Another aspect to keep in mind is the media. There is nothing like a good roid rage case to attract viewers or sell tabloid papers. Unfortunately, because of the overexposure, most of the public starts believing that bodybuilders are all a bunch of walking psychotics!

Is roid rage a side effect of anabolic steroids? Is it possible that steroids make some individuals more volatile? Or is roid rage simply an imaginative legal defense? Time will tell.

BODYBUILDING PSYCHOSIS

Despite the name, bodybuilder's psychosis is not restricted to bodybuilders. Any psychosis can be described as a psychiatric condition in which the individual has made a break with reality and cannot be held responsible for his/her behavior. There have been cases of bodybuilders experi-

encing psychotic episodes during steroid use, but given the limited research it's difficult to establish whether the episodes were drug induced or not. Consider the following cases.

A 22-year-old construction worker and bodybuilder had been using steroids for four months. At that point he began to experience severe depression which gradually disappeared. It was replaced by the more alarming symptoms of paranoia and religious delusions. An extensive search of the individual's medical background failed to find any trace of prior symptoms of paranoia. To provide further evidence that the anabolic steroids were the contributing cause, all psychotic symptoms disappeared completely when steroid usage was terminated.[34]

Case two involves a 27-year-old professional who had been bodybuilding for a year prior to seeking professional help. Before his steroid use, he had a psychiatric evaluation, and it did not reveal any major dysfunctions. The examination did find that he periodically experienced episodes of depression alternating with hyperactivity. Two weeks prior to his next psychiatric evaluation, he started steroid use. Within two days he had begun to feel irritable and hyperactive, noting a decreasing need for sleep and an overall increase in energy levels. During the following week he began to feel "good all the time", and described how he

Roid rage provides the tabloids with the potent, saleable gossip their readers seek.

had "thoughts running around his head". He also experienced an abnormal need for food and sex. A tentative diagnosis of steroid-induced hypomania was made. (This is a bizarre diagnosis because mania is defined as an emotional state characterized by intense and unrealistic feelings of elation. Hypo means low; therefore hypomania might be defined as a mild case of mania. But if the case is mild, how can it be mania?). The symptoms disappeared three to four days after cessation of steroid use. He resumed his steroid use, and the symptoms reappeared.[35] It is clear in this case that there were underlying problems before steroid use was initiated. Steroid use may simply have unmasked underlying psychiatric problems.

Case three concerns a 17-year-old high school student who had taken up bodybuilding because he was being picked on by his peers. A short time later he expressed confusion, paranoid delusions, heard voices, and was diagnosed as being a paranoid schizophrenic. Placed on antipsychotic medication, his symptoms soon disappeared. A year later he discontinued his medication and the symptoms returned. Despite restarting the medication and increasing the dosage, his condition could not be brought under control, and he required hospitalization. He then informed his doctor that he'd been using anabolic steroids. After the steroids were discontinued his symptoms subsided and he was discharged.[36]

As in the previous case, it's possible that an underlying psychiatric condition was lurking. Schizophrenia

Despite the claims of some bodybuilders, addiction to steroids is a real possibility.

often strikes its victims in adolescence, and it's possible that this disease's appearance coinciding with steroid use was a coincidence. An improvement in the 17-year-old's symptoms was seen whenever steroid use was stopped.

From the previous examples, it appears that steroids may aggravate or bring to the surface underlying psychiatric conditions. Some of the examples cited show that steroids may produce a drug-induced psychosis. Users may also have underlying conditions, such as schizophrenia, aggravated by steroid use. Factors such as drug interactions and diet may also influence whether or not a psychosis is produced. Bodybuilder's psychosis is vary rare, and could probably be avoided if steroid use is carried out under medical supervision. Because steroids have such a negative reputation there is a tendency for the scientific community to interpret any unexplained bizarre behavior in steroid users as being caused by steroids. It's not uncommon to find cases in medical literature labeled as "bodybuilder's psychosis," which in reality can be explained, simply, as examples of poor judgement.

ADDICTION

"As I said, I kept taking the stuff after retiring from the Raiders in 1985. I couldn't stand the thought of being weak. I tried to taper down. Mostly I took low dosages of Anavar and Equipoise. I thought it was stuff that would help me. But I know now I should have gone off it. I stayed too big, too mean." **– Lyle Alzado**
NFL veteran (explaining why he continued using steroids after his retirement)[12]

Why do athletes continue to use steroids after they have stopped competing? If the reason for their use has been discontinued, why not give up the drugs as well? A possible answer may lie in psychiatry. A few studies have suggested that anabolic steroids may be addictive. The World Health Organization defines addiction as a state of periodic or chronic intoxification, detrimental to the individual and to society, produced by the repeated consumption of a drug (natural or synthetic). The three main characteristics are: (1) an overpowering desire to continue taking the drug and to obtain it by any means; (2) a tendency to increase the dosage as usage continues; and (3) a psychological or physiological dependence on the effects of the drug.

Many professionals define addiction as the continuing condition whereby the body's chemical functioning has altered in such a way that its normal state is now the drug state. For the body to maintain normal functioning, the drug must be present. To make matters worse, the user's body develops tolerance to the drug. Tolerance is the condition whereby the body becomes accustomed to a certain drug dosage, and increasing amounts of the drug must be taken in order for the same effect to be produced. If the user's body is suddenly deprived of the drug, the user will undergo withdrawal symptoms. These symptoms are in the form of psychological and physiological disturbances caused by the body trying to readjust to the predrug state. Not all addictive drugs produce physical dependence. For this reason psychiatrists and psychologists have come up with the term psychological dependence, to describe the condition of psychological need for a drug.[37] The following is a good example.

A 24-year-old male weightlifter, who was admitted to a psychiatric emergency room, complained of depression and increased outbursts of anger which he felt were caused by his anabolic steroid use. The previous night he had experienced suicidal thoughts of crashing his car. He requested professional help because he felt controlled by the drugs and was unable to stop using them on his own. The patient's history revealed that he was symptom free for the first three months of his use, as he was cycling the drugs under the supervision of his physician. His desire to increase his performance caused him to stop the cycling program and regular visits to the physician. For the next nine months he took heavy doses of five different steroids.

ANABOLIC STEROIDS IN SPORT AND EXERCISE

Steroid Myths:
The responsible use of anabolic steroids

Both supporters and opponents of steroid use have been trying to "educate" the public.

In an evaluation of the patient it was found that six of the criteria set down in a diagnostic manual (DSM III) for substance dependence were met:
1. The substances were taken over a longer period of time than was initially intended.
2. He was unsuccessful in his efforts to cut down on his use.
3. He continued to use the steroids despite his knowledge that he was having emotional and marital problems related to their use.
4. He had built up tolerance to the drugs as indicated by the supertherapeutic doses taken.
5. He experienced the withdrawal symptoms of headaches, fatigue, psychomotor retardation and depression.
6. He regularly took these substances to avoid withdrawal symptoms.[38]

DEPRESSION

Depression is characterized by a withdrawal of interest in normal activities. In severe depression, the individual has low self-esteem, low libido, poor hygiene, insomnia, and loss of appetite. The intensity of the depression depends on a number of factors, one of which is physiological. If the user was on steroids for a long period of time, his/her depression is likely to be more severe than for an individual on a short drug cycle upon cessation of drug use.

How the individual comes off the steroid cycle is also important. If the user quits "cold turkey" (abruptly, without using a declining dosage) the user is creating a tremendous shock to his/her system, possibly resulting in severe depression due to: low levels of circulating hormone, high levels of circulating cortisol (which is correlated with the occurrence of depression), and grief over loss of mass. Conversely, an individual who gradually decreases the dosage towards the end of the cycle is allowing his/her system to adjust its hormone levels back to presteroid levels. This gives the individual time to adjust to the decrease in size.

SUICIDE

From what is known about the behavioral effects of these drugs, it is possible that they may have played a role in some suicides. The behavioral effects of steroids can be compounded by the method in which they are obtained. Adults have provided steroids to teens in exchange for sexual services.[39] Prostitution, whether for drugs or money, has a devastating effect on any teenager's self-esteem. The result is a witch's brew of conflicting emotions, behavioral effects, and low self-esteem combining to create a foundation that could lead to tragedy.

Many teenagers are obsessed with their body image. A teen who takes steroids to improve this image generally does not have the maturity to deal with the regressive physiological change upon cessation of the steroid cycle. The problems associated with reverse anorexia compound this situation. Some teenagers have been known to kill themselves for what, to adults, would seem to be the most trivial of reasons. For example, some have committed suicide because of mild cases of acne. Grief over loss of mass, and hence body image may be too much for some teenagers to deal with. Having seen the behavioral problems that adults may experience while on these drugs, it's clear that steroids are potentially dangerous for teenagers to use.

In the case of an athlete in a state of severe depression, the ability to think rationally is impaired. While rare, it's possible for the steroid-using athlete to experience suicidal thoughts.[38] If a bodybuilder is warned about potential behavioral side effects then the individual can recognize them in their early stages, and seek medical attention. It's essential for the bodybuilder to communicate with his/her physician, so that tragedy can be prevented.

"It's not possible to compete on the pro level of men's or women's bodybuilding without the use of anabolic steroids." — **Lee Labrada, retired pro bodybuilder (in an interview with Muscular Development *magazine*)**

Why have the psychiatric effects previously discussed rarely been reported in studies of medically supervised steroid use by athletes? One reason may be that the doses of anabolic steroids routinely used in the gym are frequently 10 to 100 times higher than those used in medical studies. Additionally, the common practice of stacking as many as five or six different types of drugs may be responsible for psychiatric effects that might not be seen if only one or two drugs were used.[34]

There is a complicating factor in studying any practice that is illegal or considered distasteful by the majority. Because of fear of persecution or public ridicule, these behaviors are practiced discreetly, and are for the most part known only by the participants. Only a select few are given glimpses of these subcultures. In the case of steroid use, few athletes are willing to reveal their secret to a physician. Hence, the psychiatric effects of steroids, although perhaps often witnessed, may rarely be identified as such by professionals.

Similarly, the psychiatric effects of anabolic steroids cannot be easily studied in the laboratory. Only by observing the effects of these drugs in natural settings, in the doses and combinations actually used by athletes, are we likely to understand them better.

PHYSIOLOGICAL EFFECTS

"As used by most athletes, the side effects of anabolic steroids are minimal. Even in those using large doses for prolonged periods of time, clinical evidence shows that any side effects are reversible."
— *Mauro DiPasquale, M.D.*[40]

There are many myths surrounding steroids and their effects, not the least of which is that steroids are always physically harmful. The key to the public's negative perception is the media's portrayal of steroids on physical health: liver cancer, sterility, and heart failure. But on what evidence are these claims based? Given the number of bodybuilders using steroids, why hasn't there been an epidemic of deaths? Is it possible that what the media has been reporting is wrong? Upon closer examination of the facts, a different story from the one presented usually emerges. This section examines how steroids affect physical development, and the side effects associated with steroid use are also discussed.

ANABOLIC EFFECT

"Guys who take steroids are healthier and more health conscious than the general population. Steroid users aren't suicidal; they're adventurers who think for themselves and who want to accomplish something noble before they are buried and become worm food. And isn't that how we all end up? As Jim Morrison put it, 'Nobody here gets out alive.'"
— *"Craig," a steroid dealer*[41]

Anabolic steroids, by mimicking the action of testosterone, increase muscle size and strength in people engaged in weight-training programs. Both testosterone and anabolic steroids bind to the androgen receptors found in the cytoplasmic fluid surrounding the nucleus of the body's cells. This binding signals the nucleus to begin protein-building activity which produces an increase in muscle size and strength. During puberty, testosterone causes the male to develop what is known as the "male physique". The male becomes bigger, stronger, and faster in a very short period of time. After puberty, the body normalizes itself to the circulating levels of testosterone and growth stabilizes. When people use steroids they are essentially forcing their bodies to go through puberty again. It's obvious why athletes would use a synthetic drug to achieve the same effects.

ANABOLIC TO ANDROGENIC RATIO

"If something about the human body disgusts you, complain to the manufacturer."
– Comic Lenny Bruce

Testosterone also has androgenic effects on the human body. These include: acne, increased growth of facial and body hair, loss of scalp hair, and a deepened voice. The majority of steroid users will experience these androgenic effects to some degree, and with the exception of acne scarring and baldness, all are usually transitory and will disappear after cessation of drug use. Steroids were developed to maximize the anabolic effects and minimalize the androgenic effects. Each drug has a ratio of anabolic to androgenic effects which describes the relative strengths and risks of the drug. A drug with a high, or positive, ratio is one in which the anabolic effects are higher than the androgenic. This positive ratio is desirable as it produces the greatest benefit with a minimum of risk. Conversely, a drug with a low, or negative, ratio should be avoided.

STEROIDS AS A BODYFAT METABOLIZER

Steroids have the ability to burn off fatty tissue without an accompanying loss in muscle mass. This allows bodybuilders who use steroids to fast before competition without losing muscle mass. In fact many bodybuilders rely as much on the drugs' fat-burning properties as muscle-building properties.

NET GAIN VERSUS NET LOSS

A popular misconception is that steroid-using athletes are like balloons, in that they inflate when on steroids, and completely deflate when they cease using drugs. It's true, most of the muscle mass gained will be lost after the drug leaves the athlete's system. The loss of mass will also be accompanied by a loss of strength. The reason is that once the drug leaves the athlete's system, the body's natural hormone level is not high enough to maintain the gains made while on the drug. There will, however, be

a net gain of muscle mass and strength, the amount of which depends on factors such as a person's genetics, whether they continue training, the diet followed, and the drugs used.

BRAIN CANCER

Cancer ranks second nationally (US and Canada) as a cause of death – only heart disease takes more lives. But what is cancer? In reality, cancer is not a single disease, but many. The human body contains more than one hundred different types of cells, each of which can malfunction and produce a characteristic type of cancer. When these cells malfunction and duplicate faster than normal, a growth of tissue called a tumor is produced. A tumor may be benign (harmless) and will not spread to other tissues. Or, it may be malignant (harmful) and may spread throughout the body producing secondary tumors. The spread of disease from one part of the body to another unrelated to it is called metastasis. Often it is the secondary cancer which is diagnosed, while the primary cancer may never be found.

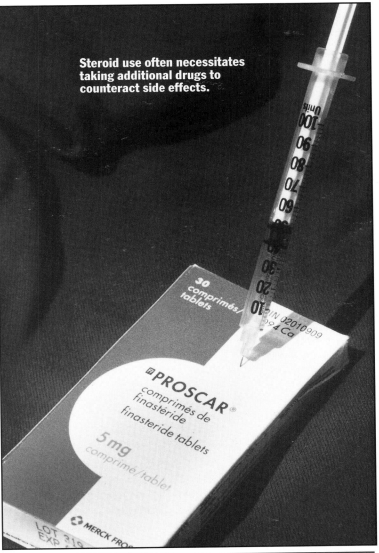

Steroid use often necessitates taking additional drugs to counteract side effects.

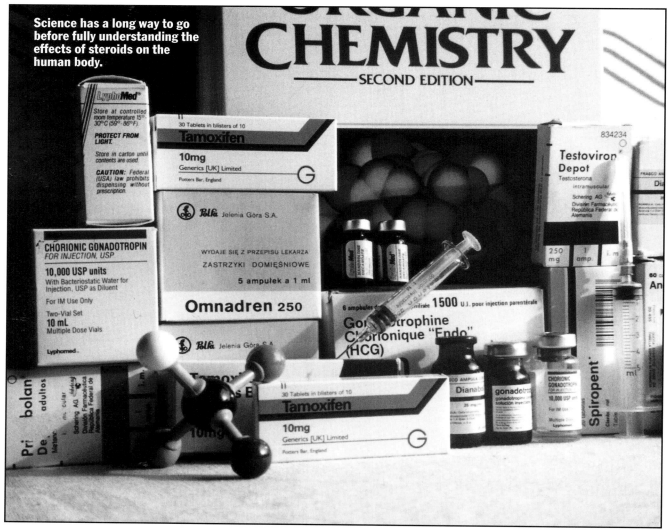

Science has a long way to go before fully understanding the effects of steroids on the human body.

The late Lyle Alzado was a professional football player (defensive end) for 15 years, and twice made all-pro. He began using anabolic steroids in college in 1969, and continued to use them throughout his career, even after he retired. He stopped using steroids in 1991 after he was diagnosed with brain cancer. Alzado maintained that his health problems were related to his prolonged and heavy use of both steroids and human growth hormone (HGH). Among the steroids he used were: Dianabol, Bolasterone, Quinolone, Anavar, Equipoise, and Depo-Testosterone. He estimated that he annually spent between $20,000 and $30,000 on steroids and HGH.[12] While Alzado's cancer may possibly be related to his drug use, other explanations may account for his disease.

Cancers are caused by a number of factors. The World Health Organization estimates that 60 to 90 percent of all human cancers may be caused by environmental agents called carcinogens.[42] For example, until its cancer-causing properties were recognized, asbestos was commonly used as insulation in buildings. Most of the early weight-training gyms were low-budget, poorly-ventilated, basement affairs. Many athletes were unwittingly exposed to asbestos filaments in the air. These types of cancers often do not develop until 20 to 40 years after exposure.

Athletes in large cities are exposed to industrial pollutants because much of their heavy training is outdoors. This air pollution is known as smog, and many of its components have been identified as carcinogenic. Even indoors, athletes have not been safe as exposure to second-hand cigarette smoke was common until recent legislation was passed in the US and Canada.

Other factors to be considered are genetics (former US President, Jimmy Carter, lost his mother, brother, and sister to pancreatic cancer), viruses and radiation. The latter is important as both training and competition often take place outdoors, where athletes are exposed to U.V. radiation from the sun. Even something as simple as age plays a role in the development of cancer. The incidence of malignancy is relatively low in youth, but increases dramatically in later life. Basically, the older we get, the greater the chance we have of developing cancer.

Given this information, it can be seen that cancer may be caused by a multitude of factors. To categorically state that cancer is caused by just one of these factors requires a substantial amount of empirical evidence. The role of smoking in causing lung cancer was proven only after a review of hundreds of thousands of case studies in which smoking was found to be the common factor. No such data exists to prove a relationship between brain cancer and steroid use, therefore there is as of yet insufficient evidence to show that a relationship exists between the two.

KIDNEY CANCER

Wilm's tumor is the most common form of kidney cancer in children, but occurs rarely in adults. A case of Wilm's tumor (kidney cancer) was reported in a 38-year-old man. This individual was a competitive bodybuilder who had used anabolic steroids as part of his training regimen. Close associates of the deceased had stated that he had taken large injections of Dianabol and consumed other steroids orally. The exact agents and their amounts were difficult to determine because the drugs had not been prescribed by a physician, but obtained from friends and trainers.[43]

Despite an intensive review of the medical literature, we have been unable to find other documented cases of Wilm's tumor associated with anabolic steroid use by athletes. While this individual died of Wilm's tumor, the rarity of the disease, together with his vague drug history, makes it likely that the association between Wilm's tumor and anabolic steroid use is a coincidental one. If there was a relationship there should be more cases cited in the literature, given the fact that a half-million Americans regularly use anabolic steroids.

LIVER FUNCTION

"Some authors or research papers about Fanconi's anemia have reported hepatocellular carcinoma [liver cancer] in association with (but not necessarily due) to steroid treatment. Yet these papers are used as references in articles written about the dangers of steroid use to healthy athletes." – Dr. Craig Brigham[44]

Anabolic steroids may cause physical side effects which are neither anabolic nor androgenic in nature. Liver abnormalities are the most commonly cited effect in the condemnation of steroid use. The liver's enzymes break down the various drugs a person may be using. When these levels are normal, the liver is able to carry out its primary function of detoxification. If these levels become abnormal, the liver's ability to perform this function can be impaired. Steroid use may lead to a condition called "steroid-induced jaundice". While this condition will clear up after the person stops using steroids, immediate medical attention is warranted as jaundice is a symptom of a liver problem.

The risk of liver cancer has been propagated by antisteroid groups as an overwhelming danger to the steroid user. There is, however, only one documented case of an athlete who used anabolic steroids dying of liver cancer.[45] This athlete had used multiple oral and injectable anabolic steroids for four years prior to his death. Orally active C-17 alpha alkyl testosterone derivatives were among the steroids used. Of 36 cases of liver tumors associated with anabolic steroid use, in all but one of the cases, the use of C-17 alpha alkyl testosterone derivatives were involved. Of these cases, 35 were patients being treated for medical illnesses, the other case involving the previously mentioned athlete. Except for the information that the athlete had not had any prior liver disease, the rest of his medical history was not given. It is not possible to conclude that steroid use alone was responsible for his cancer.

Anabolic steroid use has been associated with peliosis hepatitis, a rare form of hepatitis historically linked with tuberculosis. Peliosis hepatitis is characterized by the formation of multiple, blood-filled, cystic lesions within the liver. In one study of 23 cases of peliosis hepatitis associated with anabolic steroids, 22 of the cases had been treated with the orally active C-17 alpha alkyl derivatives of testosterone. In all 23 cases, the individuals were being treated with anabolic steroids for medical illnesses. There have been no cases of peliosis hepatitis reported in bodybuilders or otherwise healthy people.[46]

It has been found that the treatment of liver disease using the anabolic steroid stanazolol may be beneficial. Stanazolol may be of particular benefit in haemophilia where no other treatment is known to be effective, in cases of liver damage, after treatment with factor concentrates (globulins or proteins necessary for normal blood clotting).[47] It is of interest to note that antisteroid activists have cited this study as evidence for steroid-induced hypertension, but have avoided mentioning this previous finding.

HIGH BLOOD PRESSURE

"In my practice I have been using anabolic steroids with athletes for about 18 years now... The side effects I do see are acne, gynecomastia, and, very rarely, mild hypertension. In each of these cases I simply switched to a different anabolic drug and the problem went away." – Robert Kerr, M.D.[48]

Most steroid users report increased blood pressure while on a cycle. Anabolic steroids cause the body to retain fluids, resulting in a rise in blood pressure. This is transitory, and once the steroids are discontinued fluid retention ceases and blood pressure returns to normal. Hypertension can be controlled during the steroid cycle by dietary salt restriction, although occasionally a diuretic agent is also needed. For a patient with underlying cardiac or renal disease, the addition of anabolic steroids to his system can aggravate a pre-existing tendency to fluid retention. In such a case the retention of sodium and water (and with it an increase in blood pressure) presents a serious medical problem.[49] This point emphasizes the need for medical supervision when using anabolic steroids.

CHOLESTEROL

"It's very difficult to convince an 18-year-old that changes in his serum lipoproteins, resulting from anabolic steroid use, could have implications for him in his 30s and 40s." **– Andrew Pipe, M.D.**[50]

"The doctor taking care of me thought it best to have a look and found a partially blocked ventricular artery. He fixed it and I'm fine now. The blockage may have stemmed from hereditary factors – my father had heart trouble – the fact that I ate 10 to 15 eggs and 4 to 6 pounds of red meat a day for years, or that I had rheumatic fever when I was young. Not necessarily steroids." **– Larry Pacifico, world class powerlifter**[51]

Anabolic steroids have been shown to increase the ratio of LDL-C (low density lipoprotein cholesterol or "bad" cholesterol) to HDL-C (high density lipoprotein cholesterol or "good" cholesterol). This increased ratio is directly related to instances of coronary artery disease. In one study the cholesterol levels of powerlifters were recorded before, during, and after steroid cycles. Three of the athletes had used steroids for as long as eight years while the other 19 had never previously used them. The study was carried out to determine: a) if brief periods of steroid use were associated with increased total cholesterol levels; b) if prolonged use resulted in higher levels maintained by continued use; and c) if total cholesterol levels return to presteroid levels upon termination of steroid use.

The study found that powerlifters using large doses of steroids developed high cholesterol levels, and that these levels were maintained for several years by continued steroid use. Following cessation of steroid use, total cholesterol levels rapidly returned to their presteroid levels. It was also found that presteroid total cholesterol concentration was not predictive of the size of steroid-induced high cholesterol levels, nor was it found that low presteroid cholesterol levels necessarily protect against this abnormality. The increase in total cholesterol levels was in all cases caused by an increase in "bad" cholesterol concentrations. The authors of the study concluded, "Our study suggests

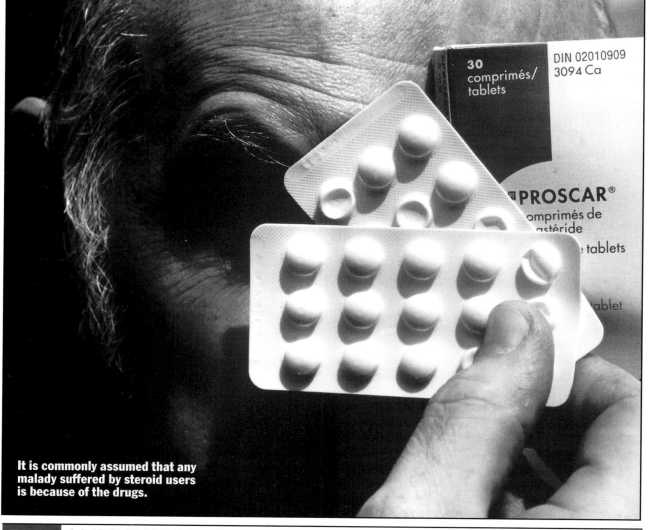

It is commonly assumed that any malady suffered by steroid users is because of the drugs.

Is getting induced with steroids like opening a modern day Pandora's box?

that another coronary risk factor (elevated total cholesterol concentration) should be added to the list of risk factors already described in athletes who use steroids, but the clinical significance of these findings remains unclear. Although steroids have been available to athletes for some 30 years, we are not aware of any report in the medical literature of coronary morbidity associated with steroid use, and an increased incidence of coronary artery disease in these athletes has yet to be demonstrated."[24] In other words, it has never been shown that there is an increased incidence of coronary artery disease associated with steroid use, nor has there ever been a report of an athlete dying of coronary artery disease directly associated with steroid use.

Commenting on the possible link between anabolic steroid use and cardiovascular disease, Dr. Charles Yesalis of Penn State University said, "Anybody who has used steroids and has any malady, it's immediately assumed that steroids caused it."

SIDE EFFECTS EXPERIENCED BY MEN

"I think the media's treatment is biased because not enough research has gone into it to know true side effects on someone's health. I know people who have done 30 to 50 cc/week and had no visible side effects, but when I did a set cycle I got gynecomastia."
– Steroid user

"I keep upping the dosage until my nipples start to hurt, then I start cutting down." **– Another steroid user (explaining how he determined his maximum dosage)**

Anabolic steroids are derivatives of testosterone, and they can be converted by the body to the female hormone estrogen. When this occurs, one or both breasts may swell and develop a feminized appearance. This condition is called gynecomastia, and is commonly known as "bitch tits". Gynecomastia can be

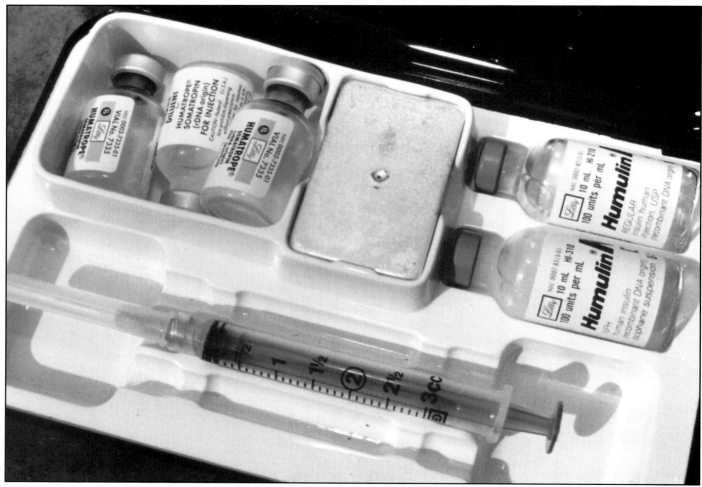

painful, but is usually transitory, with the breasts returning to normal after steroid use is stopped. For some, drugs or surgery may be required to restore a normal masculine appearance. This condition is not restricted to steroid users. It occurs infrequently throughout the male population, especially during puberty, and is sometimes associated with the use of drugs such as marijuana. Because gynecomastia can also be a symptom of testicular cancer, a prompt medical examination is always recommended for anyone with these symptoms.

A popular myth surrounding steroids is that they cause an enlargement of the penis. Some users may temporarily experience this phenomenon. It is caused by fluid retention, and will only last for the duration of the cycle. There will be no permanent gain in penis size. There will be a shrinkage of the testicles during the steroid cycle as a result of the body shutting down natural testosterone production. This shrinkage results in decreased sperm production, sometimes to the point of sterility.[52] Despite vocal claims to the contrary by antisteroid activists, this condition is in fact transitory, and both testicle size and sperm production will return to normal after cessation of steroid use. During steroid use the sex drive of the individual may increase, decrease, or remain the same.[46]

Under no circumstances should a woman use steroids while there is a possibility of pregnancy.

SIDE EFFECTS EXPERIENCED BY WOMEN

"…overt masculinization of the female, liver and kidney toxicity, are just a few of the side effects that are reported, and I don't deny that these occur. I see instances of these side effects quite often in people who come to me for the first time saying that they had been taking black-market drugs. Generally, they have been taking an overabundance of these drugs."
– Robert Kerr, M.D.[48]

Women who take anabolic steroids may experience a number of physical reactions. For example, they may experience enlargement of the clitoris. This condition does not affect the woman's sexual functioning but is permanent and can cause emotional distress. While on a steroid cycle, most women experience an increase in their sex drive which returns to its presteroid level upon cessation of steroid use. Most women also experience menstrual irregularities.[53] This latter phenomenon is also common among steroid-free female athletes involved in intensive training, whose bodyfat levels have dropped below normal.

Pregnant women present a special case. Anabolic steroid use may result in masculination of the developing fetus. The abnormally high levels of the masculinizing agents circulating in the woman's body may affect the fetus. A genetically female fetus may have its external genitalia masculinized to such an extent that visual identification of the sex of the child at birth may be impossible.[54] Under no circumstances should a woman use anabolic steroids while pregnant or while there is a possibility of pregnancy.

SIDE EFFECTS EXPERIENCED BY TEENAGERS

"I know one guy at school who still had severe gynecomastia two months after his last cycle. The guys' too embarrassed to take his shirt off in gym. He's got better breast development than half the girls. He won't see a doctor about it." — *Teenager*
(commenting on his classmate's gynecomastia)

In recent years the use of steroids by teenagers has increased dramatically. The use of steroids by this age group poses a real danger due to the fact that young people are not physically mature. Normally a person does not stop growing until the early 20s, when the epiphyseal plates (growth plates, at the end of long bones) fuse completely. Steroids cause the plates to

Whether right or wrong, opponents of drug use often refer to scare tactics.

fuse at a much faster rate, and once they have become completely fused further bone growth is impossible.[54]

Dr. Craig Brigham is a medical doctor who has done extensive research on steroids, and is a former athlete who placed second to Bruce Jenner at the 1976 Olympic trials. Dr. Brigham's comment on anabolic steroid use was that he knew athletes who had been using anabolic steroids for 20 years in a cyclic fashion. In his opinion, they were probably no more harmful than oral contraceptives.[44]

The question of whether anabolic steroids are "safe" is not a black or white issue. Like any group of drugs (i.e. birth control pills, antihypertensives, etc.) they have both desirable and undesirable effects. The key to ensuring user safety is to make sure that any drug use is carried out only under strict medical supervision. Most side effects experienced by athletes are mild and transitory, and the fatal side effects so often mentioned in the media are steroid myths.

SCARE TACTICS – ARE THEY EFFECTIVE?

"There is a whole array of diseases and medical disorders that are going to show up. And the really unfortunate thing is that by the time we find out, it will be too late for an entire generation."
— *Dr. Robert Goldman, author of the antisteroid book,* **Death in the Locker Room.**[55]

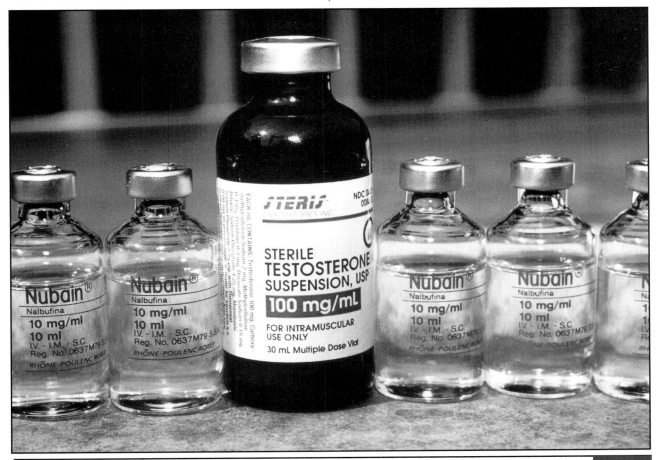

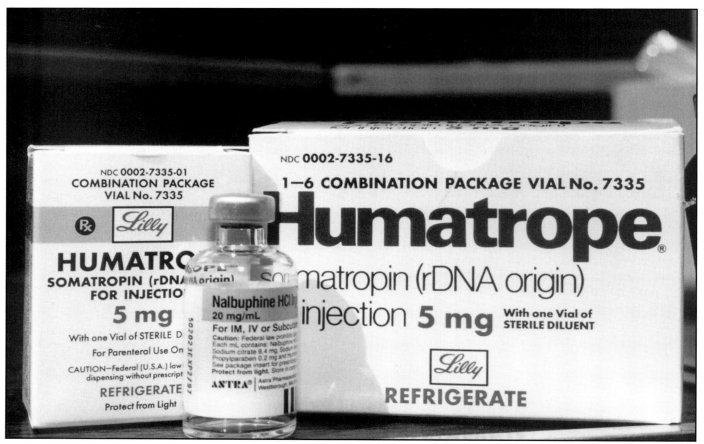

NDC 0002-7335-01
COMBINATION PACKAGE
VIAL No. 7335

℞ Lilly

HUMATRO
SOMATROPIN (rDNA origin)
FOR INJECTIO

5 mg

With one Vial of STERILE D

For Parenteral Use On

CAUTION—Federal (U.S.A.) law
dispensing without prescript

REFRIGERATE
Protect from Light

Nalbuphine HCl
20 mg/mL
For IM, IV or Subcut
Caution: Federal law prohibit
Each mL contains: Nalbuph
Sodium citrate 9.4 mg, Sod
Propylparaben 0.2 mg and
See package insert for pre
Protect from light. Store
ASTRA® Astra Pharma
Westborough M

NDC 0002-7335-16

1—6 COMBINATION PACKAGE VIAL No. 7335

Humatrope®

somatropin (rDNA origin)
injection 5 mg With one Vial of
STERILE DILUENT

Lilly

REFRIGERATE

Most drugs have negative side effects. Steroids are no exception. Before using them you should carefully weigh the pros and cons.

"The sky is falling! The sky is falling! **– Chicken Little (from the children's tale of the same name), provoking mass hysteria in the barnyard. The sky wasn't falling.**

Historically, it has been a common antidrug media approach to dissuade drug use, by exaggerating side effects and attempting to frighten the public. A classic example of this is the 1930s movie *Reefer Madness,* a US government film about the dangers of marijuana use. It graphically describes the descent of wholesome people into a psychotic, law-breaking, sex-crazed, and generally demented, drooling group of party animals. It is available in many video stores, is hilariously entertaining, and is reportedly a big hit with marijuana users. The message in this film, despite being well-intentioned, backfired, and became the source of much of the movie's unintended humor. In recent years, sports' federations have adopted a similar approach to the steroid problem. Despite little evidence that steroids have life-threatening potential when used under medical supervision, these organizations have lobbied quite successfully in the US to make steroids a controlled substance. Nonetheless, more athletes than ever before continue to use steroids, and steroid use appears to be increasing internationally.

MISINFORMATION

"We're one of the few businesses around where there is no agreed upon standard of achievement, education or behavior. To be a beautician you need a diploma. But anybody can be a journalist." **– Michael Cobden Director of the University of King's College School of Journalism, Halifax, Nova Scotia.**[56]

The following is a partial list of side effects frequently attributed to steroid use by women:
– heart attack
– liver disease
– breast cancer
– abnormal vaginal bleeding
– loss of vision

What you have just read is an example of misinformation. The above is a list of side effects associated with the use of birth control pills (which are in fact steroids, just not the anabolic kind). It does make one wonder why these side effects do not receive the same attention as side effects from anabolic steroid use. It is easy to get the facts wrong, particularly for journalists who are unfamiliar with the subject. Journalism is unlike most trades and professions in that it has no governing or regulatory body.

We live in what is called an information era. Because so much information, particularly of a scientific nature, is being constantly generated, the average individual has neither the time nor the expertise to

figure out what it all means. There is a tendency for people to depend on the mass media to give them information in simple, brief and understandable terms. Unfortunately, it can be difficult for a reporter with even the best of intentions to present an unbiased story on a difficult subject, in which he or she has no background. In such a situation a responsible reporter will endeavor to locate an expert. The reporter assumes that what the expert says is correct, and that the expert maintains an unbiased position to the subject. Even if the reporter has located the genuine article, often experts in the same field hold diametrically-opposed views on the same topic. With whom does the reporter agree?

Complicating the problem, deadlines must be met and little time is available for consultation with more than one "expert". Further complicating matters, some subjects such as drug use (steroids or otherwise), are very much in the political arena. Viewpoints that go against the grain are rarely welcomed by publishers concerned about circulation. Throw in lobby groups, who spend a great deal of time (and money) to see that their viewpoint gets the most attention, and one can see the potential for problems. All of these factors influence the media's treatment of the dangers of using anabolic steroids for improving athletic performance. It was, and still is, a classic case of misinformation.

ANABOLIC STEROIDS AND NUTRITION

Since anabolic steroids speed up the cell's metabolic processes, the body must take in a wide range of raw materials and nutrients. If these nutrients are not supplied in adequate quantities, the user's body could suffer from metabolic stress, such as hormone or other imbalances. In one study carried out by the Sport's Medicine and Research clinic of Marseille, France, it was found that athletes who had taken 100 mg each of testosterone enanthate and Primobolan depot experienced a drastic decrease in vitamin A, B complex vitamins, calcium, chromium and potassium.[57]

ANABOLIC STEROID USE AND ITS EFFECT ON GLUCONEOGENESIS

It is well known that corticosteroids not only affect nitrogen metabolism, but also induce hyperglycemia (increased blood sugar) and hypercalcemia (increased blood calcium). Studies have shown that anabolic steroids promote the attainment of a high positive nitrogen balance and a normalizing of blood sugar levels.[58] Because they have similar structures, anabolic steroids compete with cortisol (a major glucocorticoid), for the pathway in the liver which deactivates cortisol. Anabolic steroids also directly inhibit the main enzyme in this pathway, thus they inhibit cortisol metabolism.[59]

It was found that anabolic steroids cause nitrogen, potassium and phosphorus retention. The administration of steroids has been shown to result in lower blood sugar levels. By causing a conservation of protein, steroids interfere with the process of gluconeogenesis. As a consequence of the reduction in available sugar, there appears to be an increased, but less efficient oxidation of fat.[60]

Glucocorticoids are sometimes called "stress" hormones. Individuals under stress undergo physiological changes because these hormones are released in great amounts. The most obvious sign of stress is rapid weight loss, which is caused by an inadequate diet and heightened metabolism. The result is the body utilizing muscle tissue for fuel. Athletes, especially bodybuilders, use anabolic steroids to reverse this process. The outcome is an ability to reduce bodyfat levels to a minimum without sacrificing muscle size.

ANABOLIC STEROIDS AND PROTEIN

Steroids have been shown to promote the synthesis and storage of cell proteins, and stimulate the growth of tissue[3,61]. They also cause nitrogen retention. Researchers found that there was a greater improvement in the body's nitrogen balance when the administration of steroids was combined with an exercise program.[62,63] In our own study we found that steroid users usually follow a high-protein diet while on a cycle.[28] Anabolic steroid use, when accompanied by a high-protein diet and a strenuous exercise program will produce an increase in weight, strength and muscle size.[62,63]

In consuming a high-protein diet, athletes should always strive to follow a diet that is low in cholesterol and high in fiber (which itself reduces cholesterol). This is very important in athletes who use anabolic steroids, as studies show that cholesterol levels rise while on a steroid cycle.[24]

THE LEGALITIES OF ANABOLIC STEROIDS

As it stands right now, the possession or trafficking of anabolic steroids is a criminal offense in the United States. Carried to the extreme it means that if you or your friend get caught with so much as one bottle of Winstrol, you can do serious time in jail. And given the nature of America's drug war, your jail term could be lengthy. So no matter how safe you might think anabolic steroids are (as we emphasized earlier most drugs have side effects and anabolic steroids are no exception), or how much you dislike current steroid legislation, the bottom line is that they are illegal!

In Canada, things are not quite as drastic, but it's still illegal to possess them for trafficking. Personal use is not a crime, but here lies the problem. What is the dividing line between an amount for personal use and an amount for sale? So even though personal possession may not be a crime on the books, any amount could be considered trafficable if you get the wrong judge, police officer, or prosecutor. So for those Canadian and American readers out there, think twice.

Milos Sarcev

Who They Are and What They Say

BOOK TEN

10

Chapter Thirty-eight

Milos Sarcev, Charles Clairmonte and Porter Cottrell

QUESTIONS AND ANSWERS

Every year we receive thousands of letters at *MuscleMag* headquarters. While a few offer comments and suggestions (some of which cannot be reprinted here!), the vast majority are inquiries from bodybuilders, all looking for that one piece of advice that will catapult them to bodybuilding stardom. We have done our best to answer them all, but logistics prevent each and every letter from being answered. To help alleviate this, every month in *MuscleMag International,* we answer the most common questions in our various advice columns. Such regular features as Ask Bob, Wild Physique, and Wisdom of Grimek, routinely dish out tips and guidance for bodybuilders – no matter what the experience level. The following is a selection of questions and answers, drawn from over twenty-four years of *MuscleMag International.* Perhaps you'll see one of yours printed here. In any case, enjoy!

SQUATS – HOW HIGH AND HOW FAR?

Q. Should I perform my squats with my heels on a block of wood? Yes or no. Please advise. Also, who was the first bodybuilder to employ this method? Last question. How far from the squat stands should I place the block if I use one?

A. Bodybuilders almost always use built-up weight-lifting shoes or a block of wood to raise their heels during squatting. This throws most of the action on to the thighs and minimizes the work done by the hips and buttocks (provided you do not bend too far forward). Steve Reeves was the first bodybuilder to raise his heels on a block when squatting. Your last question should be obvious. One step back from the squat stands to the block is the correct distance. With a heavy weight on your back there's hardly any reason to take a walk around town!

BRINGING OUT THE LOWERS

Q. How do you develop the front of the calf over the shin bone area?

A. The best exercise to develop the tibialis or muscle covering the shin bone is to do calf raises with a high block under the heels (not the toes as in regular calf raises). Raise as high as you can and try to consciously flex and stretch the tibialis and do 10 to 15 reps until the area burns. Regular calf work, running, cycling and stretching the legs also works the area to some degree. It helps if you have a low bodyfat level to show a well-defined and developed tibialis. It's hard to show any muscle if it's covered in fat.

PEAKING THE BICEPS

Q. Is there anything I can do to build a better peak on my biceps? How do guys like Albert Beckles and Boyer Coe get such huge peaks?

A. You have to remember that both Albert and Boyer have been training for over 20 years, and in that time have done every conceivable arm exercise there is. Also, both are genetically gifted in the biceps department. If you questioned them they'd tell you their peaks came as their development improved. Favorite exercises to improve biceps peaks are concentration curls, pulley curls, supination curls, and lat-machine pulldown curls. Use a full range of motion on these biceps exercises and consciously tense the biceps hard in the fully contracted position. Also flex your biceps hard without using weights. Raise your elbow as high as you can and flex and tense the biceps until it cramps. This helps to bring out the peak too.

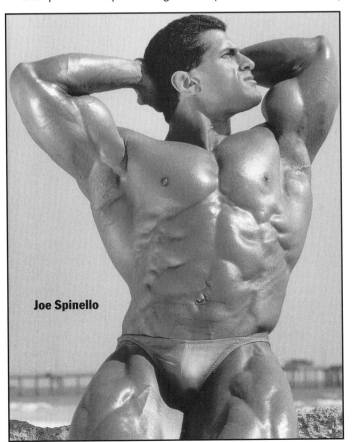

Joe Spinello

Melissa Coates

MACHINES vs. FREE WEIGHTS

Q. My friends tell me that the only way to build power and thickness is through free weights, meaning barbells and dumbells, and to stay away from machines. Is there any truth to this?

A. The old free-weight vs. machines question rears its ugly head again! Well, your friends are both right and wrong with regards to that question. It is definitely true that you need to train hard and heavy with free weights to add overall thickness to your body, but some machines are also beneficial. There is not a pro body-builder out there – or powerlifter, for that matter – who does not incorporate some sort of machine into his daily training routine. Some of the machines these days are superior to those of the old days, in the way they mimic the actual free-lift movements.

The key to adding size and thickness is to train heavy whether it's with or without the use of machines. As with life, your training needs some variety to keep your muscles stimulated and to keep your body guessing into new-found growth.

MORE VEINS

Q. I am 18 and a big fan of yours. I've been training for about a year now. My focus is on creating a more shapely and muscularly defined body – one like yours. I know that all gains come in time with patience and correct training. My question is, how do you get vascular or ripped? This might sound weird, but I would really love to have my veins show, especially on my biceps. My bodyfat is about 20 percent. Does vascularity come with time, and does it depend completely on bodyfat?

A. Vascularity is partly genetic. Some people naturally have their veins closer to the skin surface, so they are more visible. But, partly, veins show also because of a low level of bodyfat. As you said yourself, patience and hard, correct training is the answer. As months go by your body will become stronger, leaner, and yes, more vascular.

ARE SUPPLEMENTS NECESSARY?

Q. I weigh only 140 pounds at six feet in height. I'm 18 and have always been naturally thin. I see so many ads in the magazines that practically guarantee major gains in muscle size and mass. Do I need to take these supplements? Money is a problem, as I'm going to school and working part time. Which supplements do you recommend I take?

A. The key to gaining size and mass, is good eating and hard training. Supplements are just that, a supplement to your meals. To get big, you need to take in much more protein and calories than you currently do. Aim for one gram of protein per pound of bodyweight and about 30 calories per pound of bodyweight. These are minimums and you may need more.

As far as supplements go, I suggest you stick to the basics, which would be a vitamin-mineral supplement and a good-quality protein powder and/or weight-gain product. Protein and weight-gain shakes can be really useful for getting extra protein and calories because it's always easier to drink protein and calories than eat them. Try to eat four or five meals a day which contain some kind of protein (meat, fish, poultry, cottage cheese), some kind of complex carbs (rice, potato, yams, steamed vegetables, salads), and some simple carb (fruit). Then have two or three protein/weight-gain shakes between meals. The best protein products come from eggs and whey, so look for those ingredients when choosing a product.

PECTORAL IMBALANCE

Q. I am having trouble with my pectoral development. Over the past six months I have noticed that my left pec has developed better than my right pec. I don't know if this is common among bodybuilders, but it is very annoying. I bench press with elbows aligned with my shoulders, but when I use heavy weights my right elbow tends to drift downward, bringing my right lat into play. I've tried dumbells but I'm not as sore the next day. What can I do to bring my right pec up to the development of my left pec?

A. It is fairly common for one lat, pec, arm or leg to be slightly more developed than the other. The best way to bring up such asymmetrical development is through the use of dumbells or one-arm exercises. When you use dumbells you force each side to work equally hard. When you use a barbell, there is a natural tendency to let the stronger side do more work than the weaker side.

I suggest you try an all-dumbell chest routine for a while. Try flat dumbell bench presses for 4 sets of 8 to 10 reps, followed by a superset of incline dumbell presses and flat or incline flyes for another 4 sets of 8 to 12 reps. If the muscle imbalance is severe, try some one-arm pec-dek flyes or one-arm cable crossovers for 3 sets of 10 to 15 reps. This should help.

WHAT FOOTWEAR?

Q. I have been bodybuilding for a couple of years, but I am still confused about what is the best footwear to use during workouts, or is it best to train barefoot?

A. There are different ideas about what is best. For example, Vince Gironda says that one should do all forms of calf work barefoot to get a complete, full-stretch action. Most bodybuilders train in running shoes of one kind or another, while a few train in street shoes. The Barbarians have set a trend in exercising in workboots!

Your footwear is not of paramount importance in bodybuilding as it is in weightlifting, but if you are serious about bodybuilding you might as well outfit yourself with a good supporting exercise shoe. The Nike company puts out a very good weight shoe which I recommend highly. It is called the Nike Lever. Being outfitted correctly with shoes, a sweatsuit and belt is one step toward getting the most out of your training.

Jean-Pierre Fux

TO TRAIN OR NOT TO TRAIN

Q. Sometimes before my workouts I feel just too tired to train. Should I not exercise and just rest, or what?

A. It has been my experience that a good workout is just what the doctor ordered in terms of renewed energy and vigor. I guess you might use the analogy of a car sitting in traffic and getting loaded up with carbon and sludge. Once out of the city and away from traffic, the freely running car essentially cleans itself as it runs at top speed. I think the same holds true for humans. Work, deadlines, family responsibilities and stress tend to be drains on our energy. The best thing you can do to restore energy levels is to take that workout.

BICEPS GAP

Q. I have a wide gap between my elbow and biceps. Is there anything I can do to fill it in?

A. You cannot lengthen a muscle but only reshape it. It would be best to do strict preacher curls on a 45-degree bench to build the lower biceps. Make sure you go all the way to a complete stretch at the bottom, or you will take the stress away from the lower biceps area.

HITTING THE LOWER ABS

Q. What are the best exercises for my lower abs? My upper abs are pretty good, but my lower abs lack development.

A. Try lying leg raises on an incline board set at any angle greater than 20 degrees.

LOWER THIGHS

Q. How can I get more development in my lower thighs? All my development seems to be at the top of the thigh. I do squats and leg presses and leg curls for the thighs. What are the exercises that best hit the lower thigh?

A. While squats and leg presses are excellent thigh exercises, they stress mostly the upper thigh area, especially if you do your squats flatfooted. To hit the lower thigh area try doing your squats with your heels elevated on at least a three-inch block. Also, hack squats and leg extensions (concentrating on fully locking out) hit the lower thigh area too.

THE INNER PECS

Q. What's the best exercise for the inner part of the pecs, along the sternum?

A. Try close-grip bench presses, keeping your elbows to the side. The Nautilus pec-dek is also great for the inner pecs. As a final suggestion, try squeezing the pecs together at the top of your dumbell flyes and presses.

LIMITED TIME

Q. My time for training is extremely limited. Can I still build a decent physique on three or four workouts a week of 30 to 40 minutes? What exercises do you recommend I do and how many sets of each?

A. Some genetic superiors could build a fair body in 30 minutes a week but most people could not. Even an hour's workout four times a week is pushing it. You would have to make every minute count. Never rest more than sixty seconds between exercises and use a fair amount of intensity. I would suggest you superset your exercises (opposing muscle groups) to allow maximum work in the shortest period of time.

Vary your exercises to hit all regions of a muscle group.

HIGH AND SHORT LATS

Q. My lats are high and short. How can I make my lats longer and have more lower lats?

A. Unfortunately the muscle insertions that give you your high, short lat structure cannot be radically altered by exercise. What you should do is pick exercises that stress the lower lat area which will give you the illusion of larger lats. Most narrow-grip exercises tend to hit the lower lat area more than wide-grip exercises. Try close-grip pulldowns or chins using either a normal or reverse grip, narrow-grip bent rows, one-arm dumbell rows and perhaps one of the best for lower lats, reverse-grip bent rows. Use good style and concentrate on isolating the lower lat.

REAR DELTS

Q. What's a good exercise to develop the rear delts? When I do rear raises I can't seem to feel it in the rear delts.

A. If you're not feeling it in the delts when you do dumbell rear raises then you are probably using too

Ronnie Coleman strikes a pose!

much weight. Drop the weight and use better form. But to answer your question, I think the chest expander movement using a set of cables or springs is excellent, as it strongly works the rear delt in the fully contracted position. Hold the handle of the cables in a palms-facing position and pull the handles out to the sides until the arms are fully extended. For variety, try doing the movement in a bent-over position.

TO LOCK OUT OR NOT?
Q. Is it best to lock out during exercises, or should I maintain constant tension by cutting the movement short of a full lockout?

A. This varies with each exercise. You will have to figure out for yourself which exercises should be locked out and which ones should not. Personally I don't lock out on the triceps dumbell extension. But on the triceps kickbacks I lock out and squeeze. On leg extensions I lock out, but on squats I don't. It's often a matter of personal preference, and often you will have to experiment a little to find out which exercises are made more effective by locking out or not.

THE OUTER PEC
Q. I want to develop the outer part of my pecs. I seem to have plenty of muscle near the center of my chest, but things get pretty thin in the outer region. What weight-training exercises do you recommend?

A. I was always impressed by the outer pectorals of Arnold Schwarzenegger, yet he never handled more than 60-pound dumbells when he did flying motions. And this was the exercise that was giving him the wide outer pecs. 60-pound dumbells may seem heavy to you, but thousands of bodybuilders have used and still use far more than that. I know for a fact that Arnold

could have used more. The reason he only trained with 60-pound dumbells was that he concentrated on stretching all the way down.

Other great outer-pec exercises are: wide-grip bench presses, dumbell presses with a slow, full stretch, and dips performed with the chin on the chest and leaning forward.

TRAINING VERSUS DIET
Q. What's more important in a bodybuilder's success, training or diet?

A. Diet, definitely! You have to liken your body to a sports car. It won't perform optimally if it doesn't receive the right kind of fuel. Super nutrition sets you up for maximum benefit in the gym, but without the right fuel your efforts in the gym will probably be wasted. Remember, lifting weights only stimulates growth. Proper recuperation requires plenty of rest and good food. You can't have one without the other.

IS FIVE YEARS ENOUGH?
Q. Do you think it's possible to reach one's ultimate potential in five years? I've been training for longer than that and can't seem to make any more gains.

A. Even though each one of us is definitely limited by our genetics, I don't feel anyone ever fully realizes his or her potential. A lot of people have come close, but I think there are always ways to push yourself further physically. Don't give up your fight in the gym. Sometimes all it takes to break out of a training rut is a radical change in either diet or routine. One of my favorite methods of overcoming a plateau is what I call "boatloading." Try eating everything you can get your hands on for a few weeks. Of course, try to keep the nutrition content high. Potato chips and chocolate bars won't help. As for pizza, eat two or three a week! Sit down and eat something every couple of hours. While I wouldn't suggest following this regimen indefinitely, it can certainly help kick start your body into further muscle growth.

THE GREAT PUMP UP
Q. My question revolves around the importance of a pump. Is a pump necessary for muscle growth? I get a good pump most workouts, but my bodybuilding progress is slow. Please answer my question.

A. A pump is not necessary for muscle growth. There are many bodybuilders who train regularly, and for one reason or another seldom get a significant pump. Perhaps they either don't change their exercises often enough, work with low reps, or refrain from intense training. These same men do build muscle size though, proving that a big pump each workout is not necessary.

Also, as you appear to have found out, an almighty pump every workout does not by any means indicate you are getting bigger or that your muscles are on a positive growth pattern. There are bodybuilders who train very effectively and pump up to an impressive appearance by the end of each workout, only to deflate by the time they walk out of the gym. Many do this month in, month out, and still do not gain size.

One thing is sure, as a bodybuilder makes gains in the advanced stages, say 18-inch arms, he has to get a pump to take his growth to the 19- or 20-inch-arm barrier.

IF IT WORKS DON'T CHANGE IT
Q. I have been training somewhat hard six days a week, occasionally five, and for the last four months I have been making unbelievable gains everywhere. I was wondering if I will build more muscle mass training heavy every other day, or the way I am training now?

A. Do not change a thing. Basically, I am for the every-other-day split principle of training (that is: train half the body one day and rest the next. Then train the other half, and then rest again. This continues in an alternating fashion). But if you are making great gains as you say then I suggest you keep on training as you are, until progress slows down or comes to a halt.

UPRIGHT ROWS – HOW WIDE?
Q. Must the upright-row exercise be done with a narrow-hand spacing to make the shoulder area really grow?

A. The deltoid is worked with this exercise but so are the trapezius, forearms and biceps. It is generally accepted that a shoulder-width hand spacing puts more attention on the deltoid muscle and less on the aforementioned areas. Try a wider hand spacing and look for more shoulder development.

TRAINING TO FAILURE
Q. Dear Vince (Gironda), I am writing to ask you about a training principle that has received a lot of coverage lately. My question to you, Vince, and I respect your opinion, is: Do you believe in training to failure?

A. Yes, I believe in training to failure… but not in the sense that you mean. I believe in training to failure with FORM. It is useless to continue an exercise if you have to use every muscle in the body to hoist it up in bad form.

CHINS OR PULLDOWNS
Q. I have access to a chin bar and a lat machine, but I do not have time (or energy) to use both. Please tell me which is the best apparatus to use for wide lat development.

A. Each has a unique use. There is more tensile strength and nervous energy involved in chinning, but make sure that you keep the elbows back throughout

James Roberts

the entire movement. Most top bodybuilders regularly perform wide-grip chins, and there is a definite "look" about the back of a regular wide-grip chinner.

On the other hand, the lat-machine pulldown is not quite so severe a movement. It's more complete in that lighter than bodyweight can be used and the bar can be pulled right to the sternum or below. This is something which few bodybuilders can do on the chin bar because they lack the strength. Of the two movements, and in view that most top bodybuilders find them extremely beneficial, I advise you to go with the chins, but don't discount the lat machine. When you have more time you could add a few sets of pulldowns to supplement your back training.

HALTING GAINS

Q. Is there any truth to the theory that regular swimming and other mild sports like table tennis or horseback riding will interfere with my bodybuilding gains?

A. You will lose muscle size if you swim and participate in other sports regularly. I say this because your gains have taken time. This means you have to fight hard to keep your capillaries and muscle cells at their fullest. Extra nonprogressive sports activity will hold back your gains.

On the other hand, if you are blessed with a huge amount of muscle cells and gains come easily, then a moderate amount of extra sports activity will not hold back progress.

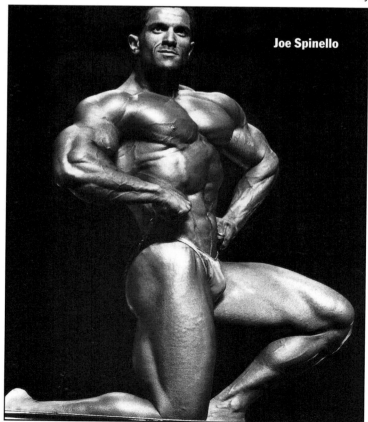

Joe Spinello

CALLUSES

Q. Is there any way I can prevent getting calluses on my hands from regular bodybuilding with weights?

A. You could wear gloves. A few bodybuilders train with light leather gloves which can be purchased at sporting goods stores. Specific weightlifting gloves may not be available at retail outlets so you may have to ask for golfer's or race-driving gloves.

LEG MASS

Q. I have been a serious bodybuilder for about a year now and cannot gain mass in my legs. I feel I am doing all the normal exercises – leg curls, extensions, squats etc. Could it be my diet? I eat as much fresh fruit and salad as I can, along with tuna and steaks. Please help!

A. If you want size in your legs, first of all you must lift heavy! Do fewer repetitions and use the heaviest poundages that you can handle. Do supersets and giant sets. You should almost feel sick after leg training.

As far as your diet goes, well, you seem to be missing an important food type – carbohydrates! Salad and fruit are great diet foods, but to put on size you need protein combined with good complex carbs. Try adding carbs three times daily to your diet. Here are some good examples: potatoes, yams, oatmeal, rice, pasta, and beans.

DO I NEED LIFTING STRAPS?

Q. Just how important are lifting straps in bodybuilding? I have friends who swear by them and friends who insist they're useless. Those who use them do not appear stronger or better built. I want to do every single thing that I can to help my muscles grow, but I'm a bit lost. I see some guys with gloves and some without. Some who strap elbows and knees, and some who never do. I do wear a belt when training, but I'm not sure if this is right or not. Please help.

A. Bodybuilding, like any sport, will always attract people who get off on buying and wearing all the latest clothing, trappings and accessories, whether useful or not. Remember, however, that if you are serious about getting those muscles to grow then you must never discount any innovation.

Common sense and intelligent trial and error must be your guide. Straps are definitely useful to the bodybuilder. They can help maintain your grip when nursing an injury or when using heavy weight. They can also help you forget the grip and concentrate on form. Try them out for yourself and see. The strapping of an injured joint, or as a safety measure when going into heavy poundage is also common sense.

Belts are a little different. While I advocate their use for the same two reasons – injury and heavy training – they can be overused and result in a weakening of the back. This can come about if you strap the belt on too tight and leave it on for the entire workout. To avoid a weaker lower back down the road, tighten your belt only for heavy work and loosen it or take it off for all other training.

THREE OR FOUR ABS

Q. Bob, please answer my question about abs. My workout buddy, John, and I have good abs. John has four distinct rows of abdominal muscles above his navel, whereas I only have three. We have been arguing on and off for months as to whether or not my three sets are the more normal shape, or if his four are. I told him that his abs are deformed because his top row is divided. I bet him ten bucks that his four-ab set-up is so freakish that it is unique. What do you say?

A. Whereas your three sets of abs are the most common formation, there are lots of fours out there. They also look good when ripped, so many bodybuilders who have the three or even two set-up wish they had the four. To be honest, you're the one who's going to have to hand over that ten!

CHEATING FOR SUCCESS

Q. I have been a reader of *MuscleMag International* for several years and have enjoyed all the articles, especially those by Greg Zulak, whom I greatly admire. Others whose training advice I respect include Dennis Weis, Don Ross, and yourself, Mr. Kennedy. My question involves the value of cheating when performing the various bodybuilding movements. After all my years of bodybuilding I am still confused. Is it better to use loose form (cheating) when exercising, or will more muscle growth result from using a very strict exercise form?

A. I am glad you like *MuscleMag* and the writers who pen the various articles. You should not think in terms of performing a cheating workout or a strict workout. Rather you should adapt your chosen style to each selected exercise, bearing in mind of course that one can get results from a variety of training styles. Tailor your style to isolate and exhaust the area you are working in the most effective manner. You should also take into consideration your allotted workout time, your efficiency, energy levels and stage of development. Your exercise style will be dictated by tuning into your feelings, listening to your body feedback and actively thinking out the effect you want to get from the exercise in question. Age and condition have a lot to do with your decision. It would be madness to throw yourself into cheating lateral raises, for example, if you haven't worked your deltoids in months.

Tom Platz

Vince Gironda adopts a loose style for some movements when he feels the need. He calls this "creative cheating." This is where body feedback is important. Champion bodybuilders do this instinctively. Before they start a set they know how they are going to approach it – heavy or light, strict or loose, fast or slow, to failure or not… it's all in the mind.

TO SITUP OR NOT?

Q. Should I do situps every day to keep my stomach flat? How many sets and reps would be enough?

A. I feel that training your abs four times per week is plenty. With a proper (low-fat) diet and a good overall workout program this will be enough to keep your stomach area nice and tight. I recommend also including some type of leg raises in your abdominal training because they stress the lower abs a bit more. It's good to have a variety of exercises for your abs, too.

WIDENING THE SHOULDERS

Q. Vince, I have narrow shoulders. I realize that I cannot widen my scapulae, but what in your opinion is the best exercise to make my delts look wider?

A. To look wider you must work on the side head. Lateral raises strongly work the side head if the little finger is kept higher than the thumb as the dumbells are raised. But I think the best shoulder broadener is the barbell upright row. To place emphasis on the side head, you must use a wide grip. Grasp the barbell with your hands 15 inches apart. Stand upright with the shoulders rounded, knees bent and the bar resting on the thighs. From this position, pull the bar up to the neck, but be sure not to hunch your shoulders. Keep them down or you will work the traps. You must keep the shoulders rounded and the elbows forward. Try 4 sets of the following reps: 10-8-6-15.

HIP REDUCTION

Q. I have been bodybuilding about 10 months and I have a couple of problems that I hope you can help me with. First, I can't reduce the size of my hips. I have tried lots of different exercises but so far nothing has worked. My training partner tells me that part of the problem is that I do heavy squats, but I love to squat; it's one of my favorite exercises. What do you suggest?

A. There is no exercise that acts as a subcutaneous fat emulsifier. Exercise builds muscle. It does not reduce it. Lack of exercise will shrink or cause muscle tissue loss. To reduce the hips you must cut out exercises that throw stress on the area like squats, half-squats, and leg presses, and do exercises that throw stress on the legs and glutes: hack slides, sissy squats, Roman-chair squats and leg extensions. Also, cut out your carbohydrates and get rid of any fat you are carrying in this area.

ALTERNATING HEAVY AND LIGHT WORKOUTS

Q. Do professionals and top amateurs train all muscle groups equally hard all the time, or do they not train some at all while they specialize on others? I am curious because when I try to follow the types of training routines so often seen in the magazines, I burn out after a few weeks. What's the real story on how the pros train?

A. No, the pros and world-class amateurs do not train all muscle groups equally hard all the time. First of all, the goal of bodybuilders should be perfect symmetry and proportions. This takes some juggling when it comes to training the individual muscle groups. Obviously, the fastest and easiest growing muscle groups will receive less sets and work than the hardest and slowest growing muscle groups. Secondly, you sometimes hear the pros say something like, "I'm training arms these days." This does not mean the pro is training only arms. It means he is specializing on his arms for six to eight weeks. During the time he is specializing on his arms (or other muscle group), he will do maintenance training for the other muscle groups, just enough to maintain their size. I suggest you have something for every muscle group in your training but only specialize on one muscle group at a time. Also, focus your training on the slow-growing muscle groups and less on the fast-growing muscle groups.

MUSCLE SORENESS

Q. After a really good workout, the next day my muscles are quite sore. Is this soreness good or bad? If it is bad, how can I prevent it and what should I do when it occurs?

A. If the soreness is so severe that you can hardly move, obviously this is not good. Besides being painful, it can inhibit your upcoming workouts. But a mild soreness is not bad, and champs claim that if you do not feel some soreness after a workout then you haven't worked the muscle hard enough to stimulate growth. Whether this is true or not is debatable. People seldom experience much soreness in their training except when resuming training after a layoff, or when doing a new exercise that stimulates the muscle fibers differently. After a few days the soreness goes away.

The best way to rid muscles of the lactic acid build-up that causes soreness is by doing lightweight, high-rep exercises to flood the muscles with blood and flush out the lactic acid. Massage is also useful in eliminating muscle soreness. If you are getting sore every workout you are probably overtraining or training too hard. Cut back on the intensity and train at a more comfortable level until your body adjusts to the training load.

Jay Cutler

Renel Janvier

TRAINING PARTNERS

Q. I have often read about the importance of training partners in bodybuilding, and also about the importance of high-intensity training by reducing rest time between sets. How can you train with a partner and still reduce time between sets? Obviously you have to wait for your partner to finish his set before you can start your set, and that's about as fast as you can go – isn't it?

A. It isn't necessary to reduce time between sets to increase intensity. That's only one way to do it. You can superset or do pre-exhaust sets of superhigh intensity with your training partner helping you through some forced reps and perhaps a few negatives. Then while you rest he can do his pre-exhaust or superset. When doing this type of training, the length of time your partner takes to do his sets is hardly long enough to allow you to rest and recuperate for your sets. You wouldn't want to go much faster than 60 to 90 seconds between his set and yours. Remember, the whole idea of having a training partner is to allow you to train with greater intensity while using heavier weights. If you train too fast you must use much lighter weights and the cardiovascular system is brought into greater play.

Decide what your priorities are. More size – via heavier weights and high intensity or greater cardio fitness and reduced bodyfat – via light weights and fast sets.

HEAVY OR LIGHT?

Q. I have been training for only three months and am confused. Should I be training heavy (reps in the 6 to 8 range) or lighter (reps in the 10 to 15 range) if my goal is to gain size and mass?

A. As a beginner you should now be able to start heavy training after a three-month break-in period. The beginner must build a base through heavy weights and strict form. Except for calves, forearms, and abs, I believe that you are right in keeping your reps in the 6 to 10 range. As you advance, you can make good gains with lighter training, but build your base first.

TENDINITIS

Q. I am 17 years old and I have been lifting weights for almost two years now. I have loved every minute of it except the time spent nursing an old knee injury. My doctor said that tendinitis had set in. She gave me some advice on how to treat it, such as icing it and taking aspirin. I know from numerous articles I have read that the main thing in treating tendinitis is rest. I haven't worked on my legs in some time. I am trying to search for the right exercise that will build the surrounding muscles in order to protect the infected joint. Is this the right thing to do?

My problem is that I have yet to find an exercise that doesn't put pressure on the knee when I work my legs. Can you help me? I don't want to give up bodybuilding – I've just started.

A. First of all, don't worry. With the right amount of exercise and rest you'll get rid of the tendinitis. Leg extensions should be the best and safest exercise for you to start with. You must do this exercise as well as all other exercises with perfect technique. Bring your legs to the upper position, stop for a second, then slowly lower. Completely control the movement. Never do fast, bouncing movements and avoid overstretching.

Try other leg exercises, but if your tendinitis flares up, use only partial movements. For instance, try hack squats or leg presses using partial movements. See if this eliminates the aggravation and gradually strengthens the muscles until you are able to do a more complete movement. Also, try not to use too much resistance too soon.

STRENGTHENING THE LOWER BACK

Q. I have been lifting weights for a number of years. In that time I have strained my lower back several times. Could you please let me know which exercises to do so as to strengthen my lower back and prevent further injury to that area?

A. No problem! The lower back is often susceptible to injury, especially when training heavy on basic exer-

Darrem Charles

cises for the legs and back. Squats, deadlifts, bent rows, T-bar rows, and cable rowing are usually the main exercises that cause injury to the lower back. This comes from using too much weight or doing the exercises in poor form. If you do squat or deadlift heavy, limit such workouts to no more than once a week, and really heavy deadlifting should not be done more than twice a month. To strengthen your lower back I recommend hyperextensions, 4 x 15 reps, good mornings, 3 to 4 x 12 to 20 reps, and the Nautilus lower-back machine. One thing about lower back work, never go to absolute failure, and never use really heavy weights. Try to get a nice pump, but never strain.

SQUATS ARE KING
Q. I have skinny legs and a small flat butt. What would be the best exercise to build up my legs and to fill out my glutes? Please advise me on sets and reps too.

A. That's an easy question to answer. Squats are absolutely the best leg-glute builder for men and women. Try doing 4 sets of 10 to 15 reps, 2 or 3 times a week. Make training progressive by adding weight to the bar, working up to as heavy a weight as you can. I suggest bodyweight for 15 reps as a minimum goal. Leg presses and leg curls will also fill the legs and glutes out.

STRETCH MARKS
Q. Are people on vegetarian diets more susceptible to stretch marks than those on normal bodybuilding diets? I ask this because since having become a

vegetarian two years ago, I have been plagued by an extensive network of unsightly stretch marks. Is there any way to reduce or eliminate this condition?

A. I don't think that a vegetarian diet would increase your likelihood of stretch marks; although, I must admit that I don't know for sure. Stretch marks are usually secondary to rapid growth, and represent a tearing of the less elastic collagen tissue. Once you have them there seems to be little you can do about them, although they do become less noticeable with time.

I have not found vitamins of any use, either in preventing or treating stretch marks. There is a cream in Europe that some people say helps both prevent and treat stretch marks. This compound, called Alphastria cream, has not been found particularly helpful in the prevention of pregnancy stretch marks (striae distensae). Plastic surgery would only be helpful if there's enough loose skin to remove. It's not much use in the pec-delt tie-in area. Tanning does nothing for the stretch marks – unless they're somewhat colored and stand out, then the tan would make them less noticeable.

GETTING RID OF BODY HAIR
Q. How do bodybuilders get rid of body hair?

A. Most bodybuilders just shave their hair off. Get a pack of those disposable razor blades. Get in the shower and shave in the shower. As soon as one razor starts to pull and drag a bit, use a new one. Be careful. Don't rush it. Don't try and shave your whole body in five minutes. Take your time so you don't nick yourself.

You can also use commercial hair removers like Neet. Test patch an area to see if you get an allergic reaction. If not, spread it over your arms, legs, chest and back if necessary; wait ten or fifteen minutes then get in the shower and rinse it off. This is a fast and convenient way to remove hair.

If you have the money, you can go to a salon and have your hair removed by wax. But this is more costly than shaving or using hair removers. One final tip, if you shave, do so three or four days before the contest. This gives small nicks and cuts a chance to heal.

OBLIQUES?
Q. It's always been my understanding that most bodybuilders want to have little if any obliques. But some lay claim to certain exercises that promote their growth. Where do you stand on this?

A. Obliques are only desirable if you have a small waist like Frank Zane. If you do not, you will ruin your taper.

CONFUSED – HEAVY WEIGHTS OR LIGHT?

Q. I am totally confused. Steve Michalik and many others, like Serge Nubret and even Arnold Schwarzenegger say that you will not build huge muscles using heavy weights. However, men like Mike Mentzer, Larry Scott, and Kal Szkalak, insist that handling progressively heavier and heavier weights will give you the utmost size. Which is true?

A. Opinions will always vary. One thing's for sure, you can waste years of bodybuilding if you don't increase your poundages. You have to push the weights at least to a certain stage. Nubret and Arnold both reached 500-pound bench presses. I can also recall seeing Arnold deadlift 600 and cheat curl near 300.

Every top bodybuilder alive can manage a 300-pound bench and squat considerably more. You simply have to push for more weight during your earlier years in the sport. Later you can moderate the weight used and learn to make the body "feel" it, even if it isn't heavy.

Best advice I can think of is try and make your workouts progressive from week to week, year to year. This does not always mean increasing poundage. You can do it by: increasing sets, decreasing rest periods, improving style, concentrating on the action, adding reps, tensing and squeezing the muscles at the conclusion of each rep, and by adding resistance to the bar.

FOREARMS

Q. My forearms are so bad I am ashamed to wear a short-sleeve shirt. I have developed a pretty good chest and even my upper arms are fair (16-1/4) but my forearms are long and skinny with virtually no development.

A. Many people have difficulty building forearms (and calves) because of insufficient cell allocation to that particular area. On the other hand, there are thick-wristed naturals like Casey Viator, Tim Belknap, Ron Teufel, and the Mentzer brothers who never need to do specific forearm work. Their forearms grow from regular exercises such as chins, rowing, curls, and pulley machines, all of which stimulate and work the forearms strongly.

People such as yourself, with a long-wrist appearance and only a small amount of development near the crook of the elbow should work their forearms regularly using the pre-exhaust system.

I suggest you alternate wrist curls with overgrip chins leaving your hands 6 inches apart, 4 sets each. No rest between sets. Rest briefly and then alternate palm-up wrist curls with undergrip chins, 4 sets of each and no rest between sets.

CANCER

Q. I have heard that exercise can cure cancer. Is it true?

A. No! Exercise cannot cure cancer, but new findings indicate that regular vigorous exercise can drastically reduce your risk of getting cancer. Numerous studies show that people who do not exercise are ten times more likely to get cancer than those who exercise strenuously. According to noted cancer researcher,

Sherilyn Godreau, Mia Finnegan, Maria Gonzales, Renita Harris and Daniella Morlanne

Dr. Ernst Van Asken, people who do not exercise run the risk of having their healthy cells turn into cancerous tissue.

TRIPLE DROP AND PYRAMIDING

Q. I really enjoy your "Ask Bob" column because you get straight to the point and answer questions head on. Please explain what the triple-drop and pyramid training methods are?

A. The triple-drop method is a system whereby weight is systematically decreased during a set to enable further repetitions to be achieved. Pyramid training involves increasing the weight each successive set and then decreasing the poundage each subsequent set. Both methods are enjoying a revival in recent years, and are used extensively by today's champs.

HITTING THE TRAPS

Q. I have a long scraggly neck, no traps, and my clavicles angle up at about 30 degrees even when I try and force my shoulders down. I want to win all the top bodybuilding titles. Please give me the two best trap-building exercises in the book.

A. The two best trap exercises are high pulls from the floor, and heavy shrugs. Your clavicle structure indicates that you are predominately ectomorphic. Bodybuilding will help you gain muscular weight, but you will probably never win Mr. Olympia.

Astrid Falconi

PRE-EXHAUST DETAILS

Q. I am currently using your pre-exhaust system and would like to know one thing. After you've done your isolation movement could you use two combination movements in superset fashion, so as to hit the muscle at different angles?

A. No! It would be better to use isolation sets to really tire the smaller muscle, and then follow immediately with only one set of a compound movement.

DOORWAY CHIN BARS

Q. Can you give me your thoughts on doorway chin bars. Are they safe?

A. Doorway chin bars unscrew to fit solidly between the uprights of any doorway. Pressure on the hard rubberized ends keeps the bar in place, not suction. If a bar is fitted properly it will hold a 300-pound man easily.

The disadvantage is that the doorway chin bar is not suited for anyone who wants to do wide-grip chinning.

TRICEPS OUTER HEAD

Q. Please list some exercises for building the outer head of the triceps because I lack development in this area. The only equipment I have is a set of barbells and dumbells, an EZ-curl bar and an adjustable bench. Thanks for any help you can give me.

A. The best exercise for the outer head of the triceps is the supine triceps extension done with a light dumbell. Lie on your back on a bench and hold a single dumbell at arms' length with your right hand. Now lower the weight slowly with your thumb facing downward until the top of the dumbell touches the left pectoral. Return to the straight-arm position (without any bounce from the weight as this can defeat the purpose of the exercise). This was a great favorite of Steve Reeves who used the exercise extensively.

SITUPS NO, CRUNCHES YES!

Q. Dear Vince, I need to lose my gut. How many situps and leg raises should I do to develop my abs?

A. None! Situps are not a good waist movement. I was the first trainer to promote crunches. They are far better than situps or leg raises. Perform 3 or 4 sets of 10 to 15 reps. To lose weight you must eat less.

TOO MUCH SUGAR

Q. I like to take sugar with my cereal at breakfast and also have it in my beverages. Is sugar so bad? I do not want to get fat.

A. The big problem with sugar is that we simply eat too much of it. Often we are unaware of just how much we eat. You may not realize it, but you're eating almost 50 percent sugar when sucrose is a number three ingredient in a box of cereal, corn syrup is a number five, or when honey is a number seven. It is beyond argument that sugar is a prime factor in tooth decay and it is also the villain in hypoglycemia. Sugar is generally accepted as contributing directly or indirectly to diabetes and heart disease. As a bodybuilder, sugar is your enemy. It has no nutritional value, yet it can cause obesity. Watch labels carefully. Look for sucrose substitutes such as corn syrup or corn sugar, and watch out for words that end in "ose" which indicates the presence of sugar. Keep clear of: soft drinks, cakes, cookies, candies, canned fruits, ice cream, jams, desserts, and syrups.

SUPERSETS – TOO SEVERE?

Q. I have heard many bodybuilders state that they only use supersets prior to an important contest. They went on to state that supersets are too severe to use during the off-season and they would soon burn out. My question is, wouldn't supersets performed with less intensity during the off-season lead to shorter workouts while keeping the muscles growing?

A. You are assuming that the superset principle can be used moderately. You should understand that the superset principle is not clearly defined. Some people superset chest and back work, two totally different muscle areas, while others superset triceps and biceps (both muscles in the upper arm). The benefit of supersetting is in the time-saving factor. And obviously, when more work is done in a shorter period of time, the benefit is increased greatly.

If you keep in mind that muscle-building gains come about from increased intensity (resulting in an increased blood flow – to pump up capillary size), while providing the system with adequate nourishment, and subsequent relaxation (to allow compensational growth to take place), you will not go wrong. No known exercises are "too severe," but discretion should be used on the number of sets performed. Too many can lead to overwork, and loss of muscle size.

VITAMIN C – HOW IMPORTANT?

Q. How important is vitamin C in the bodybuilder's diet?

A. I don't know if one could possibly single out any particular vitamin and stress its importance over another, because they are all important. But here are a few facts about vitamin C which I hope will help you. Vitamin C is an antioxidant. One of its specific roles is in promoting the formation of collagen, needed for connective tissues. And, as you may know, it is the single most important connective tissue protein in the body. Contrary to what I'm sure you have heard in the gym, the body also stores large amounts of vitamin C in the adrenal glands where it is needed to aid in the production of the hormones epinephrine and norepinephrine.

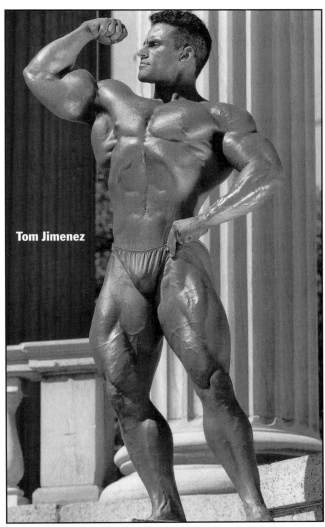

Tom Jimenez

MEDIUM-CHAIN TRIGLYCERIDES – MCTs

Q. What are medium-chain triglycerides?

A. Medium-chain triglycerides (MCTs) are special dietary nutrients derived from coconut oil. MCTs have been used for over thirty years in hospital nutrition. They contain over twice the energy of carbohydrates, and are still absorbed and metabolized as easily as carbohydrates. Your red muscle fibers (back and legs) prefer MCTs as an energy source during exercise.

MCTs have been shown to reduce bodyfat, improve the metabolism of carbohydrates and proteins, and enhance the absorption of essential elements like calcium and potassium. MCTs will give you extra energy during hard workouts and faster recovery.

TOO SMALL A WAIST!

Q. My question may seem unusual. My waist area is definitely too small. I do not want to enter contests and only wish to look good on the beach. I have tried performing side bends with a dumbell in both hands, but my oblique muscles are not thickening up. Please do not doubt that my waist is too small; several friends have pointed it out to me. My waist measures 20 inches and my chest is 43.

A. I guess there's not much hope for British bodybuilder Brian Buchanan is there? He has a 27-inch waist going steady with a 53-inch chest! Are you sure that your friends are not pointing out your waist because they admire it?

At any rate, the obliques are not really worked when you use two dumbells. You may as well use none at all because you are balancing the weight when you use two. Try sidebends with one dumbell (3 sets of 30 reps). You will also find that if you train with heavy weights in basic movements like rows, squats and deadlifts, your waistline will balance up quickly.

HOW MUCH PROTEIN?

Q. How much protein do you actually absorb at any one time? If I eat a steak with 100 grams of protein in it, how much do I really absorb and use? Is it better to take in slightly too much protein than not enough and what are the side effects of eating too much protein?

A. The amount of protein that you can digest and absorb (called bioavailability of the protein) is dependent on many factors, including the state of your digestive system, and the type of protein eaten. For example, about 90 percent of high-grade animal protein is bioavailable; while some plant proteins, because they are poorly digested and absorbed, may have a bioavailability of less than 50 percent. If you have diarrhea, then more of the protein will pass right through without being digested and absorbed.

By taking in a very large amount of protein all at once, you may overload your digestive system. The result being that you may end up losing more of the protein in your stool than you would have if you had taken in the same amount of protein over a longer period of time. For several reasons, it's probably best not to overdo protein consumption at any one meal. Most athletes who want to gain size will take their protein over several smaller meals rather than one or two larger ones – it's more efficient and you feel less bloated. As well, if your body gets too much protein all at once it will metabolize any extra protein it doesn't need at that time. So by ingesting large amounts of protein at any one time, it is simply being wasted as an expensive source of extra calories.

If a supplement says it contains one gram of protein then it usually is one gram of protein. If you take 30 grams of a protein supplement, then you will likely digest and absorb about 25 grams. Where the confusion comes in is when someone eats say 100 grams of meat or fish and thinks he is getting 100 grams of protein. High-protein foods are usually around 25 percent protein (if cooked without other ingredients).

Hamdullah Aykutlu

MOTIVATION LEVELS

Q. I was wondering, what is the best way to motivate myself to lift weights? I can't go to the gym. Could you also let me know which amino acids are the best to take, and when to incorporate them into my diet.

A. If you cannot find the reasons to motivate yourself to train, I can't do it for you. Set some goals for yourself and go after them. All bodybuilders are self-motivators – something drives them into the gym, and makes them want to train harder. You have to get that "eye of the tiger" desire.

The best amino acids are the complete amino acid complexes. Taken with your meals and in between meals they keep your blood sugar levels elevated, keep you in a positive nitrogen balance, curb your craving for sweets, help build muscle, and burn fat. Try five with each meal and two every two hours in between meals.

STICKING POINT

Q. Vince, I've come to a point where I just cannot seem to increase my workout poundages any more. I have been at a sticking point for over six months and my progress has been stalled. What can I do to get myself gaining again?

A. Adding weight is not necessarily a method of adding resistance. At least it is not the only method. Trying constantly to increase workout poundages leads to cheating; thus your muscles are working less than if lighter weights are being used. Try this trick. Do what I call 1-1/2s. For every rep, do a half rep followed by a full rep. This one and a half equals one rep. Do all your reps for every exercise in this manner. The secret is to do only 3 sets. Any more will lead to overtraining and a resulting loss of muscle tone and hormone depletion. I have found that bodybuilders always add exercises, sets, and reps when they stop improving. This never produces results. The real secret is to cut back on sets and use better form.

BETTER BICEPS

Q. I am having difficulty in making my biceps grow and respond. I haven't gained half an inch in six months. What can I do to make my biceps grow? Presently I do barbell curls, dumbell curls and preacher curls, 3 sets of each of 10 reps.

A. Try doing 21s for increased arm size. Do 7 partial barbell curls, moving the bar halfway up. Next do 7 partial reps from the top, lowering halfway down. Next

Jean-Pierre Fux

do 7 full reps. Your biceps should be pumped to the max and on fire! Try also to eat more protein. I recommend 50 grams of protein six times a day while on this biceps program. Also try taking five free-form amino acid tablets and five desiccated liver tabs every three hours. This will keep you in a positive nitrogen balance and your tissues will be saturated with protein.

OVERTONUS

Q. Vince, I've heard you use the term before but what exactly is overtonus and what happens when you get it and how is it caused?

A. Overtonus is a condition caused by too many sets, too many different exercises and, in short – overtraining. This may cause muscle loss, hormone depletion, weakness, and a smoothed-out appearance. Other effects include an inability to produce a pump and general lassitude or weakness.

ENOUGH IS ENOUGH

Q. How do you tell when you have done enough sets, and how much of a pump should you aim for?

A. The right amount of sets is the amount that produces maximum pump. To find out the right amount of sets, exercise until you are pumped to the maximum. Then continue to exercise until you begin to lose some of your pump. At this point, check back the number of sets, time tempo and repetitions required to achieve this effect. This is your personal exercise requirement level. When you lose your pump, you know you are doing too much. Next time do a few sets less.

EARLY-MORNING TRAINING

Q. The only time I can train is early in the morning before I go to work. My question is this: How do I eat before my workout? I can't get in a big meal because I train at 6:00 a.m. Also, I wanted to know if my workouts can still be productive at this hour?

A. Better you than me, that's for sure! If it was me, I think I would just give up bodybuilding right now and find a hobby that can't be done before noon!

Seriously though, you're going to have to have your large glycogen-loading meals the day before. These will fuel your early-morning workouts. Before your workout just eat something like fruit or an energy bar. You want enough in your stomach to kill the hunger pains, but not enough to make you puke after 3 sets! Another thing, try two or three cups of coffee.

With regards to productivity, yes your workouts can be productive at that hour. Absolutely! Just ask Bill Pearl!

WHERE'S THE BEEF?

Q. My question is about two different foods, meat and vegetables. Are these two food groups necessary for muscle growth? You see, I don't really like these foods and that's why I'm asking. If I have to eat them I will, but I'm hoping you'll tell me I don't.

A. Well, you don't have to eat meat but I do believe in it, and lots of it I might add. I'll usually eat a 10-ounce flank steak for a morning meal and a pound of ground buffalo later in the day (usually after training). I believe that beef builds beef. I'm made of red meat! Now, there's no science behind my theories so I'm sure you can be just as big and strong with chicken or fish. I also eat chicken and fish, but I'm mainly a red meat fan.

Now on the vegetable question, I think you should eat your greens every day because of the vitamins and fiber and all that good stuff. My problem is that I don't like them either! I mainly limit eating them to contest time. If someone makes them for me I'll eat them, but I'm too lazy to prepare them myself.

Workouts can be effective at any time of the day.

JAZZING UP TUNA
Q. I hate tuna! But I want to eat it for its good protein content. How do I get the stuff down?

A. Simple old bodybuilding trick – and I'm sure a lot of you out there have tried it – pineapple. That's it. Take a can of tuna and throw in a can of pineapple. (Make sure both are packed in water.) The pineapple kills the dry tuna taste. Great protein, great carbs, no fat.

GOING FOR THE V
Q. Whenever I do T-bar rows and dumbell rows I can really feel my lats. When I do barbell rows however, I can't seem to feel my lats at all. Do you have any idea what I'm doing wrong?

A. You might be using so much weight on your barbell rows that you're heaving and throwing the weight up rather than rowing it up strictly. Sometimes guys go so heavy that their bent-over rows look more like deadlifts. I suggest you try going lighter and concentrate on proper technique. Use a weight that allows at least 6 strict reps and then cheat out 2 or 3 extras at the end of the set for more intensity.

LACKING LOWER TRICEPS
Q. I need to build more lower-triceps thickness, especially near the elbow. What's the best lower-triceps exercise you know of?

A. You should realize first off, that you may have high triceps insertions and may be incapable of building much muscle mass near your elbows. Of course, you will never know unless you try. I think seated EZ-bar overhead extensions work the lower triceps more than the lying version; but one of the very best lower triceps builders of all is the close-grip pushup. Place your hands together so they are almost touching and directly under your chest. For real lower-triceps work make your hands into fists. Now do as many pushups as you can. Do your reps slowly, feeling the lower-triceps work. Try 4 sets of max reps of close-grip "fist" pushups and see how much lower triceps you can build.

DIET – HOW IMPORTANT?
Q. Does diet play a big part in a person's weight-training program? I'm asking this because I don't like taking all the tablets that most bodybuilders take. Are they necessary? Also, what kind of diet should a beginner follow when he starts training?

A. Yes, diet does play a major role in your bodybuilding program if you are trying for a muscular body. Most experts agree that diet is responsible for at least 50 percent of your success in bodybuilding and some experts put the figure even higher. Larry Scott and Vince Gironda think it's more like 80 percent, especially when dieting for a contest.

Food supplements are not an absolute necessity, but most bodybuilders take supplements because generally, results come a little easier and faster with food supplements. This is especially true if you are underweight and need extra protein and calories in your diet. Then protein powders and weight-gain formulas really shine.

Generally speaking, you should try to eat low-fat protein sources like fish, poultry, egg whites, skim or 2% milk, and some lean red meat. Fresh fruit and vegetables are a must. For complex carbs, try brown rice, yams, baked potatoes, and some whole grain. Keep your fat intake as low as possible. If you wish to gain weight you will of course consume more calories daily than if you are overweight and needed to shed some pounds.

Today, most bodybuilders try to eat five or six small meals a day instead of three larger ones, as is traditionally done. This allows you to digest and assimilate your food better and keeps the blood sugar levels elevated throughout the day. Eating smaller, more frequent meals also keeps your muscles constantly supplied with nutrients.

TRAINING AROUND A LOWER-BACK INJURY

Q. I just received the bad news that I have to take a whole month off my weightlifting due to a minor lower-back injury. I would like to know your estimates on how much strength I'll lose and how long it will take to regain that strength, and the best way to start back up again?

A. If you do take a whole month off, you will probably lose about 30 percent of your strength, but you should regain most of that in a month or less. However, I do not suggest you take a complete layoff, but rather change to exercises that do not stress the lower back. This will require you to perform mostly isolation exercises. For example, instead of shoulder presses for the delts, you might want to do seated laterals, keeping the back straight and no cheating. For the arms, instead of the barbell curl, you might do seated dumbell curls with your back braced against the back of a preacher bench or a wall. For legs, instead of squats, do light leg extensions and hack squats. For the chest, do bench presses to the neck with no arch. Instead of bent rows (and T-bar rows) for the lats, do lat pulldowns, which will help decompress the spine. For triceps, lying triceps extensions with an EZ-curl bar will not stress the lower back if you keep the back flat.

The point is, choose exercises that do not stress the lower back, and use strict form with no cheating, arching, or throwing the weights around. It might also be best to do slightly higher reps than normal, say in the 15 to 20 range. If you follow these tips you shouldn't lose any of your muscle size or strength.

MUSCLE SIZE – HOW FAST?

Q. How fast can muscles grow? I want to get my body in shape as fast as possible. I do not want to wait 15 or 20 years to build up my body. How many pounds of muscle can I expect to gain each month?

A. The average bodybuilder, if he trains hard and eats well, can expect to average about one pound of weight gain per month (12 pounds a year). On the other hand, with a special surge in training (change of diet, equipment, gym, atmosphere, training partner, etc.) some seemingly average bodybuilders manage to gain 12 pounds a month! Needless to say, it all depends on whether you are a natural gainer, your training intensity,

Diet is responsible for at least 50 percent of your success.

frequency, and eating habits. A bodybuilder who has a positive attitude, sets personal goals, trains regularly and hard, eats three meals a day, takes the appropriate supplements, and rests sufficiently between workouts, is going to make far better gains than the fellow who has infrequent workouts, misses breakfast, takes no supplements, plays table tennis before his workout, or goes to a club afterward.

ADDITIONAL ARM SIZE

Q. I weigh 225 pounds and have been weight training for about nine months. My best bench press is 300 pounds. My chest is 49 inches but my arms are only 17-1/2 inches. This is my problem – I can't seem to put any additional size on my arms. They need to be bigger to keep up with my chest. I have worked my arms hard, but I can't get them to grow beyond 17-1/2. Building 18-inch arms seems out of my reach. I would appreciate any help you can provide.

A. That additional inch you seek on your arms is easy! The first thing you should do is give your arms a "shock treatment." Do four alternate curls with 25-pound dumbells. Up five pounds each set until you can no longer curl. Now turn around, and work down the rack. No rest between sets, just shake your arms and take four deep breaths. Do no other biceps work and work arms three days a week only. Also, no abdominal work of any kind. The next thing you need to do is take three desiccated liver tablets every three hours. And in three weeks you will have that extra inch!

BREATHING

Q. I have read several medical references to exercises in which it is clearly stated that one must never hold one's breath. In contrast, John McCallum states that a person should hold his/her breath during the squat and other heavy exercises. What is the proper way, I'm confused?

A. John McCallum doesn't mean that you should hold your breath indefinitely, but he feels that you should squat on full lungs rather than empty ones. It is impossible to give everything to the tough part of an exercise without holding your breath. All heavy exercises involve holding the breath during the most difficult part of the movement, after which you immediately exhale.

There are many theories about breathing and exercises, but as long as you don't run into an oxygen debt there is no cause for alarm. Although not carved in stone, try to inhale/exhale for every rep of a given exercise. Not only is it a good pacing practice, but you are ensuring the body has adequate oxygen.

A DARKER, SAFER TAN

Q. What is the safest way to have a dark tan? I like the way I look with a dark tan, but with skin cancer and things like drying skin, I'm concerned about tanning in the sun. How do bodybuilders always seem to have that dark glow, even in winter? I have seen ads on sprays, creams, and pills that you can take to give the skin color, but what's the story on these? What is safe and what is not? What about canthaxanthin? Can you take this year round or not?

A. You are right to be concerned about skin cancer from tanning in the sun. I should point out to you that most bodybuilders do not have year-round dark tans. They only tan for shows and photo shoots. In the off-season and during the winter, they have very little – if any – tan at all.

The safest way to tan is to use tanning lotions and canthaxanthin. These allow you to get a tan without any exposure to ultraviolet rays. Tanning beds are your next best bet. If you do tan in the sun, start slowly – say, ten or fifteen minutes a day – and then gradually build up. Make sure you use sunscreens to avoid sunburns.

WRIST PAIN

Q. I have recently started bodybuilding. After three months of workouts I have run into a problem with my wrists and forearms. It feels like my biceps can curl more than my wrists can hold. When I do any curling exercises, I have a pain in my wrists and in the tendons

Laura
Creavalle

and ligaments of my forearms. I'm not sure if my wrists are too small (they're seven inches around), or my forearms are under-developed for the amount of weight I am lifting. In any case, the pain has forced me to stop working my biceps until I can find a solution to this problem. Any advice you could give would be greatly appreciated.

A. The problem is that your wrists aren't able to take the strain while your biceps are. The solution is twofold. First, you can support your wrists with either a splint or supportive wraps, but only in your heavier sets. Next is to eventually become inde-pendent of any supports by concentrating on your wrist and forearm strength during every workout. Pick two or three exercises that give the wrists and forearms a good workout – such as wrist curls, or reverse curls, but be sure that your wrists don't hurt regardless of which exercises you choose to do. If you feel pain, don't do that exercise – or modify it so that it still works the wrists and forearms but doesn't hurt.

SPLITTING THE PECS
Q. I want to know how to develop a split between my upper and lower pecs like some of the top bodybuilders have. Which exercises should I do to develop a split?

A. A split between the pecs is not something that can be trained for. Just as some people cannot build peaked biceps or long, full calves, most people cannot build a deep split between the upper and lower pecs. One of the best in this regard was former Mr. Olympia, Franco Columbu. Of course, until you try, you won't know if you are one of those lucky people who can build a split.

You will need to do specific exercises for the upper and lower pecs – incline presses and flyes for upper pecs, and decline presses and flyes for the lower pecs. Also, and this is very important, you must have a low bodyfat level to show any split between the pecs. Only when you have good definition will any splits be seen. Too much fat will blur the possibility of showing any upper-lower pec separation.

LACK OF ENDURANCE
Q. I like doing squats, but I get so out of breath after only a couple of reps that I'm unable to do as many reps as I'd need to work my legs. How can I train to improve my strength endurance?

A. You need to get in better cardiovascular shape. Besides running a few miles two or three times per week, try sprinting twice a week, either running or with

Hamdullah Aykutlu

a bicycle. Also, make sure that you breathe in and out with each repetition when you do your squats. Don't rush, but keep a steady rhythm when performing the exercise.

ABS – NOT EVERY DAY!
Q. Dear Vince, you said it was bad to work your stomach muscles every day. Yet many of the muscle books say you should. I have read many of your articles which have made sense to me and given me the idea that you know what you are talking about, so that is why I am asking you for advice. I would like to know if it is all right to work your stomach muscles every day?

A. Work abdominals every day and you will lose them! They will smooth out, and become bloated looking. If you work any muscle every day you lose muscle tone, and about 40 percent of your male hormone. Over-training does not produce muscle tissue – it destroys it. Work your abdominals the same number of sets and reps as you would any other muscle.

Ericca Kern

FULL CANNONBALL-SIZED DELTS

Q Perhaps you guys at *MuscleMag* can help me. I want to build high deltoids that really look impressive when I do a double-biceps pose from the back. I also have a friend who has quite impressive shoulder width. His lateral deltoids stand out well from the side, but he doesn't have fully developed shoulders when viewed from the back. Please give me advice.

A. The exercises which contribute most to building "high" deltoids when viewed from the back are the press behind the neck, the incline-bench press, and alternate front raises with dumbells. The muscle you admire is actually the frontal deltoid. Your friend seems to have spent more time on the deltoid exercises which give a longer look to the deltoid muscle.

TURNING CALVES INTO COWS!

Q. I don't have a calf machine at home, and I want to build really good lower legs. What do you advise? There are no gyms in my area, so I have to train at home.

A. Many bodybuilders train their calves with nonresistance movements like concentrated heel raises, single-leg calf raises and "burns."

We must point out that the greatest gains in calf development, made by men like Pearl, Schwarzenegger and Park, resulted from many, many sets of standing calf raises using a machine. The best nonapparatus exercise for building lower leg size is the donkey calf raise. Place your toes on a four-inch block of wood, bend over at the waist (supporting your body with your hands on a chair or bench), and have a heavy training partner sit on your lower back. Try to do no less than 20 reps and work up to the point where you are doing at least 8 sets three times a week.

FAT EMULSIFIERS

Q. I want to know if choline and inositol work in helping the body lose fat. Also, I have heard that regular doses of cider vinegar, lecithin and kelp can also help definition. What is the truth?

A. This is a difficult question to answer. The medical profession tends to frown on the usefulness of any of these ingredients as fat mobilizers. However, many bodybuilders swear by some, or all of the above — especially when taken in conjunction with a low-calorie diet. The difficulty is in knowing which, if any, of the supplements work, and whether or not any increased definition is due to the supplements, or the low-calorie diet, or to both. The answer would be more definite if some unbiased authority would arrange some strict controlled tests on bodybuilders.

TOO OLD!

Q. I am worried because I have just discovered the wonderful world of bodybuilding, but I think I may be too old to make progress in body development. My doctor says I am fit and recommended that I take up weight training to gain bodyweight, but I am 26 years old.

A. Dear me! 26 years old! One foot in the grave...

Now hear this, if you are in good physical health, you can make really fine bodybuilding progress at twice your age! Granted the ideal age to start bodybuilding would be the middle or late teens, but just because you're older doesn't mean you can't make super progress. Just make sure you start right and don't waste your time on incorrect training methods.

TOO MUCH PROTEIN?

Q. I follow a high-protein diet, trying for 50 grams of protein, six times daily. My doctor tells me this is too much and that it will put a strain on my liver. How can I get the protein I need without harming my liver?

A. Try free-form amino acids which go directly into the bloodstream. This places little or no strain on the liver, and you get all the protein you need.

CUTTING THE PECS

Q. I am a loyal reader of *MuscleMag International* and I really enjoy it. I have a problem I hope you can help me with. I have been working out for over a year and have a big chest but can't seem to get my pectoral muscles tight or cut. I do a lot of decline and incline presses and flyes, but to no avail. I am big, but not hard and tight. I would appreciate it if you could give me a few pointers.

A. If you are big but not cut, you are carrying too much bodyfat everywhere, not just in the pecs. You must lose some fat. Cut back on your calories. Your chest will be smaller, but cut and better shaped. As well, I recommend that you take amino acids, five to ten at each meal. Eat only good, nutritious foods, no junk. As for exercises, I recommend that you do more isolation exercises for your pecs, as well as trying supersets. For example, try decline presses supersetted with decline flyes, incline presses supersetted with incline flyes, or dips supersetted with dumbell pullovers.

STRETCH MARKS

Q. What are the cause of stretch marks and how can I get rid of them?

A. Stretch marks occur when your muscles grow faster than your skin. They also occur when individuals gain too much weight (usually fat), too fast. It has also been suggested that poor nutrition causes the skin to lose its elasticity, and therefore it doesn't stretch when the underlying muscle grows. The most noticeable spots are the chest and delts, particularly the pec-delt tie-in. Many authorities, including Vince Gironda, suggest that a lack of minerals, such as manganese, contribute to the condition. Once you get stretch marks it's virtually impossible, short of surgery, to get rid of them. You can reduce the chances of developing new ones by supplementing your diet with manganese, and a good mineral-vitamin tablet. Also, take extra vitamins A and E. Finally, some bodybuilders have found that vitamin E-rich creams help alleviate already existing stretch marks.

HERNIA

Q. I think I am developing a hernia. It hurts when I do squats as well as when I try other leg and ab exercises. Can I correct this problem through exercise? What should I do?

A. The first thing you should do is see your doctor and determine if you indeed have a hernia. You can prevent a hernia by strengthening the abdominal wall, but once you have one, it can only be corrected by surgery. The condition is aggravated by interthoracic pressure (holding your breath and straining). Do all your leg work sitting or lying on your back. Make sure you have no downward pressure.

MASSIVE LEGS

Q. I would like to know how to get massive leg size like Franco Santoriello. I was wondering if a person can diet, train hard and compete successfully without strong genetic potential?

A. Just as there's no real substitute for a "winning hand" dealt by genetics, there's no substitute for the basic squat when it comes to

quad growth. Whatever exercises you do for thighs — and you should be doing at least two exercises for size and one for shape — base them all around the squat. Work up to 6 to 8 sets of 10 to 20 reps in the squat before performing your shaping exercises. Treat the lower leg the same and do at least three exercises (with different foot placements) for the calves. As with squats, base your calf workout around the standing calf raise.

BUILDING THE INNERS

Q. I have two questions for you. One, how do you get the inner thighs built up, and two, will leg extensions hamper my squat strength?

A. On the first question, all you have to do is perform all your squats, leg presses and hacks with your feet wide apart. Be sure to point your toes outward and go all the way down.

As for question number two, who knows for sure? I've always done both in my leg workout, whether on the same leg day or consecutive leg days. As a

J.J. Marsh

bodybuilder you should aim for total development, and this means hitting the muscles from all angles. Perhaps leg extensions would hinder achieving a one-rep lift record on the squat, but is this what you're after? I would advise going for the maximum effect, and hitting the muscle with as many different exercises as possible.

SIDE DELTS

Q. It seems that I can't get my side and rear delts to grow with regular standing laterals and bent laterals. Is there any exercise that you recommend that works not only the side and rear head, but also the tie-in between both heads?

A. I have just the exercise to meet your needs. It's the lying one-arm lateral. You can do it either lying on the floor or off a bench. The important thing is to lie on your side and to lift the dumbell smoothly and strictly with delt power alone. Keep a slight bend in your elbow as you lower the dumbell in front of your body. To take advantage of negative resistance lower slowly and with great control. Never allow the dumbell to rest or touch the floor so that constant tension is on the delt. Keeping the little finger higher than the thumb at the top position will work the side head, the rear head and the tie-in. This happens to be Serge Nubret's favorite delt exercise and he has fantastic side and rear delts. Keep the reps in the 10 to 15 range and do at least 4 sets every delt workout. And by the way, if you lower the dumbell along the body you work mostly the side head. Lower behind the body and you hit mostly the front head, with some side head and tie-in involvement.

UPSET STOMACH

Q. Every time I take vitamins I get an upset stomach. I think I'm weird… help!

A. The reason could be the brand of vitamins, the time of day they're taken, or whether or not you've eaten. Experiment with all of these variables, and I'm sure you will find a plan that works. If not, you might want to see your doctor, especially if you have allergies or are taking prescription medicine.

MORE ON TRAINING TIME

Q. I am a businessman who enjoys pumping iron for a more muscular physique. I don't know if there are other guys out there who think like me, but I have always felt that there must be a time of the day when the "hour is ripe" to facilitate greater muscular progress. By this I mean that there must be some specific hour in the day to train so that better and faster bodybuilding results will materialize.

I continue to search for this magical hour but to no avail. In your years and years of experience what have you found to be the best time of day to train in order to obtain faster results?

A. From the time one rises in the morning, energy levels build so that by midafternoon, between 3:30 and 6:00 p.m., they are supposed to be at their peak. This energy level depends on a person's habits, the amount of sleep he or she gets, and how nutritious his or her diet is to meet the demands of the body.

On the other hand, not everyone is in a position to take time off and train at four in the afternoon. Besides, this energy build-up can be disturbed by other frustrating or emotional factors, which exact their toll on a person during the day. Therefore, there is no particular hour better suited to training than the next. Make adjustments and fit your training schedule into whatever hours are available. It's really no big deal what hour you select to train. The important thing is that you train regardless of what time you decide to do so. The ideal time is the most convenient time!

STARTING OVER

Q. My interest in bodybuilding started at age 17, and now that I'm finished having children I want to pursue bodybuilding. I need more

Darin Lannaghan

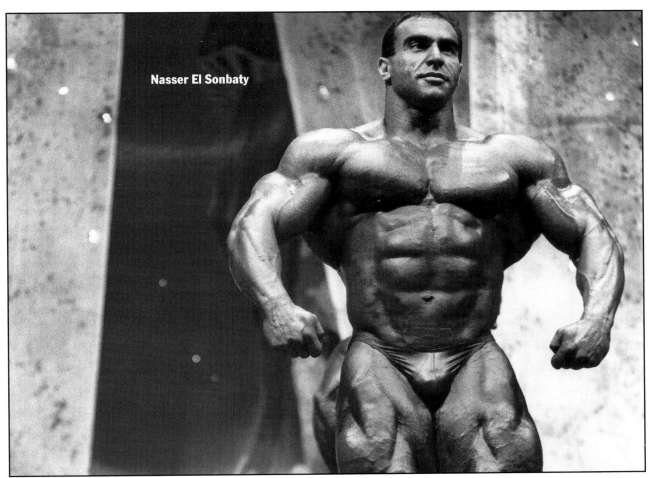

Nasser El Sonbaty

information on fat-burning, supplements, and muscle-building.

I have that hourglass body shape, where most of my mass is in the lower half, so I have to work harder to burn fat. To burn fat and build muscle at the same time seems contradictory. Could you please give me some advice? Thanks!

A. It is possible to burn fat and build muscle at the same time, but you must have a good solid plan that balances training with nutrition.

To burn fat you need to follow a low-fat, moderate-carbohydrate, high-protein diet. Try to eat at least every three hours, with your morning meals the largest, followed by decreasing meal sizes throughout the day. Take a multivitamin-mineral supplement with your meals. Also drink anywhere from six to ten glasses of water daily.

As for your training, work out with weights four or five times a week, training two bodyparts each session. Add some sort of aerobic exercise each day, (45 minutes for maximum results). I recommend separating your weight training and aerobics because if your total exercise session goes over 90 minutes, you will probably start losing muscle instead of fat. All the best and good luck!

HOW MANY CALORIES?
Q. I'm a beginner bodybuilder who needs to lose weight. Every article I've read says you need to eat up

to 7000 to 8000 calories to build muscle mass, but I need to lose fat. Is it possible to do both at the same time, or do I have to lose fat, then build the muscle mass?

A. I wish I could eat 8000 calories! Really, those articles do not apply to you or most any other women. To build muscle you do need to eat plenty of protein (approximately one to one and a half grams per pound of bodyweight), but the number of calories should range from a minimum of 1600 to a maximum of 2500 depending on your current weight and metabolism.

Don't think in terms of just losing weight. Try to change your whole body composition; replace excess bodyfat with good solid muscle tissue. When this happens you look leaner, but your actual bodyweight may not go down because muscle weighs more than fat. Finally, when a person loses a lot of weight by just doing hours and hours of aerobics and not eating enough protein, he or she often ends up with a weak body that still appears fat.

16 AND NEEDS HELP!
Q. I am a 16-year-old beginner in bodybuilding. I have been training for four and a half weeks with no positive results. Please recommend a good training program for me, along with the max amount of time I should spend in the gym. I would appreciate it if you would recommend my daily calorie intake. Thank you very much for your help.

Lee Priest

A. I'm going to answer this letter not just for the individual but for every beginning bodybuilder out there. You see, today's kids who are in the gym are not getting the right picture. They want it all, they want it now, and they don't want to sweat a drop to get it! Like this guy here who isn't getting results after four weeks of training. Come on dude, I've taken longer layoffs than four weeks. In a month I might train a bodypart only four times. How can you expect anything to happen in a month?

Now let's get a grip on reality here. I want to see some honest blood, sweat and tears in the gym. Barbells, dumbells, clanging plates, rock and roll cranking loud, and sounds of pain and groans throughout the concrete walls. That's what it's all about!

HIGH REPS OR LOW REPS
Q. Steve, I am confused about how many repetitions I should do. Some guys at the gym say never do more than 10 reps on any given set, or you will be over-training. What do you recommend?

A. So you are looking for the magic number of repetitions? I searched for years, and to be honest with you, I am not sure that I have the absolute answer. What I do know is this: Each muscle is composed of two different types of muscle fiber – fast and slow twitch. Fast twitch is identified as the explosive type

which respond best to lower reps, while slow twitch are defined as the endurance muscles which respond to higher reps. Logically, what follows is that to thoroughly train the total muscle you should incorporate both high and low reps in your sets. The following is a good rep sequence based on a 4 sets per exercise routine.

Set 1 – 12 reps with a medium weight
Set 2 – 8 reps with a heavier weight
Set 3 – 4-6 reps with your heaviest weight
Set 4 – 15-20 reps with your lightest weight

LACKS DEFINITION
Q. I don't know what to do. I'm 16 years old, 5'9" and weigh 195 pounds. I train on a three-days-on/one-day-off routine. While I've built my share of mass, I lack definition. My problem areas are my abs, thighs, and obliques. I take two aminos a day and follow a few Weider principles. Could you suggest a few exercises and a diet I could follow?

A. You weigh too much, and need to lose fifteen or twenty pounds. You didn't list your training routine, so I can't make any recommendations there. Keep your sets per bodypart to 12 or under for major muscle groups, and 8 or less for minor ones. Keep your reps between 6 and 12 for upper-body exercises, and 10 to 20 on lower-body exercises. Abs, calves, and forearms can be trained for higher reps.

I recommend that you start to do some aerobics, such as running, jogging, or aerobic classes. This will increase fat-burning and also give your physique a harder appearance. With regards to diet, cut down on your fat, salt, and sugar intake. Try to decrease your calorie intake, 300 to 500 calories below maintenance level, or the amount of calories you consume each day to maintain your present bodyweight. Aim at losing about a half to one pound per week, until you reach the desired weight you want. When your abs are hard and defined, no doubt the rest of your body will be the same.

JUST PLAIN SKINNY!
Q. At fifteen years of age, I am just plain skinny. You could say I'm at my wits end. I just cannot gain weight. I train like crazy, never missing workouts. My father says I am naturally skinny and that I'll never be really built. Please help me beat this thing.

A. If you are healthy, you will build up. You may never become a Mr. Olympia (few do!), but with hard, regular training you will get bigger and add muscle. At 15 years of age your male hormones are just kicking in. Look for good gains during the next few years. Train each bodypart twice weekly, three exercises per bodypart, 5 sets of 8 to 12 reps. Split your workout into two or three parts. Try and relax as much as possible when not training. Eat every couple of hours – cheese or meat sandwich, fruit, yogurt, nuts, eggs, and don't forget the best gainer of all – milk!

STILL IN PAIN

Q. Two years ago I was really into lifting. I would exercise four days a week training different bodyparts, but making sure I worked all major muscle groups.

I hurt my leg and had to have surgery. It has since healed and I have resumed training. Now my left elbow is giving me problems. No matter what the lift, barbell or dumbell, it still gives me great pain. Even with light weight, it still hurts. What do you suggest?

A. Any pain, whether from an old leg injury or one which gradually comes on from training, must be treated with care. Ease up on those exercises that cause pain in the left elbow. Then if you find it still hurts after a good warmup, don't train. Simply rest that arm until the pain level improves. Then, if pain continues to occur even after six weeks, see your doctor. If you can train with slight pain, then applying ice packs to the elbow after workouts will help.

WHEN TO TRAIN

Q. I am wondering if training a different bodypart every day would be the answer to my problems of gaining muscle size. I have tried working the whole body on Mondays, Wednesdays, and Fridays, but I just didn't gain. I would appreciate your thoughts on this.

A. You are thinking about changing from training each bodypart three times a week to only training each bodypart once a week. Bodybuilding researchers have determined that in most cases our muscles grow best from two workouts a week. I suggest you split your routine in three parts and train three days on, one day off, or else split your workout in two and train four days a week. In both cases you will be exercising each bodypart twice a week.

BAREFOOT

Q. I have read that you always recommend that calf work be done barefoot. I have tried this on the standing calf machine at my gym, but my feet really hurt after the first few reps. Please help me, Vince.

A. Yes I do recommend barefoot calf work, but only when the step of the calf machine is covered with a thick layer of hard rubber. You get more range and action when you train your lower legs with bare feet. In your case, however, wear proper exercise shoes, otherwise you could damage the arch of your foot. If you find that the stiffness of the sole hinders your range of motion, then undo the laces of your sneaker, and you will obtain both comfort and a full range of motion.

EXERCISE SEQUENCE

Q. Is it necessary that exercises follow a certain sequence? I like to alternate my training routine, though I actually use just about the same exercises. On one day I may begin with a press, followed by a curl, etc. And the next day I will start by squatting or deadlifting, or even do some abdominal work first in the routine. In the end I still do all the exercises I am supposed to do, so what's the difference, if any? I am asking you this question only because I correspond with a friend and he tells me that I would make better progress if I followed my exercises in a definite pattern every training day. I would if it's a must, but please advise me about this. I'm sure other readers of your column would find this question interesting.

A. I personally do not subscribe to the idea that exercises must follow any specific pattern, although there are several exercises which, when followed in a sequence, are better. I am referring mainly to leg exercises that should always be followed by some chest-expansion movements such as breathing pullovers. All other exercises can be used in whatever sequence you prefer.

The idea of proper exercise sequence where you work the middle pecs before working the upper pecs or delts before the triceps is gaining popularity, but what if the upper pecs and the triceps are the least responsive to training? Wouldn't it be better to work them early on in your training?

Jason Arntz

CHAPTER THIRTY-EIGHT - QUESTIONS AND ANSWERS

Also, many bodybuilders find that training one group of muscles completely then moving on to another group has its limitations. The congestion associated with the first group often interferes with training the second. To get around this I do one or two exercises for one muscle group, and then work the antagonistic (opposite) muscles (i.e. biceps and triceps or chest and back).

As a final point, most bodybuilders find that training the small arm muscles first interferes with training the larger torso muscles. For this reason they leave the biceps, triceps, and forearms till last. Of course, if your arm muscles are woefully weak you will have to give them priority.

100 SETS!

Q. I have a question that has been bothering me. From reading just about everything I can lay my hands on regarding bodybuilding, I have concluded that every exercise hits a muscle in a different way. Therefore, if someone just did one set of each exercise, but performed sixty to a hundred different exercises, would this give more development all round?

A. Theoretically yes! In practice, however, the first set doesn't seem to do the job of fully stimulating the deeper muscle fibers. Most bodybuilders, although not all, find that a minimum of 3 sets of a given exercise is needed to fully work the muscle for overall size, and most prefer 5 sets (some even go to 8 sets per exercise). If anyone out there is just using 1 set per exercise with a wide variety of movements, I would like to hear from them, especially with regard to the results achieved. I will gladly print the information in *MuscleMag*.

BODYBUILDING – BAD FOR THE BONES!

Q. I am fourteen years old and have been bodybuilding for five months. My mother tells me that weight training is bad for the bones and that it will stop my growth. Can you tell me if this is true?

A. At fourteen you have at least six more years of natural growth, and there is no evidence to show that weight training, or indeed any form of vigorous exercise adversely effects bone growth.

I suggest you check your condition with your doctor if there is any doubt. If you are in good, robust health I am sure he will give your weight training his approval.

FIVE-HOUR WORKOUT!

Q. I will be 15 on September 29, and I have been lifting weights for a year and one month, but it seems that I am not getting any bigger and I need help. I am trying a new method. I am lifting weights 5 hours every other day and I need to know what kind of foods I need to eat to gain weight.

A. Five hours training every other day is too much. Cut it down to two hours. Eat a varied diet including; fish, meat, vegetables, fruit, whole grains, nuts and milk. Many teenagers find difficulty gaining because their hormone levels don't kick in fully until they are about 19 or 20.

NITROGEN BALANCE

Q. I keep reading the term nitrogen balance in the different magazines. What is this nitrogen balance?

Mike Francois

A. When the body utilizes amino acids, nitrogen is liberated. Fat and carbohydrate contain no nitrogen. When amino acids are used for energy, nitrogen is eliminated in the urine. If one is on a protein-free diet, 19 gm of protein can be catabolized from the body tissues to satisfy various bodily protein needs. If you consume only 19 grams of protein, you will be in a negative nitrogen balance because the essential amino acids are not supplied by each gram of protein eaten. A large quantity of protein must be available to provide the body with the amino acids it needs. Research has shown that the average person needs about 95 gm of protein just to maintain a nitrogen balance. If enough protein is eaten to create a positive nitrogen balance, the excess will be deposited as new tissue (provided the body's muscles have been stimulated by some form of exercise). This will ensure that a growing muscle is well fed.

MILK INTOLERANCE

Q. I have been drinking a lot of milk to gain weight over the years, but in recent years it seems to cause loose bowels. I have even tried milk containing lactobacillus acidophilus, but it did not help. Is there anything I can buy to put in my milk to correct the problem?

A. There is a high percentage of people who have this intolerance to milk. About 10 percent of the adult white population is lactose intolerant and estimates run as high as 85 percent for other ethnic groups. The problems, which may not be absolute (i.e. small amounts of milk may be acceptable), range from diarrhea, gas, distension, and abdominal pain to symptoms of spastic colon.

These individuals lack sufficient amounts of an enzyme in the small intestine which breaks down the disaccharide found in milk – lactose. Lactose cannot be absorbed into the bloodstream if it is not digested into single sugars. As a consequence, the undigested milk sugar ferments, causing the previously mentioned problems.

It seems that the acidophilus milk you tried still contained enough lactose to cause trouble. You may get better results from Lactaid. This enzyme when put in milk in advance, breaks down the lactose the same way your enzyme would.

MORE THAN JUST THE BASICS

Q. I come from the old school of bodybuilding. I believe that all one needs to develop a top physique are the basics: squats, deadlifts, bench presses, etc. Why do you advocate so many isolation and what I call sissy exercises, like sissy squats and side lateral raises?

A. As I glance through pages of various muscle magazines or look at the physiques of the competitors at the contests I attend, rarely do I see a body that I consider fully developed. Every bodypart has a weak area in most physiques I see. This is because most

Melissa
Coates

bodybuilders never seem to know the proper exercise for bringing out the slow-developing portions of the muscles (weak points), which really enhance the shape of the muscle. And to be a good bodybuilder you must train for shape. The basics only work the belly of the muscle, but do nothing for the origins and insertions of the muscle. If basics worked the muscle, we would have no need for: preacher curls for low biceps development, hack slides for low thighs, lat pulldowns for lengthening the lats, dips for lower and outer pecs, cables for inner pecs, lateral raises for side delts, incline presses for high pecs, and incline side raises for rear delts. The point is, unless you do shaping exercises you will get big but not look good. You will never attain maximum size unless you include shaping exercises in your routine. Have I made myself clear?

FAST OR SLOW?

Q. I'd like to know your opinion. Should I do my reps at a fast pace (lighter weight, continued tension) or use heavy, paused reps? Personally, I feel that pausing between reps because the weight is too heavy is just another form of cheating. What's your opinion?

A. Both methods of performing reps have proved useful. Beginners should stick to one method for a few months until results stop… after which a change would be the answer.

At your stage of bodybuilding, the most important aspect of training is regularity, followed by constant efforts at making your training progressive (getting more reps and adding more weight without sacrificing style). Finally, you cannot expect to grow unless you are taking in plenty of wholesome food every day, plus getting adequate relaxation and sleep.

NEED MORE CHEST DEVELOPMENT

Q. I've got pretty good arms which just seemed to arrive after six months of training. My delts, back, and legs have developed well too, but my chest just seems to be under par. I have a fairly deep rib cage however, and do a lot of bench presses, especially with a wide grip. What am I doing wrong?

A. The bench press is a great exercise for the chest, but it is not suitable for everyone. Actually, the depth of your rib cage is a factor in holding back your pectoral development. You are not getting the needed stretch in your pectorals because the bar cannot travel low enough to really work the chest muscles. Fortunately, there are literally hundreds of workable chest exercises. If you want to keep doing bench presses, I suggest you narrow your grip to a little more than shoulder width. This will give your pectorals more stretch. If you have access to a cambered bar (similar to an overgrown EZ-curl bar), give it a try. The bar's shape allows for a full stretch at the bottom of the bench-press movement.

Other fine chest exercises are: flat and incline dumbell presses and flyes, pec-dek machine flyes, and various cable-crossover movements. Do at least 10 sets for your pecs on chest day.

EGG WHITES

Q. Over the past year I have read that top bodybuilders are using egg whites in their diet. What's the big deal?

A. For many years bodybuilders have realized that eggs are one of nature's most nearly perfect foods and actually rate highest on the PER (Protein Efficiency Ratio). In the past some bodybuilders have eaten as many as three dozen eggs a day!

The trend toward egg whites is basically twofold: low in calories and zero in fat content. Egg whites have only 17 calories compared to 100 calories for the whole egg. One egg white has 3.6 grams of protein and no fat, whereas a whole egg has 7.5 grams of fat. In an attempt to get as ripped as possible it is necessary to reduce your consumption of fat, and eliminating the yolk is an effective way.

The thought of eating egg whites may not appeal to you but actually there are a couple of ways to spice them up. You can either scramble them with bits of green onion and mushrooms or make an egg-white omelet with bits of fresh fruit inside.

WANTS SIZE NATURALLY

Q. Can you tell me how to acquire great muscle size without resorting to drugs? I am 19 years old and train on and off. I often feel tired after work and skip workouts. When not training with weights I do other sports like cricket, karate, and boxing. Can you help?

Debbie Kruck

A. I can tell you how, but you have three main problems. One, you are young and probably have a fast metabolism making it difficult for you to gain weight. Two, you skip workouts and do not train regularly. Three, you play other sports which burn up precious calories making it even harder for you to gain weight.

To get big you have to (1) train big – that means hard, heavy, progressively and regularly on a proper routine; (2) eat big – that means at least one gram of protein per pound of bodyweight per day, plus 5000 to 6000 calories a day; and (3) you won't be able to play many other sports unless you are willing to eat an additional 1500 to 2000 calories a day for all the calories you burn up playing sports.

A few key points: When I say 5000 to 6000 a day, I'm talking all good food – no junk food at all. You must eat: lean red meat, eggs, chicken, fish, baked potatoes, rice, raw vegetables, skim milk etc. and no sugar, fats, salt, processed food, etc. You must eat this way, every day, until you obtain the size you desire.

As for training, lift on an every-other-day routine, half your body one day, the other half the next. Take a day off, and then repeat the cycle. Use two exercises per muscle group, doing 4 sets of 6 to 10 reps each.

LACK OF ENERGY

Q. Is there anything I can eat or take that will give me instant energy? I have the desire to train but lack the energy to do it. Should I go off junk food or cut down on my cigarettes? I drink heavily only on weekends, but I am young (23) and must have my fun.

Occasionally, I have a whole bunch of energy but when I train, this soon runs out. Any suggestions? I sure could use some good advice.

A. Some people have more energy than others. It depends on your genetics. But in your case you are responsible for your lack of energy.

Firstly, your weekend binges have got to stop. Heavy drinking, two or three days in a row, can mess you up physically for several days. You will recover only in time to start partying again. Better to have one drink a day, every day of the week, than to go crazy on the weekend. Junk foods will kill energy levels because most are loaded with refined sugar. You need natural complex carbohydrates such as grains, fruits, and vegetables, that deliver a steady flow of energy – fuel to the system rather than a quick-fix result that comes from sugary junk food.

Finally, as for that other vice, I'm shocked that you smoke. Few things kill energy quicker than cigarettes. Cut them out completely – now. Don't even think about ever smoking again. It's so old-fashioned and a complete waste of money.

Six-time Ms. Olympia Lenda Murray.

SHOULDER INJURY

Q. I had been doing straight-arm barbell pullovers (3 sets of 10 to 15 reps) with 40 pounds as part of my workout for about a month. While I was doing them recently, I felt my shoulder pop out of place. It popped back into place when I sat up, but because the area was sore and difficult to move, I have stopped working out for a while. Is this a common injury with this exercise? Is there some way I could avoid it in the future? How long should I wait until I start to work out again?

A. For starters, I would have yourself checked out by a sports physician to make sure the injury is not serious. If he gives you the OK to return to training, start back very light, say just an empty barbell. Do 2 sets of 25 to 30 reps and do the reps very slowly and smoothly. It's very important that you use no bouncing, jerking, or momentum in your reps. Only add weight when it is comfortable to do so. The way to avoid this injury in the future is to warm up well and to avoid heavy weights in the exercise. Instead of adding weight, try to do higher reps.

FOR SUPERIOR BACK DEVELOPMENT...

Q. I've been bodybuilding for two years and have made great progress. I've studied anatomy and now have a fair knowledge about muscles. My one problem is that I can't figure out which exercise will benefit my back the most. I am big-boned and have naturally broad shoulders; therefore, having a muscle-studded back would help my physique very much. I know how to develop the latissimus dorsi and the infraspinatus, but have held off developing the other muscles of my back. I would truly appreciate it if someone can help me.

A. If you have studied anatomy, you should know that it's nearly impossible to work any of the back muscles independently. In fact, it's quite impossible for any muscle to function separately. Every muscle is dependent upon another in some way. Even biceps, which seem to be more isolated in their actions than most muscles, are still aided by the shoulders and forearms, as well as the trapezius. The muscles of the back are even more closely associated and tied together, so it's impossible for you to work the rhomboids, teres muscles, the lats, or the infraspinatus separately. All back muscles work in unison when any back exercise is done. Although it's true that one or more of these back muscles may become more involved than the others in certain exercises, all of the muscles are still, nevertheless, affected.

Therefore, in order to better work your back and obtain as much muscularity and size as you're capable of, include a variety of back exercises to activate all the muscles to a greater or lessor degree. As your back develops and improves, you will show greater mass and have the muscularity that you desire. All this, however, takes time and patience!

CANNONBALL-SIZED DELTS

Q. Recently I've gone on a deltoid binge. My problem area however, is the rear section which lacks fullness. This makes me appear somewhat round-shouldered. My side and front delts are well-built, but I need some of the magic Grimek advice to beef up the rear section.

A. Thanks for your kind thoughts. The rear deltoid can be a little stubborn to build effectively, but with proper application you can bring about plenty of growth. The best exercise is the bent-over lateral raise. Sit on the edge of a bench, with feet together. Lean forward so that your chest and abdomen rest on your thighs. Raise two light dumbells out to the side while holding this position. Try 4 sets of 10 repetitions. In addition, remember that all rowing movements work the rear delts to some extent.

HOW MANY EXERCISES PER BODYPART?

Q. How many exercises per bodypart do you suggest? I've been told that as many as five are necessary for full development. Can a bodypart be fully developed with only two or three exercises if you vary the exercises every few months?

Also, how do you avoid building the upper portion of the glutes? I think this gives a square, bulky look to the glutes. Is this a genetic factor, or from squatting? If it is from squats, can I avoid the problem by doing front squats or leg presses instead?

A. I think that two or three exercises per muscle group can give a muscle good development. However, the longer you are in the sport the more quickly your body adapts to the stresses placed on it from training, and you would need to change exercises more frequently. In other words, the advanced bodybuilder needs more variety than the beginner or intermediate. Most top bodybuilders have a repertoire of five to seven exercises for each muscle group that they can choose from – usually picking two to four exercises – for each workout. The beginner should, of course, pick only one or two exercises per muscle group, 2 or 3 sets each, and only increase his sets and number of exercises when his recuperative powers increase.

Now for your glute question. If a bodybuilder is training naturally and his glutes are getting a square, bulky look from squats, I would say this is mostly a genetic factor, although exercise style should be considered too. If you squat with a wide stance and/or in a bent-over powerlifter style, this will increase the stress placed on the glutes more than if the bodybuilder

Roland Cziurlok

squatted in a close-stanced, strict, upright style. If regular squats build your glutes too much, then try squatting on the Smith machine. And choose exercises that don't stress the glutes – hack squats, sissy squats, lunges, and leg extensions.

LACKING THIGH SWEEP

Q. I have been doing all kinds of squats and leg presses for five years, but still lack sufficient thigh sweep. Can you suggest something to stimulate outer-thigh growth? The remainder of my musculature is well developed, except for this particular area.

A. Squats with the toes pointed straight ahead or even slightly in (and feet close together – 12 inches or less) are generally regarded as one of the best for thigh sweep. Leg presses with the feet close together and toes pointing straight are also very good. Probably one of the best to develop thigh sweep is the hack squat with the toes pointed out. Also, try Smith-machine squats with the toes pointing in and out – 3 to 5 sets each.

FOREARM

Q. Bob, my forearms are very skinny and weak. I have just started bodybuilding three months ago and find that my grip is really poor. Sometimes (on curls and chins) my grip gives out before my biceps do. Is there any exercise I can do to improve my grip and build my forearms at the same time?

A. The best exercise you can do to improve your grip and to build your forearms is the barbell wrist curl. Sit at the end of a flat bench with a barbell in your hands. Hold it as you would when doing barbell curls (palms-up grip), but rest your forearms on your knees so that your wrists and hands extend past the knees. Using wrist strength only, so the forearm contracts forcibly (only the wrists move), lower the barbell and then wrist curl it up. To build your grip even more, allow the barbell to roll down so that only your fingers hold it. Pull it back into the palm of your hand then wrist curl it up again. Wrist curls are a high-repetition exercise, so aim for 15 to 20 repetitions per set. This one really burns, but that's what you want. 4 or 5 sets of 15 to 20 reps should help improve your forearms greatly if practiced twice a week.

MUSCLE-BLASTING TECHNIQUES

Q. What muscle-blasting techniques do you advise during the off-season, and which ones should be used in the precontest phase? For example, giant sets, up and down the rack, supersets, trisets, pre-exhaustion, negatives, forced reps, burns, and rest-pause reps.

A. Most top champs train heavy and basic in the off-season – straight, heavy sets on basic exercises, while always trying to handle heavier and heavier weights. The muscle-blasting techniques are saved for the precontest phase, or for specialization on a weak muscle group that doesn't respond to regular training. Supersets, trisets, giant sets, etc., are just too intense to be used year round and can lead to overtraining.

ELECTRO-MUSCLES!

Q. I am interested in improving my rate of progress in bodybuilding – fast. I do not want to find myself somewhere down the road saying, "If only I knew so and so…" I am particularly interested in knowing what you know about electronic stimulators. My main interest is: Do they work? Are they dangerous? Where can I obtain them?

A. Many gyms now have these machines available to members (usually for additional fees). Beauty parlors and health spas also use them as a trimming and slimming aid; often they are promoted as an effortless way to exercise.

Those bodybuilders who use them actually turn up the juice and flex rigorously while applying the electrical current. Their use in beauty parlors, to slim

Lee Priest

CHAPTER THIRTY-EIGHT – QUESTIONS AND ANSWERS

and trim, is limited to a far milder electrical current and customers feel no pain. Many patrons can actually relax and read a book while the treatment is being applied.

According to an information officer in the FDA's Washington Headquarters, "These devices are not approved except for legitimate medical therapy in a hospital or doctor's office." Accordingly, some government seizures have taken place in the USA. Do they work? I have tried them, but not extensively and cannot offer personal experience. Certainly no bodybuilder has built a physique using these machines. On the other hand there may be a small advantage to using these stimulators on stubborn areas. Then again, there is no evidence to show that bodies can be trimmed by stimulating the body electrically.

The medical use of these machines is to improve neural pathways in injured patients, and to reduce blood clotting in people who have undergone surgery. Regular iron-pushing is by far the best way to build an outstanding physique.

THE MOST-MUSCULAR POSE

Q. I'm 18 years old and have been training hard for two years. I have recently signed up for my first contest (a novice show, two months away), and have a question about posing. How do I do a most-muscular pose to look my best? I feel that I look good on most of the others. My double biceps from the front is the best, but I just don't feel right about the most muscular. It seems so awkward. Also, if it's not too much trouble – would you tell me what you consider to be the best color for posing trunks?

A. Basically, I feel that you should try to stay away from showing any weak areas. The same stage lighting that can do wonders for a hard, well-prepared muscle, will magnify faults. This is also true of facial expressions. A big smile and a confident look is a definite plus. However, as you should learn to pose so that you can instantly display your physique to full advantage – here are some pointers on the most-muscular "crab" pose.

Start with one foot slightly forward. Flex your legs. Bring your arms out to your sides. Rolling your shoulders forward, flex your trapezius while rotating your wrists so that your palms go downward. Flex your abdominals at the same time. Now bring both hands together in front of you, slowly flexing your pectorals, rippling your chest upward. Lock your fingers together and pull outwards, making your trapezius bulge. Hold your breath to bring out the veins. Don't lean too far forward or the shadow from the stage lights will darken the whole of your upper body. Common mistakes are to hold the hands too high or too low, or to have the elbows too close together. Remember to look forward and not down at yourself, and don't forget to smile. Check out photographs of the pros.

Remember the saying "practice makes perfect?" Get in front of the

Roland Kickinger

mirror every night between now and the contest. Rigging up two mirrors will help you see your back. A friend can help with the poses you cannot see.

As for the color of your trunks, who can say for sure? It depends on body, hair and eye color. High cut or low cut will depend on whether you have long or short legs in relation to your upper body. All I will say is get a good tan all over. Don't try any fancy carb-loading this first time out, and don't wear trunks that contrast too much with your skin color unless you have a small, well-muscled waist and great thighs.

SHOULD I GO HEAVY?

Q. I have been bodybuilding for 18 months now. I have been following a basic routine of all-round exercises including: presses, rows, bench presses, squats, curls, etc. My gains have recently come to a halt. I was wondering if I should train really heavy using 2 or 3 reps per set, or perhaps even a spell of performing singles. Please let me know your opinion through your column in *MuscleMag*. Thanks.

A. I guess every male bodybuilder has to have his fling using heavy weights so you might as well get them out of your system. But only use ultralow reps on multijoint exercises like deadlifts, bench presses, squats, etc. You will wreck your tendons and joints if you try to exceed your limit for poundages on lateral raises, dumbell curls, triceps extensions, etc.

David Dearth

Injury often occurs when we use heavy weights because in the effort to raise the poundage we move out of our normal exercise groove and bring about a tear or strain. This is why you should warm up thoroughly before making limit attempts. Personally, when I performed singles in deadlifts, squats, presses behind the neck and bench presses, I found that the practice greatly interfered with my recuperative powers. I was always totally drained the day after my workout. You may find the same thing happens in your case.

FASTING!

Q. I recently read an article on fasting, and I understand that fasting "cleanses" and "re-energizes" one's body. I'd like to try fasting, but I'm afraid of losing muscle mass! Do you think fasting is a bad idea for a "growing" bodybuilder? Have you ever tried it?

A. I've been on a grapefruit fast for three days in order to cleanse my body, and I liked how I felt after the fast. I felt healthier and lighter, and my energy level increased. I did lose a few pounds from my weight, but I think it was just because I didn't have the usual amount of food in my stomach! I still have my muscles.

I wouldn't recommend long and extreme fasting because you do need protein to keep your muscles, but a short two or three day vegetable juice or fruit fast is a good option you may want to try. Check at your local bookstore for books on fasting, and read how different fasts benefit your health.

DISTRACTIONS, DISTRACTIONS!

Q. I have a hard time keeping my concentration in the gym where I train because all of my friends train there and we always end up talking. I don't feel like answering them but that would be rude! Can you offer a few suggestions on how to deal with the problem? Thanks.

A. I have run into the same problem at Gold's Gym in Venice. I love all the people there, but I have a hard time completing a set because someone always has to "tell me something quick." When your schedule is strict, as mine is, and your time is limited, it's important to get in and get out of the gym as quick as possible while having a great workout too. One device that I have

Mia Finnegan

A. Your pain is most likely attributed to heavy poundages. I have had similar pain in the past, especially around the time of a contest. One treatment that I suggest is a deep tissue massage at a Soft Tissue Center in your area. My doctor explained to me the reason I have such pains is because the muscle surrounding the joint becomes very tense. The pain is relieved after the deep tissue massage because it releases the tension.

TORN PECS!

Q. I am a 16-year-old body-builder, and I have been training for about a year. When I started, I didn't have a clue what exercise builds which muscle. I soon found out that bench presses build the chest. Not knowing any different, I overtrained my chest, and now my left pec is developed nicely but my right pec has kind of a hole near the center, though the outside part is built.

I recently read that what I have done is torn a tendon off the bone at the center of my chest. I also read that it can only be corrected by having it operated on. All I really know is that I'm totally confused. What do you think I should do?

A. It sure sounds as though you have torn your pectoral muscle. I'm not a doctor so I cannot say for sure, but I feel you should see a sports physician as soon as possible. It's important that you take care of it quickly, as it will continue to develop in a deformed manner. Good luck! Follow through and take care of your pec.

TROUBLE WITH LEG CURLS

Q. I have trouble with leg curls because I have a weak back, and for some reason I just cannot avoid tension when I use a regular leg-curl machine. I hope you can suggest something that would help me.

A. I'm glad you understand that it's wise to seek a change when an exercise feels awkward and causes the wrong kind of tension. First of all, I assume that by a "regular" leg-curl machine you mean one that has a flat bench to lie on, and perhaps also unadjustable lift pads. Flatness of the bench may cause you to raise

found to be quite effective is a headset. Sometimes, if you have music playing in your ears, the people will know you can't hear them and they won't try to say anything. But maybe they will. The best thing is to be honest. Explain that you only have a little time to train and it's important that you get to finish your workout. I always say "You want me to win, don't you?" If you're a competitor I am sure your friends will understand — giving you the freedom to finish your workout so you can win that contest! Good luck!

MORE ACHES AND PAINS

Q. I have been training for some time now, and continually have a problem with aches and pains in my elbow and knee-joint areas. Can you suggest anything, or do I just have to lighten up my poundages?

Mike Francois

your chest and shoulders on it to avoid excessive arching of the back. If nothing helps to make the machine curls better and safer, try dumbell curls, because here you at least have an automatically correct "adjustment" vs. immovable lift pads.

Have your partner place a light dumbell between your feet as you lie on a flat bench, with your knees at the end of the bench. Move your legs up and down slowly. Stop at the top of the movement as you feel the maximum contraction in your leg biceps and squeeze your glutes, pressing your hips against the bench. Make sure the weight stays securely between your feet, and remain in complete control by holding the sides of the bench or extending your hands to the floor. Good luck!

your hips and butt, and lift pads that cannot be adjusted to fit your body measurements can result in an uncomfortable movement.

See if the gym where you train has another leg-curl machine, one with a contoured bench and adjustable lift pads. Or, if the version with the flat bench is the only one, try putting an extra pad or cushion of some sort under your stomach/hip area. As you perform the leg curls, make sure you hold on to the bench and keep

Eddie Robinson

MUSCLEMAG INTERNATIONAL'S GALLERY OF STARS

Chris Aceto

Throughout our twenty-four years of operation, *MuscleMag* has interviewed and profiled virtually every top bodybuilding superstar. In many cases the interviews were conducted before the individuals reached international status. In fact their feature in *MuscleMag* often catapulted them to higher levels within the sport.

The following is a brief look back at some of the stars that have graced the pages of *MuscleMag.* While most are competitive bodybuilders, a few have been included because of their contribution to the sport.

In most cases we give the individual's name, and a brief description (titles won, etc.) of their place in bodybuilding history. A few individuals required additional information, however, given their impact on the sport. For example, there is no way to do Arnold Schwarzenegger justice in two sentences!

As would be expected, no list is complete, and ours is no exception. Instead we have endeavored to include a representative cross-section from our twenty-four-year history. We apologize to those we may have inadvertently omitted.

Scott Abel – Like John Parrillo, Canadian, Scott Abel has developed a reputation as one of the sport's leading trainers. At last count, Scott's clients had won over 100 titles. Among the more famous bodybuilders who have sought Scott's advice are Laura Binetti, Lenda Murray, Vince Taylor, and Laura Creavalle.

Chris Aceto – Although not a major contest winner, Chris has established himself as one of the leading authorities in the sport. Many of today's top champs have relied on Chris's wisdom to get into their all-time best shape. Among the champs he has trained are Bob Paris, Vince Comerford, David Dearth, and Laura Creavalle. In fact Laura enjoyed Chris's advice so much that she married him in 1991!

Dinah Anderson – Dinah was one of the more successful female competitors of the mid-1980s. Her string of 10 consecutive firsts is among the longest in the sport's history. Included in this record run was the USA National Championships.

Dinah Anderson

Mike Ashley and Janice Ragain

Mike Ashley – With two of the best arms in the business, Mike has won such prestigious contests as the USA Nationals and the Arnold Classic. He is also one of the few pros to maintain that his physique was built without the help of performance-enhancing drugs.

Charles Atlas – Throughout our twenty-four-year history, *MuscleMag* has featured articles pertaining to the history of bodybuilding. And while not a bodybuilder in the modern sense, Charles Atlas, nevertheless, had a profound influence on the development of what was called "physical culture" in his day. With his "America's most perfectly developed" body, and strongman demonstrations, Atlas became an international figure from the 1920s onward. His most famous claim to fame was his magazine ad featuring a teenager "getting sand kicked in his face". Between 1928 and 1972, some 6 million people bought Atlas's training courses.

Aaron Baker – Aaron turned pro in 1990 after winning the prestigious Mr. USA title. A brief foray in the WBF was followed by Aaron's reinstatement in the IFBB. His first year in the IFBB (1993) was mediocre, but after his spectacular third-place finish at the '94 Ironman, it was obvious that Aaron would soon make his mark. Aaron established himself

as one of today's top pros by placing second at both the 1995 South Beach Pro Invitational and '95 Ironman, and sixth at the Arnold Classic.

Samir Bannout – The "Lion of Lebanon" reached the zenith of his career in 1983, when he won the Mr. Olympia title. During his heyday, Samir packed an ultraripped 195 pounds on his beautifully symmetrical physique.

The Barbarians – Two of the more colorful individuals to be featured in *MuscleMag* over the years are the Barbarian brothers, Peter and David Paul. With their lumberjack clothes and construction boots, the Barbarians gave bodybuilding a unique shot in the arm. Bit parts in the movie *D.C. Cab,* and 500-pound reverse-grip bench presses seemed to only add to their legend.

Doris Barrilleaux – One of the true pioneers of women's bodybuilding, Doris has been promoting the benefits of weight training for over 35 years. With her boundless energy and youthful enthusiasm Doris is presently active as an IFBB representative.

Laura Bass – Laura was born in Livingston, New Jersey, and among her titles are the New Jersey State Championships and the 1991 Jr. USA Championships. Besides her success in bodybuilding, Laura holds degrees in business and physical education.

Nicole Bass – With her 6-foot frame and 185 pounds of muscularity, Nicole was one of the largest competitors on the women's bodybuilding scene in the late 1980s and early 1990s.

Shelley Beattie – Besides winning the 1990 Emerald Cup and USA Nationals, Shelley placed third at the 1992 Ms. Olympia, and most recently has appeared as "Siren" on TV's *American Gladiators.*

Aaron Baker

Shelley Beattie

Albert Beckles – Like heavyweight boxing champ, George Forman, no one is quite sure how old Albert really is. Suffice to say he was winning pro bodybuilding contests while in his 50s! The "Ageless Wonder" has won just about every contest there is, including Mr. Europe, Mr. Universe, the Night of Champions, and numerous Grand Prix events. Albert is living proof that age isn't a barrier to winning, provided you have the will and determination.

Tim Belknap – Standing 5'2" and weighing 180 pounds, Tim Belknap was one of the most muscular competitors back in the early 1980s. In short order he won such titles as Mr. Illinois, Mr. America, Mr. World and Mr. Universe. Besides his bodybuilding success, Tim was an inspiration to millions, as he showed that an athlete with diabetes could be just as successful as those without the disease. Although he attempted a comeback in the early 1990s, Tim has since retired from competitive bodybuilding.

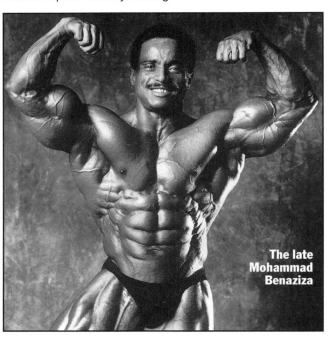

The late
Mohammad Benaziza

Mohammad Benaziza – One of the more tragic twists of fate in the bodybuilding world occurred on October 4, 1992, when just hours after winning the Dutch Grand Prix, Mohammad Benaziza died of a heart attack. Although the media frenzy claimed anabolic steroid abuse, the more likely cause was an electrolyte imbalance brought on by diuretic-induced dehydration. At a height of only 5'2", Mohammad had won eight pro shows before his tragic death. It's ironic that a man supposedly representing the epitome of health would die of a heart attack at only 33 years of age.

Francis Benfatto – Born to an Italian father and French mother, Francis won his first contest at age 23. In 1987 he placed second to Lee Labrada at the World Championships, turning pro soon after. Standing 5'7", Francis weighed a solid 190 pounds in contest

condition, and is known for his outstanding symmetry.

Laura Binetti – One of Canada's most successful pro bodybuilders, Laura has won such events as the Canadian Championships, her class at the 1989 North American Championships, and the 1994 Canada Pro Cup.

Laura
Binetti

Paula Bircumshaw – This outspoken female bodybuilder followed up her 1989 British Championships win with a fourth-place finish at the 1991 Jan Tana Classic. Her most memorable appearance, however, was the 1992 Ms. International, where after placing eighth, Paula walked onstage and gave obscene hand gestures to the judges. She was promptly given a two-year suspension and only time will tell if Paula decides to return to competition.

Steve Brisbois – This 1986 Mr. Universe winner is originally from Timmins, Ontario, Canada. With his nearly flawless symmetrical physique, Steve regularly placed ahead of opponents outweighing him by 75 pounds or more. Among his best pro placings are two fifths at the Arnold Classic.

Sharon Bruneau – With her combination of muscularity, symmetry, and athleticism, this Vancouver, British Columbia native won the 1991 North American Championships, and placed fourth at the 1992 Ms. International.

Sharon Bruneau

Andreas Cahling – Sweden's first pro bodybuilder, Andreas, first came to the public's attention after winning the 1983 Mr. International. Although his pro career fell short of expectations, Andreas has developed a very successful business catering to bodybuilders, and his posing suits are considered some of the best available. His ad can be seen in *MuscleMag* and other bodybuilding publications.

Roy Callender – When he competed back in the late '70s and early '80s, Roy was known for his huge muscle size. A native of Barbados, Roy later moved to Montreal, Canada, which served as his base of operations until the mid-1980s. Among his wins were the amateur and pro Mr. Universe titles. Roy is presently living in the Canadian province of Newfoundland, where he operates a gym in the town of Stephenville.

Kim Chizevsky – This 5′8″ female bodybuilder has won such titles as the 1990 AAU Southern Illinois Championships, the NPC Mid-West Grand Prix, 1992 NPC Junior Nationals, North American Championships, 1993 Ms. International and the 1996 Ms. Olympia.

Charles Clairmonte

Boyer Coe – Few bodybuilders have been competing as long as Boyer Coe. He entered his first contest in 1963 and competed up until the early 1980s. A ten-year hiatus was followed by a third-place finish at the 1994 Masters Olympia. In his illustrious career, Boyer has won such titles as Mr. America, Mr. World (six times), Mr. Universe (five times), and the World Cup.

Ronnie Coleman – Besides being a full-time police officer, 230-pound Ron has won the 1991 World Championships and placed fourth at the 1994 San Jose Pro Invitational. He went on to have a successful competitive season in 1996, winning the Canada Pro Cup in Montreal for a second consecutive year and placed second to Flex Wheeler in both the South Beach Invitational and Night of Champions.

Franco Columbu – This native of Sardinia, an island off the coast of Italy, first came to the United States in 1969. Besides being a chiropractor, Franco became famous as Arnold Schwarzenegger's training partner and best friend. He's also one of bodybuilding's more successful competitors, having won such titles as Mr. International, Mr. World, Mr. Europe, and Mr. Olympia (twice).

Ms. Olympia 1996, Kim Chizevsky.

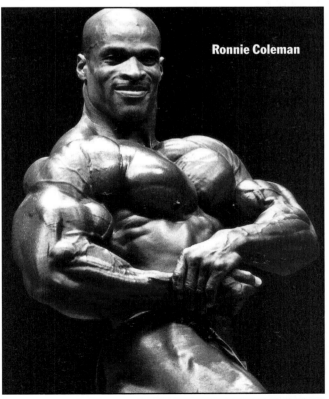

Ronnie Coleman

Mike Christian – Even though Lee Haney dominated bodybuilding in the 1980s, he was forced to the limit on numerous occasions by Mike Christian. Standing 6′1″ and weighing 245+ pounds in contest condition, Mike was one of the larger competitors during the 1980s. Besides his Olympia placings, Mike has won such contests as the World Championships, the Pro World, and Pro Mr. USA. In recent years Mike has been devoting most of his time to his highly successful "Platinum Everywhere" clothing line.

Charles Clairmonte – With two of the greatest arms in the business, and a reputation for showing up ripped, Charles has won the NABBA Pro Mr. Universe, and placed third at the 1995 Arnold Classic.

Charles Clairmonte, Porter Cottrell
and John Sherman

Laura Combes – One of the pioneers of women's bodybuilding, Laura won the 1980 Ms. America. With a level of muscular development never seen before on a woman, Laura set the standard for things to come. In fact her physique was years ahead of its time. Her death in 1989 shocked and saddened the bodybuilding community.

Vince Comerford – One of the biggest, thickest, and most graceful men to ever compete is the "Blond Myth", Vince Comerford. Also called the "Pit Bull" of bodybuilding, Vince has placed as high as second at the USA Pro Championships and third at the Night of Champions. At his best, Vince sported 20-inch arms and a 50-inch chest, all on a 5'5" frame.

Chris Cormier – Nicknamed "the Real Deal", because of his resemblance to heavyweight boxing champ, Evander Hollyfield, Chris won the overall at the 1993 USA Nationals. He followed this up with a sixth-place finish at both the 1994 and 1995 Mr. Olympia, placing eighth in 1996.

Selwyn Cotterill – Weighing between 255 and 280 – depending on the time of year – Britain's Selwyn Cotterill is one of the biggest bodybuilders on the pro circuit. Among his achievements are the 1988 British Heavyweight Championships and the 1988 European Sundown Cup. Since turning pro, Selwyn has placed fourth and fifth at two European Grand Prix contests and sixth at the Niagara Falls Grand Prix.

Porter Cottrell – Full-time firefighter and world-class bodybuilder, Porter is known for the pleasing symmetry of his physique. He has won such contests as the Chicago, Pittsburgh, and Niagara Falls Pro Invitationals.

Laura Creavalle – Although born in Guyana, Laura emigrated to Canada thirteen years later. With wins at the World Championships and Ms. International, Laura

Chris Cormier

is considered one of the top female bodybuilders in the world. In 1994 she placed a very controversial second behind Lenda Murray at the Ms. Olympia. She followed this up by claiming the 1995 Ms. International. Most feel it's only a matter of time before Laura captures female bodybuilding's most coveted title.

David Dearth

Laura Creavalle

Candy Csencsits – One of the true pioneers of women's bodybuilding, Candy lost her battle with breast cancer in January of 1989. In her short 33 years she accomplished more than what most accomplish in a lifetime. Besides being a pro bodybuilder, she was a model, school teacher, health-food store owner, and IFBB official. In addition she was one of the sport's more knowledgeable individuals, holding degrees in nutrition and psychology. Her death was felt throughout the bodybuilding world.

Marlon Darton – Standing 6'3" and weighing 250, Marlon is one of the sport's larger but least well-known pro bodybuilders. With 22-inch arms and a 58-inch chest, Marlon has won such titles as Mr. America, Mr. World, and Mr. Universe.

Joe DeAngelis – A former native of Elmer, New Jersey, Joe won such contests as Jr. Mr. World, Mr. North America, Mr. USA, and the 1991 AAU Mr. America. In contest condition, Joe weighs 224, at a height of 5'11".

David Dearth – Another former member of the now defunct WBF, David won the middleweight class at the 1989 NPC Nationals, and placed seventh at the 1995 Ironman Invitational and 12th at the 1995 Arnold Classic.

Greg Deferro – Called "Rocky" because of his striking facial resemblance to actor Sylvester Stallone, Greg was one of the larger competitors back in the early 1980s. He first came to bodybuilding prominence with his win at the IFBB Mr. International contest.

Paul DeMayo – Nicknamed "Quadzilla" because of his 30+ inch thighs, Paul won the 1994 USA Nationals. At only 5'10", Paul weighed 253 pounds on the night of the contest. Although he earned his pro card, Paul took 1995 off to focus on business interests. He intends to compete in the future.

Berry DeMey – Nicknamed the "Flexing Dutchman", Berry was one of the top stars in the early to mid-eighties. A stint in the short-lived WBF was followed by reinstatement in the IFBB.

Dr. Mauro DiPasquale – With his numerous books on drug and supplement use in sports, Dr. DiPasquale has become one of the more well-known individuals in the sport. Realizing that many athletes would continue to use performance-enhancing drugs, no matter what the potential side effects, Dr. DiPasquale decided to write a series of unbiased books on the subject. In addition to his books and newsletter, Dr. DiPasquale has a monthly feature in *MuscleMag* called Doctor's Corner.

Chris Dickerson – Chris's long and successful career reached a climax with his win at the 1982 Mr. Olympia. In addition to the Olympia, Chris won such titles as Mr.

Chris Dickerson

America, Mr. Universe, and numerous Grand Prix titles. In fact Chris won more titles than any other bodybuilder in history. Known for his outstanding symmetry and elegant posing, Chris routinely beat competitors outweighing him by 30 or 40 pounds.

Paul Dillett – Few bodybuilders have made such an impression on the sport as Canada's Paul Dillett. Weighing over 270 pounds in contest condition, Paul is considered to be one of the most genetically gifted bodybuilders of all time. Many rate his potential as being the equal of Sergio Oliva. After winning the 1992 North American Championships, Paul turned pro and went on to win two European Grand Prix events.

Shane DiMora – After winning his class at the 1986 NPC Nationals, it was expected that Shane would do well in the pros, but a severe pec injury sabotaged his plans. Although he did manage a second-place finish to Mike Ashley at the 1987 Detroit Grand Prix, his pro career has since been put on hold.

Paul Dillett

The late Debbie Dobbins

Debbie Dobbins – One of the saddest days in *MuscleMag's* history was when we heard the news of the tragic death of Debbie Dobbins. With two *MuscleMag* covers to her name, and a growing popularity in the fitness world, Debbie's career was skyrocketing. Debbie was training for the Ms. Galaxy contest when she died in a house fire on New Year's Eve in 1993. To honor her memory *MuscleMag* ran a special page tribute to her in each issue, for the remainder of the year.

Lance Dreher – Famous for his outstanding back and arms, Lance won both the amateur and pro Mr. Universe titles.

Dan Duchaine – Like Dr. Mauro DiPasquale, Dan Duchaine has become famous writing about anabolic steroids. The main difference between the two being Dr. DiPasquale's emphasis on the medical side of things, and Duchaine's focus on the "how to" of steroids. Duchaine's books, *the Underground Steroid Handbook,* and *Numbers 1 and 2,* have sold over a hundred thousand copies worldwide.

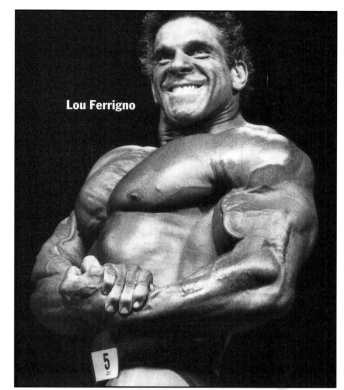

Lou Ferrigno

Marla Duncan – Besides winning the 1990 Ms. Fitness USA Championship, Marla has her own monthly column in *MuscleMag International.* She has been on the cover of over 25 magazines, and is kept busy with such endeavors as seminars, guest appearances, and personal training.

Carla Dunlap – Few women bodybuilders have accomplished as much as Carla Dunlap. Besides being one of the sport's pioneers, Carla won the 1983 Ms. Olympia and is an accomplished broadcaster and personal trainer. Although retired from competition, Carla is still devoted to the sport and trains nearly every day.

Tony Emmott – Tony was a popular competitor for over 20 years. Included in his wins are the NABBA Mr. Universe and Mr. World titles.

Cory Everson – Without a doubt Cory Everson has established herself as female bodybuilding's greatest star. Before she retired in 1990, Cory had won the Ms. Olympia contest no less than six times. Cory's domination was due to her combination of symmetry, muscularity, and presentation. In short, she combined the best features of bodybuilding without taking on a masculine appearance. When other competitors began looking like males, Cory retained her femininity and the bodybuilding public loved her for it. Since retiring she has appeared in a number of films, served as a TV color commentator, and most of all, still does her part for the promotion of women's bodybuilding.

Jeff Everson – This former Mr. America contestant is best known for his stint as editor of Joe Weider's *Muscle and Fitness,* and as husband to female bodybuilding's greatest star – Cory Everson. Since leaving *Muscle and Fitness,* Jeff has won the Masters USA Nationals and become involved with MET-Rx supplements.

Lou Ferrigno – Next to Arnold Schwarzenegger, Lou is bodybuilding's most famous star. Standing 6'5" and weighing between 275 and 300 in contest shape, Lou has won both the Mr. America and Mr. Universe titles. After retiring in 1977, Lou went on to star as TV's *Incredible Hulk,* and in the 1980s he starred in such movies as *Hercules* and *Cage.* In 1992 the competitive urge returned and big Lou turned up at the Mr. Olympia in the best shape of his career. A poor placing that year was followed by a second-place finish at the 1994 Masters Olympia. With his patented ability for gaining muscle mass, many feel Lou's best years are yet to come.

Dave Fisher – This former Canadian, now living in California, made his mark on the bodybuilding world by winning his class at the 1991 North American Championships. His best finish has been sixth at the 1995 Ironman Invitational. Dave now owns a bodybuilding retail store.

Bertil Fox – Called "Foxy" by his fans, Bertil was one of the thickest and most popular competitors on the pro circuit in the early to mid-eighties. Originally from the island of St. Kitts, Bertil won such titles as Mr. Britain, Mr. Europe, and Mr. Universe.

Ben Weider, Mike Francois and Arnold Schwarzenegger

Alá Gurley

was over 40 years ahead of his time, as it wasn't until the 1970s before the rest of bodybuilding caught up! In 1984 he teamed up with Robert Kennedy to write the best seller *Unleashing the Wild Physique*. Besides his writing career, Vince has helped thousands of actors and actresses get in shape for the movies.

Paul Jean-Guillaume – One of the top pros in the late 1980s, Jean gained a reputation for training without the help of performance-enhancing drugs. In his short career he won the World Amateur Championships, and placed well in a number of Grand Prix events. At his best he weighed 170 pounds in contest form (at a height of 5'8").

Alá Gurley – Alá was born in Cape Cod, Massachusetts, and won both the 1990 NPC USA Nationals, and World Championships.

Lee Haney

Michael Francois – With only five years of competition behind him, Mike has won all three pro events he entered. This includes the 1994 Night of Champions and 1995 Arnold Classic. Standing 5'9", Mike weighs an awesome 244 pounds in contest condition, and many feel it's only a matter of time before he wins the Mr. Olympia.

Johnny Fuller – This 1980 Mr. Universe winner weighed a solid 195 during his competitive career, despite standing only 5'6". A former powerlifter and boxer, Johnny was a regular fixture on the Grand Prix tour in the early 1980s.

Rich Gaspari – Famous for his rock-hard contest appearance, Rich rose quickly through the bodybuilding ranks. He won the Junior Nationals at 20 years of age, and within two years had claimed both the USA Nationals and World Championships. Throughout the 1980s Rich was right in the middle of things at the Mr. Olympia, placing second to Lee Haney on three different occasions. Although in a state of semi-retirement, it's possible New Jersey's super kid may return to the Olympia.

Vince Gironda – Called the "Iron Guru" of bodybuilding, Vince has operated his gym "Vince's" for over 50 years. With his dogmatic approach and sometimes seemingly "too direct" style, Vince is one of bodybuilding's more famous characters. He started his career as a stuntman in movies, and later developed a reputation for his outstanding muscularity. In fact Vince

Lee Haney – With his eighth consecutive Mr. Olympia victory in 1991, Lee Haney established himself as one of the greatest bodybuilders ever. And while he may never fill Arnold's shoes in the entertainment field (who can?), few can argue that Lee wasn't the best at what he did. Weighing 250+ pounds in contest shape, Lee overwhelmed opponents with his sheer size and muscularity. Since his retirement in 1991, Lee has devoted his time to various business interests, including training former heavyweight boxing champ, Evander Holyfield.

Ian Harrison – Originally from West Yorkshire, England, this 260-pound pro has won such titles as the British Championships, Junior Mr. Britain, and 1988 Junior Mr. Universe.

Ian Harrison

Dave Hawk – Nicknamed "Killer Hawk," Dave became famous as a teenage USA National champion.

Oscar Heidenstam – When he died in 1991, Oscar left behind a lifetime of bodybuilding achievements. Besides cofounding the NABBA (National Amateur Bodybuilding Association), he was instrumental in the forming of the WABBA and NABBA International. Later he was editor and publisher of *Health and Strength* magazine. Among his bodybuilding achievements were the 1937 Mr. Britain, and a second-place finish at the 1952 Mr. Universe. A bodybuilding supporter to the end, he attended over 50 contests a year.

Manfred Hoeberl – Manfred stands 6'5", weighs around 320, and sports a chest in the 60-inch range. Although he has never won a major bodybuilding contest (his best was a 4th at the 1989 German Amateur Championships), like Vic Richards, he is besieged by promoters and fans. Manfred is one of the top competitors on the World's Strongest Man Tour, and has won the World Muscle Power and Europe's Strongest Man Championships. With his 25+-inch arms, Manfred draws a crowd wherever he goes.

Bob Hoffman – Called the "father of modern weightlifting", the late Bob Hoffman devoted much of his life to physical fitness and in particular, weightlifting. Among the organizations he founded or helped develop were, the Weightlifting Hall of Fame, *Strength* magazine, and the AAU (American Athletic Union).

John Hnatyschak – This New Jersey policeman came to bodybuilding prominence when he won the 1984 USA Nationals and World Championships. Although

never having won a pro contest, he placed fourth at the '87 Night of Champions and third at the '88 Chicago Grand Prix.

Negrita Jayde – Negrita has been a multi-Canadian women's champion, and has placed as high as third in the World Championships.

Renel Janvier – Renel earned his pro card by winning the light heavyweight division of the 1988 World Championships held in Brisbane, Australia. Originally from Haiti, Renel has developed a reputation for competing in absolute ripped condition.

Dr. Arthur Jones – Although not a competitive bodybuilder, Dr. Jones is without a doubt one of the most influential figures in bodybuilding history. With his line of Nautilus equipment, Dr. Jones introduced the controversial one-set-per-bodypart training style. Among his more famous followers are Mike Mentzer and Casey Viator. Besides his bodybuilding interests, Dr. Jones has one of the largest private collections of wild animals in the world.

Robert Kennedy – Since emigrating to Canada in the early 1970s, British-born, Robert Kennedy has established himself as one of the most influential figures in bodybuilding history. With his unique combination of perseverance and genius, Bob created *MuscleMag International,* and turned it into one of the greatest bodybuilding magazines in the world. For many, operating a best-selling magazine like *MuscleMag* would suffice, but not Bob. Throughout his long career

Hamdullah Aykutlu and Bob Kennedy

in the iron game, Bob has also written or cowritten over 40 books on his favorite subject – bodybuilding and physical fitness.

Nimrod King – One of the greatest bodybuilders to ever come out of Canada is 1989 United States Pro champion, Nimrod King. Originally from Trinidad, Nimrod moved to Canada in 1972. Besides the Pro win, Nimrod has won such contests as the Canadian Championships and Junior Worlds.

Tonya Knight – Tonya is one of the most popular female bodybuilders on the pro scene. Besides winning the Ms. International title, Tonya had her own column in *MuscleMag International* called KnightTime. She was also a regular on TV's *American Gladiators* in the early '90s.

Irvin Koszewski – Most bodybuilders are remembered for the titles they won, but Irvin has gone down in history for his amazing abdominals. During his competitive career (which started in 1948) Irvin "Zabo" Koszewski won more awards for best abs than anyone in bodybuilding history. Even today at 70 years of age, Irvin "Mr. Abs" Koszewski still does hundreds of reps daily for his abs.

Lee Labrada – With his numerous Grand Prix victories and second-place finishes to Lee Haney at the Mr. Olympia, 5'6" Lee Labrada has established himself as one of the greatest bodybuilders in history under 200 pounds. Even though he weighed just 180 pounds in contest condition, Lee brought new meaning to the term "finished". Realizing that the trend in the '90s was size, Lee decided to retire after the 1995 Arnold Classic.

Anja Langer – Often called the "Katerina Witt" of women's bodybuilding, Anja was one of the sport's top stars in the late '80s and early '90s. Her combination of muscularity, femininity, and creative posing, earned her second place at the 1988 Ms. Olympia.

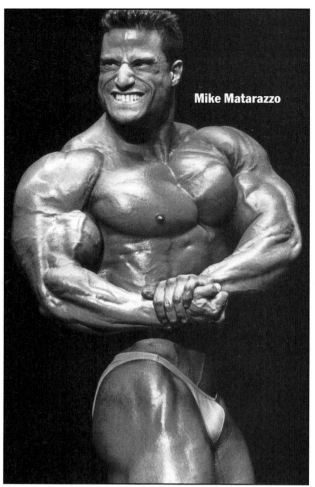

Mike Matarazzo

Kevin Levrone – When you think of genetic superiors, such names as Arnold, Sergio, Dorian and Dillett come to mind. Now another name can be added to the list – that being Maryland's Kevin Levrone. This 245-pound behemoth has won such prestigious events as The Arnold Classic, Night of Champions, and San Jose Pro Invitational. In 1994 he placed a respectable third behind Shawn Ray and Dorian Yates at the Mr. Olympia, placing second in '95 and third in '96. Besides his bodybuilding success, Kevin was an accomplished powerlifter, with such impressive lifts as a 600-pound bench press and 800-pound squat.

Ron Love – If they gave awards for perseverance, then Ron would have a house full. To give an idea of Ron's dedication to the sport, he competed in no less than 18 contests throughout 1989. He gathered a host of 5th-, 6th-, and 7th-place finishes, and a victory at the Niagara Falls Pro Invitational. With his cannonball-sized delts, Ron was one of the larger pros on the scene in the late '80s and early '90s.

Joe Weider, Kevin Levrone and Arnold Schwarzenegger

Mike Mentzer

Mike Mentzer – To anyone new to the sport, Mike is perhaps most famous as a writer and trainer. But back in the late '70s, Mike was one of the sport's most feared competitors. Mike won such contests as the Mr. America, Mr. Universe, two Grand Prix titles, and placed second to Frank Zane at the 1979 Mr. Olympia.

Mike's greatest claim to fame is his popularizing of the "Heavy Duty" system of training. The style is based heavily on the theories of Dr. Arthur Jones. Although no top contest winner has claimed to have used Mike's system solely for training, many of today's stars (including Dorian Yates and Lee Labrada) have been heavily influenced by Mike's writings.

Johnnie Morant – This 260-pound pro bodybuilder won the heavyweight division at the 1989 USA Championships.

Andreas Munzer – If not for Arnold Schwarzenegger, the late Andreas might well have been Austria's most famous bodybuilder. Weighing around 240 in contest condition, Andreas developed a reputation for his outstanding muscularity. The terms "ripped," "sliced," and "cut," didn't do the man justice, as Andreas had striations on his striations! In fact many bodybuilding writers started using the term "Munzered," to describe competitors who displayed extreme muscularity.

Lenda Murray – No sooner had the reign of six-time Ms. Olympia Cory Everson ended, when women's bodybuilding found a new queen – Lenda Murray. Lenda was born in Detroit and her first major athletic ambition was to become a Dallas Cowboy cheerleader. Numerous try outs brought her down to the final 45, but

Mohamed Makkawy – Mohamed burst on the bodybuilding scene with his 1976 Mr. Universe win. After emigrating to Canada, Mohamed became a regular competitor on the Grand Prix tour, winning numerous titles in the process.

Mike Matarazzo – One of the biggest bodybuilders currently on the scene, Mike has won such titles as the 1988 Atlantic States Championships, 1989 Massachusetts Championships, and the 1991 USA Championships. Although he hasn't performed as well as expected on the pro circuit (he placed second at both the 1993 Pittsburgh Pro Invitational and 1997 Toronto Pro Invitational) Mike remains one of the sport's more popular competitors given his 22-inch arms and seemingly yard-wide shoulders.

Rachel McLish – Another of women's bodybuilding pioneers, Rachel was also the sport's first Ms. Olympia, which she won in 1980. Although small by today's standards, Rachel nevertheless helped guide women's bodybuilding in its earlier days. Many feel with today's emphasis on mass, a return to Rachel's type of physique might be in order.

Ray McNeil – One of the most promising young bodybuilders to come along in years, Ray was allegedly shot and killed by his wife, bodybuilder Sally Marie McNeil, on Valentine's day in 1995. Ray's best win was the 1991 North American Championships.

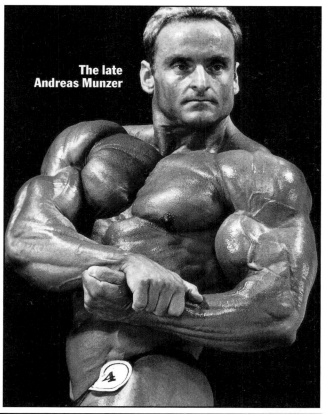

The late Andreas Munzer

Dennis Newman

midsection and stupendous chest. Although in his fifties, Serge still sports a physique that could hold its own in a Mr. Olympia lineup.

Sergio Oliva – When lists are drawn up outlining the top bodybuilders of all time, the Cuban-born Sergio Oliva is usually at or near the top. In his prime he was one of the few bodybuilders to beat Arnold Schwarzenegger in competition. With three Mr. Olympias and a host of other titles to his credit, Sergio is easily one of the sport's all-time greats. Even by today's standards, Sergio is regarded as "Mr. Genetic Potential." In fact it was his freaky development that earned him the nickname "Myth," early in his career.

Danny Padilla – In 1975, Danny Padilla, a virtual unknown, came from nowhere to win the Mr. USA title. The following year he captured both the Mr. America and Mr. Universe titles. A brief appearance in *Pumping Iron* and Danny was soon recognized as one of the greatest bodybuilders in the world. He reached his best condition ever at the 1981 Mr. Olympia, but managed only fifth in what has gone down in history as the most controversial Mr. Olympia ever (the winner was Franco Columbu). Danny retired from the sport soon after-

one of the selection committee members said Lenda's thighs were too big. Cheerleading's loss became body-building's gain. Early advice from pro bodybuilder, Ron Love, convinced her to try bodybuilding, and the rest, as they say, is history. Her first major win, the 1989 North American Championships, earned Lenda her pro card. Not being one to waste an opportunity, Lenda won six consecutive Ms. Olympias from 1990 - 1995.

Susan Myers – With her 5'1", 114-pound physique, Susan captured the lightweight class at the 1989 USA Nationals. Although diminutive in height, Susan looks much heavier given her thickness and muscle density.

Dennis Newman – One of the fastest rising stars in the sport of bodybuilding is California native Dennis Newman. In short order he won the NPC Teen USAs, 1991 San Jose Super Bowl, 1991 Muscle Mania and the 1992 Mr. California. After winning the overall at the 1994 USA Championships, it seemed but a formality that Dennis would clean up on the pro ranks, but fate intervened. He was diagnosed with leukemia, however, he's overcoming the hurdle and vows to be back on the scene in no time.

Serge Nubret – Considered by many to be one of the greatest bodybuilders of all time. This former Mr. Universe was immortalized in the 1975 documentary *Pumping Iron,* where he placed second to Arnold Schwarzenegger. Serge was famous for his rippling

Serge Nubret

wards, but made a comeback in 1989. Showing the form that made him famous, he placed second at the Gold's Gym Classic, third at the Night of Champions, and made the top five in several European Grand Prix events. Given his eighth-place finish at the 1994 Masters Olympia, and his relatively young age (mid-forties), many feel that Danny could still cause trouble on the regular pro circuit.

Cathey Palyo – One of the more outspoken female bodybuilders of the late '80s and early '90s, Cathey won the 1988 Ms. International.

Tony Pearson

Bob Paris – With his outstandingly symmetrical physique, Bob captured both the USA National and World Championships. His book *Beyond Built* is one of the sport's best sellers.

Reg Park – Reg is one of the sport's true legends. Besides winning three Mr. Universe titles and starring in a remake of *Hercules,* Reg was the inspiration of millions, including a young Austrian named Arnold Schwarzenegger.

John Parrillo – Called the "most knowledgeable person I've ever met" by *MuscleMag* writer, Greg Zulak, John has become famous over the years for training some of the sport's top pros. With his reputation growing by leaps and bounds, it wasn't long before John received his own column in *MuscleMag International.* John's words of wisdom can be found each month in Parrillo Maxx.

Thierry Pastel – In recent years the name Pastel has become synonymous with rock-hard abs. But in a way,

John Parrillo

such compliments are doing Thierry an injustice as his 5'2" physique is loaded with quality. A protegee of France's Serge Nubret, it's not surprising that Thierry is the epitome of refinement. And, like Lee Labrada, he can hold his own with any of the competitors who outweigh him by 50 pounds. After winning numerous NABBA events, Thierry joined the IFBB and won the 1990 German Grand Prix.

Bruce Patterson – One of the fastest rising stars on the Canadian bodybuilding scene, Bruce has won the New Brunswick, Regional, and Canadian Championships. In addition, he received his pro card by winning the overall at the 1994 Pro Canada Cup. Standing 5'10" and weighing 265 in the off-season, Bruce promises to be one of the best young bodybuilders in the pro ranks.

Bill Pearl – Bill is one of the sport's more enduring athletes. In a competitive bodybuilding career that began in 1952 and ended in 1971, Bill won such titles as Mr. America and Mr. Universe (no less than four times!). Famous for his early morning workouts, Bill has trained many of the sport's all-time greats, including 1982 Mr. Olympia, Chris Dickerson. To this day, Bill is involved with the sport, either as a personal trainer, selling food supplements, or writing magazine articles.

Tony Pearson – Tony won the 1978 Mr. America, only to lose the Mr. Universe qualifying posedown to Tom Platz. He later went on to win the NABBA Mr. World, WBBG Mr. Olympus, and pro Mr. Universe. Perhaps Tony's best accomplishments were his string of couples championships with such female stars as Shelley Gruwell, Carla Dunlap, Tina Plakinger, and Juliette Bergman.

Tom Platz – Called the "Golden Eagle" for his blond hair and eagle-eyed determination, Tom was one of the sport's more popular competitors in the early 1980s. Although massive all over, Tom's legs are considered the greatest of all time. In fact many feel his outstanding leg development overshadowed his upper body, thus keeping him from winning bodybuilding's greatest titles. Even though Tom won the World Amateur Championships, it was his stellar performance at the 1981 Mr. Olympia that brought him superstardom. After placing much lower than expected (third behind Chris Dickerson and winner Franco Columbu), Tom won the hearts of millions with his dignified acceptance of third place. After retiring from the sport, Tom went on to become public relations director of the short-lived WBF. In recent years he has established himself as one of the sport's most successful business personalities.

Sue Price

Gladys Portugues – Although a top female body-builder in the early to mid-1980s, Gladys became more famous after marrying actor/martial arts champion Jean-Claude Van Damme.

Sue Price – This Chicago native won the 1994 Jan Tana Invitational and placed sixth in her first Ms. Olympia appearance. She also won her weight class in such contests as the 1987 Collegiate Illinois and 1990 Midwest Grand Prix.

Lee Priest – Australia's Lee Priest is considered one of the largest, yet shorter men on the scene. He was also one of the youngest men to compete in the Mr. Universe contest – at 17 years of age! Standing 5'4" and weighing a rock hard 185 to 190 pounds, Lee placed third at the 1995 Ironman Invitational and ninth at the 1995 Arnold Classic. He went on to place second at the 1997 Ironman

Jim Quinn – With his 285 pounds of "vascularity" spread over a 6'2" frame, Jim is one of the larger bodybuilders on the pro scene. After winning the 1990 North Americans, Jim joined the short-lived WBF, but has since rejoined the IFBB.

Mike Quinn – Mike is one of the more durable pros on the scene, having won his first title, Mr. Bay State, in 1979. Two years later he was Teenage Mr. America. Over the next few years Mike won such titles as the NABBA Mr. Universe and 1987 USA Championships, and placed as high as sixth at the Mr. Olympia.

Janice Ragain – Janice was one of the sport's more popular stars between 1986 and 1989. She turned pro after placing second in the 1985 World Championships.

Shawn Ray – Although history shows that Dorian Yates won the 1994 Mr. Olympia, many in attendance felt that second-place finisher, Shawn Ray, was just as deserving of the title. In five short years, Shawn has established himself as one of the sport's premier players. Known for his almost perfect symmetry, Shawn has won such contests as the American Championships and Arnold Classic.

Jim Quinn

Steve Reeves – An idol to millions of bodybuilders, Steve won such prestigious titles as Mr. America and Mr. Universe. He later became one of the first body-builders to carry his success over to the movies. In the late 1940s and early 1950s, Steve became famous the world over with his *Hercules* movies. Still in great shape, Steve has started a third career as a promoter of his "Power Walking" style of physical fitness.

Bill Reynolds – When he died in 1992 of heart failure, Bill Reynolds left behind a legacy of bodybuilding writing. Bill started his writing career with *MuscleMag* in the early 70s, and soon was writing for such magazines as *Ironman* and *Muscle Training Illustrated*. After being spotted by Joe Weider, Bill's writing talents were put to work, first as editor of *Muscle and Fitness,* and later as editor-in-chief of *Flex*. Besides his association with magazines, Bill wrote or ghost wrote dozens of books.

Such famous bodybuilders as Tom Platz, Lee Haney, Samir Bannout, and Rachel McLish had books written for them by Bill. He also wrote a number of highly successful books that appeared under the Weider name. Bill's death left a void in the bodybuilding world; one which will not easily be replaced.

Denise Rutkowski

Sandy Riddell

Victor Richards – Weighing between 280 and 300 pounds in hard condition, California's Vic Richards is one of the most popular bodybuilders in the world. He is in constant demand for seminars and posing exhibitions, and his appearance at a contest is guaranteed to produce a sellout. What's remarkable about Vic is that he has never won a major amateur contest, let alone entered a pro bodybuilding competition! Vic is living proof that when it comes to popularity, mass is still king.

Sandy Riddell – This former firefighter from Arizona first came to bodybuilding prominence in the fall of 1989 when she placed a close second to Cory Everson at the Ms. Olympia contest. In recent years she has shown her athletic ability by competing in the Ms. Galaxy contest.

Eddie Robinson – This 5'7", 220-pound competitor has won such contests as the 1985 teen USA championships, the 1986 Junior Nationals, and the 1989 NPC Mr. USA title. Like many top pros, Eddie spent time in the short-lived WBF federation, but has since rejoined the IFBB.

Robby Robinson – Robby is considered one of the sport's enduring legends. In a competitive career spanning over 20 years, Robby has won such prestigious contests as the Night of Champions, Mr. America, Mr. Universe, and the 1994 Masters Olympia. Although picking a "best" bodypart is difficult, Robby is considered by many to have the greatest arms of all time.

Don Ross – The late Don Ross was one of bodybuilding's most respected personalities. Don had won the coveted Mr. America title, and also wrote the highly successful book *Muscleblasting.* Known for his incredible muscularity, Don was often called "Ripper Ross".

Denise Rutkowski – Standing 5'5" and weighing 140 in contest condition, Denise has won such contests as the USA Nationals and Jan Tana Classic.

Franco Santoriello – This popular bodybuilder has won such titles as the 1989 NPC Nationals and World Cup. Franco usually competes at a ripped 210 pounds and attributes much of his success to the Cybergenics line of supplements.

Milos Sarcev – A native of Yugoslavia (now Bosnia – Herzegovina), Milos won that country's bodybuilding championship in 1987. Since coming to the USA, Milos has earned his pro card and has since won the '97 Toronto Pro International.

Reid Schindle – In the late 1970s and early 1980s, one man symbolized Canadian bodybuilding – Reid Schindle. With five, first-place finishes in the Canadian championship's heavyweight division, Reid reached almost "Schwarzenegger-like" popularity in Canada. Only a lack of being able to get super-ripped prevented Reid from going on to win the World Championships.

Sonny Schmidt – Currently one of the top pros on tour, Sonny hails from Australia, and regularly competes at a bodyweight of over 240 pounds He won the 1995 Masters Olympia.

Larry Scott – Not only was Larry bodybuilding's first Mr. Olympia (1965 and 1966), but he was also the first bodybuilder to win all three of the sport's top titles: the Mr. America, Mr. Universe, and Mr. Olympia. Larry was famous for his outstanding arm development, particularly his long, fully peaked biceps. Over the years the preacher bench has been renamed the Scott bench, in honor of Larry. Larry still finds time to train, and resides in Salt Lake City, Utah.

Anja Schreiner – Born and raised in Bad Wimpen, West Germany

Milos Sarcev

Championships. Among his most distinguished body-parts are his 29-inch thighs.

Joe Spinello – This 5'6", 205-pound Canadian, has won such titles as Mr. Montreal, Mr. Quebec, the Canadian Championships, the World Championships, and placed in the top ten in four pro events.

Daryl Stafford – Bodybuilding for over 20 years, Daryl is a perfect example of how perseverance pays off. After placing second, three times in the past, Daryl finally won the light heavyweight class at the 1993 NPC Nationals. Although only 5'6", Daryl competes at a ripped 198 pounds of muscle.

Sonny Schmidt

(now Germany), Anja is considered to be the epitome of what a female bodybuilder should look like. Her symmetrical physique is complemented by blue eyes and long wavy blond hair. After winning the WABBA Ms. World Championships, Anja joined the IFBB, where she has placed as high as third at the Ms. Olympia, and second at the Ms. International.

Arnold Schwarzenegger – It's safe to say that Arnold is the most famous bodybuilder of all time. With seven Mr. Olympia titles to his credit (a record finally broken by Lee Haney in 1991) he's also regarded as the greatest bodybuilder ever. After establishing himself as the sport's top star, Arnold set his sights on Hollywood. Using the same determination that brought him seven Mr. Olympias, Arnold is now the number one box office draw in the world. Besides his bodybuilding and acting accomplishments, Arnold has written or cowritten numerous best sellers including *The Education Of A Bodybuilder,* and *Arnold's Encyclopedia Of Modern Bodybuilding.*

Marjo Selin – Marjo has been one of the world's top female bodybuilders for over a decade. She is also a regular member of the *MuscleMag International* family with her monthly "Repping With Marjo" column.

John Siembida – John won his class (light heavy-weight) at both the 1989 Canadian and North American

Roger Stewart – Although he hasn't won a major bodybuild-ing title, Roger Stewart is one of bodybuilding's most sought after stars. With his boyish good looks and beautifully proportioned physique, Roger is in big demand for photos. In fact, the issues of *MuscleMag* with Roger on the cover have been some of our biggest sellers.

Gary Strydom – With numerous Grand Prix titles to his credit, including four in 1989, Gary was one of the more successful bodybuilders in the late 1980s. After a couple of dismal Mr. Olympia placings, Gary, like many

Larry Scott

other pros, left the IFBB and joined the WBF. Although he has since rejoined the IFBB, Gary has yet to compete and regain his contest-winning form.

Vince Taylor – Without a doubt, Vince is one of today's top bodybuilding stars. In his illustrious career he has won such contests as the Night of Champions, Arnold Classic, numerous Grand Prix titles, and the '96 Masters Olympia.

Gary Strydom

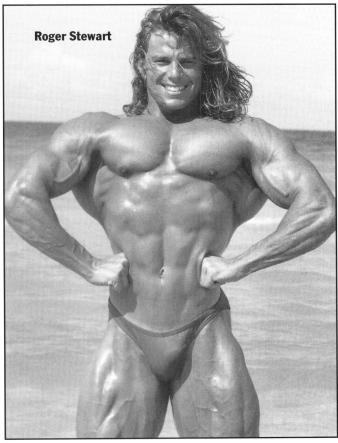

Roger Stewart

emerge on the scene in recent years. After his second-place finish behind Paul DeMayo at the 1994 NPC Nationals, Craig went on to win the '96 USAs.

Kathy Unger – A top female bodybuilder famous for her combination of muscularity and femininity, Kathy won the 1989 Women's Amateur World Championships.

Ben Weider – As president of the IFBB (International Federation of Bodybuilders) Ben is the senior statesman of the sport. Together with his brother, Joe, this Canadian has brought bodybuilding from an obscure level to one of the world's more popular sports in terms of practicing members and countries involved. For example, the 1994 World Championships held in Shanghai were watched by over 600 million people. And now with bodybuilding's recent acceptance as a Pan American sport, most feel it's only a matter of time before Ben's dream – bodybuilding as an Olympic sport – becomes reality.

Tom Terwilliger – A native of Long Island New York, Tom used his vast knowledge of nutrition and almost flawless symmetry to capture the light heavyweight class at the USA Nationals.

Ron Teufel – Often called the "Golden Boy" of bodybuilding, Ron won his weight class at the Mr. America competition. He left bodybuilding in 1982, only to re-emerge in 1988. After a comeback attempt met with limited success, Ron decided to retire.

Henderson Thorne – Originally from Barbados, Henderson moved to Canada when he was 14 years old. Known for his incredible workout poundages, Henderson is one of the best bodybuilders to ever come out of Canada, and has won the 1989 World Games. On the pro circuit he placed second to Porter Cottrell at the 1993 Niagara Falls Pro Invitational, fifth at the New York Night of Champions, and cracked the top six at numerous Grand Prix events.

Craig Titus – This 225-pound, Texas-based bodybuilder is regarded as one of the most promising stars to

Daryl Stafford

Joe Weider – Often called the "Master Blaster" or "Trainer of Champions", Joe, with the exception of Arnold Schwarzenegger, is bodybuilding's most dominant personality. His leadership and perseverance have nourished the sport of bodybuilding for decades, advancing it to where it is today. He has also been publishing magazines and bodybuilding-related books since the early 1940s. Besides his monthly publications (*Flex, Muscle and Fitness,* and *Shape),* Joe runs Weider Enterprises, an organization specializing in bodybuilding-related products.

Flex Wheeler – In five short years, Flex has won just about every title available in bodybuilding. Only the Mr. Olympia has escaped his grasp, and in 1993 he gave Dorian Yates a scare by placing second. Weighing in the 245-pound category, Flex is considered by most to have the

Vince Taylor

Flex Wheeler

greatest combination of size and shape of the pros currently competing. A car crash in 1994 nearly ended his life, but within a year he was back onstage. He won both the 1995 Ironman and South Beach Pro Invitationals, and placed second to Michael Francois at the Arnold Classic. He went on to win the Arnold Classic in 1997 as well as the San Jose Pro Invitational and Ironman Pro Invitational.

Jusup Wilkosz – Jusup was one of bodybuilding's most promising stars back in the early 1980s. With his rugged 230-pound physique, Jusup won both the

Jusup Wilkosz

amateur and professional Mr. Universe titles. Perhaps his most famous trademark was his full, but neatly trimmed beard.

Frank Zane – Another of bodybuilding's legends, Frank reigned as Mr. Olympia from 1978 to 1979. Frank is one of the few bodybuilders to have defeated Arnold Schwarzenegger in competition (1968 Mr. Universe). Not having the greatest genetics for building mass, Frank had to concentrate on totally refining his physique, and in many ways he was the forerunner of today's ripped competitors and superposers. Today he runs the highly successful Zane Haven, a bodybuilding camp for those interested in the personal attention of a former Mr. Olympia.

Troy Zuccolotto – With his dense, rock-hard physique, backed up by 21-inch arms, Troy easily won the 1989 USA Nationals. In recent years he has been seen frequently on the *American Muscle Magazine* show.

The Photographers – Although not an all encompassing list, the following are some of the many individuals whose photographic talents have graced the pages of *MuscleMag* over the years: Paul Goode, Garry Bartlett, Bert Perry, Ralph DeHaan, Artie Zeller, Kevin Horton, Per Bernal, Doris Barrilleaux, Irvin Gelb, Jim Amentler, Alex Ardenti, Steve Douglas, Reg Bradford, Paula Crane, John Campos, Greg Aiken, Bill Heimanson, Denie, Dick Falcon, Gino Edwards, Mitsuru Okabe, George Greenwood, Robert Nailon, Wayne Gallasch, Robert Kennedy, Rick Schaff, Steve Neece, Jason Mathas, Mike Neveux, John Butler and Chris Lund.

Arnold Schwarzenegger

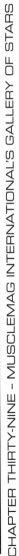

GLOSSARY

Abdominals – The series of muscles located on the lower midsection of the torso. They are used to contract the body forward through a range of six to eight inches.

Acupuncture – The ancient Chinese practice whereby the body's well-being is controlled by pressure points. Acupuncture involves stimulating these points with long needles.

Aerobic Exercise – Any long-lasting exercise that can be carried on within the body's ability to replenish oxygen in working muscles.

AFWB – The American Federation of Women Bodybuilders. This organization is an affiliate of the IFBB, and is responsible for organizing and running women's bodybuilding contests in America.

AIDS – Short for Acquired Immune Deficiency Syndrome. AIDS is caused by a virus and is contracted by the exchange of bodily fluids. There have been some cases of bodybuilders contracting AIDS from the sharing of needles (used for anabolic steroid injections).

Amenorrhea – Absence of menstrual periods due to a low bodyfat percentage. This condition is not dangerous and is common in such sports as gymnastics, bodybuilding, and track and field.

Amino Acids – Called the "building blocks of life," amino acids are biochemical subunits linked together by chemical bonds to form polypeptide chains. Hundreds of polypeptides, in turn, linked together from a protein molecule.

Anabolic – Metabolic process whereby smaller units are assembled into larger units. For example, the combining of amino acids into protein strands is a form of anabolism.

Anaerobic Exercise – Any high-intensity exercise that outstrips the body's aerobic capacity and leads to an oxygen debt. Because of its intensity, anaerobic exercise can only be maintained for short periods of time.

APC – The American Physique Committee. This federation is responsible for organizing and running men's amateur bodybuilding contests in America. It is also an affiliate of the IFBB.

Arm Blaster – Short, curved metal training apparatus used for bracing the arms when performing exercises such as biceps curls.

Arthritis – Chronic condition marked by an inflammation of the tissue surrounding the joints.

Asymmetric Training – Any exercise that targets only one side of the body. One-arm dumbell curls, lateral raises, or triceps extensions, are all examples of asymmetric training.

Back – The series of muscles located on the dorsal region of the body. The back muscle complex includes the latissimus dorsi, spinal erectors, trapezius, rhomboids and teres minor and major.

Barbell – One of the most basic pieces of bodybuilding equipment. Barbells consist of a long bar, collars, sleeves, and associated plates made of steel or iron. They may be either adjustable (allowing the changing of plates) or fixed (the plates are kept in place by welded collars). Barbells average between five and seven feet in length, and usually weigh between 25 and 45 pounds.

Basic Exercises – Exercises that work more than one muscle group simultaneously. Basic exercises form the mainstay of a bodybuilder's mass-gaining routine. Examples include: bench presses, shoulder presses, squats, deadlifts, and bent-over rows.

Belt – Large leather support worn around the waist by bodybuilders. Weightlifting belts are usually four to six inches in width and provide support to the lower-back muscles and spine.

Biceps – Flexor muscles located on the upper arm. The biceps are composed of two "heads," and are responsible for bending the lower arm towards the upper arm.

Biofeedback – Any physiological or psychological symptom given off by the body. The best bodybuilders are those who recognize such biofeedback signals and use them to improve their training, eating, and competitive preparation.

BMR – Short for Basil Metabolic Rate, the BMR is the speed at which the resting body consumes energy (calories).

Bodybuilding – Competitive or noncompetitive subdivision of weight training in which the primary goal is the improvement of one's physique. For most, the objective is not competition but for those who do compete the final placings are determined by a panel of judges who look at such physical qualities as muscle size, shape, symmetry, bodyfat percentage, and presentation (posing).

Bodyfat Percentage – The ratio of fat to bodyweight. For most bodybuilders, 8 to 10 percent is the off-season goal, while 2 to 4 percent is the competitive goal.

Breathing Pullovers – Specialized exercise important to a bodybuilder as it stretches the rib cartilage, producing a large rib cage and therefore, a larger chest measurement.

Bulking Up – Bodybuilding term which refers to the gaining of 30 to 40 pounds of bodyweight over a short period of time. This practice has become less common, given the increased number of competitions, and the demand for guest posers on a year-round basis.

Burn – Unique term to the sport of bodybuilding describing the feeling a muscle gets as it's exercised. Burns are partial reps done at the end of a set when performing full reps is impossible.

Bursae – Flat sacks filled with fluid. They support and protect joints.

Buttocks – Another term referring to the gluteus maximus, medius and minimus, extensors and abductors of the thigh at the hip joint.

Cables – Long wire cords attached to weight stacks at

one end and a hand grip at the other. Cable exercises keep tension on the working muscle throughout a full range of motion.

Calves – Also called "lowers" and "bodybuilding's diamonds," the calves consist of the soleus and gastrocnemius muscles located on the backs of the lower leg bones. The calves are similar to the forearms in that they are composed of extremely dense muscle tissue. Their function is to flex the feet.

Carbohydrate Loading – The practice of depleting and replenishing the body's glycogen levels in the weeks leading up to a bodybuilding contest. This technique allows bodybuilders to saturate their muscles with stored water, thus making the muscles fuller and harder.

Cartilage – Connective tissue that acts as a shock absorber between bones. It's found wherever two bones articulate over one another.

Chalk – White, fine-grained powder, used to improve the grip on a barbell or dumbell. Chalk is formed from the shells of dead marine microorganisms.

Cheating – An advanced training technique that consists of utilizing fresh muscles to assist in the completion of an exercise, when the muscle being trained is nearing fatigue.

Chelation – The process by which protein molecules are bonded to inorganic minerals, making them easier to assimilate by the human body.

Chest – The large pectoral muscles located on the front of the upper torso, responsible for drawing the arms towards the center of the body.

Cholesterol – Naturally occurring steroid molecule involved in the formation of hormones, vitamins, bile salts and the transport of fats in the bloodstream to tissues throughout the body. Excessive cholesterol in the diet can lead to cardiovascular disease.

Circuit Training – A specialized form of weight training which combines strength training and aerobic conditioning. Circuit training consists of performing 10 to 20 different exercises, one after the other, with little rest between sets.

Clean – Weightlifting technique whereby the barbell is hoisted to shoulder level using the arms, legs, hips, and lower back. The competitive version is called the "clean and jerk."

Collar – Small, round, iron or plastic clamp, used to anchor plates on a barbell or dumbell. In most cases collars are screwed on but some versions are held in a spring-like manner.

Compound Exercises – Any exercise that works more than one muscle group. Popular compound movements include: bench presses, squats, shoulder presses, and bent-over rows.

Compulsory Poses – Seven poses that are used to compare contestants in a bodybuilding contest. They include: side chest, rear lat spread, front lat spread, front double biceps, rear double biceps, side triceps, abdominal and front thigh.

Cortisol – Catabolic hormone released by the body in response to stress (of which exercise is one form). Cortisol speeds up the rate at which large units are broken down into smaller units (catabolism).

Cut – Competitive term used to describe the physical appearance of a bodybuilder. To be "cut," implies that you are in great competitive shape, with extremely low bodyfat levels.

Cycle Training – Form of training where high intensity workouts are alternated with those of low intensity. The technique can be applied weekly or yearly.

Decline Bench – Bench used to work the lower and outer pectorals. Decline benches require the user to place their head at the low end and their feet at the upper end of the bench.

Definition – Another term to describe the percentage of bodyfat carried by a competitive bodybuilder. A bodybuilder with good definition shows a great deal of vascularity and muscular separation.

Dehydration – Biological state where the body has insufficient water levels for proper functioning. As the human body is over 90 percent water, athletes must continuously replenish the water lost during intense exercise.

Density – Term used to describe the amount of muscle mass carried by a bodybuilder. It generally refers to muscle thickness and hardness.

Descending Sets – An advanced training technique involving the removal of weight at the completion of a set, and then performing additional reps with the lighter weight.

Diet – A term that refers to a fixed eating pattern. In general usage it usually means to try and lose weight.

Dislocation – Type of injury where the end of one bone (called a "ball") slips out of a hollow indentation (called the "socket") of another bone. It is usually accompanied by tearing of the joint ligaments, which makes the injury so painful.

Diuretics – Any natural or synthetic chemical that causes the body to excrete water. In most cases the drug interacts with aldosterone, the hormone responsible for water retention. Some bodybuilders use diuretics before a contest as it improves their muscularity. But diuretics also flush electrolytes from the body (one of their functions being the control of heart rate), therefore it is a dangerous practice and a few pro bodybuilders have died of diuretic-induced heart attacks.

Down the Rack – An advanced training technique involving the use of two or three successively lighter dumbells during the performance of one set.

Dumbell – Short bars on which plates are secured. Dumbells can be considered the one-arm version of a barbell. In most gyms, the weight plates are welded on, and the poundage is written on the dumbell.

Ectomorphs – Body type characterized by long thin bones, low bodyfat levels, and difficulty in gaining muscle mass.

Endomorphs – Body type characterized by large bones and an excess of bodyfat.

Endorphins – Chemicals released by the brain in response to pain. Often called "natural opiates," endorphins decrease the individual's sensitivity to pain.

Epiphysis – Locations on bones at which growth takes place. They fuse by the late teens or early twenties, but they can prematurely close in young teens by anabolic steroid use.

Exercise – In general terms, any form of physical activity that increases the heart and respiratory rate. In bodybuilding terms, an exercise is one specific movement for one or more muscle groups (i.e. bench press, squat, curl, etc.).

Flexibility – The degree of muscle and connective tissue suppleness at a joint. The greater the flexibility, the greater the range of movement by an individual's limbs and torso.

EZ-curl Bar – Short, S-shaped bar used for such exercises as biceps curls and lying triceps extensions. The bar's unique shape puts less stress on the wrists and forearms than a straight bar.

Fast-Twitch Muscle Fiber – Type of muscle fiber that is adapted for rapid but short duration contractions.

Fluid Retention – Bodybuilding term refering to the amount of water held between the skin and muscles. A bodybuilder "holding water" appears smooth, and his muscularity is blurred.

Forced Reps – An advanced training technique where a training partner helps you complete extra reps after the exercised muscles reach the point of fatigue.

Fractures – Complete or partial break of one of the body's bones.

Free Posing – Held in round three of a bodybuilding contest, free posing consists of individual poses set to the bodybuilder's personal choice of music.

Free Weights – Term given to barbells and dumbells. Free-weight exercises are the most popular types performed by bodybuilders.

Genetics – The study of how biological traits or characteristics are passed from one generation to the next. In bodybuilding terms it refers to the potential each individual has for developing his or her physique.

Giant Sets – An advanced training technique where four or more exercises are performed consecutively. In most cases the term refers to exercises for one muscle group, but bodybuilders have been known to use exercises for four different muscle groups.

Gloves – Specialized hand apparel worn while working out. Gloves help prevent blisters and the build up of calluses.

Glycogen – Primary fuel source used by exercising muscles. Glycogen is one of the stored forms of carbohydrate.

Golgi Tendon Organ (GTI) – Stretch receptors located at the ends of muscles. They terminate muscular contraction when too much stress is placed on the muscle.

Gravity Boots – Specialized boots fitted with an attachment device that allows the user to perform various exercises while hanging upside down on an overhead bar.

Gym – Although this can apply to almost any exercising venue (i.e. high school gym), for bodybuilders the term refers to a weight-training club.

Gynecomastia – Condition characterized by a swelling of the nipple region in males. It may occur naturally at puberty, but in most cases the term applies to the condition brought on by anabolic steroid use. From a biological viewpoint, the condition occurs after excessive amounts of testosterone (or anabolic steroids), is broken broken down into estrogen (a feminizing hormone), which then stimulate estrogen receptors in the breast region. Gynecomastia is also known as "bitch tits."

Hamstrings – The leg biceps located on the back of the upper legs, responsible for curling the lower leg to the upper leg. The hamstrings are analogous to the biceps in the upper arm.

Head Straps – Leather or nylon harness that is placed over the head allowing the user to attach weight and train the neck muscles.

Heavy Duty – Training style developed by former Mr. Universe, Mike Mentzer. Much of Mentzer's theory is based on the works of Dr. Arthur Jones, and involves performing just one or two high intensity sets for each muscle group.

Hypertrophy – Biological term that means muscle growth. Muscles do not grow by increasing cell number but increasing the size of existing muscle fibers.

IFBB – International Federation of Bodybuilders. First founded in 1946 by Joe Weider, the IFBB is the largest bodybuilding federation in the world and the fifth largest sporting federation.

Incline Bench – Bench where the body is tilted back with respect to the vertical. Incline benches are primarily used to work the upper-chest region.

Injuries – In bodybuilding terms, injuries are any damage to bone, muscle, or connective tissue. The most common bodybuilding injuries are muscle strains.

Instinctive Training – One of the most advanced training techniques, it means training according to how you "feel." In short, you deviate from the normal routine and train according to intuition. It takes many years of experience to become fine-tuned with your body and train instinctively.

Intercostals – Small, finger-like muscles located along the sides of the lower abdomen, between the rib cage and obliques.

Isolation Exercises – Any exercise aimed at working only one muscle. In most cases, it's virtually impossible to totally isolate a muscle. Some common examples are: preacher curls, lateral raises, and triceps pushdowns.

Isometric – Type of muscle contraction where there is no shortening of the muscle's length. Isometric exercises were popularized by Charles Atlas.

Isotension – Exercising technique where continuous stress is placed on a given muscle. Extending the leg by contracting the quadriceps, and holding the position for 10 to 20 seconds or more, is an example of isotension. Bodybuilders make use of the technique during the precompetition phase as it improves muscle separation.

Isotonic – Type of muscle contraction where the contracting muscle shortens. The muscle may also be lengthening, as when doing a "negative." Most bodybuilding exercises are examples of isotonic contraction.

Joint – The point at which two bones meet. Most joints have a hinge-type structure which allows the bones to articulate (bend) over one another.

Lactic Acid – A product given off during aerobic respiration. Lactic acid was once thought to be strictly a waste product, however recent evidence suggests that a version of lactic acid called lactate is used by the liver to replenish glycogen supplies.

Latissimus Dorsi – Called the lats, these large fan-shaped muscles are located on the back of the torso, and when properly developed give the bodybuilder the characteristic V-shape. The lats function to pull the arms down and back.

Layoff – Any time spent away from the gym is called a layoff. It can be referred to as a training vacation.

Ligament – Fibrous connective tissue that joins one bone to another.

Lymph System – Parallel system to the cardiovascular system, responsible for collecting and removing waste products from the body. The system's fluid is called lymph, and collects at nodes found in the neck, armpits, and groin.

Mass – Term used to describe the degree of muscle size. A bodybuilder carrying great muscle size would be referred to as massive.

Massage – Recovery technique that involves a forceful rubbing, pinching, or kneading, of the body's muscles. Massage speeds up the removal rate of exercise byproducts, helps athletes relax, and improves performance. The most popular forms of massage are Soviet and Swedish.

Mesomorphs – Body type characterized by large bones, low bodyfat levels, and a greater than average rate of muscle growth.

Muscularity – Another term used to describe the degree of muscular definition. The lower the bodyfat percentage the greater the degree of muscularity.

Muscle – The series of tissue bellies located on the skeleton that serve to move and stabilize the body's various appendages.

Nautilus – Type of exercise equipment invented by Dr. Arthur Jones. Nautilus machines employ a wide assortment of cams, pulleys, and weight stacks, to work the muscle over a wide range of movement.

Negatives – A portion of the rep movement which goes in the same direction as gravity, but the user concentrates on resisting it. In most cases negatives are the downward part of an exercise. For example, during barbell curls, the downward part of the exercise is the negative half of the movement (the upward, curling part, is the positive phase).

Neuromuscular System – The combination of nerves and muscles that interact to control body movement.

Nutrition – The art of combining foods in the right amounts so the human body receives all of the required nutrients. In bodybuilding terms, eating to gain muscle size, yet reduce bodyfat levels is considered proper nutrition.

Nutrients – The various minerals, vitamins, proteins, fats, and carbohydrates, needed by the body for proper maintenance, health, and growth.

Off-Season – Competitive bodybuilding term used to describe the period of the year primarily devoted to gaining muscle mass.

Oil – Mineral or water-based liquid used by bodybuilders to highlight the muscles while onstage. Most bodybuilders use vegetable oils as they are absorbed by the skin and give it a better texture.

Olympia, Mr. and Ms. – The top professional contest in men's and women's bodybuilding. The Mr. Olympia was first held in 1965 (won by Larry Scott) and the first Ms. Olympia was held in 1980 (won by Rachel McLish).

Olympic Barbell – The most specialized and refined barbell in weightlifting. Olympic barbells weigh 45 pounds and are made from spring-steel.

Overload – Term used to describe the degree of stress placed on a muscle. To overload means to continuously increase the amount of resistance that a muscle has to work against. For bodybuilders the stress is in the form of weight.

Overtraining – The physiological state whereby the individual's recovery system is taxed to the limit. In many cases, insufficient time is allowed for recovery between workouts. Among the more common symptoms are: muscle loss, lack of motivation, insomnia, and reduced energy.

Peak – This can mean the degree of sharpness or shape held by a particular muscle (usually the biceps), or it may refer to the shape a bodybuilder holds on a given contest day. A bodybuilder who has "peaked" is in top condition (i.e. full, vascular muscles and a low bodyfat percentage).

Peliosis Hepatitis – Liver condition often associated with anabolic steroid use. As of yet no hard medical evidence exists to support the claims that steroids do in fact cause the disease.

PHA – Short for Peripheral Heart Action, PHA was first developed by 1966 Mr. America, Bob Gajda. The training style involves grouping sets of exercises into sequences, each one aimed at a different muscle group. PHA is one of the best methods of combining weight training and aerobics.

GLOSSARY

Plateau – A state of training where no progress is being made. Plateaus usually occur after long periods of repetitious training. Breaking the condition involves shocking the muscles with new training techniques.

Plates – Small to large cast-iron weights that are placed on a barbell or dumbell. Plates on average range in size from 1-1/4 pounds to 100 pounds. The most common plates in bodybuilding gyms weigh 5, 10, 25, 35, and 45 pounds.

Posedown – Final round in a competitive bodybuilding contest, whereby the top three to six contestants match poses in a posing free-for-all.

Posing – The art of displaying the physique in a bodybuilding contest. Posing consists of mandatory poses used to compare contestants, and free posing where the individual combines favorite poses to highlight strong points, deemphasize weak body parts and let their personality show through.

Posing Trunks – The small one- or two-piece suits worn by competitors in a bodybuilding contest. Posing trunks allow the competitor to show as much of his or her physique as possible.

Positives – Part of the rep movement that goes against gravity. In barbell biceps curls, the positive phase would occur during the curling of the barbell. The lowering of the bar is the negative phase.

Poundage – Another term used to describe the weight of a barbell, dumbell, or machine weight stack.

Powerlifting – The competitive sport that utilizes three lifts – the squat, deadlift, and bench press. The objective is to lift more than your opponent both in the three individual events, and in total.

Precontest – Period of the year devoted primarily to refining muscle size and shape. Bodybuilders, on average, devote the last three months before a contest to this type of training.

Pre-exhaust – Advanced training technique first described by *MuscleMag's* Robert Kennedy. The technique involves fatiguing a desired muscle with an isolation movement, and then using a compound exercise to stress the muscle even further. Pre-exhaust is ideal for eliminating the "weakest link in the chain" effect, often encountered during compound exercises.

Prejudging – Section of a bodybuilding contest where most of the actual judging takes place. Although the competitors may go through their free-posing routines, most of the emphasis is placed on the compulsory rounds.

Priapism – The persistent and often painful erection of the penis that sometimes occurs with steroid use.

Priority Training – Training strategy where an individual devotes most of his/her energy to targeting weak muscle groups.

Proportion – Term used to describe the size of one muscle with respect to the whole body. A bodybuilder with good "proportions" would have all his/her muscles in balance with regards to muscle size.

Protein – Nutrient composed of long chains of amino acids. Protein is primarily used in the production of muscle tissue, hormones, and enzymes.

Psychological Warfare – Any verbal or behavioral strategies employed by competitors to interfere with their opponents' preparation or competition.

Pump – Biological condition where an exercised muscle swells and becomes engorged with blood.

Pumping Iron – Term coined by bodybuilders to refer to their sport. The name was immortalized by George Gains and George Butler, in their 1975 documentary, *Pumping Iron.*

Pumping Up – The practice of performing light exercise just before walking onstage. Bodybuilders pump up to give the muscles a temporary size increase.

Pyramiding – Training technique where weight is added for the first couple of sets, and then decreased for the remaining sets. Bodybuilders may also perform a half-pyramid technique where the weight is only added or decreased for the given number of sets.

Quadriceps – Commonly known as the "thighs," the quads are the large, four-headed muscles located on the front and sides of the upper legs. They are analogous to the triceps, and are the extensors of the legs. Their primary function is to extend the lower leg forward (bringing the upper and lower legs to a locked-out configuration).

Repetition – Abbreviated "rep" in gyms, this simply refers to one full movement of a particular exercise.

Resistance – The amount of force being placed on a muscle. In bodybuilding circles it refers to the amount of weight being lifted.

Rest/Pause – A training technique where the user completes one set, and then rests about 10 seconds before starting the next set. The technique is based on the biological fact that a muscle recovers about 90 percent of its strength within 10 to 15 seconds. Rest/pause allows the bodybuilder to maintain the use of heavy weight for their sets.

Ripped – Another term to describe the percentage of bodyfat carried by a competitive bodybuilder. A ripped bodybuilder has a very low fat percentage (2 to 4 percent).

Routine – Another word for program, schedule, agenda, etc. It refers to the complete number of sets, reps, and exercises performed for a given muscle or muscles on a particular day.

Set – Term referring to a given number of consecutive reps. For example, 10 nonstop reps would be called 1 set of 10.

Shocking – Training strategy that involves training the muscle with a new form of exercise. Shocking techniques are used to "kick start" muscles that have become accustomed to repetitious training routines.

Shoulders – The deltoid muscles – anterior, medial and posterior – located at the top of the torso. The deltoids are responsible for elevating and rotating the shoulder girdle.

Sleeve – Short, hollow, metal tube fitted over both ends of a barbell. The sleeve allows the plates to rotate on the bar, thus reducing the stress on the user's wrists.

Slow-Twitch Muscle Fiber – Type of muscle fiber adapted for slow, long duration contraction. The spinal erectors of the lower back are primarily composed of slow twitch muscle fiber.

Somatotype – Term referring to an individual's body characteristics including such things as muscle size, bone size, bodyfat level, and personality.

Soreness – The mild pain felt in muscles after a workout. It is primarily caused by a build up of lactic acid, and usually appears 12 to 24 hours after exercising.

Spinal Erectors – Two long, snake-like muscles located at the center of the lower back. The spinal erectors help maintain posture by keeping the upper body perpendicular with the floor.

Split Routines – Any routine where different muscle groups are worked on separate days. The most common bodybuilding split routines are four- and six-day splits.

Sponges – Sponges are used to protect the hands from blisters and callouses. Many bodybuilders find sponges more convenient to work with than gloves.

Spot – In short, a helping hand when performing a particular exercise. A spot is provided by a training partner when you fail during an exercise. In most cases it involves providing a few pounds of upwards pressure to keep the barbell, dumbell, or machine handle moving.

Staggered Sets – An advanced training technique where the user adds sets for a weak muscle group between their regular training exercises. For example, many bodybuilders with weak calves add extra calf training between other muscle groups. In many cases, the calf exercise is performed instead of taking a rest.

Steroids – Synthetic derivatives of the hormone testosterone that allow the user to gain muscle mass and strength more rapidly. In addition to their muscle-building effects, steroids (anabolic) increase the oxidation rate of fat, thus giving the user a more "ripped" appearance.

Sticking Point – The point during an exercise where the user is in the weakest biomechanical position. In other words, this is the most difficult part of the movement. The sticking point is usually close to the bottom of the exercise.

Straps – Long, narrow pieces of material used to increase one's gripping power on an exercise. Straps are wrapped around the lower forearm and bar in such a manner that as the user grips the bar, the straps get tighter. They are used on such exercises as deadlifts, shrugs, and chins.

Stretching – Form of exercise where the primary goal is to increase flexibility. Stretching is also an excellent way to warm up the body and prepare it for more stressful forms of exercise.

Stretch Marks – Red or purple lines caused by thinning and loss of elasticity in the skin. In most cases the marks are the result of rapid muscle growth, but gaining large amounts of fat can also cause them. The most common site for stretch marks on bodybuilders is the pec-delt tie-in. There is no effective means of prevention or treatment.

Strict Form – Training technique which involves performing exercises in a slow, controlled manner, and through a full range of motion, without the aid of a partner or cheating techniques.

Stripping Method – An advanced training technique where the individual removes a few plates at the end of a set and forces out extra reps. The technique allows the user to force a muscle past the point of normal failure.

Supersets – Advanced training technique where two exercises are performed consecutively without any rest. Supersets may consist of exercises for the same muscle group (i.e. dumbell curls and barbell curls) or exercises for different muscle groups (i.e. triceps extensions and biceps curls). If performing supersets for different muscle groups, bodybuilders usually pick opposing muscle groups (triceps-biceps, quads-hamstrings, chest-back, etc.).

Supination – Technique where the palms start off facing the body during a dumbell curl, and rotate outward as the dumbell is raised. At the top of the movement, the palms are facing upward. The technique takes advantage of the wrist-rotating properties of the biceps.

Supplements – Any form of vitamin, mineral, protein, or other nutrient, that is taken separately or in addition to, normal food. Supplements come in many forms including: tablet, capsule, powder, oil, or plant material.

Sweat Bands – Small pieces of material, usually cloth, wrapped around the forehead to absorb sweat.

Symmetry – In bodybuilding terms this refers to the overall look to the body. Symmetry is closely related to proportion. A bodybuilder with good symmetry would have no overdeveloped or underdeveloped muscle groups.

Tanning – Biochemical reaction where the skin releases pigment upon exposure to sunlight (or artificial tanning light). Bodybuilders tan for complexion as the darker color improves skin appearance in a contest or photo shoot and highlights muscularity.

Tendinitis – Form of inflammation involving tendons and the points where they attach to muscles and bones. Tendinitis is usually caused by overstressing a particular area. Bodybuilders often get tendinitis in the biceps-tendon region.

Tendon – Tough cord of connective tissue that joins a muscle to a bone.

Testosterone – Androgenic/anabolic hormone responsible for such physiological effects as: increasing muscle size and strength, facial hair growth, scalp hair

GLOSSARY

loss, decreasing sperm production (males), and increasing aggression levels. Although both sexes have circulating testosterone, males have it in greater concentrations.

Training Diary – Daily journal or record kept by bodybuilders. Diaries are useful for keeping track of such items as weight, exercises, sets, reps, calories and overall motivation levels.

Training Partner – Any individual who matches you set for set during your workout. Training partners allow you to go for that extra rep. They also serve as a sort of coach on days when you just don't feel like working out.

Training to Failure – Any form of exercise where you terminate a set only after the muscle cannot contract for additional reps. Most bodybuilders train to positive failure and then have a training partner help them perform a few extra reps.

Triceps – Extensor muscles of the upper arm. The triceps are composed of three "heads," and work opposite to the biceps in that they extend the lower arm to a locked-out position.

Trisets – Similar to supersets but involving the use of three different exercises for the same muscle group.

Twenty-one's – Advanced exercise technique where you perform 7 half reps at the bottom of the movement, 7 half reps at the top, and finish with 7 full reps.

Universal Machine – The most common type of training apparatus (not counting free weight) found in bodybuilding gyms. The machines may train one muscle group, or have numerous stations to train the whole body.

Vascularity – The degree of vein and artery visibility. In order to be "highly" vascular, a bodybuilder must have an extremely low bodyfat percentage.

Visualization – Relaxation technique performed by clearing the mind, and then concentrating and focusing on particular goals. For bodybuilders, common visualization goals include an upcoming contest, workout, or a new training strategy.

Warmup – Any form of light, short duration exercise that prepares the body for more intense exercise. Warming up should involve increasing the heart and respiratory rate, and stretching to prepare the muscles for exercise. A good warmup helps prevent injury.

Weight – This term refers to the plates or weight stacks themselves, or it can be used to describe the actual poundage on the bar.

Weight Class – Generally speaking, men's bodybuilding competitions are subdivided into four categories called weight classes: light, medium, light heavyweight, and heavyweight. Women's events have two divisions, lightweight and heavyweight.

Weightlifting – A general term used to describe the exercise form involving the use of weights, or an Olympic event. The competitive version involves two lifts – the snatch, and clean and jerk.

Workout – The program or schedule of exercises performed on any given day. Bodybuilders refer to exercise as "going for a workout."

Wraps – Long pieces of material (usually a first aid bandage) that bodybuilders wrap around weak or injured bodyparts. Wraps keep the area warm and provide extra security. Many bodybuilders wrap the knees during squats, and the wrists during bench presses.

Brandi Carrier

GLOSSARY

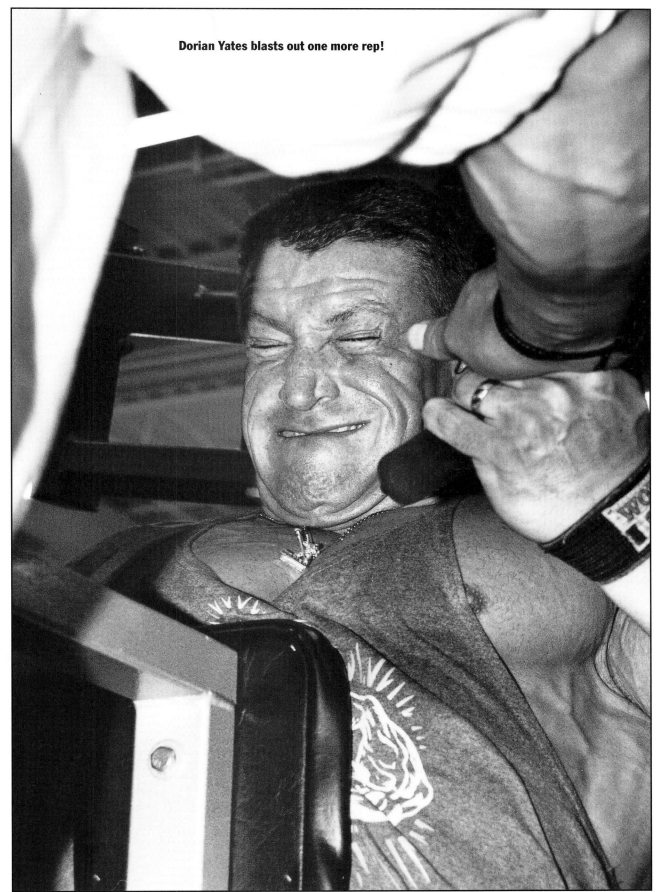

Dorian Yates blasts out one more rep!

REFERENCES

CHAPTER SIXTEEN:

1. Cox News Service. "How to Recognize and Deal With Increased Stress." *The Montreal Gazette* (November 5, 1992), D3.
2. Singer, Robert; Murphey, Milledge; and Tennant, Keith. *Handbook of Research on Sport Psychology.* New York: Macmillan Publishing Co., 1993.
3. "Perspectives." *Newsweek* (February 18, 1991), 23.
4. Cafarelli, E., and Flint, F. "The Role of Massage In Preparation For and Recovery From Exercise." *Sports Medicine.* 14:1 (1992).
5. Beard, Gertrude. "A History of Massage." *The Physical Therapy Review.* 32:12 (December 1952).
6. Messi, Carolee. "The Massage Therapist In Rehabilitation." *Rehabilitation Nursing.* 14:3 (May 1989).
7. Callaghan, Michael. "The Role of Massage In the Management of the Athlete: A Review." *British Journal of Sports Medicine.* 27:1 (1993), 28.
8. Birukov, A. A.; Krakhmaleva, I. I.; and Koshcheeva, T.I. "Massage as a Means of Treating Aggravated Osteochondrosis of the Spine in the Training of Athletes." *Soviet Sports Medicine.* 7:54-55 (1984), 119.
9. Brainum, Jerry. "Lactate." *Muscle and Fitness.* 50:5 (May 1989), 146.
10. "Perspectives." *Newsweek* (April 10, 1989), 17.
11. Turin, A. M. "The Influence of Pneumo-vibromassage On An Athlete's Neuromuscular System." *Soviet Sports Medicine.* 6:30 (1982), 20.
12. Birukov, A. A. "Training Massage During Contemporary Sports Loads." *Soviet Sports Medicine.* 6: 71-73 (1971), 42.
13. Sikowitz, Peter. "Marathoner Wishes He Had Known Benefits of Massage Early In Career." *The Montreal Gazette* (March 14, 1990), D7.
14. Jacobs, Miriam. "Massage For the Relief of Pain." *The Physical Therapy Review.* 40:2 (n.d.)
15. Wiktorsson-Moller, et al. "Effects of Warming Up, Massage, and Stretching On Range of Motion and Muscle Strength in the Lower Extremity." *The American Journal of Sports Medicine.* 11:4 (n.d.), 249.
16. Habib, Marlene. "Therapist Says Massage Is Just What Aching Muscles Need." *The Montreal Gazette* (November 8, 1989), D7.
17. Wright, James. "Soviet Restoration Techniques." *Muscle and Fitness.* 52:1 (January 1991), 129.
18. Birukov, V. A. "Restorative Massage For Decathloners Following Speed Training." *Soviet Sports Medicine.* 1:52-53 (1989), 11.
19. Advertisements, Uvalux International Inc., P.O. Box 214, Innerkip, Ontario, Canada, N0J 1M0.
20. Dubrovsky, V. I. "Use of the Vacuum Massage." *Soviet Sports Medicine.* 7:35 (1975), 162.
21. McCall's, M. "Dream Bill." *The Globe and Mail* (December 4, 1993), DI.
22. Yessis, Michael. "The Sauna: Rapid Recovery Aid." *Muscle and Fitness.* 50:10 (October 1989), 70.
23. Sobolevski, V. I. and Shukhardin, I. O. "The Sauna as a Means of Restoration During Intense Training of Swimmers." *Soviet Sports Medicine.* 15-17 (1980), 49.
24. Trifonov, Y. M., and Alekperov, I. M. "Heat Baths as a Means of Rehabilitation and Increasing the Functional Reserves of the Body." *Soviet Sports Medicine.* 10:29-32, (1978), 4.
25. Levitski, P. M.; Bikova, V. S.; and Pauhina, V. P. "Musical Accompaniment In Physical Culture In Sports." *Soviet Sports Medicine.* 4:32-33 (1985), 59.
26. Embleton, P. and Thorne, G. *Steroid Myths; The Responsible Use of Anabolic Steroids.* St. John's, Newfoundland, Canada: Thorton Publishing Ltd., 1991.
27. "Perspectives." *Newsweek* (June 4, 1990).

CHAPTER THIRTY-SEVEN:

1. Hoberman, J. and Yesalis, C. "The History of Testosterone." *Scientific American.* (February 1995), 76-81.
2. McKim, W. and Mishara, B. *Drugs and Aging.* Toronto: Butterworths Publishers, 1987.
3. Murad, F. and Haynes, R. "Androgens." *Goodman and Gilman's The Pharmacological Basis of Therapeutics.* 7th ed. New York: Macmillan, 1986.
4. Dodds, E. "Ancient Apothecaries and Modern Biochemists." *The Lancet.* (February 16, 1946), 221-224.
5. Brainum, Jerry. "Anabolic Madness." *Muscle and Fitness.* 48:10 (October 1987), 92.
6. News and Comments: "Anabolic Steroids: Doctors Denounce Them But Athletes Aren't Listening." *Science.* 176:30 (June 1972).
7. Oakley, R. *Drugs, Society and Human Behavior.* 2nd ed. St. Louis: C.V. Mosby Company, 1978.
8. Reuters. "Nurmi Won With Drugs in Olympics, Swedes say." *The Globe and Mail* (December 14, 1990), A19.
9. Boje, O. "Doping." *Bulletin of the Health Organization of the League of Nations.* 8 (1939), 439-469.
10. Pearl, B. "Think Twice About Steroids." *Muscle and Fitness* 48:6 (June 1987).
11. The David Letterman Show, NBC. December 26, 1990.
12. Alzado, L., and Smith, S. "I'm Sick and I'm Scared." *Sports Illustrated.* 75:2 (July 8, 1991), 20-27.
13. *Physician's Desk Reference,* 1988.
14. "Sport In Brief: An Anabolic Spray." *The Globe and Mail* (December 5, 1990), A13.
15. Logan, G. "Jets' Cadigan: I'll Do Anything to Succeed." *Newsday* (March 28, 1988).
16. McKim, W. and Mishara, B. *Drugs and Aging.* Toronto: *Butterworths Publishers,* 1987.
17. Burkett, L. and Faldutor, M. "Steroid Use by Athletes in a Metropolitan Area." *The Physician and Sports Medicine.* 12:8 (August 1984).
18. Mathas, J., "The Steroid Guru." *MuscleMag International.* (July 1989).
19. Hatfield, F., Dr. *Anabolic Steroids – What Kind and How Many.* Van Nuys, Calif.: n.p. (n.d.)
20. Murray, T. "Male Bodybuilder Tests Positive for AIDS After Sharing Needles for Steroid Injections." *The Medical Post.* 25:8 (August 8, 1989), 17.
21. Hynes, M. "Francis Took a Sledgehammer to Fragile Illusions About Sport." *The Globe and Mail* (March 4, 1989), A17.
22. Goldman, R. *Death In The Locker Room: Steroids, Cocaine, and Sports.* Tucson: The Body Press, 1987.
23. Smith, W., Dr. "Catch Me If You Can, How The Pros Beat The Drug Test." *MuscleMag International.* (December 88/Jan. 89).
24. Cohen, J., Noakes, T. and Spinnler Benade, A. "Hypercholesterolemia in Male Powerlifters Using Anabolic-Androgenic Steroids." *The Physician and Sports Medicine.* 16:8 (August 1988).
25. Kerr, R. "A Plea From An Experienced Physician." *Muscle and Fitness.* 45:2 (February 1984), 190.
26. Cowley, G. and Hagar, M. "Can Hormones Stop The Clock?" *Newsweek* (July 16, 1990).
27. Friedl, K. and Yesalis, C. E. "Self-Treatment of Gynecomastia in Bodybuilders Who Use Anabolic Steroids." *The Physician and Sports Medicine.* 17:3 (March 1989).

28. Embleton, P. and Thorne, G. "Anabolic Steroid Users In Atlantic Canada (Survey Results)." Unpublished manuscript. Newfoundland: Memorial University of Newfoundland, January 1991.

29. Reynolds, B. "Coming Clean." *Flex.* (May 1990).

30. Bubb, J. "One Man's Story." *MuscleMag International.* (April 1988).

31. Neff, C. "Mighty Tough Cowboys." *Sports Illustrated.* 69:16 (October 1988), 102.

32. Conacher, G. and Workman, D. "Violent Crime Possibly Associated with Anabolic Steroid Use." *American Journal of Psychiatry.* 146:5 (May 1989), 679.

33. Embleton, P. and Thorne, J. *Steroid Myths: The Responsible Use Of Anabolic Steroids.* St. John's, Newfoundland: Thorton Publishing Ltd., 1991.

34. Pope, H. and Katz, D. "Affective and Psychotic Symptoms Associated With Anabolic Steroid Use." *American Journal of Psychiatry.* 145:4 (April 1988).

35. Freinhar, J. and Alvarez, W. "Androgen-Induced Hypomania." *The Journal of Clinical Psychiatry.* 46:8 (August 1985).

36. Annitto, W. and Layman, W. "Anabolic Steroids and Acute Schizophrenic Episode." *The Journal of Clinical Psychiatry.* 41:4 (April 1980).

37. Bootzin, R. and Acocella, J. *Abnormal Psychology: Current Perspectives*, 4th ed. New York: Random House Inc., 1984.

38. Brower, K.; Blow, F.; Beresford, T.; and Fuelling, C. "Anabolic-Androgenic Steroid Dependence." *The Journal of Clinical Psychiatry.* 50:1 (January 1989).

39. Cowart, V. "National Institute on Drug Abuse May Join in Anabolic Steroid Research." *JAMA.* 261:13 (April 7, 1989).

40. DiPasquale, M. *The Medical Post* (June 13, 1989).

41. Nassif, D. "Steroid Underground." *Muscle and Fitness.* 45:2 (February 1984), 93.

42. Tortora, G., and Anagnostakos, N. *Principles of Anatomy and Physiology*, 2nd ed. New York: Harper and Row Publishers Inc., 1978.

43. Prat, J.; Gray, G.; Stolley, P; and Coleman, J. "Wilm's Tumor in an Adult Associated with Androgen Abuse." *JAMA.* 237:21 (May 23, 1977).

44. Cowart, V. "Physician-Competitor's Advice to Colleagues: Steroid Users Respond to Education, Rehabilitation." *JAMA.* 257:4 (January 23/30, 1987).

45. Overly, W. L., et al. "Androgens and Heptocellular Carcinoma in an Athlete." *Ann Intern Med.* 100:158 (1984).

46. Haupt, H. A. and Rovere, G. D. "Anabolic Steroids: A Review of the Literature." *The American Journal of Sports Medicine.* 12 (1984), 469-484.

47. Greer, I.; Greaves, M., Madhok,; R.; McLoughlin, K.; Porter, N.; Lowe, G.; Preston, F.; and Forbest, C. "Effect of Stanazolol on Factors VIII and IX and Serum Aminotransferases in Haemophilia." *Thrombosis And Haemostatis.* 53:3 (June 24, 1985), 386-389.

48. Kerr, R. "A Plea From An Experienced Physician." *Muscle and Fitness.* 45:2 (February 1984), 188.

49. Fruehan, A. and Frawley, T. "Current Status of Anabolic Steroids." *JAMA.* 184:7 (May 18, 1963).

50. Zanyk, L. "If Not Steroids, Then What?" *Canadian Pharmaceutical Journal.* 122:8 (August, 1989).

51. Hatfield, F. "The Last Word On Steroids." *Muscle and Fitness.* 45:2 (February 1984), 87.

52. Eidelsberg, J. and Ornstein, E. A. "Observations on the Continued Use of Male Sex Hormone Over Long Periods of Time." *The Journal of Clinical Endocrinology.* 26 (1940), 46-53.

53. Strauss, R. H.; Liggett, M. T.; and Lanese, R. L. "Anabolic Steroid Use and Perceived Effects in Ten Weight-Trained Women Athletes." *JAMA.* 253:16 (1985), 2871-2873.

54. Bowman, W. C. and Rand, M. J. *Textbook of Pharmacology.* 2nd ed. Toronto: Blackwell Mosby Book Distributors, 1980.

55. Litke, J. (AP) "Athletes Paying Price for Using Steroids." *The Evening Telegram.* St. John's. (August 3, 1991), 22.

56. Arnold, G. "Ethics Issue Is Bothering Journalists." *The Evening Telegram.* St. John's. (July 28, 1990), 18.

57. Pardee, R. "Dietary Problems of the Steroid User." *Muscle and Fitness.* (November 1984).

58. Albanese, A. "*Anticatabolic Applications of Newer Anabolic Steroids.*" 96:9 (September 1968).

59. Goldman, B. *Death In The Locker Room.* n.p.: HP Books, 1984.

60. Butler, A.; Talbot, N.; McLachlan, E.; Appleton, J.; and Linton, N. "Effect of Testosterone Proportionate On Losses Incident to Inadequate Dietary Intake." *Journal of Clinical Endocrinology.* 5:8 (1945).

61. Kruskemper, H. *Anabolic Steroids.* New York: Academic Press, 1968.

62. Bowers, R. and Reardon, J. "The Effect of Anabolic Steroids On Strength, Aerobic Capacity and Selected Antrhopometric Measures." Thesis. Ohio: Bowling Green University, Ohio, 1971.

63. Stepaniak, P.; Furst, J.; and Woodard, D. "Anabolic Steroids as a Countermeasure Against Bone Demineralization During Space Flight Aviation." *Space, and Environmental Medicine.* (February 1986).

Lee Priest

INDEX

Contributing Photographers
Greg Aiken, Jim Amentler, Alex Ardenti,
Doris Barrilleaux, Garry Bartlett, Per Bernal,
Reg Bradford, John Butler, Paula Crane,
Ralph DeHaan, Denie, Gino Edwards, Dick Falcon,
Irvin Gelb, Kevin Horton, Robert Kennedy, Chris Lund,
Jason Mathas, Robert Nailon, Mike Neveux,
Mitsuru Okabe, Rick Schaff, Artie Zeller